FODOR'S GUIDE TO THE
CARIBBEAN, BAHAMAS
AND
BERMUDA 1963

FODOR'S GUIDE TO THE

CARIBBEAN, BAH

A comprehensive handbook of t

693 pages of text; map of the We

12 city plans; illustrations in col

MAS AND BERMUDA

1963

slands and the Spanish Main;

ndies; 25 island and country maps;

nd black and white.

EUGENE FODOR

editor

DAVID McKAY COMPANY, INC.-NEW YORK

Travel Books Edited by Eugene Fodor

1936 ON THE CONTINENT
1937 IN EUROPE
EUROPE IN 1938

In Yearly Revised Editions

AUSTRIA 1963

BELGIUM AND LUXEMBOURG 1963

BRITAIN AND IRELAND 1963

FRANCE 1963

GERMANY 1963

GREECE 1963

HAWAII 1963

HOLLAND 1963

ITALY 1963

SCANDINAVIA 1963

SPAIN AND PORTUGAL 1963

SWITZERLAND 1963

YUGOSLAVIA 1963

GUIDE TO EUROPE 1963

GUIDE TO THE CARIBBEAN,
    BAHAMAS AND BERMUDA 1963

MEN'S GUIDE TO EUROPE

WOMAN'S GUIDE TO EUROPE

JAPAN AND EAST ASIA 1963

INDIA 1963

Printed in the Netherlands - Mouton & Co., The Hague

TABLE OF CONTENTS

FACTS AT YOUR FINGERTIPS

BY WAY OF BACKGROUND

TABLE OF CONTENTS

THE ISLANDS AND THE SPANISH MAIN

TABLE OF CONTENTS

TABLE OF CONTENTS

TABLE OF CONTENTS

TABLE OF CONTENTS

TABLE OF CONTENTS

TABLE OF CONTENTS

TABLE OF CONTENTS

TABLE OF CONTENTS

Color pictures are published by courtesy of: Alcoa (photos Fritz Henle) — Bahamas Development Board — Bermuda Trade Development Board — B.O.A.C. — Wendell P. Colton Co. — French Line — Fritz Henle — Jamaica Tourist Board — Netherlands West Indies Tourist Bureau.

Black and white photographs by courtesy of: Fritz Henle — Bermuda News Bureau (photo John Weatherill) — Bahamas News Bureau — Cuban Tourist Commission — Jamaica Tourist Board — Inter Talk — Puerto Rico News Service — Department of Tourism, Virgin Islands — Netherlands West Indies Tourist Bureau — Office Départemental du Tourisme, Fort de France, photo Willy Robert — The U.K. Commissioner for the West Indies.

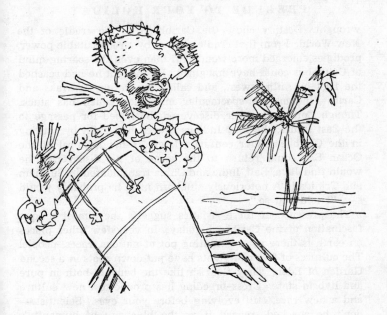

PRELUDE TO YOUR HOLIDAY

Practical Planning for a Year-round Eden

(*Political upheavals in Cuba have given a black eye to the whole Caribbean area—unjustly so. No parts of the world could be safer and more enjoyable than the some forty islands which remain the perfect tourist paradise.*)

"I saw so many islands that I hardly knew to which I should go first." The year was 1492. The writer, Christopher Columbus. The place: the Caribbean Sea.

The problem of choice, so succinctly stated by the first tourist, remains. So do the golden beaches, the crystal water, the sapphire bays, and blazing blue skies which dazzled the discoverer along with "the soil, so beautiful and rich, the mountains, full of trees, so lofty that they seem to reach the sky, the singing nightingales, parrots, birds of a thousand sorts . . ." These pristine marvels, duly noted in the Admiral's journal, remain unchanged, as though untouched by five centuries of violent history. This is the first miracle of the Caribbean.

The second, paradoxically, is the wonder of what man hath

wrought. Destiny chose the Caribbean as the cradle of the New World. From that cradle, rocked by an inscrutable power, prodigies emerged more wonderful than even the soaring mind of Columbus could have imagined. He thought he had reached the East by sailing west, and called the native Arawaks and Caribs "Indians", a spectacular misnomer which has stuck. Though Columbus never discovered the hoped-for passage to the East Indies, the East Indians proved him right by settling in the Caribbean four centuries later. If the Admiral of the Ocean Sea could return to the scene of his discoveries, he would find Java, Bali, India and China transplanted in Surinam and Trinidad. A notoriously stubborn man, he probably would say, "I told you so."

The presence of these Asiatics suggests the almost unique fascination of the Caribbean today. In very few other places on earth is there such a melting pot of nations, races, people. The cultures of five continents have put down roots in a second Garden of Eden. They flourish like the banyan, both in pure and hybrid state. Cross-breeding has produced a new culture and a new race, still evolving before your eyes. Scientists— don't be shocked—regard it as the blueprint of humanity's future.

Meanwhile the present meets the past at every turn in the Caribbean. Nowhere will you find such a happy marriage of Old World charm and New World efficiency as in this strategic area over which the major powers of Europe battled for three centuries. It was the colonial cockpit of the world. Germán Arciniegas likened it to "a gaming table, where the crowns of the kings of Europe were the stakes and the pirates rolled the dice."

When the tumult and the shouting of Napoleonic Europe died away, the West Indies were officially parcelled out at the conference table. The lion's share went to the lion which had spawned such cubs as Raleigh, Drake, Morgan, Rodney, Hood and Nelson. But the rights of lesser nations were respected to the extent that America and Canada still have half of Europe at their doorstep. This is a temptation to the tourist, almost as strong as the call of the beach.

Mosaic of Living Cultures

If you are looking for European flavor you won't be disappointed. Bermuda, the Bahamas, Barbados are as British as Big Ben; so are British Guiana, Jamaica, the British Leeward and Windward Islands. Generally speaking, their people, both black and white, are charming. They may not be as aggressive as Drake and Hawkins, but we personally have never found them "stand-offish, coldly reserved" or in any way resembling the dehumanized cold fish of anti-British caricature. In Guadeloupe, Martinique and the independent Black Republic of Haiti, you'll find the manners and morals of France along with the language, *fantaisie,* culture, and (*Dieu merci!*) the incomparable cuisine of la Belle Marianne. *Les Filles de Couleur,* incidentally, are a match to their Paris cousins.

Curaçao, Aruba, Bonaire, Saba, Sint Maarten and Surinam are full of pink-faced, tow-headed Dutchmen, the gabled roofs of Amsterdam, the round fat cheeses of Edam, good strong Holland gin, and the exotic foods and faces of Indonesia and West Africa. The Swedes have left their mark on St. Barthélemy, the Danes on St. Thomas and St. Croix, but the Negroes on these American Virgin Islands look and walk like cowboys and girls of the golden west.

Fundamentally Latin, Puerto Rico, Venezuela, Columbia and Panama remain forever imbued with the music, color, and violence of Spain. The last is usually suppressed or smouldering behind dark eyes in a manner which kindles a certain sympathetic spark among tourists.

Negroes, both pure-blooded and mixed, make up about 90 per cent of the population on most West Indian islands, and it is fascinating to observe the ways in which they have adapted themselves to the dominant culture patterns of Europe as well as the manner in which they have affected such patterns.

In addition to the enduring cachet of Europe, you may look forward to a persistent Amerindian influence in Venezuela and Colombia and the matchless exoticism of a place like Surinam. Here you will see Dutch burghers, graceful Javanese women gliding along in Batik skirts, and half naked Djukas trampling the banks of ochre rivers in tribal dances whose throbbing rhythm is the primordial heartbeat of Africa. In Trinidad you will hear the tinkling of Hindu temple bells, the brazen clangor of Christian belfries, the cry of the muezzin from a minaret calling the faithful of still another sect to prayer. This is not done for the edification of tourists; it is all part and parcel of the rich mosaic of living culture which the Caribbean offers.

Where is It?

Lying roughly between 10 and 22 degrees of north latitude,

3

this most romantic of seas is shaped most unromantically like an old shoe. The Greater Antilles: Cuba, Hispaniola (Haiti and the Dominican Republic), and Puerto Rico form its instep. The Lesser Antilles curve down to describe the toe. The coasts of Venezuela and Colombia make the sole. Central America is the heel and counter. North of the instep in the Atlantic Ocean are Bermuda and the scattered Bahamas where Columbus made his first landfall, Ponce de Leon searched for the Fountain of Youth, and Blackbeard the Pirate had his lair.

The Caribbean is 1700 miles long, 700 wide. Most of its islands are washed by the Atlantic on the windward side providing the tourist with exhilirating surf bathing in addition to the unruffled placidity of tropical lagoons. All the islands are swept by the trade winds, that never failing air conditioner which keeps them comfortably cool even in summer. Together with the Bahamas, Bermuda and the northern coast of the Spanish Main they share a year round temperature which fluctuates between 65 and 89 degrees.

On and Off Season

The Caribbean is one of the few areas in the world where you can count on good weather the whole year through with its corollaries of good swimming, good fishing, good sailing. Snow is unknown in these parts. This is a claim which cannot be made, incidentally, by such renowned resorts as Monte Carlo and Mallorca. The summer "rainy season", which evokes memories of Sadie Thompson and the unrelenting downpours of *Rain*, means occasional refreshing showers in the Caribbean, nothing more except in the inaccessible mountain interior of Dominica or on Grand Cayman. You will be fairly warned of any rain problem in the text on individual countries in this guide.

Meanwhile nothing should deter you from planning a budget vacation during the "unfashionable" summer season. Between mid-April and December prices are lower, and you can pick and choose among hotels which would be booked to capacity in winter. If the nightlife is duller, the days are more brilliant with the flowering trees, orchids and other exotic flora of the region in glorious full bloom. The Caribbean is at its smoothest and clearest, a vast diaphanous blue lake for swimmers, sailors, fishermen and that growing army of subaqueous explorers who only come up for meals. The West Indies offer escape from the heat and humidity of a North American summer as well as a refuge from winter's snow and sleet.

4

PRELUDE TO YOUR HOLIDAY

At any season the Caribbean provides amenities and attractions of enough diversity to suit any taste. The tourist attached to worldly pleasures has a wide choice of plush hotels, fancy restaurants, luxury shops, posh nightclubs, dance terraces under the stars, gambling casinos, kidney-shaped pools, yacht havens, horse racing, polo, and other charms and distractions of international society; all this and the tropics too. San Juan, Puerto Rico flashes into the mind when one thinks of gaiety with an international accent; so do Bogota, Caracas, Port of Spain and the Gold Coast of Jamaica. Havana, once among the gayest of Caribbean capitals is currently in the doldrums. Castro, who began by inviting tourists, has succeeded in making his island paradise rather uninviting.

For the escapist there are islands in the sun where one can bask alone on a palm-fringed beach, far from the gadding crowd and the beaten path on which it gads. The British Virgins, Anguilla, St. Vincent, St. Lucia, Bonaire, St. John, Grenada and the Grenadines were made for getting away from it all.

There are resorts for mountain climbers, horseback riders, water skiers, croquet players, stunt fliers, baseball fans, amateurs of cricket and cockfighting, sociologists, gardeners, folklore addicts, hunters, deep sea fishermen, skin divers, all sorts of sportsmen, and even those gentle inactive souls who are content to soak up the sun and enjoy the scenery without walking all over it.

There are the quiet family resorts where the management has thoughtfully provided kiddie pools, playgrounds, nurses and even special restaurants for your children. We think affectionately of the Piscadera Bay Club on Curaçao, Puerto Rico's Treasure Island, Barbados' Paradise Beach Club, Parque Ramfis, the Hamaca and Embajador Hotels in Santo Domingo, and the new Trinidad Hilton with its Tobago-shaped pool for Tobago-sized tots.

Shopping, anyone? This favorite indoor sport is fully covered, country by country, below. But if you're planning your trip with shopping as your chief activity, know that the happiest hunting grounds are in St. Thomas, Haiti, Jamaica, Curaçao and Panama.

When it comes to shopping, the West Indies are quite simply the merchandise mart of the world. All the luxury products of Europe, the Far East and Latin America are here at prices that justify that superbly feminine remark: "I couldn't afford not to buy it!" Price tags on watches, jewelry, cameras, fabrics, clothes are often 50 per cent and more below their U.S. counterparts. Warning: You'll find everything you've ever wanted to buy and a lot of things you haven't thought of until you've seen them beckoning in the island bazaars.

In short, there is something for every known type of vacationist in the Caribbean. From the tourist point of view El Dorado has materialized at last, and you'll find it between Bermuda and the Spanish Main. You must make the same choice as Columbus, a choice that has been complicated by nearly 500 more years of the human story. This *Guide to the Caribbean, Bahamas and Bermuda* has been prepared to help you choose wisely. We have combed the beaches, shopped the shops, checked the hotels, sampled the food, drunk the rum, driven over the roads, and even dived to the depths of the Caribbean to bring you the most complete guide possible to this fabulous vacationland. If we have missed a good guest house, "a little place where they cook the most divine fish", or anything else between Bermuda and Bogota, won't you please let us in on your own discovery?

$$\star\ \star\ \star$$

The present guide, result of five extended trips throughout the Caribbean area, would not have been possible without the active cooperation of many people engaged in tourist promotion of this fabulous "Mediterranean of the Western Hemisphere".

One of the most energetic of these was Mrs. Lee Karwick, a former Director of the Caribbean Tourist Association, whom we met in Ocho Rios on our first trip in 1955. Mrs. Karwick's enthusiasm helped to crystallize our own intention to produce this guide. She has been an unfailing source of cooperation throughout the four years of the guide's preparation. She literally paved its way, and we wish to acknowledge our debt of gratitude to her with very special thanks, recognition and fond friendship. This spirit of wholehearted CTA cooperation is being carried on by Mr. Nicolas Craig, general manager, and Miss Jane H. Condon, his deputy.

No conventional list of "acknowledgments" could adequately express our gratitude to the many key personalities of Caribbean tourism who helped us in our task.

It is a very great pleasure for us to thank these friends individually, for in doing so we retrace the Caribbean journeys which they helped to make memorable. Hopping from island to island we wish to thank especially:

PRELUDE TO YOUR HOLIDAY

Mr. W. J. Williams, director of the Bermuda Trade Development Board and Mr. D. Colin Selley, publicity director, both in Hamilton. Mr. J. C. Forbes, manager of the New York office, who lent a helping hand in checking our information.

In the Bahamas, Hank Jones, former press chief of the Nassau Development Board's office, and his assistant, Ray Glist, gave valuable help in our researches. The company of Hank and his charming wife, Dori, was an added source of enjoyment during our stay in Nassau.

In Jamaica, that dynamo, the Hon. Abe Issa, as chairman of the Tourist Board, mobilized his island's most efficient information "machine". We had the privilege of being taken in tow by Mr. V. C. McCormack, director, and the talented Fred Wilmot, his press officer. Abe also made us welcome in his home with his family.

Haiti was a real thrill, thanks mainly to the gracious M. Roy, a former president of the Tourist Commission, and his beautiful wife, who manages the pleasant Beau Rivage. M. Jaques Honorat, the Director General of the Commissariat du Tourisme, and Madame Honorat honored us with the hospitality of their home, in the elegant Haitian tradition—a rare treat. M. Paul Baussan, manager of the Cacique Island Resort, was a great help as was Luckner Lazard, the well-known painter.

Our visit to the Dominican Republic would have injected a discordant note into this enumeration of uninterrupted pleasures, had it not been for Mr. and Mrs. Kurt Peyer now in Jamaica. These outstanding figures in the local tourist industry erased all evidence of the indifference which we noticed in the attitude of tourist officialdom. Our thanks also go to Mrs. Vaught, press attachée of the U.S. Embassy in Santo Domingo, and to Mr. José M. Lovaton.

Puerto Rican energy and cordiality are an old story to us, of course. It was good to see our friends Rafaelo and Olga Benitez Carle. Rafaelo, the former director general of the Puerto Rico Department of Tourism, delegated Sr. Suárez to help us. Mr. Morton Sontheimer, president of the Puerto Rico News Bureau, and Rick Wellen, press officer, gave us their eager assistance in San Juan, while Don Short did likewise in New York. We are indebted also to Frank Ledesma, former Acting Director.

Our Virgin Islands story is one of efficient achievement when at work and enchantment when at play. Harry Goeggel, the genial and knowledgeable Assistant Commissioner of Commerce for Tourism, and his charming assistant, Mrs. Symons, produced a treasure-trove of information and material. Harry also introduced us to his family and we left the Islands enriched by new friendships. Incidentally, we can vouch for Harry's authority on rum (see chapter contributed by him); we sampled some in his company...

The Leewards provided us the pleasure of meeting Miss Maginley, Secretary of the Antigua Tourist Information Office, who guided and documented us on this enchanting piece of real estate; Mr. Ivor MacLaren, of the new Antigua Tourist Information center in New York, who was also indispensable. We also met scores of old and new friends there. St. Kitts and Nevis were altogether new to us, but we intend to return. In this most recent edition we are indebted to Mrs. Flavila Tosch, head of St. Croix and Virgin Islands Tourist Bureau, and to Mrs. Margaret Lenci, Manager of the Virgin Islands Tourist office in New York.

Guadeloupe and Martinique, familiar French islands, now hold promise of entering the tourist picture in a big way. M. de Gentile, Executive Director of the Tourist Commission, Mr. Parfait of the Banque Martiniquaise also Mr. Parfait, owner of Hotel Berkley, and Mr. Pierre Lacascade, owner-manager of Dole-les-Bains and of the new airport restaurants in Guadeloupe, were all very helpful.

We visited only two islands in the Windwards this time: St. Lucia and Grenada. The latter was an unforgettable experience as we were able to stay with friends whom we already knew or just met; they made us feel as if we belonged to this fascinating island. Mrs. Anderson, a *grande dame*, and her son Basil offered us an insight into a way of life that is rare nowadays even in these parts. Mr. Otway, a member of the Tourist Board and of B.W.I.A., showed us around and gave us the benefit of his knowledge of local lore.

We have a particular attachment to Barbados, since we literally owe our life to the balmy effects of the Barbados coast, where we recovered from a serious illness. We therefore returned with great anticipation to see our good friends Jock Mitchell and his wife, Peta of the Colony Club. Mr. Paul Foster, general manager of the Barbados Tourist Board, gave us his most willing cooperation, while Mr. J. Cecil Ince, district manager of B.W.I.A., was our distinguished guide. Mr. George Hunte, publisher of the *Bajan Magazine,* was a pillar of support of our project.

We made repeated stops in Trinidad, an old acquaintance,

where our trip was organized most effectively by Bob Cook, then sales promotion manager of B.W.I.A. Among the numerous friends we fondly remember was Mrs. Erica Hawkins, who joined us in exploring every nook and corner of this fascinating big island. Mr. John E. Probst, director of P.A.A., and his wife were, as usual, most hospitable. Don Bain, general manager of the Trinidad and Tobago Tourist Board, is another old friend who deserves our special gratitude, and so does Stephen Goerl, head of the advertising and public relations agency representing the Islands in New York. He, more than anyone else, was an unfailing source of information and help concerning the Islands.

In Surinam, the greatest help was given by Mr. H. A. Van Eyck, general manager of the Travel and Tourist Board, and by Dr. M. M. Van Poll, of the Government of Surinam.

Caracas was one of the highpoints of our whole trip, owing to the presence there of our very good friends, the Wenzels. Peter is manager of P.A.A. and as such was able to mobilize everything and everybody on our behalf. Thanks to these friends, we also had an interesting insight into the social life of the Venezuelans. Mr. Emerico Wohl, managing director of the newspaper *El Diario,* also helped us kindly. Dr. C. Padilla, director of tourism, was good enough to brief us and provide documentation and photographic material. Senor G. G. Perez provided us with hotel information.

Mr. A. J. Seymour, chief information officer in Georgetown, British Guiana, gave us his full cooperation.

Our visit to Bogotá was made at the time of the C.T.A. Conference, where our host was Mr. Ernesto C. Martelo, president of C.T.A. and manager of the Empresa Colombiana de Turismo. His talents for organization and flair for gracious Latin hospitality, made our stay a delight. He was most ably assisted by Messrs. Benito Lopez Uribe and Gregorio Obregon, who gave us the full benefit of their knowledge and advice in the preparation of our chapter on Colombia.

In Barranquilla, Sr. Galo Dugand and his attractive wife as well as Gus Romea, then director of El Prado Hotel and his delightful American wife Margaret, made us feel at home with traditional Spanish cordiality.

When thinking of our visit to Curaçao, we instantly recall Jimmy Leander, the jovial officer of the Curaçao Tourist Bureau whom Mr. Evertsz, director of the Tourist Committee, delegated to show us around. Jimmy's knowledge of local lore and his entertaining presentation of it make him one of the most popular tourist officials anywhere, and the figure of this big cheerful Dutchman appears in many a travel book.

We must also thank Colonel and Mrs. Taber, well known travel agents, who also provided us with a great deal of valuable advice and information.

In Aruba, Mr. Michael Kuiperi, director of the Aruba Tourist Office, eagerly cooperated, with the enthusiasm and efficiency that are characteristic of this booming island.

We would also like to thank Mr. Gus Iraola of the James C. Seix Co. for his assistance in our revision of Cuba.

For our latest information about Panama we are indebted to Mrs. E. de Arias, Public Relations Manager of Panama Hilton, who very kindly made corrections and additions to the material published in the first edition. The Government tourist office in Panama has been extremely lax in providing information.

The number of tourist industry executives representing the various Caribbean countries in New York who gave unfailing support and effective assistance is large. Among them are:

Mr. A. H. Mossman, vice-president of Wendell P. Colton Co., as well as Messrs. Robert Montgomery and Thomas C. O'Connell and in particular, Miss Barbara Schaefer of the same organization, for her thorough correction of our section on Panama.

Mr. A. Michael Finn, of Hill & Knowlton Inc., representing the Bahamas Development Board in New York.

Our very particular thanks go to Mr. Paul E. Knapp, former director of advertising and public relations for Alcoa Steamship Company, and his assistant, Mr. Charles A. MacKenzie, who placed at our disposal their photographic archives, known to be the richest collection of photographs of the Caribbean area. Most of their pictures were taken by the famous photographer, Fritz Henle, who also contributed a chapter on photography to this book.

Mr. Louis F. Bouman, former director of the Netherlands West Indies Tourist Bureau in New York, has our gratitude for his prompt and efficient cooperation.

Miss Frances Niles and Mr. Eugene Phillips, of Delta Airlines, went out of their way to attend to our problems in the spirit of public service so typical of this company.

Mr. Miguel Pombo, manager of Avianca in the U.S.A., gave us a last-minute assist with pictures, maps and kindred problems.

But this year's thorough-going revision could not have been

carried out so successfully but for the most conscientious and effective cooperation of Mrs. Tandy N. Van Doren for whose untiring efforts we are most grateful.

Finally, Mr. and Mrs. Boyriven of Paris extended welcome assistance to the editor in preparing the present edition for the press.

In Europe, Mr. Arthur Taylor, manager of the Bahamas Development Board in London, was a source of great help and so were Mr. H. Hensser, photographic officer of B.O.A.C. in London, and Mr. R. J. Gelink, of K.L.M.'s public relations service in The Hague.

Mr. Ben Holt, public relations manager of Pan American World Airways in Paris generously assisted us in the final phase of our fact-finding efforts.

Our life-long friend George Frank, managing director of Milbanke Travel Ltd. in London, lent us a willing hand with our various problems in Britain.

Finally, we wish to thank all the other hotel managers, tourist office executives, tour managers, Calypso singers, steelbandsmen, taxi drivers, bar tenders, porters, and all the indispensable cogs that make the wheels of Caribbean tourism turn. Their unfailing courtesy and good nature helped to make all our trips a pleasure and constitute a major reason for looking forward to the next one.

Blessed by all the gifts that sea, sun and sand can bestow, the people of the Caribbean, Bahamas and Bermuda have also that additional asset without which the rest is nothing: we refer to their inborn sense of hospitality.

In conclusion, all critical appraisals in this guide, whether favorable or adverse, are based on the editor's personal experience. We feel that the first responsibility of a guide is to inform, and on occasion protect the reader, rather than to praise indiscriminately. All adverse comments are made in the spirit of constructive criticism and in the hope of stimulating improvements where they are needed. We are always happy to receive letters from readers whose opinions are at variance with ours, and always ready to reappraise factors in the constantly changing tourist picture and revise our own opinions when the situation warrants it. In the meantime the editor assumes sole responsibility for all the judgments in the book.

11

FACTS AT YOUR FINGERTIPS

FACTS AT YOUR FINGERTIPS

WHAT'S WHERE

The myriad islands and countries in the vast expanse of the Atlantic-Caribbean region, have been organized in this guide in such a way as to orient the reader and facilitate island hopping in logical sequence from the U.S.A. and Canada. A glance at your four-color map of the Caribbean will immediately familiarize you with the great S curve formed by the lands of this region.

The garden island of *Bermuda,* English-speaking British Crown Colony, begins the S in the middle of the Atlantic. From there, you curve southwest to the *Bahamas,* lovely "isles of perpetual June", another British colony, and then eastward to the four large islands that make up the *Greater Antilles.* These are *Cuba,* a Spanish-speaking independent republic currently going through a phase of complete sovietization which has scuttled the tourist trade, at least for the moment; *Jamaica,* a splendidly developed island, now independent and member of the British Commonwealth; *Hispaniola* and *Puerto Rico.* The large island of Hispaniola is shared by two independent countries: the French-speaking Black Republic of *Haiti,* which occupies the western third of the island; and the *Dominican Republic,* whose official language is Spanish. An hour's flight eastward across the Mona Channel will take you to Spanish and English-speaking *Puerto Rico,* once a poor ward of the United States, now a flourishing commonwealth with wonderful tourist hotels and facilities.

A short hop from Puerto Rico lie the *Virgin Islands,* three American ones (St. Thomas, St. John and St. Croix) and a host of British ones. These relaxed and scattered islands lead you into the third curve of the S which now sweeps southward in an archipelago known as the *Lesser Antilles.*

These are divided into three separate groups: the *Leeward Islands* (because they are farther west or to the lee of the others), the *Windward Islands,* and *Barbados.* The Leeward Islands, north to south, are *Anguilla* (British), *St. Martin* (French and Dutch), *St. Barthelemy* (French), *Barbuda* (British), *Saba* and *St. Eustatius* (Dutch), *St. Kitts, Nevis,*

Antigua, Redonda, and *Montserrat* (British), *Guadeloupe, Désirade, Marie Galante* and *Iles des Saintes* (French) and *Dominica* (British). *The British Leewards* are now gradually developing, but still escapist havens; their official language is English.

The Dutch islands are known as the *Dutch Windward Islands* because they are to the windward of *Curaçao, Aruba* and *Bonaire* (see below), but don't let this spoil your fun. They speak, eat and treat Dutch, and offer unusual opportunities to get away from it all.

Guadeloupe and her Gallic satellites speak French with a soft creole accent as does Martinique, the top island of the Windwards, which now continue the Antillean arc southward. Guadeloupe and Martinique are full départements of France with representatives in the French parliament.

The rest of the *Windward Islands* are all British, members of the still-born West Indies Federation, and all delightful spots for an escapist holiday. They are *St. Lucia, St. Vincent* and *Grenada.* Between the last two stretches a handful of island jewels, known as the *Grenadines,* a superlative area for cruising and relaxing.

Barbados lies about 90 miles east of St. Vincent, like a solitary sheep dog guarding the whole flock of the Windwards. Most British of islands in character and appearance, Barbados is the main island of "Little Eight" of British West Indies after the secession of Jamaica and Trinidad and Tobago.

One hour southwest of Barbados by plane is little *Tobago* ("Crusoe's Island"). Twenty minutes farther and you are in the land of Carnival par excellence: *Trinidad,* rich with oil and asphalt, athrob with Calypso and steel band music, and proud of its new status as a newly independent member of the British Commonwealth.

A two hour flight southeast from Trinidad's capital, Port-of-Spain, and you are on the *Spanish Main,* as the northern coast of South America is called. Specifically, you are in Georgetown, *British Guiana,* an English-speaking enclave of the South American continent. East of British Guiana is *Dutch Surinam,* one of the most fascinating stops on your tour, and east of that is *French Guiana,* just barely beginning as a tourist area.

From here the S swings across the Spanish Main through oil-rich *Venezuela* to refinery-rich *Curaçao* and *Aruba,* which, along with *Bonaire,* compose the most important group of the Dutch West Indies. Colorful and cosmopolitan, these islands speak Papiamento and Dutch and, as in Holland, have another language: English.

Back on the Spanish Main, cultivated *Colombia*, most Spanish of all Latin American countries, continues our S curve westward to *Panama*, the final serif on this imaginary letter, a Spanish-speaking Central American republic with a celebrated canal and a ten-mile-wide corridor occupied by a rich, English-speaking uncle with a permanent lease on the property.

CHOOSING YOUR VACATION SPOT

Beginning at the top of the S, here are more than 40 resort possibilities and what they have to offer in a nut shell.

Bermuda. Main season is April through Labor Day, but there's a good secondary season extending to November. Price range from very expensive to moderate. Choice between active social life or tranquillity. Superior facilities for sailing, fishing, tennis, golf and skin diving. Shopping very good for liquor and British imports. A sedentary resort, suitable for long stays and family vacations. Many new hotels are already opened or in construction. The new Bermudiana and the Carlton Beach have already made a difference.

The Bahamas offer striking contrast between fancy, exclusive clubs, big hotels (gay and social) and simple accommodation. Excellent fishing and sailing. Shopping for liquor and British goods saves a good bit of cost of trip from Florida, but the Bahamas are not for the budget-minded. Prices: very expensive to moderate. There are new resorts developing here, particularly in Nassau, and on Paradise Island, where Huntington Hartford's much publicized *Ocean Club* is both operating and expanding at the same time.

Cuba had three main facets, before Castrofication: (1) Gay Havana with gambling, the mambo, high-priced vice, delicious Bacardi rum and mammoth posh hotels at reasonable rates; fascinating sight-seeing in historic capital with remarkable modern additions. (2) Modern, well-equipped beach resorts. But tourism to Cuba was wiped out by Castro. Americans can not go to this unhappy land as we go to press. (3) Provincial Cuba, beautiful, historic and very inexpensive.

Jamaica has topnotch accommodations and facilities but, until recently, was no place for tourists on a budget. Montego Bay and Ocho Rios are two of the poshest resorts anywhere, gay, luxurious and social. Port Antonio follows close behind

17

but is less dressy, more sporty. Mandeville, English hill station, is cool, rather dull, but the exception to the rule on budget; it's cheap to medium priced. Relaxing hill atmosphere attracts the elderly. Kingston, busy capital, very hot in late spring, summer. Excellent hotel situation. Resort estates very elegant and can be expensive, perfect for golf, riding, fishing and swimming. Baby sitters provided in most hotels. Transportation by taxi and limousine an expensive item as resorts are widely dispersed. However, resort and hotel facilities are rapidly expanding. Wonderful shopping in free-port and in-bond shops, very well stocked. Despite lovely scenery and splendid resorts, parts of capital and native towns dab and depressing.

Haiti. An independent country now. Most exotic, very rewarding, plenty of accommodation from simple, low-budget to luxurious. Not ideal for children, as pasteurized milk is scarce and so are beaches. Nightlife, folklore, food, painting and human interest all touched with a special creole exoticism. Abscene of racial discrimination. A major shopping center: well-stocked free port stores and excellent local artisanship in mahogany, sisal, metal, painting. Very good brandy-like rum, and French-creole cuisine is outstanding.

Dominican Republic. Main assets are de luxe hotels at sensible prices; a handsome modern capital with unsurpassed Spanish colonial buildings; modern sanitation, excellent water and milk, and special playground facilities for children. Now that the crisis following the elimination of Trujillo has subsided, and diplomatic relations have been resumed with the United States, the Dominican Republic is once more welcoming American tourists. There is a lot to be welcomed by: hotels and casinos are reopening at a fast pace, and there is a lively night life in Santo Domingo—a city which may very well take honors as one of the most sophisticated and international in the Caribbean, a prize once held by Havana.

Puerto Rico offers a wonderful variety of vacation possibilities, and has been having a Florida-like boom in its tourist business. Hotels range from very expensive and luxurious to modern low-cost guest house types. Excellent gambling casinos under government supervision, not publicized. You can have vacation at moderate expense here if you rent your room on European plan and take meals outside or in hotel coffee shops. There are several excellent, medium-priced mountain resorts, good for family holiday. Transportation by *publicos* very inexpensive. Topnotch facilities for sports, especially fishing, skin-diving and golf. Old San Juan wonderful for sightseeing. Good restaurants and native cooking. Becoming more and more popular with the middle income group. Unique combination of Spanish and Yankee atmosphere, charming, optimistic and free from tensions.

U.S. Virgin Islands. St. Thomas is topflight resort for vacation with lots of social activity or for a rest in an environment ranging from comfortable to de luxe; for complete escapism plus either luxurious or basic amenities (St. John); for a pleasant relaxing holiday (St. Croix). Price range is from expensive to moderate; low-cost meals and accommodation are hard to find. Some of the most recent improvements include a new jet airport on St. Croix, improved facilities in the *Virgin Isle Hilton* and at *Bluebeard Castle* and new hotels in St. Thomas. Shopping is the best in the Caribbean: biggest choice, lowest prices. You can find a variety of accommodation: slick and chi chi: elegantly dignified; picturesque, the last in delightful family-type guest houses. St. John has the only U.S. offshore national park; can be visited only on horseback or rough-going jeep. Sailing, fishing, skin-diving are outstanding. Excellent for family vacation, though some hotels do not admit children in winter season.

British Virgins. Until now, a backwater area chiefly known by yachtsmen, but there are now signs that it is beginning to develop. Three new hotels have opened on Tortola Island and Beef Island now has an airstrip with regular service from other islands. The Trellis Bay Club on Beef Island has become an important refueling and repair station for yachters and can accommodate guests as well. There are also hotels on Beef Island and Marina Cay. Ideal for sailing, fishing, skin-diving and getting away from the social whirl. Waters of the British Virgins are among best cruising grounds for yachtsmen.

Anguilla. Now accessible by *Leeward Island Air Transport* service as well as boat service, this island has terrific beaches, good fishing, hotels where you can get room and board for less than $5 a day. It's an inexpensive hideaway for hardy escapists, the kind that don't mind roughing it. Riding trails abound on this island.

St. Martin. A lovely island, half Dutch, half French, now in process of development, but still quite unspoiled and not expensive. Accessible by air. Free port shopping in both French and Dutch capitals. A swank 150-room hotel, *The Dutchman's Walk,* should be open by the end of 1963.

St. Barthelemy. An undeveloped daughter of France, most difficult of access. A group of millionaires is said to have chosen it as the ideal spot to develop their own private Shangri-la. David Rockefeller is building here. In the meantime, there's no accommodation unless you want to dicker for a room in the home of one of the native whites of Swedish-French origin.

Barbuda. Accessible by small sloop that has to dart through a rift in the reef, this is a primitive island, inhabited mostly by smugglers, visited primarily by sportsmen who stay at *Coco Point Lodge.* Wild pigs, deer, duck and pigeon are the quarry. Make arrangements for transportation and accommodation in Antigua.

Saba. Most exciting part is getting there by boat through a rough sea, but the trip can soon be made by air with construction almost completed of an airstrip. After that the rest is silence. Quaint, picturesque, photogenic, Dutch. Recommended only for a day's excursion, but very inexpensive if you want to be really alone.

St. Eustatius. Also Dutch, accessible by air from St. Kitts. Agriculture, ruins of past history, inexpensive government guest house. For the excursionist or escapist.

St. Kitts. Oldest British colony of the West Indies and fun to explore, especially Brimstone Hill, Gibraltar of the Caribbean. Three hotels in minuscule capital of Basseterre charge too much to put this island in the rock bottom category. A government hotel project is planned. Meanwhile St. Kitts is for excursions only.

Nevis. Dramatic scenery, good beaches, two small but attractive hotels with moderate rates. Very British. Nelson slept here. Good place for escapists and honeymooners.

Antigua. Fast growing British tourist island with big hotel developments moving in. Island has cluster of extraordinary beaches and good resorts ranging from exclusive Mill Reef Club to medium-priced hotels with solid comfort. Good sanitary conditions. Historically interesting (Nelson's Dockyard), and a yachtmen's paradise with best charter facilities and repair services in Lesser Antilles. Ideal for family vacation, one of best spots in Caribbean for children.

Montserrat. An English island, inhabited by the Black Irish, which is to say Negroes who speak English with an Irish brogue. There's one inexpensive hotel, several boarding houses where you can get bed and board for as little as $3. Abundance of good fruit, food and drinking water. But every rose has its thorn; Montserrat's is malaria. Still, with caution and mosquito repellent, this is a grand place for complete escape and roughing it.

Guadeloupe. Big French island with superb scenery and pretty girls. One new hotel has opened and more are planned for the very near future. Wonderful French and creole food, especially at La Pergola. Good but undeveloped beaches. Sailing, fishing, mountain climbing, and good shopping for French merchandise.

Desirade. Former leper colony, now an extremely picturesque place for the hardy to explore.

Marie Galante. Interesting for Sunday excursion to see foulard and madras folk costumes, but the lone hotel probably won't tempt you to stay overnight.

Iles des Saintes. Extremely picturesque, a favorite week-end spot for Guadeloupiens. Very inexpensive. A good bet for escapists and the adventurous.

Dominica. For the adventurous. Accessible by air BWIA. Very rainy, full of grand, untamed scenery. Although British in tradition, the natives speak a French patois. A curiosity is the Carib reservation where a hundred or so pure-blooded Indians are all that remain of this vanishing race. There are few hotels, all inexpensive. But better make it a day's excursion.

Martinique. Another big French island with wonderful scenery and great "human interest" appeal. French atmosphere. Attractive women. Limited hotel accommodation. The two first-class establishments are expensive, but worth it. *Cuisine française.* Good but undeveloped beaches. Except for Lido hotel, not recommended for a family vacation. Atmosphere is more vivacious than restful. Interesting excursions (St. Pierre, Trois Islets, birthplace of Napoleon's Josephine). First rate shopping spot, especially for French perfumes, liqueurs, crystal and other luxury products of the mother country plus local rum.

St. Lucia. An ex-British isle with lovely scenery, a new 70-room hotel, other acceptable medium-priced hotels and guest houses, good beaches, excellent sailing, the yachtsmen's paradise, charter and repair facilities. A rewarding spot for a quiet, reasonable holiday.

St. Vincent. A delightful volcanic island, now in the "Little" West Indies, accessible by air from Grenada, St. Lucia, Dominica, Barbados, Fort de France, Port of Spain. Four excellent hotels, several simple ones with prices ranging from moderate to inexpensive. Wonderful center for sailing south to the Grenadines. Swimming and snorkeling also outstanding. Good for a family holiday, heaven for the aquatic sportsman.

The Grenadines. Designed by nature for yachtsman and snorkeler, especially among the incomparable islets called the Tobago Cays. Three of the islands have a hotel a piece, simple, even primitive, but with rock bottom rates, cheapest in the Caribbees. For escapists who can dispense with luxury, the Grenadines are perfect.

Grenada. In a popularity contest for most beautiful of all Caribbean islands, this candidate would probably win by a wide margin. A few hotels and guest houses, moderately priced. A new luxury hotel has just opened and is beginning to make a difference. Assets are scenery, swimming, fishing, and spear fishing. Recommended for a restful, holiday. Children are welcome.

Barbados. Best resort island in the Lesser Antilles, and the most British of all. Has three large beach resort areas, plenty of medium-sized and small hotels, residential clubs and guest houses with a big price range from expensive to cheap. Expanding at a fast pace. Bridgetown, the capital, is hot, Caribbean coast is just right, Atlantic coast is breezy and bracing. The East and South-West coasts are the least expensive. You can have an entertaining holiday here at the beach-front hotels or just settle down in guest house or apartment for a restful family vacation. Help is cheap. Shopping for British goods and British tailoring is satisfactory.

Trinidad. Exciting, febrile island, proud of its newly won independence. Absolute tops for human interest, mixture of races, calypso music and steel bands. Active social life, entertainment, outstanding Carnival. Only one ocean front hotel so far. Expensive. A Hilton hotel opened recently with two swimming pools, part of a new drive to stimulate tourism. Hot and humid in summer. Good shopping for British and East

Indian goods, but not cheap, except for duty-free in-bond shops, which are dependable.

Tobago. Trinidad's political ward and weekend resort. Lots of dancing and steel bands on weekends. Rest of the time it's a quiet relaxing place, good for fishing and snorkeling, ideal for children and quiet holidays. There's a famous bird sanctuary and undersea gardens. Hotels range from plain and comfortable to deluxe, prices from moderate to expensive.

British Guiana. Practically no tourism.

Surinam. An independent, associated partner of the Netherlands. First resort hotel now in operation. Top attraction is trip by Alcoa bauxite freighter up Commewijne or Cottica rivers into the heart of the jungle and through the Djuka country where Bush Negroes dance on the river banks in tribal rituals as old as Africa. Accommodations in Paramaribo are medium-priced. Cuisine is Dutch with East Indian additions. Except for jungle trips, Surinam is recommended for the ethnologist, or the jaded traveler who wants something different and not in the luxury category.

French Guiana. Tourism is a thing of the future, to begin shortly with the completion of the *Montabo,* first luxury-class hotel, just as Devil's Island is a thing of the past. There's much talk about both.

Venezuela. Independent, gradually stabilized, Spanish-speaking, oil rich, Indian-tinged republic. Ultra-luxurious hotels, restaurants, night clubs in bustling Caracas, the capital. Coastal resorts and offshore islands good for aquatic vacation. An expensive country, at one time the most expensive in the world. However, a magnificent chain of government hotels, heavily subsidized, are scattered throughout the country and special tours, also subsidized, make this visit an economical one.

Curaçao. This is the place where everybody comes to shop. The stores are loaded with merchandise from all over the world at free port bargain prices. Colonial Dutch atmosphere in Willemstad, perhaps the most picturesque port in the Caribbean. Cosmopolitan population, speaking Papiamento and Dutch, two official languages. Most important cruise stop for shopping. *Curaçao Intercontinental Hotel* is attracting longer-term clientele. There's a residential club and good business hotel. Rates are medium-priced to expensive. Second largest oil refinery in world accounts for Curaçao's solid spic-and-span prosperity, but they pay through the nose for it when the trade winds shift. Some good swimming and sailing, some night life tailored to Latin American tastes. But the shops and quaint Willemstad are the chief attractions.

Aruba. A twin brother of Curaçao, it has an even bigger refinery. One new de luxe hotel has helped to establish it as a resort island, several smaller ones, wonderful beach. Price range is expensive to moderate. Excellent place for a family holiday, scrubbed and spotless as a Dutch tile.

Bonaire. The second largest of the Dutch ABC group, an ideal inexpensive retreat for escapists and flamingo watchers. A new resort hotel just opening. Good for children too. Accent is on water sports and wholesome pleasures. But accommodations are limited at the moment, so reserve ahead if you want to comb the beaches in comfort.

Colombia. Beautiful Spanish-speaking country, the most intensely Spanish of South America, offers a holiday in three dimensions: (1) coastal resorts of Cartagena, Barranquilla, and Santa Marta; the first is the oldest and best-preserved Spanish town in South America, and all three cities have good resort facilities. (2) "Swiss mountain" holidays in and around Bogotá with opportunity for climbing in the rarefied air of the capital at 8,600 feet plus the attractions of a big modern city. (3) Jungle trips and big game hunting in the southeastern provinces. Vacation costs are moderate to inexpensive owing to favorable rate of exchange. There are excellent bargains in the shops in emeralds, native handicrafts, fashion and men's wear.

Panama. Independent Spanish-speaking republic, a good shopping center, a luxurious ultra-modern hotel. Prices are expensive to moderate. Excellent fishing on Caribbean side. Fascinating excursions to primitive Indian villages. Apt to be steamy and rainy. Don't bring the children. Check on conditions before booking. A new push to attract tourists is on. A new arrangement about the Canal may be in the making, too. We hope Uncle Sam's popularity will improve along with these moves.

WHEN TO GO?

The Caribbean "season" is a winter season extending generally from December 15 to April 15. Paradoxically, this season is at once the most fashionable the most expensive and the most popular time to cruise the Caribbean or laze on its golden beaches, far from winter's icy blast. Most hotels, especially the luxury resorts, are booked to capacity at this time, and you should make your reservations two or three months in advance. Hotel prices are generally at their highest at this period. These prices are indicated in the practical information under each individual country, along with the summer prices and occasional "between season" prices which obtain in a few resorts. Comparing winter hotel rates with those for the summer, sometimes from 20 to 40 per cent lower, will suggest the chief advantage of "off season" summer travel.

There are others. The flamboyant and other flowering trees are at the height of their glory in summer, and so are most of the flowers and shrubs of the West Indies. The water is clearer for snorkeling, smoother in May, June and July for sailing in the excellent cruising grounds of the Bahamas, the Virgins and the Windward Islands. In addition, you have a much wider choice of hotel accommodations and an atmosphere which is generally less "social", less dressy, more relaxed.

The Caribbean climate, air-conditioned by the trade winds, approaches the ideal of perpetual June. Average year round temperature for the region is from 78 to 83 degrees F. The extremes of temperature are 65 degrees low, 95 degrees high, the latter registered in Trinidad in July and August. Thus, if you are trying to escape summer heat, don't plan to do it in Trinidad, though it must be added that the heat is no worse than it is in New York. As every American knows, it isn't the heat, but the humidity that makes you suffer, especially when the two go hand in hand. Remembering that a humidity range of from 70 to 75 per cent is the most comfortable, here are a few yearly averages to guide you: Cuba 75, Haiti 63, Puerto Rico 76, Antigua 69, Montserrat 67, Martinique 81, Guadeloupe 82, Dominica 67, St. Lucia 78, Barbados, 67, Grenada 75, Trinidad 79, Coast of Venezuela 79. You can therefore anticipate mild discomfort in the French West Indies, Trinidad and Venezuela when this humidity rate is accompanied by higher temperatures, but you will not be caught in anything resembling the frightful summer heat waves of the temperate zone.

Most of the humidity readings are taken in the island capitals. Remember that most Caribbean islands are mountainous, and the altitude always offers an escape from the latitude. When it's 90 in the sun in Port-au-Prince, Haiti, it's a good ten degrees cooler on the heights of Kenscoff above the capital. Kingston, Jamaica, and Fort-de-France, Martinique are two cities which can swelter in summer, but climb a thousand feet or so and everything is fine.

What about such unpleasant things as rainy seasons and hurricanes. You don't have to worry about either. 'Urricanes do 'appen; everybody knows that, especially around Cuba, Haiti, Dominican Republic, the Bahamas and Guadeloupe. They sometimes sweep over the Windward Islands, but the warning service is now so highly developed that planes can change in mid-flight to avoid any disturbances, and everything can be battened down ashore. The rainy season, except on Dominica and Grand Cayman, consists mostly of brief showers interspersed with sunshine. You can dismiss this bugaboo from your mind in planning your trip.

There is one important exception to the general disposition of seasons among the countries covered in our guide. This is Bermuda, floating in its mid-Atlantic waters far from the Caribbean *hoi polloi*. In Bermuda, the fashionable season is April through August, with people flocking to this breezy paradise from the warmer climes of the U.S. and Canada. In the winter months Bermuda turns from a flower garden into a windswept, rainswept onion patch. Better go south.

Generally speaking, the bill of entertainment fare is more tempting in the winter months. The great climax of excitement on most islands, notably Trinidad, the U.S. Virgin Islands, French West Indies, the fabulous Caribbean, is Carnival. This traditionally precedes Ash Wednesday, and therefore occurs usually in February or late January. If gaiety is what you're looking for, then Carnival time is the time to come. The events indicated in the calendar below may help determine your plans. The *Caribbean Tourist Association* will provide you with a news letter each December, listing specific dates for events throughout the coming year.

CALENDAR OF EVENTS

JANUARY. Gay New Year's celebrations and parades on all islands and on Spanish Main; *Antigua:* Parade of Clowns and Steel Bands; *Aruba:* Public Audience at Governor's House, "Dandee" Roving musicians serenading private residences, Opening of Basketball season; *Barbados:* Traditional celebration, Steel Bands, Mummers, Open air concerts, Choir competition at Kensington, Yacht Races, Police Band concerts twice a week, Masked Costume Ball at Marine Hotel, Big Flower Show, Trooping the Colors at Garrison; *Curaçao:* Fireworks, dancing and music in the streets; *Haiti:* Independence Day, Official ceremonies and concerts; *St. Kitts, Nevis:* Masquerade Parade and Steel Bands; *Grenada:* Yacht Club

FACTS AT YOUR FINGERTIPS

Regatta, Horse Racing at Turf Club; *St. Lucia:* Excursions to neighboring islands, Dances at Club; *St. Vincent:* Steel Bands parade, Dances at private clubs, Discovery Day, Beach Picnics and dances; *Puerto Rico:* Holiday Season, Three King's Day, Parades, Open House at City Hall, Strolling singers. Patron Feast Day of San Sebastian, Daily Parades and Street Dancing; *Trinidad:* Horse Racing and Cricket at Queen's Park, Savannah; *British Guiana:* Horse Racing; *St. Croix:* Three King's Day Festivities; *Martinique:* Carnival and Parades; *Bonaire:* "Divine Enfant", Children's religious Flower Parade.

FEBRUARY. *Aruba:* Carnival, pre-elections, Costume Balls, Coronation of Carnival Queen; *Puerto Rico:* Feb. 2, *La Virgen de la Candelaria,* sugar harvest festival with lighting of bonfires; late Feb.-early March, season of Puerto Rico Symphony Orchestra, open-air concerts all over island. Carnival, Parades with Floats, Sailing Regattas; *Trinidad:* Calypso Tents open every night, Carnival; *Curaçao:* Carnival, Dancing and Parades; *Barbados:* West Indian Art Exhibition at Museum, Motor Boat Races, Water Skiing Competition, Steel Band Competition, Children's Carnival, Shrove Tuesday "Jump Up" parties, Valentine Ball, Kennel Club Show; *Martinique:* Carnival, Parades, Balls, Ash Wednesday, Funeral of King Carnival; *Dominica:* Samedi Gras Dance, Union Club, Carnival, Parades, "Running" in Streets; *Grenada:* "Jour Ouvert" Mask and Disguise Parties, Steel Band Parades, Carnival and Coronation of Queen; *Haiti:* Carnival, Parades, Costume Balls, Coronation of Queen; *St. Lucia:* Carnival, Selection and Crowning of Queen, Parades and Competitions, Prizes and Awards to Steel Band Competitors; *Netherlands Antilles & Surinam:* Carnivals Parade of Floats, Costume Balls; *St. Vincent:* Carnival, Competition of Steel Bands, Coronation of "Miss St. Vincent", Parades, Dances at Clubs and Hotels, Bamboo Melodians at Hotels; *Jamaica:* Ash Wednesday, Public Holiday; *St. Croix:* Annual Donkey Races by St. Choix Donkey Club; *St. Thomas:* Annual Open Golf Tournament.

MARCH. *Puerto Rico:* March through May, Puerto Rico Theatre Festival, featuring original Puerto Rican dramas and ballet performances in Old San Juan. Inter American Skeet Tournament at Club Metropolitano, Anniversary Celebrations of University of Puerto Rico, Open House, Exhibits and Conferences. Annual Invitational Tennis Tournament at Caribe Hilton Hotel, Celebration of Abolition of Slavery; *Tobago:* Horse racing at Shirvan Park, Goat races at Bucco Point; *Barbados:* Bi-weekly outdoor Police Band Concerts, Horse Racing at the Garrison Race Track; *Columbia:* St. Joseph's Day.

APRIL. *Aruba:* Opening of Soccer Season, Sports Car Races; *Barbados:* Children's Easter Costume Parade, Easter Monday, Kite flying competition at Garrison Savannah; *Guadeloupe:* Easter Sunday Soccer game between Martinique and Guadeloupe, classic sports event of the year; *Puerto Rico:* Opening of State Game Fishing Tournament, Jose de Diego's Anniversary, Holy Week, Pageants and Processions, Majestic Floral Monuments, Passion Play in San Juan, visitation to the Seven Churches on Holy Thursday. Orchid and Garden show; *Haiti:* Pan American Day Official Celebration and Concert; *St. Thomas:* Virgin Island Carnival, Parade of Floats, Steel Bands, Coronation of King and Queen, Competition Awards, Dances at Hotels, Yachting Regatta; *St. Croix:* Easter Monday Horse Racing; *Trinidad, Tobago and Grenada:* Celebration of Queen Elizabeth's Birthday, Dances, Concerts, Military Parade, Colonial and Honor Awards; *Netherlands Antilles & Surinam:* Celebration of Queen Juliana's Birthday, Dances, Sports

Events, Parades and Fireworks. *St. Kitts:* Good Friday kite flying competition. *Everywhere:* Easter Services and fashion parades.

MAY. *British Guiana:* Horse Racing; *Haiti:* Agricultural Fair, Flag and University Day, School Parades; *Martinique:* Celebration of birth of Jeanne d'Arc, Agricultural Fair; *St. Vincent:* Big Drum Dancing and Saraka in Grenadines; *Puerto Rico:* Armed Forces Day, Parades, Exhibits, Demonstrations, Air Maneuvers, Open House at Military Posts, Memorial Day, *British West Indies and Bermuda:* Empire Day, Public Holiday and Celebrations.

JUNE. *All over Latin America:* Celebration of Corpus Christi Religious Processions; *Puerto Rico:* Casals Festival featuring orchestra and chamber music from works of Schubert, Mozart and Bach. Famous featured soloists. Farm and Animal Fair, Dog Show, University of Puerto Rico Theatre, Patron Feast Day of San Juan Batista, tradition decrees spending night of June 23 on beach, Public parties and bonfires on beach, street dancers and concerts, Basketball Season opens; *Barbados:* Water Polo; *Aruba:* A.S.U. Olympiad (soccer, basketball, baseball, tennis, calisthenics and water sports), Election of best Sportsman of the year, St. John's Day, "Deri Gai", Folklore Ceremones; *Trinidad:* Mid-Summer Horse Racing at Queen's Park Savannah; *British West Indies and Bermuda:* Queen Elizabeth's Birthday, Ceremonial Parades and Honor Awards.

JULY. *Barbados:* Polo Season Opens; *Trinidad:* Soccer Season Opens, Caroni Bird Sanctuary Opens, Hosein-Moslem Festival, Religious Moslem 3-day Festival with Procession and Music; *Surinam:* Commemoration of Abolition of Slavery, Folk music and Parades; *Puerto Rico:* U.S. Independence Day, Sports car races at Ramey Air Base, Road and Drag races, Patron Saint Festival of Virgin del Carmen, Night-time ceremony of carrying Virgin on decorated barge to sea to assure good luck and welfare of fishermen, Patron Saint Festival of Santiago Apostol, Old traditional Ceremonies and Festival of 16th Century, Commonwealth Day Celebrations in *Loiza Aldea,* Parades and Parties, Speedboat races in Condado Lagoon; *St. Croix:* Horse Racing; *Guadeloupe and Martinique:* Bastille Day, Parades of Troops, Fireworks, Public Festivities, Schoelcher Holiday Honoring Abolition of Slavery. *St. John,* V.I.: 4th of July Festival.

AUGUST. *Barbados:* Horse Racing at Garrison Savannah; *Grenada:* Horse Racing at Turf Club; *St. Vincent:* Excursions to Grenadines and Falls at Balaine; *Surinam:* Kermesse d'Été (Fair), Native boat races, sports events, bazaars; *St. Thomas & St. Croix:* Yacht Club race to Tortola; *Trinidad & Tobago:* Discovery Day, Bicycle races and sports, Aug. 31, Independence Day; *Puerto Rico:* Anniversary of Don Juan Ponce de León (First Governor), "Paso Fino", Horse Races at Salinas, Santo Cristo de la Salud Festival, in Old San Juan. *Aruba.* Pilgrimage from Oranjestad to Alta Vista Chapel; *Colombia:* The 15th, Feast of the Assumption; *Guadeloupe:* Parish Feasts; *St. Lucia:* Fete La Rosa, First Christian Saint of New World Celebration; *Jamaica:* Aug. 6, Independence Day; *Antigua:* 1st Monday, Carnival Week, calypso, steel bands.

SEPTEMBER. *St. Lucia:* Opening of Hunting Season; *U.S. Virgin Island:* Labor Day, Horse Races; *Puerto Rico:* Patron Saint Festival of Lady of Montserrat, Dancing, Fireworks, Fairs, in Salinas Sailing, Regattas, Fishing competitions; *Jamaica:* Annual International Fishing Tourney at Port Antonio.

OCTOBER. *British Guiana:* Horse Racing Season; *Colombia:* Professional International Baseball Championship; *St. Lucia:* Harvest Church Festival;

Trinidad: Devali-Indian Festival; *Puerto Rico:* International Baseball Season Opens, Game Fishing Tournament Opens, Senior Golf Tournaments, Coffee Harvest Festival's "Queen of Coffee" election starts; *Haiti:* Dessaline's Death, Official Cermonies; *Tobago:* Autumn Horse Racing at Shirvan Park; *Everywhere in the Caribbean:* Columbus Day celebrations.

NOVEMBER. *Puerto Rico:* Discovery Day Honoring Christopher Columbus, Discovery of Puerto Rico Nov. 19, 1493; *Colombia, Guadeloupe, Haiti, Martinique, Puerto Rico, St. Vincent, Trinidad & Tobago:* All Saints Day, Illumination of Cemeteries with candles;*Barbados:* Horse Races at Garrison Savannah, Turf Club Horse Racing, Annual "Poppy" Dance at Marine Hotel; *Antigua:* Prince Charles' Birthday Celebration, "Dockyard" Day, Colorful "Beating of Retreat" by Police Band; *Jamaica:* Constitution Day; *Puerto Rico* and *U.S. Virgin Islands:* Thanksgiving Day; *Martinique* and *Guadeloupe:* Nov. 11, Armistice Day celebrations.

DECEMBER. *Barbados:* Annual Agricultural Exhibition; *Netherlands West Indies:* St. Nicholas Day, with St. Nick Parading through the streets on Dec. 5, Kingdom (Autonomy) Day, Celebrating end of colonial status Dec. 15; *Haiti:* Discovery Day with Official Ceremonies and Concerts Dec. 6; *Colombia:* Religious Celebration of "La Purissima Conception", Dec. 8; *Puerto Rico:* Dorado Beach Invitation Golf Tournament; Patron Saint festival of Our Lady of Guadeloupe in Ponce; Duck Season Opens Dec. 15-31; *St. Croix:* Coronation Ball, Horse racing and Costume and Lantern Parades, Steen Bands, jig and quadrille dancing competition from Dec. 23 to 31, Horse Racing; *Trinidad:* Horse Racing; *West Indies:* Boxing Day; *Everywhere:* Christmas Celebrations, Parades, Fireworks, Public trimming of community Christmas tree, Concerts, Carol singing, Fetes at all hotels, New Year Fiestas, Masquerade Balls.

HOW TO GO?

All the fishnets of the Caribbean combined could hardly equal the intricate web of air and sea routes spread out over the Caribbees. Few areas are better served, and almost every type of transportation is in the act from the modern jet planes and turbojets down to old sea scows that tramp between the islands. When you look at a transportation map of the Caribbean area, you might come to the conclusion that the sky and the seas would be black with planes and ships. But you'll hardly be conscious of planes at all, except at the airport as you arrive or leave. And the ships, even when they pass at the rate of 20 a day, as they do steaming into Willemstad Harbor, always look as though the tourist bureau had put them there as a finishing touch to the Caribbean scene. To help you plan your trip, we here list regularly-scheduled air and sea transportation along with a variety of cruise combinations by both plane and ship.

THE AIRWAYS

Most of the nuggets of the Caribbean's new golden age are air-borne. Air gateways to the region are New York, Miami,

Montreal, New Orleans (serviced by *Delta*), Houston (by *Braniff*), San Francisco, Los Angeles, Boston, Philadelphia and Baltimore. The air situation could not be more dynamic than it is.

Pan American is flying its Boeing 707's, 721's and Douglas DC-8's (all jets) from New York to Caracas, Bermuda, Trinidad, Puerto Rico, the Dominican Republic, Jamaica, the Virgin Islands, the French West Indies, Barbados, Curaçao, Panama, out through both the Leeward and Windward Islands, the Guianas and Nassau. *BOAC* is employing mainly 707's and Britannia Turbojets on its Caribbean runs. When you get to the planning stage of your trip with a travel agent, check on the types of plane available, and see that you get the most comfort for your money.

Types in current use on inter-island Caribbean runs include pressurized four-engine Super Sevens (DC 7B's and DC 7C's), Super Sixes (DC 6B's), the British Viscount (Turbo-jets with minimal vibration), Constellations and Super-Constellations. These are the most luxurious planes in general service at the moment. Also in service are the non-pressurized four-engine DC-4's, work horse of World War II, not recommended if you have a heart condition or susceptibility to mountain sickness; modern, two-engine pressurized Convairs (240 and 340) and the two-engine non-pressurized DC 3's and C-46's.

Cutting Costs. Fares are constructed to give you a small sliding discount according to the length of your trip. Therefore it will pay you to purchase your ticket initially to the most distant point you plan to visit. *Do not buy your transportation piecemeal.* Do take advantage of the 10 per cent discount on round trip. And check very carefully with your agent about stop-over privileges so that you can see the most for your money. See separate information on stop-over privileges.

Off-season Fares to the Caribbean are generally in effect from April 15 to December 15. Excursion fares exist to numerous points, and island-hopping possibilities increase all the time. Here, for ready reference, are lists of standard fares, excursion rates, and island-hopping prices in U.S. Dollars.

FACTS AT YOUR FINGERTIPS

STANDARD PROPELLER FARES (*Courtesy of Pan American Airways*)

From	To	First Class OW	First Class RT	Economy Class OW	Economy Class RT
New York	Barbados	214.00	385.00	141.00	270.00
,,	Barranquilla	211.00	395.00	142.00	265.00
,,	Bermuda	80.00	144.00	58.00	105.00
,,	Bogota	249.00	464.00	157.00	294.00
,,	Caracas	226.00	407.00	160.00	302.00
,,	Santo Domingo	140.00	252.00	91.30	178.60
,,	Curaçao	202.00	364.00	139.00	264.00
,,	Havana	109.00	213.00	83.70	162.40
,,	Jamaica	161.00	297.00	106.00	205.00
,,	Maracaibo	213.00	399.00	160.00	302.00
,,	Nassau	115.00	223.00	78.70	153.00
,,	Panama	211.00	395.00	142.00	265.00
,,	Port au Prince	161.00	297.00	106.00	205.00
,,	Port of Spain	226.00	407.00	158.00	289.00
,,	St. Croix	124.65	224.75	84.05	165.35
,,	San Juan	108.65	195.75	70.30	140.60
Miami	Barbados	174.00	314.00	123.90	232.70
,,	Bogota	165.00	296.00	100.00	180.00
,,	Caracas	179.00	323.00	133.00	240.00
,,	Santo Domingo	96.00	173.00	61.00	110.00
,,	Curaçao	159.00	287.00	110.00	198.00
,,	Havana	25.00	45.00		
,,	Jamaica	76.00	137.00	56.00	107.00
,,	Nassau	25.00	45.00	20.00	36.00
,,	Panama	127.00	227.00	85.00	151.00
,,	San Juan, P.R.	70.30	126.75	47.85	95.70
Montreal & Toronto	Barbados	231.00	409.00	153.00	294.00
,,	Bermuda	99.00	183.00	66.00	132.00
,,	Trinidad	243.00	431.00	170.00	313.00
,,	Curaçao	231.00	422.00	159.00	297.00
,,	Nassau	126.00	247.00	91.00	177.00
Toronto	Nassau	116.00	227.00	79.00	153.00

Approximate Jet Surcharges:

New York	Nassau	$10	New York	Barbados, Trini-	
New York	Montego Bay	$10		dad or Caracas	$15
New York	Bermuda	$10	New York	San Juan, P.R.	$8
			Miami	San Juan, P.R.	$5

Rock Bottom Note: Three major airlines, *Trans-Caribbean, Eastern,* and *Pan American* have reduced their New York-Puerto Rico fare to $57.75 one way, $115.50 round trip; on thrift jet flights daily. PAA also has thrift jet flights Miami-San Juan at $43.95 one way, $87.90 round trip.

EXCURSION FARES (*Courtesy Pan American Airways*)

New York-Puerto Rico-Dominican Republic-Haiti-Jamaica-Miami-New York, 30 day excursion, available all year in both directions and from any point en route: $239 first class; regular economy fare $205.00.

31

New York-Santo Domingo, 30-day excursion, available all year round in both directions: $140 economy class.

New York-Jamaica-New York, 30 day excursion, available from April 15 to December 15 in both directions: $210 first class; excursion at $129, $186 economy class.

New York-Nassau-New York, 30 day excursion, available April 15 to December 15 in both directions: $170 first class; $131 economy class.

New York-Jamaica-New York, 17 day excursion, available April 15 to December 15 in both directions: $162 economy class.

Miami-Jamaica-Miami, excursion, available April 15 to December 15 in both directions: $69 (17-day) economy class, $92 (30-day) first class.

New York-Jamaica-Colombia-Panama-Miami-Nassau-New York, 45 day excursion, available all year in both directions. An economy class ticket is only $260.

New York-Jamaica-Barranquilla-Cartegena-Medellin-Cali-Bogota 45-day excursion $269.

Montreal-Nassau-Kingston, Jam. 30-day excursion available from April 15 to December 15: $213 tourist class.

Montreal-Toronto-Antigua-Barbados-Trinidad-Tobago-Nassau-Jamaica 30-day excursion available from April 15 to December 15: $293 economy class.

New York-Bermuda 8-day excursion $85 (Oct. 31-Dec. 18 and Dec. 30-March 1).

New York-Bermuda-Nassau-Miami 30-day excursion $170 first class (Apr. 15-Dec. 15).

These are typical of attractive excursion rates offered by major Caribbean carriers. New excursion fares are announced frequently. In connection with its new Miami-Jamaica route, Panama Airways is offering: Miami-Kingston-Panama-Miami; Caribbean Triangle 30-day excursion: $112.50. Check latest information on excursion rates with your travel agent before booking.

ALL ABOUT STOP-OVERS

by DAVID GOLLAN

(The writer is Executive Editor of two North American travel industry publications, The Travel Agent *and* Interline Reporter. *His background includes extensive experience in airline rates and tariffs.)*

If you're flying to the Caribbean always ask the airline of your travel agent to outline all the possible stopovers covered by the fare he charges you.

You'll be pleasantly surprised at the way a straight round-trip can be broadened in scope at little or no additional fare into a very comprehensive island-hopping circle trip.

FACTS AT YOUR FINGERTIPS

Your destination will determine the variety of stopovers available but the examples we're going to discuss will give you an idea of what lies in store.

Take a roundtrip ticket from New York to Curaçao in the Netherlands Antilles. It's entirely possible to fly nonstop both ways; however, if you wish to sample a wider variety of attractions, it's easy to arrange numerous stopovers en route without paying a penny more.

For instance, you can fly first to San Juan. After a stopover at Puerto Rico, you can continue to Santo Domingo, Dominican Republic and Port-au-Prince, Haiti. The Haitian city has long been a shopping favorite for cruise passengers sailing and winging around the Caribbean.

Leaving Haiti for Curaçao, the next stop is Kingston, Jamaica. Air service between these islands is frequent; reservations well in advance are suggested however.

Between Kingston and Curaçao, yet another en route stop is in order. This is at Aruba, the increasingly popular resort island with long stretches of beach and modern hotel accommodations.

Then follows the short hop from Aruba to Curaçao, the turning point on the itinerary.

What about alternate routings between New York and Curaçao? It is possible to fly first to Miami thus adding Florida as a stopover on the Curaçao itinerary. Then you may continue via Grand Cayman island and Montego Bay to Kingston where the first routing is picked up to Aruba and Curaçao.

Any or all of the intermediate stopovers can be omitted, of course. It is entirely up to you. You purchase a ticket to one destination and add whichever en route stops you prefer from the selection available.

Miami also can be added to itineraries which include Puerto Rico. You may fly first to the Florida city, then wing across to Puerto Rico and continue around the islands mentioned earlier until arrival at Curaçao.

How about circle trip possibilities on your New York/Curaçao ticket? By combining the two routings outlined you can come up with this itinerary: New York, San Juan, Santo Domingo, Port-au-Prince, Kingston, Aruba, Curaçao, Kingston, Montego Bay, Grand Cayman, Miami and New York. All this for the roundtrip ticket plus a few dollars federal tax on the Miami/New York domestic flight.

The example we've just outlined doesn't exhaust all the stopover possibilities between New York and Curaçao but space prevents us from doing so. Ask your travel agent to go into it in more detail.

If you purchase a roundtrip ticket from New York to Kingston or Montego Bay, you can cover most of the ground traveled by Curaçao passengers between New York and Jamaica. The stopovers are basically the same.

One of the most popular circle trips enables the island-hopper to travel from New York via Bermuda to Antigua and then wing West to San Juan, Kingston and Montego Bay. Homeward bound, Nassau may be added to the itinerary. Surprisingly, the extra fare runs around $10. To appreciate the scope of this trip, pinpoint New York and Antigua on the map. Then move across to Jamaica. Look how far off your direct route Jamaica is. Yet, you are entitled to all this additional mileage for only a few extra dollars.

Here is a tip from a veteran traveler who has been burned himself for not following the simple rule. Always reconfirm your onward or return reservations. This is especially important in some of the smaller Caribbean islands because service is not always frequent and the seating capacities of the aircraft are small.

Failure to reconfirm can result in your entire itinerary being wrecked while you try and secure space on the next plane and attempt to change your hotel bookings at the height of the season. When you arrive at a new island, reconfirm at once. And just to be on the safe side, visit the airport or city ticket office the day prior to your departure. Reservations have a habit of going astray in the Caribbean.

How about stopovers on a New York/Port of Spain ticket? Here are just a few of the bonus routings available. Leaving New York it is possible to fly via Bermuda to Antigua then continue to Barbados. Next comes the short flight to Port of Spain, Trinidad's bustling capital.

However, alternate routings exist between Antigua and Trinidad which enable the visitor to sample some of the smaller islands.

Dominica and St. Vincent both can be added or you may travel via Martinique, St. Lucia and Grenada. It also is possible to fly from New York to San Juan and stop at St. Croix before reaching Antigua. The fare is exactly the same although you broaden the itinerary considerably. Another interesting stopover which may be added on certain Antigua/Barbados routings is Guadeloupe.

Passengers purchasing a New York/Port of Spain ticket have

perhaps the widest scope in planning their itineraries. The routings described earlier between New York and Curaçao may be incorporated. The passenger merely continues from Curaçao to Port of Spain. On some tickets an intermediate stop at Caracas, Venezuela is in order, thus enabling you to add South America to your itinerary.

The circle trip possibilities are limitless on a ticket to Trinidad. Let's explore just one possibility. Leaving New York the passenger can fly to Miami, Grand Cayman, Montego Bay, Kingston, Aruba, Curaçao, Caracas and Port of Spain. Homeward bound, he can visit St. Vincent, Barbados, Dominica, Antigua and Bermuda. Note: some excursion fares don't include Caracas as a stopover.

These bonus stopovers are not just confined to tickets from New York. If you're traveling from Chicago, Miami, the West Coast and other areas of the United States or Canada, check locally for the permissable routings from your hometown.

And here's another tip which you might find profitable to keep in mind. If you're visiting one Caribbean island and decide to visit another area not on your original itinerary, don't buy new tickets without first having the airline check your existing coupons.

Often, the fare you paid initially will cover your changes in itinerary.

ISLAND-HOPPING

Here are some sample island-hopping fares, provided through courtesy of *British West Indian Airways*. These will give you an idea of how you can see more without paying more. In other words, extra islands at no extra price. There are scores of other possibilities. Write to *B.W.I.A.*, 20 McAllister Hotel Arcade, Miami 32, Florida, or *Caribbean Tourist Association*, 20 East 46 Street, New York. Fares below are tourist class.

FROM MIAMI
(Returning direct or via same islands)

Grand Cayman, Miami $59, 17-day excursion, April 15-Dec. 15. Regular all-year fare $89.70

Grand Cayman, Montego Bay, Kingston, Miami $69, 17-day excursion, April 15-Dec. 15. Regular all-year fare $107.00

Grand Cayman, Montego Bay, Kingston, San Juan, St. Thomas, St. Kitts, Antigua, Miami. Regular all- year fare $163.70

Montego Bay, Kingston, San Juan, St. Thomas, St. Kitts, Antigua, Martinique, St. Lucia, Barbados, Miami $184, 30-day excursion, April 15-Dec. 15. Regular all-year fare $232.70

Montego Bay, Kingston, San Juan, St. Thomas, St. Kitts, Antigua, Martinique, St. Lucia, Barbados, Grenada, Port-of-Spain, Tobago, Miami $204, 30-day excursion, April 15-Dec. 15. Regular all-year fare $240.00

FACTS AT YOUR FINGERTIPS

FROM NEW YORK

(Returning direct or via same islands)

Nassau, Montego Bay, Kingston, New York $207.40

Bermuda, San Juan, St. Thomas, St. Kitts, Antigua, New York $208.60

Bermuda, San Juan, St. Thomas, St. Kitts, Antigua, Martinique, St. Lucia, Barbados, Grenada, New York $270.00
30 day excursion April 15-Dec. 15.

Bermuda, San Juan, St. Thomas, St. Kitts, Antigua, Martinique, St. Lucia, Barbados, Grenada, Port-of-Spain, Tobago, New York $289.20
30 day excursion April 15-Dec. 15. tourist $248.00

FROM NEW YORK
(Circle Trips)

Bermuda, San Juan, St. Thomas, St. Kitts, Antigua, Kingston, Montego Bay, Nassau, New York $218.60

New York, Jamaica, San Juan, St. Thomas, St. Kitts, Antigua, Martinique, St. Lucia, Grenada, Trinidad, Tobago, Barbados, Dominica, Bermuda, New York 30-day excursion Apr. 15-Dec. 15 $258.00

Nassau, Montego Bay, Kingston, New York $182*, 17-day excursion, April 15-Dec. 15. Regular all-year fare $225.00*

Antigua, Guadeloupe, Dominica, Martinique, St. Lucia, Barbados, New York $226, 30-day excursion, April 15-Dec. 15. Regular all-year fare $270.00

Antigua, Guadeloupe, Dominica, Martinique, St. Lucia, Barbados, St. Vincent, Grenada, Trinidad, Tobago, New York $248, 30-day excursion, April 15-Dec. 15. Regular all-year fare $289.00

Bermuda, Antigua, St. Kitts, St. Thomas, San Juan, Kingston, Montego Bay, Nassau, New York. Reular all-year fare $218.60**

Bermuda, Antigua, Barbados, Port-of-Spain, Tobago, Grenada, St. Vincent, St. Lucia, Martinique, Dominica, Guadeloupe, St. Kitts, St. Thomas, San Juan, Kingston, Montego Bay, Nassau, New York $258**, 30-day excursion, April 15-Dec. 15. Regular all-year fare $299.00**

* Jet Economy Class.

** Jet-prop Economy Class incl. $10.00 for Jet Service Jamaica-New York.

LIST OF AIR CARRIERS SERVING THE CARIBBEAN AREA
AIRLINES OF MAJOR IMPORTANCE FOR THE REGION

Air France
683 Fifth Avenue,
New York 22, NY.
1020 Rue Ste. Catherine Ouest,
Montreal, Quebec.
Bord de Mer,
Fort de France,
Martinique.
Calle Trocadero 59,
Havana, Cuba.
Grand Hotel,
Pointe a Pitre,
Guadeloupe.
Boite Postale No. 1161
Dante Destouches,
Port au Prince, Haiti.
Hotel La Rada,
San Juan, Puerto Rico.

St. Martin-Guadeloupe (DC-4s).
Guadeloupe - Martinique - Barbados - Puerto Rico - Trinidad - Br. Guiana - Surinam - Cayenne (Fr. Guiana) (DC-4s).
Paris - Lisbon - Santa Maria - Point a Pitre - Caracas - Bogota - Lima (Boeing 707 Jets).

JOIN THE

BOAC Escape Club

TO THE CARIBBEAN

Daily get-aways to Bermuda, Nassau and the Bahamas, and Jamaica

Escape from the humdrum, in BOAC comfort. BOAC Cabin Service is deservedly world-famous. Quite rare. Traditionally British. And ever so relaxing.

Ask your Travel Agent about BOAC's many low-cost tours. Or call BOAC.

ALL OVER THE WORLD

B·O·A·C

TAKES GOOD CARE OF YOU

BRITISH OVERSEAS AIRWAYS CORPORATION
Offices in all principal cities

SOLD AND SERVICED IN 111 COUNTRIES

. . . and you can swim with it, too!

Dinner clothes or diving gear . . . it makes no difference to the Mido Ocean Star. It takes to water like a marlin, adds its own note of elegance to the most elegant surroundings. Mido has developed a revolutionary one-piece case, which makes Ocean Star 100 % water-proof and gives it the slim silhouette your fashion sense demands. Self-winding. Shock-resistant. Unbreakable mainspring.

Mido Watch Company, Bienne, Switzerland.
Mido Watch Company of America, Inc., 580 Fifth Avenue, New York 36, N. Y.

Available in stainless steel,
Midoluxe and 18 ct gold

THE WATCH YOU <u>NEVER</u> HAVE TO WIND

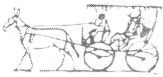

Avianca
6 West 49 Street,
New York 20, N.Y.

N.Y. - Miami - Jamaica - Baranquilla - Bogota - Quito - Lima (720-B's).
Frankfurt - Paris - Madrid - Lisbon - San Juan - Baranquilla - Bogota (720-B's).
Bogota (720-B's).
Miami - Bogota (720-B's).

BOAC
Airways Terminal,
Buckingham Palace
Road, London S.W.1,
England.
530 Fifth Avenue,
New York 36, N.Y.
Place Ville Marie,
Montreal 2, Canada.

London - Bermuda - Barbados - Trinidad - Caracas (Britannias).
N.Y. - Nassau - Montego Bay - Kingston (Rolls Royce 707).
N.Y. - Bermuda (Britannias, Rolls Royce 707).
London - Bermuda - Trinidad - Caracas - Bogota (Britannias).
Miami - Montego Bay (Viscounts).
Montreal - Jamaica (Britannias, Rolls Royce 707).

BWIA
530 Fifth Avenue,
New York 36, N.Y.

London - New York - Antigua - Barbados - Trinidad.
Antigua - Barbados - Trinidad.
Miami - Grand Cayman - Jamaica - San Juan - Antigua - Barbados - Trinidad.
Belize - B. H. - Jamaica.
San Juan - St. Thomas - St. Kitts - Antigua - Dominica - Martinique - Guadeloupe - St. Lucia - Barbados - St. Vincent - Grenada - Trinidad.
Barbados - Grenada - Trinidad - Georgetown - B.G.
Trinidad - Tobago.
(Boeing 707, Britannias, Viscounts, Dakotas, Herons).

Cunard Eagle Airways
15 Lower Regent
Street, London S.W.1.
441 Park Avenue,
New York, N.Y.
Queen Elizabeth
Hotel,
Montreal, Quebec.
12 McAllister Arcade
Miami, Florida.

New York - Bermuda (Viscounts).
Miami - Nassau (Viscounts).
Bermuda - Nassau (Viscounts).
Miami - Nassau - Bermuda - London (707's)
Montego Bay - Kingston - London, via Nassau and Bermuda (707's).

Eastern Air Lines
10, Rockefeller Plaza,
New York 20, N.Y.
1409 Peel Street,
Montreal, Quebec

N.Y. - Washington - Bermuda (DC-7Bs and Super Constellations).
N.Y. - Puerto Rico (Jet Electras, DC-8Bs and DC-7B air-coaches).
N.Y. - Bermuda (DC-8's).

KLM Royal Dutch Airlines
609 Fifth Avenue,
New York 17, N.Y.
International Aviation Building,
Montreal, Quebec.

New York - Curaçao - Caracas (Convair 880 jet, 3 days a week each direction) (Connecting flight to Aruba).
Miami - Kingston - Aruba (DC-6s, 3 days a week each direction, with connection to Curaçao).
Miami - Havana - Kingston - Aruba - Curaçao (DC-6s - twice a week in each dir.).
Curaçao - Aruba (Convairs, DC-6s - several flights per day).

Curaçao - Caracas (Convair 880 jets, DC-6 - four times a week).

Curaçao - Bonaire (Convair - daily flights).

Curaçao - Barranquilla (Convair - twice a week).

Curaçao - Maracaibo (DC-6s - twice a week).

Aruba - Maracaibo (DC-6s - twice a week).

Curaçao - St. Maarten - St. Kitts (Convairs - twice a week).

Curaçao - Caracas - Paramaribo (DC-8 jet - once a week).

Curaçao - Port of Spain (Trinidad) - Georgetown (British Guiana) - Paramaribo (Surinam) (DC-6s - three times a week).

Amsterdam - Frankfurt - Zurich - Madrid - Lisbon - Paramaribo - Caracas - Curaçao - Panama City - Guayaquil - Lima (DC-8 jets) (twice a week between Amsterdam and Curaçao; once a week Curaçao/Lima).

Pan American
135 East 42nd Street,
New York 17, N.Y.
1450 City Councillors Street,
Montreal, Quebec.

New York or Boston - Bermuda (Jet).

New York or Boston or Baltimore/Washington or Philadelphia - San Juan (Jet).

New York - Port of Spain (non-stop) (Jet).

Miami - Caracas (non-stop) (Jet).

New York - Caracas (non-stop) (Jet).

New York - Santo Domingo (non-stop) (Jet).

New York - Curaçao - Panama City (Jet).

New York - Antigua (non-stop) - Point-à-Pitre - Barbados - Port of Spain - Georgetown - Paramaribo (Jet).

Miami - Montego Bay - Kingston - Baranquilla - Panama City (DC-6Bs).

New York - Montego Bay (non-stop) (Jet).

Miami - Montego Bay - Kingston - Port-au-Prince - Santo Domingo - San Juan - St. Croix - Antigua - Fort de France (Jet/Piston).

Miami - San Juan (non-stop) (Jet).

Miami - San Juan - Curaçao - Caracas - Port of Spain (Jet).

New York or Miami - San Juan - Caracas - St. Croix - Antigua - Point-à-Pitre - Barbados - Port of Spain (Jet).

Miami - Curaçao - Caracas - Port of Spain (Jet).

San Francisco or Los Angeles or Miami - Panama (Jet) - Baranquilla - Maracaibo - Caracas - Port of Spain - Georgetown - Paramaribo - Cayenne (DC-6Bs).

San Francisco or Los Angeles - Panama (Jet).

Houston or New Orleans - Panama (Jet).

Miami - Havana (Piston).

Miami - Nassau (Piston).

The "El Interamericano" to South America, serviced by Panagra, flies through the Caribbean starting from New York, Washington and Miami by way of Panama and Cali (Colombia).

FACTS AT YOUR FINGERTIPS

TCA (Canadian)
730 Fifth Avenue,
New York, N.Y.
Place Ville Marie
Montreal 2, Quebec

Toronto - Tampa - Nassau - Montego Bay - Kingston.
Toronto - Bermuda - Antigua - Barbados - Trinidad.
Montreal - Bermuda - Barbados - Trinidad - Antigua (DC-8's all flights).

LINES OF REGIONAL IMPORTANCE

Bahamas Airways
Bay Street,
Nassau, Bahamas.

Miami - Nassau (Viscounts).
Fort Lauderdale/West Palm Beach - Out Islands (DC-3, Grumman Goose).

Caribair (Caribbean Atlantic Airlines)
Loiza Street Station,
San Juan, P.R.

San Juan - Santo Domingo (DC-3's).
San Juan - St. Thomas.
San Juan - St. Croix (DC-3's, Convairs), regular daily shuttle service on these two routes.
St. Thomas - St. Croix - St. Martin - Guadeloupe (DC-3's).

CDA Dominican Airlines
P.O. Box 59-2137,
Miami Int'l Airport
Miami 58, Florida.

Santo Domingo - San Juan.
Santo Domingo - Miami.

COHATA (Haiti)
Bowen Field,
Port-au-Prince, Haiti.

Local runs only out of Port-Au-Prince: Cap Haitien, Jacmel, Cayes, Jeremie, Hinche, Gonaives.

Guest (Mexican)
Paseo de la Reforma
51, Mexico City.

Mexico City - Havana - Mexico City (Britannias).
Montego Bay - Havana - Montego Bay (Viscounts).
Mexico City - Miami - Bermuda - Santa Maria (Açores) - Lisbon - Madrid - Paris (DC-6s).
Mexico City - Panama City - Caracas (Lockheed Constellations).

Iberia
Avenida America 2,
Madrid, Spain.
518 Fifth Avenue,
New York 36, N.Y.

Madrid - Santa Maria - San Juan - Caracas - Bogota (DC-8s).

LACSA (Costa Rican)
P.O. Box 1531,
San Jose, Costa Rica.
238 Biscayne Blvd.,
Miami, Florida.

Panama City - Grand Cayman - Miami (Convair 340s, DC-6's).

LIAT (Leeward Islands Air Transport)
Plymouth, Montserrat, BWI.
St. Mary's Street,
St. John's, Antigua,
BWI.

Antigua - Dominica - St. Lucia - St. Vincent - (D. H. Herons).
Antigua - Barbuda (Bonanza).
Antigua - Montserrat - St. Kitts - St. Martin - Anguilla - St. Thomas.
Antigua - Montserrat.
St. Kitts - Nevis.
St. Kitts - St. Eustatius.

Mackey Airlines
Broward County International Airport,
Fort Lauderdale,
Florida.

Florida - Bahamas Out Islands - Nassau - Havana (DC-4s and DC-3s).

St. Vincent Govt. Air Service
c/o John H. Hazell Sons & Co. Ltd.,
Kingston, St. Vincent.

St. Vincent - Trinidad.
St. Vincent - Barbados - Dominica (Grumman Goose).

TACA
Moisant International Airport,
New Orleans, La.
Edificio Taca, Tegucigalpa, D.C., Honduras.

New Orleans - Panama City (Vickers Viscounts).

Trans Caribbean Airways
375, Park Ave.,
N.Y. 22.

New York - San Juan (P.R.) - Aruba, (N.W.I.) (DC-6Bs and DC-8's).

Transcontinental (Argentinean)
International Airport
Miami, Florida.
Cerrito 1117,
Buenos Aires.

South America - Caracas - New York (Britannias).

TAN (Honduras)
Edificio Salame,
Tegucigalpa D.C.,
Honduras.

Miami - Central America - South America, by way of Panama - Bogota (DC-6s).

Varig (Brazilian)
634 Fifth Avenue,
New York, N.Y.
P.O. Box 243,
Porto Alegre.

New York - Santo Domingo - Port-of-Spain.
Miami - Santo Domingo - Caracas - Port-of-Spain (pure jet Caravelles on all routes).

VIASA (Venezuelan)
1271 Avenue of the Americas,
New York, N.Y.
160 S.E. Third Avenue,
Miami, Florida.
Edificio Auto Comercial,
La Plaza Altamira,
Caracas.

Miami - Caracas (Convair 880-M's).
New Orleans - Caracas (Convair 880-M's).
Caracas - Curaçao (DC-8's).

FACTS AT YOUR FINGERTIPS

AIR CRUISES

There are hundreds of these aerial package deals, sponsored by nearly all the airlines that serve the Caribbean area. Air cruises have many advantages. They are economical (far less expensive than the more leisurely cruises by ship). They reduce travel time to a minimum, allowing you precious extra hours for sightseeing and enjoying the tropics, even if you're on a short vacation. They are package deals which include hotel reservations in de luxe or first class hotels so that you are assured of the reservations and can budget your trip more easily. In addition they provide you with companionship, which you can take or leave, but this is usually an advantage for people who are traveling alone. An important added economy is the saving in taxi fares between airports and resort destinations. We know from experience that these expenses can become a major item in your travel budget. These jitney fares are included in the all-over price of your air cruise.

Your tour rates normally include all airport transfers and sightseeing, all charges for planning and operational expenses, standard "run-of-the-house" hotel accommodations, or superior accommodations on a more luxurious cruise, and all meals. Usually not included in the rates are airline transportation, tips, laundry, wines, liquors, mineral waters and other restaurant extras, passports, landing and tourist cards and personal expenses. Your airline will arrange to procure the necessary tourist cards for you, however. Before you tip at the hotel, check to see if the service charge has already been added to your bill.

Nearly all the major air carriers and all travel agents who serve the Caribbean cooperate in weaving the air cruise web. Here are a few typical possibilities, culled from hundreds, just to give you an idea of the repertory.

AMERICAN AIRLINES combines with Pan American to offer attractive package deals from Chicago, San Francisco, St. Louis, Philadelphia, Washington, Miami and New York to Antigua, Barbados, Guadeloupe, Haiti, Jamaica, Nassau, Puerto Rico, Trinidad and the Virgin Islands. A two-week "Holiday on Wings", including five nights on Haiti, four on Puerto Rico (at the famed *Dorado Beach Hotel*), would cost $575.14 from Chicago (for each of two people travelling together). From New York, the cost would be $479. A week in Bermuda can be as little as $53.25, plus air fare.

AMERICAN EXPRESS has many air cruises including 14-day tours from Miami or New York, hopping to almost any group of islands you can name. Sample jaunt could include Barbados, Trinidad, Tobago, Grenada and Antigua; sample price would be $451 for a single during the "off-season",

FACTS AT YOUR FINGERTIPS

including air transportation by BWIA. Or you can juggle the islands around any way you wish: four days and three nights on St. Croix, at *Estate Good Hope,* would cost 82.50 for a single; add another four days at *Caneel Bay Plantation* on St. John ($66.00), and you come out with a week in the sun for $148.50, plus air fare.

AVIANCA's 720-B jets and Super Constellations service Jamaica and Colombia thrice weekly from New York and Miami. Features in Jamaica are 6-night/7-day package tours—hotels with Modified American Plan—for as low as $88 in Montego Bay; $102 in Ocho Rios. Air transportation not included, but transfers to and from the airport and hotel are. In Colombia, a 14-day tour of five cities — Bogota, Cali, Medellin, Cartagena and Barranquilla—will cost $233 for each of two travelling together. This price is based on hotels using European Plan. Round trip air fare from New York to Bogota is $305.90 economy class. From Miami it drops to $180.

BRITISH WEST INDIAN AIRWAYS covers the best of the West Indies in its *Caribbean Carrousel.* Air cruises range from a 10-day Jamaican rest cure to a 22-day circuit that includes Puerto Rico, Trinidad, Tobago, Barbados, and Martinique. Minimum cost of the 22-day trip is $403 (April 16 to December 14), $510 during the winter season. Air transportation must be added to these figures: $204 from Miami, $246 from New York (April 16 to December 14).

THOS COOK & SON, oldest of world-wide travel agencies, offers many itineraries. One of the most interesting is a two-week air cruise from New York or Miami to Puerto Rico, Trinidad, Tobago, Barbados and Antigua. Minimum land costs is $185. For total cost add air fares from New York or Miami: $278 economy class from the former; $260 from the latter, round trip.

DELTA AIRLINES, one of the most imaginative operators in the Caribbean area, has a number of cruises of more than usual interest. Among the most popular, especially with women, is the *Delta Dream Vacation,* not a conducted tour, but a special cruise in which ground transfer service, hotel accommodations, sightseeing trips and even nightclub visits are provided for with a handy book of coupons. Delta's equipment is all jets. Write to Tour Department, Delta Air Lines, Atlanta Airport, Atlanta, Georgia for brochures and advice on Delta's package tours.

CUNARD EAGLE AIRWAYS specialize in Bermuda holidays, putting its clients up in state at the popular Princess Hotel. Eight days and seven nights of holiday here will cost you only $166 including the air transportation from New York. Smooth-riding, prop-jet Super Viscounts are the planes you'll fly on. Special rates and programs for honeymooners. Here's your chance if you've been thinking of taking the plunge.

EASTERN AIRLINES has many "Mix and Match" tours to the Caribbean, Bahamas and Bermuda. A good bet is the 14-day Caribbean Island Hopping Air Cruise to Jamaica, Haiti, the Virgin Islands and Puerto Rico, staying at luxury hotels for a cost of $384 per person, on the basis of double occupancy. Eastern also offers bargain transportation New York - Puerto Rico, as low as $99.50 round trip.

EMBASSY TOURS INC. in conjunction with BOAC offer holidays in Nassau, Bermuda and Jamaica at irresistible prices. Seven days and six nights in the Bahamas, for example, can cost as little as $73. Add $129 round trip economy fare from New York; $232 first class.

ONLY THE SUN COVERS THE CARIBBEAN BETTER THAN PAN AM

There's no reason under the warm sun why you can't see *all* of the Caribbean on your holiday. Pan Am serves more islands than any other airline — and by choosing your Pan Am Jet route closely, you can often see many of them at no extra fare!

Puerto Rico, St. Croix, Antigua, Guadeloupe, Martinique, Barbados, Dominican Republic, Haiti, Jamaica and Nassau — these are just some of the wonderful islands you can visit on Pan Am.

With Pan American, you also enjoy the Priceless Extra of Experience.

Choose first-class *President Special* or low-fare *Rainbow* Economy service on every flight. For reservations, call your Travel Agent or Pan Am.

Enjoy the Priceless Extra of Experience on the World's Most Experienced Airline

INTERNATIONAL
of Schaffhausen

Timekeeper to the world

.. for those who want the best

recommended for their magnificent reliability and performance, as well as for their elegance. Sold and serviced by the leading jewellers all over the world.

Ref. 601 AD DE LUXE 18 ct. gold, AUTOMATIC, 21 jewels, waterresistant, shock-protected and non-magnetic, dial solid gold 18 ct. with raised gold figures and gold hands. (Same model available without calendar, Ref. 601 A)

International Watch Co.

SCHAFFHAUSEN/SWITZERLAND

Of all the ships that
cruise the Caribbean

Only two

were designed and built
specifically for Caribbean cruises

The *Santa Rosa* and *Santa Paula* are in a class by themselves! Unlike the many ships that cruise the Caribbean on a part-time basis, the twin "Santas" were planned and built for full-time Caribbean cruising, *all year 'round*. For your complete cruising pleasure, nothing else!

These seagoing resorts provide more "living room" per passenger than any other ship. The La Playa Deck is a gay tropic "beach" featuring the largest outdoor pool afloat and all deck sports. High on the sunny promenade deck, the panoramic Seaview dining room is bright and spacious. Accommodations are superb, service unsurpassed.

The 20,000-ton *Santa Rosa* or *Santa Paula* sails on a 13-day cruise from New York every Friday. Visiting Curaçao and Aruba, La Guaira (Caracas), Kingston, Port-au-Prince, and Fort Lauderdale. Minimum rates from $395 to $495, depending on season. See a Travel Agent.

Also 17 to 19-day *Casual Cruises* to the Caribbean
26 and 31-day *Jewel Box Cruise Tours* to South America

Beginning January, 1963—the first of four NEW "SANTAS" cruising to the Caribbean and the Pacific Coast of South America!

GRACE LINE
3 Hanover Square, New York 4, N. Y.   Digby 4-6000

THE MOST FAMOUS NAME IN CARIBBEAN-SOUTH AMERICA CRUISES

FACTS AT YOUR FINGERTIPS

INTERNATIONAL TRAVEL BUREAU of New York features *Sunny Lands Air Tours* in conjunction with Caribair, BOAC-Cunard Eagle, Avianca and other airlines. Among their novelties: a 5-day tour of Panama, staying at *El Panama Hilton Hotel*; cost, including transportation, from $310.60. Another novelty: a 4-day, 3-night visit to little known Grand Cayman Island, a change for wonderful off-beat escapism from $189.35 including night coach flights between New York and Miami, tourist flights between Miami and Grand Cayman. Cost of the round trip flights alone would normally run $162.60, which will give you some idea of the economy angle of air cruises.

K.L.M. ROYAL DUTCH AIRLINES, famous for food and service, offers two Caribbean tours. The Bon Bini Holiday Tour takes in the Dutch islands of Curaçao, Aruba, and Bonaire, with four different itineraries planned for four days, eight days, 10 days, or a combination of air and sea travel. During the busy winter season, the Bon Bini tours start at $266 from Miami and $316 from New York, including tourist air fare. The Caribbean Island Hop combines an air trip from New York or Miami to Curaçao, and return, with approximately two weeks aboard an inter-island cargo ship that carries passengers. The ship stops and lets the passengers ashore in Aruba, Jamaica, Costa Rica, Colombia, and sometimes Haiti. In Curaçao, the passengers stay at the luxurious Curaçao Intercontinental Hotel. The 14-day tour from Miami starts at $365, including tourist air fare; the 18-day tour from New York starts at $470, including tourist air fare.

PAN AMERICAN AIRWAYS is appropriately named when it comes to the Western Hemisphere, and their clippers blanket the Caribbean skies. Their thrift class fare of $115.50 round trip from New York to Puerto Rico is the basis for bargain "Holidays in Puerto Rico" of seven days and six nights with accommodations at the *El San Juan* hotel. Transportation is by jet, of course, and this tour can be combined with any number of tours to other exciting islands. Costs, all inclusive, start as low as $198.50 for the 7-day holiday.

TRAVELTYME TOURS teams up with Trans Caribbean and Pan American to offer a galaxy of glamorous cruises by air. One that caught our fancy for variety and down-to-earth price is the 16-day jaunt to St. Croix, Antigua, Martinique, Barbados, Tobago, Trinidad and Curaçao. This comes to $299 minimum price plus $278 round trip air ticket (economy class) from New York. These tours also have that highly desirable built-in feature: private car hire for transfers and sightseeing at no additional cost. This is on a double basis. If you want a car just for yourself, you will have to pay extra.

SEAWAYS

Bermuda, the Bahamas and the entire Caribbean are well served by regularly-scheduled passenger ships and cargo freighters. Many of them are run by lines you may be unfamiliar with, but they are all experienced at navigating in these waters.

All times and rates given below are for round trip voyages. One way rates upon request from the shiplines themselves.

ALCOA. A special word should be said here for Alcoa, one of the great names in the Caribbean. They operate regularly scheduled freighter cruises carrying up to twelve passengers from New York, New Orleans, and Mobile to the glamor ports of the Caribbean. These cruises range in length from 11 to 35 days. Fares range from $250 to $665, depending upon length and itinerary.

Ore-ship cruises from Mobile and Texas to Trinidad, Dominican Republic and Surinam are also available on Alcoa's air-conditioned bauxite ore carriers, sailing frequently, accommodating 12 passengers in attractive outside staterooms.

Alcoa is also your carrier for one of the most fascinating adventures in the Caribbean: a trip from Trinidad to Surinam and up the rivers into the jungle interior, inhabited by Bush Negroes who live as they did before they were brought here from Africa. If time permits, you can visit their villages while your ship loads bauxite. The trip is made on shallow draft air-conditioned bauxite ore freighters, carrying from 4 to 12 passengers in outside staterooms with private bath. You eat with the ship's officers. Round trip voyage, Trinidad to Surinam takes about six days and costs $125. Reservations can be made through your travel agent or any Alcoa office. Passengers wishing to sail from Trinidad for the *Jungle Cruise* and who are arriving in Trinidad by alternate means of surface transportation or by air, need only specify their arrival date and the approximate length of time desired between arrival and departure.

Alcoa Steamship Company's addresses are 17 Battery Place, N.Y.4, and 1 Canal St., New Orleans 12, La. Brochures on request.

Now here's an alphabetical rundown on other carriers who serve the Caribbean area with regularly-scheduled sailings:

BLUE STAR LINE (3, Lower Regent St., London) has services from the United Kingdom once every three weeks to Curaçao and Balboa en route to Los Angeles, San Francisco, Seattle, Victoria and Vancouver. Cost to Curaçao or Balboa varies from £107 to £144.

BOOTH LINE (17 Battery Place, N.Y.) has monthly sailings on freighters from New York to Antigua, Guadeloupe, St. Kitts, Dominica ($175 one way), St. Lucia, St. Vincent, Barbados, Grenada, Trinidad, Martinique and British Guiana ($200 one way).

EASTERN STEAMSHIP CORP. (Pier 3, Miami, Fla.) *S.S. Evangeline* makes weekly (every Friday) 7-day cruises from Miami to Port Antonio, Kingston, Port-au-Prince and Nassau, from $160 up. Beginning December 15, 1962 (and on every Saturday thereafter), the *S.S. Ariadne* will make 7-day trips from Miami to San Juan and St. Thomas, from $185 up. Also the *S.S. Bahama Star* on twice-weekly cruises to Nassau from Miami every Monday and Friday, from $54 for a 3-day cruise. All ships are air-conditioned.

FRENCH LINE (610 Fifth Ave., N.Y.) has a Europe to West Indies service from the port of Le Havre to Pointe-a-Pitre or Fort de France, Barbados or Trinidad, La Guaira, and San Juan, Puerto Rico. Ships are the *Antilles* and the *Colombie* and they sail twice monthly. Rates from Europe to Martinique are $315 first class, $224 cabin class. Month's tour, 15 days at sea, 15 days in port. Food is the best French cuisine, nothing better.

ELDERS AND FYFFES, LTD. (15 Stratton St., London W.1) sails fortnightly from United Kingdom to Barbados, Trinidad and Jamaica. Ships are *S.S. Golfito* and *Camito*. Minimum fare: £106.

FACTS AT YOUR FINGERTIPS

FURNESS BERMUDA LINE (34 Whitehall St., N.Y.) *The Queen of Bermuda* and the *Ocean Monarch* are the famed royal barges that transport you from dirty New York to the flowery isle of Bermuda. Weekly sailings Saturday, arriving Monday morning, minimum rate, $130 round trip. Or you can take the 6-day "Liv-Aboard" cruise, living on the ship with all meals provided. Two and one-half days for Bermuda, shopping and sports, $160 and up. Bermuda-Nassau and West Indies Cruises come with beautiful memories built in. From Feb. 5-March 22, 1963, the *Ocean Monarch* will sail on four cruises from Florida.

GRACE LINE (3 Hanover Square, N.Y. 4). Two beautiful new ships, the *Santa Rosa* and the *Santa Paula* provide weekly service between New York, Curaçao, La Guaira, Aruba, Kingston, Haiti and Port Everglades, Florida. The ships, both with outdoor swimming pools, are floating palaces. All rooms outside with private bath. Minimum fare for 13-day round trip is $395.

The Grace Line also has three combination passenger-cargo ships with accommodations for 52 travelers, air-conditioned staterooms (all outside with private bath) and outdoor tiled swimming pool. These attractive boats ply between New York, La Guaira, Puerto Cabello, Guanta, Maracaibo, Barranquilla and Cartagena, and frequently make Baltimore and Philadelphia ports of call on the return trip; 17 to 19 days.

Ships of the same type link New York with Venezuela and Colombia on their South American service. Minimum fare between New York and Venezuela is $275; between New York and Colombia $250. You can count on comfort, efficiency and excellent service from a line that has long specialized in this area.

GRIMALDI SIOSA LINES (44 Whitehall St., N.Y.) provides regular passenger service to and from Southampton and Dominica, St. Lucia, St. Vincent, Barbados, Trinidad, Antigua, Venezuela, Curaçao, and Kingston. The same line also has service between Mediterranean ports (Napels, Genoa, Cannes, Barcelona) and Trinidad, Venzuela, Martinique and Guadeloupe.

HAMBURG-AMERICA LINE links the Dominican Republic, Haiti and Jamaica with Hamburg, Bremen and Antwerp on cargo passenger trips. Limited passenger facilities.

ITALIAN LINE (24 State St., N.Y. 4) has monthly sailings from Mediterranean ports to Panama, Venezuela, Colombia, and Dutch West Indies. Sample fares: Naples to La Guaira $375 cabin class; $245 tourist. To Curaçao, $375 cabin class, $255 tourist. To Cartagena: $440 cabin; $275 tourist. To Cristobal, $475 cabin class; $275 tourist.

JOHNSON LINE (2 Pine St., San Francisco) is a reputable Swedish line with sailings every two weeks from Vancouver B.C., Seattle, Portland, Ore, San Francisco and Los Angeles to Panama and Curaçao. Accommodations on motor cargo vessels for 12 passengers. Rooms have private baths; food and cleanliness are Scandinavian, so no complaints.

LYKES BROS. STEAMSHIP CO. (1300 Commerce Bldg., New Orleans) links Houston, Galveston and Lake Charles with the Caribbean by montly sailings to San Juan, Mayaguez, and Ponce, Puerto Rico, Colombian and Venezuelan ports. This trip averages 23 days, costs $450. Ships are cargoliners, so itineraries and schedules are on the flexible side. For the time being, former regular sailings to Havana and Santiago, Cuba have been discontinued, although they may be taken up again in the future.

FACTS AT YOUR FINGERTIPS

MOORE-McCORMACK LINES (2 Broadway, N.Y. 4), another famous name in American shipping, makes Barbados and Trinidad ports of call on its voyages from New York to South America with their two new luxury liners.

P & O ORIENT LINES (25 Broadway, N.Y. 4) links London and Le Havre with Trinidad and Panama on its U.K.-North America service between England, Los Angeles, San Francisco.

PACIFIC REPUBLICS LINE (214 California St., San Francisco) sails semi-monthly between Los Angeles and the Canal Zone en route to South America. Ports of call include Cartagena ($270/$320, Puerto Cabello ($340/$390), Trinidad ($435/$485), Maracaibo ($375/$425), La Guaira ($335/$375). Larger fare is for full season (Nov. 1 through end of February). Off season fares are the first figures indicated.

PACIFIC STEAM NAVIGATION CO. (30 James St., Liverpool 2 and 34 White-hall Street, N.Y. 4) has a fortnightly service with a fleet of modern, luxurious cargo/passenger liners from Liverpool, England to Bermuda, Bahamas, Cuba, Colombia and the Panama Canal Zone and then on to the West Coast of South America.

PENINSULAR & OCCIDENTAL STEAMSHIP CO. (P.O. Box 1349, Miami 1, Fla.) links Miami and Nassau on Tuesday and Friday sailings at 5 p.m. Minimum fares are $24 one way, $39 round trip; $54 three-day cruise. All outside staterooms. They will take your car too. Rates on request.

ROYAL MAIL LINES, LTD. (Leadenhall St., London E.C.3 and 34 Whitehall St., N.Y. 4) have cargo vessels with limited passenger space sailing between the United Kingdom and (via the Panama Canal) Nassau, Kingston, Curaçao, Aruba, Colombia, Dominican Republic, Haiti, Panama, Puerto Rico and Venezuela, and to U.S. west coast ports.

ROYAL NETHERLANDS STEAMSHIP COMPANY (29 Broadway, N.Y. 6) has excellent Caribbean passenger services. You can sail from New York every Friday in modern cargo vessels carrying 4 to 12 passengers to Curaçao (5 days), Aruba (6 days), La Guaira (7 days), Maracaibo (9 days), Puerto Cabello (11 days). One way fares to these ports are $190 with private shower and toilet; $150 without these facilities. Last stop on this route is Trinidad 13 days), with fares of $230 and $190 respectively. Sometimes (better check beforehand), these ships return to New York via Florida ports, and the round-trip fare for this 26-day cruise is $475.

Another service also leaves every other Friday from New York and follows the same route except that Haiti replaces Curaçao, Aruba and La Guaira. Fares are about the same.

There are two other routes from New York, again leaving every other Friday. The first stops at Curaçao, Aruba, La Guaira, Guanta, Georgetown and Paramaribo, and returns to New York. At a price of $525 per person, round trip, for 33 days, this is an extremely popular service.

The remaining route from New York is one-way only, and visits Santo Domingo, Port-au-Prince, Cape Haitian, and Kingston. Fares to all destinations are $140 with facilities; $110 without.

From New Orleans every other Thursday to Maracaibo (6 days), La Guaira (8 days), Puerto Cabello (10 days): $190 and $150. On to Guanta (12 days) and Trinidad (13 days): $230 and $190. On to Georgetown (16 days): $260 with facilities, $210 without. Return is via Tampa and Mobile to New Orleans; round-trip cost is $525.

FACTS AT YOUR FINGERTIPS

Also from **New** Orleans, sailings every other Thursday to Aruba, Curaçao, La Guaira, Puerto Cabello, Carupano (Venezuela), Panpatar (Venezuela), Trinidad and Paramaribo—15 days in all. Prices are similar.

There are also sailings every four weeks from Amsterdam and Southampton via Madeira to Trinidad, Paramaribo and Georgetown. Fares range from $255 to $455. This service is by one-class steamer—*Oranjestad* or *Willemstad*.

Also every four weeks, the *Oranje Nassau* and *Prins der Nederlanden* (one-class, 116 passengers) link Amsterdam and Southampton with Barbados and Trinidad ($295 to $465), La Guaira, Curaçao and Aruba ($320 to $525), Kingston, Port-au-Prince (optional), Puerto Limon and Cartegena ($350 to $590).

SAGUENAY SHIPPING LIMITED (1060 University St., Montreal, Canada) provides an important link between Canada and the Caribbean, also between the United Kingdom and the Caribbean.

There are weekly sailings on cargo liners (up to 12 passengers) from Montreal and Halifax to Trinidad with alternate calls at Georgetown, British Guiana and Bridgetown, Barbados. Round trip (about 25 days) from Montreal costs from $330 to $385.

There are sailings every ten days from Montreal to Santo Domingo, Venezuela and Trinidad. Also fortnightly sailings from Montreal and Halifax to Hamilton (Bermuda), San Juan (Puerto Rico), Basseterre (St. Kitts), St. John's (Antigua), Plymouth (Montserrat), Roseau (Dominica), Castries (St. Lucia), Kingstown (St. Vincent), and St. George's (Grenada). This coverage of the Leewards and the Windwards takes about 35 days, costs between $500 and $585 for the round trip.

Saguenay also has fortnightly sailings from Montreal and Halifax to Santiago de Cuba and Kingston, Jamaica, with alternate calls at Port-au-Prince and the Canal Zone (Cristobal). Count on 25 days and from $330 to $385 for this round trip from Montreal.

There are fortnightly westbound sailings from London to Trinidad, Barbados and British Guiana. Also fortnightly sailings from London to San Juan, Kingston and Santo Domingo. These are on freighters accommodating up to 12 passengers. Rates for the Trinidad, Barbados passage are from £80 to £115 (December through April), from £60 to £90 (May through November). Year round rates for the San Juan, Kingston, Santo Domingo voyage are from $80 to $130.

There is fortnightly service between Liverpool (or some other U.K. west coast port) and Port of Spain, Bridgetown and Georgetown as well as direct monthly sailings to Kingston via this line.

UNITED FRUIT COMPANY (Pier 3, North River, N.Y. 6) has a number of freighter cruises to Middle America. Ships are restricted to not more than 12 passengers each, enough for good company but never a crowd. Arrivals and departures and ports of call of these ships depend on cargo, so passengers should be prepared for changes involving sailing time, routes, etc.

From New York there is a 16-day cruise every Friday to the Panama Canal and Puerto Bolivar, Ecuador at $385 per person. A 12-day cruise can be taken every Wednesday to Jamaica and Honduras at $295 per person. There is also a weekly excursion to the Panama Canal with several days for sightseeing on the Isthmus of Panama and return. Cost is $275 per person, not including stay in Panama. From New Orleans there is a weekly 19-day cruise to Jamaica, the Panama Canal and Ecuador at

FACTS AT YOUR FINGERTIPS

$450 per person. All fare quotations are for double cabins with private showers and toilets. Some ships have single cabins at slightly higher fares. Folder and details furnished upon request.

C.A. VENEZOLANA DE NAVEGACION (Pier 10, North River, N.Y.) takes 4-6 passengers on its cargo vessels every Friday from New York to La Guaira, Venezuela.

WATERMAN LINE (P.O. Box 51420, New Orleans, La. or 19 Rector St., N.Y.) sails every Wednesday evening from New Orleans to San Juan, Puerto Rico, arriving the following Monday. One way fare is $105 with private bath, $97.50 with connecting bath.

SOURCES OF INFORMATION

The fountainhead of information on the Caribbean is the Caribbean Tourist Association at 20 East 46 Street, New York City. Air and Marine Travel Service at 355 West 57 Street, New York, can also provide you with information. They are the foremost travel agency for the Caribbean area, and Thaddeus Hyatt, the director, is a well of up-to-the-minute knowledge on the West Indies.

Many of the countries and islands in the region covered by our guide maintain information offices in New York City. They can supply you with news of the latest developments and attractive illustrated brochures designed to tempt you southward and seaward. Here are their addresses and names of directors:

Antigua Tourist Information Center, 9 Rockefeller Plaza, N.Y. Mr. Ivor MacLaren.
Aruba Tourist Bureau, 609 Fifth Avenue, N.Y., Mr. Jack Waugh.
Barbados Tourist Board, 750 Third Avenue, N.Y. 17, Mr. Wendell P. Colton, Jr.
Bermuda Trade Development Board, 620 Fifth Avenue, N.Y. 20, Mr. John Powers.
Colombia National Tourist Board, 608 Fifth Avenue, N.Y., Mr. Julius Siefken-De Perly.
Curaçao Information Center, 1270 Avenue of the Americas, N.Y., Mr. Lloyd N. Newman (also represents Bonaire and Dutch Windwards).
French Government Tourist Office, 610 Fifth Avenue, N. Y. 20, Mr. Andre Alphand
Haiti Government Tourist Bureau, 30 Rockefeller Plaza, N.Y. Mr. Romeo Barrella.
Jamaica Tourist Board, 630 Fifth Avenue, N.Y. 20, Mr. Sam Levy.
Nassau Bahamas Development Board, 620 Fifth Avenue, N.Y. 20, Mr. Frank Ramey.
Panama Government Tourist Board, 750 Third Avenue, N.Y. 17.
Puerto Rico Department of Tourism, 666 Fifth Avenue, N.Y. 19, Mr. Kenneth Wright.
Surinam Tourist Bureau, 10 Rockefeller Plaza, N.Y. 20, Mr. John H. Nelson.
Trinidad & Tobago Tourist Board, 48 East 43rd Street, N.Y. 17, Stephen Goerl Associates, Inc.
Virgin Islands Government Information Center, 16 West 49th Street, N.Y. 20, Mrs. Margaret Lenci.

For the following, the addresses of the Caribbean Tourist Association, 20 East 46 St., N.Y., is given as the "tourist information office": Dominica, Grenada, St. Barthelemy, St. Kitss-Nevis-Anguilla, St. Lucia, St. Vincent.

FACTS AT YOUR FINGERTIPS

Some operators who have outstanding tours to the Caribbean include:

Air & Marine Travel Service, 353 W. 57 St., New York City.
American Automobile Association, Miami, Fla.
American Express Co., New York City.
Cartan Travel Bureau, 108 No. State St., Chicago, Ill.
Thos. Cook & Son, New York City.
Delta Air Lines, Atlanta, Ga.
Embassy Tours, 147 W. 42 St., New York City.
Happiness Tours, 6 East Monroe St., Chicago.
Hilton Tours, P.O. Box 1007, Vallejo, California.
International Travel Bureau, New York City.
Safaritours, Inc., 7805 Sunset Blvd., Hollywood, Cal.
Trans Caribbean Airways, 200 West 57 St., New York City.
Travel Plans Tours, 88 Eglinton Avenue, Toronto, Canada.
Traveltyme Tours, 501 Fifth Avenue, New York City.
United Tours, 329 E. Flagler St., Miami, Fla.

HOTEL RESERVATIONS

In reserving hotel rooms, your travel agent is an invaluable help. If he's on his toes, he knows which hotels are already booked to capacity, which ones are in the throes of renovation, which ones are about to be invaded by the veterinarians' convention.

If you are planning a fairly long stay, say a week or more, in a single place, you may prefer to reserve directly through the hotel representative nearest your home.

MISCELLANEOUS

 PASSPORTS, VISAS, HEALTH CARDS. Except for Venezuela, which requires both a valid passport and a visa (apply to Venezuelan consul or through your travel agent) passports and visas are not necessary for any of the countries mentioned in this guide. Tourist cards are required for Haiti, the Dominican Republic and Colombia. These can be bought through your carrier or travel agent. You should also be equipped with a birth certificate, proof of naturalization if you are a naturalized citizen, or some official documentary proof of identification.

So many places (Antigua, Aruba, Barbados, Panama, Dominican Republic) require a vaccination certificate, and Uncle Sam insists that you have one before you can re-enter the United States. So get that scratch as soon as possible, and have it duly recorded by your doctor on the International Health Certificate which your agent, air or ship carrier will procure for you. Stash this in your purse or wallet. It's a handy, in fact a necessary part of your travel baggage. You can, of course, have the smallpox vaccination on a doctor's letterhead or a plain piece of paper certified by Public Health Authorities. But you must have it, and the date of innoculation must be within three years of the time the certificate is used or you'll have to submit to inoculation on the spot, a big waste of time.

Specific travel document requirements are listed in the main text of the guide under each country.

FACTS AT YOUR FINGERTIPS

 PACKING. The smart, sophisticated traveller usually packs light. It pays to do so if you're going by air. Your baggage allowance is 44 pounds in tourist class, 66 pounds in first. Drip dry summer cruise clothes are a boon, but remember that nylon can be hot in the tropics. The dacron cotton combinations or the new tazlon fabrics dry just as fast and just as smooth, and they're pleasantly cool to wear. Saks' Fifth Avenue has a $10 taslon shirt for men that's perfect. It can get cool in the hill towns of the tropics after the sun goes down. Better take along at least one sweater or medium warm jacket, even a top coat if you're the chilly type. If you are going to a posh resort, you will want tropical dinner clothes. Check hotel listings under individual countries. In general it's safe to plan your wardrobe as you would for Florida or Southern California.

To reiterate our main advice: When in doubt leave it out.

 SHOPPING. You are going to one of the greatest bazaars of the civilized world. In addition to Swiss watches, German cameras, French perfumes, English China at unheard of bargain prices, you will find cruise clothes, swim suits, sports shirts, dinner jackets, frocks, sweaters, Bermuda shorts, slacks, linen jackets, evening gowns and everything your heart can desire in the sartorial line. Much of it is imported from Britain. All of it is far less expensive than it is in your home town. So if you forget something or pack too lightly, you will have a perfect excuse to indulge yourself. Shopping is one of the main pleasures of the Caribbean area, and we have listed the shops and their offerings in detail under the individual countries. *Tip:* If buying extra clothes makes you overweight for the return trip, you can offset this by mailing used clothing back home.

 CUSTOMS REGULATIONS. *Arriving.* The islands and countries to which you are going are happy to have tourists, and customs formalities are simple. Unless otherwise specified under the individual countries, you can bring in anything for your bona fide personal use.

Returning Home. If you are a resident of the U.S. you can import $200 worth of purchases duty-free providing you have been outside of the U.S. for 48 hours and not already used this exemption within thirty days. Puerto Rico counts as American soil, so don't let a stopover there invalidate your 48 hour exemption privilege. The Virgin Islands' free port status exempts it from this restriction. Your exemptions include one gallon per person (five fifths)) of alcoholic beverages and 100 cigars.

Duty-free Goods

Despite the cut in the duty-free purchasing allowance, the Caribbean is still a good buy for American tourists. The allowance is double that for other areas ($100).

But of the $200 allowance for the Caribbean, $100 worth of goods must be purchased in the U.S. Virgin Islands.

Canadian residents who have been out of their country for at least 48 hours may import $100 worth of purchases duty free if they have not used this exemption within the previous four months.

Unsolicited gifts of less than $10 value may be sent into the U.S. duty free. Not more than one gift may be sent to the same person, and liquor, perfumes and tobacco are not included in this category. Packages should be marked: "Gift, value less than $10." These gifts do not reduce your $200 exemption, so this regulation is of great help to travelers who are near their duty-free exemption limit. The regulation is also a godsend for those whose luggage is already near the weight limitation allowed by the airlines.

 MONEY. You will be dealing with pounds sterling, Dominican and Colombian pesos, Haitian gourdes, British West Indian (Beewee) dollars, Dutch West Indian guilders, Venezuelans bolivars, French francs. Exchange rates for these currencies are given under each country. Almost without exception you can use American and Canadian dollars, exchanging them at the current rate, throughout the West Indies. American and Canadian travellers checks on reputable banks or agencies are as good as gold throughout the area, and always welcomed by shopkeepers. Cost of these checks is one per cent of their amount (i.e. $10 for $1,000 worth of checks), which is tantamount to cheap money insurance. No one else can cash the checks, and if you lose them the money is replaced.

 INTERNAL TRANSPORTATION. The problem of getting about in the islands and countries of your choice is fully discussed under each country with information as to public services, taxis, sightseeing tours and car rental with and without chauffeur. Generally speaking, it will not pay you to take your own car to the Caribbean. Cars can be taken into the countries in this guide, with the exception of Bermuda. Cruise passengers can reserve rented cars in advance, arranging to pick up a car at one or all of the scheduled ports of call. This can be done any time prior to sailing through the steamship companies, travel agents, or representatives of Hertz. Hertz delivers cars to the dock.

171.5
13.0
201.0
―――――
385.5

INSURANCE. You can insure almost anything in this world. The Virgin Isle Hotel (see section on the Virgin Islands) even insures you against bad weather. Baggage insurance can be arranged through your travel agent; in fact he is only too anxious to sell it to you. You can take out a personal floater for all your possessions for the duration of your trip. We collected twice, once on a camera, once on a raincoat, and that more than made up for about ten years of premium payments.

 TIPPING. This is one of the few obnoxious problems of tourism. On airlines (God bless'em) you don't have to worry at all: no tipping. On ships it's absolutely obligatory, and should be done in proportion to services received and cost of the voyage. Some travelers stick to 5 per cent of the cost of the ticket to cover all tipping exigencies. This would not be enough on a luxury cruise where you are waited on hand and foot by personnel who depend on you as much as you depend on them. On a luxury cruise, we would tip our steward at the rate of a dollar a day. The dining room steward will be happy with $10 to $15 at the end of the voyage, the deck steward with $2. Your cabin steward should get $10 for doing up a double stateroom on a week's cruise; $15 for ten days to two weeks. If you used public bath-rooms, the bath attendant gets $2. Tip the wine steward in accordance with the frequency and quality of his services: $3 if you have wine habitually, more if he goes to a lot of trouble to please you with various vintages. The barman should get 12 % of the bar bill. Generally speaking, your tips on a luxury cruise should add up to 10 per cent of the ticket cost, 12 per cent if you are very well satisfied, as high as 15 if you've had the royal treatment.

In second class or on a cargoliner, the 5 per cent is more in line, but still a little low in our opinion. Here your obligations will be to waiter, room steward, and, depending on how much tucking into deck chairs you get, the deck steward. On our last "luxury" freighter cruise (14 days) we tipped the dining room steward $10, cabin steward the same, deckchair boy $2, and all beamed. These tipping suggestions are made on the basis of a single person. Two can tip half again as cheaply as one. In other words a $15 tip to waiter and cabin steward for a couple; $3 for the deck steward.

A number of Caribbean hotels (all indicated under individual countries) have adopted that excellent European habit of adding a service charge to your bill. In this case you have nothing to do but smile when it's time to leave. Many of these hotels are still on that wonderful, old-fashioned 10 per cent arrangement too, something that Europe and America have long since forgotten. Throughout the West Indies, however, you can still tip 10 per cent in most restaurants and not be taken for a piker or the exploiter of the downtrodden. In the luxurious hotels, nightclubs, and restaurants, however, the expectation is 12 to 15 per cent of the bill. Don't forget the chambermaids, "boots" and the other remarkably cheerful and usually underpaid slaveys who do the dirty work. Give the maid a dollar for a stay of three or four days, $2 if you stay a week. The boy who shines your shoes will be overjoyed with half a buck for a couple of days' polishing, a dollar for a week. Don't give more than that or they'll follow you home.

The important thing to remember in this whole tipping problem is the human relationship involved. Tip what you feel you can afford for services received, and give the money as a friendly gesture with a "Thank you for all your help." A tip given in this way does more for international good will and the human soul than any amount of money thrown down with a grumpy or disdainful attitude.

ELECTRIC CURRENT. 110 to 120 volts A.C. is the general rule throughout the Caribbean, the Bahamas and Bermuda. Here are the exceptions: St. Kitts, St. Lucia, St. Vincent and Grenada in the British West Indies all of which have 230 volts A.C. Antigua has both 110 A.C. and 220 D.C. The Castle Harbour Hotel in Bermuda has 220 volts; rest of the island is on 110. The French West Indies have 110 volt alternating current, but they use European plugs so you will need a converter plug there for your razor, traveling iron or other electric appliances.

WATER AND MILK. Tap water is safe and there is pasteurized milk available in the following places: Aruba, Bahamas, Barbados, Bermuda, Curaçao, Colombia, Dominican Republic, Jamaica, Puerto Rico, Martinique, Trinidad and Tobago (in hotels), St. Thomas, St. Vincent, Colombia (in large cities), Venezuela (in large cities), Panama (except for small villages).

FACTS AT YOUR FINGERTIPS

Boil water and milk or drink mineral water and canned milk in the following places: Antigua, rural areas of Bonaire, British Virgins, Cayman Islands, Guadeloupe, parts of rural Martinique (ask for locally-bottled *Didier* mineral water), Montserrat, St. Kitts, Nevis, St. Lucia, rural Trinidad and Tobago, away from the larger cities of Venezuela and Colombia, in rural Panama and in all three of the Guianas. Port au Prince has pasteurized milk in limited quantities. To be on the safe side travel with powdered milk if the kids come along.

CRUISING THE CARIBBEAN

by LEE KARWICK

(A newspaper woman and former Executive Director of the Caribbean Tourist Association, Lee Karwick knows the Caribbean like the back of her hand. To prepare this article for us on Cruises, she made a special voyage to many of the places which she knows so well.)

No other waters in the world can offer you the cruising pleasure of the Caribbean.

Four short days out of New York you will find yourself in sub-tropical golden sunshine and sapphire seas where no island or country is more than a day apart.

Ships have been sailing the Caribbean for more than four hundred years—galleons, Spanish caravels, pirate schooners, Yankee clippers, battleships, freighters and pleasure yachts.

Now, for the pleasure of the traveler, there are the fabulous cruise ships, floating palaces that carry him luxuriously from one port to another. Or, for the budget conscious, sturdy freighters that offer a more intimate kind of trip, calling at tiny out-of-the-way places or even extending into the jungle where the nights are filled with cries of monkeys and parrots.

There are at least three hundred passenger ships sailing the Caribbean during the winter months and because the trade winds keep the temperature rise at only ten degrees, many of them sail the year around.

Whichever type of ship you choose, it will go full speed ahead to get you into the Caribbean Sea as soon as possible. From then on it will cruise slowly around the area, depending upon the number of ports to be made and the amount of time you have.

The ships have planned their itineraries well so that you will arrive at the time most comfortable for you and have longer lay-overs in ports which have greater attractions. And they try to vary the itinerary so you will have the pleasure of completely different stops.

The first days out are spent getting a sun tan and resting up. Then one morning you will find that the ship has taken on a new look. The sea, the weather, and the shipboard tempo have changed. Then you will know that the Caribbean has worked its golden magic and your cruise has really begun.

There are approximately thirty-one islands and countries in the Caribbean and each stop is completely different from the last. There are Jamaica with its British influence, Haiti so French and so different, Curaçao, the bristling seaport, La Guaira backed by the Andes mountains, and Grenada and St. Thomas with their beautiful harbors.

There is a marvelous choice of both itinerary and transport to meet every time schedule and every pocketbook.

Least expensive and considered by many to be the most interesting, are the intimate twelve-passenger freighters which stop at even the tiny islands.

If you love the sea and want to learn all about a ship, the freighter is your answer. You can watch the loading and unloading of cargo, get acquainted with the officers who will usually be pleased to show you around.

On Working Ships

The freighter is fundamentally a working ship and hours aboard are governed by the crew, so lunch is served at noon and dinner at five. Passengers eat in the dining room with the officers and the food is good, if not fancy, since seamen are known for their hearty appetites.

Rooms on the freighters are excellent and there is a sun deck and a public lounge. Clothes are informal. Slacks or Bermuda shorts are perfect during the day and in the evening. For the women, simple cotton dresses are right. Women should remember that while they may go on the sun deck or top deck to sun bathe in jackets and bathing suits, it is a working man's ship and they should dress accordingly.

Next in line are the combination freighter-passenger ships which carry from thirty to eighty passengers. These ships are on scheduled runs to specific islands and countries, taking from ten to fifteen days. Meals are similar to those on the large passenger ships and include specialties not offered on the small freighters.

There is more activity aboard these ships including a swimming pool and movies. Some even have a cruise director and a small band for dancing, but here again life is informal.

There is an excellent side trip from Trinidad on the Alcoa

Ore Freighters across the Caribbean Sea to Surinam. It takes about a week round-trip. The ship goes to Surinam, on the coast of South America, one of the most interesting places in the Caribbean. She goes up the Surinam river and then travels up the Cottica River to the bauxite mines at Moengo.

This is a trip into the jungles on an ocean freighter and as you slowly go up the river, the jungles are within your reach. You pass the native villages of the Djukas and Amerindian Tribes. Many of the natives will follow along in their native dug-out canoes calling for soap or coins. At night you can hear the monkeys and parrots screeching through the jungles.

As you get farther up the river a tug boat takes over to pull your ship through the narrow river passages with their hairpin turns. When you arrive at Moengo you can visit the open bauxite mines or hire a car to take you to St. Laurent in French Guiana where you will see the outcasts of the former Devils Island prison (if time permits).

On your return the next morning down river, you may see suddenly over the tree tops the funnel of one of your sister ships coming up. As you round the bend she will have run right up on land to give your ship room to pass.

Another fascinating trip is the Grace Line's "Jewel Box Casual Cruise" which lasts thirty-one days and takes you through the great locks of the Panama Canal and down the west coast.

Flying and Cruising

There are also regular Caribbean cruise ships which leave weekly from New York, such as the Grace Line's "Santa Rosa" and "Santa Paula".

Another popular combination is to fly to Puerto Rico and pick up the small cruise ships of the Bergen Line. The Bergen Line's "Meteor" sails frequently starting December 22, calling at ten to fifteen ports. Stops are at St. Thomas, St. Kitts, Guadeloupe, Martinique, St. Vincent, St. Lucia, Montserrat, Grenada, Trinidad, Barbados, Antigua, St. Maarten and return to San Juan, Puerto Rico.

There are also regular cruise ships out of Miami, Florida. The Eastern Steamship Corp.'s "Bahama Star" goes to Nassau twice weekly and the "Evangeline" stops at Port Antonio, Kingston and Port-au-Prince.

Of course the Transatlantic Lines have their well-known ships cruising the Caribbean. You have only to select your time, your budget and the nationality of the ship. Cruises run from ten days to a grand Caribbean cruise of 24 days. Ten-day cruises to four ports start at about $255, with 15-day cruises to six ports, $360, and the Grand Caribbean Cruise of 24 days and fourteen ports, about $550.

These include such famous ships as the Swedish American Line "Gripsholm", the Home Line "Homeric", the Cunard Line "Mauretania", North German Lloyd "Bremen", Holland American Line "Statendam" and "Rotterdam", The Canadian Pacific "Empress of Canada", the Zim Line "Jerusalem", the Norwegian America Line "Oslofjord", and many others equally as good.

All of them will have just about everything: swimming pools, both indoors and out; fabulous luncheon buffets on deck; entertainment; dancing; movies; competitive sports; lectures on the ports visited; steam baths and masseurs.

The cruise director and his staff will be there to help you have a marvelous time, from asking you to dance to finding you partners for bridge. Most important of all, the director handles all the shore excursions. You can purchase the entire package of all port tours or you can purchase a separate tour for each port.

Of course your wardrobe must be more extensive for a cruise of this type than for one aboard a freighter. You should have shorts and sport shirts, bathing suits with jackets, daytime summer clothes for shore excursions and evening clothes. A cruise is a grand opportunity for people who like to dress up, especially the Captain's dinner which is the climax of the trip. And don't forget to bring a costume for there is sure to be some kind of a costume party.

Shopping's No Problem

Cruise ships could almost be called "shoppers" ship since there are no problems with overweight and you can shop to your heart's content. U.S. travelers are permitted to take back $200 worth of gifts, duty free, if they have been out of the country more than 48 hours.

Since the Caribbean is a shopper's paradise, by all means plan to buy a large basket, an excellent catch-all for your loot. The market in Nassau has about the best collection of straw baskets. It will simplify your going through Customs since you will have all your purchases in one place.

There won't be a port where you will be able to resist buying something. A good rule to remember is that islands which belong to a European country will have all the best gifts that are made in the home country at lower prices. So, for example, if you are in a Dutch island, all the lovely things of Holland can be bought cheaper. The French islands will have French perfumes, wines and crystal, and the British, the woolens, china and silverware.

In addition to the local tourist products which are excellent in Colombia, Puerto Rico and Venezuela, some ports are either free ports or have "in bond shops". In the free ports, like the Dutch and U.S. Virgin Islands, all imported merchandise is sold at duty free prices.

The "in bond" ports are where tourist merchandise is sold duty free. Haiti is a fine example of this type of port. Barbados and Jamaica have "in bond shops" but all merchandise purchased must be delivered to your ship. They have arranged this so well that you will usually find your purchases in your cabin by the time you leave the port.

If at the last moment you find you have forgotten a present for someone, the shop aboard the ship has lovely things from the country of its origin plus little "finds" from the different ports.

Cruising the Caribbean can offer you many things. If it's your first trip, it is an excellent way to see the islands and countries where you may wish to stay on your next trip. If you've made one cruise, plan another and another so that each itinerary takes you to different places. Or if you liked the first one so much, take it again, the same time, the same places with the same friends. You'd be surprised how many people do this each year. There were 300 Caribbean cruises last year, and the number grows as more and more people discover this extraordinary vacationland.

If you write to the New York office of any of the shipping lines indicated in the cruise list below, they will send you handsome brochures describing their accommodations, amenities and prices. These brochures may seem to exaggerate the charms of the cruise ships, but this is one case where the reality exceeds the dream. There's only one pleasure greater than thumbing through these illustrated pamphlets, and that's putting yourself in the picture. The various lines vie with each other to please you, and it would be invidious of us to single any one out for special praise.

And now to choose your cruise. All sailings from and to New York unless otherwise indicated: [1] New Orleans, [2] Galveston, [3] Everglades. Prices are approximate.

FACTS AT YOUR FINGERTIPS

Dep. Date	Cruise Days	Min. Prices	Ship and Line	Itinerary
Dec. 1	7	$150	*Italia* (Home Lines)	Nassau.
Dec. 3	14	$385	*Nieuw Amsterdam* (Holland-America Line)	Port-au-Prince, Montego Bay, Curaçao, Bridgetown, Guadeloupe, St. Thomas.
1Dec. 3	44	$900	*Del Sud* (Delta Line)	Houston, Bahia, Rio de Janeiro, Santos, Buenos Aires, Santos, Rio de Janeiro, Curaçao.
1Dec. 7	12	$355	*Rotterdam* (Holland-America)	St. Thomas, La Guaira, Curaçao, Port-au-Prince.
Dec. 7	13	$395	*Santa Paula* (Grace Line)	Curaçao, La Guaira, Aruba, Kingston, Port-au-Prince, Fort Lauderdale.
Dec. 7	18	$445	*Santa Monica* (Grace)	Santo Domingo, Puerto Cabello, La Guaira, Maracaibo, Barranquilla, Cartagena, Baltimore, Philadelphia.
Dec. 7	26	$800	*Santa Luisa* (Grace)	Cristobal, Balboa, Buenaventura, Callao, Salaverry, Guayaquil, Buenaventura, Canal Zone.
3Dec. 8	4	$95	*Franca C* (Atlantic Cruise Line)	Port-au-Prince.
Dec. 8	7	$150	*Italia* (Home)	Nassau.
3Dec. 9	10/12	$295* $3601)	*Argentina* (Moore-McCormack Lines)	St. Thomas, Martinique, Barbados, Trinidad, San Juan, Nassau, Port Everglades*, New York (1).
3Dec. 12	8	$175	*Franca C.* (Atlantic Cruise)	San Juan, St. Thomas, Port-au-Prince.
Dec. 14	43	$1,080	*Rio Tunuyan* (Argentine Lines)	Rio de Janeiro, Santos, Montevideo,/Buenos Aires, Santos, Rio de Janeiro, Trinidad, La Guaira.
Dec. 14	13	$445	*Santa Rosa* (Grace)	Curaçao, La Guaira, Aruba, Kingston, Port-au-Prince, Fort Lauderdale.
Dec. 14	18	$445	*Santa Sofia* (Grace)	Santo Domingo, Puerto Cabello, La Guaira, Guanta, Maracaibo, Barranquilla, Cartagena, Baltimore.
Dec. 15	7	$150	*Italia* (Home)	Nassau.
Dec. 20	14	$250	*Gripsholm* (Swedish-American Line)	San Juan, Castries, Port of Spain, La Guaira, Curaçao, Port-au-Prince.

FACTS AT YOUR FINGERTIPS

Dep. Date	Cruise Days	Min. Prices	Ship and Line	Itinerary
3Dec. 21	13	$325	*Franca C* (Atlantic Cruise)	St. Thomas, Guadeloupe, St. Lucia, Trinidad, Grenada, La Guaira, Curaçao, Port-au-Prince.
Dec. 21	12	$275	*Oslofjord* (Norwegian America Line)	St. Vincent, Guadeloupe, St. Thomas, San Juan, Cap Haitien.
Dec. 21	13	$495	*Santa Paula* (Grace)	Curaçao, La Guaira, Aruba, Kingston, Port-au-Prince, Fort Lauderdale.
1Dec. 21	16	$390	*Stella Polaris* (Clipper Line)	Nassau, San Juan, St. Thomas, St. Martin, Kingston, Grand Cayman, New Orleans (terminates).
Dec. 21	18	$445	*Santa Barbara* (Grace)	Santa Domingo, Puerto Cabello, La Guaira, Maracaibo, Barranquilla, Cartagena, Baltimore, Philadelphia.
Dec. 21	26	$800	*Santa Maria* (Grace)	Cristobal, Balboa, Buenaventura, Callao, Salaverry, Guayaquil, Buenaventura, Canal Zone.
Dec. 21	31	$1,110	*Brasil* (Moore-McCormack)	St. Thomas, Bahia, Rio de Janeiro, Santos, Montevideo, Buenos Aires, Santos, Rio de Janeiro, Barbados, San Juan.
Dec. 22	7	$170	*Italia* (Home)	Nassau.
Dec. 22	13	$325	*Olympia* (Greek Line)	New York, San Juan, St. Thomas, La Guaira, Curaçao, Kingston, Haiti.
Dec. 22	17	$560	*Argentina* (Moore-McCormack)	Nassau, Cristobal, Cartagena, Barbados, Martinique, St. Thomas, San Juan.
1Dec. 24	44	$900	*Del Mar* (Delta Line)	Houston, Bahia, Rio de Janeiro, Santos, Buenos Aires, Santos, Rio de Janeiro, Curaçao.
Dec. 28	13	$445	*Santa Rosa* (Grace)	Curaçao, La Guaira, Aruba, Kinston, Port-au-Prince, Fort Lauderdale.
Dec. 28	18	$445	*Santa Monica* (Grace)	Santo Domingo, Puerto Cabello, La Guaira, Guanta, Maracaibo, Barranquilla, Cartagena, Baltimore.
Dec. 28	43	$1,080	*Rio de La Plata* (Argentine)	Rio de Janeiro, Santos, Montevideo,/Buenos Aires, Santos, Rio de Janeiro, Trinidad, La Guaira.
Dec. 29	9	$220	*Italia* (Home)	Nassau, Port-au-Prince.

Dep. Date	Cruise Days	Min. Prices	Ship and Line	Itinerary
1963				
2Jan. 5	3	$165	*Franca C* (Atlantic Cruise)	Nassau.
Jan. 4	12	$345	*Gripsholm* (Swedish-America)	St. Thomas, San Juan, Cap Haitien, Nassau.
Jan. 4	26	$800	*Santa Luisa* (Grace)	Cristobal, Balboa, Buenaventura, Callao, Salaverry, Guayaquil, Buenaventura, Canal Zone.
Jan. 4	13	$395	*Santa Paula* (Grace)	Curaçao, La Guaira, Aruba, Kingston, Port-au-Prince, Fort Lauderdale.
Jan. 4	18	$445	*Santa Sofia* (Grace)	Santo Domingo, Puerto Cabello, La Guaira, Maracaibo, Barranquilla, Cartagena, Baltimore, Philadelphia.
Jan. 5	9	$225	*Olympia* (Greek)	New York, Haiti, Kingston, Nassau.
1Jan. 7	16	$390	*Stella Polaris* (Clipper Line)	Cap Haitien, St. Thomas, La Guaira, Curaçao, Kingston, Grand Cayman, New Orleans (terminates).
2Jan. 8	8	$175	*Franca C* (Atlantic Cruise)	San Juan, St. Thomas, Port-au-Prince.
Jan. 11	13	$445	*Santa Rosa* (Grace)	Curaçao, La Guaira, Aruba, Kingston, Port-au-Prince, Fort Lauderdale.
Jan. 11	18	$445	*Santa Barbara* (Grace)	Santo Domingo, Puerto Cabello, La Guaira, Guanta, Maracaibo, Barranquilla, Cartagena, Baltimore.
Jan. 12	7	$150	*Italia* (Home)	Nassau.
Jan. 12	24	$550	*Oslofjord* Norwegian-America)	St. Thomas, San Juan, St. Kitts, Nevis, Guadeloupe, St. Lucia, Barbados, St. Vincent, Trinidad, Aruba, Cartagena, Panama Canal Zone, Kingston, Port-au-Prince, Nassau.
Jan. 15	13	$325	*Olympia* (Greek)	New York, San Juan, St. Thomas, Grenada, Trinidad, La Guaira, Curaçao.
2Jan. 17	9	$200	*Franca C* (Atlantic Cruise)	Nassau, Port-au-Prince, San Juan, St. Thomas.
Jan. 18	7	$170	*Queen Frederica* (Nat'l Hellenic American)	Nassau.

Dep. Date	Cruise Days	Min. Prices	Ship and Line	Itinerary
Jan. 18	26	$800	Santa Maria (Grace)	Cristobal, Balboa, Buenaventura, Callao, Salaverry, Guayaquil, Buenaventura, Canal Zone.
Jan. 18	13	$445	Santa Paula (Grace)	Curaçao, La Guaira, Aruba, Kingston, Port-au-Prince, Fort Lauderdale.
Jan. 18	18	$445	Santa Monica (Grace)	Santo Domingo, Puerto Cabello, La Guaira, Maracaibo, Barranquilla, Cartagena, Baltimore, Philadelphia.
Jan. 19	7	$150	Italia (Home)	Nassau.
Jan. 24	19	$475	Empress of England (Canadian Pacific)	Port-au-Prince, Kingston, Montego Bay, Cristobal, Cartagena, Curaçao, Kingstown, Barbados, Fort-de-France, Frederiksted, San Juan.
Jan. 24	21	$610	Stella Polaris (Clipper)	Nassau, Cap Haitien, St. Thomas, St. Kitts, Martinique, St. Lucia, Trinidad, Aruba, Kingston, Grand Cayman, New Orleans (terminates).
Jan. 25	7	$170	Queen Frederica (Nat'l Hellenic American)	Nassau.
Jan. 25	13	$470	Santa Rosa (Grace)	Curaçao, La Guaira, Aruba, Kingston, Port-au-Prince, Fort Lauderdale.
Jan. 25	18	$445	Santa Sofia (Grace)	Santo Domingo, Puerto Cabello, La Guaira, Guanta, Maracaibo, Barranquilla, Cartagena, Baltimore.
Jan. 26	7	$150	Italia (Home)	Nassau.
2Jan. 26	13	$325	Franca C (Atlantic Cruise)	St. Thomas, Guadeloupe, St. Lucia, Barbados, Grenada, La Guaira, Curaçao, Port-au-Prince.
Feb. 1	26	$800	Santa Luisa (Grace)	Cristobal, Balboa, Buenaventura, Callao, Salaverry, Guayaquil, Buenaventura, Canal Zone.
Feb. 1	13	$495	Santa Paula (Grace)	Curaçao, La Guaira, Aruba, Kingston, Port-au-Prince, Fort Lauderdale.
Feb. 1	18	$445	Santa Barbara (Grace)	Santo Domingo, Puerto Cabello, La Guaira, Maracaibo, Barranquilla, Cartagena, Baltimore, Philadelphia.
Feb. 1	43	$1,080	Rio Tunuyan (Argentine)	Rio de Janeiro, Santos, Montevideo,/Buenos Aires, Santos, Rio de Janeiro, Trinidad, La Guaira.

FACTS AT YOUR FINGERTIPS

Dep. Date	Cruise Days	Min. Prices	Ship and Line	Itinerary
Feb. 1	7	$170	Queen Frederica (Nat'l Hellenic American)	Nassau.
Feb. 2	7	$170	Italia (Home)	Nassau.
Feb. 8	7	$170	Queen Frederica (Nat'l Hellenic American)	Nassau.
Feb. 8	13	$495	Santa Rosa (Grace)	Curaçao, La Guaira, Aruba, Kingston, Port-au-Prince, Fort Lauderdale.
Feb. 8	18	$445	Santa Monica (Grace)	Santo Domingo, Puerto Cabello, La Guaira, Guanta, Maracaibo, Barranquilla, Cartagena, Baltimore.
Feb. 9	7	$170	Italia (Home)	Nassau.
2Feb. 9	14	$350	Franca C (Atlantic Cruise)	San Juan, St. Thomas, Guadeloupe, St. Lucia, Trinidad, Grenada, La Guaira, Curaçao, Port-au-Prince.
Feb. 14	14	$350	Empress of England (Canadian Pacific)	Frederiksted, Antigua, Fort-de-France, Port-of-Spain, Aruba, Montego Bay.
Feb. 15	7	$170	Queen Frederica (Nat'l Hellenic American)	Nassau.
1Feb. 15	22	$630	Stella Polaris (Clipper)	Nassau, San Juan, St. Thomas, St. Kitts, Guadeloupe, Curaçao, San Blas, Cristobal, Montego Bay, Grand Cayman, New Orleans (terminates)
Feb. 15	13	$495	Santa Paula (Grace)	Curaçao, La Guaira, Aruba, Kingston, Port-au-Prince, Fort Lauderdale.
Feb. 15	18	$445	Santa Sofia (Grace)	Santo Domingo, Puerto Cabello, La Guaira, Maracaibo, Barranquilla, Cartagena, Baltimore, Philadelphia.
Feb. 15	43	$1,080	Rio de la Plata (Argentine)	Rio de Janeiro, Santos, Montevideo,/Buenos Aires, Santos, Rio de Janeiro, Trinidad, La Guaira.
Feb. 16	7	$170	Italia (Home)	Nassau.
Feb. 22	7	$170	Queen Frederica (Nat'l Hellenic American)	Nassau.

FACTS AT YOUR FINGERTIPS

Dep. Date	Cruise Days	Min. Prices	Ship and Line	Itinerary
Feb. 22	13	$495	*Santa Rosa* (Grace)	Curaçao, La Guaira, Aruba, Kingston, Port-au-Prince, Fort Lauderdale.
Feb. 22	18	$445	*Santa Barbara* (Grace)	Santo Domingo, Puerto Cabello, La Guaira, Guanta, Maracaibo, Barranquilla, Cartagena, Baltimore.
Feb. 23	7	$170	*Italia* (Home)	Nassau.
2Feb. 23	13	$325	*Franca C* (Atlantic Cruise)	St. Thomas, Guadeloupe, St. Lucia, Barbados, Grenada, La Guaira, Curaçao, Port-au-Prince.
Mar. 1	43	$1,080	*Rio Jachal* (Argentine)	Rio de Janeiro, Santos, Montevideo, Buenos Aires, Santos, Rio de Janeiro, Trinidad, La Guaira.
Mar. 1	7	$170	*Queen Frederica* (Nat'l Hellenic American)	Nassau.
Mar. 2	7	$170	*Italia* (Home)	Nassau.
Mar. 2	16	$400	*Empress of England* (Canadian Pacific)	San Juan, St. Thomas, Pointe-a-Pitre, St. Lucia, Barbados, La Guaira, Curaçao, Kingston, Nassau.
Mar. 9	7	$170	*Italia* (Home)	Nassau.
2Mar. 9	13	$325	*Franca C* (Atlantic Cruise)	St. Thomas, Guadeloupe, St. Lucia, Trinidad, Grenada, La Guaira, Curaçoa, Port-au-Prince.
1Mar. 11	18	$440	*Stella Polaris* (Clipper)	Nassau, San Juan, St. Thomas, Guadeloupe, St. Lucia, Curaçao, Kingston, Grand Cayman, New Orleans (terminates).
Mar. 16	7	$170	*Italia* (Home)	Nassau.
Mar. 20	15	$375	*Empress of England* (Canadian Pacific)	San Juan, St. Thomas, Fort-de-France, Kingston, Curaçao, Montego Bay, Nassau.
Mar. 22	43	$1,080	*Rio Tunuyan* (Argentine)	Rio de Janeiro, Santos, Montevideo,/Buenos Aires, Santos, Rio de Janeiro, Trinidad, La Guaira.
Mar. 23	7	$170	*Italia* (Home)	Nassau.
2Mar. 23	13	$325	*Franca C* (Atlantic Cruise)	St. Thomas, Guadeloupe, St. Lucia, Barbados, Grenada, La Guaira, Curaçao, Port-au-Prince.

FACTS AT YOUR FINGERTIPS

Dep. Date	Cruise Days	Min. Prices	Ship and Line	Itinerary
Mar. 30	7	$170	*Italia* (Home)	Nassau.
Apr. 5	10	$230	*Bergensfjord* (Norwegian America)	Cap Haitien, San Juan, St. Thomas.
Apr. 5	43	$1,080	*Rio de la Plata* (Argentine)	Rio de Janeiro, Santos, Montevideo,/Buenos Aires, Santos, Rio de Janeiro, Trinidad, La Guaira.
Apr. 6	6	$145	*Italia* (Home)	Nassau.
2Apr. 6	13	$325	*Franca C* (Atlantic Cruise)	St. Thomas, Guadeloupe, St. Lucia, Trinidad, Grenada, La Guaira, Curaçao, Port-au-Prince.
Apr. 9	7	$170	*Queen Frederica* (Nat'l Hellenic American)	Nassau.
Apr. 12	10	$245	*Italia* (Home)	Nassau, Port-au-Prince.
Apr. 17	12	$275	*Bergenfjord* (Norwegian America)	Guadelope, Barbados, Dominica, St. Thomas, San Juan.
Apr. 19	43	$1,080	*Rio Jachal* (Argentine)	Rio de Janeiro, Santos, Montevideo,/Buenos Aires, Santos, Rio de Janeiro, Trinidad, La Guaira.
2Apr. 20	8	$175	*Franca C* (Atlantic Cruise)	San Juan, St. Thomas, Port-au--Prince.
Apr. 27	7	$170	*Italia* (Home)	Nassau.
2Apr. 28	4	$95	*Franca C* (Atlantic Cruise)	Port-au-Prince
May 4	7	$170	*Italia* (Home)	Nassau.

1 New Orleans   2 Galveston   3 Port Everglades

SEA-AIR CRUISES

These were designed especially for tourists who want a taste of the special relaxation and luxury of shipboard life, but cannot afford the time for an extensive cruise. Your travel agent can arrange for you to go one way by sea, the other by air.

Here's a typical sea-air cruise offered by the *Panama Line* from New York to Haiti and Jamaica: You leave New York on

64

Friday, have three full days of cruising at sea, arriving in Haiti the following Tuesday. After three days and four nights in Haiti, you fly to Jamaica on Saturday, enjoy four days and five nights on that wonderful resort island, then fly back to New York on Thursday, the 14th day of your trip. These itineraries can be reversed: fly down, sail back.

The Panama Line's ships, incidentally, have outdoor pool, all outside rooms with private bath and every luxury you expect from a tropical cruise ship. Minimum rates (round trip) are $504 in winter, $445 in the summer season. A similar sea-air cruise is offered by the same to Haiti, the Dominican Republic, Puerto Rico and the U.S. Virgin Islands. Same time (two weeks) and approximately the same cost.

BY WAY OF BACKGROUND

MEET THE PEOPLE

Polychrome Pageant of Races

BY

WILLIAM W. DAVENPORT

(William W. Davenport is a contributing editor of "Fodor's Guide to Europe," author of books on Austria, Belgium, and Scandinavia for the American Geographical Society, and his latest "Guide to Paris" (Doubleday & Co.). A world traveler, Mr. Davenport has covered every inch of land and water between his former home, Hawaii, and Paris where he now resides.)

In the beginning were the Arawaks, a copper-colored race whose gentleness is suggested by two consolations which they bequeathed to posterity: tobacco and hammocks. The latter impressed Columbus and revolutionized the sleeping habits of sailors, who, before the discovery of this flexible beautyrest mattress, were accustomed to bedding down on a hard deck. The Arawaks introduced the western world to another joy:

the sweet potato, which they spent most of their time cultivating. A peace-loving agricultural people, the Arawaks were no match for the fierce warrior Caribs who swept northward from Paraguay like an Amerindian reincarnation of the Huns, conquering everything in their path. Their favorite cut of meat was roast leg of man, and we have some gruesome gastronomic reports as to how they found Frenchmen the tenderest, Spaniards the fattest, and Englishmen the stringiest of cuts. They also added a word to the Indo-European vocabulary: their own tribal name *caribe*, which is Spanish for cannibal.

The Arawaks were a pushover for both Caribs and for those even more relentless white-faced warriors who began to show up with cross and sword at the turn of the 16th century. Forced to work in mine and field by the Spaniards, the enslaved Arawaks languished and died like animals in captivity. Long before the term genocide was invented, the Spanish conquistadores provided a classic illustration of the term by wiping out two million Arawaks within the course of a single century.

The Caribs were more reluctant to lie down and die. The near extermination of this race took almost three centuries of the uncombined efforts of the white invaders, bent upon civilizing and Christianizing the Caribbean in the name of Spain, England, France and Holland. You will find a hundred or so pure Caribs today on the island of Dominica where they live in a Carib village, making baskets, canoes and cassava flour just as their ancestors did. Wide-cheeked, black-eyed, straight-haired and skin the color of brass, they have a striking resemblance to the Mongols of Asia.

Although few pure-blooded Caribs and even fewer Arawaks remain in the West Indies, the features of these vanishing races do not vanish at all but reappear in the faces of those children of European and Indian blood whom the Spanish call *mestizos,* "mixed." As a result you will see people in the Caribbean with a Eurasian look that suggests the Malay Peninsula or the Philippines. You will also find the stamp of the aboriginal in the Black Caribs and the Arawak-Maroons, descendants of Amerindian and Negro unions. In Venezuela and Colombia, Indian tribes like the Guagjiros and Cocinas fared better than the Caribs and the Arawaks, and you will find a stronger persistence of Indian feature and culture in these countries than anywhere else.

The Spanish conquistadores were looking for cities of pure gold and fountains of youth, but the El Dorado of the West Indies came with silver plumes, millions of them floating over endless fields of sugar cane. With Europeans developing a voracious taste for sugar and with the soil and climate of the Antilles ideal for raising cane, the economic destiny of the West Indies was set. But who was to perform the back-breaking labor of planting and harvesting this golden crop under the burning rays of the tropic sun? No white man, whether *hidalgo*, gentleman or *seigneur* was going to do it. The Arawaks couldn't stand the gaff; they either died or had to be killed off by their impatient masters. The Caribs were most uncooperative. The Spanish found the key to the problem on the Gold Coast of Africa which was to furnish the West Indian plantations with Negro slaves and make the Caribbean rich beyond the maddest dreams of the conquistadores. Less than two decades after Columbus discovered America, the first Negroes were brought to the West Indies. Stronger than the Arawaks, more docile (at first) than the Caribs, these kidnapped Africans could work for ten or twelve hours a day in the fields and exhibited commendable reserves of strength at the flick of an overseer's whip. The trickle of slaves in the 16th century became a steady flow in the 17th, a flood in the 18th, engulfing the West Indies in a dark tide of humanity which is now the broad basis of the world's most colorful population.

It would be beyond the scope of this guide to discuss the vicious circle of sugar, slaves and rum which brought unparalleled riches and misery to the Caribbean colonies of England, France, Spain, Holland and Denmark before slavery was abolished in the 19th century. The greed and cruelty of some planters ended by reaping a whirlwind of violence where sugar had been sown. The most notable of slave uprisings was on Saint Domingue where, with voodoo drums beating out a tattoo of revenge, the slaves rose against their French masters in a revolt that was to create the Black Republic of Haiti.

At all events, the immorality of slavery could not survive the tocsin of "Liberty, Equality and Fraternity" which rang in the 19th century nor the humanitarian pressures which were to abolish it in the West Indies by 1834. By that time there were hundreds of thousands of Negroes and mulattoes in the Antilles, and the broad basis of the Caribbean population was and remains the dusky shade of Africa.

It remained to add one more basic ingredient to the pot in which red white and black were now irrevocably mixed. The last infusion was Asiatic. Thousands of East Indians, both Moslem and Hindu, came in from the teeming Eastern colonies of Holland and Britain to fill the labor vacuum created by emancipation. The Indonesians added saffron to the pot. A sprinkling of Chinese throughout the Islands and the mixture was complete.

This *pot au feu* still boils merrily away, giving the West Indies a human savour that few other places can match.

The atavistic recurrence of both East and West Indian features in the people of the Caribbean is just one aspect of an incredibly rich racial heritage. The possible combinations and recombinations of ancestral genes in this area staggers the imagination. The Caribbean is more than a melting pot; it's the world's biggest Mendelian laboratory. The experiment, however, is uncontrolled. The subjects, unlike caged guinea pigs or mice, have long since taken over the experiment with a basic human zeal which is obviously shared by Englishmen, Frenchmen, Spaniards, Portuguese, Dutchmen, Danes, Swedes, Irishmen, Chinese, Indonesians, Indians East and West, to say nothing of the already polyglot Yankees and half the tribes of Western Africa.

Today's Caribbean population, though basically Negro, is often sufficiently mixed to keep ethnologists busy from now until the end of time. While the professors assemble their data, the experiment shows no signs of stopping. Its most interesting results so far are to be found in that light *café au lait* category, known in the West Indies as Creole.

The French Islands and Haiti have a widespread Afro-French dialect called creole, which anyone planning to stay a long time in these islands ought to learn if he wants to get to the heart of this polyglot situation. Papiamento is another new language, evolved by the inhabitants of Curaçao from Dutch, English, Spanish and Portuguese, and so advanced now as a means of expression that newspapers are published in it. Without a little study, you will not be able to understand any of the patois or dialects which are evolving as living languages in the Caribbean. But that need not disturb you. English is a lingua franca throughout the area. All the hotel keepers, travel agents, waiters, taxi drivers with whom you come into contact will speak and understand it.

One of the fascinating aspects of the islands is the manner in which the Negro tongue has adapted itself to the exigencies of English, French and Dutch, softening and thickening those languages in much the same way that the sauce is thickened by long simmering in a creole stew. You will be fascinated with the broad a's, clipped cadences and sing-song intonation of English as spoken by the Negroes of Barbados, Jamaica or

Trinidad. Puerto Rico and the Dominican Republic speak fluent Spanish with occasional overtones as resonant as the throb of a Voodoo drum. As for Haiti, Martinique and Guadeloupe, the language is French with a difference. The fleshy lobe of the African uvula was never designed to purr that impossible French "r". In this section of the world, creole is pronounced cweole.

Although absorbing the European manners, morals and speech of the ruling whites, the Negro has not renounced his own birthright of African rhythm and music which hold these islands forever in their spell. The fascinating thing about the Caribbean is the way in which two and more cultures are in perpetual interaction, one enriching another in a continuing sea change.

As for the "ruling" whites, their political power is inevitably being vitiated by the forward march of democracy, and the color bar is being lowered in the wake of evolving political equality. Generally speaking, however, the whites remain firmly ensconced in the economic saddle as administrators, businessmen, plantation managers, merchants, hotel keepers. The social bar between the privileged and underprivileged still has important color connotations, for the economically underprivileged in the Caribbean, with few exceptions, are colored. Except for Haiti, the French West Indies, and the Dominican Republic, all of which have a creole elite, the colored people with whom the average tourist comes into contact will be taxi drivers, porters, servants and Calypso serenaders.

The white minority consists of the highly competent managers of the resort hotels; the clannish shop-keeping, shipping, hotel-keeping aristocracy of the British islands, the go-getting, progressive, Americanized *Latinos* of Cuba, Puerto Rico, Venezuela; the erudite Latin elite of Colombia, and the exclusive and snobbish upper crust of Spanish-American society; the thrifty, conservative Dutch businessmen of Aruba and Curaçao, the cultivated ultra-conservative French businessmen and officials of Martinique, so insular, so suspicious of outside influence as to constitute a major obstacle to tourism. In general, however, the whites who own most of the land, control most of the business of the West Indies, are welcoming and friendly to tourists, a shining example of enlightened self interest. There is no cynicism intended in this remark. Your editor made five extensive trips to the Caribbean, and knows of few areas where the hospitality is more sincere.

FROM COLUMBUS TO CASTRO

Unquiet Cradle of New World History

"Civilization as we know it" began in the New World on October 12, 1492 when the caravels of Columbus hove to in the Bahamas. There had been earlier civilizations, of course, riding in canoes that were faster than the caravels, incising its cultural records on the walls of caves, reaching heights of splendor in the Aztec kingdom of Mexico, the Inca empire of Peru. But these could not withstand the cunning and the reckless courage of the Spaniards. Driven by an age-old mad obsession for gold, enrolled, incongruously enough, under the banner of the Prince of Peace, the Spaniards advanced everywhere with fire and sword. Within a decade of the first landfall, Columbus had discovered Cuba, Hispaniola, Jamaica, Trinidad, all of the lesser Antilles, Panama and the mainland of South America, claiming them all with their heathen peoples for their Catholic Majesties, Ferdinand and Isabella of Spain, still flushed with their victory over those more civilized infidels, the Moors.

FROM COLUMBUS TO CASTRO

The Spanish Colonial Era

Columbus died, in bitter disappointment and official disgrace, in 1506. Seven years later Balboa discovered the Pacific from a peak on that narrow isthmus which a nation still undreamed of was to pierce with that passage to the Indies which Columbus had sought in vain. A decade later Hernando Cortes had conquered Mexico, Francisco Pizarro had subdued Peru, and the gold of the Incas was being transported across Panama from the Pacific to the Caribbean and thence to the coffers of Spain. Simultaneously Alonzo de Oneda was exploring the gulf coast of North America with its great river delta, and Governor Ponce de León of Puerto Rico, searching for the fountain of youth, stumbled upon Florida and death in the form of a poison-tipped Indian arrow.

In 1522, Gil Gonzales Davila induced the conquered Cacique of Nicaragua and 9,000 of his subjects to submit to one of the more impressive mass baptisms of history. Other Indians were more recalcitrant, fearing that if they went to a Christian heaven, they might meet the Spaniards there. One cannot blame them for hesitating. In spite of the protests of such a humane priest as Father Bartolomé de las Casas, the Spaniards wiped out a whole race of two million Indians within the space of a single century. They were most unsatisfactory workers, these Indians. The Spanish, having found that sugar cane from the Canaries would grow in their new possessions, were forced to bring in Negro slaves to work the field. Father de las Casas approved, an interesting commentary on the morality of the day.

As the 16th century moved into its sixth decade, Imperial Spain held the golden key of the New World. The Spanish monopoly was almost complete. As early as 1494, Pope Alexander VI had given his official blessing to Spanish conquest by establishing the line of demarcation which divided the "non-Christian world" between Spain and Portugal. The line, drawn with a rather sketchy knowledge of New World cartography, assigned everything to Spain with the exception of a coastal slice of Brazil.

History is full of ironies. The pope who thus divided the New World did his part in dividing the Old by having a number of strictly illegitimate children and behaving generally in a most unpopish manner.

Martin Luther was a boy of 11, Henry VIII of England a babe in arms when the line of demarcation was drawn. Within half a century another line was drawn, and Europe was split asunder by the Reformation. In 1558 the daughter of Henry VIII and Anne Boleyn ascended the throne of Protestant England, deadly enemy of Spain. This was no legitimate sovereign, said the Catholics, this was the bastard of a liaison not only illicit but unholy. Bastard or not, the Virgin Queen's star was rising. The days of Spanish hegemony were numbered in the Old World and the New. The period of Spanish exploration and conquest was over. It was time for history to bring on the buccaneers.

Privateers, Buccaneers, Pirates

The first two freebooters to appear were gentlemanly proto-types of countless scoundrels to come. Their names were Drake and Hawkins. Their position on the high seas was highly ambiguous. To the Spanish they were pirates out and out, and history says amen. To the English they were privateers, almost an anagram for pirates, on the business of Her Majesty the Queen. If they attacked the Spanish, it was an aggressive act of self defense, the best method of staving off a Spanish assault. The sea of operations was the Caribbean. Hawkins contented himself for the most part with slave-running, buying Negroes on the Guinea coast and selling them to the Spanish colonists in defiance of the Spanish king. Drake's method was more direct. There was gold in the galleons of Spain, treasure piled high in the cities of the Spanish Main, and he meant to get them for God, for Country and for Queen, all three of whom were Protestant.

He attacked with religious zeal, with infinite audacity and courage. As red-haired as the Queen, he had the kind of personality that compelled faith, obedience, devotion. He was 26 years old and the Caribbean was his oyster. More precisely, it was an oyster bed, full of priceless pearls, some of them as big as acorns. He lay in wait for Spanish galleons, striking at them from hidden bays. Like a swift bird of prey, he pounced and plundered. With each attack, another load of bullion was lost to Spain. Drake's most romantic coup was a night attack on a mule-train plodding along the Camino Real of Panama, carrying the gold and jewels of Peru across the isthmus to Spanish ships waiting on the Caribbean shore. There were more than 200 mules in the caravan, each one with a fortune on its back. Drake got it all, every pearl and emerald, every shining nugget down to the last speck of gold dust. The treasure went to England, not to Spain.

At a New Year's reception, Elizabeth wore part of the booty, a splendid brooch of Muzo emeralds that set off her red hair to perfection. The Spanish ambassador simmered with rage. Two days later, he boiled over. For Drake's name led the New Year's honors list. Thenceforth and forever more in history, this plundering pirate would be known as *Sir* Francis Drake.

Not only knighted, but equipped with 30 ships and more than 2,000 armed men, Sir Francis attacked two of Spain's strongest Caribbean bastions, Santo Domingo and Cartagena. He took them both by the same stratagem, landing men at night and surprising the Spaniards from the rear. To add insult to injury, he captured Cartagena on Ash Wednesday. Pious Spaniards were convinced that God was punishing them for past transgressions with these visitations of the Devil in the form of Drake. Both cities were plundered, their churches pillaged, their citizens forced to pay huge ransoms or see the towns go up in flames.

It was 1585. The Spanish, fed to the gills with undeclared wars, began to build a great Armada that would put a stop to these outrages forever. Like a bolt of lightning, Drake struck the harbor of Cadiz and set fire to the Spanish ships. Not until Pearl Harbor would there be such a stunning surprise again. Admiral Santa Cruz of the Spanish fleet had a heart attack. King Philip was almost paralyzed by the shock. It took him three years to get the Armada into ship shape again. The rest is a simple historical statement, sung out in chorus by every English, American and Canadian grammar school boy since the event itself: "1588: The English under Drake defeated the Spanish Armada."

Britannia Rules the Waves

It is customary at this point to say that the power of Spain was broken forever. This is an over-simplification. But there is no question that the era of Rule Britannia was at hand. And Drake was merely the first of a pack of English sea dogs who were to bay the moon of the Caribbees for another century at least.

Among the more famous were Blackbeard the Pirate (real name: Edward Teach) and Sir Henry Morgan. The first operated out of New Providence in the Bahamas, that Cromwellian colony where pirates consorted with puritans and you could hardly tell one from another. There was no mistaking Blackbeard, however. His coal black beard was plaited into a series of braids. He swaggered about with three braces of pistols, his mad febrile eyes shining in the glow of lighted matches, which he stuck under his hat. He was fond of sticking matches under the nails of his victims too, and so was Henry Morgan, as mean a fellow as ever plowed the Caribbean, though an English gentleman withal.

Morgan's career was a 17th-century parallel of Drake's. His name was anathema marantha to the Spaniards. Operating out of Port Royal, the "Babylon of the West" on English-captured Jamaica, Morgan occupied and pillaged the colonial cities of Spain: Granada on Lake Nicaragua, Santa Maria de Puerto Principe of Cuba, Portobello, which he captured by forcing nuns and monks to precede his men up the scaling ladders of the fortress, and Panama City itself. Since England and Spain were ostensibly at peace, this was pure piracy. Madrid protested to London. Henry Morgan was summoned to England, put on trial, sentenced to imprisonment in the Tower, released and knighted! He ended his days in Jamaica as Lieutenant Governor of that thriving colony. Uncrowned king of Port Royal, he sat in that doomed and wicked city, drinking rum and piously contributing portions of his pirate loot to the local church. There in 1688 Sir Henry died in the odor of sanctity, four years before Port Royal with its unbearable burden of wickedness sank beneath the waves.

Blackbeard and Morgan were but two of the Caribbean's famous English sea-dogs. There were Newman and Jackman, preying on the Spaniards and even planning to establish a Central American republic of buccaneers!

Piracy was by no means a British monopoly. There were the noble Frenchmen, Pierre Belain d'Esnambuc and Urban de Roissey. Their headquarters was the tiny island of Saba. In the neighboring waters they took so many prizes that Cardinal Richelieu got interested in the game. He bought $50,000 worth of stock in a new French company to exploit les *Isles de l'Amérique*, commissioning Esnambuc to colonize, plunder, privateer, in short, make profits. France's hat was in the Caribbean ring. So was Holland's. The famous Dutch seaman, Piet Heyn, fell upon the Spanish fleet off the Cuban coast and took five million dollars worth of booty home to Amsterdam. For this and other services to his country, Pirate Heyn became Admiral of the Netherlands.

All these, if you like, were national pirates, respected and rewarded citizens of their countries, which they were enriching at the expense of unhappy Spain. There were other buccaneers, freebooters whose only flag was the Jolly Roger, whose only loyalty was to captain and mates. Their ragged clothes were stained with blood and rum. Anything in the Caribbean was fair game for these cut-throats: any ship, and settlement, any woman, regardless of race or religion. Tortuga and the Virgin Islands swarmed with pirates. They lived on rum and smoked pig, *a la bucana*, whence the name buccaneers. Nothing in *Treasure Island* or the wildest fancies of fiction could equal the reality of this democracy of bandits, cutting a swathe through the West Indies as they cut the throats of their victims. Epic binges, epic orgies were the order of the freebooter's day. They made the 17th century the most colorful of the Caribbean; call it the cycle of the corsairs.

Rum, Sugar and Slaves

As the 17th century drew to a close, it was clear that the economic stakes in the Caribbean were high. The freebooters' days were numbered. It was time now for another kind of piracy, legalized, organized on a national scale. In other words, war. Exhausted Spain, plundered alike by English, Dutch and French, now watched as her three principal tormentors began to torment each other. Between 1665 and 1702 there were at least eight separate wars among the three upstart powers which had challenged Spain's monopoly.

The stakes were sugar, rum, coffee, cocoa, and cocoa-colored slaves. Europe had developed an insatiable hunger for the first four items. The West Indian plantations could not get enough of the last. The life blood of the plantations was black slave labor. Forty "factories" were operating on the coasts of Africa. These were actually concentration camps where captured Negroes were held pending transportation to the West Indies. The British owned about half the factories. The Dutch owned the rest. Native African chiefs cooperated by selling their prisoners of war to the enterprising slave traders. The British salved their conscience with this; by shipping these unfortunate blacks to the nice plantations of the West Indies, they were saving them from a far worse fate in Africa. At the end of the 17th century about 75,000 slaves a year were being shipped from the gold coast of Africa to the cane fields of the Antilles. Negro slaves in good condition brought about 18 pounds sterling a head, or the equivalent in sugar and rum, in the markets of the West Indies. So slavery itself was big business, to the tune of nearly $7,000,000 a year. The fact that the slaves were so valuable was used by apologists of the trade to counter abolitionist charges of "the horrors of the middle passage". After all, reasoned the apologists, no planter was going to pay good money for merchandise damaged in transit.

It was on the slave trade and the plantation system that the economic prosperity of the West Indies was built. Never in the history of the world had there been a colonial economy as rich as this one based on slavery and sugar. "Rich as a creole" became the new simile of wealth in London, Paris, Amsterdam. This was the wealth over which the powers of Europe squabbled for a hundred years. In the end the whole structure was brought down by emancipation. The institution of slavery could not withstand the principles of the French Revolution or the humanitarian ideals that spread through Europe in the 19th century.

The Age of Revolt

The Negro slaves of Saint Domingue sounded the tocsin of revolt with their voodoo drums, and the fall of the fabulously rich French plantisocracy was no less dramatic than the fall of the Bastille. The second republic in the New World came into being, a black one, Haiti, resuming its original Indian name, defying Napoleon, and, miraculously, surviving. By 1834, slavery was abolished everywhere in the West Indies. The plantations were in the doldrums. The beautiful islands of the Caribbean lay in abject poverty with their dusky legacy: millions of emancipated blacks. There were the sun and the surf, the beaches, the splendid mountains, the climate. But, although all of Europe was stirred by a new romantic interest in Nature, the idea of exploiting its beauties for tourism still lay a century in the future.

The libertarian passions of the 19th century, however, spread like a brush fire through Latin America. Here the great leader was Simón Bolívar of Venezuela. Under his inspired direction, half the continent of South America was liberated from the Spanish yoke. He is the father of five countries: Venezuela, Colombia, Ecuador, Peru, Bolivia, the last one named in grateful memory of El Libertador, the Liberator.

President Pétion of the fledgling republic of Haiti had helped Bolívar with money and men during the early days when the liberating revolution had bogged down in what looked like hopeless defeat. And what of that other fledgling republic, prototype of them all, the United States of America? The Monroe Doctrine was promulgated, warning the powers of Europe and especially Spain that America would take the dimmest view of Old World interference in the affairs of the Western Hemisphere.

This famous and much-maligned doctrine was brought into play in 1898 when all America echoed with the cry, "Remember the *Maine!*", the U.S. battleship which was blown up, some said at the instigation of William Randolph Hearst, in Havana Harbor. The dogs of the Spanish-American war were unleashed. It was Spain's expiring gasp in the golden world over which she had once ruled alone. Cuba became an independent republic. Ceded to America was Puerto Rico, the land of Ponce de Léon, an abject little island, an orphan, an "insoluble problem", the "stricken land." Within half a century it was to pull itself up by its bootstraps to the status of a thriving commonwealth, 20th-century pace setter for the Caribbean.

The Present-Day

What is the political status of the Caribbean as this century forges ahead in its sixth decade? The era of intervention when the United States took steps in Haiti, Santo Domingo, Nicaragua "to protect our interests" now seems one with that of piracy and the slave trade. Whatever the provocation, Uncle Sam and the Western democracies of Europe seem determined to let this once-turbulent area forge its own destiny. That destiny moves inexorably in the direction of independence and self government.

Moving from Bermuda southward, the "colonial" situation looks like this at press time:

Bermuda and the Bahamas swim in the Atlantic, aloof from the Caribbean and from all concern with Caribbean politics, independence movements and the like. They are British colonies with a British-appointed governor. They elect their own local legislature, and they are perfectly content with arrangements as they are.

Cuba, largest of the Caribbean islands, has been an independent republic since 1898. Currently in the throes of a communist revolution, Cuba's status is that of a distant Soviet satellite. Her man of the hour, Fidel Castro, admittedly is leading the country toward complete sovietization—a policy which has obliterated tourism. Cuba is out of bounds for Americans for the time being, and all of those who know Cuba cannot help but experience a feeling of deep loss at not being able to visit this beautiful country.

Haiti, always a problem, still foments from time to time, and the Dominican Republic which shares the island of Hispaniola is no longer in the doghouse with the American Republics. With Trujillo dead, fundamental changes are taking their unavoidable course.

Jamaica is the largest and most populous of Britain's Caribbean possessions. It became an independent member of the British Commonwealth only recently and is now hopefully building its future in line with some ambitious plans for development.

Puerto Rico is a self-governing Commonwealth with full autonomy, a status the islanders achieved by popular vote in 1952. Puerto Ricans have their own constitution, elect their own legislature and governor, and are represented in Washington by a commissioner who has the status of a United States congressman. The Puerto Ricans also enjoy the benefits of United States citizens without the liability of paying federal income taxes. It's a case of having their tortilla and eating it too. Most Puertoriqueños are highly satisfied with the current arrangement, though there is some agitation for full statehood in the United States and a small minority which wants secession and complete independence. The secessionists are losing ground at the moment while advocates of Puerto Rico as the 51st state in the Union have been gaining support in view of the recent admission of Hawaii.

The United States Virgin Islands, bought from Denmark in 1917, elect their own unicameral legislature, have a governor appointed by the President of the United States. Operating under an organic act signed by President Eisenhower in 1954, they enjoy all privileges of American citizens except for representation in the U.S. Congress. The Virgin Islander is a focus of envy among his Caribbean cousins, since he enjoys high standards of living and wages and even the benefits of American federal relief payments when unemployed. The Virgin Islands' free port status was guaranteed in the purchase agreement with Denmark. We know of no Virgin Islander who wants to jeopardize those free port privileges by agitating for independence but sentiment is growing in favor of statehood.

Martinique, Guadeloupe and the rest of the French West Indies belong to France. They are full departments of France with Paris-appointed prefects, elected representatives in the French National Assembly in the Council of the Republic and in the Assembly of the French Union. Since all the inhabitants of the French islands are citizens of the French Republic, there

Carnival is the climax of Caribbean fun

is little agitation for independence from the mother country.

The Netherlands Antilles (Dutch West Indies) are an integral part of the Kingdom of the Netherlands, having the same rights of citizenship as the Dutch living in Holland. The governor is appointed by the Queen. The local legislature or "Staten" is elected by universal suffrage on a basis of proportional representation: 12 members from Curaçao, 8 from Aruba, 1 from Bonaire, and 1 from the Dutch Windward Islands.

Venezuela, Colombia and Panama are independent republics. The Panama Canal Zone, a strip of land which includes five miles on each side of the canal, is leased to the United States at an annual rent of $430,000 a year, and administered by an appointed Governor who is also President of the Panama Canal Company.

The British Status-Seekers

The string of British Leeward and Windward islands curving like a vertebrate spine from the Virgins down to Barbados are the backbone of the British West Indies, the latest experiment in self government that misfired.

The West Indies Federation which started in April 1958 when Princess Margaret formally opened the first Federal Parliament in Trinidad, has been dissolved in May 1962.

Jamaica, Trinidad and Tobago its two major components, each gained separate independence with full membership in the British Commonwealth.

In the meantime the British Leeward and Windward Islands, now called the "Little Eight", are wrangling and muddling under the leadership of Barbados, to reach an agreement on federation on this reduced scale.

While high hopes faded somewhat the "Little Eight" may ultimately be able to achieve political consolidation and economic security through cooperation with each other and the Commonwealth.

This new development is not the first sea change of the Caribbean, nor will it be the last. No matter how static the weather in this lovely part of the world, the human story remains dynamic, ebbing and flowing, mysterious and inexorable as the tides of the sea.

Christmas shopping in a native quarter

THE LIVELY ARTS

They Got Rhythm They Got Music

The outstanding cultural contribution of the Caribbean is in music and the dance. The West Indies throb with rhythm from the Bahamas to the Spanish Main. And although there is a good deal of Amerindian influence in that music, especially in Venezuela, Colombia and Panama, its essential beat was established centuries ago in the jungles of Africa, and it remains irrepressibly African. Seldom in history has there been such a triumph of art over circumstance. The music of the Negro, kidnapped, deported, enslaved, has conquered not only the Caribbean but the world.

Whatever the faults of the Spaniards as colonists, they loved music, and it is significant that they adapted both Indian and African tribal music to their own uses. They also retained and adapted the dance forms of the peoples whom they conquered and enslaved. The British and the Dutch, Protestants for the most part, found these native gyrations conducive to sin and repressed them, often with puritanical severity. Music and the dance thus flourished on Latin-American soil, but languished in the Anglo- and Dutch-American colonies. It is significant that the most important musical developments on British Caribbean islands, Calypso and steel bands, came late and in defiance of the authorities. Calypso, which is discussed at length in our chapter on Trinidad, also had strong connotations of social criticism, another example of the whirligig of time bringing in its revenges against official suppression. A similar "revenge" may be observed in the unbridled exuberance of the Trinidad Carnival (see below), the hottest annual blowout in all the West Indies.

Indian Dance Dramas

History tells us that the Indians on Santo Domingo (now the Dominican Republic) charmed the Spanish conquerors with graceful dances, performed to the accompaniment of drums and vocal music. These do not survive in the islands where the Spanish all but exterminated the dancers, but you can see Indian ceremonial dancing in Venezuela, Colombia and Panama. You will be more likely, however, to see Spanish-Indian dances like the *Joropo* of Venezuela, the superbly graceful *El Tamborito* of Panama, the *Cumbia* of the mountain Indians of the Colombian coast. These and many more furnish sufficient evidence that the Indians adapted the dance forms of the conquering Spaniards, absorbing them easily into their own highly-developed dance tradition. When you watch certain dances of the Caribbean with that incredibly fast staccato stamping which the Spanish call *zapateos*, you won't know where the Amerindian influence leaves off and Flamenco takes over. One thing is certain: the combination is exciting and even compelling, for you are dealing with two races, each with rhythm in its national soul. Most interesting of all the combinations are the dance dramas of Venezuela, both Indian and mestizo, which are being rescued from obscurity by the Venezuelan Ministry of Folklore to its everlasting credit and to the advantage of all lovers of the dance. The mestizo dance dramas are splendid, a kind of opera-ballet in which the story is unfolded by a singer as in the Indian areitos. Whatever the story, the whole production is an argument in favor of the blending of diverse cultural elements into something beautiful and new. In this sense, the mestizo dance dramas are typically and symbolically Caribbean.

Enter Africa

If this is a happy blending, the combination of Spanish with African music and dance form is an ideal marriage. Its offspring, if you like, are on constant display, not only in the West Indies but all over the world. It is in fact almost impossible to conceive of modern jazz and popular dance without reference to the contribution of Africa, and specifically of the African slaves who were dragged to the New World within two decades of Columbus's discovery.

When you are in the Caribbean you are at the focal point of that incredible rhythmic energy whose vibrations have reached to every corner of the civilized world. Although pure African dance forms remain intact among the Bush Negroes of Surinam, the Africans in Latin lands embraced Spanish music with even more enthusiasm than the Indians had shown. And what Spaniard worthy of the name could remain insensible to the throbbing of a jungle drum? To the insistent rhythms of these drums, the Spanish added the exotic Moorish wail of their own melodic tradition. Out of the plantation shacks and into the ballroom came the drums of Africa. The *rhumba* was born; the *conga,* the *guaracha*, the *mambo*. In Paris a master of orchestral color heard the smouldering relentless rhythm of this Afro-Cuban music, set it down with symphonic effects, and brought down the Salle Pleyel, Carnegie Hall, and all the temples of serious music in America and Europe. Half the world still thinks Ravel invented the Bolero. But it came from Cuba out of Africa and Spain. You will see it performed as a ballroom dance in Havana, sinuous and slow, danced by the children of a double race whose heritage is a double dose of rhythm. As for the rhumba, when you see it danced by the uninhibited Cubans it is doubtful if you will recognize the polite little box step you learned at dancing school.

Unlike the Cubans who embraced African music *con mucho gusto*, the Puerto Ricans tend to look down their noses at hybrid dance forms. The country dance called *seis* remained uncorrupted by African rhythm, and it exists today both as a communal dance for six (hence the name, *seis*) or as a ballroom exercise for two. It is charming to see this gay stamping dance, rather reminiscent of the *sardanas* or the *jotas* danced by rural communities in Spain.

In spite of Puerto Rico's "purity", an Afro-Puerto Rican song and dance routine did develop shortly after the turn of this century. This is the *plena*. It has a rhumba-like rhythm, amusing lyrics, and offers the performer a chance to improvise and engage in a certain amount of pantomime. In many ways the plena wil remind you of a Spanish version of calypso, which certainly must have had an effect on the Puerto Rican development. Subject matter for the plenas ranges from the pangs of unrequited love to current events and the high cost of living. A sugar company lawyer from New York became the subject of a plena when he fell into the sea during a sugar strike and was eaten by a shark. The composer of the plena was very gay about the tragedy; his sympathies were with the strikers. You will find a quatrain from this particular plena in the chapter on Puerto Rico. As you can see, any subject is suitable for a plena.

The Merengue

One of the dance legacies of the African slaves is the *merengue*, which you will see danced and may dance yourself in nightclubs and restaurants all over the Caribbean. It is especially popular in Haiti, the French West Indies and the Dominican Republic, where it is presumed to have originated. The French merengue is smoother and more elegant than the Spanish variety, which is on the sultry side. The basic rhythm of the merengue recalls the rhumba and the paso doble (Spanish two step) and has a strange limping motion, the weight being concentrated on one foot. This striking characteristic of the merengue is said to derive from the limping of slaves who were forced to drag a ball and chain with one foot. This explanation is more romantic than scientific, and would be more accurately applied to the conga, which may very well derive from the rhythmic inhibitions imposed upon a chain gang.

Martinique and Guadeloupe are fond of the merengue, but on these islands the *danse du pays* is the red hot, uninhibited and decidedly erotic beguine, described in our chapter on the French West Indies. A striking contrast to this is the old world mazurka, which is danced here with a sort of clinging-vine creole charm, the girls swooning in their partners' arms as the dance comes to an end. Waltzes, quadrilles, and even the minuet are still danced on all the islands with certain individual island variations on these figures from another century and another world. It is obvious enough that slaves, peering into the candlelit ballrooms of the great plantation houses, saw these dances and adopted them. The creole elite of the Republic of Haiti certainly danced every figure that Europe had to offer, and continues to do so.

These dances are hardly typical of the Black Republic, however. For here everything throbs to the rhythm of Voodoo drums, and the African influence is strongest of all. Even the mulatto aristocracy drops its elegant Parisian manner at the first beat of the drum. On with the dance; let joy be unrefined! The average ballroom dancer in Haiti is like some coffee-colored Nijinsky, a natural genius of the dance. Voodoo dancing is described in the chapter on Haiti. You should also attend one of those Saturday night hoe downs called *bambouches*. Among the country dances performed at these fêtes are the *congo* and the *martinique*. These are variations of the stately quadrilles danced by our grandfathers under crystal chandeliers. Grandfather would never recognize them now.

Haiti is the most fascinating of all the Caribbean countries from the point of view of dance and African folklore. While there, you should not miss a program of the Bacoulou Dance Troupe and the National Folklore Group which perform regularly at the Theatre du Verdure in Port-au-Prince.

This is an outstanding example of the conscious revival of a rich folklore, one which other countries would do well to emulate. Roger Albert has already taken important steps to preserve the dances of Martinique. The University of the West Indies in Jamaica is doing yeoman service in this field, and folklore societies are being formed throughout the Caribbean area. Venezuela has gone farthest of all in organizing a government Folklore Ministry. These recent developments are encouraging to all who would like to see a rich and unique cultural heritage preserved.

Afro-English Developments

The English may have tried to suppress African music and dancing, but if you think they succeeded you need only go to Trinidad, especially at Carnival time. Shango, a pagan religion, officially repressed, flourished in secret with all its ceremonial dances and trances. Africans converted to Anglicanism turned "Onward Christian Soldiers" into a Shango shindig. The dancers kicked up their legs in ecstasy. Vicars threw up their hands in horror.

Calypso and steel bands (described in the chapter on Trinidad) became the rage, not only on this island but throughout the British West Indies and beyond to America and Europe. A hot dance, King Sailor, was created by the cool cats of Trinidad to go with Calypso music. When this hit Harlem, bop was born. Jump-up, another Afro-T'dadian invention, couldn't be more accurately named. At Carnival time the whole island is jumping and you will be too, up and up until sheer exhaustion chains your feet to the ground. At that point you can watch the tribal ecstasies of the bongo and the shango or the incredible acrobatics of the limbo in which the dancers writhe under a low horizontal bar, supine *without touching the floor*. There is no scientific explanation for limbo dancing; it has to be seen to be believed, and the dancers must be literally "possessed" by the dance in order to perform it.

Carnival at Trinidad opens the floodgates of African folklore. Even the British succumb to the dark tide that pours forth. Nor should Britain's so-called "unadaptability" be overstressed. For not only do they dig their annual carnival, they also sent a steel band to the coronation of Queen Elizabeth. It played "God Save the Queen" as it's never been played before, a wonderful testimony to the African absorption of Western melody. Steel bands can play anything from "Rock of Ages" to Rock 'n Roll. This suggests the essence of Caribbean culture: it is adaptive, inventive, and full of a *joie de vivre* which transcends race, color, and previous conditions of servitude.

Pre-Columbian Art

Although less widely known than music and the dance, Caribbean art and architecture have made a cultural contribution sufficiently interesting to warrant the attention of the tourist especially in music and the dance. The purest examples of American art are those which were fashioned before the arrival of the Europeans. Although the most striking examples of pre-Columbian art are to be found in Mexico and Peru, the Caribbean tourist will find many examples of it in the Caribbean islands and especially in the museums of Colombia and Venezuela. The celebrated Gold Museum in Bogotá is a treasure trove of Amerindian artifacts, works which reflect a dynamic plastic skill and a manual dexterity which latter seems always to have been one of the outstanding Indian skills. A fascinating survival of this technical craftsmanship may be seen on Dominica where the cleverly-woven baskets and the hand-carved "dugout" canoes of the Caribs are made in exactly the same manner as they were before Columbus came. More widely known are the Indian jewelry and figurines. But the insatiable appetite of dealers and collectors for "pre-Columbian stuff" has just about depleted the stock of these handsome primitive bronzes and ceramics. You will find more Indian objects for sale in New York and Paris than you will in the Islands, but a visit to the Caribbean museums indicated in the geographical text of this guide will provide you with an introduction to the art which flourished here before it was modified by European influence.

Architecture

That influence first makes itself known to the tourist in the surviving examples of Spanish colonial architecture, which imparts so much charm and *cachet* to Latin American cities. The initial style, trembling between the Middle Ages and the Renaissance, set the tone for all subsequent architecture in the New World. The cathedral of Santo Domingo in Santo Domingo begun as early as 1496 and completed in the middle of the 16th century, is a fascinating melange of Gothic and Renaissance elements. The interior has groined Gothic arches and heavy piers terminated by attenuated vaults. The exterior is pure Plateresque, decorated with the fantasy of Renaissance Spain, a fantasy which was to burgeon into the baroque but which is here restrained by a certain classicism, reflected in Romanesque arches, Corinthian columns, and a frieze in the Roman manner. The Alcazar of Diego Columbus, built in the early 16th century and handsomely restored in the 20th, has the open loggias and other Italian features of Renaissance palaces in Florence or Barcelona.

The oldest vestiges of Spain in the New World are thus redolent of the Renaissance plus that special Hispanic addition, the exotic Moorish touch which scholars call the mudéjar influence. If you want to see a superlative example of this, visit La Fortaleza, the Governor's Residence in Puerto Rico. Its Moorish dome, entrance gate and Arabian Nights windows are designed harmoniously to create one of the handsomest buildings in all America.

Spanish Baroque

About the middle of the 17th century, the baroque style which was engulfing Europe as a reaction against the rigid "classicism" of the Renaissance, was brought to the New World. Nobody, not even the Austrians, took to the baroque the way the Spanish did. In the New World they let themselves go in an orgy of curving lines, rich ornamentation, decorative painting and sculpture, gold and silver filigree and convoluted form. The Indians, many of whom were craftsmen employed by the Jesuit fathers and other builders of the New World, took to this style like ducks to water, embellishing it wherever

THE LIVELY ARTS

possible with motifs from their own civilization. Negroes who had carved strange idols in the depths of Africa got into the act. Statues of saints, altars, columns, arches were lavishly carved all over Latin America in stone and gilded wood, rivalling the art of the mother country, often surpassing it in sheer decorative exuberance. Criollo craftsmen like Vásquez of Colombia rose along with countless other artists to express their devotion to Christ and the Virgin in paint and polychrome wood. To appreciate this 17th-century flowering, you should see Vásquez's work in the churches of Bogotá, full of religious art which can stand comparison with the leading works of the Spanish school.

For a later efflorescence of the Hispano-American baroque, go to Havana's cathedral and study the splendidly-decorated facade designed in the 18th century by Pedro Medina. This striking cathedral is, in a sense, the last gasp of the baroque. The swing back to classicism was already underway when Pedro conceived his sinuous labyrinth of stone. There are enough examples of the new trend in Havana itself: the church of El Templete, almost like a Doric temple; the Jesuit seminary of San Carlos, whose cloisters are a marvel of 18th-century austerity; the Supreme Court of Cuba, and the handsome city hall of Havana, designed in 1776 by Pedro Medina himself, a genius who could bend with the wind and construct master-pieces in more than one style.

It was this neo-classic style which provided the whole Car-ibbean area with its domed capitols, its arcaded streets, its Roman porticoes, its Greek facades, its general look of re-strained elegance which you will find throughout the West Indies in the Plantation Great Houses, similar in style to those of the southern United States.

The Victorian obsession with gingerbread detail made its mark in the Caribbean with results that are quaint and amusing, especially on the British islands, but the taste for classicism persists in contemporary architecture, especially in the monolithic skyscrapers of Caracas and Havana and in the increasingly functional hotel architecture of Puerto Rico, St. Thomas, Colombia and Aruba.

The tourist's favorite architecture, however, will be found in the domestic field: in the old Spanish houses of Cartagena, Havana and San Juan and in the colorful ultra-modern villas all over the Caribbean which have adapted the traditional grille work of balcony and *reja* to the eclectic tastes of our own times.

THE LIVELY ARTS

Painting

In the field of painting, Haiti has now dominated the entire Caribbean area for more than a decade with the vigorous "primitive" art movement which is described in detail in a subsequent chapter on the Black Republic. While this movement breaks into splinter groups and diverges into what critics are fond of calling its "decadence", its original inspiration seems unimpaired. That inspiration, like the Voodoo impulse behind Haitian music, is essentially African.

Almost without exception, the influences on original Caribbean art have been the influences of the conquered or the enslaved. In Central America and on the Spanish Main where the Indians were not subjected to the ruthless genocide that characterized Spanish occupation of the Islands, painting, architecture and sculpture are marked indelibly with the Amerindian stamp. The didactic work of revolutionary Mexican painters which stunned the art world with its bold forms and hot colors in the 1920's is the most celebrated example of this. You will find spiritual affinities with these Mexican painters throughout Latin America, especially in such an oeuvre as that of Luis Alberto Acuña, a Colombian painter whose original talent expressed itself in notable studies of Indians and mestizos, subject matter which the Europe-trained painters of his country, long under the spell of Goya, preferred to ignore. Indian influences, though less pronounced, are also visible in the work of the Venezuelan, Tovar y Tovar, who painted epic canvases, dramatically depicting the major episodes in Bolivar's struggle for independence. These pictures, in the Caracas Museum of Fine Arts, show that the painter had assimilated all that Europe could teach in the arrangement of battle scenes, but their distinctive "Venezuelan" color owes as much to the Indians as it does to the historical subject matter.

In the Antilles, the leit-motif is African. Haiti and Cuba are the leaders in exploiting this vein of blue gold. The Negroes themselves, the disinherited mestizos, and the poor white "guajiros" take the place of dispossessed Indians under the brush of Cuba's leading painters. Alberto Peña, Antonio Gattorno, and the sculptress Rita Longa found their inspiration far from the precincts of Havana's elite. Gattorno, discovered and promoted by Cuba's most famous adopted son, Ernest Hemingway, painted the guajiros with more subtlety but no less power than Orozco and Rivera brought to the peons of

Mexico. Other Cuban artists who have made more than a parochial contribution to art are Victor Manoel, who led a revolt against the academic restrictions that were strangling Cuban painting; Carlos Enríquez, a vivid painter of the Cuban landscape; René Portocarreo, whose social indignation and glowing impasto suggest the early work of Rouault; Jorge Arche and Eduardo Abela, whose work, inspired by Rivera's example, seems somewhat dated now; Maria Capdevila with her stunning, simplified portraits of Negroes, and Cundo Bermudez, a "neo-primitive" who depicts his stiffly-posed subjects against Cuban landscapes which are recorded with surrealist clarity and detail. African sculpture, by way of Picasso, has exerted a marked influence on the work of Wilfredo Lam and Amelia Pelaez, two modern Cuban painters who have lived and studied in Paris. The best place to see the work of all these painters is in the Ministery of Education in Havana, which has long sponsored one of the most important art movements in the Caribbean area. Museums and galleries which sell island paintings are indicated under individual countries in the text of this guide.

A special word on a recent development in Caribbean art should be said for the painting of Jamaica. Here too the dominant influence is African, specifically Afro-Haitian. It is not to be expected that it will have the flair and originality of the more spontaneous Haitian movement, and there is no question that it has undertones of British respectability and even formality. Less vehement, less violent than the painting of Haiti and Cuba, it is nevertheless deeply sincere and technically competent. You can see it on display at Abe Issa's *Myrtle Bank Hotel* in Kingston. Prices are more moderate than those for the works of the better-known Haitian and Cuban painters, and you may very well make some personal discoveries among these young Jamaican artists.

You may make some discoveries on other islands too. Nobody ever heard of Haitian art before 1944. And look at it now!

CALYPSO GASTRONOMY

Creole Variations on an International Theme

It would be false to pretend that the Caribbean's chief claim to fame is its food, but you can eat very well in the West Indies. The tendency is strong among the big hotels to serve an unimaginative meat and potatoes diet garnished with peas of a poisonous green shade, dyed with more than a pinch of sodium bicarbonate, and topped off with gelatinous ice cream. This, say the hotel proprietors, is what the tourist wants. The professional euphemism for this sort of fare is "continental cuisine" or "international cuisine". No restaurateur would dare to serve it on the Continent, and no truly international palate would put up with it for more than a single meal. It is not what the tourist wants, and even if it were, this would be no excuse for suppressing the tasty and spicy native dishes which adventurous tourists will want to try. We have described many of these native dishes below under the countries which make a specialty of them. You can do the cause of tourism a favor by asking for them if they don't appear on the menu, and help dispel the canard that tourists want nothing but steaks and chops.

CALYPSO GASTRONOMY

Having registered this complaint, we must add that there are certain hotels and restaurants throughout the Caribbean which will satisfy the most discriminating gourmet. They are listed, country by country, under the Food, Drink and Restaurants sections.

Caribbean and Atlantic waters abound with all the fruits of the sea, and you should be on the lookout for such delicacies as Bermuda lobsters, the fish chowders of Hamilton and Nassau, conch fritters and turtle pie (two specialties of the Bahamas), and *pescado horneado con almendras,* Cuba's superb baked fish with almonds, in which the chief ingredient is pompano, sole, or snapper. The Moro crabs and the *langostinos* (fresh water prawns) of Cuba are high on any gourmet's list, just about at the top of ours.

Pescado Santo Domingo is a Dominican Republic creation of sea bass, elaborately prepared and served cold as a delicious *hors d'oeuvre.* The Dominican Republic has also contributed to the gourmet's pleasure with *Sopa Hamaca,* one of those splendid Spanish stews in which lobster and cubed fish meet happily with rice, potatoes, tomatoes, onions, garlic, pimientos, shredded cabbage and olive oil. The Jamaicans have a way of stuffing lobsters with a heavenly concoction of chopped onions, mushrooms, bread crumbs and grated cheese, then baking the whole affair to a golden brown. Another Jamaica specialty is "Stamp and Go", delicious codfish fritters, which are served either with fried plantains or boiled green bananas.

Our top favorite for general culinary excellence is Haiti. Here the basic cuisine is French, and there are creole additions that could even teach the French a thing or two. Still in the seafood department, try the Haitian *hûitres marinées,* a remarkable variation on the oyster cocktail in which the succulent mollusks have been pickled to death. The Haitians also turn out a superb shrimp and avocado salad, which you will see on the menu as *crevettes et avocats vinaigrette.* Their greatest contribution, however, is *homard flambé,* flaming lobster, beautifully seasoned and set afire, not with cognac or armagnac, but with the local Barbancourt rum.

The waters surrounding Puerto Rico literally teem with lobsters, huge shrimps, and crabs, and you can't go wrong on this island when you order *pescado. Pescado Guisado,* the Puerto Rican fish stew, combines white fish with shrimps, conch meat, onions, leeks, garlic, parsley, tomatoes, bay leaf and seasoning to produce a rich and savory result that can stand the inevitable comparison with *bouillabaisse. Asopao,* the famous rice stew of Puerto Rico, reaches its zenith when the chief ingredient is shrimp, crab or lobster instead of the more conventional chicken.

Seafood is one of the greater joys of the Lesser Antilles too. Here top honors go to Martinique and Guadeloupe, those creole outposts of *la cuisine française*, and to St. Lucia, now British but keeping its French accent in the kitchen. The best lobsters in the whole Caribbean seem to gravitate to the pots of St. Lucia and the St. Lucians treat this king of the sea in an appropriately royal manner. If you are skeptical of the highly-touted French touch, try *Acra l'en Mori* on Guadeloupe or Martinique. They're nothing but fish cakes, but they are good enough to rival the best *quenelles* of Paris or Lyon.

The tiny oysters of Trinidad and the flying fish of Barbados are two obligatory items for any *fin bec* visiting these two islands. Both have a unique flavor, both are delicious.

The turtle steaks of the Cayman Islands rank at the very top along with Cuba's moro crabs, Barbados' flying fish, and St. Lucia's *langouste,* which is to say among the outstanding seafood delicacies in the world. Colombia is famous for its *paella* and Aruba and Curaçao for Dutch food and East Indian *Rijsttafel.*

Island Specialties

If you see *calaloo* on any menu in the West Indies, don't hesitate. This is the queen of creole soups, the royal progenetrix of the famous crab gumbo of New Orleans. It's made with crab, okra, tomatoes and onions, seasoned with thyme, bay leaf, and ground chili peppers. After half an hour or more of simmering, you have a soup that's super duper.

Sans coche, the *king* of creole soups takes us out of the fish and into the meat market. It is made with beef, pork and pig tail and 15 other ingredients which you will find listed in our chapter on Trinidad, and it's a meal in itself unless you have an appetite like Krushchev and Gargantua combined.

When it comes to soups that are meals in themselves, you also have your choice of Trinidad pepperpot (chicken, pork and corn beef!), creole pea soup, Puerto Rico's *sopa de cebolla* (a delicious cheese and onion concoction), and Cuba's *sopa de judías coloradas*, a terrific black bean soup made with ham and garnished with sliced hard-boiled eggs and lemon.

Wherever the Spanish go *arroz con pollo* goes too and so does roast suckling pig, a delicacy you may find on the menus of Cuba, Puerto Rico or the Dominican Republic under its

Spanish name: *léchon asado*. The latter is unctuous and crisp at the same time, perfectly delicious, and definitely not recommended if you've got a liver. *Arroz con pollo* is, of course, chicken with rice and some 15 other ingredients including saffron, that special seasoning that turns Spanish rice to gold. You'll find it in all the *paellas* of Puerto Rico. If you want Spanish-style chicken *without* rice, try Cuba's *guisado de pollo,* a chicken stew made with potatoes, green peas, olives, pimientos, onions, olive oil and white wine. If you're a vegetarian, or merely jaded with meat, the *aguacates rellenos* (stuffed avocados) of Cuba are just the dish for you. The halved avocados are stuffed with a marinade of potatoes, carrots, green peas, asparagus and beets, then slathered over with about an inch of fresh mayonnaise and chopped egg. Served cold, this makes a wonderful lunch with iced Cuban coffee, or a planter's punch if you prefer.

The East Indian curries of Trinidad are hotter than any curry you ever had at home. There are some milder curries in Saint Lucia, a good island for crab back (cooked and restuffed in shell), calaloo and chicken pelau, a tender chicken and rice stew with typical creole sauce. There are a number of variations of creole sauce. Some like it hot; some like it cold. If you're attached to it, you can make it yourself with canned tomatoes, sliced olives, chopped green pepper, celery, and onion, salt and pepper. Put it all together, pour it over fish, put it in the oven, and you have a creole dish.

You'll hear references to "peas and rice" in calypso songs throughout the islands. The islanders go for this combination in much the same way as Venetians go for their beloved *risi bisi,* which is substantially the same dish. It consists of pigeon peas, chopped onion, chopped tomatoes, olive oil, rice, salt and pepper. In Bermuda they call it Hop'n John, and add thyme and Portuguese sausage or bacon to the recipe. There are many variations. It's a kind of basic creole dish, and it's very good. Pigeon peas are also combined with pork in Puerto Rico's *Gandules.* Latin Americans love this dish, and are also fond of *habichuelas,* red beans, and various kinds of tamale such as *hallacas* and *pasteles* combined with pork or chicken and steamed in banana leaves.

By the time you've sampled all this, you'll probably be ready for a nice grilled steak with green peas, french fried potatoes and ice cream. There is something to be said for it after all, and you'll find some first class steak places listed under the countries you plan to visit. As for the ice cream, try the wonderful coconut variety served in a coconut shell. You'll find this in Cuba, Jamaica, everywhere where there are coconut trees and cream, and it is something to write home about. Most of the luxury hotels do offer sumptuous island desserts like baked bananas with coconut cream, and these are good enough to warrant a subsequent diet if necessary. All the exotic fruits of the tropics are available, of course, and you can eat all the mangoes and papayas you want without watching your waistline. Sorry, the same thing cannot be said for bananas, especially when they start pouring on the grated coconut, melted butter, cinnamon and heavy whipped cream. Still, a sweet tooth must be served, and it's well served, especially in the Spanish islands, with *yema doble* (a little Puerto Rican mixture of sherry, sugar and six egg yolks), *panatela,* coconut tarts and other delicious explanations of why Spanish women lose those adorable figures as they get older.

So much for whetting your appetite. And now to wet your whistle with one of the truly great products of the West Indies, that distilled sunshine which used to be called moonshine, and which the British colonists called "comfortable waters". We are referring, of course, to Demon Rum. This is the national drink of the Caribbean, an important factor in the region's past and present economy, and one good reason for going to the West Indies. There are many types of this sugar cane juice, and each has its partisans. Our personal preference happens to be for the mellow, brandy-like rum Barbancourt of Haïti, distilled according to the old formula of the French who introduced the art to Saint Domingue as the Black Republic was once called. But feeling can run so high about rum, especially after one has been sampling the various types, that we have asked an expert, our good friend H. W. Goeggel, to discuss this subject for our guide with the authority and the objectivity of an expert.

RUM

Distilled Sunshine of the Antilles

BY

HARRY W. GOEGGEL

(A pioneer in the tourist development of Puerto Rico and the Dominican Republic, Mr. Goeggel is now Commissoner of the Virgin Islands Department of Tourism and Trade.)

Rum is the most widely known export of the Caribbean area and the West Indies. This by-product of the manufacture of sugar is one of the most popular and versatile drinks ever devised to comfort the human race. The simplicity of its manufacture accounts in large measure for its popularity. It requires no great plants, no long ageing period, none of the fuss and feathers that attend the distillation of Bourbon, Rye or Scotch.

As the cane is ground, the molasses is separated from the natural cane sugar juices, and this is the basis from which rum is made. Rums are produced by a distillation and a fermentation process, both of which you'll have a chance to see when you visit the rum-producing West Indian islands. Most fermentation rums contain molasses and caramel ingredients in addition to the basic cane juice or syrup. These are the heavy or "blackstrap" types of rum.

The lighter and more refined rums are those from which most of the molasses has been removed, leaving a pure cane juice base. This highly-appreciated type comes in both dark and light varieties.

All rum has a pungent, pleasant odor; this is particularly true of the blackstrap variety. It is reminiscent of the fragrance that pervades a sugar mill at grinding time.

The rums of the world are many, but none are so renowned as those of our Caribbean area. They first came to the attention of the world in the early days of the sugar exploitation era from 1650 to 1700. In the 18th century New England became famous for its rums, made there from imported West Indian sugar and molasses.

Rum has never had any regard for race, creed, color or social position. It transcends these distinctions. Theme of a thousand rousing sea chanties, it was the favorite drink of the pirate, the buccaneer, the sea captain, the sailor, the merchant, the planter, the slave. When the English Admiral Edward Vernon, called "Old Grog" because he wore a grogram coat, gave orders to dilute his sailors' rum, he added a new word to the language. Grog Shops sprang up in every seaport of the Caribbean and along most waterfronts of the civilized world. They're still popular, and hot grogs (rum with water) still give comfort to men who never heard of Vernon. Grog became the official drink of the Royal British Navy. The crews of English ships still drink toasts to Her Majesty the Queen in strong West Indian rum.

The rums of our Caribbean Islands vary just as much as their cultures, their scenery, and their history. Perhaps the most famous are the rums of Cuba, highly distilled light-bodied rums, known the world over by the trademark *Bacardi*, the family name of an outstanding distiller. Since Castro, almost all the light-bodied rums today come from Puerto Rico including Bacardi, originally associated with Cuba. Seventy-five per cent of the rum consumed in the United States are rums from Puerto Rico. This white rum is the basis for the celebrated daiquiri and bacardi cocktails. The daiquiri was invented at the turn of the century by engineers of the Daiquiri Mining Company. Scene of their brilliant experiment was a little Havana bar known as La Florida. Here one fine weekend they hit upon the idea of mixing the juice of fresh-squeezed limes with some simple syrup and rum of the light-bodied type known in Cuba as Carta Blanca. When these ingredients were shaken up with fine shaved ice and poured into a whisky sour glass, a wonderful new cocktail was born and immediately christened in honor of the mining company. One engineer's invention begets another. When grenadine was added to the mixture as before, the bacardi cocktail made its debut. It is not known how many millions of daiquiris and bacardi cocktails were consumed by thirsty American tourists during the years of prohibition. But there has been no noticeable decline since repeal. These cocktails, now served in bars all over the world, have never lost their popular appeal.

Varieties of Rum

There are many other popular rum drinks, of course, but before preparing them it's a good idea to know a little about the best types of rum to use. We'll go over them briefly in alphabetical order so as not to ruffle any island feelings.

Barbados Rum is a finely-distilled liquor of the so-called "brandy type". Slightly heavier than Cuban and Puerto Rican rums, it is nevertheless light enough to be used in daiquiris. Its color is light brown, its flavor is clear, and its unobtrusive bouquet is such as to make it a perfect mixer. In other words, you don't taste Barbados rum in cocktails. But don't worry; it's there all right. Since Barbados rum is such a good mixer, it's very popular, especially with the ladies. It is probably the most widely-used rum in the islands for ordinary cocktails and mixed punches.

Cuban Rum, already mentioned, is distilled mostly from pure cane juice. A yeast culture is used in the distillation process with results that are unsurpassed for lightness and sweet flavor.

Demerara Rum is a horse of quite a different color. It is dark brown and heavy-bodied. This type is made in British Guiana and Trinidad. It has a pungent flavor and a strong bouquet, redolent of molasses. The smell of Demerara rum is the quintessence of the sugar and spice islands. It is delicious and very potent. Some brands (Hudson's Bay Demerara and Lemon Hart Demerara) run as high as 151 proof, so hold onto your hat. This is the blackest of the blackstrap rums mentioned above; in fact it is popularly known as black rum because of its deep color. Highly prized by experts for its virile flavor and potency, the high-proof bottled varieties bring relatively

101

high prices. The general run of Demerara is inexpensive, however, to such an extent that it is the drink of the working man in our islands. In this respect, Demerara rum is like snails; you find it in the poshest clubs and bars and in the poorest shacks. The effect on the human organism is the same: stimulating, comforting, and if you take too much, stupefying. There are notable differences within the Demerara type. Some distillers use fruit juices as flavoring agents. The juices of various tree barks are also used. Maybe that's what gives it its bite! You can have a good time trying to detect the secret agents, but don't let the idea run away with you.

Jamaica Rum comes both in light and dark varieties, but there is no difference between the two as to potency and piquancy of flavor. The bouquet is strong and distinctive. Jamaicans are very proud of their rums, ascribing their excellence to such factors as the traditional use of the pot still, special qualities of climate, water and soil, slow fermentation, and an unusual ageing process in white oak casks and vats. The making of Jamaican rum is as much of a ritual as the production of French wine. The law forbids the infusion of any bark, fruit or other "impure" element into the liquor, even as a coloring agent. So when you hear connoisseurs talking about the "purity" of Jamaica rum, they are referring to the fact that it is made exclusively from cane juice, molasses and other by-products of Jamaican sugar cane. Surprisingly enough the aroma of many Jamaican rums suggest an infusion of spices or herbs, but it all comes from the cane, you may be sure. A good deal of the heavy aromatic rum of Jamaica is exported to England where it is blended and aged in the colder climate of the north, emerging as the world-famous London Dock Rum. There are at least 30 different brands of Jamaica rum including Myers whose 30-year-old "Mona" is the rum equivalent of Napoleon brandy.

Haitian Rum, highly regarded by connoisseurs, is distilled like brandy in the finest French tradition. The famous Barbancourt distillery which produces our favorite rum is now unfortunately making no more, only bottling what has been made before. A good tip is to stock up on it if you have the chance, because it will soon disappear from the shelves, and a sad farewell we tender it. Try this rum neat in a brandy snifter. It has a splendid and subtle bouquet and the true unadulterated flavor of molasses. Perhaps the finest compliment paid to Haitian rum is that the French, who taught the Haitians how to make it, are the biggest importers of the local product.

RUM

French rums of Martinique and Guadeloupe are dark, heavy-bodied, and seem almost like a cross between Jamaica and Demerara varieties. The French call it Rhum, of course, and one of their great contributions to humanity is the famous rum-soaked cake, Baba au Rhum. Certain of the Martinique rums have a fascinating dry, smoky flavor. The local Rhum Clément is admired by experts and so is Rhum St. James, pronounced with a short *a* in this department of France.

Leading brands of light-bodied dry flavored Puerto Rican Rums are marketed as *White Label* (pale or colorless) and *Gold Label* (a deep golden) somewhat more flavorsome than white, often used in punches, hot drinks and the traditional holiday eggnog. The white leads in versatility and popularity. It blends readily with citrus juices, e.g. the daiquiri, rum sour and carbonated mixers. Best known brands are: Bacardi, Boca Chica, Carioco, Don Q, Maraca, Merito and Ronrico.

Virgin Islands Rum is in between the heavy blackstrap type and the light Cuban-Puerto-Rican variety. It has an aromatic bouquet and a delightful not-too-heavy molasses flavor. Not widely-known outside of St. Thomas, St. John and St. Croix, it has come as a pleasant and distinctive surprise to rum connoisseurs visiting the islands. There are half a dozen excellent brands including Cruzan St. Croix and Government House. The latter is 125 proof; sip slowly. Cartegena rum also has its admirers.

Varieties of Rum Drinks

There are literally hundreds of rum cocktails, swizzles, highballs and punches. Every island, every bar has its specialty. A popular cocktail success, running third to bacardis and daiquiris, is the Presidente, which uses the same ingredients as a Manhattan except that a dark, or Carta de Ora, type of rum is substituted for the whisky. This Carta de Ora rum, not to be confused with the blackstrap type, is the favorite type for highballs, blending perfectly with soda, ginger ale, 7-up or any of the usual complements including good old aqua pura. The Cuba Libre is now world-renowned, a chic name for rum and coca cola. It's most effective when a dark rum is used.

As the subtleties of this distilled liquid sunshine are appreciated, more and more of our visitors are ordering rum mists and rum on the rocks. Connoisseurs of rum use it as an after-dinner liqueur, especially when the rums are old and mellow—twenty years of age and more—and too precious to be mixed. They have been compared many times for delicacy of flavor, aroma and bouquet with the famous brandies of the world.

When it comes to long cool drinks, the most famous by far is the Planter's Punch. Here the heavy blackstrap type of rum comes into its full glory, mixed with native fruit juices, garnished with pineapple and other exotic items, served in a tall glass with plenty of ice, and sometimes lightly sprinkled with cinnamon, nutmeg or some other magic dust of the spice islands. There are many variations from island to island on this classic drink. We still savor the memory of one in Bermuda in which three different rums, Barbados, Jamaica and Demerara, were blended with lime juice, pineapple juice and half an ounce of grenadine. In Trinidad, it's made with the juice of half a lime, two ounces of Demerara, a teaspoonful of grenadine, and, since this is Trinidad, a generous dash of Angostura bitters. The rest is ice and soda water and plain, old-fashioned refreshment.

These are just three of many possible variations on the basic theme of rum. They demonstrate once again the wonderful versatility of this liquor. In a way it's like calypso; you can improvise as you go along. Many hotels now make a practice of bringing you basic ingredients: rum, lime juice, pineapple juice, Angostura and other suggestions, and letting you mix it yourself.

Sometimes a masterpiece results from the constant experimenting that goes on. One, which has received and richly deserves the accolade of connoisseurs is the now-famous Virgin Island Banana Daiquiri. This is made by a special recipe in which a whole tree-ripened banana is added for each drink. It is mixed in a Waring blendor which completely liquefies the banana. You start with ambrosia and end up with nectar.

Many readers will be familiar with the flavor of rum in fine cakes, Life Saver candies, and that other life saver, the famous Hot Toddy which is the most pleasant curer of colds in cold winter climates. But the best way to learn about rum is to visit the West Indies. Sample it on a white sandy beach, under the shade of a palm tree, listening to the surf roll in. A smiling native boy will bring you a long cool drink, perhaps a medium light rum poured into the shell of a freshly hollowed-out, chilled pineapple. As you sip this wonderful concoction through a straw you'll know why we call it "the liquid sunshine of the Caribbean".

BLOSSOMS IN THE SUN

The Dazzling Floral Beauty of the Caribbean

For all but the color blind, the trees, shrubs and flowers of the Caribbean are one of the chief attractions of a voyage to these Islands and countries in the Sun. For gardeners and real lovers of flowers, the Caribbean is the Garden of Eden, full of all the exotic wonders that God created in the beginning to delight the heart of man, and full of man's own handiwork in the important fields of cultivating and landscaping.

For the budget-minded garden lover, summer in the Caribbean offers a golden opportunity. For in June, July and August, prices are at their lowest while the island trees and blooms of the Caribbean are at the height of their glory.

Starting from the top, let us begin with the most spectacular blooms of all, those which burst like celestial fireworks from the flowering trees of the tropics. Perhaps the most familiar of all, though custom cannot stale its flaming beauty, is the Flamboyant tree or flamboyán if you prefer the Spanish version, which is just as common in the Caribbean as the tree itself. In Jamaica and Panama, you'll hear it called the Royal

BLOSSOMS IN THE SUN

Poinciana; in Venezuela, the acacia. In Surinam and Trinidad, it's called the flame tree. Even its official botanical name, *Delonix Regia,* suggests that splendor of its scarlet blooms with their attenuated orchid-like petals capturing every ray of the tropic sun. Sometimes growing wild in solitary splendor, more often cultivated in a superb avenue of trees, the flamboyant sheds its leaves when it blossoms. New leaves appear almost at once, however, and the tender green foliage sets the scarlet flowers off to maximum advantage for eight weeks and more in summer.

The sight of these flame-colored flowers against the brilliant blue of the Caribbean sky is one of the indelible memories of the West Indies. Photographers will want to shoot the flamboyant from every angle. The tree blooms in Jamaica and Puerto Rico in May, June and July. In Trinidad and Venezuela it reaches its height as early as April or May. In Surinam and the other Guianas, the blossoms don't appear until September. Let this schedule serve as a guide if you want to see this most spectacular of trees in bloom. The Royal Poinciana sets the tone for the whole color scheme of summer in the Caribbean.

Next in popularity to the poinciana is the fragrant frangipani tree with its velvety star-shaped flowers, red, creamy white, sometimes pale pink, occasionally yellow. These blooms have a strong sweet fragrance. It reminded the first European explorers of a popular Renaissance perfume called Frangipani after the chemist who produced it. Hence the name, imported from Italy, but appropriately exotic for this lovely flowering tree. Called plumeria in Hawaii, it has long been famous in the Pacific as an ideal flower for making leis. The frangipani flower fades quickly, however, once it is picked, and, as its edges darken the sweet smell of the blossom becomes fetid. This may explain why its fragrance, so delightful on the tree, has never been successfully captured in a true frangipani perfume. Both leaves and clustering flowers of the frangipani grow at the extremity of the branch so that the interior boughs of the tree will remind you of Shakespeare's "bare ruined choirs". If you live in a tropical clime, a branch of the tree broken off and stuck in dry soil with good drainage immediately becomes another tree.

Cut the frangipani, even slightly, and a sticky, milky sap emerges almost as though the tree were bleeding milk. This milk has been used by natives as a poultice, but it should not be taken internally. If you are travelling with children, you should warn them against eating or licking this sap and against

106

any consumption in any form of the oleander, whose sap is so deadly that it has been known to poison people who ate chops that had been grilled over a fire of oleander wood.

You will find this beautiful plant, incidentally, in all its pink or white glory, used everywhere as a windbreak in Bermuda. The frangipani, to return to a less noxious beauty, blooms in Trinidad from November to January, but you will find it in full flower further north (in Jamaica, for example) from May through July. As a matter of fact, this fragrant tropical beauty seems to burst into flower whenever it feels like it. We have seen the same clump of frangipanis gaily blooming in the spring and again in the early winter of the same year!

Shower of Gold

Third in our own private popularity poll is the dazzling Shower of Gold, or *Cassia Fistula* to use its highbrow academic name. This majestic tree, often growing to a height of 40 feet, is well named. Its yellow buds and petals, cascading downward, really do look like a golden shower. The bark of this tree has long had a commercial use in the fabrication of dyes, and it has medicinal properties that have produced various purgatives, astringents and cough medicines wherever the tree is found. But nothing can compare with its purely ornamental function. You will find it at its peak throughout the Caribbean from April into June, and we predict that your camera will be busy trying to record this splendid shower tree, its golden clusters forming a striking contrast with luminous green leaves and a sky of perfect blue.

Other flowering trees to watch for are the Immortelle trees, which we have always known as *Erythrina Cresta Galli* or, more commonly, the coral tree. But immortelle is most appropriate, for we once saw one of these trees putting out its cock's comb blossoms even after it had been chopped down, sawed up and burned in a fire! Haiti is one of the places to see this tree. It also thrives in Jamaica, Puerto Rico, Dominica, Venezuela, Colombia and everywhere that coffee is produced. For the immortelle is a favorite tree for shading the smaller trees on which coffee, cocoa and spices are grown, a fact which is reflected in popular names for the Mountain immortelle in Trinidad: coffee mama and cocoa mama.

Two of the most outstanding plumed monarchs of the Caribbean are the Jacaranda tree, a fabulous beauty from India and Ceylon with bell-shaped violet flowers and fern-like

107

A latter-day version of the glory that was Spain

leaves; and the Pride of Burma, whose gold and vermilion inflorescence makes it one of the most prized ornamental trees in the world. You'll find it in Jamaica, Trinidad and elsewhere in the Caribbean where it blooms from early winter right through to the following fall. Not as commonplace as the Poinciana, the *Amherstia nobilis*, to use its botanical name, has to be sought for. But it is well worth the search.

Almost as rare is the bombax or silk cotton tree whose silky red tassels appear in June and remain through July. But the commoners are as beautiful as the aristocrats in this part of the world, in which context we think especially of the African tulip tree with its cups of crimson and gold, and the ubiquitous *Brassaia,* growing all over the islands with its grey bark, glossy green leaves, and stunning, deep red, spiky flowers. These bloom in early summer and are a flower arranger's delight, since they last and last, long after they have been cut from the tree. Do not hesitate to cut them. The Brassaia is another one of those indestructible tropical trees; like the Banyan, it would take over your garden—and your house if you didn't keep it under control.

These are but a few of the myriad flowering trees which clothe the Caribbean islands with a mantle more varied than Joseph's coat of many colors. Their effect is intensified by an equal number of flowering vines and shrubs: the bignonia or orange trumpet vine; the popular Bougainvillea, tumbling over walls in great splashes of vivid red, purple or white; Hibiscus, king of all tropical shrubs, its large and showy flowers coming in many subtle shades of red, yellow, white and pink; plumbago with its lovely blue blossoms; thunbergia, a wonderful aromatic yellow-flowered vine whose tender dark green stalks end up by becoming woody tree trunks, and crape myrtle, the blooming East Indian shrub which grows here as successfully as it does in Dixie.

You will, of course, see every variety of palm tree in the islands. Perhaps the most majestic are the stately royal palms which line some of the handsomest avenues of the tropics. Cuba is the Pearl of the Antilles in this department. As you fly over the island, you'll see these trees everywhere, like millions of matchsticks stuck into the soil. When you're on the ground, these "matchsticks", soaring 50 and 60 feet in regal splendor, give the whole place an air of nobility and grandeur.

Less formal, equally appealing are the graceful coconut palms which fringe the beaches, their stiff fronds rustling in the breeze, their great clusters of fruit, green, golden, or brown, promising the pleasures of crisp white nut-meat or, if you prefer, gin and coconut water. Many of the Caribbean's trees are as pleasing to the palate as they are to the eye. The avocado leaps to mind at once; the mango (pronounced with a broad a in this region), queen of tropical fruits; the bread-fruit, brought to the West Indies by Captain Bligh of the mutinous *Bounty*; the sapodilla, tamarind, the guava, the paw paw, which may be more familiar to you as papaya; the wide-spread banana trees with their great, ragged, fringed leaves, offering a delicious fruit which is one of the chief products of the area. The cashew nut tree, the macadamia, and the pomegranate are three more which offer special delights to the eye, the stomach, and the soul. Nor should the olfactory nerves be neglected. Remember the Spice Island, Grenada, with its nutmeg trees (*myristica fragrans*), its cinnamon, camphor and clove trees, and that climbing orchid which produces vanilla beans both here and on rainy, aromatic Dominica.

The three c's, solace to the human race, grow profusely in the Caribbean too: coffee, cocoa, and cola. The coffee trees are beautiful: miniature affairs, not much higher than a bush, with glistening green leaves and the shiny red berry which will be burned by the sun to a dark brown bean. The cola nut tree is a tall evergreen, in the kernel of whose fruits is the narcotic essence of so many medicines and drinks. Still another tree with medicinal properties is the towering eucalyptus, splendid aromatic sentinel of the tropical forest.

Orchids Drip from Trees

As for flowers, you will be enchanted by the blooms which almost every island can boast. Tourists from temperate climates will be fascinated to see the most expensive and exotic denizens of hot house and city florist shop growing in dazzling profusion in their native soil. The famous lilies of Bermuda flash upon the inner eye as an outstanding example. The epiphytic glories of the floral world feed upon the tropic air. You will see orchids, not in constrained corsages, but in great sprays, literally dripping from the trees. The variety is staggering: Cattleyas, vandas, dendrobiums, oncidiums, almost every kind of orchid that is known. The orchid garden at Balboa, Panama Canal Zone, has more than 400 varieties of epiphytes in a single collection. Colombia's Medellin bills itself as "the Orchid City of the World".

A great floral favorite is the anthurium, hardy but exotic

BLOSSOMS IN THE SUN

perennial with its striking waxen spathe, blood red, sometimes pink or white, punctuated by its yellow priapic anther. You will also be tempted to "sport with Amaryllis in the shade", especially here where the red and tigrish blossoms of these bulbous plants are beautiful beyond compare.

Less exotic perhaps, but no less charming, are the African lilies (*Agapanthus Africanus*) with their arresting blue flowers; the bright, showy cannas, bigger and more numerous here than they are at home; huge Shasta daisies; flaming poinsettias, which grow here not in pots but in fields or massed together as a scarlet ornamental band to set off a lawn; hydrangeas, those popular shrubs with the pink, white or blue flowers that are called *hortensias* throughout Latin America; African violets, periwinkles and brilliant, slightly wicked-looking zinnias. These last annuals, the alphabetical rear guard of any floral check list, are among the most common glories of West Indian gardens.

The gardens of the Caribbean, both private and public, and the magnificent rain forests of all the mountainous islands, will be pilgrimage goals for all tourists with horticultural and botanical interests. Botanical gardens like the Hope and Castleton establishments in Jamaica offer the botanist a special opportunity for floral research. At the same time, these gardens are places of beauty and tranquillity which will appeal also to tourists whose knowledge of flowers is only rudimentary. Even if you don't know a dendrobium from a dandelion, it is doubtful if you'll be able to resist the charm of a place like Haiti's Kenscoff Gardens, for example, where carnations, blue larkspur, snapdragons, gladioli, Shasta daisies and Chinese asters spread out in mountain meadows as far as your eye can reach.

Almost every British island in the Caribbean has its botanical garden, beautifully organized and maintained, reflecting the traditional English love of flowers and shrubs, a love which seems to have been intensified by transplantation to tropic soil, just as the flowers themselves seem larger and more brilliant than their temperate counterparts. These botanic gardens, usually providing highly qualified guides, are indicated in the text of this book under each individual country, as are the various agricultural experimental stations, rain forests, and other preserves where the giant tree ferns, bamboos, mahogany trees and other floral glories of the tropics grow in a setting that will remain among the most vivid memories of your Caribbean tour.

REPERTORY FOR SPORTSMEN

From the Sea Depths to the Mountain Tops

BY

PATRICK ELLAM

(Patrick Ellam, born in England and a New Yorker at present, is the author of the "Sportsman's Guide to the Caribbean" and "Sopranino"; the latter an account of his crossing the Atlantic in a nineteen-foot sailboat. Mr. Ellam also writes for "Sports Illustrated", "Travel" and "Yachting Magazine".)

The 2500 square miles of islands and sparkling blue water stretching southeast from Florida to the Spanish Main constitute the Elysian Fields of the Western Ocean as far as the sportsman is concerned. This happy hunting ground abounds with fighting fish and game, and offers the tourist the best natural conditions for many sports, especially those which are practised in, on or under the sea. The great increase in Caribbean tourism has brought with it a corresponding development of sports amenities and guide facilities. These are indicated under the separate country guides in this book. Here we present an over-all picture of the Caribbean sports potential.

Every now and then a sports writer visits one or other of the islands and promptly comes out with an article announcing it as the most fabulous place for fishing, or hunting, or what-have-you, that he has ever seen. Having visited them all we would not go that far but a fair overall rating would be "definitely good".

For some sports such as fishing and yachting they offer conditions that are as good as, or better than, any available anywhere else in the world. For others, such as flying and deer hunting, there are places to delight the keen sportsman, while for an all-around vacation there are spots where you can get such things as tennis, golf and water skiing up to normal standards but with the added attraction of year-round sunshine and colorful surroundings.

In different places there are facilities available for engaging in 14 sports yourself, ranging from obvious ones such as horse riding and spear fishing to more exotic ones like surf riding and alligator hunting. Then there are 10 spectator sports to see, from baseball and horse racing to jai-alai and cock fighting, with fine opportunities to look at a good game of cricket or soccer.

With so much to see and to do, and with so many islands to choose from, it would be impossible to cover every single facility that is available in this short chapter. So we'll concentrate on those places that are best for each particular sport. Some sports, such as baseball, need no introduction. Others, such as jai-alai, will be new to many readers, so we'll describe them briefly.

The sportsman who is going to charter a yacht needs more information than the boxing fan going to the local match, so we'll have to give that more space. But for easy reference we'll keep them all in alphabetical order.

Alligator Hunting

Along the South coast of Jamaica there are swamps and marshes where alligators are plentiful (actually they are crocodiles but they are called alligators there) and they can be taken in two ways. You can shoot them at night or catch them alive by day. However the shooting is more interesting since you do that yourself, whereas catching one requires a team and you wind up as a mere spectator.

It is not easy to shoot one, as you have to fire from a standing position in a small boat, but a good full-bore rifle shot should get at least one in an evening (we saw 12 and bagged one 8 feet long). And either way there are two reliable guides available.

Dennis Cooke operates his night service out of the *Casa Blanca Hotel* in Montego Bay (Tel. 2880. Cables: Greentours), though he specializes in catching them alive (the largest he has taken that way was 12 feet, while the largest shot weighed half a ton). And Dr. Baillie arranges either day hunts or night shoots from the *Blue Water Fishing Club* at Whitehouse Cables: Sportfish), both he and Cooke working in the swamps not far from his lodge.

Your guide takes you to the lake by car, collecting a couple of native boatmen on the way. There he loads rifles, pistols, ammunition, sandwiches, drinks, an outboard motor, a car head-light and a battery into a good stout punt and you chug away from the dock with a small dinghy in tow.

Just after dark he cuts the motor and takes-up a sitting position forward with the light, while you stand amidships with a rifle (.303 Lee Enfield) and the boatmen pole you across the shallows from aft.

Suddenly the light flashes out across the still, black water, swings a little and stops. One round eye glows red on the surface about 100 yards away, moving rapidly towards the mangroves. Then it's up to you. You have time for one quick shot before he gets there and disappears. But normally you get several chances and by midnight you should have your alligator. Then you drape him over the dinghy and tow him home, to be made into shoes, purses, belts and other useful trophies.

Night shoots must be done in the non-moon period or when the sky is overcast, which happens more often during the summer, while day hunting is only done in the winter, when there is less water in the swamps. Either way it pays to write your guide well in advance to set a date when the conditions will be right.

A night shoot costs around $70.00 for two, while a day hunt costs the same for up to 5 people. Each guide provides every-thing you need, including guns and ammunition, but it's a good idea to take your own mosquito repellent (those pests can be fierce in the swamps for about an hour just after sundown).

Baseball

San Juan, Puerto Rico has regular scheduled matches (Win-ter League) from mid-October to mid-February, when they compete with Venezuela and Panama for the Caribbean title, while at Santo Domingo, Dominican Republic, they have intermittent matches, year round, and compete against the other Latin American countries.

The game is a very big thing locally (there have even been baseball divorces in San Juan) being played at night and drawing large, enthusiastic crowds. In each case the stadium is in the city and any taxi driver can take you there, while the dates and times of the games are published in the local newspapers.

Boxing

Interesting—for atmosphere—are the occasional amateur matches held in the *Drill Halls* at Barbados and Trinidad, with a good-natured crowd rooting for the local boy and the honor of the island at stake. To catch one of those, or the ones in Santo Domingo, you have to watch the local papers.

Car Racing

Since 1954, when it was first held, the annual *Speed Week* at Nassau in the Bahamas has already become an event of international importance, with two Open races (plus one for residents of the island) for Class "C" sports cars.

Held on Windsor Field Road Course, a fast 3.5 miles with good escape areas, the two main events are the *Governor's Trophy* (100 miles) and the *Nassau Trophy* (200 miles). The Week is normally held early in December but it is advisable to write ahead to the *Nassau Developement Board*, which cosponsors it, for the exact dates.

Cock Fighting

Cock fights are held at Havana, Cuba (3 times a week), Port au Prince, Haiti and San Juan, Puerto Rico (on Saturdays and Sundays) and Santo Domingo, Dominican Republic (on Sundays) in organized cockpits that operate on an admission basis.

The main interest lies in betting on the matches but since they are usually conducted in a foreign language it is best to keep your stakes down to a dollar or two unless you are conversant with it.

Cricket

Cricket matches are held every Saturday afternoon from January through April at Kingston in Jamaica, Barbados,

Trinidad and Grenada with the more important ones (including occasional 'Test Matches' against England, Australia, etc.) towards the end of the season.

Often there are several matches on the same afternoon but any taxi driver will know where the best one is. When you get there, go to the members' enclosure, where you will be welcomed as a visitor, introduced to the players (who include some of the world's best) and given a run-down in the game by an expert.

Fishing

Some of the finest fishing in the world is to be found in this area and there are five places where reliable guides with good boats and full equipment are always available: Bimini, Nassau and Andros in the Bahamas, Whitehouse in Jamaica and San Juan in Puerto Rico.

Bimini is a tiny island devoted entirely to game fishing, the main center being *Neville Stuart's Bimini Fisherman's Club* (Address: c/o *Chalk's Flying Service,* 368 N.E. 57th Street, Miami 37, Florida). It is highly organized, with at least three charter boats available and more called over as required. Lying right on the edge of the Gulf Stream, it has already produced over three dozen world records.

The skippers are thoroughly experienced and their boats are fully equipped with all kinds of tackle so that all you have to do is step aboard and go right out to fish, while the club also maintains six skiffs with outboard motors and native guides for bone fishing. The latter provide excellent sport, especially from December through March when the heavier ones are running.

In Nassau, *Bobby Symonette* has some 25 individually-owned charter boats at the *Yacht Haven* (P.O. Box 1216. Tel. 4014) available on a daily or weekly basis. The fishing grounds are along the North coast of the island, within 5 miles of the dock, and they have been doing very well, particularly with wahoo. There they have annual winter and summer tournaments, plus a wahoo roundup that usually starts in December. All are open to visitors and full details can be had from the *Nassau Development Board* which sponsors them.

In Andros, Kenneth Sundin keeps two or three charter boats at his *Lighthouse Club* (Address: c/o P.O. Box 758, Nassau) and gets more over from Nassau as they are needed. He also has skiffs with outboards and native guides for inshore work and, while the sea fishing is not as good as it is at Bimini or

115

Nassau, he offers a good variety, with bone fishing on the flats and river fishing for tarpon in 14-mile long Fresh Creek.

In Whitehouse, Jamaica, Dr. Baillie runs the *Blue Water Fishing Club* (No Telephone. Cables: Sportfish), a very comfortable fishing lodge right on the sea. He has two good boats with experienced skippers, one British and one Jamaican, and has been getting a good number of marlin (124 raised in 117 days) as well as wahoo and other game fish. He also has a couple of skiffs with outboards and guides for fishing the Black River and the Coberata River near his lodge. To reach his place you go to Montego Bay and then either rent a car or charter a light aircraft for the 40-mile run to Whitehouse.

And finally there is San Juan, where Art Wills runs *Caribe Anglers* (P.O. Box 1133. Tel. 3-0616) just across the bridge from the Yacht Club. He has three good boats with guides and all kinds of tackle available on a daily basis, though unlike the others he prefers not to make any reservations in advance.

There you normally reach the blue water from 1 to 4 miles from the harbor entrance but when the rains have been heavy you may have to go as far as 10 miles to get clear of the outflow from the river. However they are doing pretty well and during one week in October they got 13 blue marlin, 3 Allison tuna and one sailfish in four days of fishing, while 9 world records were set in that area in one year. Art also keeps two 24-foot Chris Crafts at his dock for local fishing in and around San Juan Harbor.

The current charter rates per day are: Bimini $75-100, Nassau $50-60, Andros $100, Whitehouse $70-80 and San Juan $65, while the skiffs run close to $25 a day everywhere. In all cases except Wills' you should write at least a month ahead to be sure of getting a boat, while for Bimini at the peak of the bluefin tuna run (in the last couple of weeks of May) you should double that.

Everything is provided and there is no need to take any tackle with you. However it is a good idea to take along a polaroid eyeshield, especially for bone fishing. For the best times of the year to fish each area, see the Fishing Table below (bone fish are there all the year round, in each case).

FISHING TABLE		
	Dolphin:	December–March
	Grouper:	Year round
	Sailfish:	November–April
ANDROS.	Tarpon:	Year round
Barracuda:	Year round	Wahoo:	November–April

White Marlin:	November-April

BIMINI.

Amberjack:	November-April
Barracuda:	Year round
Bluefin Tuna:	May 7 to June 7
Blue Marlin:	May-August
Bonito:	April-May
Dolphin:	February-June
Kingfish:	March-June
Sailfish:	January-April
Wahoo:	February-June
White Marlin:	May-August

NASSAU.

Albacore:	December-September
Allison Tuna:	December-May
Barracuda:	Year round
Bonito:	May-September
Dolphin:	December-March
Grouper:	Year round
Kingfish:	January-June
Wahoo:	November-April

SAN JUAN.

Albacore:	June-August
Allison Tuna:	June-November
Amberjack:	June-August
Barracuda:	June, July
Bluefin Tuna:	July, August
Blue Marlin:	March-November
Bonito:	April, May
Dolphin:	March-June
Kingfish:	November-December
Grouper:	Year round
Sailfish:	August-October
Tarpon:	May-July
Wahoo:	July, August
White Marlin:	October, November

WHITEHOUSE.

Albacore:	December-March
Blue Marlin:	December-March
Dolphin:	December-March
Kingfish:	April, May
Sailfish:	April, May
Wahoo:	November-March

Flying

Both Jamaica and Aruba have active flying clubs where reliable American and British aircraft are available at reasonable rates, while the former also has facilities for cross-country flying.

The *Jamaica Flying Club* has its hangar and club house at Pallisadoes Airport just outside Kingston, with several private planes and one club machine (two-place Cesnas, Cubs and such) available for charter to visitors, while the Civil Aeronautics Department in Kingston will give you an oral examination on the local regulations and endorse your flying license for use in Jamaica in a couple of hours.

There you can fly locally over the flat plain by the sea, or you can make your way over the mountains to Boscobel airstrip near Ocho Rios, on the North shore of the island. That is only 40 miles but it is best to have a bit of height in hand over the ridge, as it is quite unsuitable for landing on. Boscobel strip is fully 3,000 feet long and easy to get on to but there is a bad bump just beyond the eastern end of it, so that when taking-off it pays to level-out and make a left turn over the sea before you get that far.

From there you can run down the coast to Montego Bay, where there is a full-sized commercial airport, and then South across the mountains again to a small Cub strip near Whitehouse, though we have not landed on the latter and it would be advisable to get local advice before attempting it. Cub strips run small in those parts.

If you have not flown over a large tropical island before, you will find it quite impressive. The visibility is normally excellent (fog is unknown there) providing a clear view of the high, jagged, green mountains that fall sharply down to yellow beaches, with white breakers and the deep blue sea.

The *Aruba Flying Club* at the airport near Oranjestad has four similar club planes and several private ones for charter, and the Director of Civil Aviation will okay your flying license for local use but there it is a matter of strictly local flying around the very small, flat island.

In both places the aircraft are sound and properly maintained, though none of them are very new, and charter for around $10.00 an hour. Some may have non-standard equipment, such as Willy Priestnell's *Ercoupe* in Jamaica, which is fitted with regular rudder controls in place of the interlocked system.

The best time to go is from November through June but write ahead to make the arrangements and don't forget to take your flying license. Expect ground winds of 30 M.P.H. and more towards midday, with consequent bumps over mountain areas. Watch out for the occasional thunderstorm or cumulo-nimbus cloud and give both a wide berth.

Golf

There are six 18-hole golf courses available to visitors in the islands, of which three are up to championship standard. Those are at the *Bahamas Country Club* in Nassau, Bahamas (set amid mahogany trees beside the sea, with a special club house for visitors), the *Constant Spring Club* at Kingston, Jamaica (high in the foothills about 5 miles out of town) and the *St. Andrews Club* at Maraval, Trinidad (also in the foothills and probably the best of all).

The other three are the *Belmont Manor* and *Riddle's Bay* courses in Bermuda; and the *Dorado Beach* course, laid out by Trent Jones, situated north of San Juan.

In a less serious vein, San Juan, Puerto Rico, has two interesting 9-hole courses. One is at the *Berwind Country Club* about a mile and a half from town and the other is laid-out around the ancient *Morro Castle* in Old San Juan (worth a visit if only for the hole that is played through the moat, down a grass fairway between stone walls). In the U.S. Virgin Islands, there are two good 9-hole courses: one on St. Thomas, and the other at *Estate Carlton,* on St. Croix.

And finally there are the *Montego Bay Country Club* in Montego Bay, Jamaica, and the *Rockley Golf and Country Club* just outside Bridgetown, Barbados, where visitors are welcome to use the 9-hole courses. The rest are either strictly private clubs or small and very casual.

The courses are open year round, with green fees varying from $2.00 to $4.00 and caddies at around $1.50, and for a casual game you can rent a set of clubs to save weight on your baggage.

Horse Racing

The principal tracks are *Quintana* and *Las Casas* race courses in San Juan, Puerto Rico (racing 3 times a week between them, all the year round), and *Hobby Horse Hall* in Nassau, Bahamas (twice a week from January to April).

Occasional meetings are also held at Kingston in Jamaica, Barbados, Bermuda, Trinidad and Santo Domingo in the Dominican Republic (check the local newspapers for dates) which, though smaller, are colorful and good for an afternoon's fun.

Horse Riding

Horses are available for casual hacking in most of the islands but there are three places of real interest to the keen horseman. First, there is Pat Tennyson's *Good Hope Ranch* near Falmouth in Jamaica, where you take your pick of 75 horses and ride over 200 miles of marked trails or make expeditions into large tracts of unexplored territory immediately adjoining his estate.

That is a well-organized dude ranch run on a package-deal basis, with everything provided (including room, food and rum) for around $25.00 a day. His horses are mostly half-bred of native mares and imported stallions, and he caters to competent horsemen, providing gymkhanas, paper chases, cattle roundups and guides for expeditions into the nearby Cockpit country, which is still largely unexplored.

Next there is *Manuel Casseres' Riding Academy* at Sabana Llanas, Rio Pedras, about two miles from San Juan, Puerto Rico (Tel. 2-2374). That is a haute ecole establishment specializing in the *Paso Fino,* a highly-bred horse peculiar to Puerto Rico with a short-striding, highstepping gait so smooth that you can ride around with a full glass of water in your hand

119

without spilling a drop. Instruction in his classes costs about $2.00 a lesson.

Good Hope Ranch is only open in the winter and there you have to write at least two months ahead for reservations. The others are available all the year round, though from November to June the weather is better. For any serious riding take your warm weather gear and be in training.

Mountain Climbing

Most of the islands are high and mountainous but little climbing has been done and only in three places can you find guides. For the keen climber, the best of those is Soufrière village in St. Lucia, where the two bottle-shaped Pitons rise almost sheer out of the sea. Though not very high, the Petit Piton (2,400 feet) is very steep all the way, with a bare top from which you get a fine view, while the Grand Piton (2,300 feet and wooded) offers a slightly easier ascent and nearby Morne Gimme (3,145 feet) a very easy one.

To get to Soufriere from Castries (the Capital) take the M.V. "Crompton" that runs down the coast 4 times a week. There Miss Eudoxie, manageress of the *Phoenix Hotel* (primitive but clean) can get you English-speaking guides for around $6.00 a day who use cutlasses as axes but know how to handle a rope. In fact one of them saved a friend of ours on the Petit Piton recently.

Next you have Kingston, Jamaica, where the Blue Mountain (7,500 feet) offers a mild expedition well worth making. To arrange this, you first telegraph Malcolm Macdonald at *Penlyne Castle*, Mavis Bank, giving him a few days to round-up and rest the necessary mules, then telegraph Whitfield Hall, Penlyne Castle, Mavis Bank, for rooms.

Then you drive 17 miles up the foothills to Mavis Bank, meet Mr. Macdonald and go on by mule to *Whitfield Hall* (a small, clean hostel at 4,200 feet) for the night. And from there you can take the mules to the peak and back to Mavis Bank in one day. Though not strictly a climb, it is a fascinating trip with a truly fine view from the top.

Take all the food and drink you need (except water) for the two days and allow an extra mule to carry them. Mules are $7.15 a day each (with guides) and bunks at Whitfield Hall are $1.00 a night. Telegrams are very cheap but should be reply-paid.

Polo

Polo is played at Montego Bay in Jamaica on Sunday afternoons all through the winter and at Barbados (on the Savannah Race Course) on Wednesdays and Saturdays about 5 p.m. from September to January.

In Santo Domingo, Dominican Republic, games can be had all year round on the grounds opposite the hotel *El Embajador*.

Sailing

There are three places where you can rent a small boat for day sailing but though the weather is good from November through June, the winds are often strong, with sudden squalls that make it unsafe for beginners outside the shelter of the harbors.

In Nassau, Bahamas, the *Yacht Haven* has a couple of boats and the boat yard 100 yards eastward has two more. All are native sloops of around 20 feet that are well suited for sailing between the low, sandy islands and picnicking on the beaches close-by.

At Christiansted in St. Croix the *Comanche Club* has four 16-foot native sloops with Comet rigs suitable for sailing in the picturesque harbor, while in San Juan, Puerto Rico, *Art Wills* has a few 14-footers for local sailing at his dock across the bridge from the Yacht Club.

None of the boats are outstanding but they are adequate for the job and cheap enough (at around $1.50 an hour). But take a raincoat along and remember the sun reflects off the water while the breeze feels cool, so that you can get sunburned before you know it.

Soccer

In Port au Prince, Haiti, soccer is the most popular spectator sport, with regular night games throughout the year often drawing highly enthusiastic crowds of 20 to 25 thousand people. It is also played in Trinidad, usually on Saturday afternoons from July to December, though there they call it football.

Soccer is a fast, exciting game with simple, easily-followed rules and well worth seeing when you have the chance. Dates, times and locations of matches are listed in the local newspapers.

Spear Fishing

Spear fishing is no longer permitted in Bermuda or the Bahamas but there are still two places, St. Thomas and Tobago, that offer excellent fishing under ideal conditions (80-degree water and fine visibility) with boats and equipment for doing it.

In St. Thomas there are two setups. For beginners, Randy Boyd runs a regular school at *Harmon & Clerk Boats* (Tel. 395) between the airport and the town. He supplies all necessary equipment and gives scheduled lessons twice daily at 10 a.m. and 2 p.m., taking you up as far as the use of the aqualung.

Then for experts there is *Claude Caron's Tackle Shop* in town where you can rent aqualungs and large refill cylinders for longer trips and the *Yacht Haven* where you can charter sea-going vessels (see 'Yachting') to take you to the outlying islands. There the fishing is very good (one team got 800 pounds of fish, 200 pounds of lobsters and a 275-pound turtle in 5 days) but you are on your own and must be able to look after yourselves in the water.

In Tobago, Commander Jack Crook has a launch and some equipment for rent at the *Bluehaven Hotel* (Tel. 190. Cables: Bluehaven). He has no aqualungs but if you take your own he can get cylinders of air over from nearby Trinidad, given a little notice.

There is also a local man, Cecil Anthony, who lives at Buccoo on the North side of the island. He has 2 boats with outboard motors and some equipment and is highly recommended as a guide, having worked with several visiting experts. The best way to contact him is through Commander Crook.

Once again the fishing is very good, with plenty of reef fish and some grouper (a couple of visiting spear fishermen got two of 87 and 280 pounds in two days), the best spots being along Buccoo Reef and around Bird of Paradise Island.

Lessons in St. Thomas cost $7.00 each, while a guide with a boat and basic equipment in Tobago runs around $25.00 a day, but for any kind of expedition involving a larger boat, rental of aqualungs and so on, it is best to write well in advance to get the exact cost and make the arrangements. You can do local inshore work all the year round but for offshore trips it has to be November to June, when there are no hurricanes in the area.

In all the remoter spots there are sharks, barracuda, sea eggs and fire coral, all of which need watching. The sharks seldom cause any trouble but the barracuda are a pest, hanging around just out of range to snatch any fish you shoot.

The sea eggs are easy to spot as they are large and black but the fire coral, which has a powerful sting that can cause cramps, is orange in color and hard to distinguish from other varieties. Altogether it is a good idea to avoid touching any coral that looks remotely like it and make a point of leaving the water an hour before sundown.

It is worth while replacing the line on your gun with 12 feet of 1/16″ stainless steel cable that will not cut on coral. Never stay in the water when bleeding or with a bleeding fish. Always carry a knife and never fish alone.

Surf Riding

From December through April the Trade Winds send great rolling waves sweeping over the shallow sand bars in beautiful Maraccas Bay, in Trinidad, providing good conditions for surf riding. This is a fine, romantic sport and while there are no organized facilities, it is quite easy to arrange for yourself.

First you go to any lumber yard in Port of Spain and have them cut you a four-foot length of cedar about 15 inches wide, with one end (the front) rounded-off. They charge about 70 cents a board but make sure they don't leave any rough edges or splinters. Then you drive or take a taxi (making a deal on the price first) over the scenic mountain road to the sweeping white sand bay.

Now, to get started. Wade out to the first sand bar, where the water is waist deep, face the beach and wait for a wave that is just about to break as it reaches you. Then launch yourself with a jump down its steep front face, keeping the rear end of the board at your waist and the front end as flat on the water as you can without actually letting it go under. You can steer by tipping the board down on one side and make longer runs as you get better at it but be careful not to go out too far, as the sea is definitely rough.

Swimming

The swimming is very good in all the islands but the beaches do vary considerably in quality (from pure white sand to almost black) and also in accessibility. However some are excellent, with white sand and crystal-clear water within easy reach of the hotels.

Antigua has a fine one at Fort James. Barbados has several along its western shore and an exceptional one at the *Crane Hotel* on its eastern side. Bermuda has Great Bay, Horseshoe Bay and others strung along its South coast. West Bay Beach on Grand Cayman runs for six miles without a break. The North shore of Jamaica is studded with well-known ones such as Doctor's Cave, Discovery Bay and Tower Isle. Nassau is made of sand, with beaches to spare, and St. Croix has two good ones at Jack's Bay, Cramer Park and Sandy Point. On all islands, as new resorts and hotels are opening, the beaches are improving.

One tip, though. In tropical waters, watch out for sea eggs. The white ones don't matter but the black ones the size of baseballs with eight-inch spikes all over them really aren't worth standing on. But they are quite easy to see, so it is just a matter of being careful, and while painful (we've stepped on some) they are not serious.

Skin Diving and Snorkeling

The latest rage all over the Caribbean is skin diving—with and without aqua-lungs. Many resorts which once made their claim to fame on swimming and boating prospects, now brag about the number of old wrecks waiting to be explored below their crystal clear waters, and the breathtaking underwater coral scenery. Tobago Island was early on the bandwagon, and well she might be because her underwater coral formations and schools of colorful tropical fish make these waters some of the most rewarding for skin-diving explorers. In the Virgin Islands, St. John offers a special attraction in the skin diving tours of the wreckage of the French luxury liner, the *Rhône,* which went down a hundred years ago in a hurricane. There is also an underwater marked trail, pointing out unusual coral formations, at Trunk Bay on St. John. Both Nassau and Bermuda offer lessons for beginners at about $8 an hour and organized skin-diving tours operate out of the Coral Island Club in Bermuda to visit the hulks of an estimated 1000 ill-fated ships which lie deep in the offshore waters. You may even find a billboard or two posted far beneath the surface advertising the steaks and seafood at some local restaurant or the nightlife at some cabaret. There are restrictions, however, on spear fishing (see above).

Water Skiing

Water skiing is spreading rapidly through the islands but as yet there are only a few places where regular schools with boats, equipment and competent instructors are always available.

One is San Juan, Puerto Rico, where Barron Rowsen and Victor Schreibmann work out of the *La Rada Hotel* on the Condado Lagoon, a large expanse of flat-calm water almost entirely free of traffic that, with the year-round sunshine, provides ideal conditions for beginner or expert alike.

The second is Nassau in the Bahamas, where four instructors operate independently from the *British Colonial Hotel, Fort Montagu Beach Hotel, Emerald Beach Hotel* and *Paradise Beach*, the best-known being Bruce Parker (at the Colonial) who trained most of the others. There again you can ski all the year round, though the water is choppy at times, making it better for the expert than the beginner.

The third is Bermuda, where Bill Williams has his school opposite the *New Bermudia Hotel* and operates in Hamilton Harbour, which is fine most of the year but rather cool for our tastes in the winter.

Rates run around $4.00 for lessons and $1.50 for tows in those places, with all the equipment you need provided. Elsewhere you can get the occasional ride but usually on an amateur basis.

Yachting

There are three good cruising grounds in the area: The Windwards and Leewards, the Bahamas and the Virgins. In each one there are yachts for charter while, if you have a sea-going boat of your own, you can easily reach the Bahamas in her and the lucky few who have suitable craft and plenty of time can reach the others.

It is an easy run from Miami to Bimini (a port of entry) and across the flats to Nassau, whence you can cruise the out-islands of the Bahamas, which offer plenty of good anchorages, though the waters are mostly shallow and the charts are rather unreliable. To reach the other areas from America, the best route is the open-water passage via Bermuda. Otherwise you are faced with an interminable beat to windward that can be very tiresome indeed.

The Windward and Leeward Islands (stretching from Antigua down to Trinidad) offer the finest cruising ground of all, with the Trades just about on the beam all the way and plenty of interesting places to visit, and they also have the best-organized charter setup.

That is in Antigua, where Commander Nicholson has a fleet of six auxiliary yachts from 50 to 100 feet, suitable for parties of 4 to 6 people, at his base at English Harbour (Tel. ask by name). Each yacht has an experienced British, American or Swedish skipper and full crew, and maintains daily contact with the base by radio-telephone. You are welcome to help run his ships if you want to but if you are pressed for time they will make night runs from island to island while you

sleep. His skippers know the islands well and besides advising
you on the best places to visit to suit your tastes, they act as
guides and make arrangements for you ashore.

Among the islands that you can visit are Guadeloupe,
Dominica, Martinique, St. Lucia, Barbados, St. Vincent, the
Grenadines, Grenada, Tobago and Trinidad. If your time is
limited you can make a one-way run. They use Martinique
and Grenada as pick-up points besides Antigua (all three have
good air services) and you can start or finish your trip at any
one of them without extra charge.

In most cases the islands are barely thirty miles apart, so
that you can see from one to another. Between them the Trade
Winds blow strongly and you bowl along, rising and dipping
over the ocean swells, the ship silent except for the creaking
of her gear as she strains to the wind and the swishing of the
water past her hull.

Then you come under the lee of the next island, where the
wind falls calm and you slide up towards the next port, with
perhaps the motor humming away to get you there before
nightfall, though often it is more fun to leave it silent and
glide into harbor by moonlight on the last of the breeze.

In the Bahamas and Virgins the setup is rather different,
with smaller yachts (of 40 to 50 feet) each individually-owned
and skippered by her owner, assisted by the charterers. They
are suitable for parties of 2 to 4 people and many of them are
well-run, though they vary considerably as you would expect,
which makes selection more difficult. For the Bahamas it is
best to write to Bobby Symonette at the *Yacht Haven* in Nassau
(P.O. Box 1216. Tel. 4014) who can advise you on the boats
currently available there, while for the Virgins you write to
the *Charter Boat Association* in St. Thomas for folders on the
individual boats and make your own choice.

In each case the yachts are normally chartered for a weekly
fee, plus fuel, food, port charges and so on, but if you select
a boat to suit the size of your party the total cost will usually
be around $35.00 per person per day. The everlasting tropical
sun and flying spray play havoc with paintwork and cordage
alike, while the cost of maintaining a yacht down there is very
high, so that the general standard of appearance and finish is
poor, by American standards. However they are serviceable
enough and on the whole they are well suited for the work
they have to do. They are available from November through
June, though the better ones are booked-up 3 to 4 months

ahead, so that you have to write in good time to make the arrangements.

Boats to Charter

To charter a schooner, ketch, sloop or Sailfish for a few hours' sail to a three-weeks' cruise or to book for a regularly scheduled trip around the best cruising areas, see the addresses below:

Antigua, W. I.

V. E. B. Nicholson & Sons
P.O. Box 103
St. John's

Bahamas

Jack Cashin
Charmain, Inc.
2237 Delamere Dr.
Cleveland 6, Ohio
Charmain

Nassau Yacht Haven
Nassau
All others

Barbados

Mr. Robin MacFadden
Colony Club
The Carlotta

Mr. Peter Philips
Miramar
St. James
Morna

A. D. A. Cottingham
c/o Colony Club
St. James
Connemara

Mr. Victor Goddard
c/o Goddard & Son
Bridgetown
Ecstasy

Gene Tinker
Aquatic Club
Bay St.
Pas de Loup, Skin Diving

Leslie Wotton
West Coast Aquatic Sports
Sandy Lane Hotel
Do-it-Yourself

Keith Pilkington
c/o Coral Reef Club
St. James

Royal Barbados Yacht Club
Bridgetown

Barbados Cruising and Sailing
Club
Bridgetown
Others

Bermuda

Earl Wilkinson
Spanish Point
Pembroke West

Howard Simmons
Cox's Hill
Pembroke

Howard Powell
Mills Creek
Fairylands
Pembroke
Half, Full-Day Cruises

Bermuda Holiday House
Reid St.
Hamilton
Two-and-a-Half-Hour Cruises

Florida

Clippership Cruises
Suite 414A
DuPont Plaza Center
Miami
Cutty Sark

Tradewind Cruises Ltd.
P.O. Box 774
Coral Gables
Carefree

Fatima Travel Inc.
Midtown Plaza 3
Washington, N.J.
In December: Room 904
Chamber of Commerce Bldg.
141 N.E. Third Ave.
Miami 32
Columbus Cruises

Windjammer Cruises Inc.
P.O. Box 1051
Miami 32
Windjammer Cruises

Tom Burnett
P.O. Box 36-6301
Miami
Blue Goose

Jamaica

A list of the names and addresses of boat owners is available from any Jamaica Tourist Board office in the U.S. and Canada (New York officie is Suite 1614, International Bldg., 630 Fifth Ave.).
Fishing yachts

Puerto Rico

Turismo International
Darlington Apts. Bldg.
P.O. Box 1820
San Juan
Explorer

Hal Underhill
69 Luisa St.

San Juan
Day Sails

St. Lucia

Vagabond Cruises, Ltd.
P.O. Box 260
Castries
Schooner Voyageur,
Lady Phyllis, Viemas

Virgin Islands

St. Croix Yacht Club or Sailor's Center
Christiansted, St. Croix

Blue Water Cruises
P.O. Box 748
St. Thomas
Schooner Caroline

St. Thomas Charter Boat Assoc.
P.O. Box 2247
23 Sailing Yachts &
6 Power Yachts

P.O. Box 1203
St. Thomas
Yacht *Rambler*

Yachting Facilities

For those cruising in their own boats, facilities are available at Antigua, Barbados, Bermuda, Grenada, Kingston (Jamaica), Nassau, St. Lucia, St. Thomas and San Juan (Puerto Rico) and most recently in the beautiful British Virgin Islands where Trellis Bay is becoming a popular stop over for yachters. The northern Bahamas are also developing yacht facilities which are a convenient stop over for yachtsmen setting out from Florida on their way to the southern islands.

In Antigua, *Commander Nicholson* provides light repair facilities and water at English Harbour, which is well sheltered even in a hurricane, while food can be bought in St. John's.

In Barbados, the best anchorage is off the *Royal Barbados Yacht Club,* where light repair facilities can be obtained, while for major repairs there is a lift in the Careenage of Bridgetown harbor suitable for yachts of any size, with mechanical repair work, food and water available.

In Bermuda, *Bert Darrell's Yacht Yard* at Hamilton can haul yachts up to about 50 feet and make all kinds of repairs, while food and water are available in the town.

In Grenada there is good shelter with food, water and light repairs available at the *Grenada Yacht Club* in St. George's harbor.

In Kingston, Jamaica, there are marina facilities, repair facilities, food, water and marine railways for yachts up to 60 feet at Port Royal, just across the harbor.

In Nassau, the *Yacht Haven* provides marina facilities, food and water, while *Symonette's Boat Yard* can haul yachts of any size and has complete repair facilities.

In St. Lucia, *Privateer Marine Services* can do mechanical work and some hull repairs at the Petit Carenage just outside Castries, which is well sheltered even in a hurricane, while food and water can be obtained in the town.

In St. Thomas the *Yacht Haven* provides sheltered dockage with water and light repair work, while food is available in the nearby town of Charlotte Amalie.

In San Juan, Puerto Rico, the *Yacht Club* has sheltered dockage with food, water, light repair facilities and a slipway for boats up to 40 feet.

THE PHOTOGENIC ISLANDS

A Famous Photographer's Hints

BY

FRITZ HENLE

(A world-renowned photographer, Mr. Henle has published a dozen travel-photography books of which the most recent is "The Caribbean, A Journey With Pictures" with text by P. E. Knapp.)

For the photographer, the serious amateur, and even the dilettante, the West Indies are a paradise. You will feel like a modern Columbus, not hunting for new lands and treasures, but for new visions which please the eye. Conditions for photography are practically the same wherever you go—down to Trinidad or up to Nassau or west to Cuba and east to the Virgin Islands. It is not the light that makes the islands differ one from the other, nor the skies with their puffy white clouds, nor the sea in its myriad shades of blue and turquoise. It is the physical appearance of the islands themselves and the people who inhabit them which make them different one from the other. None of the islands seem to be alike. Wherever you go, there is something new to shoot: people of every pigment, costumes of every color, historic ruins, and monuments too strong to crumble, living architecture plainly reflecting its Spanish, French, Dutch or even Moslem origin.

And the people! They too are a mixture of many races with the happy faculty of blending racial elements into beautiful finished products. The women of Martinique alone are a sight you will never tire of photographing. Proud in their colorful costumes, they are the most gracious of models. The East Indians of Trinidad are also fascinating subjects. So are the Caribs who gave this beautiful part of the world its name, though only a tragic few remain today. Wherever you go you will find faces, costumes and customs which you will want to capture forever on film. In addition weather conditions are just about ideal in the West Indies. Here there is hardly a day without sunshine and you can count on taking pictures eight hours a day. There are many days when you can photograph the most beautiful sunset. If you are a newcomer, take your light meter or consult the one which is built into your camera. You will find you get steady readings day in day out. Eventually you will become so accustomed to the brilliant clear light that you will rarely have to take a meter reading.

A Few Technical Tips

But, since correct exposure is your basic condition for a good picture, get yourself thoroughly acquainted with your readings first. At present film speed readings you will discover that you can permit yourself very fast exposures even on color film. On professional Ektachrome you will find for instance that at stop 16 you can conveniently expose with 1/100 of a second. Imagine, what this means! An exposure of 1/250 of a second at an f stop of about 11. At 8 you arrive at the almost fabulous reading of 1/500 of a second. In other words, you can use a medium f stop and yet count on taking very fast moving subjects at a very fast exposure. An f stop of 8 means at the same time a field of a vast depth of focus. All this is a great advantage to the professional and amateur alike.

Since the West Indies are warm all year round, your first thought must be the purchase and care of your film. If you buy it in New York, Paris or London, or locally in San Juan, Puerto Rico, you know it is fresh. This is of vital importance. Film already close to the expiring date taken to these warm climates is likely to disappoint you.

A camera is a completely mechanical thing, but if it could

raise its voice it would give you a lot of warning signals. Exposure to heat alone is enough to make your camera boil. When it has some precious film inside (precious on account of the already exposed part and equally precious on account of the exposures it still will have to register) excessive heat can effect the final results, producing off color effects, odd patterns, and greyer than normal emulsion.

How can you avoid excessive exposure of films and cameras to heat? It is quite easy. First of all, never leave them out of your sight. Keep them with you on the plane, not in the baggage compartment where there is no way to control the exposure to heat. On arrival at the airport, suitcases may be mercilessly exposed to the sunshine which we greet with joy coming from a cold climate. But, inside the suitcase temperature may rise to over 100° F. A fine beginning for you, basking in the sun and thinking of a pleasant vacation—a poor beginning for your film which is supposed to record it. On arrival, wherever you go by car, by boat, on horseback, keep your equipment and films in the shade. Never put it into the nice dark trunk of your car, nor the glove compartment. Simply use common sense. Let those trade winds touch your case.

Your camera should have a lamp shade. It is not only protection against the sun, which may hit your lens and make your exposure a lightstricken fatality, but it staves off two other enemies: dust and sand.

When it comes to sunlight, treat your film as well as you do your skin. Your skin is under a layer of fine suntan oil, which acts as a safety filter. It will give you the lovely gradations of brown you want to show off later when you return to your shivering family and friends. Your filter over your lens will do comparable things for your pictures, make them look more sunny—soft, warmer, more attractive. To enhance contrasts, to emphasize moods, the use of filters is indispensable for black and white films. A medium yellow filter will help produce a rich effect. A stronger orange filter results in deeper skies, whiter clouds, seas whose surf becomes a more brilliant foaming white substance.

Plan to purchase new film supplies in the big trading centers with free-port facilities or on U.S. territory, such as Kingston, Port-au-Prince, San Juan, St. Thomas, Willemstad, Panama.

Do not buy film on the Leewards, Windwards, the French Islands, or Venezuela; it is too expensive and very often not fresh enough. (We paid over US $15 for a 100 ft., 16-mm.

A trading schooner like this, loaded with island merchandise, takes you back to the 18th century. You take it with 20th-century infra red film which captures all the contrasts of tone offered by the wine dark sea, the snowy spindrift, the hull, billowing sails and the dramatic sweep of Caribbean sky.

The most luxurious way to cruise the Caribbean is by yacht, your own or one you've chartered. To photograph your proud possession under full sail, use a fast shutter speed, 1/500 seconds if possible. Even with a yellow or orange filter, a fast film will enable you to stop down to 8 or 11, depending on your meter reading.

A musician to his finger tips (like all true Caribbeans), Geoffrey Holder (below) sums up all the rhythm of his native Trinidad as he strikes a drum and, incidentally, an unforgettable pose. Note the texture of the sun-bleached wall, and remember that palm trees aren't the only background in the Caribbean.

West Indian history has left a thousand romantic monuments to tempt the photographer. This bust of Lord Nelson, sculptured from wood, has been weathered by 15 decades, but still looks proudly over Antigua's English Harbor which the naval hero commanded long before Trafalgar. The Nelson Dockyard, now being restored, is full of photogenic subjects.

St. Croix's delightful harbor of Christiansted has looked like this for centuries. The prospect of five schooners in the foreground was enough to lure the photographer up the mast of a sixth to snap this picture at the risk of his neck.
Note the play of light on the housetops of the town. It's this sort of thing that will have you running out of film.

A portrait on infra red film can be an exciting experiment, especially when composed against the West Indian sky. Remember that this is a very slow film and must be used with a deep red filter. At Stop 8 your fastest speed will be 1/25 seconds. Steady on!

Few plane trips offer air view possibilities as dramatic as the flight over Henry Christophe's Citadelle in Haiti. To get a shot like this your shutter has to be set at extreme speed (not less than 1/500 sec.) because of your closeness to the subject. Fast film like Kodak Tri-X still gives you a stop of f 11.

Kodachrome roll in Antigua). You will find everywhere the same labels you are used to: *Kodak, Ansco, Gevaert* and *Perutz, Ilford*; all the familiar marks. They are all good; only the very expert will tend to make some real distinction. With most of these films you find your speeds which give you your meter settings. For the very beginner there is a small chart telling you how to expose under different light conditions.

What has been said on still photography is equally applicable to movies. In addition, here is *one* basic suggestion. Take a tripod along for your movie camera and avoid handheld footage. It will flicker and shake on your screen when you project it. The tripod need not be heavy, but should be tall enough to reach conviently to eye level. Your fixed position on the tripod will prevent stooping, fatigue and "motion happiness". A movie camera was not invented to be moved itself (except in specific instances where panning is necessary) but to record the movement of its subjects.

As you know, your movie film comes in sealed metal containers. The same is true of most of the film used for still photography. There obviously is a reason, so accept it like a doctor's prescription and seal your films back into their containers once they have been exposed. It is the best protection against any climatic influence. The advantages of cool and dry storage cannot be over-stressed.

Feast for your Camera

Generally there is more beautiful weather in the West Indies than in any other part of the world, and this is one of the reasons why no excursion to the Caribbean can possibly disappoint you as a photographer, as a human being who loves to see. Which of the West Indian islands are the most photogenic? Bermuda is a gem, so are the Bahamas. The beaches and bays around Nassau are heaven to be on, to swim in, perfect for relaxing and forgetting the noise of this century. But to a photographer, Jamaica has more to offer. The sea blends into the mountains and the mountains into the sky. Wherever you go in the "Queen of the Antilles" there are truly West Indian scenes: natives sailing, fishing, trading, harvesting. Harbors like Port Antonio will remind you of the Italian Riviera. The beach at *Tower Isle* is unique, unlike any other place. In Kingston there is a flower market, a feast for your color camera, though the hefty flower girls may not like your interference. A friendly smile and, better yet, a small purchase may put them in a cooperative mood.

THE PHOTOGENIC ISLANDS

A little jump on your map and you arrive where excitement really begins—Haiti. Highlights? The island is full of them: Markets like the "Iron Market"; fortresses like "The Citadel", Mad Emperor Christophe's unanswered challenge to Napoleon, one of the architectural wonders of the world. And the Haitian women, graceful and strong in their lovely costumes; they are wonderful subjects with their shy yet penetrating eyes. The fragrance of Africa and Europe mingles in the tropical setting of the most mountainous island in the West Indies leading down to the turquoise blue Caribe.

Again a small jump on your map—yet centuries away and you are in Puerto Rico. San Juan is the most lovely Spanish town in the West Indies. Calle de Cristo and San José, El Morro, La Fortaleza, they are just highlights among a guided tour full of stars. From El Yunque with its rain forest you can see the Virgin Islands lining the horizon to the East.

Going there involves a jump from Spain to Scandinavia. The Virgins' climate is unequaled and their physical beauty has few parallels. Quaint are the names of the towns: Charlotte Amalie, on St. Thomas, Christiansted and Frederiksted on St. Croix, still evocative of the Danish monarchy, though the islands have been under the U.S. flag since 1917.

Now your next step is really a big one, physically and mentally, because Saba can be reached only by boat. It is a crater in the sea—four square miles of rough and luscious mountains with a thousand people dwelling in the tiny houses perched on the edges of the extinct volcano or built right into its crater. What a sight once you get close! What a field day for your camera, once you have been safely set ashore from the crash boat being manipulated by the Caribbean's most experienced seamen.

"The Blue Peter" the Caribbean's only regular luxury passenger schooner may pick you up on its sail to St. Eustatius of Rodney infamy. Once, in the times of the American Revolution it was called the "golden rock of the Caribbean"; it was so rich by its trade. Now all you can photograph are the ruins which Admiral Rodney's sailors left behind—a thoroughly succesful effort of destruction.

"Blue Peter" sails you into St. Kitts, past a mighty fortress, the once unconquerable Gibraltar of the Caribbean—Brimstone Hill.

Then history leads you on again to Nevis, birthplace of Alexander Hamilton. Be careful with the consumption of your remaining film. You still have Dominica ahead of you with

134

its breathtaking mountains and the tragically few remnants of the Caribes.

Then you are close to Fort de France, Martinique. A big town, Paris-type stores, speeding cars and lots of commotion. All this seems remote once you get into the mountains and to the most cruel of them all—"Mt. Pelée", the murderous vulcano. A modern Pompeii is in your view finder, but the reminders seem more tragic, more horrible. St. Pierre and a crucifix with the heat-damaged image of Christ; excavations of a city where 30.000 died in three minutes: these are melancholy mementoes for your camera to record.

Looking south you see the mountains of St. Lucia. None are more exciting, more typical than the Pitons. And none have been more often photographed.

Try to stop on Bequia and the infinitely beautiful and remote chain of islands called the Grenadines. In Bequia you may find trading schooners being repaired or even being built anew on the beach. Others take off under full sail to islands in all directions: to Barbados, Martinique, Grenada, Trinidad, following a time table of romantic place names. And with luck and good planning you too may sail into Port of Spain, Trinidad, just in time for Carnival. The two days of splendor, for which Trinidadians seem to live all year round are about to begin. A festival of mad beauty, where everybody joins and everybody tries to surpass everybody else's fantastic-gigantic-romantic costume.

As a photographer here you have your final test of strength and will power. There is a picture, wherever you look, but there is just not enough film to take them all. Carnival is like a motion picture, a super spectacle. Plan for it. Have a little script in your mind and photograph your story as *you* have seen Carnival—in long shots and close-ups, and possibly extreme close-ups and medium long-shots. This way you will capture Carnival, the soul of the Caribbean, a living document which, like this fascinating region itself, will have very few rivals for color, excitement and human interest.

THE ISLANDS
AND
THE SPANISH MAIN

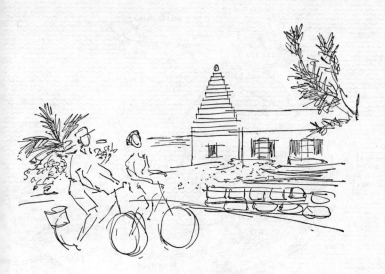

BERMUDA

Mid-Atlantic Magnet

BY

DAN BEHRMAN

(Dan Behrman is a regular contributor to Fodor's Modern Guides, and contributes to the English language edition of "Réalités." He has a broad background of world travel, has made many trips to Bermuda, and knows the island intimately.)

Bermuda is ... no, it's simpler to begin by explaining what it isn't. Bermuda is not in the Caribbean and it is not part of the West Indies. This is very important to remember when you meet a Bermudian and it is one of the reasons why we couldn't put a short, snappy title on this book.

It is not a tropical island where genteel living is practised in an air-conditioned facade hiding picturesque shanties and slums. Bermuda homes are picturesque, but they are definitely not shanties and the colony is one of the few places in the world without slums. It is not a postcard paradise seething with violent undercurrents. In recent years, Bermuda has seethed mainly about the introduction of motor cars for its roads and votes for its women. It is not a series of plantations where the old families sit on their verandahs and watch the

139

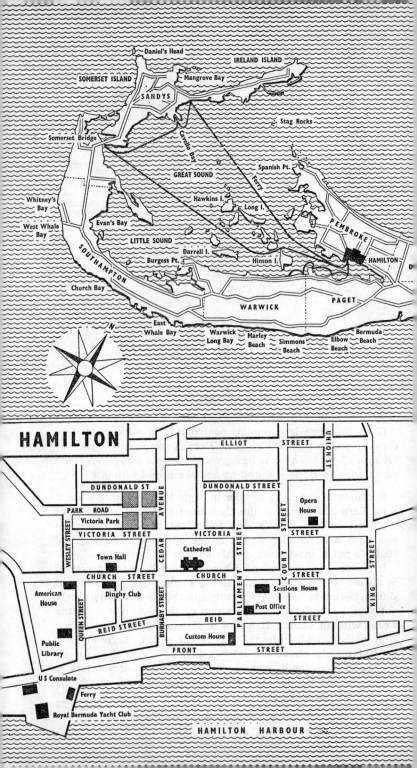

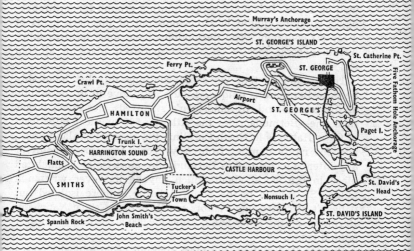

BERMUDA

0   1   2   3   Miles

Murray's Anchorage

ST. GEORGE'S ISLAND

Ferry Pt.

St. Catherine Pt.

ST. GEORGE

Crawl Pt.

Airport

ST. GEORGE'S

Five Fathom Hole Anchorage

HAMILTON

Paget I.

Trunk I.

HARRINGTON SOUND

Flatts

CASTLE HARBOUR

St. David's Head

SMITHS

Tucker's Town

Nonsuch I.

ST. DAVID'S ISLAND

Spanish Rock

John Smith's Beach

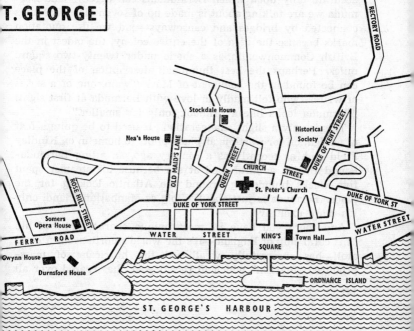

T. GEORGE

RECTORY ROAD

Stockdale House

Nea's House

OLD MAID'S LANE

Historical Society

DUKE OF KENT STREET

ROSE HILL STREET

QUEEN STREET

CHURCH

STREET

St. Peter's Church

DUKE OF YORK ST

DUKE OF YORK STREET

Somers Opera House

WATER   STREET

KING'S SQUARE

Town Hall

WATER STREET

FERRY   ROAD

Gwynn House

Durnsford House

ORDNANCE ISLAND

ST. GEORGE'S   HARBOUR

BERMUDA

banana or the sugar cane harvest come in. The old families
of Bermuda open their shops in Hamilton every morning and
wait on trade. It is not a happy hunting ground for anthropol-
ogists studying quaint local customs out of the dark heart of
a far-off continent. The Bermudians have some local customs,
but they come mostly from that quaintest place of all, old
England.

The trouble is that we could continue this list inevitably
because Bermuda is unique. Like a ship hove to in the middle
of the ocean—and, by landsmen's standards, not much larger
than one—Bermuda rides the Atlantic 568 nautical miles east
of Cape Hatteras in North Carolina, the closest mainland point,
and 666 nautical miles from New York, the closest point of
any interest. This makes Bermuda the most isolated inhabited
place in the world about which anyone has ever written a
guide. St. Helena in the South Atlantic is more isolated but
it hasn't attracted any visitors worth noticing since Napoleon.
Bermuda, on the other hand, drew 170,000 according to the last
annual count.

Next to its isolation, the most striking geographical characteristic about Bermuda is that there is so little of it. "The
Bermudas or the Somers Islands", to use their official name,
actually consist of a hundred-odd islands (some estimates go
over 300 but no one ever seems to have bothered to make an
accurate tally upon which Bermudians can agree). The Bermuda we are talking about is made up of seven "large" islands
connected by bridges and causeways—and we use quotation
marks because the area of the entire colony, the oldest in the
British Commonwealth, is a shade under twenty-two square
miles. Perhaps the best thumbnail description of the place
can be found in the comment of Mark Twain, one of a series
of writers who fell madly in love with Bermuda at first sight:
"Bermuda looks like a fishhook, only it's smaller."

This is only a slight exaggeration. It used to be quite a feat
of navigation for wartime airplane pilots to home in on Kindley
Field and, as recently as a century ago, an ailing Bermuda-
bound British admiral died at sea because his steamer spent
five weeks blundering around the Atlantic looking for the
place. Bermuda is just about as big as Manhattan Island, only
it's more exclusive.

And there you have its most unique characteristic of all.
This coral chip of England—it's the world's northernmost coral
atoll—has successfully weathered the hurricane of mass-
produced "tourism" which in recent years has roared over all

the other playgrounds of the elite from Palm Beach to Porto-fino. Geography, of course, helps a great deal in this respect. Since no one can drive to Bermuda, this means that there are no trailer camps, motels, drive-in restaurants or billboard-infested highways marring the islands. Cars have appeared over the past decade, true, but their dimensions are limited to pint-sized British standards and their speed is kept down to a pace not much faster than the horse-powered carriages they have replaced. A stubborn visitor can bring a car to Bermuda but the regulations are carefully designed to make him regret it.

But more than mere geography is involved in keeping Bermuda what it has always been. The atmosphere of the islands is as bewitching today as it was when Sir George Somers came ashore in 1609 in a shipwreck which was to be immortalized by Shakespeare in "The Tempest" set on an enchanted island. And it is this atmosphere which has enabled Bermuda to preserve its character even though it is only one and a half hours from New York by jet and less than two days by ship. Anyone can come to Bermuda today very easily and you can run into your next-door neighbour there... except that he will be talking like an FFB (a member of the First Families of Bermuda) and so will you. Don't underestimate the power of Bermuda's spell.

The spell is composed of one part climate, one part landscape and one part history and people. Blended carefully for 350 years, these ingredients have produced modern Bermuda with 45,000 people and 1,500 varieties of plants flourishing on the summit of a drowned volcano once believed to be inhabited only by devils.

The climate is... Bermudian. No other adjective can describe it. A good thousand miles north of the tropical West Indies, Bermuda seldom swelters in the summer and never freezes in the winter. The weather is always spring although, as writer Mary Johnson Tweedy has noted, Bermudians talk about an "early spring, a late spring or an unusual spring." It works out to a climate offering swimming most of the year to visitors and a chance for tradition-loving natives to toast Christmas in front of a crackling Yule log... usually after sunning themselves in their gardens.

Nor is there any other adjective but Bermudian for the landscape. Seascape might be a better word for it because no part of Bermuda is more than a mile from the sea (the "mainland" consisting of the seven major islands is 22 miles long by road, but never more than two miles wide and, in some places, no more than ten yards wide). The Bermudian palette begins with clear sea over coral. Then, at the water's edge, the blues and greens are transformed into pink by the sand—actually coral ground into powder by the waves—of the beaches. On top of this natural canvas, the Bermudians have painted their island. Flowers, vines, trees in blossom and shrubs grow not only in gardens but overflow onto walls and alongside lanes and roads. It's as though the island had been laid out by an omnipotent landscape architect (for example, Bermudians plant oleanders as windbreaks!). The exuberance of blossoming Bermuda contrasts with the soft pastels of its architecture. Bermudians stick mainly to pink with variations never going beyond a pale gray under perennially white roofs. And no-where, too, do houses integrate as well into the landscape, for the Bermudians saw limestone right out of the landscape to build their homes. Weaving through all this are unhurried English lanes which create the same impression as they do in the mother country—one of bucolic peace and seclusion on a populous island. The Bermudians are very proud of their roads. There isn't a straight stretch of more than 500 yards in the whole colony.

Colonized by Accident

Bermuda's history and people are inseparable. The story of its accidental colonization by Sir George Somers and his ship-wrecked companions is pure Robinson Crusoe and the resource-fulness of the pioneers has been matched by their descendants. Bermudians have tried everything in their eventful past from growing onions to running blockades in order to make their living. When one form of economy died out, they were always able to invent another. They usually had to, as well: compe-tition from Virginia ruined the tobacco plantations of the early settlers and that was only the first of a long string of mishaps. At one time during the 19th century, things were so bad on Bermuda that the local belles had to take down their mosquito nets in order to wear them as gowns to balls. The point of this, of course, is that they went to balls just the same. That was—and still is—Bermuda even though the mosquitos are gone and a $30,000,000-a-year tourist trade has put an end to hard times. The colony now proclaims itself "the biggest dollar-earner per square yard in the British Commonwealth." False modesty has never been a Bermudian failing.

This has resulted in one of the world's highest standards of living for Bermuda's population, approximately one-third white and two-thirds colored (the word Negro is never used in Bermuda). Since 95 per cent of Bermuda's food has to be imported—Bermudians never took to farming and present-day production of fruits and vegetables in the colony is mainly in the hands of 2,000 Portuguese immigrants from the Azores—the cost of living is also one of the highest in the world for people who live there all year round. But, while segregation is subtly practised in Bermuda, economic equality has been achieved to a far greater extent than in many places where advanced social ideas are still far ahead of wages. Even political agitation takes on a tranquilized Bermuda tone and the serene surface of the colony is seldom troubled by ripples any more serious than, for example, a polite colored boycott of movie theaters.

As we said, Bermuda's present prosperity is founded on tourists. England ruined the Bermuda ship-building industry when steam took over the seas and oversized Texas ruined truck farming by growing "Bermuda onions" with a great deal more space at its disposal. But no one has been able to duplicate the aristocratic elegance which Bermuda can offer a visitor.

This elegance is reflected everywhere—in shops, in hotels and guest houses where careful informality is the rule, in sports of the more aristocratic variety such as sailing, deep-sea fishing, golf and tennis, and in the visitors themselves. Bermuda naturally draws travelers mainly from the United States and Canada, plus a titled few from England, who are seeking a form of relaxation fast disappearing elsewhere in the rest of the world, summed up succinctly by Bermudians as "off-island." And it is likely that more and more of them will be buying tickets to the place described three centuries ago by poet Andrew Marvell, the place . . .

> "Where the remote Bermudas ride
> In the ocean's bosom unespied."

To anyone who has ever tried to wangle a last-minute reservation on Bermuda during the height of the spring season, the most amazing fact in the colony's short history is that no one wanted any part of it for a good hundred years.

Bermuda's discoverer is unknown, but the credit for naming the islands goes to Juan de Bermudez, a Spanish navigator who sighted it shortly after Columbus' voyages to the New World (the name, "La Bermuda", first appeared on a map in 1511). Bermudez never tried to do anything more than land hogs on his find and a later attempt by a Portuguese explorer to colonize it for the King of Spain was a thorough failure. True, the reputation of Bermuda was certainly not one to encourage settlers: the 16th century seamen called it the Isle of Devils, a reputation earned for it by its jagged reefs ready to rip the bottom out of a clumsy caravel blown within reach by a gust of wind.

The first Englishman to set foot on Bermuda was an unwilling visitor, Henry May. May's adventure, as related by Hudson Strode, began when he boarded a French ship in Santo Domingo in December 1593. With its crew roaring drunk, the ship foundered and a boatload of survivors, including May, reached the islands where they lived until May 1594. By that time, they had built a small boat of Bermuda cedar, in which they were able to sail to Newfoundland.

The next Englishman was Sir George Somers, and he was equally unwilling. Sir George was in command of a fleet of nine vessels carrying 500 passengers which sailed from Plymouth in June 1609, to relieve the starving colony of Jamestown. On the night of July 25, "a stern, a dreadful storme and hideous" broke, separating Sir George's flagship, the 300-ton Sea Venture, from the rest of the fleet. After an "Egyptian Night of three daies perpetual horror" with everyone aboard taking turns at the pumps, the leaking *Sea Venture* was beached on a Bermuda reef and its party was saved on July 28, now Bermuda's national holiday.

Devils Were Swine

They quickly saw that Bermuda did not deserve its reputation: "the fairies of rocks were but flocks of birds and all the devils that haunted the woods were but herds of swine." Still, Sir George did not lose sight of his original mission. With native cedar and everything that could be salvaged from the Sea Venture (whose wreck was recently discovered by a skin diver and identified), the colonists built two small vessels, the Deliverance and the Patience, and sailed for Virginia in May 1610. They left behind them two trouble-makers who hid in the woods because they were afraid they would hang in Jamestown. Somers reached Virginia and returned to Bermuda for supplies, but he died there in 1610. His nephew buried his heart in Bermuda and sailed for England, leaving the islands in the hands of this pair and a third man. They reigned as the "The Three Kings of Bermuda", the title of a story written about them by Washington Irving, but they almost annihilated each other when they discovered a huge lump of ambergris.

BERMUDA

This quarrel was settled in 1612 with the arrival of Richard Moore, a tough ship's carpenter and the island's first governor. He sent the ambergris to England and dethroned the three kings who barely escaped hanging.

Moore and his sixty settlers had been sent out by the Virginia Company but the islands were soon given to the Bermuda Company whose first governor was the notorious Daniel Tucker in 1616. Tyrannical Tucker put the settlers to work by marching them to their jobs at dawn and he had no hesitation about hanging anyone who disagreed with him. He even drove five Bermudians to the point where they slipped away from the islands in a two-ton smack, which they had built as a fishing boat for the Governor's pleasure, and reached Ireland forty-two days later with only a sun-dial as a compass. Tucker was replaced in 1619 by Governor Nathanial Butler who introduced parliamentary government the following year when the first General Assembly was called.

The experiences of the Bermuda colonists in the early 17th century must have made many of them wonder if the Spanish had not been right after all. Ambergris and whaling were a disappointment and tobacco had been a failure. By 1639, Bermudians were even emigrating to the West Indies and to America.

In 1684, this sorry state of affairs came to an end when Bermuda was taken away from the Company and turned over to the Crown. Now the Bermudians could fish, build ships and sail, occupations at which they proved themselves highly competent.

Soon, their main trade was raking salt from islands in the West Indies which they traded in America for food supplies. The advantage of this industry was that Bermudian captains could leave their slaves to gather salt while they engaged in the West Indies trade in all of its aspects, including privateering and piracy. At one time, the governor himself was reaping a fortune from piracy.

Commerce, a common outlook on the rights of colonies, and blood ties drew Bermuda quite close to America by the outbreak of the Revolutionary War. There was little doubt as to where the sympathies of the Bermudians lay, but a sternly Loyalist governor with the backing of the Royal Navy kept them from giving vent to them. This was doubly painful to the islanders: they were wounded in their principles and they were almost starving. By forbidding them to trade with the rebels, England had cut them off from their food supply.

BERMUDA

Food and Gunpowder

Bermuda needed food and America needed gunpowder. In 1775, resourceful Bermudians proposed a deal in which they offered the contents of the Royal Magazine at St. George in return for provisions. The Continental Congress accepted and then it was up to the Bermudians to make good. On the night of August 14, a band of conspirators sneaked into the powder magazine. One story, told by Walter B. Hayward in his *Bermuda Past and Present*, maintains that they stole the keys from under the governor's pillow. At any rate, they did roll 100 kegs of gunpowder across the governor's front lawn and thence to Tobacco Bay on the northern tip of St. George's Island where whale boats took them out to an American frigate which ran the precious loot to Boston. Bermudians like to say that their powder was used in the Battle of Bunker Hill.

This daring raid taught England the strategic value of Bermuda. After a golden age of privateering in which many a respectable Bermuda fortune of today was founded, the War of 1812 broke out and the British used Bermuda as a port of embarkation for their invasion armada carrying the troops who were to capture and burn Washington. When the war ended, the boom continued for Bermuda whose ships monopolized the trade between the United States and the British West Indies which had been barred to American vessels. When this ban was lifted in 1822, however, the Bermudians fell upon dreary days. Their shipyards became silent for no one wanted sailing vessels in the new era of steam. Old Bermuda seamen were driven ashore into idleness. The main activity on the islands was the building of a huge British naval base intended to turn Bermuda into "the Gibraltar of the West" directed mainly against those upstart ex-colonies on the mainland. The base, however, was built by convicts who were carefully isolated on hulks and came ashore only to be buried (some 2,000 died, mainly of yellow fever, on the job). Strode narrates that one of them was allowed to settle in Bermuda where he eventually became the colony's first carriage-driver.

There was still one last fling in store for Bermuda before she was to take on her awesome respectable air of today. The Civil War saw another blockade on the American coast but, this time, directed against the British. England needed cotton and the South needed everything. The two met in Bermuda where cargoes were transshipped aboard blockade runners bound for Southern ports. It was a dangerous game and the stakes were high. Skippers, pilots and seamen were rolling in money and spent it in Bermuda where, so the story goes, shopkeepers just swept their gold into the backrooms because they didn't have time to count it. There weren't even enough beds on Bermuda for the crews of the blockade-runners—the available ones were rented in shifts.

Then the Civil War ended and so did Bermuda's short-lived prosperity. It was at this point that the colony took to truck-farming for the dinner tables of New York where "Bermuda onion" became a household word. But there was even less future in onion-growing than in blockade-running because Texas started to raise vegetables and the United States slapped a protective tariff on them ... to protect Texas from Bermuda!

Bermuda's troubles, though, were almost over. When the onion boats returned to Bermuda for new cargoes, they began to carry tourists for ballast. It wasn't an ideal way of traveling by any means, but the passengers were soon convinced that Bermuda was worth it. Early visitors such as Mark Twain and William Dean Howells quickly appreciated it and spread the good news in their writings (beginning with Shakespeare, Bermuda has always been well-served by writers). After the First World War, the tourist industry got into full production with the help of Prohibition in the United States. Bermudians themselves have never been heavy drinkers in the colonial tradition, but their waterless islands were able to slake the thirst of a great many Americans. In those days, too, Bermuda was also a favorite stopping-place for rum-runners playing tag with American revenue men.

With the outbreak of the Second World War, the merry-makers disappeared to be replaced by tourists in uniform. It was hands across the sea, and the United States was given a 99-year lease on bases in Bermuda. Since nothing but a flying boat had ever been able to land in the colony, the Americans proceded to change the map of Bermuda, constructing an air field on St. David's Island which had been inhabited by the most insular of all insular Bermudians.

The current invasion of Bermuda by American and Canadian visitors who can't find anything like these twenty-two square miles anywhere on their huge continent is the latest and the most peaceful chapter in the history of the colony. It is one which, fortunately, does not seem likely to close.

Man-Made Islands

Coral polyps began the process of building Bermuda on top

of a drowned mountain millions of years ago, but the job was only completed by man in 1941. The finishing touch was placed on present-day Bermuda in a huge land-fill operation creating a World War II air base which, while it certainly is no beauty spot, comes in very handy at present as a flight deck for tourist-laden airliners.

The Kindley Field land fill also symbolizes the ever-present hand of man in the geography of Bermuda. Before he came—and Bermuda was the last place in the temperate zone to be inhabited—there was virtually nothing. The coral polyps were just about the only true natives of Bermuda.

That is why you can't separate Bermuda from the Bermudians. Over the past three-and-a-half centuries, they have built it with their own hands (Bermuda only celebrated the 350th anniversary of its settlement in 1959). When they first came, they found only a deserted string of coral atolls, a freak of nature in the middle of the Atlantic. Since then, they have made Bermuda—not only its houses but its vegetation and its scenery as well. It took an unusual breed of men to do this, marooned without a drop of underground water or a single river. Bermudians are still unusual.

They live on a string of seven islands, a green fishhook with Main Island forming its shaft and barb. The western tip of the hook begins with Ireland Island and continues over Lilliputian bridges through Boaz, Watford and Somerset islands. The world's smallest drawbridge, opening only wide enough to let the mast of a sailboat slip through, connects Somerset to Main Island. Then, to the east, the road continues to St. George's and St. David's islands. With their highest natural point peeking only 259 feet out of the sea, these Bermuda islands lie on about the same latitude as Madeira and Charleston, South Carolina. Their exact position, in case you ever plan to try to find this marine needle-in-a-haystack in the biennial Newport-to-Bermuda yacht race, is 32 degrees, 14 minutes and 45 seconds north latitude and 64 degrees, 49 minutes and 55 seconds west longitude. If you hit this reading right on the nose, you will come under Gibb's Hill Lighthouse, the highest man-made point in the colony.

Seven islands are complicated enough for this doughty speck of coral, but the founding fathers of Bermuda compounded the confusion by dividing them into nine parishes in order to be able to perpetuate the names of the generous British noblemen who staked the Bermuda Company. From east to west, these parishes are St. George's (named after Sir George Somers who

150

was responsible for Bermuda's settlement), Hamilton, Smith's, Devonshire, Pembroke, Paget, Warwick, Southampton and Sandys. The town of Hamilton is the metropolis of Bermuda and, as you might expect, it is not very big (by stretching, it manages to spread over half a square mile). As you might also expect in this delightful never-never land, it is not in Hamilton Parish, either. In 1815 it replaced the town of St. George as the capital of Bermuda and St. George never got over the shock. Things might have been even more confused if Daniel Tucker, one of the island's earliest governors, had had his way. As Hudson Strode relates, he rigged the original survey of the islands so that "a fatte and lustye soyle in a most delicate enlarged valley" would fall to him. But the Bermudians, an independent lot even in those days, managed to get rid of him although his name survives in Tucker's Town where the Mid-Ocean Club, the most exclusive spot in exclusive Bermuda, is located. It was here that Churchill, Eisenhower and Laniel met in 1953 and Eisenhower and Macmillan met in 1957.

While no one has laid claim to them, the reefs surrounding Bermuda are another very important factor in its geography. On the south shore, the best side for bathing, they come as close as half a mile or less from the coast. To the north, they are further out at sea but it is this coral ring which gives Bermuda its protected waters enjoyed by man and fish alike. The reefs help Bermuda attract tourists today to balance its economy and they were also an important asset in the past when ship-wrecking was one of the ways in which the industrious islanders kept body and soul together.

During their colorful history, they have also tried whaling, salt-raking, privateering, piracy, blockade-running and even honest navigation with varying degrees of success. As a matter of fact, they were willing to try anything except farming which, of course, was the reason why the lords and the earls wanted to settle Bermuda in the first place. For Bermudians have always hated farming. They brought in slaves—another of Governor Tucker's ideas—but the slaves soon became Bermudian to the point where they hated farming, too. In 1830, a census showed one plow in the entire colony and it was no great blow to the Bermudian economy when the slaves, mostly servants or boatmen, were emancipated four years later. This early abolitionism, by the way, did not prevent Bermuda from siding enthusiastically with the Confederacy during the American Civil War... when a bold Bermudian skipper could

make the equivalent of $5,000 (in pounds sterling, not Con-
federate money) for running the Northern blockade. Fortunately, the Portuguese immigration we mentioned earlier has
given Bermuda a population of hard-working farmers harvesting fruits and vegetables on 900 acres of farmland while white
and colored Bermudians harvest the annual bumper tourist
crop.

Of Boom and Bloom

The first American tourist to come to Bermuda was a
Massachusetts minister and part-time poet, the Reverend
Michael Wigglesworth, who arrived there in 1663 more dead
than alive. He had been in pretty poor shape at the start and
the month-long trip didn't improve matters (it was Mark
Twain, still in the days before airlines and the Queen of
Bermuda, who pointed out that Bermuda was heaven . . . and
you had to go through purgatory to reach it). But seven months
on Bermuda made a new man out of him—the Reverend
returned to Massachusetts, remarried twice and raised a huge
family.

Efficient though they may be in playing host to the hundreds
of thousands of Americans who have followed the Reverend
Mr. Wigglesworth, the Bermudians are not a race of hotel-
keepers and waiters. They are hospitable as only a people
who have made an inhospitable soil bloom can be. The atmosphere of that Bermudian institution, the "guest house", proves
this time and again.

The Bermudians are actually the descendants of a hardy
line of seafarers going back to the first settlers. Bermuda
cedar (virtually the symbol of the island until it was ravaged
in 1945 by a scale pest) was ideal for boat-building and Bermuda ships long showed their heels to all rivals in the trade
between New York and the West Indies. As for her seamen,
they roamed the world and they were responsible for much of
the garden-like appearance of modern Bermuda. Three hundred
and fifty years ago, only seventeen native varieties of plants
could be found in Bermuda. There were about 130 others
which had been brought in from the mainland by birds or
drifting seaweed and that was all.

It's hard to believe today for anyone who has ever taken a
heady trip through any patch of Bermudian countryside rife
with red hibiscus, scarlet royal poinciana and breathtaking
bougainvillea. They came from just about everywhere in the
sea-chests of Bermuda's navigators. The Bermuda Easter Lily,

for example, was brought back early in the 19th century from the Japanese Liukiu Islands. Exporting Easter Lily bulbs to the United States and Canada was once one of the nearest things to an industry in Bermuda, but it has waned in recent years. Mary Tweedy tells how another Japanese plant, the loquat, reached Bermuda when a ship carrying some of these evergreens had to put into St. George's Harbor in distress. The hibiscus, which blooms all year round, came from Hawaii and the West Indies. Poinsettias came from Mexico and royal poincianas from Madagascar. As for the bougainvillea, Mrs. Tweedy believes it reached Bermuda via Gibraltar.

All in all, there are now 1,500 varieties of plants flourishing in this botanical garden. Trees are a part of the Bermuda scene and their roots go deep into its history. The cedar (actually a species of juniper) supplied the needs of Bermudians for centuries from the cradle to the coffin. The Bermuda palmetto put roofs over the heads of the first settlers who fed on its berries (the reference to berry eating in "The Tempest" is supposed to be another proof that Shakespeare had Bermuda in mind although the subject is still good for an argument). Thomas Moore, another literary tourist, wrote a poem about a Bermuda calabash tree which is still standing a century-and-a-half later.

When the first Bermudians landed, they found even fewer fauna than flora. There were nothing but tortoises, insects and some wild hogs who had probably been left there by Spanish or Portuguese vessels (the hogs enjoyed fleeting glory when they graced early Bermudian coins which are now highly prized by collectors). There were also cahow birds who unfortunately were as tame as they were tasty. They wandered around beaches watching their next of kin being plunged into cooking pots until their own turn came up and, to no one's surprise, they became extinct very shortly. However, a cahow appeared in Bermuda in 1906 and, since then, a few dozen of them have been found in the islands of Castle Harbor which are now their sanctuary. Making up for their present-day scarcity are the many varieties of migrators who stop in Bermuda on their way to distant destinations. And some of them, as happens to migrating tourists, like Bermuda so much that they stay there all year round.

Saw-It-Yourself Architecture

The birds and the flowers may come from all points of the compass, but the most charming aspect of the Bermudian landscape—its architecture—has no parallel anywhere. It was mothered by necessity when settlers learned to their sorrow that cedar walls and palmetto roofs could not weather mid-Atlantic winds. So, unlike their fellow colonists on the American mainland (Bermuda used to consider herself part of the *fourteen* American colonies), they abandoned wood and turned to the soft windblown limestone under their feet to build homes as functional as any steel-and-glass cube and far more pleasant to behold in this setting.

Bermuda houses are literally sawn out of their backyards, the "quarry" becoming a garden in many cases once the house has been completed. This coral limestone, cream-colored at first and then hardening and turning a pale gray with age, is used for roofs as well as walls. The walls are a simple matter, just blocks of stone assembled as they are anywhere else (the Bermudians no longer need to use tortoise oil for mortar). It should be pointed out, though, that Bermuda limestone walls remain standing for centuries only on Bermuda. An American once tried importing limestone from the islands in order to improve his social status in New England. His house was a great curiosity when it was completed and even more of a curiosity when it cracked and collapsed with the first winter frosts. The old houses of Bermuda are a quiet testimonial to the colony's mild weather.

The roofs are made of "slates" which are nothing less than limestone sliced into inch-thick shingles and laid on over cedar beams. In many an old house, the beams sag with age producing a gingerbread-cottage effect which a new owner is always careful to preserve. A Bermuda roof is supposed to do more than just keep the rain out: its steep slopes and clever terraces are designed to lead every drop of water falling onto the house into a tank which serves as a water supply system. Without rivers or a rainy season, Bermuda must depend upon the sky for its water. While the colony receives sixty inches of rain a year, a downpour never lasts very long. This explains why every roof in Bermuda is white: by law, it is lime-washed regularly in order to guarantee the purity of Bermudian drinking water.

The Water Problem

Water used to be a serious problem on the islands with everyone suggesting solutions. The American historical novelist, the late Kenneth Roberts, even brought a dowser from New England to try to find underground water. His name was

Dream view from a Bermuda balcony

BERMUDA

Henry Gross. A man of extraordinary gifts, he dowsed three wells in dry Bermuda, and all produced pure water in great quantity. Finally, before World War II, an ingenious Bermudian had the idea of drilling horizontally into hills to tap rain-water in suspension. He struck water—it's now called "Watlington water" in his honor—which can be used for bathing and washing but which is not very pleasant for drinking. Bermuda houses still have their tanks holding from 15,000 to 100,000 gallons although water is now being stored under homes instead of in picturesque barrel or dome-shaped tanks.

Through painful trial-and-error, early Bermudian builders learned enough about the laws of aerodynamics to build low roofs with short eaves as protection against occasional hurricanes, not nearly as frequent as on the Florida coast. This led to an inverted-tray type of ceiling in order to give sufficient height to interior rooms.

The Bermuda Homes

In general, Bermuda houses are monuments to the island's living conditions of the past and present. In many homes, for example, the main rooms face the lawn while the kitchens overlook the sea. This room plan, while surprising at first sight to the visitor who comes hundreds of miles to see the sea in Bermuda, was highly satisfactory to Bermudian seamen who wanted to rest their eyes on grass in between voyages. The thickest chimneys in a Bermuda house are always to the southeast to strengthen the wall which bears the brunt of hurricanes. Strange minaret-shaped structures alongside houses were originally built as "butteries" where food could be stored in the pre-refrigeration era. They are now used as bath houses or studios. Fireplaces inside are either ankle or waist-high, depending upon whether they were intended to be used for heating or cooking. And the big room downstairs in many an old Bermuda home goes back to the days when privateers needed a handy place to cache their hauls away from the eyes of inquisitive customs officers.

Stately old Bermuda homes are among the most rewarding sights of the island and some have been opened to visitors. Glencoe, where Woodrow Wilson stayed, is even a guest house. Both Verdmont and the President Henry Tucker House, handsome examples of 18th century Bermudian architecture, are open to the public.

Bermuda's architecture already tells you a great deal about Bermudians. They are loyally English—their startling homes

Hire a surrey and see the Bahamas

are basically nothing more than English cottages adapted to unheard-of conditions—but they can be very Bermudian when necessary.

These islands are free of hay fever, snakes, income taxes, a public debt, and a great many other amenities of mainland living on both sides of the Atlantic. The Bermudians have every intention of keeping them this way.

First Families

The job of preservation is firmly in the hands of the First Families of Bermuda. This is a merchant aristocracy—the names of the shops on Front Street in Hamilton read like a Bermuda Social Register—but it is an aristocracy just the same. With no inheritance taxes, the FFBs (malicious friends sometimes call them the "forty thieves") maintain their hold on their pint-sized empires. Their scions have every reason to stay on Bermuda and continue doing so. A property qualification for voting (to be eligible, a man needs to hold real estate worth £60) also helps them keep their grip, but not in the way you might think. Bermuda is so rich that more than 5,000 voters, half of them colored, can qualify for the polls. The hitch is that a man can vote in any parish where he is worth those £60 and this gives the FFBs a legal opportunity to vote in all nine parishes in some cases (fortunately, distances aren't great on Election Day). When they are not voting or sitting in parliament or tending to their affairs, the FFBs wisely enjoy all the facilities for pleasure which bring visitors to Bermuda, although no Bermudian has ever been caught swimming in winter. A tightly-spun web of clubs, flower shows, yacht races, dog shows and other closed-circuit social events help to keep the ruling class of Bermuda together.

This may look like a shocking state of affairs on paper, but it is actually a case of benevolent "despotism." There are no beggars among what have been called Bermuda's "prosperous poor" and there is no proletariat. There is only one factory in the colony and it comes as no great surprise to learn that it turns out perfume. The Bermudians themselves were taking things easy on their islands long before the tourist trade arrived. The colony, for example, lies in the heart of one of the richest fishing grounds in the Atlantic but there is no organized commercial fishing industry. Independent fishermen go out when they feel like it, and the rest of the time Bermuda eats food imported from the mainland. Everything, for that matter, is imported and customs duties (not paid by visitors coming for a short stay) are the main source of government revenue. None of this may sound very democratic, but no one really wants to change things on this mid-ocean Utopia.

As They Like It

For another characteristic of the Bermudians is their dislike of change whenever it can be avoided. The Bermuda Parliament first met in 1620 in St. George (making it the oldest in the world next to those of England and Iceland) and it is still presided over by a bewigged speaker in its present home at Sessions House in Hamilton. Wigs are the rule, too, in the Bermuda Supreme Court which also occupies Sessions House. The chief executive of the colony is "His Excellency, the Governor and Commander-in-Chief of the Bermudas, or Somers Islands." Official functions, when the governor comes out in his state carriage, are a leading event in Bermuda where relations between the representative of the British Crown and his subjects have improved enormously since the days when Bermudians expressed their disapproval of the governor by putting him into jail.

This love of tradition has led to the survival of a great many customs in Bermuda. They can be found first of all in cooking, always the richest treasure house of folklore in any country. The uniquely Bermudian combination of tough English mariners living on sub-tropical islands is expressed perfectly in Bermuda's Sunday breakfast of codfish and bananas ("sliced avocado pears make a nice finishing touch if available," says one recipe!). Cassava pie, whose origin is said to go back to a year when ordinary flour was not available, is a pillar of the Bermuda Christmas dinner which also includes American roast turkey and English plum pudding. More appreciated by non-Bermudians are the colony's fish dishes such as Bermuda lobster (actually a crawfish) and baked rockfish or red snapper. Bermudians also have a weakness for sharks: they eat them or else they use them to manufacture shark's liver oil barometers (when the oil in a bottle turns cloudy, it predicts the weather).

Island customs are reflected in the cuisine everywhere in Bermuda. The Bermudians faithfully observe Guy Fawkes Day on November 5 like true British subjects, but they have concocted a sweet potato pudding which is eaten in Bermuda, and nowhere else, when the fireworks go off. The most charming dish of all is the Bermuda wedding cake, a confection which unfortunately cannot be enjoyed by honeymooners from the mainland who still account for 21 per cent of all visitors. To tell the truth, there are two cakes in a Bermuda wedding, one for the bride and one for the groom. To assure the future prosperity of the couple, the bride's cake is covered in gold leaf and the groom's cake in silver leaf. Traditionally, these cakes used to bear cedar seedlings which were then planted after the ceremony but other trees are now used to replace the blighted cedars.

Another holiday which the Bermudians celebrate in their own way is Good Friday. On this occasion, just about every youngster in Bermuda flies a kite, often in contests to judge the biggest or the most beautiful kites. The story of this tradition is supposed to go back to a Bermudian who had trouble explaining Christ's ascension to Heaven to a Sunday School class. So the teacher and his class climbed a high hill on Good Friday and he launched a kite bearing a likeness of Jesus Christ. Once it had reached the end of its string, he cut it loose and the kite soared out of sight in the sky. To this day, Bermuda's children launch kites on Good Friday to show how well their predecessors remembered the lesson.

Rich in home-made and English customs (such as driving cars on the left side of the road) Bermuda is relatively short of the African folklore permeating islands further south. This is probably explained by the economic well-being of Bermudians of all colors, for picturesqueness is too often a gaudy facade for poverty. However, Africa does penetrate Bermuda in the form of the "gombeys", those groups of dancers wearing colorful costumes and head-dresses who parade to the rhythm of drums at Easter and Christmas. But, in a truly Bermudian paradox, another custom among the island's colored population is to go out on Christmas—and sing carols.

Add all these together—the gombeys and the FFBs, the staid clubs and the dazzling gardens, the sleepy stone houses and the bustling traders, the bewigged judges and the cassava Christmas pie—and you have Bermuda, a mixture to be found nowhere else on earth and whose proportions have been set once and for all.

Of course, there are now GIs from the American air base in the bars, the colony is in the throes of its biggest building boom of all time, and it looks as if the automobile is here to stay. But Bermuda itself will not change basically, at least not if the Bermudians can help it. They know when they are well off.

BERMUDA

PRACTICAL INFORMATION FOR BERMUDA

 WHEN TO GO? Bermuda is one of those rarities, a year-round vacation resort. Winter months are balmy and summer is seldom sweltering. The result is that the old Bermuda season concentrated mainly around Easter has stretched to the entire year with many hotels never closing. In general, however, the colony is less crowded during "winter" and some hotels offer reductions running to about 10 per cent if you come between November and April.

The climate of Bermuda is its main natural resource. The year-round temperature average is 70 degrees with summer lasting from late April to the middle of November. Over 65 years, though, the average temperature in Bermuda's hottest month, August, has been only 85.8 degrees with a refreshing 10 degree drop at night. The "cold" months from December through March offer thermometer readings in the low 70's and in the 60's, but even then you can count on many days with enough sun for the beach. Humidity is high, with all that water on all sides, but rainfall comes in spurts and a rainy day is an event. Bermuda's 60 inches of rain a year are spread out over all twelve months and there is no rainy season to be avoided. Bermuda has experienced only six hurricanes in the past twenty-three years. Swimming is excellent from late April to the middle of November and the temperature of the sea seldom goes below the low 60's even in winter when it's still a good idea to bring a bathing suit to Bermuda.

College Week. An excellent time for students to come to Bermuda, either in organized groups or with their parents. It draws some 3,000 students to Bermuda over a period ranging from three to five weeks and coinciding with college spring vacations in the United States. Group rates bring the cost, including transportation, of a week's trip down to a figure running from $200 to $300, depending upon where students decide to stay (in general, they bunk up with three or four to a room). During this period, every Monday is College Day on Bermuda with games and contests, including matches allowing Harvard men or Princetonians to pit their skill against Bermudian soccer and rugby teams. There is also a free boat trip every Wednesday from Hamilton to St. George with entertainment on board. Last year's college week festivities were enlivened with jazz sessions, featuring combos from leading men's colleges competing for prizes. Another new feature is College Week Revue, the student's own off-Broadway threat in the middle of the Atlantic. Every fall, the Bermuda Trade Development Board issues a list of hotels and guests houses accepting student groups and offering special rates for College Week, beginning in March.

 WHERE TO GO? Don't be fooled by Bermuda's small size. Though the colony is only 22 miles from tip to tip, it offers a huge variety of atmosphere. Somerset is rural, Hamilton is lively, St. George is quietly historic, Tucker's Town is exclusive and yet it's not much more than an hour's drive from one end to the other of the colony. Your choice of where you will stay in Bermuda will determine the type of vacation you will have. It can be a lazy rest in a small cottage next to a deserted beach or it can be a wallow in the luxury of a huge hotel with something going on nearly all the time. Making up your mind with the help of this guide and a good travel agent before you go is very important, as it is often hard to change

159

BERMUDA

once you are on Bermuda. You won't have a car, not even a rented one, and reservations are made well in advance, especially during spring.

The Highlights of Bermuda. The main sightseeing destinations in the colony are Hamilton, the capital and the biggest "city"; old St. George where history has been preserved for three centuries; Somerset for gracious Bermuda country living; and Harrington Sound with its caves and its two remarkable aquariums—one natural and the other built by the government. You can see Bermuda by taxi, bus, bicycle, auxiliary-powered bicycle, horse carriage, ferry, or excursion boat. You can also see it underwater with a diving helmet or aboard a glass-bottomed boat. While not a free port, Bermuda offers some wonderful shopping, especially in Hamilton, where English articles are offered far below their cost in the United States. Products of other European countries and Bermuda's own handiwork are also good buys. For sportsmen, the onion patch has golf, fishing, tennis, water ski-ing, sailing, swimming and skin-diving.

 HOW TO GO? Since Bermuda is an island—and surrounded by more water than nearly any other place on earth—your choice of transportation is rather limited. It's either by air or by sea although, in both cases, a wide variety is offered. Air travel is fast—Bermuda is only 1½ hours from New York by jet—and frequent, an important factor for the person who wants to waste as little time as possible in getting to his final point of relaxation. Sea travel, however, is not too time-consuming. It's only a forty-one hour run from New York to Hamilton or St. George aboard the *Queen of Bermuda* and the *Ocean Monarch*. Travel by ship is slightly more expensive than air travel in a comparable class, but you have two days of living included with the ticket. In the case of the Furness liners, it's virtually Bermuda living because the Queen has become a part of the colony for all intents and purposes.

You can travel to Bermuda on your own or else take advantage of the many package tours which are now being offered. In either case, you will probably find it wise to use an experienced travel agent. If he arranges your transportation or books you on a package tour, his services should cost you nothing. On the other hand, if he takes care of your hotel accommodations, transfers and other arrangements, his commissions will not cover his expenses and he will usually have to add a service charge. Since Bermuda tends to be expensive, a well-informed travel agent often can save you money by avoiding unpleasant surprises.

171.5
13.0
201.0
─────
385.5

WHAT WILL IT COST? Like most of the good things on earth, Bermuda comes high. This is a place where everyone, not just the tourists, lives well and you shouldn't expect to profit from a bargain economy based on cheap wages and misery. On the other hand, Bermuda makes a point of giving you your money's worth in quality. The tourist industry is far too important to the colony's economy to be sabotaged by shoddy service or elastic price scales (the commercial honesty of the British is always appreciated by a traveler anywhere under the Union Jack). Bermudians don't want to have to go back to growing onions.

In the end, too, you just about break even on a Bermuda vacation. While hotel and restaurant prices may be higher than in certain other spots, transportation costs are low because of the colony's conveniently short distance from its American and Canadian visitors. This isn't true, of course, for Englishmen, but the English who go to Bermuda don't worry about price.

BERMUDA

The cost of a Bermuda vacation, though, is basically up to you. Hotels and guest houses offer a complicated series of plans—*European Plan* with only the room, *Bermuda Plan* with room and breakfast, *Modified American Plan* with room, breakfast and one meal and *American Plan* with room and all meals—and some have arrangements allowing you to eat elsewhere. Figuring this out on the basis of rates and restaurant prices is something like filling out an income tax return. In general, we can say that a room and meals for one person on Bermuda can run from $9 to $25 a day—the range runs from a room in a private home with inexpensive eating in Hamilton to the most expensive hotels on the island. Dinner in most Bermuda restaurants and hotel dining rooms runs from $4 to $7. There are restaurants in Hamilton where the tab is only $3. Lunch amounts to $1 or $2 if you don't overeat.

As a general rule, a room-and-meals budget of $16 a day per person (based on double-room rates) or roughly $100 a week should allow you to live quite comfortably on Bermuda. Of course, you can be comfortable for less . . . and for more.

Then comes that item usually hidden as "miscellaneous" in the family budget. On Bermuda, it probably will not amount to as much as in the average resort because Bermuda living is not high living in the flashy sense. Still, there are incidentals and they do add up.

Count on about $3 for your transfers to and from the airport and add $2.85 for the Bermuda stamp tax which everyone must pay on leaving. Drinks are slightly lower than in the United States. A bathhouse at the beach runs between $0.75 and $1 if it is not provided by your hotel.

Taking a trip around Bermuda by taxi will cost between $7 and $9.50 depending on the mileage. The same trip by boat is $9 with lunch and a rum swizzle usually thrown in.

Greens fees at golf courses amount to $4 or $5. Some hotels have free tennis courts for guests; at others, it can cost from $1 per person per half day to $2 per hour. A skin-diving lesson is about $8, water skiing behind a speedboat is $5 per lesson.

If you pedal a rented bike, it will cost you $7 a week. The fee goes up to $21 a week if there is a motor to help your pedal. Tobacco and cigarettes are about the same as in the United States. So is film for your camera (prices of Kodachrome include processing).

Night life is not at all of the tomorrow-we-die variety. Most of the big hotels have orchestras and entertainment and you probably won't paint the colony red very often because the entertainment moves from one hotel to another during the week. Hotels providing evening entertainment charge a modest $1 cover charge. This isn't Pigalle.

 WHAT TO TAKE? Unless you are planning to dress for dinner—with a different dress—every night, it's no problem to travel light to Bermuda. If you go by air, it's a necessity, especially if you want to have some breathing space on your weight allowance for what you will buy in Hamilton (whose shops, fortunately, are well experienced in shipping purchases home in accordance with customs regulations). Even if you go by ship, don't go overboard (figuratively, that is) with your luggage. Remember, Bermuda taxis are of the British variety and you haven't got much of a chance of putting a steamer trunk on the roof of an Austin.

CLOTHING. This depends mainly upon when you go to Bermuda. From May to the middle of November, summer clothes are all anyone needs.

BERMUDA

From the middle of November to the middle of December, your wardrobe should be divided between lightweight summer clothes and light woolens whenever there is a nip (by Bermuda standards) in the air. From Christmas to April, it's spring clothes and then, in April, you have to pack keeping in mind the likely possibility that summer can come any day. A raincoat of the kind that can be easily folded into a bicycle basket or under your arm is fashionable in Bermuda all year long ... and so is a bathing suit.

Women. Of course you need Bermuda shorts, slacks and sports clothes, especially if you are bent on golfing or playing tennis, but remember that they are among the best buys in Bermuda. Evening dresses should be simple and at least one pair of shoes should be sensible for walking. Daytime dresses should be classic, too ... this is a British colony. Take along all the usual bathing and beach paraphernalia, of course, not forgetting your own particular formula for sunburn protection (there are enough lobsters in Bermuda as it is). Remember, too, that your husband is almost bound to go out sailing or fishing and that you will want to go along. Use nylon or orlon whenever possible because laundries and dry-cleaners operate at a leisurely Bermudian tempo.

Men. At last, you won't feel self-conscious in your Bermuda shorts. To tell the truth, you'll feel self-conscious in anything else, especially shorter shorts. Otherwise, the Bermuda-length variety can be worn anywhere save to an official reception by His Excellency, the Governor. The suit you have on your back when you land in the colony will probably be enough to see you through the more formal demands of Bermuda day and night life. Then, of course, the requirements include slacks, tennis and golf clothes if you plan on using them, bathing trunks, sailing and fishing togs, sport shirts and jacket and, though not essential, a dinner jacket is usually worn for dining and dancing on Thursday and Saturdays at the larger hotels and clubs.

 PASSPORTS. Citizens of the United States or Canada do not need a passport to enter Bermuda for a stay of less than six months. Upon their return home, U.S. citizens need proof of their citizenship, such as a valid or expired passport, a birth certificate or a voter's certificate which can be obtained from your local Board of Elections. Canadian citizens need no papers if they return directly to Canada but they must possess proof of their Canadian citizenship if they plan to return via the United States. Americans and Canadians are not required to show proof of smallpox vaccination within the past three years, but this is demanded of all visitors coming from Europe, Africa, South America and Asia. Immigration officers check to ensure that travelers have a return ticket to their point of departure or ultimate destination.

Bermuda requires no visas, except for citizens of Iron Curtain countries.

ANIMALS. It's a lot less easy for them. Most hotels and guest houses do not accept dogs or other pets. The ones that do require that you ask permission in advance and two of them tack a $15 charge on their bill to cover costs of fumigation after Rover leaves. The airlines carry them as a favor at excess baggage rates of 31 cents a pound and the Furness liners stipulate that they must be crated and kept out of the owner's cabin and all public rooms. Even if a dog or a cat swims to Bermuda he still needs a veterinarian's certificate stating that he doesn't have any contagious animal disease, that there has been no rabies within a radius

162

BERMUDA

of 50 miles from his home address for the past year and that he has an anti-rabies vaccine less than a year old.

Parrots, parakeets and similar birds need health certificates stating that they have had psittacosis examinations within six months (three months if they have been newly purchased).

And now you see why the first settlers of Bermuda didn't find very many animals there.

 BY SHIP. In prewar days, the glamorous twins of the Furness Bermuda Line, the *Queen of Bermuda* and the *Monarch of Bermuda*, were the only way of reaching the colony. As a result, to many Americans, these ships became part of the traditions of Bermuda and many a Bermuda honeymoon began on a North River pier. Today, the Queen of Bermuda is still an institution while the Monarch of Bermuda has been replaced by a new vessel, the *Ocean Monarch*.

There is regular steamship service to Bermuda only from New York, although cruises are occasionally routed there from other American and Canadian ports. The Queen and the Ocean Monarch sail from Piers 95-97 at the foot of West 55th-57th Streets in the afternoon and arrive in Bermuda on the morning of the second day, only some 40 hours later. Schedules are carefully designed to allow for weekend travel. The Queen, for example, usually leaves New York at 3 p.m. on Saturday, arriving in Hamilton Monday morning. When the Ocean Monarch is routed via Bermuda, she often sails at 5 p.m. on Friday to arrive in Bermuda, most of the time at old St. George, on Sunday morning. Most of the time, too, it is possible to use either of these Furness Liners as your hotel in Bermuda (the Queen sails for New York on Wednesday and arrives Friday).

Passengers are allowed 20 cubic feet of baggage, which is more than you could possibly need. Both ships have swimming pools and entertainment. Fares start at $130 for a round trip and go up to $250 for de luxe cabins. All first-class cabins have private baths. Children under one year are carried free. They pay quarter-fare between one and three and half-fare between three and twelve.

You can have your cake and eat it—that is, you can gain time and still enjoy shipboard living—by taking an air-sea combination trip. The rate here is one-half the round-trip steamer fare for accommodations on board plus $58 or $72 for the airplane fare, depending upon whether you fly in tourist or first class.

 BY AIR. Bermuda first appeared on the world's commercial airways map as a stopping-place for the pioneer transatlantic service started by Pan-American with its Clipper flying-boats. Then, once land planes were able to span the Atlantic, it almost disappeared from the map. Happily, the Kindley Field air base, which had been roundly condemned by so many old-line Bermudians as a blot on the colony's peaceful landscape, came to the rescue by offering civil air facilities. Bermuda now has excellent airline service bringing it closer to New York than most of America. *Pan American, BOAC* and *Eastern Airlines* now have jet service between New York and Bermuda, flying time 1½ hours. *Cunard Eagle* flies from New York with turbo-prop Viscounts in 2½ hours.

The usual regulations governing international air travel apply to flights to Bermuda. Baggage allowance is 44 pounds in tourist class and 66 pounds in first with excess baggage being carried at the rate of 31 cents a pound.

BERMUDA

From New York City, there are daily flights to Bermuda on no less than four airlines—*BOAC, Eastern Air Lines, Pan American* and *Cunard Eagle*. The round trip fare from New York is $105 in tourist class and $144 in first with a $10 surcharge for jet flights.

Pan American also runs several flights a week directly from Bermuda to Boston (the fare is the same as from New York), and during the spring season adds up to 18 jets a week to accommodate the usual invasion of college vacationers.

From Washington, *Eastern Air Lines* offers direct flights several times a week and a daily flight with a connection in New York. *Cunard Eagle* also has several direct flights every week from Washington and Baltimore to Bermuda.

Finally, you can start out from Miami and reach Bermuda via Nassau aboard *BOAC* and *Cunard Eagle*. The fare is $152 in first class and $119 tourist.

BOAC and *Cunard Eagle* have regular once a week flights from Montreal. *Trans-Canada Airlines* also flies once a week from Montreal to Bermuda and several times a week from Toronto. *Eastern Air Lines* flies regularly from Montreal and Ottawa. Round trip fare is $132 in tourist class and $183.60 in first.

If you happen to be starting from somewhere else, there is also a rather wide choice of airlines landing on the minute colony. *Trans-Canada Airlines* and *BWIA* (British West Indian Airways) fly from Barbados and Trinidad; *Venezuelan Airlines* from Caracas, Barranquilla and Europe; *BOAC, Cubana, Guest, Cunard Eagle* and *KLM* from Europe: *Cubana Airlines* from Havana; *KLM* from Curaçao; and *Iberian* from Puerto Rico via Havana from Europe.

 CUSTOMS. While customs revenues are the main source of income for Bermuda's government, it is the Bermudians who foot the bill. As far as the visitor is concerned, he can bring in anything for his own personal use including cameras and sports equipment. Each visitor is allowed to take in 100 cigars, 100 cigarettes, one pound of pipe tobacco, one quart of liquor and one quart of wine. Since cigarettes, when bought by the carton, and liquor are cheaper in Bermuda, it would be carrying coals to Newcastle to try to bring in any more. While there is a 25 per cent duty on radios, a portable is considered as an item for personal use and can be brought in without any charge. But duty must be paid on gifts brought in for Bermudians.

 MONEY. While American and Canadian dollars are accepted everywhere in Bermuda, the colony has its own currency which is exactly the same as that of England in value and almost the same in appearance. The Bermuda pound is worth $2.80 in U.S. currency and $2.74 in Canadian currency. There are twelve pence in one shilling and twenty shillings in one pound.

The principal monetary unit is the pound sterling, which is worth $2.80. There are 20 shillings in a pound. Each shilling is worth 14¢. There are 12 pence in each shilling. Pence is the plural of penny and each penny is worth a fraction more than 1¢. Paper money is in denominations of five pounds, one pound, 10 and 5 shillings. Coins are *half-crown*, which is 2 shillings 6 pence; *florin*, which is 2 shillings; *shilling, sixpence, three-pence, penny* and *half-penny*. The abbreviations are £ for the pound, s or a dash for the shilling, d for the penny.

BERMUDA

Here is a handy conversion table:

American	Bermuda	American	Bermuda
.01	1 d.	1.00	7 s. 2 d.
.03	3 d.	$ 2.80	£ 1.
.07	6 d.	5.00	£ 1. 15 s. 9 d.
.10	9 d.	10.00	£ 3. 11 s. 5 d.
.14	1 s.	14.00	£ 5.
.28	2 s.	20.00	£ 7. 2 s. 10 d.
.35	2 s. 6 d.	50.00	£17. 17 s. 1 d.
.50	3 s. 7 d.	100.00	£35. 14 s. 3 d.

In Britain you will often see and hear the expression "guinea." This means £1.1.0. But there is no note or coin for it. (One guinea is $2.94.)

You are not allowed to take Bermuda bank notes out of the colony nor can you bring in English bank notes. Since prices are quoted everywhere in dollars, the best way of handling the Bermuda currency system is to try to ignore it.

ELECTRIC CURRENT. Bermuda has 110-volt 60-cycle alternating current, as is usually the case in Canada and the United States, which means that you won't have any trouble with your electric razor. There are two exceptions, however: the Furness Line ships and the Castle Harbour Hotel which use 220 volt 60-cycle direct current.

TIPPING. It's about the same as in the United States—that is, between 10 and 15 per cent in hotels and restaurants. Service charges are seldom included in your bill.

MAIL. Postal rates for first-class airmail to Canada and the United States are 10 cents per half ounce from Bermuda. First-class mail goes at 7 cents for the first ounce and 5 cents for each additional ounce. Airmail postcards are 7 cents and ordinary postcards a nickel. For the jumbo variety, the tariff is 10 cents by air and 7 cents by sea. There is a general postoffice in Hamilton with branches in all parishes. It costs 4 cents to mail a letter in Bermuda.

Telegrams. Cables to the United States and Canada cost 25 cents a word by ordinary rate and $2.59 for a 22-word night letter. There are cable offices in Hamilton and at Kindley Field, but they can be sent from most of the big hotels as well.

Telephone. A long-distance call to the East Coast of the United States is $4.50 (station-to-station) for the first three minutes and $2 a minute if you keep talking (the rates for the Middle West and the West Coast are slightly higher).

TRANSPORTATION

Cars. In 1946, Bermuda half-heartedly entered the automobile age and it still isn't sure whether it was a good idea. Cars on the island are restricted to 14 horsepower (English rating and not much bigger than a Hillman) and a 20 m.p.h top speed (15 in towns). A family can have only one car and it can change cars only once every five years. Only a visitor who stays at least 30 days on Bermuda even has the right to drive. There are no cars for rent and it's illegal to bring in a car more than six months old.

Taxis. Fringe-topped little English cars are driving the Bermuda carriage

BERMUDA

to extinction. Fares run about 50 cents a mile and go up 25% after midnight. The daily rate is $17 for an 8-hour day.

Buses. They go almost everywhere very cheaply (from Hamilton to St. George or to Somerset takes an hour with a 60-cent fare) but they are crowded during rush hours. Bus tours are also available. For complete information dial 1-3927, 1-4333 or 1-6371. Two tours are noteworthy. One goes from Hamilton to Somerset, leaving Monday at 11:45 a.m. for an extensive tour of the Western parishes. The $6.25 charge includes lunch. The other popular tour leaves Hamilton every day except Thursday and Sunday at 10:30 a.m. for St. Georges. The $6.75 fare includes admission fees for Crystal or Leamington Caves, the Perfume Factory, Devil's Hole and the Aquarium.

Ferries. From Hamilton, there's a frequent service across the Harbour to Paget and Warwick and five trips a day to Somerset. The fare is 14 cents to Paget, for example and 40 cents to Somerset and the boats are about as fast as land transportation. Bikes are carried free and there is a very small charge for motor-assisted bikes (14 cents to Somerset, for example).

Bicycles. The time-honored way of getting around Bermuda on holiday. Muscle-powered English bikes rent as follows: $1.50 for 3 hours (the minimum period); $2 a day, $7 a week and $28 a month. With a 1-horse-power auxiliary motor (sufficient on flat stretches and needs help on hills), bike rates are: $5 a day, $21 a week, $60 a month. No one under 16 can ride a powered bike. Bicycles are for rent just about everywhere. There are tandems, too: $3 a day and $10.50 a week if you do all the work, or $4 a day and about $14 a week with a motor.

Remember, the keep-to-the-left rule applies to bicycles, too.

Carriages. There is only about one dozen left and they're not very easy to find (it's best to hire one through your hotel). Rates are: $2.82 an hour for a carriage for two and $4.23 for a carriage for four. By the mile, it's around 85 cents for the first mile and 28 cents the rest of the time. Drivers have schedules of rates for specific trips and it's wise to ask to see them.

From the Airport. Taxi rates from Kindley field are about $1 to St. George, $3 to the city of Hamilton and $5.50 to Somerset Island. The airport limousines charge $1 per person to St. George and Castle Harbour and $1.15 to points around Hamilton. Many hotels will meet guests at the airport.

SPORTS

SWIMMING. One of Bermuda's main industries. It's always good from late April to mid-November and there's even a chance of using a bathing suit in the winter. The water is clear, running the scale of blues and greens, and clean even in the harbour. Bermuda's best beaches, either long stretches of sand or small coves, are on the South Shore, but you can swim from docks anywhere. Not many hotels or guest houses have their own beaches but most of them have arrangements with beach clubs for their guests.

The colony is equally suited for underwater swimming as well. You can either rent a diving helmet and go for a walk along the bottom of the sea, hire an aqua-lung outfit and learn skin-diving (price for lessons, $8 an hour). Organized Skin Diving tours led by trained guides for viewing reef scenery or wrecks operate out of the Coral Island Club in Flatts. All

166

BERMUDA

are unforgettable experiences in Bermuda's reefs (which can also be enjoyed from a glass-bottomed boat on a cruise over the "sea gardens"), where more than 1,000 wrecks are lying.

Spear fishing is miraculous—but the government wants to keep it that way. You can only use a hand spear—no guns or projectiles of any kind—and you are limited to no more than two fish of any one species a day. Using an aqua-lung in spear-fishing just isn't done in Bermuda, either.

SAILING. Bermuda's traditions of seamanship are reflected in the huge number and variety of sailboats available to visitors. They start with small, sail-yourself craft. (Cape Cod, Knockabouts, Snipes or Comets) renting for $20 a day or $12 a half-day. Sailboats with a skipper can be chartered for parties up to 8 for $24 a day or $5 an hour.

There are sailing races on Thursday and Sunday afternoons and *International Race Week* comes late in April or early in May.

The ocean yacht race from Newport to Bermuda is in June, bi-annually. Through your hotel, you can make arrangements to charter a boat for watching races. The *Bermuda Dinghy Races,* in particular, are an amazing sight. These are boats measuring 14 feet and one inch but crammed with enough sail to drive a man of war. The crew keeps busy bailing and shifting lead ballast in what is usually a vain attempt to stop this marine monster from turning over . . . but it's great fun.

Outboard motor boats are available on Bermuda for $4 an hour or $20 to $35 a day, depending upon their size.

GOLF. There are four eighteen-hole golf courses on Bermuda: the *Mid-Ocean Club* (open to non-members only on Wednesday and Friday); the *Belmont Manor Golf and Country Club;* *Riddell's Bay Golf and Country Club* and the *Castle Harbour Hotel.* There is a 9-hole course at the *St. George Hotel,* and a public, nine-hole Queen's Park Golf Course.

Golf is in season all year round in the colony. Clubs can be rented in Bermuda but the quantity is limited. Green fees run around $5 daily. An introduction by a member is necessary in most of the big clubs, except Belmont Manor.

All golfers agree that the championship Mid-Ocean course is a must.

TENNIS. Bermudians never stop reminding you that it was an American visitor, Mary Outerbridge, who introduced tennis into the United States in 1874. There are tennis tournaments all year round and a wide selection of courts. *Ariel Sands, Belmont Manor, Castle Harbour, The Briton* and the *Mid-Ocean Club* have courts for the free use of their guests. Courts can be hired at the Tennis Stadium in Pembroke, *Elbow Beach Surf Club, Princess Hotel, Pink Beach Club* and the *Inverurie Hotel.*

FISHING. Whether you cast for bonefish from a dock or go out for barracuda aboard a deep-sea fishing boat, your luck will probably be as good in Bermuda any day of the year. The fishing is as good as it was in 1610 when Sir George Somers "in half an hour took so many fishes with hookes" that he was able to feed his company of 150. Since then, 335 varieties of fish have been caught along the reefs of Bermuda and 267 more in the open sea. In the past three years alone, two dozen world record catches have been landed in Bermuda waters.

Light tackle for shore fishing can be rented for $2.50 a day or $10 a week. Fishing boats supply tackle to their guests on a charter.

The Bermuda deep-sea fishing boats go out of Somerset, St. George,

BERMUDA

Pembroke and Southampton for tuna, white and blue marlin, dolphin, wahoo, amberjack, barracuda and bonito... to name a few. Charter rates are $75 a day for up to 6 persons or $50 a half-day. The *Pompano Beach Club* has its own 38-footer.

Reef fishing is done from smaller cruisers at rates running about $7.50 a person for a party up to six for a half-day. Here, the fisherman can count on yellowtail, bonito, amberjack, snappers, porgy, hind or mackerel.

SPECTATOR SPORTS. Loyally British Bermuda plays cricket, football (American soccer) and rugby. Bermudians get excited about all of them.

The sport of kings is now in the saddle again with the recent reopening of Shelly Bay Race Track, a major tourist magnet.

 CLOSING DAYS AND HOLIDAYS. Leisurely Bermuda shops close on Thursday afternoons and quite often for lunch. Legal holidays in the colony are New Year's Day, Good Friday, Empire Day (May 24), the Queen's Birthday in June, Cup Match Days (usually Thursday-Friday before the 1st Monday in August when the big cricket matches are played), Armistice Day, Christmas and Boxing Day (December 26).

BLOSSOM TIMES. The main event for flower-lovers is the Bermuda Floral Pageant held the last week in April. Flowers are always in bloom on Bermuda: bougainvillaea most of the year; hibiscus all year; Bermuda lilies from January to June; oleanders from May to October; passion flowers from spring to fall; poinsettia from November to February; purple morning-glory and royal poinciana in spring and summer.

CHURCHES. Most parishes have Anglican and Roman Catholic Churches. There are Presbyterian churches in Hamilton and in Warwick Parish. Also in Hamilton, a Methodist and a Christian Science church. While there is no synagogue, Jewish services are held at the U.S. Air Force base on Kindley Field and visitors are welcome.

CHILDREN. No baby carriages for rent and no diaper service in the colony. Baby sitters at $.75 to $1 an hour are available everywhere. Certain cottage colonies, in particular, offer attractive rates for youngsters and this vacation-housing formula is a good one for ex-Bermuda honeymooners returning with a brood. Reef-protected waters offer safe bathing and there is plenty to do for the younger generation.

RADIO AND TELEVISION. Two radio stations and a TV station (Bermuda claims to have the world's highest percentage of TV set ownership).

 NEWSPAPERS AND READING MATTER. Bermuda has two dailies of its own, the *Royal Gazette* in the morning and the snappier and more-Americanized *Mid-Ocean News* in the afternoon. There are several magazines, ranging from the serious *Bermudian* which mirrors colony life and delves into Bermuda history to *This Week in Bermuda* and *Preview* which tell you everything that goes on. New York morning papers arrive in Hamilton late the same day. Evening and Sunday papers are a day late.

HEALTH AND EMERGENCIES. Despite all the flowers, there is no hay fever on Bermuda (because there are no weeds). The colony has also been free of polio. There are are 40 doctors and 20 dentists in the colony and a modern 100-bed hospital, King Edward VII Hospital in Paget.

BERMUDA

HOTELS

Bermuda may have once grown onions, but these days it is hotels, guest houses, cottage colonies, beach clubs, housekeeping cottages and homes-with-a-few-spare-rooms which flourish best of all on its soil. At the last count, there were a good seventy hotels or other forms of full-time tourist accommodations on the island with nearly 100 private homes taking guests as well. Obviously, making a choice is a matter deserving serious thought, all the more so because the Bermuda hotel is more than just a bed to sleep in at the end of the day. On the contrary, you will probably find yourself in the orbit of your hotel most of the time, whether for meals, swimming, night life or sports.

Geographically speaking, all but a dozen-odd Bermuda hotels (we use the word here to describe accommodations in general) are clustered in Pembroke and Paget parishes on both sides of Hamilton Harbour. This makes them extremely convenient for shopping expeditions to Hamilton and also for partaking in the life of the colony which is centered around its capital (by Bermuda standards, they are a good haul from the airport, but they were built when steamships docking in Hamilton were carrying all the tourist trade). There are a few guest houses on Somerset Island (part of Sandy's Parish) which offer peace and quiet along with a convenient and inexpensive ferry service to the "excitement" of Hamilton, and a few more on the road into Hamilton. To the east, a rim of hotels, including some of the best in the colony, has grown up around Harrington Sound. In St. George's Parish, just across the water from the airport, there is only one hotel but it's an institution as much as hostelry.

In listing Bermuda's accommodations, we have adopted a criterion based mainly upon size. Facilities and prices, as you will note, can be quite comparable in guest houses and cottage colonies. In most cases, we have to limit ourselves to sample rates because most Bermudian hotels have a complicated price system based on how many meals you eat, the time of the

169

year, whether or not the room is air-conditioned, how many beds in the room ... and probably the license number of the taxi which brought you.

There are only a few hotels in Bermuda which do not practise racial discrimination. They include Glenview Lodge, Sunset Lodge, the Cannville Hotel, the Imperial Hotel, the Plaza, Swanston House, and the Sapphire Bay Cottage Colony. Religious discrimination, however, is limited mainly to certain clubs.

Many of the places we list have swimming pools. This may sound odd, considering that water is never more than a mile away in Bermuda, but few hotels are built on beaches. Distances from the nearest swimming facilities are a good thing to keep in mind.

Finally, here is a key to the plans used in Bermuda (all daily rates given are per person in a double room): AP-American Plan—room and three meals. MAP-Modified American Plan—room, breakfast and dinner. BP-Bermuda Plan—room and breakfast. EP-European Plan—room only.

DE LUXE

MID-OCEAN CLUB. A very dignified and elegant landmark in Tucker's Town, Smith's Parish. Private beach, a world-famous golf course, two tennis courts and history (two mid-Atlantic conferences). About 68 guests and very exclusive (you need an introduction by a member). Spacious public rooms, period furniture, cozy settees. Has a very relaxed air. Rates (MAP) - $16 to $25.

ELBOW BEACH SURF CLUB. Though there's room for 411 in the hotel and 16 cottage units, it has a cozy, club-like atmosphere in its public rooms. Excellent site in Paget Parish a ten-minute taxi ride from Hamilton. A large luncheon terrace overlooking its own beach, perhaps the most popular on the island. The beach is lovely; it's under steep cliffs, and cabins are available to outside guests. This may be considered its only setback for those who might prefer a quieter and more isolated beach—there are plenty of playful youngsters (GIs) who lend animation to the place. Dancing, tennis (both for

practice and for tournaments) and a swimming pool. Rates (MAP). Double rooms in the hotel run from $17 to $25. In cottage units, it's Bermuda Plan and $15 per person per day. Also offers a "honeymoon package" from November 1 to March 15. Rates per couple, even on second honeymoons, run from $200 to $250 (MAP) including bike rentals and tips for seven days.

CASTLE HARBOUR HOTEL. This is the biggest in the colony—500 guests. All by itself on Harrington Sound with a 180-acre garden. The architecture is somewhat austere and the decoration of the public rooms tends to be old-fashioned, but it is the most self-contained resort in Bermuda: swimming pool, private beach five minutes away, nightly dancing, tennis, golf and boating. A favorite spot for young New York lawyers and doctors on their honeymoons.

Rates (MAP). In season from $18 to $26. Suites are $65 a day for two.

THE REEFS BEACH CLUB. Here, in Southampton Parish, 65 guests live in cabanas built on a cliff overlooking a private beach (there are

BERMUDA

no phones in the rooms, which is a bit of a disadvantage because the cottages are scattered. Dancing four times a week (not very formal) and a cocktail lounge in the clubhouse.

Rates (MAP). $16 in the main buildings, $18 to $21 in the cabanas.

PINK BEACH COTTAGE COLONY. On the South Shore beach of the same name in Smith's Parish with cottages for 50 guests. Two tennis courts, a beach reserved for guests and not far from the Mid-Ocean golf course. Food is excellent and very plentiful. The Duponts are regular clients here and so are many film stars. The manager is Mr. E. Lerigo, former assistant manager of the Reefs.

Rates (AP). From $20 to $25, depending upon type of cottage.

CORAL BEACH CLUB. Cottages for 90 guests spread over a mile of spacious grounds on Paget's south shore. Private beach and five practise and competition tennis courts. This is a very lovely place with a small, intimate lunch terrace and good period furniture in the main house. An introduction by a member is needed. (Also owned by the Coral Beach management: The Horizon, the Newstead, as well as Waterloo House). Dancing on Thursdays and Saturdays with formal dress preferred.

Rates (AP). $18 to $25.

PRINCESS HOTEL AND COTTAGES. In Pembroke Parish right on Hamilton Harbour, the Princess, recently air-conditioned, is the social center of Hamilton. It's only a seven-minute walk from town and shopping, but its private launch offers free transportation to the beaches. Nightly shows and dancing are very popular in this old hotel with a young spirit and the food is reputedly good. The cottage colony next to the hotel (350 guests in all) is right on the water and a pleasant contrast to the bustle of the main house, presently being extended.

Rates (MAP). From $16 to $22 (or $9 to $15 without any meals).

NEW BERMUDIANA. Overlooking Hamilton Harbor, one of the newest hotels, a steel and glass palace with 233 air-conditioned rooms replaces its old namesake which burned down in 1958. Swimming pool, and lavish sunken gardens where the hotel's nightlife is staged stick pretty much to the traditions of the old Bermudiana, long one of the most popular rendez-vous for dining and dancing. 175 rooms have harbor view and the rest face on the gardens. Guests of the Bermudiana have exchange meal privileges at *Harmony Hall*, in Paget, under the same management. A social hostess organizes entertainment if you wish. This up-to-date hostelry has many firsts including wall to wall carpeting everywhere, colored tile baths, game rooms, an arcade of fashionable shops and its very own Turkish baths.

Rates: (MAP). $16 to $27.

CARLTON BEACH. Recently built on Bermuda's spectacular south shore, this ultra-modern hotel rises on a seaside promontory flanked by twin bays. With 28 acres of ground between Boat Bay and Sinky Bay, the hotel is just south of Gibbs Hill lighthouse. In the shape of an arc, the hotel is designed so that each of its 200 double rooms opens directly onto a private balcony overlooking the sea or one of the two bays. It is operated by the Hotel Corporation of America. Beaches, tennis courts, swimming pool and substantial shopping area are other amenities and a marine and fishing inn is built on one of the two bays.

Rates (MAP). $18 to $25.

FIRST CLASS SUPERIOR

PALMETTO BAY COTTAGE COLONY. An old country home and 11 cottages on the edge of Harrington Sound in Smith's Parish. Dancing three times a week and a cocktail bar. There's a sand beach on the Sound and free water-skiing and sailing. The atmosphere here is informal with something going on all the time. 42 guests.

Rates (MAP). $14 to $20 in season.

ARIEL SANDS. A private beach and salt-water pool on the South Shore in Devonshire Parish. There's a main house, where the rooms are rather antiquated, and 34 air-conditioned cottage accommodations. Tennis court, cocktail lounge and dancing once a week. 70 guests.

Rates (MAP). $21 in season.

ST. GEORGE HOTEL. An enchanting old Victorian-style hostelry (built in 1907) and with a style and atmosphere quite in keeping with historic St. George which it dominates from a wonderful hilltop site. The atmosphere is heightened by the 17th-century costumes of the staff. It has a tremendous indoor swimming pool; special staff to take care of children; a private beach with free transportation; a 9-hole golf course and free services for touring, fishing and cruising. Many U.S. Air Force transient dependents stay here while the men stationed at Kindley Field like it for dining and dancing. It has recently been completely renovated with a new laundry, a cocktail lounge and elevators.

Rates (MAP). From $12 to $18. Also a "family plan" for families of three or more: the first person pays from $16 to $22 and all the others pay half.

BELMONT MANOR HOTEL AND GOLF CLUB. Somewhat away from it all in Warwick Parish, 15 minutes by ferry from Hamilton and on spacious grounds above Great Sound. An 18-hole golf course, considered the third best in the colony, tennis court, heated swimming pool, and dancing every night but Sunday for its 225 guests. It has many Canadian patrons.

Rates (MAP). Double room with bath starts at $17 in season. With connecting bath, it's $13. A cottage for two can be had for $42 a day (for two persons).

LANTANA COLONY CLUB. Near the very quaint Somerset Bridge in Sandys Parish way out west. All accommodations have a kitchen, private patio and air-conditioning. There are bay windows in the lounge and a terrific view. The cottages are spread over a wide area which is covered with attractive trees and local flora that do much to give a pleasing appearance. Swimming in Great Sound or in a pool. 68 guests.

Rates (MAP). From $18 to $20 in 1-room villas and $20 to $22 in 2-room cottages.

THE LEDGELETS. Right next to the Lantana Colony Club in Sandys and the same ownership. A smaller version (24 guests) with six air-conditioned cottages and a main lodge. A sand beach on Ely's Harbour and a swimming pool. Free rowboats for guests and sailboats (Snipes and Comets) for hire. Guest privileges at Lantana.

Rates (MAP). $17 to $20.

INVERURIE HOTEL. At the water's edge in Paget overlooking Hamilton Harbour and near Darrell's Wharf. Not too big—170 guests— and with very comfortable rooms. Dancing on a pleasant terrace overlooking the water, tennis and easy swimming (just dive in from the terrace). Noted for its shows. The ferry station is nearby.

Rates (MAP). From $15 to $21.

CAMBRIDGE BEACHES. A village of 28 cottages on 25 acres in Sandys Parish on Somerset Island with two big beaches and some smaller ones on Mangrove Bay and Long Bay. Sailboats, speedboats and fishing cruisers available. Dancing twice a week, a bar and a cocktail lounge. 98 guests.

Rates (AP). $18 to $24 a day (higher figure is in a 2-room cottage).

HARMONY HALL HOTEL. Very charming. Modern, and with attractive gardens. The rooms look like Bermuda cottages. Dancing every night in the Gombey Room. In Paget

Parish, a short walk from a south shore beach 8 miles long. 126 guests. New additions include extensive renovations to the main buildings which have a new cocktail lounge and lobby. Two huge cabanas (like motels) nearby accommodate 64 additional guests. 35 new cottage units of Italian architectural design have also been opened.

Rates (MAP). $14 to $18.

HORIZONS. A restored old house in Paget with cottages on well-kept grounds. Swimming pool and privileges of Coral Beach Club four minutes away by bike. 62 guests.

Rates (MAP). $14 to $20 (same rates in cottages accommodating from two to eight persons).

FOURWAYS INN. It's 250 years old but this Paget guest house has been well modernized and air-conditioned. Lots of local and steady clientele. It's exceptionally charming—Royal Stuart Hunting tartan and Bermuda Parish crests are used as decoration elements. There's a Pegleg Bar, a small swimming pool and a dining-room all in copper and wood where excellent candle-lit dinners are served. 30 guests.

Rates (MAP). $16 to $20 in season.

POMANDER GATE CLUB. One of the few cottage colonies in Paget Parish near Hamilton. A main guest house and cottages for 33 guests are on the water's edge with eight acres of gardens behind them. There's a pool and a dock for swimming. Atmosphere is quiet, hospitable (the owners have cocktails with you every night) and tasteful.

Rates (MAP). $15 to $20. $3 less for Bermuda Plan.

FIRST CLASS REASONABLE

SHERWOOD MANOR HOTEL. This small hotel is in Fairylands, a Pembroke Parish residential district for Hamilton a mile-and-a-half away. It offers its 44 guests excellent cuisine, a private sand beach on Great Sound, air-conditioning, two bars, Saturday night dancing and boating facilities.

Rates (MAP), from $14 to $18 in season.

POMPANO BEACH CLUB. This is mainly for fishermen and water sportsmen. It's on the south shore in Southampton Parish not far from Somerset. Swimming is from an ocean beach or a flat terrace. Dancing twice a week. For fishermen, there are a deep-sea fishing boat, a glass-bottom boat for reef fishing, and small dinghies. Other pastimes include aqua-lung diving (with an instructor), snorkeling on the reefs and water-skiing. Cottages accommodate 46 guests.

Rates (MAP). $17 to $20 in season and $60 for a suite for four. American Plan can be had for an additional $2.

ROSEDON. Superior guest-house living with air-conditioned rooms and a private swimming pool for 44 guests in Pembroke Parish a short walk from Hamilton. Ample grounds.

Rates (BP). $11.50 in season.

FARAWAY COTTAGE COLONY. This vacation hamlet has large rooms in a dozen cottages and a main house on the South Shore of Warwick Parish a 15-minute taxi ride from Hamilton. Among the amenities are a private beach a 5-minute walk away and a heated fresh-water swimming pool. Good cooking. Dancing once a week. 42 guests.

Rates (MAP). $14 in the main house, $18 in a 1-bedroom cottage.

GLENCOE. Woodrow Wilson once stayed in this old Bermuda home before it became a guest house. It's on Salt Kettle Point in Paget Parish and it has its own sand beach and a bar. 44 guests. Rates (MAP). $14 to $18.

WATERLOO HOUSE. In Pembroke with the front lawn on Hamilton Harbour and a small swimming pool. Cocktail lounge and Coral Beach club privileges (a 15-minute taxi ride). 55 guests.

Rates (AP). $13 to $21. $1 less for MAP and $3 less for BP.

173

MIZZEN-TOP. This is a small cluster of 6 cottages (room for 19 guests) in Warwick Parish on a hill overlooking Great Sound where there's a private dock for deep-water swimming. The Belmont Manor Golf Course is just across the road.

Rates (MAP). $14, BP deduct $5, EP deduct $6.

DEEPDENE MANOR. A handsome old Bermuda house with room for 40 guests on Harrington Sound (swimming terrace) in Smith's Parish.

Rates (MAP). $12 to $19. A seven-day honeymoon package runs to $245 per couple including bicycles, 2 dinners out and an outboard motorboat for a day.

WHITE SANDS. A Paget guest house with a private ocean beach on Grape Bay and a cocktail lounge. Children are welcome (in the rooms, not the cocktail lounge).

Rates (MAP). $16 to $20. It's $5 to $11 more for a child added to a double room depending upon his size.

NEWSTEAD. Across the harbour from Hamilton in Paget. Cocktail lounge and Coral Beach Club privileges. 55 guests.

Rates (MAP). $14 to $20, and $3 less for BP.

MODERATE

CORAL ISLAND CLUB AND HOTEL. In Hamilton Parish (not Hamilton city) on Harrington Sound. Eighty-five guests and its own sand beach. Quiet with an attractive verandah and very pleasant rooms. Dancing and a floor show in season. A nice place.

Rates (MAP). In season from $11 to $12. Or $9 to $10 BP.

BRITON HOTEL. This is a hotel in a beautiful garden on Langton Hill in Pembroke Parish. Its 60 guests are high above Hamilton. Dancing to a calypso band several times a week. A large-size swimming pool and also a tennis court.

Rates (MAP). $13 to $16.

SALT KETTLE HOUSE. On Salt Kettle Point in Paget opposite Hamilton.

Three small cottages (12 guests) and very charming. Deep-water swimming in two bays on the grounds. Kitchen facilities.

Rates (BP). $6 to $10.

BUENA VISTA. Across the bay from Hamilton in Paget Parish with a small private beach. Reasonable. 46 guests.

Rates (AP). $12 to $15.

LOUGHLANDS. A ten-minute walk in Paget from Elbow Beach. 24 guests. Quiet.

Rates (MAP). $12 to $14. $9 to $10 on Bermuda Plan.

FORDHAM HALL. This is a quiet hotel in Pembroke. The guest capacity is 20, and the food is very good. The hotel is open all year round; prices are reasonable and moderate. BP plan.

Rates (MAP). $12. $8 with just breakfast and $7 with just the room.

BAYSWATER. Swimming from a private dock on Pitts Bay in Pembroke Parish near Hamilton. 21 guests.

Rates (BP). $8 to $11.

MOUNT ROYAL. Small (15 guests) and casual on a hill in Paget.

Rates (BP). $7 to $8.

EMPIRE CLUB. In the heart of Hamilton and convenient for shopping. 30 guests in air-conditioned rooms. The patio is its best feature. Dancing to steel or calypso bands.

Rates (EP). $6.50 in season. Add $1 for breakfast.

INEXPENSIVE

Kenwood Club. This is a good place for the budget-minded visitor. In the heart of Hamilton's shopping district, 65 guests.

Rates (EP). $4.35 to $5. $1.50 more with breakfast.

Kerri. On a quiet street in Pembroke and handy to downtown Hamilton. 11 guests.

Rates (BP). $7 to $9.

Richmond House. Equally close to downtown Hamilton. 10 guests.

Rates (BP). $5 to $9 in season.

Tallent Villa. In a Pembroke residential area near Hamilton and not far from north shore swimming. 12 guests.

Rates (BP). $6 to $7.

Chelmsford. In Pembroke on Hamilton Harbour. Swimming dock. 16 guests.

Rates (BP). $6 to $8.

Oxford House. Five minutes walk from Hamilton shops. 22 guests.

Rates (BP). $7 and up.

Avonmoor. On a hill in Pembroke Parish and close to Hamilton. 12 guests.

Rates (BP). $6 to $7. Add $2.50 for MAP, $4 for AP.

Trevelyan. Handy to Hamilton and beaches by bicycle in Paget. 12 guests.

Rates (BP). $7 in season ($8 in the "honeymoon cottage").

The Gables. Small (12 guests) and simple on Harbour Road in Paget Parish.

Rates (MAP). $9.50 to $10.50 or $3.50 less with just breakfast.

Campbell Corner Guest House. Only 12 guests in this house on Salt Kettle Point on the Paget side of Hamilton Harbour.

Rates (BP). $6.50 to $7.50.

Greenbank. On Salt Kettle in Paget Parish with a terrace for swimming.

Rates (BP). $6 to $8 in season.

Grandview. In Devonshire, not far from South Shore beaches. 16 guests.

Rates (AP). $11 to $12; less $1 for MAP, less $4 for BP.
Special family rates.

Glendon. Only 11 guests here in Warwick Parish. Very reasonable.

Rates (AP) $8 to $10; MAP deduct $1; BP deduct $3 to $4.

HOUSEKEEPING COTTAGES

This is the nearest thing to taking a house and doing it yourself. The advantage of the housekeeping cottage for a family is that it can be used for a short stay without the attendant trials and tribulations of finding a maid or getting up to make breakfast every morning.

BERMUDA COTTAGES. In all, 38 individual cottages in Paget, Warwick and Southampton Parishes on or near the South Shore (12 are grouped in a development at Marley Beach). Ten are small studio cottages for two while the others have living-room, kitchen, bath and anything from one to four bedrooms. They run either on a special Bermuda Plan (breakfast and picnic lunch) or European Plan with maid service in both cases. Twenty have air-conditioned bedrooms. All are within walking distance of swimming facilities. The mailing address: Bermuda Cottages, Paget Parish. 130 guests and they can bring dogs.

Rates $11 and $14 in season on the Special Bermuda Plan; $10 and $14 on European Plan. Children are about half-price. Cottages can be rented by the month from November 1 to March 15 and from June 1 to September 30.

CAPISTRANO-HARRINGAY. Capistrano is on a hill estate, Harringay is on Harrington Sound and both are in Smith's Parish (the mailing address). Capistrano has one cottage and four apartments; Harringay has two cottages and a room in the main house. All have kitchens (a maid is available for cooking dinner at $1.50 an hour). The swimming is at Harringay on the sound and some fine restaurants are nearby. Accommodates 18 guests.

Rates (EP) about $9 in cottages and $7.50 (BP) in the main house.

CORAL COTTAGES. Near Harrington Sound in Smith's Parish and not far from the Breakers Beach Club. Five cottages and 14 guests.

Rates (EP). $17 per couple (with maid service).

BERMUDA

MONTGOMERY APARTMENTS AND COTTAGES. Five apartments and six cottages on three sites in Paget Parish about five minutes or less from Elbow Beach. Maid available for extra services or baby sitting at $1 an hour.

Rates (BP). $7 (in main house) to $9 and up. Minimum of three to a cottage.

SEA HORSE COTTAGES. Four are on Grape Bay in Paget and there is an apartment in Fairylands (address is Box 343, Hamilton). The cottages are 100 yards from a beach.

Rates (EP). $11. Add $1.50 for breakfast.

TEUCER PLACE. Two cottages and three apartments on a 12-acre estate on Somerset Island in Sandys Parish. Deep-water swimming on the grounds. Three hours of maid service a day. A cook for dinner available at 70 cents an hour.

Rates (EP). $7.50 to $9.50 ($2.50 less without maid).

VACATION COTTAGES. Individual cottages in three parishes (address: Box 271, Hamilton). Some are near the Belmont Manor Golf Course.

Rates (EP). $9 to $11.

SOUTH CAPERS COTTAGES. Newest of Cottage colonies on its own private south shore beach in Paget parish. Three separate units built around a swimming pool offer spacious accommodations for 24 guests. All apartments are air-conditioned, equipped with telephones and radios, and maid service is available. Small apartments consist of bed-sitting room plus kitchen and bath. Deluxe suites have living room opening onto porch plus bedroom.

Rates (EP). $22 to $25 for two.

FURNISHED HOUSING

Most of the time furnished houses have to be rented at least a month. Prices per month range from $150 to $350 for a one-bedroom house to $600 to $1,000 for a very comfortable place with five or six bedrooms. Food is slightly higher than in the United States. Maids receive from $25 to $35 per week. The Bermuda Trade Development Board can supply you with a list of real estate agents.

ROOMS IN HOMES

This is one way of staying in Bermuda on a close budget. There are about 90 homes offering rooms or apartments, mainly in Hamilton and Pembroke and Paget Parishes. Rates run around $5 or $6 a day per person with breakfast.

RESTAURANTS

Since very few hotels or other accommodations in Bermuda operate on a full *pension* basis, there is usually at least one meal a day which is to be eaten away from your base headquarters. This does not mean, though, that you have to spend all your time looking for restaurants. Picnic lunches are a standard item in most places (where they can be had for $1 to $1.50) and they are the obvious thing for a day on the beach. Nevertheless, you will certainly want a few meals out for a change of atmosphere (certain hotels have grouped themselves into a dining pool allowing you to eat in any one of them on your basic rate) or else you may decide not to cut an excursion short by hurrying home for dinner.

Most of Bermuda's restaurants, like everything else, are in Hamilton and its adjoining Pembroke and Paget parishes. Further away from the city, the restaurants are usually in hotels or cottage colonies, but they do make an effort for a transient trade.

In general, Bermuda restaurants offer a mid-Atlantic compromise between American and British cooking—plenty of steaks and chops—with the local color provided by seafood which is usually excellent. Typical Bermuda dishes exist, but they are not always found in restaurants and hotels where the cuisine has been adapted to the taste of the North American guest.

The tab for dinner in Bermuda usually runs between $5 and $7 with a cover charge of about $1 in many places offering entertainment as well. Here we offer a sampling of the best-known eating places throughout the colony.

Note: reservations are often a wise idea for dinner.

HAMILTON AND HINTERLAND

EMPIRE CLUB. The Hofbrau Restaurant in this hotel on Queen Street is a favorite for Austrian food. Cocktails in the new Jungle Room. Dinner: $1.75-$4.75. Lunch: $1.75.

ACE OF CLUBS. At Front and Parliament Streets. Buffet lunch $2.25, buffet dinner $5. Good cuisine.

PENTHOUSE CLUB. Up above Hamilton and very elegant. Flambé specialties. A la carte.

THE WATERFRONT. Right on the harbour and one of Hamilton's newest restaurants. Fish tanks and shells are part of the decor.

FOURWAYS INN. Candlelit dining in Paget next to a swimming pool, $5; Buffet lunch $2.50.

Working westward, you might try in Southampton:

THE POMPANO BEACH CLUB. Excellent seafood. $3.75-$4.75.

THE WATERLOT INN. An old home with a terrace on the water and right below Gibbs Hill Lighthouse. You have a good chance of getting into a dart game in the bar. $4.50.

SOMERSET ISLAND

BELFIELD-IN-SOMERSET. An old Bermuda cottage serving tea and such local dishes as fish chowder for lunch. No dinner.

SUMMERSIDE INN. A quiet place near the ferry landing. Reasonable prices. Dinner: $3.

HARRINGTON SOUND AND TUCKER'S TOWN

ARIEL SANDS. This is on the way in Devonshire Parish. A cottage colony on the south shore. Shakespearean in its name and in its Caliban Bar. $4.

DEEPDENE MANOR. Near the aquarium on Harrington Sound. Cocktails at the Boathouse. $4.50.

PALMETTO BAY. Same location. Very picturesque Yardarm nautical bar. $4-$4.50.

THE BREAKERS CLUB. In Tucker's Town and romantic. Boula soup and shrimp-filled avocado among the specialties. $4-$5.50.

PINK BEACH. Also in Tucker's Town and in keeping with the lavish surroundings. Charcoal-broiled steaks. $6.50.

PLANTATION. Seafood, especially lobster on Bailey's Bay near the Leamington Caves. $3-$5.

TOM MOORE'S TAVERN. An old house on Bailey's Bay built in 1652 where poet Tom Moore is supposed to have come for inspiration. Walls are papered with quotations, of course. Lobster also a specialty. $2.95-$5.

ST. GEORGE

ST. GEORGE HOTEL. Waiters in 17th Century garb and dinner for $4.50. There's an orchestra at night, but we put it here because it's a favorite spot for lunch when touring old St. George.

GUNPOWDER CAVERN. The old magazine from which Bermudians stole powder for the American rebels is now a bar and restaurant. Underground atmosphere and very historical.

EATING FOR LESS

Most of the lower-priced restaurants (dinner from $1.75 to $3) are in Hamilton.

Among them are the *Buckaroo, Elisabeth's Tea Cosy* (home cooking), the *Hideaway* (upstairs on Reid Street for a light lunch), and *The Spot* (if you're in a hurry). *Queen's Cafe* is a Chinese restaurant, despite its name.

WITH DANCING AND SHOW

Here, the big hotels and the more glamorous cottage colonies make their bow.

BELMONT MANOR. On Hamilton Harbour and dinner in the Warwick Room. $5.

CASTLE HARBOUR. Dancing in the Rendezvous Room in Bermuda's biggest hotel in an isolated beauty spot. $4.50-$5.

CORAL ISLAND CLUB. Long John Silver welcomes guests to the Pirate's Den on Flatt's Inlet leading into Harrington Sound.

ELBOW BEACH SURF CLUB. Dancing in Paget with a sea view. For the younger set, $4.20-$4.90.

FORTY THIEVES CLUB. The largest and newest night club to open on the island, imports 'name' entertainers from the United States and can seat 350 people.

HARMONY HALL. In Paget. There's a native floor show in the Gombey Room four times a week. $4 and up.

INVERURIE HOTEL. Dancing on the water's edge in Paget. $4-$5.

LANTANA COLONY CLUB. A very spectacular setting in Somerset. $5.

PRINCESS HOTEL. Pink palace outside Hamilton with a native floor show. $4-$6. Very popular with the younger set, particularly with the Air Force boys.

THE REEFS BEACH CLUB. On a cliff overlooking the south shore in Southampton. $4.50-$5.

SHERWOOD MANOR. In Fairylands, Hamilton's suburb. Indoor dining at *Le Monaco*, a French restaurant, and outdoors around the *Lobster Hole*. $4.50 and à la carte.

SHOPPING

This delightful pastime looms large among the colony's attractions. All the best shops in Bermuda are clustered around Front Street in Hamilton where visitors are served by Triminghams and Goslings and Butterfield and other members

They say it with artificial flowers in Cuba

of the island's aristocracy. There are branches in St. George, too, and in certain hotels.

What to buy? Well, as a general rule, it can be said that judicious shopping should enable you to recoup a good part of your fare to Bermuda. Savings are extremely high on articles brought in from Great Britain and also from the Continent. Liquor is so cheap compared to New York that you wonder why anyone does his drinking in a Manhattan bar when it would be so much more economical to lose a weekend in Bermuda. It should be emphasized, too, that shopping in Bermuda, as in England, is quality shopping. Prices are low because of customs regulations, not because of sleazy workmanship aimed at the one-time tourist customer.

Here are some of Bermuda's leading shops and what they have to offer:

SMITH, the abbreviation for H. A. & E. Smith, Ltd. with a main store in Hamilton and gift shops scattered almost all over. Smith's specializes in English dresses, blouses and skirts but this colony-sized version of a department store also sells you anything from Bermuda shorts to golf balls. Mark Cross doeskin gloves, for example, are $3.98 instead of the $9 stateside price.

MASTERS, LTD. Another Hamilton shop with just about everything including French perfumes (40% lower than in the United States), English cutlery and gloves, Swiss watches particularly those of the International Watch Co., and Midó (at a 55% saving), German clocks, French Limoges china ... and Bermuda calypso records. On Front Street.

TRIMINGHAM'S. They've been doing business under the same management since 1844 in Hamilton and now they have branches at St. George, Somerset and Castle Harbour. Also a wide selection of Bermuda bargains including doeskin gloves, perfume, English handbags and Indian Madras sportswear.

CECILE, a "maison française" in Hamilton with a Castle Harbour branch and specializing in cash-

meres from England, and sportswear from Italy.

CALYPSO, the Hamilton birthplace of Bermuda Calypso fashions—slacks, blouses, skirts, etc.—at a healthy saving compared to American department store counters.

BAMBOO GATE. Something different—it's on Harbour Road in Paget and it goes off the beaten path in materials such as batik Madras shorts, straw hats or Italian plastic flowers.

THE BERMUDA SHOP. Specializing in Bermuda shorts, of course, on Reid and Queen Streets in Hamilton, but it also has a wide selection of cashmeres at the usual Bermuda savings.

ASTWOOD-DICKINSON. One of Bermuda's leading jewellers and well-stocked with Piaget, Omegas, Patek Philippes and other aristocratic timekeepers. An Omega Constellation in Bermuda is $310 instead of $500.

A. S. COOPER. While we're on the subject of jewelry, we might mention this Front Street shop in Hamilton which has a large selection of stones imported from Brazil as well as Christian Dior costume jewelry from Paris. Cooper's is also a good place for Dutch crystal-

179

Relaxed luxury is the keynote of Jamaica

BERMUDA

ware, continental fabrics and English bone china. Prices of Wedgwood Jasper Ware, for example run from $1.75 to $15.51, as compared to $3 to $23.50 for similar pieces in the United States.

THE BERMUDA CIGAR STORE, in new quarters opposite the Bank of Bermuda, with cigarettes, of course, but also English briar pipes at half the price you're accustomed to paying for them. Swiss watches are also available here on Front Street.

HILDRED, a children's shop on Queen Street with warm English woolens for the younger set.

WILLIAM BLUCK & CO. Another landmark in Hamilton—it first opened its doors in 1844—and it is one of the colony's leading specialists in china, from England and the continent, and antiques. The Hamilton shop is on Front Street West and there's a St. George branch on York Street.

VERA P. CARD LTD. Also worth noting for china as well as linens and Swiss watches. On Front Street in Hamilton with a branch at the Castle Harbour Hotel.

PENISTON-BROWN CO., LTD. They have so much French perfume that they need three stores in Hamilton to sell it—one on Front Street next to the cable office and two on Queen Street (one of the latter handles Guerlain exclusively). As a rule, perfume in Bermuda is just half as expensive as in the United States, but be careful of limitations on how much you can bring in.

ENGLISH SPORTS SHOP. A good place for English wool for both sides of the family with Shetland jackets at less than $50 and cashmere sweaters starting at $17. At 26 Front Street opposite the "Queen of Bermuda"—when she's in port, of course.

STUART'S STORE. Here camera fans will be able to take advantage of Bermuda's favorable tariffs on imported cameras. It's on Reid Street in Hamilton and there are also cameras for rent.

Liquor in General. Well-organized Hamilton shops well aware of American tastes sell it by the gallon (five fifths) in handy packages designed to fit U.S. customs regulations. Standard brands of Scotch are a 50 per cent saving at $16 a gallon and so are Canadian whiskies. You do even better with English gins—$12 instead of $28.50 a gallon. These bargain rates apply to French brandies and cordials as well: for example, Remy Martin VSOP is $25 instead of $45 for five bottles and Grand Marnier $20.50 instead of $44.80.

Among Bermuda's leading liquor stores are *Frith's* with three shops—on Front and Reid Streets in Hamilton, on York Street in St. George and at Mangrove Bay on Somerset Island; *J. F. Burrows* on Front Street with branches in Paget West and St. George; *J. E. Lightbourn & Co.* at Hamilton and St. George; and *Gosling's,* Bermuda's oldest business concern (open since 1822) in Hamilton, Somerset and St. George.

In addition to these Hamilton shops and their branches, there is shopping to be done outside the capital, especially for typically Bermudian items.

The *Cedar Shop* in Somerset, for example, has articles ranging from monograms to salad bowls in Bermuda cedar. The *Sea Breeze* shop opposite Spittal Pond in Smith's Parish on the way to St. George goes in for local color with Bermuda shirts and shell jewelry. Out at this end of the colony, there is also a perfume factory where the fragrance of Bermuda is bottled.

Finally, Scotland and Ireland are neighbors in Somerset with the *Irish Linen Shop* and *Loch Lomond* (the latter a gift shop with budget prices).

BERMUDA

EXPLORING BERMUDA

Bermuda offers a great deal in a small package, a package which must be opened carefully and enjoyed at a leisurely Bermudian rate. Exploring the colony is something like browsing through old prints in a sleepy bookshop: as soon as you try to hurry, you miss everything. There is something to be savoured, if nothing more than a glorious sea view or a lonely beach or an intimate glimpse of a garden behind a country lane, on virtually every one of Bermuda's 12,000-odd acres. There are no quick tours of Bermuda because people in a hurry don't go there.

There is no point in setting out in search of Bermuda, armed with maps, cameras, guidebooks, conversation manuals, comfortable shoes and a determined expression. This is one place where touring has not been transformed into the most exhausting occupation forced upon modern man. No, Bermuda is to be seen in quiet side trips at the relaxing rate of bicycles, boats or cars limited to twenty miles per hour on the open road. Then, after a few days, you suddenly realize that you have seen it without even trying.

Despite its midget size, Bermuda offers a tremendous amount of variety. Through an accident of history, its capital was transferred from St. George to Hamilton only 150 years ago, producing the present-day contrast of busy Hamilton with St. George, quick-frozen in time. Through an accident of geology, its postage-stamp landscape is rich in natural wonders.

The move of the seat of government to Hamilton was made in order to bring Bermuda's capital into a more central location. Hamilton is the hub of the colony's transportation services, whether by land or sea, and most resort life is concentrated in Hamilton's Pembroke Parish and in Paget Parish on the other side of Hamilton Harbour. Almost invariably, it is here that a visitor is introduced to Bermuda.

Within 180 acres, Hamilton manages to be a capital, a shopping center, a port and also, the most difficult of all, a pleasant place for historical sight-seeing. All of this is tucked between a hillside and the sea with no waste space. There is no dockside area: you just cross Front Street and you are aboard the Queen of Bermuda.

A relative newcomer to the colony, Hamilton was only incorporated as a town in 1793 (it was named for Governor Henry Hamilton, not for the Marquis of Hamilton who gave *his* name to Hamilton Parish to the east). That explains why most of the jewel-like city's points of interest go back to the 19th century when it took on its present shape.

The Bermuda Visitors Service Bureau, on the waterfront right next to the ferry terminal is as good a starting point as any for a tour of Hamilton. Only a few yards away is Albuoy's Point where the city has managed to squeeze a public park between the sea and the Bank of Bermuda. Albuoy's Point is the home of what is often called the true capital of the colony, the Royal Bermuda Yacht Club founded in 1844 in a meeting under a calabash tree.

Turning inland at Heyl's Corner (named after Bermuda's leading drug store and the busiest traffic spot in the colony), a few steps take you to the Public Library and the Par-la-Ville Gardens. The library, with a famed century-old rubber tree in its frontyard, was once the handsome home of W. B. Perot, the Bermuda postmaster who put the colony on the philatelic map by making his own stamps by hand and signing them. Inside the library is the Museum of Bermuda History (open from 10 to 1 and 2 to 4 on weekdays, except Thursday afternoons) with a collection of old Bermuda cedar furniture, silver, china and a copy of George Washington's letter in which he thanked the daring raiders who stole the powder from the Royal Magazine. Also of historical interest is Perot's original postoffice which has been restored nearby.

Here, you are only two blocks away from the salient point on Hamilton's skyline, the Bermuda Cathedral, a modern Gothic structure dedicated in 1894 and replacing Holy Trinity Church which had burned ten years previously. In all, there are no less than ten churches in or around this minute city.

Its secular rival on the skyline is Sessions House where the colonial House of Assembly meets under the Jubilee Clock Tower (the jubilee was that of Queen Victoria). The Bermuda Supreme Court is also housed here and the sessions of both of these august bodies are open to visitors. Bermudians take their parliament as seriously as some Latin countries take their churches. In other words, visitors should dress in keeping with the decorum of the House of Assembly (the House meets on Monday, Wednesday and Friday afternoons).

The executive branch of the colony's government is housed in another series of imposing buildings on Front Street behind the Cenotaph Memorial to Bermuda's dead of the First World War. Its main attraction is the governor's Throne, a big Bermuda cedar chair in the Legislative Council Chamber, the upper house of the colony's Parliament. The governor's offices are here, but his residence is at Government House on the north shore. Continuing along Front Street, whose name changes to East Broadway, you come to the Wreck Museum at Inglenook, offering a page of Bermuda history with gold bars, arms, jewels ond other treasures from unfortunate ships which came to grief on the colony's reefs.

Westward by Ferry

The easiest excursion to make out of Hamilton is westward toward the tip of the fishhook. This is usually done by going out aboard one of the little government ferries plying Great Sound (the only way to get any perspective in Bermuda is to take a boat) and then returning to Hamilton by taxi or bicycle. It is no problem to put a bike aboard the ferry and part of the trip back is along a car-free cycle path laid out on the roadbed of Bermuda's short-lived railway.

The ferry's first stop is Ireland Island, once a Royal Navy base and now a free-port area where the colony is endeavouring to encourage light industries. You will probably want to disembark at Somerset which has clung to all the charm of old rural Bermuda. The community itself is built around Long Bay and Mangrove Bay and it includes some fine examples of old Bermudian homes. One of them, Belfield-in-Somerset has become a tea-room specializing in dishes bearing such Bermudian names as hop'n john and syllabub (tea, of course, is served as well). Somerset is also an excellent place for picnicking—even old Fort Scaur has been turned into a picnic ground. East of the fort are the Cathedral Rocks where the sea has carved a temple of pillars and arches.

From Somerset, the road to Main Island goes over the world's smallest drawbridge. (We saw a fair-size cuttlefish chasing a lobster in the crystal-clear water beneath the bridge.) The draw consists of a plank lifted out of the center by obliging passers-by whenever a sailboat wants to pass from Ely's Harbour into Great Sound. After running through the middle of Main Island past Little Sound and the U.S. Navy Base on Evans Bay, the road then splits, and we advise you to take the branch running along the south shore with its coral necklace of beaches. If you want the best view on the island, you must go up to Gibbs Hill Lighthouse although you can look at it from below. The light is perched on a cast-iron shaft 117 feet high built on top of a 245-foot hill and it is visible 40 miles away. It went into operation in 1846, making it one of the oldest lighthouses in the world (at the time of its construction, steel was not yet in common use). The Gibbs Hill Lighthouse came as a blessing to mariners, but it ruined the local salvage industry. In *Bermuda Past and Present*, Walter Hayward tells of how the rector of nearby St. Ann's Church reacted when he was informed that a ship was on the western reefs. Said the parson: "The congregation will remain seated until I take off my surplice and then, boys, we'll all start fair."

Back in Hamilton, you can catch up on your shopping while you plan your next expedition. It probably will be eastward although you can spend a pleasant hour or so going out on the Pembroke side of Hamilton Harbour, a residential area favored by modern Bermudians, to Spanish Point, stopping off on the way back for a look at the ducking-stool on the north shore, one of the ways in which old-time Bermudians kept their wives under control.

Eastward from Hamilton

East of Hamilton, the two principal objectives are Harrington Sound and St. George. It's wise, though, not to attempt both in the same day. Remember, you came here to get away from the rush.

On the way out to Harrington Sound along the south shore, you can stop at the Botanical Gardens in Paget Parish for a wide selection of Bermuda's marvelous variety of plants grouped handily into one place. Further out is Verdmont in Smith's Parish, an elegant Bermuda house of the 18th century which has been completely restored by the Bermuda Historical Monuments Trust and furnished with a noteworthy collection of antiques. Inland, on the Middle Road (which you might take coming back if you have the time for a detour) is Old Devonshire Church, of which parts go back to 1716. One of the strangest features of the old church, which has now been restored, is the use of shipknees to strengthen it, proof that ship's carpenters had a hand in its building.

Further along the shore road is another relic of Bermuda's past, a rock bearing the date 1543. It is known as Spanish Rock and its inscription is believed to have been left by a passing Spaniard or Portuguese navigator. Then you reach Devil's Hole near Harrington Sound. This is nothing less than a natural fish pool in which angel fish, turtles, groupers and a couple of 12 ft. shark frolic as if they were in an aquarium. Your admission fee gives you the right to drop a baited line into Devil's Hole. Both fish and turtles will always take it, rising out of the water before letting go. Hooks, you see, are not allowed and the sport is theirs as much as it is yours. (Our wife thought she was landing a shark.)

From here, you can wander eastward past the Mid-Ocean Club and Tucker's Town, the sanctuary for American and Canadian millionaires (the road takes you past the Spittal Pond bird sanctuary as well). Then you can circle northward to at least one of the caves on the eastern end of Harrington Sound. Both Crystal and Leamington caves are famous for white crystal stalactites and stalagmites.

Back along the north shore, you soon reach Flatts where Bermuda has displayed one of the world's finest aquariums for more than thirty years. It is a haven for tropical fish collected not only in the happy hunting grounds off Bermuda (where Beebe made his pioneering bathysphere dives) but from all over the world and brought to the colony by generous donors. Adjoining the aquarium is a museum with more fish (these are mounted) and a zoo housing monkeys, exotic birds, penguins, flamingos and giant turtles from the Galapagos.

On your trip to Harrington Sound, as well as on all your other excursions, always take along a bathing suit, by the way. You never know when an unexpected cove will appear.

By this time, you have had a good look at present-day Bermuda and you are ready for a trip to its past—that is, a trip to St. George. You probably didn't realize it, but you were only a few hundred yards away from the 17th century if you came in by air on Kindley Field which has been constructed opposite St. George's Island.

Historic St. George

St. George is the most remote point of major interest from Hamilton. It will take you anywhere from forty-five minutes to an hour-and-a-half to reach it, depending upon whether you go by taxi, put-put (auxiliary-engined bikes are now rented in the colony), bus or bicycle. No matter how you get there, you will end up on foot because not even a miniature British car is at home in some of the lanes and alleys of St. George.

It is the proud boast of St. George that it is the oldest continuous Anglo-Saxon settlement in the New World. It was founded in 1612. Jamestown was settled five years earlier but Bermudians point out that the first Virginians had to abandon their colony. St. George has been inhabited ever since its founding although it fell asleep when the capital was moved to Hamilton and it is only now waking up from its long slumber which protected its old walls from the zeal of 19th century builders. The awakening of St. George is being carried out, however, as a careful restoration in which its past atmosphere, down to the town crier, is being brought back to life. Even the street names in St. George evoke the flavor of its past... names like One Gun Alley, Old Maids Lane, Shinbone Alley, Blockade Alley and the King's Parade.

One way of beginning a tour of St. George is to start from the King's Parade, or King's Square (there is a Visitors' Service Bureau on the square) with a look at its pillory and stock. A favorite tourist pastime is photographing your husband inside the stocks although the original users never considered them very amusing. The Town Hall, a recent replica of a building constructed in 1782, is on the square and so is the State House, neither recent nor a replica. It is believed to be the oldest stone building (and therefore the oldest building) on Bermuda. It was built in 1619 with the help of turtle-oil-and-lime mortar and it is used today as a Masonic Lodge at an annual rental of one peppercorn a year.

Just around the corner from King's Square is York Street, St. George's shopping centre, where many Hamilton stores have branches. York Street is more famous, though, for ancient St. Peter's Church, believed to be the oldest Anglican church in the Western Hemisphere. The St. Peter's you see has gone through four centuries of architectural alterations and restoration since it was opened in 1612, but its altar dates back to 1624 and the silver communion service received as a gift from King William III in 1684 is still used. St. Peter's has a secular history as well—it was here that the first Bermuda parliament met.

Right across the street from St. Peter's is the Globe Hotel, recently converted to a small museum housing mementos of the Civil War. It is open daily, admission free. Built in 1700 by Governor Samuel Day, it was occupied during the Civil War by a Confederate agent and it became the headquarters for the Confederates' blockade-running operations out of Bermuda (St. George is said to be the only place in the world where the Stars and Bars received an international salute). At one time in its colorful career, it was also used as a hotel.

From here, you can browse a few yards west and then cut over to Water Street where the 18th century Tucker House stands (this particular Tucker was Bermuda's colonial secretary during the American Revolution). Its interior, which has been tastefully restored, is a flashback to Bermuda living during one of its most gracious eras. The kitchen of the Tucker House is also of historical interest: it was the home at one time of J. H. Rainey, a slave who escaped from the South and served as St. George's barber (Barber's Alley is named after him) until he returned home to sit as the first colored member of the House of Representatives during Reconstruction days.

Further to the west, you reach Old Maid's Lane, the name that has stuck to Duke of Cumberland Lane. Here was the home of Tom Moore on Bermuda and it was here that he wrote his "Odes to Nea" with the wife of one of his neighbors, yet another Tucker, in mind. The poet stayed only a few months on Bermuda with an easy job as Registrar of the Court of Vice Admiralty. He left in April, 1804, turning his job over to a deputy who proceeded to steal everything he could grab, leaving the poor poet saddled with debts. Think of his sad fate when you hoist a drink in *Tom Moore's Tavern.*

Style of Good Queen Anne

Wandering back toward the center of St. George, you will soon reach Queen Street, where the early 18th century architecture is steeped in the style of good Queen Anne. Near the head of the street on Printer's Alley stands the Old Rectory, a little cottage given its present appearance in 1703 by a pirate named George Dew who reformed to such an extent that he became a Vice-Admiralty judge.

Your next stop will probably be the St. George Historical Society building on the corner of Duke of Kent Street and Featherbed Lane. Its entrance steps, narrow at the top and wide at the bottom, are a perfect example of the "welcoming arms stairs" found in old Bermuda architecture. It is an historical museum, of course, and it also is the home of the Featherbed Alley Print Shop. Here, a printer in 18th century costume shows visitors relics of the early days of printing in Bermuda and runs the replica of an old hand press.

No visit to St. George is complete without a pilgrimage to nearby Duke of York Street (everything here is "nearby") and Somers Garden. In this little park, the heart of Sir George Somers was buried in answer to one of his last wishes. There is a simple stone column surrounded by flowers and palm trees to perpetuate the memory of Bermuda's founder.

St. George, when it was the capital of the colony, lived under the protection of a ring of forts intended to keep intruders, particularly the all-conquering Spanish, away from the islands. In all, only two shots were ever fired in anything resembling anger from these forts, but that does not make them any less fascinating for a prowl through military history. They are easily reached along the Circular Drive which you can pick up on the outskirts of the town.

The first is Gates Fort, named after Sir Thomas Gates who was one of the men leading the original Sea Venture band of settlers. It was built between 1612 and 1615 by Governor Moore. Nearby is Building Bay, where the "Deliverance" was launched in 1610.

Next is Fort St. Catherine, a much more ambitious undertaking where battlements and thick walls were added conscientiously down through the centuries from the day when its foundations were built in 1613. St. Catherine's offers not only a wonderful view of the sea it once commanded but also a collection of dioramas explaining in 3-D the history of St. George with the help of a guide in red-coated uniform. Fort St. Catherine overlooks Sea Venture Flat where Sir George Somers was shipwrecked and it was on the beach below the fort that the survivors came ashore.

Beyond the fort is Tobacco Bay, the scene of the American Revolution gunpowder raid. The kegs of stolen powder were loaded here after they were liberated from a magazine near Fort St. Catherine. The magazine is now known as the Gunpowder Cavern and, like everything else in St. George, it has been beautifully restored—in this case, to the point where there is a bar and restaurant for the restoration of visitors as well.

From St. George, you can finish the job of girdling Bermuda by taking a ferry to St. David's Island, stopping off to visit St. David's Lighthouse marking the colony's extreme eastern tip, or just enjoying the view of St. George from the sea. The St. David's islanders were once among the most picturesque of all Bermudians (they were reputed to be a mixture of Negro and Irish) and they kept very much to themselves. The Kindley Field air base put an end to their isolation and led to the introduction of another picturesque species of humanity, the American GI.

BAHAMA ISLANDS

Cays of the Kingdom

BY

FRANK O'SHANOHUN

(A well-known British journalist and publicist, Frank O'Shanohun commutes between London and the Bahamas, and is as familiar with Nassau as he is with Fleet Street.)

No islands in all the seven seas can boast such a distinguished roster of tourists as this wonderful archipelago that stretches 800 miles from Florida southeast almost to the Dominican Republic. Christopher Columbus leads the list. San Salvador, smack on the 24th parallel of north latitude, was his first landfall in the New World. Thinking he had reached an island off the coast of China, he went ashore on October 12, 1492 and claimed it for their Catholic Majesties of Spain, never dreaming that history would award it to those infidels, the Protestant Majesties of England. But—what a disappointment —there was no gold! It was shining over the explorer's head, but it took the 20th century to find this commodity in the sky.

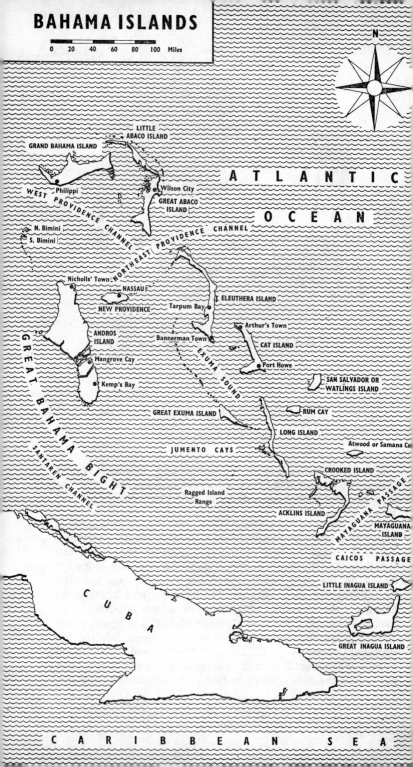

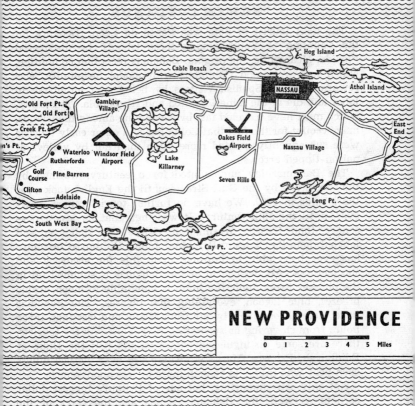

Old Fort Pt.
Old Fort
Creek Pt.
n's Pt.
Waterloo
Rutherfords
Golf
Course
Pine Barrens
Clifton
Adelaide
South West Bay

Gambier
Village

Windsor Field
Airport

Cable Beach

Lake
Killarney

Oakes Field
Airport

Seven Hills

Cay Pt.

Hog Island

NASSAU

Athol Island

East
End

Nassau Village

Long Pt.

NEW PROVIDENCE

0 1 2 3 4 5 Miles

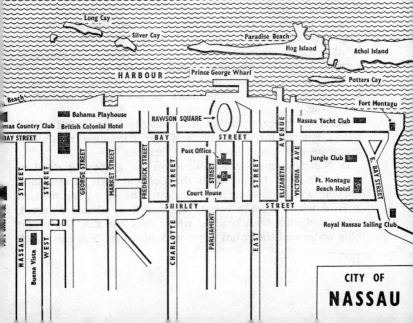

Long Cay

Silver Cay

Paradise Beach

Hog Island

Athol Island

HARBOUR   Prince George Wharf

Potters Cay

Fort Montagu

Beach

Bahama Playhouse

mas Country Club   British Colonial Hotel

BAY STREET

NASSAU
STREET
WEST
STREET
Buena Vista

GEORGE STREET

MARKET STREET

FREDERICK STREET

STREET

RAWSON SQUARE

BAY   STREET

Post Office

CHARLOTTE

PARLIAMENT

STREET

Court House

SHIRLEY   STREET

STREET

EAST

ELIZABETH

VICTORIA AVE

AVENUE

Nassau Yacht Club

Jungle Club

Ft. Montagu
Beach Hotel

Royal Nassau Sailing Club

E. BAY STREET

CITY OF
NASSAU

BAHAMA ISLANDS

The next tourist of note was Ponce de León. Looking for the Fountain of Youth among these islands, he discovered Florida. Meanwhile, the original Bahamas reception committee, which had welcomed Columbus with model hospitality, was rewarded by its Spanish visitors by being sent en masse to labor and die in the mines of Cuba and Hispaniola. This news, which must have traveled fast by canoe vine among the islands, may account for the fact that Columbus and other early tourists were subsequently greeted more often than not by volleys of poison-tipped arrows.

The Bahamas lay unpopulated for a century, warmed by the sun, laved by the Gulf Stream until the English took over the islands in 1629. We have no further tourist report, however, until the 18th century. It was then that no less a personage than George Washington visited the Bahamas and labeled them the "Isles of Perpetual June". No tourist brochure has ever been able to improve upon this for accuracy and succinctness. All the charm of the Bahamas is summed up in the phrase. From June, the jump is inevitable to moon, tropic breezes, blue lagoon, everything that pleases. The Bahamas have them all one hour by air from Miami and less than three hours from shivering or sweltering New York. As for tourists, there are some distinguished names on the list: the Duke of Edinburgh, Princess Margaret. There are over 300,000 others each year who prefer to remain more or less anonymous.

Not only self-supporting, but one of Britain's biggest dollar earners as well, the Bahama Islands are the Cays of the Kingdom.

Many people think of the Bahamas as just Nassau. In fact, there are about 700 islands and nearly 2,000 cays and rocks in the island chain, scattered like a handful of pearls in turquoise waters extending across an area of 70,000 square miles. They all lie along the path of the Gulf Stream and have a steady year-round temperature of between 70 and 80 in the shade.

Light sea breezes prevent the humidity experienced in the island resorts farther south and the Bahamian rainfall is moderate and spread over May to October.

In Nassau there is not a neon sign nor a hot dog stand in sight. You can trot through the Colonial style streets in a horsedrawn, fringed surrey. You can land at a huge modern airfield which is only twenty minutes from almost deserted, white and pink sand beaches where only the sun, the bright blue water and the palms share your pleasure. You can watch

On mid-Atlantic golf greens or in the Colonial Secretariat in Hamilton where the Governor formally opens Parliament with his annual Throne Speech, life in Bermuda remains deeply, delightfully British.

You can get your boat in shape for a cruise or just laze in
the sun the whole year round in the palm-studded Bahamas.
Water (72° in winter) is unsurpassed for boating, bathing.

or take part in yachting, swimming, fishing, water skiing, skin diving, golf, tennis, boxing, riding and motor racing. And in the Out Islands—the lightly inhabited resorts on the fringes of the group—you can live in hotels, clubs or a simple camp.

The main Out Islands can all be reached by regular flights from Nassau and no journey on these services takes more than an hour and a half. Nassau has one of the finest fleets of charter boats in the Caribbean and these may be hired, complete with expert Bahamian skipper and crew, for cruises to the islands.

The Out Islands have something for everybody. The Biminis, for example, boast the best game fishing in the world. Marlin, Sailfish, Dolphin and Swordfish are all found there. Fishing, incidentally, is magnificent all over the Bahamas. As of 1962, the International Game Fish Association listed 60 world record fish caught here. At Cat Cay, a small island south of Bimini, twenty-one fishermen once caught between them forty-nine Tuna weighing a total of 21,105 lb. in one day during a competition. An International Tuna fishing contest is held here each year.

The Exuma islands are well known for their wonderful cruising grounds. The islands, spread out like the diamonds in a duchess' tiara, are among the most exotic in the world with a range of almost indescribable colours caused by varying depths over different types of sea bottom. When the sun is reflected through these waters they record a dozen tints of blue, green, yellow and gold.

Eleuthera, another of the islands, was the first to be colonised by white settlers. Today, its way of life has not radically altered from those times, except that half a dozen hotels have been developed along its 100 miles or so. These range from traditional, old world inns to contemporary club houses. All blend into the landscape, however, and any suspicion of "holiday resort" atmosphere has been carefully avoided. At Cotton Bay on the island a championship golf course has been designed by a world famous golfing architect. Always in sight of the sea, the course has accommodation consisting of separate bungalows, a restaurant and bar, and a small harbour for visiting golfers who arrive in their cruisers.

Other romantically named islands—Grand Bahama, Abaco, Andros, Crooked Island, Ragged Island, Inagua, Long Island, Mayaguana—all have their own particular personalities, but what they have in common is a peace and tranquility unequalled elsewhere—no crowds, no screaming headlines, no traffic jams. The people are friendly and the islands have an informal type of beauty giving the impression that man has never set foot on them before.

Pirates Expelled, Commerce Restored

The Bahamians, as well as being friendly, are a rugged bunch. From buccaneering in the 17th century they successively tried, with varying results, wrecking, gun-running and bootlegging. As one of Great Britain's oldest colonies they must have tried the Mother Country's patience on more than one occasion. In 1696 someone complained to King Charles II that the Bahamas were one of the "chief places where pyrates resort & are harbourd" and so, in 1717 (Governments didn't work any faster in those days) an energetic governor of the Bahamas—one Captain Woodes Rogers, the first Royal Governor—hanged a handful of pirates, pardoned a lot more and chased the rest away. He then adopted the Colony's present motto "Pirates expelled, commerce restored", which to this day sounds more like a telegram than a motto.

The repeal of Prohibition finally convinced the Bahamas that respectability was a virtue. Today, Nassau is like an elderly aunt trying very hard to be respectable but with a closet full of skeletons. Tourism is the main industry, although the average Bahamian businessman's eye will catch a little of its lost gleam if you mention real estate, which is having a boom of its own. Liberal tax laws (for those mad enough to want to work in such a paradise there is no income tax, no profit tax, no capital gains tax; no death duty is payable on real estate and only a small tax is levied on personal property) have attracted a good deal of international finance business. Many U.S. "off shore" companies and "suitcase companies" are registered here and investment trusts and banks abound. The urge to supply liquor, however, has not entirely deserted the Bahamians and the number of liquor stores per hundred yards in Nassau must be among the highest in the world. Prices well below those on the mainland send most visitors away at the end of their vacations weighed down with bottles.

As something like three hundred thousand tourists arrived last year it can be safely assumed that the Bahamians know a thing or two about providing the right facilities. A group of shrewd businessmen—known locally as the Bay Street Boys—were responsible for setting up the official Development Board which has increased tenfold the tourist count since 1949 when only 32,018 people visited the islands. Most of the present day visitors are American, although the number of Canadians and

Britons is on the upgrade. Nassau has for long been a winter resort for rich British tourists and residents but bargain air fares are now pulling in budget tourists as well.

None of this means that the amenities of the area have been spoiled. The fact that many islands can accommodate visitors avoids any great concentration of tourists in one spot and it is always possible to find a deserted beach.

Looking for a Wife?

The population of the Bahamas consists (at the last census) of 39,338 men and 45,503 women, a comfortable discrepancy if you are looking for a wife. The racial groupings are roughly as follows: African 61,627, Mixed 12,361, European 10,709, Others 144. The coloured population, like almost everywhere else, is increasing owing to the improving conditions. A recent economic survey showed that the Bahamas enjoy a general overall standard of living higher than any other country in the Caribbean.

Both the Duke of Edinburgh and Princess Margaret have visited the Bahamas in recent years and thoroughly enjoyed its informal atmosphere and friendly people. Princess Margaret visited the Bahamas twice before her marriage and spent her honeymoon in the Caribbean area. The Colony has another link with the British Royal family for the Duke of Windsor was Governor here for some years. It must be one of the few British colonies to have had an American woman as its Governor's lady.

The Bahamas offer the beauty of semi-tropical islands; a canopy of periwinkle blue sky with gleaming masses of lazy clouds, surf-pounded reefs and sandbanks, masses of bougainvillaea pouring wildly over pink walls, secluded lagoons and long stretches of powdery beach, whispering casuarina trees leaning with the wind, shady little streets guarded by rows of stately royal palms, nights scented with jasmine, and bright with the twinkle of southern stars.

Well could the Canadian poet Bliss Carman write of Nassau:
"The trade winds fan her forehead, in everlasting June,
She reigns from deep verandahs above her blue lagoon".

History of Boom and Slump

You can't really understand the people of the Bahamas unless you know at least a little of their history. The geography of the region has had a strong effect in shaping the development of the Islands and their people.

There is little arable land or pasture, although there is a

good deal of timber, and the undeveloped islands are covered in scrub and conifer with a scattering of salt marshes. There are no important mineral deposits except salt, although two U.S. oil companies are drilling for oil from an offshore well off one of the islands.

Two facts of fundamental importance emerge if you take a close look at the Bahamas—that they have close natural ties with the southern part of the United States and that they are unable to support a sizeable population on their own agricultural output.

These two facts have played a major part in the history of the Bahamas, a copy-book history of boom and depression.

The islands were discovered by Columbus in 1492 (the day is still a national holiday) when he made his first landfall in the New World. About 1509, the Spaniards, to whom the Pope had granted the concession, transported the native Indians to work in the mines of Cuba and the mainland. Fairly soon, as a result, the Bahamas were depopulated and disappeared for a century from history. In 1629 King Charles I of England, threw the islands in with Carolina in a grant to his attorney-general, Sir Robert Heath, but the first real English settlement was made 18 years later by an ex-governor of Bermuda, William Sayle, who was looking for a religious refuge, and by the Eleutherian Adventurers— a group of merchants from London —who settled on Eleuthera and made an attempt to establish the first republic in the New World.

The land was poor, the settlers quarrelled; they set up a timber trade with England but soon fell back on wrecking. And so in 1670 the Bahamas were taken over by the Lords Proprietors of Carolina.

They made very little difference except to introduce a system of government—some aspects of which still survive today. The settlers disliked the kind of work that could wring a decent living out of the rocky soil; what wrecking couldn't supply piracy could. The Bahamas became notorious as a den of pirates—including Blackbeard himself—and suffered frequent reprisal raids from the Spanish and French. Not until 1718 did the Bristol seaman, Captain Rogers, with the backing of London merchants, take over the rights of the Proprietors and, appointed Governor of the Bahamas by George I, set out with a force of 100 soldiers and routed the pirates. Some were hanged, some were pardoned and some fled. The rest of Rogers' life and money was spent in an attempt to put the islands on a businesslike footing.

BAHAMA ISLANDS

An American Naval Squadron captured Nassau for a while in 1776 but in 1782 the Spaniards took over again. One year later, however, Nassau and the Bahamas were finally and irrevocably returned to Great Britain when an English Colonel re-took the town.

The American War of Independence opened with an ammunition raid by the rebels and for one day the islands flew the American flag. Loyalists with their slaves began to move to the Bahamas attracted by generous grants of Crown land. They trebled the population and created the situation in which negroes outnumbered their white masters. Settlement of the other islands began and there was a period of destructive social friction between the aristocrat loyalists and the all-but-pirate natives.

There was a stop to trade when the Napoleonic wars closed the American market, and there was emancipation of the slaves in 1838.

In 1861 the American Civil War began and the Bahamas boomed again. England wanted Southern cotton, the South wanted arms. Nassau lay nicely in between these two desires and fantastic activity and profits resulted. But in 1865 it was all over, the bubble burst, and there was nothing to show but the Royal Victoria Hotel and a few public works.

Boom turned to slump once more. For 50 years the Bahamas suffered depression, although a number of minor industries were introduced and by the beginning of the 20th century modest prosperity had returned. It was about this time that the Bahamas Government first began to woo the tourist. A winter steamer service to Miami began and another hotel was built.

But the first World War put a stop to that, and at the end of the war the sturdy Bahamians were once again pulling in their belts and preparing for another period of blank depression. But once again fortune favoured them and their luck turned. This time it was Uncle Sam who did the trick—by establishing Prohibition.

Rum and Tourist Boom

It didn't take long for the Bahamians to discover that rum-running was even more profitable than gun-running. Plenty of good liquor was imported from England and re-exported in fast motor boats from quiet coves and creeks to the U.S. mainland. The Bahamas treasury grew fat on liquor duties and was able to get new hotels built and increase transport services.

BAHAMA ISLANDS

Luxury tourism began to develop and the advantages of the liberal tax laws also attracted millionaires in the twenties. The second World War brought large Royal Air Force contingents and American ferrying bases.

Since 1946 the Bahamas have seen their real and apparently permanent boom—in tourism, in real estate, and in finance. It is on tourism, however, that the Colony really depends for its livelihood.

Before the Second World War, the tourism on which the islands basically depended had been a matter only for the rich, and that for only three or four months every winter. In 1949, however, a group of white businessmen gained control of the House of Assembly in an election (the group is now The United Bahamian Party) and determined to put tourism on a more popular footing and to provide all year round employment for the local people. They injected new life into the Development Board and voted large sums to promote the islands and advertise them as an all year resort. Tourism boomed and the boom got bigger each year. In six years the number of vacationers visiting the Bahamas increased from 32,000 to a quarter of a million. The industry continues to grow.

Today the whole economy is geared to providing all the usual—and off-beat—things that tourists like to see in an English colony with its tradition and occasional glimpses of benevolent feudalism. The consequences of this tourist boom have been far-reaching.

It has obviously produced good profits for the Bay Street merchants who sell luxury goods. But it has also produced a very large amount of new employment and put the Treasury in funds (no financial help from Great Britain is required by the Bahamas) and stimulated a building boom which has made construction the third largest industry in the islands.

The cost of living has risen, although, like most other places, if you take the trouble to pick up some local knowledge, you will be able to get along far more cheaply than just accepting everything at first sight.

Politically, the Bahamas are stable although the general strike of 1958 did lead to the recognition of trade unions. The government, modeled after the English system, is composed of a Governor, representing the Crown, an Executive Council (not more than 9 members), a nominated Leglislative Council (11 members), and an elected House of Assembly (33 members elected from 15 districts). The creation of new electoral districts has narrowed the gap between white and coloured parties. It is very possible that in the coming elections in the islands, a coloured majority party will be elected. Relations between the races in the Bahamas however is no problem. There is no segregation on colour grounds and there has clearly been a good deal of inter-marriage. If anything, a change in the balance of power stems from the opinion, commanding a good deal of white sympathy, that heretofore, too much power and too large a share of the boom were going into too few hands.

The Social Network

But this is an age-old problem everywhere. The average Bahamian is a happy, easy-going character who loves to laugh and, in any case, it should not be imagined that wages are low. A Nassau taxi driver, for instance, can make a hundred dollars a week. Generally speaking, all sections of the Bahamian population get on well together, and there is a good deal of loyal friendship and traditional association between the coloured people and the white community. Politics sometimes produce a few sparks, but even in the House of Assembly when members are hurling contempt at each other's policies, tradition breaks through when members assemble weekly wearing morning dress and toppers.

The apex of Nassau's social life is Government House, high above the town where the Union Jack is flown and furled each day with customary ceremony. Here sits his Excellency the Governor of the Bahamas, Sir Robert Stapledon, K.C.M.G. representing Queen Elizabeth the Second. A gilt-edged invitation to cocktails or dinner is never overlooked, even by Nassau's elite.

From Government House, the social network extends to Nassau's merchant aristocracy "the Bay Street Boys" who provide the driving force that has developed the Colony's economy to its existing healthy state. Living in gracious houses on the fringe of Nassau, with an average of two cars in the garage, mixing their cocktails and often dressing for dinner, they represent a rugged slice of the community that has worked fantastically hard and is now earning what they consider a just reward. Among them are several who have earned the title of The Honourable—a traditional method of address to those who belong to the Legislative Council, a kind of miniature House of Lords. Ever since 1728 when the Bahamas House of Assembly was constituted, the governmental system has adhered very closely to the procedure and traditions of the British Houses of Parliament.

Then there is the community consisting of the international set. Some of these have winter houses in the Bahamas; some come as regular visitors. This section includes many American stars from films and television. Dr. Milton Eisenhower is seen on the golf course sometimes. Juan Trippe of Pan-American has an interest in an Out Island property. American tycoons Louis Rice Wasey and Wallace Groves also have Out Island interests. Huntingford Hartford, U.S. millionaire (A & P chain stores) has bought Hog Island off Nassau where he transformed 700 acres of sand and marsh into a $25 million resort aptly named "Paradise Island". Early in 1962 this extravagant resort-hotel held its debut complete with 1,000 guests from the international set, champagne and fireworks. The estate of the late Swedish millionaire Axel Wenner-Gren has an 11 million dollar investment in the Lighthouse Club on Andros, which is beginning development of 800,000 acres, an area larger than the State of Rhode Island. Clint Murchison Jr. sunbathes on Spanish Cay; Standard oil heiress Marion Carstairs and her half brother Francis Francis bought Whale Cay and Bird Cay; Alcoa chairman Arthur Vining Davis built the exclusive Rock Sound Club on Eleuthera and laid out Cotton Bay Golf Club (among members are Laurance Rockefeller, General Nathan Twining). Howard Hughes controls Cal Say, closest Bahamian island to Cuba.

From England Lord Beaverbrook, the famous British press lord is a regular visitor. Nancy, Lady Astor, her son Lord Astor, the Earl of Dudley, Lord Rootes of motor car fame, Lord Dunmore, Lord Wilton are just a few of the names from Debrett's who enjoy the winter sunshine of the Islands. Eunice, Lady Oakes (widow of Sir Harry Oakes whose murder in Nassau during the war still intrigues the world press) lives here.

Native Life and Color

Native life in the Bahamas, despite the tourist boom, goes on in a time-honoured way. The Bahamians are great sailors and a look at the busy waterfront of Nassau will provide evidence of the dependence of the local population on sea traffic. Work boats of all shapes and sizes tie up there every day with vegetables and fish, passengers and poultry, heaped in seeming confusion upon their decks. All this varied freight is carried to and fro, back and forth from the Islands to Nassau harbour—hub of the Bahamas.

BAHAMA ISLANDS

Native Bahamians, live, love and die mostly in the "over the Hill" district of Nassau. Some houses are obviously unsanitary and in need of re-building but by and large there are fewer slums than in most Caribbean communities. Running water is still at a premium in some households but strenuous efforts are being made to improve matters. Like many coloured peoples, the Bahamians are not naturally energetic and the self-induced effort required to raise one's own standard of living is not in every case forthcoming. However, many new Government-supported housing schemes are under consideration which would help create modern dwellings for much of the native populace.

In the Out Islands, where urbanite temptations are very scant, life is simpler. Fishing, boat building and other traditional work is the mainstay, and although some of the communities live in very unsophisticated conditions, there is little of the squalor that can characterise urban and crowded areas where many people are herded into comparatively small spaces.

Moreover, a recent survey comparing the Bahamas with Jamaica, Antigua, Barbados, Trinidad, Cuba, and Haiti has shown that the Bahamas enjoy a much higher overall standard of living than those islands. This includes distribution of income, wages, conditions of work, unemployment, education, health, housing and public utilities.

You will seldom meet a native Bahamian in the bar or restaurant of your hotel. There is virtually no colour bar but the prices there are fairly high and, in any case, the Bahamians prefer their own bars and eating places. There are, however, several bars and restaurants in Nassau where you will notice coloured people and, of course, the night spots "over the hill" will be thronged with them thoroughly enjoying themselves. You will also find them wearing their best clothes, crowding the churches on Sundays—and singing, it always seems, slightly flat.

To see the natives at their most native you ought to watch, or join in, the Junkanoo Parade which is held on Boxing Day and again on New Years Day. A kind of Bahamian Mardi Gras, it starts at 3 a.m. and goes on for hours. Wearing garish costumes and head-dresses, natives weave and dance up and down Bay Street to the music of bongo drums and calypso. Origins of Junkanoo are shrouded in the mists of time, but it is obviously some kind of celebration to invoke the good spirits' aid for the coming year and chase away the bad ones.

Native Bahamians have their own food specialities, and some

of these are worth trying. Conch (a kind of large shell fish) comes in a variety of ways—as delicious chowder, hot and spicy and extra good if you lace it with sherry, and as fritters. You should try green turtle soup; peas and rice, fried with onions, salt pork and herbs—this dish is almost a staple diet of the natives. Green turtle pie, baked Andros crabs or chicken roasted Bahamian style are some of the best known dishes.

The space age has come to the Bahamas as another aspect of its boom time. Cape Canaveral blasts off long-range missiles from its launching pads, and the scientists there like to keep a track on where those high-explosive man-made toys go after firing. The Bahamas happen to lie right across the firing arc of America's "four hundred million dollar shooting gallery" and a series of tracking stations have been set up to watch the performance of the rockets as they roar across the sky, finally to drop like falling stars into the sea 5,000 miles or so from the firing point. Grand Bahama, Eleuthera, San Salvador, and Mayagüana all contain tracking stations manned by Air Force officers and men and employees of Pan-American World Airways and the Radio Corporation of America who tend the electronic brains which track, guide and probe the missiles' behaviour during their flight.

The range, between shoots, is a drowsy chain of sunny islands but when geared up for action it is a humming complex of electronic gadgets connected by a submarine cable so that all data is instantly presented back at Cape Canaveral.

So there is a brief cameo of life in the Bahamas today. You will find them a pleasing blend of old British tradition and customs with modern American standards of living and entertainment. For all the attention paid to U.S. visitors however, the Bahamians have been careful to preserve their own way of life, and, despite the tremendous developments that are taking place, to keep intact the characteristic charm and peace of Nassau and the beautiful out islands.

PRACTICAL INFORMATION FOR THE BAHAMAS

HOW TO GET THERE. Nassau is the communications centre of the Bahamas, although there are two air services direct to Out Islands from the States. The Bahamas are the nearest British possession to the U.S.A. Nassau is less than one hour by air, and overnight by boat, from Miami. The rapidly expanding tourist industry has overtaxed the transportation facilities in recent years, and the Bahamas Government has met the challenge with the construction of a new boat-passenger station in Nassau Harbour, and with the construction of the modern International Airport at Windsor Field, one of the finest in the area.

BAHAMA ISLANDS

By Air. From New York: Daily by *B.O.A.C.* and *P.A.A.* jet service in 2½ hours (4½ by non-jet), or by *Eastern* or *National Airlines* to *Miami.*

From Miami: Daily flights by *P.A.A., Cunard Eagle* and *Bahamas Airways* in less than one hour and by *Mackey Airlines* via Fort Lauderdale.

From West Palm Beach and Fort Lauderdale by *Mackey* and *Bahamas Airways.*

From Tampa and St. Petersburg by daily *Mackey* flights.

From Palm Beach, Fort Lauderdale, Tampa and St. Petersburg: By *Mackey Airlines* daily.

From Toronto: By *T.C.A.* via Tampa with directs flights and a minimum of five weekly flights throughout the year.

From Montreal: Weekly flights (Thursdays) by B.O.A.C. via Bermuda.

From London: By *B.O.A.C.* via New York and Bermuda; *Cunard Eagle* via Bermuda.

Bahamas Airways maintains scheduled services to several of the Out Islands from Florida and *Mackey Airlines* flies to Bimini and Grand Bahama. *Bahamas Airways* also operates an extensive inter-island service from Nassau with regular stops at 27 Out Island settlements.

Unlimited charter service is available from *Bahamas Airways* and *Bahama Air Traders, Ltd.,* based in Nassau.

By Sea. Twice weekly sailings by the *S.S. Florida* and the *S.S. Bahama Star* from Miami to Nassau. Weekly sailings by *M.S. Italia* from New York. Occasional sailings by the *Queen of Bermuda* and *Ocean Monarch.*

Overnight boats from Miami to Nassau bring passengers, heavy baggage and motor cars as well as freight. No duty is payable on cars unless they remain in the Colony over six months when American cars pay 25% of value and Canadian cars 10% (plus 7½% War Tax), however, a cash deposit must be made. Visitors are granted the courtesy of a free temporary driver's license, and remember it is left-hand driving here.

Canadian National Steamships operates a freight service between Montreal and/or Halifax and Nassau.

There is also a regular freight service of *Royal Mail Lines* between England and Nassau, and irregular calls by *Pacific Steam Navigation Company's* steamers.

Apart from airline offices and travel agents, the Bahamas Development Board maintains several offices overseas where full information about transportation and all facilities in the Islands can be obtained.

They are situated at:

307 British Empire Bldg., 620 Fifth Avenue, New York 20.N.Y.

608 First National Bank Bldg., 351 E. 2nd St., Miami 32, Fla.

1230 Palmolive Bldg., Chicago II, Ill.

Adolphus Hotel Arcade (1406), Dallas 2, Texas.

1341 Biltmore Hotel, 515 Olive Str., Los Angeles, 13, Calif.

707 Victory Bldg., 80 Richmond St. W., Toronto 1, Ontario.

Lufthansa Bldg., 10/A Old Bond Street, London, W.1, England.

Headquarters of the Board are at Bay Street, Nassau, Bahamas. Cable address, *DEVBOARD, NASSAU.*

BAHAMA ISLANDS

CURRENCY. The currency of the Bahamas is based on the British Pound but American and Canadian money is accepted everywhere. Prices are usually shown in dollars.

But it is an economy for American and Canadian tourists to exchange their dollars for Bahamian bills, and pay the British prices quoted in hotels, shops and restaurants in Bahamian currency.

	Bahamian		*U.S. or Canadian*
Notes:			
	4 shillings (Green)	equal	56 cents
	10 shillings (Red)	equal	$ 1.40
	One Pound (Grey)	equal	2.80
	Five Pounds (Blue)	equal	14.00
Coins:			
	Halfpenny (½d)	equal	About a half cent
	Penny (1d)	equal	About one cent
	Threepence (3d)	equal	Four cents
	Sixpence (6d)	equal	Seven cents
	Shilling (12 pence) (1/—)	equal	Fourteen cents

GETTING ABOUT. Apart from using your flat feet or hiring a cab there are several means of locomotion available to you in Nassau.

You can hire a Surrey for a leisurely look at the town. You can't miss them, there are several ranks at central points.

You can also hire a car, motor scooter or bicycle. But for heaven's sake remember to drive on the *left*. Speed limit is 20 MPH in the city, 30 MPH elsewhere. Hertz-Rent-A-Car recently opened a branch in Nassau.

Also, beach hotels have no-charge limousine services into town.

SPORTS. *Swimming* is perhaps the first sporting idea that hits any visitor to the Bahamas. There are beaches everywhere, but one not to be missed is Paradise Beach on Hog Island, just off Nassau. You can get there from the quayside at Rawson Square in a boat. The fare is 50c. and admission to the beach $1. New York grocery millionaire Huntington Hartford who owns most of the island has re-christened it Paradise Island and is constructing a club, hotel, yacht basin, golf course and other facilities which will make it one of the finest in the Nassau area.

Spear fishing, *skin-diving* and *water skiing* are three other activities not to be missed in Nassau. Contact Underwater Tours, Ltd., at the Nassau Beach Hotel, or Bahamas Watersports, at the Emerald Beach Hotel.

If you want to go *deep sea diving* (you don't need to be an expert) call on Mr. and Mrs. Hartley on their yacht "Carioca" which is based at Nassau Yacht Haven. They will take you out for a half day trip for $7.50 per person and introduce you to a world beneath the water which is fascinating and fun.

Another kind of undersea exploring (without getting wet) is to be found in a trip to the sea gardens in a glass bottomed boat. These boats make their trips from the Prince George wharf.

For *golfers* there are 18 hole courses at the Bahamas Country Club, Lyford Cay, and Paradise Island.

INCRES IS AT HOME ON THE CARIBBEAN!

As year 'round Caribbean cruise specialists of long standing, we know what sun-worshipping vacationers like . . . and it's all yours on the ship designed for cruising, the air conditioned m/s VICTORIA! All cabins have private facilities. You're served by cruise-trained all-Italian personnel. Facilities are truly elegant, with 2 outdoor swimming pools, two-story theatre, magnificent public rooms. And the fun goes on night and day, directed by an experienced, permanent American cruise staff!

M/S VICTORIA

Exciting, Well-Balanced Caribbean Cruises with Ample Time to Enjoy Each Port!

Visiting variously throughout the year: St. Thomas, San Juan, Kingston, Jamaica; Port-au-Prince, Haiti; Nassau; Bermuda; Trinidad; Guadeloupe, Curacao, Aruba, Antigua, Barbados, Grenada, St. Lucia

Incres Line

CRUISES BEYOND COMPARE

Incres Line, 39 Broadway, New York 6, N. Y.

BAHAMA ISLANDS

Tennis is to be had all over the place—most of the big hotels have courts. But the two most popular sporting pastimes in the Bahamas are boating and fishing, which are discussed below.

CALENDAR OF EVENTS. The Bahamas have a crowded calendar of events during the year. Fishing tournaments are held from January through August. These include the Winter Fishing Tournament, Cat Cay White Marlin Tournament, Coral Harbour Club International Fishing Tournament, Bimini Marlin-Tuna Club's White Marlin Tournament, Bimini Big Game Fishing Club White Marlin Tournament, the same club's Tuna Tournament, the Annual Bahamas International Tuna Tournament—highlight of the angling year—the annual Bahamas Summer Fishing Tournament and three Blue Marlin Tournaments—two at Bimini and one at Cat Cay. In December there is the annual Wahoo Round Up.

Sailing, too, has pride of place every year. From the International 5.5 metre Championship races at the Nassau Yacht Club the season goes on to the annual Miami-Nassau ocean power boat race, the Round Nassau Ocean Sweepstakes, the Out Island Regatta, the Fort Lauderdale-Cat Cay cruise, the Miami-Nassau ocean race for yachts and the Nassau Cup Race.

There are several golf tournaments and in late November and early December racing motorists of the world congregate in Nassau for the annual Speed Weeks held on Oakes Field.

Many air-conditioned cinemas show up-to-date movies all the year round. Several other peculiarly British occasions are observed like the Queen's Birthday, and Empire Day on 24 May. Discovery Day (12 October) is also a Public Holiday.

HOTELS

Nassau has just about everything in the hotel line from old fashioned hostelries which were operating during the American Civil War to ultra-modern air-conditioned pleasure domes like the Emerald Beach and Nassau Beach Hotels. Exclusive private clubs abound in Nassau and the Out Islands, but there are plenty of more modest places too.

BRITISH COLONIAL. 300 Rooms. On the ocean a few steps from Bay Street, Nassau's shopping centre. Two private beaches, fresh water swimming pool, tennis courts, private golf course. Catering to habitués, this hotel is known for atmosphere and service. Good food and cocktails, nightly entertainment and dancing. Nightclub atmosphere in the La Cage Room; piano entertainment in the Britannia Bar and Hong Kong Room. Coffee house for food at popular American prices. Casual wear during day but wear your best at night. Air conditioned. Daily Rates: Summer Modified American Plan (Room, 2 meals). Single rooms with Bath $19 up,

Winter $23 up. Manager: Gordon M. Anderson.

BUENA VISTA. A small hotel with 15 rooms, (was once a Bahamian mansion) operated by the same management as Cumberland House. Known for its gourmet meals.

Rates: Summer Continental Plan (light breakfast) $5, Winter European Plan $14 up.

CARLTON HOUSE. Right off Bay Street. 67 Rooms. Popular with the "locals" for lunch and dinner. No dancing and about 10 minutes from beaches. Friendly atmosphere, dress informal. Food good, but unpretentious. Rates: Summer M.A.P. $11-$15, Winter $16-$20.

BAHAMA ISLANDS

COLUMBUS. 20 Rooms and 20 apartments. Within walking distance of beach. Dress informal, Modern building in heart of town. Rates: Summer European Plan $5-$7, Winter $5-$8.

CUMBERLAND HOUSE. 25 rooms. A small hotel serving some of the best food in Nassau—gourmet's delight. Continental and Bahamian cuisine, but fairly expensive ($6-10 a meal). Discreet atmosphere. Dress: lunch informal, but semi-formal and formal for dinner.

A few blocks from city and beach, charming patio and gardens. Rates: Summer M.A.P. $16 up, Winter European plan (Room only) $14 up. Run by two very capable lady restaurateurs V. Lorraine Onderdonk and Hedwig Hauck.

⅄ DOLPHIN. 67 Rooms. One of Nassau's newest. Airconditioned on the ocean front. Large windows with private balconies. Swimming pool, cocktail lounge, nightly calypso. Dress informal but wear a collar and tie for dinner. Food good. Rates: Summer M.A.P. $16 up, Winter $22 up.

√ EMERALD BEACH. 300 Rooms. On lovely beach a few miles to West of Nassau. Very chi-chi decor, air-conditioned with your own control knob to twiddle. Has a beach club, Calypso lounge and Jubilee Terrace. Nightly dancing and shows. Good standard of cuisine. Has 6,000 square foot Convention Hall and is popular for such meetings. Tennis, water ski-ing, sailing, fishing. Private boat pier. Dress: casual for lunch, but best bibs for dinner. Rates: Summer M.A.P. $20 up, Winter $30 up.

⅄ MONTAGU BEACH has 200 rooms, including luxurious poolside cabanas. On private beach to East of Nassau. Swimming pool with glass windows through which drinkers in bar can peer mistily at mermaids in swimsuits. All sports, cocktails in gay After Deck Bar or with dancing on hibiscus patio. Enter-

tainment and dancing in new Empire Room supper club. Cuisine is excellent, with a Yorkshire chef who makes that famous pudding. Gay atmosphere, sports clothes during the day, but on the dressy side for dinner and dancing. Rates: Summer M.A.P. $20 up, Winter $30 up. Manager: David Richardson.

LUCERNE. 21 Rooms. Two blocks from the Dock and half a block from Bay Street. Rooms with or without baths, breakfast only served. Rates Summer E.P. $3 without private bath, Winter $5. Lowest rates in town.

MAYFAIR. 52 Rooms. Modern, facing Nassau's harbour entrance. Air conditioned, bar, swimming pool. Rates: Summer M.A.P. $13 up, Winter $20 up.

√ NASSAU BEACH. 278 rooms. This hotel is just four miles from town. Swimming pool with bar for snacks. Lamplighter Room for dinner-dancing. Good cuisine—among the best in Nassau. Entertainment nightly in the new "Rum Keg" cocktail lounge with native musicians. New Out Island Bar is bang up to date. Dress up for evenings. Rates: M.A.P. $20 up, Winter $30 up.

OLYMPIA. 24 Rooms. Across the Street from British Colonial. Air conditioned. Snack luncheons. Bar. Rates: Summer Continental Plan (Room, Breakfast) $6 to $8 up, Winter $10 to $12.

PARADISE ISLAND. Recently opened resort area once called Hog Island, near Nassau. Comprises a 52-room hotel, the *Ocean Club* (minimum daily rate: $45), superb tennis courts, golf course, and swimming pool. Frequented by international set. Luxurious. Owned by George Huntington Hartford, U.S. millionaire.

PRINCE GEORGE. 53 Rooms. In the heart of the city, a great favourite with local businessmen. Almost every day the leading Bay Street merchants and politicians may be discovered lunching there. Good plain food. Overlooks harbour. Cocktail lounge air conditioned, entertainment in winter. Sports clothes during day and informal suits at nights. Rates: Summer M.A.P. $13 up, Winter E.P. (Room only) $13 up.

ROYAL ELIZABETH. 41 Rooms. Overlooking harbour. Patio dining on the waterfront. Swimming pool. Informal clothes at all times. Cocktail lounge. Rates: Summer M.A.P. $12 up, Winter E.P. $8 up.

ROYAL VICTORIA. 130 Rooms. Nassau's oldest, was Confederate Army H.Q. for a while during that well known struggle on the mainland. Full of character with impeccable atmosphere. Lovely old building set among famous botanical gardens. Has everything, bars, swimming pool, garden suites, all air conditioned. Recently acquired by the Treadway Inn chain, the stout old Victorian landmark has undergone considerable face-lifting. A new Queen's Court has been built and there is an up-to-date nightclub which fits alongside the swimming pool. There is a new Treadmill Room Supper Club with entertainment and dancing, and for the daring there is a new tree house in the garden where guests sip cocktails twenty feet in the air. Excellently run with many Europeans on the staff. Cuisine is first class, especially the Sunday night cold buffet which is as good to look at as to eat. If you prefer ocean bathing to the pool, the British Colonial beach where free privileges are granted to hotel guests, is a few minutes walk away. Dress is fairly formal unless you eat at the pool. Dinner needs your best—a black tie if you fancy it. Rates: Single $16-$20, double $28-$32. Manager: Roy Russell.

TOWNE. 48 Rooms. New, half a block from Bay Street. Coffee shop patio, swimming pool, bar. Rates: Summer E.P. $6 up, Winter $8 up.

WINDSOR. 36 Rooms. Centre of shopping district, two blocks from beach. Ba-Ma cocktail lounge and restaurant—good food and native entertainment nightly. Features steaks and roast beef ($5 to $7). Rates: Summer M.A.P. $12 up, Winter E.P. $14 up.

RESIDENTIAL CLUBS

BAHAMAS COUNTRY CLUB. 60 Rooms. You need to be proposed for membership. 18-hole golf course, tennis courts, restaurant and bar. Excellent cuisine since arrival of manager Rico Heller, an experienced Swiss hotel executive. Dress for dinner. Rates: Summer M.A.P. $16.50, Winter $24.

PILOT HOUSE CLUB. 50 Rooms. A gay informal place opposite Nassau Yacht haven. Much used by local gentry and international sportsmen and fishermen. Racing drivers headquarters during Speed Week. You'll meet lots of friendly people here. Bar, garden suites, swimming pool. Food adequate (but improving) including local dishes. Dress informal but no shorts at dinner, please. Run by a charming and delightful English couple, Denis and Peggy Hickman. Rates: Summer M.A.P. $15 up, Winter $19 up.

BALMORAL CLUB. 88 Rooms. On the ocean front five miles from Nassau. Excellent cuisine. Attractive. Informal dress but add a little extra for dinner. Rates: Summer M.A.P. $17, Winter $26.

GROSVENOR CLUB. 10 suites. You need to be a member. Centrally located. Swimming pool. Cocktail bar, all indoor sports, squash, badminton, Golf membership at Nassau Country Club. Rates: E.P. suite for 2 people Summer $10 up, Winter $25 up.

LOFT HOUSE CLUB. 25 Rooms. Worth a visit. Beautiful garden, swimming pool. Food is very good. Old Bahamian building. Rates: Summer B.P. $8-$10, Winter E.P. $15.

CORAL HARBOUR CLUB. 67 rooms and suites and a marina which can accommodate 150 boats; one of the island's newest. Located 15 miles outside Nassau, the Club has swimming pool, shuffle board. Completely air-conditioned . Limited accommodations during summer. Rates: Winter M.A.P. $30 up, Summer E.P. $8.

LYFORD CAY CLUB. An all new plush resort-residential area on the western tip of New Providence, about 17 miles from Nassau. Features an 18-hole golf course, club house, yacht marina, residential clubhouse with 50 luxury rooms, bar lounge, tennis courts and 1,200 foot beach front. All rooms in club front on ocean and have balconies. Open only to members and the membership is exclusive. Inquiries should be directed to Lady Ann Orr-Lewis, 5 Chesham Mews, Belgrave Square, London S.W.1.

There are also specialised Clubs in Nassau including the *Lawn Tennis Club*, the *Nassau Yacht Club* and the *Royal Nassau Sailing Club*. You need membership in all these.

Nassau also has a good selection of smaller hotels, apartment houses and guest houses. Details can be obtained from the Development Board Office.

In the summer, dress rules are relaxed almost everywhere.

Nassau also boasts a Casino—open only in the winter. Incidentally local Bahamians are not allowed to play. It is called the *Bahamian Club* and is just out of town. It contains an excellent restaurant for dinner and dancing. French cuisine of the highest standard with lots of vintage wines. An intimate continental atmosphere. Try to get a Bahamian friend to take you there—he can watch you lose your money. Its quite in the best French tradition and you really need to wear a black tie.

RESTAURANTS AND NIGHTSPOTS. There are several good bars and restaurants in Nassau that will provide you with an evening's amusement of one kind and another. Nightspots are nearly all situated "over the hill" in the native part of the city. Some of them look slightly sinister, but by and large they are relatively harmless and you are quite safe in taking a wife, or a date, to them. As everywhere, cab drivers know them all, and can outline their respective merits to you. Nassau cab drivers are courteous, helpful and usually amusing.

The background in all cases is calypso, goombay music, bongo drums, steel bands and the like. In some of them, when the boys really get going, you need ear plugs. Why worry, you'll have a good evening out anyway.

At many of them you will see the famous limbo dancing—which consists of a kind of high jump in reverse. Performers wriggle to the frenzied beating of bongo drums, underneath a bar which gets lower and lower. Has to be seen to be believed.

BLACKBEARDS TAVERN on Bay Street does a nice line in charcoal broiled steaks. Nice cosy bar and lots of amusing characters about the place. Food not cheap but good. Plenty of entertainment including George Symonette, famed Bahamian pianist.

THE ARDON is a complete contrast. Be on your best behaviour when you dine at this lovely and gracious Bahamian house. Dinner is served in elegant surroundings to a background of French and Spanish songs by Jean. Fine food.

BA-MA. If you like exotic drinks

served in coconut shells and scooped out pineapples try this one just off Bay Street. Good food, too, and calypso going hot and strong.

THE CAT AND FIDDLE CLUB is worth a visit. Two miles out of town, it puts on sensational native floor shows.

CLUB CONFIDENTIAL at Ardastra Gardens lives up to its name. More fire dancing and what are described as "torrid routines".

COCONUT PALM is another late spot. Serves delicious conch fritters. Candlelight conversation and dancing too.

THE JUNKANOO CLUB is on the waterfront side of Bay Street in mid-town. An amusing oval bar. Good floor show with pretty dancers. Voodoo decor and plenty of noise and fun. Good beat for dancers even if they have two left feet. Don't miss it—it's very accessible.

RED CARPET INN. You will find an old English setting here. Just around the corner on Bay Street. Good food and native music.

SILVER SLIPPER is another nightspot "over the hill". Dancing and native entertainment under the stars.

GOLDEN DRAGON. If you like Chinese food, try this restaurant. Superb Chinese cooking—also American and Bahamian.

DIRTY DICK'S is a favourite rendezvous bar on Bay Street for tourists. It opens early in the morning—about 10 a.m. Serves sandwiches and is very informal. Music.

NEW DEVELOPMENTS. A number of large scale resorts and real estate developments are in various stages of completion in New Providence. *Coral Harbour* on the south shore, is in its fourth year of development. It is a self-contained well-appointed club and community which brings a new dimension to resort life and opens new vistas for those seeking something different. The harbour boasts a turning basin of 1000 feet in diameter, two docks and 1500 feet of sheltered seawall fitted with mooring pilings.

The club has 12 different outdoor-indoor areas for wining and dining and is the centre of the resort's social and yachting activities. The area has been developed by Mrs. Leonora B. Hopkins of Atlanta, and her son and daughter, Lindsey Hopkins, Jr., and Mrs. James McKillips.

The recently opened *Lyford Cay* residential colony is about 17 miles from Nassau and includes thousands of acres of beach, slopes and heights. The natural beauty is being preserved during the creation of residential areas. A network of scenic drives is planned, an 18-hole golf course (available to members and guests only), and modern municipal services for residents. The developer of the Lyford Cay residential colony is Mr. E. P. Taylor C.M.G. of Montreal.

SHOPPING

Nassau is the shopping centre of the Bahamas. You will find the odd boutique at hotels in the Out Islands but the only real place to buy is on or near Bay Street in Nassau.

There you will be greeted with traditional Bahamian politeness in many stores that have been owned by the same families for generations. Fine merchandise from all over the world is available at prices usually well below those you would pay in the States. This is because no taxes are levied on goods sold in Nassau.

The goods are mainly imported from Europe; china, cutlery,

leather, fabrics and liquor from England; glass, silver and jewelry from Scandinavia; watches from Switzerland; cameras from Germany, perfumes from France.

At Rawson Square, just off Bay Street, there is a picturesque open air market selling straw goods and other native craftwork. Straw bags, hats—the big ones, admittedly must be very difficult to pack—dolls and a variety of things you would never dream of seeing made in straw. Native art in the Bahamas does not, it must be admitted, provide many exciting collectors' pieces. There seems to be no traditional source of paintings, sculpture or similar culture. Mention must be made, however, of an Englishman called David Rawnsley who, in recent years, has started *The Chelsea Pottery* at the top of Parliament Street. The pottery is Nassau's art centre. Rawnsley, a well known artist in London, has encouraged and trained native Bahamians in painting, sculpture and ceramics, and already his students have produced much fine work. Go and browse through the exhibit rooms and look at the work on display.

Even a cursory glance along Bay Street will convince you that liquor is big business in Nassau. And no wonder, for gin that costs $5.20 in New York sells at $2.00 in Nassau; Scotch at $3.50 instead of $6.47. All the liquor stores on Bay Street, or thereabouts, and the shops in hotel foyers have the most dazzling display of drinks, and they are all good. Don't try to buy table wines in the Bahamas, however. The climate is not the best one for cellaring, and once removed from air conditioning they go to pieces very quickly. It's unlikely that you will ever get them home in drinkable condition. A charming introduction to the Bahamas, by the way, is the glass of Planter's Punch with which you are greeted at the airport. It is impossible to detail all the stores in Nassau, but here is a selection of some—there are many more and they are all entirely reputable.

THE NASSAU SHOP. It's Bay Street's biggest. You'll love their display of English menswear. Lovely woollens from Scotland, and almost everything in the clothing line. Also Swiss watches, including Piaget's ultra-thin automatic timepieces.

THE ISLAND SHOP, Bay Street. Has a wonderful collection of Irish linen clothes, cashmeres from Scotland, English shirts and calypso print dresses.

ENGLISH CHINA HOUSE, Bay Street. Royal Worcester, Doulton, Wedgewood, Spode, Crown Derby, Minton, Staffordshire-products with all these famous names are displayed for you to see. Great savings too—for instance a china set costing $57 in the U.S. will only set you back $33 here.

Other stores in the same line of business are *Treasure Traders Ltd., Kelly's Hardware Co., General*

BAHAMA ISLANDS

Hardware Co. and *John & George and Co.*

SOLOMON'S MINES, Bay Street. An astonishing collection of pipes, cigars, cigarettes, tobacco and everything the smoker needs from ashtrays to beer steins. Much fine china and a varied display of figurines. Copenhagen porcelain and Swedish and Waterford glass.

FRANCIS PEEK LTD., George Street. A wonderful collection of antiques shipped from England and Europe. Run by Sir Francis Peek, an English baronet, who's an expert collector and finds many splendid things from all over the world. Open winter only.

MADEMOISELLE, Bay Street and at leading hotels. Jaeger separates, Madras blouses and shorts, cottons and laces by well known continental designers, doeskin gloves from England, swimwear, evening wear, African prints. All this and lots more for you mademoiselle—or madam.

SUN 'N SEA. We saw a unique reminder to take home with you after a visit to Nassau here. It was a series of glass-like plastic items with examples of marine life set in them. Sea horses, lovely shells, and delicate seaweed caught for posterity in cigarette boxes, key rings, jewel boxes, lighter stands and lamps. Quite unusual and prices start from $1.00. Also available elsewhere in Nassau.

French perfume, like that other liquor you drink, is to be had in overwhelming profusion in Nassau. *Lightbourn's Perfumes, The City Pharmacy, Cole-Thompson Pharmacies, The Perfume Shop, The Nassau Shop, The Paris Shop* and *Vanité* have every perfume you have ever heard of—and several you haven't. Prices are low—a $25.85 bottle of Arpège costs you about $12.50. Do try some Bahamour. It's sold only in the Bahamas, is of top French quality, and makes an acceptable souvenir of a Nassau vacation. It comes as perfume or toilet water.

STEWARTS, Bay Street. Parisian swimwear and fashions.

MOSELEYS LTD. A selection of cameras to delight the professional and the amateur alike. Considerable savings over U.S. prices in almost every range. We were intrigued with the Minox Camera, the smallest one in our experience. Fits in the palm of the hand—ideal for spies, yet it has every modern refinement. You can carry it on your key ring.

The Camera Shop, John Bull, The International Camera Shop and *The Carib Shop* also sell cameras.

Time doesn't matter in the Bahamas, but you might like a good Swiss watch for when you get home. *The City Gift Shop, The Nassau Shop, John Bull, The Carib Shop* and *Treasure Traders* all sell them. Rolex, Mido, Zodiac, Piaget, Girard-Perregaux, every world famous name is represented at prices about one third lower than those in the U.S.

FRANÇOISE at Bay and George Streets. We saw many distinctive fabrics including some figure flattering Swiss designs.

BAHAMAS RECORDS LTD. Available at most gift shops are several recordings of local artists—a particularly nostalgic and unique reminder to take home with you. Most of the best local stars you will have heard at your hotel and during that night club crawl are on these discs. They make a very unusual present, too.

AMBROSINE, George Street. Has an unusual collection of Oriental brocades and rare silks. You are bound to admire the coats, dresses, robes, pajamas, shorts and shirts from Hong Kong. An unusual buy. Also cashmere sweaters with matching doeskin skirts from Vienna.

BAHAMA ISLANDS

CORAL REEF, Parliament Street. Here we did see some examples of locally made pottery. For example Bahamian pepper and salt shakers decorated with sea shells and pretty stones.

MAYFLOWER, Post Office Square. Pure Irish linens are a good buy in any British colony, and this shop specialises in table cloths, handkerchiefs and the like. Beautiful hand embroidery, and don't forget linen packs flat so it's not much trouble to take with you.

NATCHA'S, Bay Street. Has imported an expansive array of day and night time sandals from Fredelle of Italy. Straw and leather, low heeled and high, and much cheaper than back home.

THE LINEN SHOP on Parliament Street also stocks linen.

JOHNSON BROS, New Rawson Square. A truly Bahamian shop specialising in tortoise shell earrings, brooches, bangles, paper knives, all kinds of shell jewelry for men and women. If you walk upstairs you can see an enormous tank on the balcony full of great tortoises and turtles swimming lazily about.

CAPRICE, Charlotte Street. An arresting display of Irish fashions from Dublin. Dresses, blouses and skirts, in hand woven light weight wool.

THE WINDSOR SHOP, Parliament Street. Has soft wool stoles in lovely pastels from England.

Don't expect to bargain with the sales people in Nassau's stores as you can at the stalls in the native market place. The price marked on the merchandise is the price you will pay. It's usually lower than the U.S. anyway.

Stores are open from 9 a.m. to 5 p.m. except on Fridays when they close at noon. Some stay open until 9 p.m. on Saturday nights.

Most Nassau shops will mail goods to any part of the world. Liquor stores will deliver bottles (carefully packed) to hotel, ship or aeroplane.

SAILING

Some of the best sailing and Cruising in the world is found in the Bahamas.

Everything a cruising visitor wants to know about Bahamian waters is contained in the excellent *Yachtsman's Guide to the Bahamas* published by the Development Board. This 200 odd page book is a "must" for any sailor visiting the area.

The Development Board can also supply a detailed list of charter boats available for both cruising and fishing. Many of these boats and their captains can be contracted at the Nassau Yacht Haven.

The Circular Cruise

Perhaps the best way to introduce sailing in the Bahamas is to take you on an 1400 mile circular cruise of the Islands. First the visiting sailor should follow the rule of using the four C's effectively: charts, compass, communications and common sense. And don't forget the Yachtsman's Guide.

A suggested starting point is West Palm Beach, Fla., with West End, Grand Bahama, the first stop in Bahama waters.

BAHAMA ISLANDS

Then comes a run to Walker Cay, northernmost of these British Resort Islands, followed by a trip down through the island settlements of the Abacos.

The trip can be broken by a visit to Nassau, with Spanish Wells, Harbour Island and the communities of Hatchet Bay, Governor's Sound, and Rock Sound on Eleuthera next on the agenda. An exploration of the Exuma cays leading to George Town is also suggested.

Returning from the Exumas, another stop at Nassau is suggested and then the homeward portion of the voyage—first to Fresh Creek on Andros, then up to the Berry Islands for a leisurely survey and on across the Bahama Banks to Gun Cay, Cat Cay and Bimini before heading back to Miami.

This could be done in about 20 days if weather permits. Such a schedule, however, would permit only fleeting visits to the numerous island settlements well deserving more extensive exploration. It also calls for some running at night.

Once in the Bahamas at no point along the suggested route is the visiting yachtsman more than a day's run from Nassau and is always within 60 miles of supplies of gasoline, diesel fuel and provisions.

The numerous harbors and protected anchorages which sheltered pirate sloops, provided havens for blockade runners and offered hideaways for whiskey-laden motorboats in the prohibition era are still there, unchanged and unchanging, awaiting rediscovery by the crusing yachtsman.

For the islands to be visited along this route, U.S. Navy Hydrographic Office charts 944; 26 A, 26 B, 26 D and 26 E should be included. Sets of the detailed charts compiled by Harry Etheridge will make navigation and pilotage easier—these are available in Nassau and Miami.

Pinpoint accuracy in plotting courses in the Bahamas isn't absolutely essential. Most inter-island voyages are short ones, and seldom is the yachtsman out of sight of an identifiable shoreline or navigational beacon for more than an hour at a time.

Two radios are best to handle the communications situation properly—a ship to shore radio-telephone equipped with both the Nassau (2190) and Miami (2031.5) crystals and a reliable battery portable for standard broadcast.

Should an emergency arise, the radio-telephone can get the Bahamas Rescue Service or the Coast Guard into action within minutes, and the portable proves handy for checking weather reports and newscasts.

Common sense assumes the sailor follows Coast Guard requirements concerning life jackets, fire extinguishers, flares and signaling equipment, fresh water, food, and reserve supplies of fuel and motor oil.

A convenient starting point for a Bahamas circle cruise is West Palm Beach, springboard for the trip across the Gulf Stream to West End, Grand Bahama, one of 19 ports of entry for the Bahamas.

Most of the year, the crossing of the Gulf Stream is an effortless run of 53 nautical miles. When the wind swings to the northern quadrant, however, a big sea can build up fast and make the voyage both wet and uncomfortable. Common sense again comes into play, and a check of weather reports is advisable before departure.

The northward flow of the Gulf Stream varies from almost zero to nearly five knots, according to location and wind direction. Under most conditions, a two-knot average can be figured for navigational purposes. Heading for West End from the Lake Worth inlet near West Palm Beach, a 10-knot cruiser can make the trip in a shade over six hours on a corrected course of 110 degrees.

Fourth largest of the Bahama Islands, Grand Bahama has an area of 430 square miles and a population of only about 4,600.

Crossing the Gulf Stream

Perhaps the best time to cross the Gulf Stream is at night, timing departure to arrive at West End shortly after daybreak. It is usually cooler and the wind is not as strong as during the daytime. Not shown on the charts but one of the best navigational aids to yachtsmen approaching West End is a new radar tower at Bootle Point, about five miles southeast of West End. The top red light on the 420 foot tower is flashing and the other two, at 100 foot intervals, are steady. The lights can be picked up while the lights of West Palm Beach are still visible off the stern.

The Grand Bahama Hotel, a sprawling installation which is the Bahama's largest Out Island resort, has gas, diesel fuel, water and ice and 350 air-conditioned rooms for visitors who want accommodation ashore. It also has a gigantic swimming pool and an 18-hole championship golf course.

Newest facility at West End is the *Diamondhead Club*, which has more than five feet of water at its docks and can accommodate about 20 yachts. There are six guest rooms, bar, lounge, gift shop and liquor store and gas and fuel. The *West End Servicenter* (Esso) has gas, fuel, water, ice and mechanics who can handle minor repairs. *Hope Bight Lodge* offers good food and accommodation ashore.

From West End, it is a run of about 48 miles to Walker Cay, northernmost of the Bahamas at the tip of the Abaco chain, on a course of 53 degrees. With 10-15 feet of water over most of this route, it can be travelled easily after dark, but the approach to Walker Cay should be done in daylight, following the white paths cleared through the dark grass by propellers.

Walker Cay also has a 250-foot radio mast, which may be picked up easily halfway from West End. *The Walker Cay Club* dock is protected by a stone breakwater on the ocean side, and has space for six or seven 50-foot boats in addition to cruisers maintained by the club. The club has gasoline, diesel fuel and 110 volt electricity at the dock and cubed and crushed ice from purified rain water. Ashore, accommodation includes 16 double rooms with showers and a swimming pool.

It is about a 70 mile run southeast to Green Turtle Cay, the next major settlement in the Abacos, but along the way are numerous interesting islands and harbors.

Because of the numerous islands, cays and occasional rocks which dot the area, night running is not recommended without a knowledgeable local guide.

Only about six miles from Walker Cay are Grand Cays, which has the first central international port facility to accommodate boats and amphibious planes in the northern Bahama Islands. The new installation includes an official port of entry, a fuel station and a newly built government dock which accommodates vessels of six foot draft at low mean tide.

Fishing enthusiasts find their sport varied and exciting at Carter Cays, another 20 miles to the ESE. There is a shallow white sand bank near the harbor entrance, which should be passed to the SE. Carter Cays also have a 250-foot radio mast, which can be easily distinguished up to 20 miles away at night, three miles in the daytime. There's a strong tide in the main channel, which has 20 or more feet of water, but near the settlement on the SE shore there's fine anchorage in 5-15 feet.

Another 250-foot radio mast with fixed red lights marks Allan's Cay (also called Pensacola Cay, since the two were separate cays until joined by a hurricane some years ago) which is about 21 miles from Carter Cays. Though lacking facilities, this is an excellent harbor with 7-9 feet of water.

Both the Carter Cays and Allan's Cay radio installations

have plenty of white light at ground level.

Next major stop is the settlement of New Plymouth at Green Turtle Cay, about 25 miles on down the Abacos from Allan's Cay.

Shore accommodation, provisions, gas, diesel fuel, water and ice may be obtained at New Plymouth.

Green Turtle Cay has three fine harbors which offer excellent shelter and deep water—each capable of handling yachts up to six feet. The principal harbor at Settlement Creek has a recently constructed new entrance.

The curving approach is indicated by markers to be kept to starboard coming in. The markers have reflectors for night navigation and the outside marker has a flashing red light which is visible four miles away. The channel is 40 feet wide and a deep turning basin, its edges clearly discernible, enables yachts drawing a shade over 4 feet to anchor little more than a dinghy-length from the docks.

Under consideration is a plan to blast a channel through from Settlement Creek to Black Sound, a perfect anchorage with up to 15 feet of water. The present entrance is marked with small stakes and requires some caution although boats drawing 7 feet can make it at high water.

White Sound, only a couple of hundred yards farther north, can handle yachts up to 6½ feet at high water and also offers good shelter in water up to 15 feet.

Green Turtle Cay has several excellent beaches. Supplies and provisions may be obtained at several well stocked stores. Gas, water and diesel fuel are available.

Accommodation is available at the *New Plymouth Inn, Bluff House Club,* and other cottages. There is more than 7 feet of water at the Government Dock, but better protection is offered at docks up Settlement Creek which have about 5 feet.

Three Good Harbors

Another 20-odd miles farther brings three of the most interesting settlements in the Bahamas, located within five miles of one another. Man of War Cay, Hope Town and Marsh Harbor all have excellent harbors, good holding ground and fine facilities but the three communities are considerably different.

Running down from Green Turtle Cay, Man of War Cay is the first target. Its double harbor, branching at right angles from the channel entrance, is one of the best in the Bahamas and offers excellent shelter even during hurricane weather.

A living relic of the Spanish Renaissance, Trinidad, Cuba preserves the charm of an older day while monolithic ultra-modern apartments proclaim the 20th century in Havana.

Variety is the spice of Jamaica's tourist menu whether you're rafting
with a native boatman on the swirling Rio Grande or strolling
through the botanical wonderland of Kingston's Hope Gardens.

The entrance is straight in, marked by a five-mile flashing white light at the eastern end of Dickie's Cay, and has a shade less than five feet of water at low tide. Care should be taken not to come in too fast, for a right angle turn is required and the water shallows off fast if you overrun the channel.

The settlement of Man of War Cay includes numerous American citizens who have built homes there and lies up the western channel which has 6-9 feet of water in the anchorage and six feet at the Government Dock.

The Eastern harbor at Man of War has fewer houses nearby but deeper water—12 to 15 feet—and the protection is better should the weather turn bad. Supplies, some gas and fuel, and fresh vegetables may be obtained there but the yacht needing provisions might better wait until reaching Marsh Harbour, on the mainland of Great Abaco only five miles away.

The passage is an easy one in deep water on a course of 240 degrees but approaching Marsh Harbour the point should be given about 250 yards clearance. Keep about 75 yards off the cays and NW shore until about opposite the town dock. The harbor has 6-9 feet with over 5 feet at the several docks.

A marina at Marsh Harbour can haul boats up to 150 feet and has a machine shop for both gas and diesel repairs. Gas, diesel, oil, water and ice may be obtained, but on Sundays and holidays the 110 v. generator is shut down until dusk. Current plans call for extending the Government dock 50 feet and adding electricity. The new *Great Abaco Club* here has 22 rooms and overlooks a beautiful white sand beach. Here also is the new *Treasure Cay Club* with 40 comfortable rooms and a sheltered marina for boats up to ten feet draft.

Provisions and a fairly complete line of marine necessities may be found in the settlement. A new restaurant has a varied menu and if given advance notice can handle groups of yachtsmen. A new laundry, in the other half of the same building, offers laundry and dry cleaning in one day on special service.

Hope Town, with its candy-striped lighthouse a beckoning finger to yachtsmen, is the next stop. This is another fine harbor offering protection even in heavy weather, with nearly 20 feet of water and good holding ground. The channel will handle boats up to 7 feet with little trouble. Approaching on a course of 135 degrees, the channel is easily discernible. White sand left by dredging should be left to starboard and in the harbor entrance the deepest water is on the side toward the lighthouse.

There are two mangrove-bordered creeks south of the harbor

proper and the western creek is a fine anchorage for boats drawing up to six feet.

Hope Town also has a plenty of provisions and facilities, with 7 feet of water at the Government dock. Gas, diesel fuel and kerosene plus bread, fresh fruits and vegetables may be obtained, and the fishing nearby is excellent. Accommodations here include the 20-room *Elbow Cay Club,* the 8-room *Hope Town Harbor Lodge,* the 10-room *White Sound Club,* and the *Coral Cottage.*

Running from Hope Town to Little Harbour poses no problems although the yachtsman down to his last bottle of scotch might well be sure it's secured. The swell runs unchecked in from the ocean between islands and can produce periods of fancy rolling with little warning.

Approaching from the north, the entrance to Little Harbour is a bit hard to find. It's hard to distinguish between the reef and beach which shelters the eastern side of the entrance and Tom Curry's Point, which forms the other side. The gap in the ocean reef is both wide and deep—16 feet plus at LW—but shouldn't be attempted when there is a rage.

The entrance has been marked by stakes, but they can be a bit confusing and can appear like markers warning of a shallow spot because the bottom in that section is sandy and bright.

The proper approach is between the stakes, following them around in almost a semicircle.

Beware the Boilers

Six miles south of Little Harbour is the fishing settlement of Cherokee Sound. Heading there, the yachtsman should stand about a mile offshore to avoid the Boilers, a heavy-breaking reef a little more than a mile south of the Little Harbour Light. Cherokee has about 6 feet of water but, aside from a supply of stores, has few facilities for yachtsmen.

From Cherokee, skippers should stand about a mile offshore the balance of the 28 miles to Hole in The Wall on the southern tip of Great Abaco for the shore is rocky, steep, and devoid of any shelter. At Hole in The Wall, shelter from winds from the northern quadrant may be found in 9-12 feet, but it's not a good spot to be in when the breezes shift to the south.

Great and Little Abaco and the numerous islands which fringe both the eastern and western coasts offer excellent cruising areas. In addition to fishing and turtling, the residents conduct lumbering operations and grow fruits and vegetables.

By this time, the cruising yachtsman may be pining for the bright lights, of Nassau. If so, he can break the "circle cruise" by heading for the Bahamas capital. It's a run of 49 miles across the deep ink-blue waters of the Northeast Providence Channel on a course of 190 degrees from Hole in The Wall.

Next objectives are Spanish Wells and Harbour Island, two island settlements nestling just off the northern tip of Eleuthera about 50 miles to the north and east of Nassau.

Yachtsmen may leave Nassau Harbour by either exit, heading up just north of Rose Island and the cays which dot the passage toward Spanish Wells, northernmost of the Bahamas' eastern islands. It is safer to continue in deep water and travel the pass which lies between Great and Little Egg Islands.

The approach to Spanish Wells is well marked and poses no problems. Supplies of all types may be obtained there.

Spanish Wells harbor is long, narrow and usually crowded. The concrete Government dock is about 600 feet long but lacks fenders or pilings which would make it more attractive as a place for yachtsmen to dock. Diesel fuel, gas, parts and frozen foods may be purchased and accommodation ashore is available at the *St. George's Hotel.*

On the trip to Dunmore Town, Harbour Island, peace of mind is worth the price of a reliable native guide to handle your craft on the inside passageway. It's possible to go around the outside in deep water, standing well off the reefs, but this can be pretty rugged going with a swell and onshore winds.

The entrance to Harbour Island channel is marked only on the north side and hard to see on a northern approach until you're almost past. The bar can be in pretty ill humor without being raging. There is a stake SW of the entrance which should be approached, left to starboard, and then head for the Eleuthera mainland. About 300 yards out, swing right for the settlement at Dunmore Town with about six feet of water. An eye should be kept out for the occasional shallow spot.

The Government dock at Dunmore Town is spacious, with more than 6 feet of water at the end. It has electricity, water, and fuel may be obtained.

If you're heading back for Spanish Wells and want to save the price of a pilot and yet avoid pilotage problems, time your departure with that of the mail boat from Dunmore Town. It draws more than 6 feet and most cruisers are safe if they stick close to its wake.

Harbour Island, with a population of about 2,000, is a resort popular with Bahamians as well as foreign visitors. Accommodation is varied and includes the *Pink Sands Lodge, Picaroon Cove Club, Sunset Inn, Little Boarding House* and *Up Yonder*. Its beach of fine pink sand on the ocean side is one of the sights which shouldn't be missed.

THE ELEUTHERA COAST

Continuing south from Spanish Wells to explore the 100-mile long, pencil-thin island of Eleuthera, time and distance can be saved by utilizing Current Cut, which separates Eleuthera from Current Island.

Leaving Spanish Wells, the channel rounding the eastern end of Charles Island, which forms the south border of the harbor, is well marked and there is at least 7 feet of water all the way. Arrow-topped stakes indicate the channel more than half way, then continue west to the end of Charles Island before swinging southwest on a course which will clear the north end of Meek's Patch by about a half mile. Running two miles SW will carry you to the south end of Meek's Patch, where it's a straight run south of 6½ miles to the entrance to Current Cut.

Unless a boat has adequate power, capable of at least ten knots, it is best to wait for slack tide before attempting to buck the tidal flow at Current Cut, for it whisks through at up to 7 miles an hour and can turn up a tricky chop off the entrance. There is plenty of water, however.

There are some sand bars SE of Current Cut, but they're plainly visible and can be avoided with little trouble. Once clear, yachts may head direct for Harchet Bay on a course of 105 degrees.

The entrance to Hatchet Bay, which was blasted through the limestone cliffs, isn't easy to spot until almost south of the passage, which is only 90 feet wide. There's a flashing white eight-mile light just west of the entrance and the flashing red range lights located on buildings across the harbor, line up on an approach course of 22 degrees.

The harbor is spacious, deep and virtually landlocked, making it an ideal shelter in any kind of weather. There's 16 feet in the entrance channel and up to 30 feet inside, with numerous good anchorages.

The Harrisville Company, which operates the dairy and poultry farm at Hatchet Bay, has installed a huge dock with a minimum of 9 feet of water.

Gas, diesel fuel, and water are available and the Harrisville Company will lend a mechanic to effect emergency repairs.

Fresh eggs, milk and chickens are available here, but the company store stocks virtually anything needed including liquor and ice. Limited accommodations ashore are now available.

Easing down the Eleuthera coast to Governor's Harbour, a run of 16 miles to the SE, the trip can be broken by investigating several interesting bays and inviting beaches. Deep water runs in close to shore, so the voyage poses no problems. Midway between Hatchet Bay and Governor's Harbour is a landing strip and U.S. military installation which has a rash of radio and radar masts and outdoor lights. These can be picked up more than 15 miles away and aren't shown on the charts.

Governor's Harbour, though lacking in facilities for yachtsmen, is well worth a visit. The settlement is more than 300 years old and once was the capital of the Bahamas.

The harbor has been dredged recently and six feet of water may be found in close to shore on a clear, sandy bottom. Gas, diesel fuel, water and all kinds of goods may be obtained ashore but have to be ferried out.

Ashore, a wide range of accommodation is available. They range from *French Leave*, with 50 rooms facing the ocean, to modest boarding houses. *Belmont, Buena Vista* and *Buccaneer Club* are other spots for the yachtsman who wants to spend a night ashore.

From Governor's Harbour to Tarpum Bay is about 12 miles, again in deep water which runs in close to shore without danger of reefs or shoals. There is a dock at Tarpum Bay but not any shorefront facilities for yachts. The anchorage is good holding and usually quiet in prevailing winds. Tarpum Bay is a tranquil community, with several tall stone buildings scattered along the hillside overlooking the harbor, and cottages for shore stays.

Continuing on the route to Rock Sound, another nine miles, head out from Tarpum Bay on 205 degrees to pass the light beacon to the westward. This will eliminate having to keep a lookout for shoals and coral patches. From the beacon, steer direct for Poison Point (152 degrees) which forms the southern side of the entrance to Rock Sound, running to within a half mile before heading directly east. This course carries 10-18 feet and avoids the sand bars stretching out from Sound Point.

After passing the three rocks off Starve Creek, watch for

them to line up and then head for the settlement on 30 degrees. In addition to the Government Dock at Rock Sound, there is a stone dock owned by the *Three Bays Company* and a yacht dock maintained by the *Rock Sound Club* which has 110 volt electricity, water, gas and diesel fuel. There is 6-8 feet of water off each.

If the yachtsman intends to cruise the Exuma Cays before heading back to Nassau, Rock Sound is a good spot to take inventory and add whatever supplies will be needed. *The Rock Sound Grocery,* handy to the dock, carries the best supply of provisions including prime Angus beef raised nearby on an experimental farm. Marine equipment and fishing gear is available at the *Rock Sound Hardware,* which can also hustle up mechanics if repairs are needed.

The Rock Sound Club, with accommodation for 100 guests, makes a pleasant overnight stop. It has a bar, lounge, large swimming pool, tennis courts, and other entertainment.

Leaving Rock Sound, head on 295 degrees 4½ miles from Sound Point to pick up Davis Buoy. Pass north of Davis Buoy, then swing to 250 degrees to head down to Powell Point. Along the way, which carries 8-15 feet, there are several dark grassy patches, and eyes should be kept peeled for a couple of rocky spots.

The 250-degree course will bring the yachtsman into the mile-deep waters of Exuma Sound for the 26-mile run across to Highborne Cut, just to the north of Highborne Cay, one of the gateways to the Exumas. Highborne Cay is easily identified, having three conspicuous hills discernible several miles distant. Rounding the northern tip about a quarter-mile off, there is at least 12 feet. Some low, flat rocks should be given 200 yards clearance to the south. Continue SW to give Highborne about 2 miles clearance before heading on south.

Cruising the Exumas

The Exumas stretch for nearly 100 miles and offer excellent cruising grounds. There are many beautiful beaches, fine harbors with good protection, and unmatched fishing. Settlements are few and rather primitive with no modern facilities, so yachts should be virtually self sustaining for the period they plan to spend in the Exumas.

Fine help for the helmsman is a set of charts of the Exumas, by Morton Turtle, available at *Nassau Yacht Haven.* They cover the area accurately and indicate the best routes for craft drawing as little as three feet.

BAHAMA ISLANDS

No attempt will be made here to detail all of the Exuma Cays. Pilotage is easy, and as a general rule, standing two miles west of any of the islands in the chain will keep yachts in 9-15 feet of water.

Safe navigation into harbors can be done by eye, not only in the Exumas but throughout the Bahamas. Judging the depth of water by the color is a reliable method—that and a good lookout and caution on the throttles. In the deeps of the Exuma Sound the water will be a deep, almost ink blue. On the edge of the bank it changes to a bright intense blue in about 10-15 fathoms.

With sand or marl bottom, the blue fades to a deep green in 25-35 feet of water, to a pale green in 10-20 feet, and a bright, almost colorless green in 6 feet or less. If the water is noticeably green and you draw less than 6 feet, there's plenty of depth.

Over rocky bottom, the bright blue of 10-15 fathoms becomes a dark green and in shallower water over grass or rocks the lighter green takes on a brownish hue. Coral heads in grassy areas usually are surrounded by a ring of white sand and should be avoided.

The Staniel Cay Yacht Club, at Staniel (or Stanyard) Cay, is about 43 miles south of Highborne Cay and is the only place at which gasoline, diesel fuel, water and supplies may be obtained between Nassau and George Town, Great Exuma. Located roughly halfway between the two, it's a "must" stop for most yachts cruising the Exumas.

Along the way to Staniel, cays with such interesting names as Oyster, Lobster, Saddle, Wax, Shroud, Hawksbill, and Cistern slide by, each with an appeal of its own.

Harvey Cay, just west of Staniel, has a six-mile flashing white light. Approach Staniel on 110 degrees, bearing on the white building with red roof on the point at the south end of the settlement. The channel, with 12-18 feet, will be picked up about a half mile offshore. *The Staniel Cay Yacht Club* has space for several yachts drawing up to 6½ feet, a bar, lounge and accommodation ashore.

Another 25 miles, down past Great Guana Cay, finds the yachtsman near Galliot Cut, perhaps the best spot to venture back into the waters of Exuma Sound for the balance of the trip to George Town. The Galliot Cut channel may be picked up about a mile W and SW of Little Farmer's Cay and has 9-12 feet. There's 15-20 feet inside Galliot Island and several excellent anchorages. The cut is straight, but the tide is very strong.

It is 35 miles to George Town, almost all in deep water. Approaching the harbor, steer about midway between Channel Cay on the inside and Conch Cay outside, favoring the latter. There is a bar, marked by a stake which should be kept to starboard. Steer for Simmons Point until it's about 200 yards away, then head for the beacon on Stocking Island. The deep channel runs close to the island with 16 feet. When the entrance to Stocking Island harbor comes abeam you may alter course and head direct for George Town.

The settlement, located on the Tropic of Cancer, plays host to the native skippers of the Bahamas and visiting yachtsmen from many nations each spring when the Out Island Regatta is conducted in George Town's harbor.

At the Government Dock there is 8 feet and craft drawing more than 4 feet may tie up at the *Peace and Plenty Inn,* where comfortable overnight accommodation may be obtained. Gas, diesel fuel, and water may be purchased in George Town or at the *Stocking Island Club,* which has a fine sheltered harbor and 7 feet at the dock. Groceries and liquor can be bought in town and a mechanic is available for minor repairs.

The return trip to Nassau can be as leisurely and as interesting as the trip down. Coming back to Nassau from Highborne Cay offers no problems, although the yachtsman may want to continue north and see the few cays missed earlier.

This time the approach to Nassau will be through the eastern entrance to the harbor, about 32 miles across the Yellow Banks. There's plenty of water, but it is advisable to keep a lookout for the occasional shallow spot. The course is 295 degrees for 20 miles, then 354 degrees for the final 12 miles.

Return Trip

After another break in Nassau to refuel and add provisions, the homeward portion of the cruise completes the circle trip. First step can be a run of 60 miles directly north to pick up the western shore of Abaco. There are numerous cays offshore worthy of exploration and good harbors and anchorages will be found on the mainland of Great Abaco.

It's an area where you may sail for days and sight only an occasional native fishing boat, so it's well to have the yacht well supplied again before leaving Nassau. Using the same navigational methods employed in the Exumas, boats drawing up to 6 feet will have no trouble.

BAHAMA ISLANDS

Sole spot where supplies and provisions may be obtained is the *Sandy Point Fishing Camp*, which has gas and diesel fuel, water and 110 volt electricity, plus a bar and restaurant and accommodation for overnight visitors. There are several small stores in the settlement where additional provisions may be obtained.

The Government Dock at Sandy Point is rather exposed and yachtsmen planning an overnight stay might better tie up at the Fishing Camp dock just around the point or anchor up the harbor in the channel, which can handle boats up to 6 feet. There are reefs and shoal water lying off the western coast of Abaco in this vicinity and some caution is advised on the approach.

Heading back, altering course to the SW will open up the Berry Islands for exploration. This chain of more than 30 large cays flanks the eastern edge of the Great Bahama Bank and offers many good harbors. There is plenty of water to within a couple of hundred yards of any of the islands along their eastern edge.

Worthy of a visit is the *Berry Island Club*, on Frazer's Hog Cay. The approach from the SE point of the island is well marked and has 9 feet at low water. In addition to fuel and water, the club has electricity on the dock and there is a bar and restaurant, plus accommodation ashore which ranges up to four-bedroom furnished homes. Fishing is excellent throughout the area. It is convenient to Nassau and on course for craft coming from Miami.

Before returning to Florida, a visit to Andros Island should be included. Fresh Creek, with its *Lighthouse Club* having accommodation for 100 guests, is the showplace of this island which is the largest in the Bahamas. It is a run of a shade less than 50 miles from Frazer's Hog Cay on a course of 185 degrees.

With a minimum of 7 feet in the entrance channel, the approach to Fresh Creek is an easy one. The Outer marker is a flashing white light on a steel light tower about a mile off shore and located at the southernmost tip of several rocky cays. Keep this beacon to starboard and stay between the can buoys the rest of the way in, favoring the north side at the entrance to Fresh Creek. There is 12-16 feet in the harbor and boats drawing 8 feet may tie up at the *Andros Yacht Club* docks, which is part of the Lighthouse Club operation. The tide can be very strong.

Gas, diesel, water and 110 volt electricity are available at the AYC dock and fuel is also available at Coakley Town, the native settlement on the northern bank of Fresh Creek.

The next homeward leg confronts the yachtsman with the longest run of the cruise so far—about 130 miles from Fresh Creek up the coast of Andros and on the Northwest Channel Light, across the Bahama Banks and up to Bimini.

The reef along Andros' eastern shore is second only to Australia's Great Barrier Reef. A northbound yacht drawing up to 5 feet can poke along inside the reef if leisurely exploration of the coast is desired, but a lookout should be kept on the bow or wheelhouse.

It is considerably easier to stand out about five miles from the Fresh Creek outside buoy, then set a course direct for NW Channel Light on 335 degrees. An automatic pilot can take a lot of strain out of running on these long stretches when no sharp lookout is needed. For calculating running time, it is about 50 miles from Fresh Creek to NW Channel Light.

Passing NW Channel Light with its open frame tower on port, head directly west for 47 miles to pick up Sylvia Buoy. The water on the banks is about 12 feet deep, so no problems are encountered. From Sylvia Buoy, it is about 17 miles to Gun Cay on 292 degrees and another nine miles up to Bimini.

Bimini merits its status as a mecca for fishermen and has fine facilities for visitors. *Brown's Dock, Weech's Dock* and the *Bimini Marina* are the favored spots for yachtsmen to tie up, although there is considerably more dock space and a number of fine protected anchorages in case of a blow. Gas, diesel fuel, water and electricity are available and supplies of all kinds may be obtained.

Accommodation ashore may be had at the new *Bimini Gateway Hotel*, at night a brilliantly-illuminated landmark on the southern tip of North Bimini, at *Anchors Aweigh, Bimini Big Game Fishing Club, Brown's Hotel, The Compleat Angler* or the *Seacrest Hotel*. The newest guest facility is the attractive *Sunshine Inn*, with 40 air-conditioned rooms, a dining room and swimming pool. It is located in South Bimini.

Entering Bimini Harbor, the yachtsman should head for South Bimini's range lights or several isolated coconut palms a bit further south. The channel runs roughly parallel to shore and only about 300 yards out. It is close enough inshore so the docks on North Bimini's eastern shore may be seen.

Heading for Miami, a run of 46 miles, the corrected course is 254 degrees to complete the Bahamas circle cruise.

BAHAMA ISLANDS

FISHING

The Development Board also publishes a comprehensive Fisherman's Guide to the Bahamas. In addition the board maintains a Fishing Information Bureau which will provide full details of facilities and fishing spots. Address it c/o P.O. Box 818, Nassau, Bahamas.

It makes no difference what time of the year the angler chooses to take a vacation, every month is a fishing month in the Bahamas.

There is no better way to enjoy the wide variety of fish and fishing provided by this island area than to cruise the Out Islands aboard a charter boat, living on the craft throughout the trip.

Troll over a fresh section of ocean, fish a new reef or work a different bonefish flat every day. When night approaches the skipper will head for a sheltered anchorage in some sandy cove or picturesque harbour of an uninhabited cay.

When the party wants a break in the daily routine there are curving sandy beaches to be explored and afterwards there will be swimming in the crystal clear water while the crew spreads a picnic lunch under shady palms.

The fishing in these areas is so varied that no two days need be alike. Over the reefs are amberjack, grouper, mutton snapper, mackerel, jacks, yellowtail and the ubiquitous barracuda waiting to take a trolled bait, a drifted live bait or any of the many artificial lures cast with plug, fly, or spin-tackle.

Along the "drop-offs" and farther out in the deep water are wahoo, kingfish, dolphin, bonito, blackfin tuna and Allison tuna in their respective seasons. And there is always the even chance of raising a marlin, sailfish or mako.

On the flats are bonefish; up winding creeks in the deep holes of creek or bay or under overhanging ledges of mangrove cays there are wily grey snapper, all to be caught on light tackle and natural or artificial lures.

There are fish for every kind of salt water trolling gear from 3 to 39-thread line and for the three forms of casting—plug, fly and spinning.

Charter rates are reasonable and expenses low when a party of four divides the cost of a charter boat for an Out Island cruise of a week, ten days or a fortnight, living and eating aboard the boat.

In single-engine boats of 36 to 40 feet the cost for a week's cruising and fishing, including food and fuel, will range from $18.00 to $22.00 per day per person.

The cost of twin-engined boats of 40 to 60 feet will run higher, averaging between $25.00 to $28.00 per day per person for a week's trip.

For the casual angler who prefers to live ashore and go fishing when the spirit moves him, there is excellent accommodation on several islands in the Bahamas. All can be easily reached from Florida or Nassau by boat or plane.

The western edges of the Great and the Little Bahama Banks provide a chain of fine fishing spots not far from Florida's lower east coast. These are Bimini and Cat Cay, approximately 50 miles across the Gulf Stream from Miami, West End, Grand Bahama, 60 miles from Palm Beach, and Walker's Cay, Abaco, 100 miles east of Stuart, Florida.

Bimini and Cat Cay, nine miles to the south, are known the world over for the size and variety of their game fish.

Some of these fish, such as bonefish, barracuda, grouper, snapper, permit and tarpon, are present the year around. Others—amberjack, bonito, dolphin, both species of marlin, bluefin tuna, mako, sailfish and wahoo—are seasonal.

At West End, the *Grand Bahama Club* has put the Gulf Stream end of the island of Grand Bahama back on the angling map. This area is a happy hunting ground for light tackle enthusiasts and has the same kind of fish and fishing as in the Bimini-Cat Cay area.

Walker's Cay, in the Abaco chain, is the northernmost of the inhabited islands of the Bahamas and is a port of entry for yachts and commercial craft clearing for the northern Bahamas from the port of West Palm Beach, Florida.

It is best known for blue marlin, dolphin, kingfish, sailfish, wahoo and white marlin. World record catches of kingfish, sailfish and wahoo have been registered from here. Both the reef fishing and bonefishing are fine.

Bimini, Cat Cay and West End can be reached from Miami and from Fort Lauderdale and West Palm Beach by scheduled flights.

Walker's Cay—as well as Bimini, Cat Cay and West End—also can be reached by chartering amphibious planes based at Miami, Fort Lauderdale and West Palm Beach.

Nassau has fine ocean fishing in the Northeast Providence Channel to the north and the Tongue of the Ocean to the west. It has a charter fleet that compares with any in the world.

Across the Tongue of the Ocean to the west of Nassau is Andros Island, the largest island in the Bahamas.

The Lighthouse Club offers bonefishing on adjacent flats,

casting for tarpon in the creek and deep water fishing for all the pelagic species of salt water gamesters common to the Bahamas.

To the north of Nassau is the Island of Great Abaco with its string of cays along the Atlantic ocean offshore from the mainland. The two cays that now offer accommodation for anglers are Elbow Cay, 90 miles north of Nassau and Green Turtle Cay, 110 miles from the capital city.

Fifty-six miles north of Nassau on the lower west coast of Great Abaco a new fishing territory has been thrown wide open to anglers through the *Sandy Point Fishing Club* at Sandy Point. There is fine reef fishing, practically virgin deep water fishing and numerous bonefish flats within a few minutes of the camp.

To the east of Nassau at distances varying from 50 to 70 miles is the 90-mile-long island of Eleuthera and two smaller islands—Harbour Island and Spanish Wells. They lie off the northern end of Eleuthera and offer bonefishing on the flats, deep water trolling in the Atlantic ocean and fine reef fishing along the southern edge of the Northeast Providence Channel.

Briny Monsters of the Bahamas

The fish you will meet in the Bahamas include:

Blue Marlin—generally found well off shore. He likes solitude and plenty of room. Once hooked the marlin is an awe-inspiring sight, throwing its broad-shouldered body clear of the water and crashing back in a welter of spray. Trolling is the accepted method of angling with a whole fish—usually bonefish—as bait. Tackle ranges from 9 to 39-thread outfits. "Blues" are sighted throughout the year but the summer months find them in their greatest numbers. The world record stands at 742 pounds.

Bluefin Tuna—a mammoth member of the mackerel family. Lean and hungry it is the star attraction in the Bahamas during May and early June, when it passes Cat Cay and Bimini on its annual trip to the herring ground northwards. Tuna travel in schools numbering from four to forty. The strike of a bluefin tuna is a tremendous spectacle and it puts up a dogged battle. Tuna fishing is arduous and the game is rough on boat, tackle, crew and angler.

White Marlin and *Sailfish* can be treated together. Both are found in same water, take the same kind of baits and have similar tricks. They are present in Bahamian waters all the year round—in considerable numbers from January to April.

When hooked they take to the air in a series of twisting leaps and also indulge in a little "tail walking". The method of angling is similar to that for blue marlin.

Wahoo—a beautiful fish with vivid colouring which, alas, fades almost as soon as you get him out of the water. The wahoo is among the best marine game fish, and in the Bahamas, December, January and February are the best months to hunt it. It has two outstanding characteristics—a strike like a sledge hammer and sizzling speed. The world record wahoo of 133½ pounds was caught off Nassau and nine other records are credited to Bahamian waters. The wahoo performs best on high tackle, 6 to 9-thread line being adequate for old hands, 12 to 15-thread for beginners.

The *Dolphin* with it blue, green, and bronze flecked body is the most brilliant fish of them all. It is an active, voracious fish that travels in schools which are always on the move. It has incredible eyesight and can spot its prey at enormous distances. When hunting it takes to the air in long, graceful leaps. When a dolphin is hooked it stages an acrobatic display which calls for skill and good tackle. Dolphin are curious, and will follow a hooked member of the school right up to the boat, and several dolphin may be taken out of one school. Many have been taken on spinning tackle, plug casting gear and fly tackle under these conditions. Many record dolphins have been taken in the Bahamas.

Kingfish—a fine food fish with excellent game qualities. It is a member of the mackerel family and is a worthy opponent when taken on light tackle. They are met in the deep ocean, along the "drop offs" or in on the reefs. Trolling slowly over reefs, or drifting live bait across the grounds are usual methods of angling. Spoons, feathers or cut baits near the bottom work well. Spinning tackle or plug casting gear can also be used. Kingfish go over 70 pounds, but the average is nearer 20 pounds.

Ocean Bonito and *Blackfin Tuna* invade the Bahamas from May to September. Both species charge headlong into shoals of smaller fish gulping their prey by the mouthful and leaving bits and pieces of the victims scattered on the water. Flocks of sea birds feed on these remains and their diving and skimming is the telltale sign that boatmen look for when seeking these large members of the mackerel family.

Allison Tuna come and go in Bahamian water with no definite rhyme or reason. They have been caught in January, March, June and August. There is always a chance that some may be lurking below or on the flanks of a school of bonito or tuna. Average weight of an Allison is about 30 pounds but they go up to 150 pounds.

Barracuda—the tiger of the sea with its rows of teeth and a mania for murder. It is an all round game fish, abounding in all Bahamian waters and taking live baits of any kind or almost any kind of artificial lure. They come in all sizes—the world record is 103¼ pounds caught off Grand Bahama.

Amberjack—is found from December to April around wrecks or where the sea fans wave in tidal currents among irregular rocks on a sandy bottom. The amberjack is tireless with a good turn of speed. When hooked it heads for the bottom and zig zags among the rocks—usually followed by other members of the school. Live bait is best but artificial lures will also attract the smaller fish.

Bonefish—a doughty little fellow with a strong following of anglers. A bottom grubber, it frequents shallow flats, and can be taken with conch, crab, shrimp, crawfish and sometimes artificial lures.

Permit is a comparatively new star in the game fish firmament. It is a slab-sided powerful fish and is usually found over flats or reefs feeding on the bottom. It is one of the strongest fish for its size in the Bahamas.

Tarpon—are present in small schools in many parts of the Bahamas. Mostly, they are found in harbours and deep creeks. 60 to 70 pounders have been caught and reports of fish in excess of 100 pounds have come from the Out Islands. Average weight is about 30 pounds. Feeding grounds and habits of tarpon vary in different localities and local advice on these is usually required. Fly rod, plug casting or spinning gear may be used.

Reef fishing differs considerably from deep water angling and offers a pleasing change of pace. For the larger varieties of reef fish, such as *snappers* and *groupers* it is usual to troll slowly with a 24 thread linen line which is carried close to the bottom by a heavy, specially shaped sinker. A whole fish or a large strip is used for bait. Snapper up to 20 pounds and grouper up to 75 pounds are caught in this fashion.

EXPLORING THE BAHAMAS

New Providence

Although only 21 miles long and seven miles wide, New Providence is the most important island in the Bahamas group because it contains the capital city of Nassau. It was named after William III of England who had been Prince of Orange Nassau before occupying the throne.

If, like the majority of Bahamas visitors, your vacation starts at Nassau, you will either reach New Providence Island by sea at Prince George wharf or by air at Windsor airport—the most modern airfield in the Bahamas.

Your first impression of the Bahamas will be one of flower scented breezes. Bahamian flowers are gay—purple and red bougainvillaea; yellow and red hibiscus; pink, white and red oleander and royal purple passion flower—their mingling perfumes give a subtle fragrance to the southeast trade winds.

Next you will notice the characteristic architecture. Bahamian houses all have a traditional look. The old ones were built of the island limestone and have upper porches that hang out over the street. To protect the home from the sun, wide verandahs were built in graceful wooden construction and louvers were used to permit cooling breezes to enter. Georgian and Federal styles are the keynotes of Bahamians architecture. The best way to see them is just to stroll around Nassau's charming streets or go leisurely in a surrey.

Nassau is grouped around Bay Street—the bustling shopping centre of the Island. Focal point of Bay street is Rawson Square in which are located the Government administrative and legislative buildings. The House of Assembly is here too, and the Supreme Court. If the House is in session you can attend its sitting when it meets with all the pomp and tradition of the Mother of Parliaments. Admission can also be gained to the Law Courts where the highest standards of British justice prevail. At the back of the Post Office, with its statue of Queen Victoria, is a fine garden containing the Public Library and museum. This octagonal building dates back to 1799 and was originally built as a gaol.

There are three old forts well worth seeing in and around Nassau. The largest is Fort Charlotte. Named after the wife of King George III, it was built in about 1790. Despite the fact that it mounted some 42 guns, plus a battery on the water front, it has to be reported that the fort never repulsed an invader nor fired a shot in anger. It was built by Lord Dunmore, last Royal Governor of New York and Virginia. It has many grim dungeons and underground chambers and cheerful Bahamian guides who will show you round.

Fort Montagu was built in 1741 to guard the eastern entrance to Nassau Harbour and was captured by the Americans in

1776 during the War of Independence. It was captured again in 1782 by the Spaniards, but finally recaptured by the British a little later. It was named after the Duke of Montagu and built by a famous engineer of the period who was under contract for less than three dollars a day.

Finally, there is Fort Fincastle, also built by Lord Dunmore, who named it after his second title, which was Viscount Fincastle. It suffered the same fate as Fort Charlotte, in that it was never used in earnest.

All these forts are easy to reach from Bay Street.

Most of the Bahamas are relatively low lying, but Nassau itself is built on a hill. Surmounting this hill, close to Fort Fincastle, is a large water tower. Although, oddly enough, built to hold water, this 126 ft. tower which is 216 feet above sea level makes a fine vantage point to view the city and surroundings, and it has been equipped with a modern elevator.

Also close to Fort Fincastle is the Queen's Staircase, a flight of 65 steps cut in the solid rock of a deep limestone canyon. The steps were built by slave labour about the same time as the Fort and were designed as an escape route for the troops garrisoned there. Not far from the Royal Victoria Hotel is Government House, home of the Governor. In front of it stands a fine statue of Christopher Columbus—who landed on San Salvador centuries ago and discovered the Bahamas.

Several miles to the east of Nassau's Bay Street is Blackbeard's Tower. The crumbling ruins are said to be the remains of a watchtower used by the notorious pirate Edward Teach —in other words, "Blackbeard" himself.

Ardastra Gardens, outside Nassau, are among the loveliest in the Island. Hedley Edwards, who runs them, has planted an extensive collection of tropical flowers and shrubs. It is here, too, every day at 11 a.m. and 4 p.m. that you can see his famous squad of parade ground Flamingos—he calls them the Bahamas Battalion. The Flamingo is the national bird of the Bahamas, and Hedley has trained a squad of about fifty birds to go through a drill routine. It is really quite a sight and the children will love it. Flamingos come from Inagua Island about 300 miles from Nassau—there is a sanctuary there which holds an estimated 50,000.

The water front at Nassau is always worth a visit. Fishing boats tie alongside every day and you can see them unloading giant turtles—which are put into large tanks in the fish market —and a weird collection of tropical fish and enormous lobsters. The straw market is near the water front, just off Rawson

Square, and it is no exaggeration to say that every visitor to the Bahamas sooner or later goes there and buys a hat or bag.

Paradise Beach, just across Nassau Harbour, is world famous —and well earned fame it is, too. Boats will take you across from the water front and they operate all day at frequent intervals. New Providence is ringed with lovely beaches. Lyford Cay and the Coral Harbour Club are two projects that are worth seeing but you will need a car or a cab to get there.

A popular day out with visitors is the all-day island cruise aboard the "Show Boat" which sails from the Nassau Yacht Haven. The cruise includes entertainment and dancing on board, and a barbecue lunch in some quiet lagoon. A stop for swimming, diving and water-skiing is also on the programme. Free rum punch is also dispensed so things get better as the day progresses!

There are a number of scheduled tours of Nassau and the Island. You can get details of them from the following agencies —*Playtours, R. H. Curry and Co. Ltd., Bahama Holidays Ltd.* and *East Bay Rentals.*

The Out Islands

Why the "Out" Islands? Nassau is the capital and everything else is "out" and "away" from Nassau, the hub of the Bahamas wheel.

They are becoming increasingly popular with visitors and it is our intention here only to mention the main ones that have suitable accommodation for tourists. Many of the smaller islands are private and you can only go to these by invitation.

While Nassau continues to occupy its place as the cosmopolitan centre of international society and tourism, developments in the Out Islands are attracting increasing numbers of visitors who seek a quiet haven away from the "madding crowd".

All the places mentioned are served by regular services of *Bahamas Airways.* Aircraft may also be chartered. Details of these, and of other flights, may be obtained from the *Development Board office* on Bay Street. This office will also provide up-to-date details of accommodation rates. These range from six dollars a day (European Plan) in small hotels to 27 dollars in the more luxurious places in the summer. Winter rates are somewhat higher. There is, however, accommodation for all tastes and pockets in the Out Islands—simplicity or luxury, you can take your pick.

BAHAMA ISLANDS

ABACO

Abaco and its cays form the northern group of the Bahama Islands. In company with several others of the Islands, Abaco once enjoyed great prosperity from the sea, from farming and from the timberlands of the mainland.

Green Turtle Cay, as its name implies, was famous in bygone days for the excellent turtle caught in surrounding waters and shipped abroad. Pineapple growing was also the source of considerable wealth at one time, and there are several large residences still standing which recall those prosperous days.

In the last few years an ever-increasing number of visitors have "discovered" the Abacos, creating a new source of livelihood for the industrious people of the islands, whose ancestors were among the first of the Loyalists to leave New York City in 1783.

At Green Turtle Cay there are four excellent resorts. Largest of them is the *New Plymouth Inn*, named for the chief settlement on that cay, with eleven bedrooms and detached lounge and dining room. Also in the village is the *Green Turtle Cay Fishing Camp*, and across the harbour is an 8-room establishment known as *The Other Shore*. On a ridge, overlooking the ocean and a fine wide beach is the cottage colony *Long Bay Estates*.

In the picturesque fishing village of Hope Town is the *New Hope Lodge* and *Yacht Marina* with 20 bedrooms in one and two-bedroom cottages. The resort specializes in catering for family vacations, and families with as many as six children can occupy a cottage without being crowded. The cottages can be rented on the American Plan or on a housekeeping plan; those who select the American Plan eat family style in a spacious, airy dining pavilion.

The area surrounding Elbow Cay, where Hope Town is located, is perfect for day-trip exploring.

Five miles to the north is Man-O-War Cay, where numerous American and Canadian executives have built private homes as vacation hideaways. The cay is the seat of a thriving boat-building industry, and Abaco boats are known throughout the world.

Lying on the edge of the Northwest Providence Channel is Sandy Point where four years ago the *Sandy Point Fishing Camp* was opened, consisting of four duplex cottages and a club house.

Newest hotel on Abaco is the *Great Abaco Club* on the beach at Marsh Harbour. It has 22 double rooms and is located only a few miles from the new airstrip.

The whole of the Abaco area, like the rest of the Bahamas, is a fisherman's paradise, and all the resorts mentioned maintain fleets of fishing craft equipped either for bonefishing or deep-sea trolling.

There is also wild hog hunting.

ANDROS

Andros Island, haunt of the 18th-century pirates, is the largest of the Bahama group, having an extreme length of just over 100 miles.

A low, thickly wooded island, it is divided into three parts by three wide cuts, known as North Bight, Middle Bight and South Bight.

It is the only island in the Bahamas which has a native folklore, the chief characters of which are the Chickcharnies, who are fairies of great benevolence unless they are crossed or slighted.

The Chickcharny has great influence for either good or evil and is said to nest in pine trees. To compensate for the fact that Chickcharnies dwell in trees, Andros also has the elusive Lusca, a mythical half-dragon, half-octopus that lives in caves. This creature pulls unwary wanderers into his cave with his long tentacles and devours them.

Bleached bones found in the caves from time to time may be thought to be those of pirates who once headquartered on the islands, or early settlers seeking refuge from a storm, but they are really the remnants of a Lusca feast, according to legend.

The four-foot high mobile anthill, called a Yahoo, makes a speciality of stealing children, another local superstition.

About four miles back from the mouth of Fresh Creek, Spirit Island is said to be the home of the souls of all departed Andros Islanders.

The flats of Andros provide excellent bonefishing and so it was natural that the first resort to be opened in the island should be a camp devoted primarily to the sport of fishing. Andros also provides good duck shooting in season.

The Bang Bang Club has accommodation for 12 persons. There are a dozen boats and several guides available for bone-fishing and nearby reef fishing, and the club also has its own private bathing beach.

About seven years ago the Swedish multimillionaire industrialist, Dr. Axel Wenner-Gren, joined the ranks of major Out Island developers with the construction of his luxurious *Lighthouse Club* and the *Andros Yacht Club* at Fresh Creek.

Named *Andros Town* by Dr. Wenner-Gren, his resort community is among the most lavish in the Bahamas. Set against a background of lush tropical beauty, the Lighthouse Club is the hub of activity at Andros Town. Each spacious room has a bath and dressing room, with the most handsome appointments, and in addition, a private terrace commanding a view of the sparkling Bahamian waters.

There is a modern salt water swimming pool, and a few steps from the club a beautiful sandy beach, palm-shaded and surrounded by native thatched huts.

Most of the sporting activities of Andros Town are centred around the Yacht Club which offers boats, guides, tackle and bait for the many varieties of fish available in the vicinity, as well as guides and equipment for shooting during the season.

The Yacht Club offers a gift shop, world-wide telephone service, a commissary, power hook-up for yachts, fuel, ice and water and medical facilities.

BERRY ISLANDS AND BIMINI

One of the new resorts to brighten the Bahamian scene is the *Berry Island Club Hotel* and *Yacht Club* on Frazer's Hog Cay, just 30 miles north-west of New Providence.

The hotel has 12 double rooms, each with bath, private patio and screened verandah. There are four double rooms available at the Yacht Club, which also has a dining room, bar and lounge. Homesites on the island are offered for sale to members.

The marina has a 250-foot dock. The fishing is excellent, and bonefishing boats are available.

Bimini, on the other hand, is perhaps the oldest and certainly one of the most famous of Bahamian resorts. The spectacular gamefishing first brought Bimini into prominence among sportsmen.

The people of Bimini refer to their home as a "magical" isle. It is, they maintain, a place that has been singularly blessed—where yesterday can be forgotten and today takes care of itself.

Bimini has three large resorts. Newest and largest is the 40-room *Sunshine Inn* in South Bimini. Next is *Avis-Bimini Gateway* with 26 double rooms and Club apartments with 11 two-bedroom suites. Third largest is *Anchors Aweigh Hotel and*

Marina with 34 rooms. Other hotels are *Compleat Angler,* 24 rooms; *Browns Hotel* and apartments, 26 rooms; and the *Sea Crest* and *Ocean Hotel* and apartments. *Ocean View* and the *Bimini Fisherman's Club* also have accommodation.

Bimini is a virile and important segment of the ocean-bounded Bahamas archipelago. There tranquility is as tangible a part of the atmosphere as the sun and the multi-hued sea.

There are many things to do and to be discovered on Bimini. None, except the big game fishing, requires a great expenditure of effort.

ELEUTHERA

The native name of Eleuthera was Cigatoo, and it is thought that its present name was given to it by the early settlers who sought religious freedom there, choosing the Greek word "Eleutheros" meaning free.

Tiny Cupid's Cay, the oldest portion of the settlement, was once an island, but today it is connected to the mainland by a narrow causeway.

The tranquil community of Governor's Harbour, lies quiet and sleepy, a monument of old world charm combined with tropical vacation pleasures.

Groves of casurina trees and rustling coconut palms towering above verdant foliage enhance the setting. Located at the midway point of slender, 110-mile long Eleuthera, Governor's Harbour reaches from the eastern to the western shore, bridging the crest that runs the length of the Island.

On each side of this crest are two of the settlement's guest houses; *Belmont*, overlooking the lovely harbour, and *Buena Vista* which commands a magnificent view of the ocean. In the village itself is the *Buccaneer Club*, and nearby is the unique *Antique Gift Shop* open from November 1st to May 31st.

Across the ridge from the village, along one of the most beautiful beaches in the Bahamas is the completely remodelled resort of *French Leave*, owned and operated by former Broadway and Hollywood actor Craig Kelly.

It is a long, rambling inn with 50 rooms facing the sea, and is one of the major Out Island hotels.

Another of Eleuthera's resorts is the *Rock Sound Club*, near the settlement of that name. The club, which offers both cottages and rooms with private bath, is set in an estate of approximately 6,500 acres. It is owned by Mr. Arthur Vining Davis. At the nearby beaches of Half Sound and Winding Bay there are cabanas for the use of guests, and smart English cars may be hired.

BAHAMA ISLANDS

A few miles distant is the *Cotton Bay Club* with the first land-locked harbour in the Bahamas. Cotton Bay also has a golf club.

Rock Sound was a traditional place for wreckers. In fact, a hundred years ago the locals were known as "Wreck Sounders".

EXUMA

One of the most memorable experiences to be enjoyed in the Bahamas is to cruise through the lovely islands of the Exuma range. Every year the Out Island Regatta for native workboats is held in George Town Harbour, an exhilarating affair, with few rules and great enthusiasm.

George Town has the *Peace and Plenty Inn* with 20 furnished bedrooms all facing the sea and overlooking a patio. Across the harbour is the *Stocking Island Yacht Club* which is operated in conjunction with Peace and Plenty Inn.

GRAND BAHAMA

Game fishing, skin-diving, golfing on a nine-hole "pitch and putt" course, shuffle board, swimming, cycling—all these and many other vacation pleasures are available to guests at the *Grand Bahama Hotel* at West End, Grand Bahama Island.

The 350-room resort is the largest in the Bahamas. It has recently been completely rebuilt and is now a link in the Jack Tar chain of U.S. operated hotels. New additions are a protected yacht harbour, swimming pool, convention facilities and a golf course.

At the Grand Bahama Hotel, you can spend your days just lazing beside the pool—the largest in the Bahamas—or explore the beaches and wooded paths for sea shells, tropical birds and wild orchid plants.

You can play croquet, shuffle board, badminton, indoors or out, volley ball, tennis, bowl, or do a bit of skeet shooting.

Bicycles are available for sightseeing trips along the picturesque shoreline, and into the nearby village of West End.

You can climb aboard one of the club's skiffs, take a picnic lunch and fishing pole, and cruise to nearby Sandy Cay, Wood Cay or Indian Cay, for the day.

Within three minutes by boat from the Club's dock are some of the Atlantic's most fruitful areas for bonefishing, reef-fishing and deep-sea fishing. Expert native guides, tackle, bait, and a fleet of 15 modern fishing cruisers are available to anglers for full days or half days in these virgin waters.

Skin-diving and spear fishing just developed at the Club,

has opened a new world of intrigue and charm for visitors to the island.

HARBOUR ISLAND

Harbour Island, one of the gems of the Bahamas, is also one of the original Island resorts. The settlement is called Dunmore Town after a former Governor of the Bahamas, the Earl of Dunmore.

The Island is only about one mile and a half square, but its large harbour, facing the Eleuthera shoreline, is one of the finest in the Colony.

The popularity of Harbour Island as a resort, over a period of many years, has resulted in the construction of some of the finest guest accommodation in the Bahamas.

Pink Sands Lodge consists of 20 one and two-bedroom cottages on a 40-acre estate, overlooking the ocean and the beach. There is a dining-room, indoor and outdoor terraces, a lounge and library.

The Picaroon Cove Club has three main buildings overlooking the fascinating harbour. There are 20 double rooms, all with private bath, contained in the principal buildings and five outlying cottages. On the beach is the *Dunes Club*, maintained for use of guests at Picaroon Cove.

The beach itself is one of the distinguishing features of Harbour Island, being a delicate pink colour derived from pulverized shells washed in by the tides.

The Little Boarding House, with 12 rooms, is the oldest resort, and two other smaller establishments are *Sunset Inn* and *Up Yonder*.

SPANISH WELLS

On a sandy little island called St. George's Cay lies Spanish Wells, forming the narrow winding channel that leads outwards to the ocean from Harbour Island. During recent years the *St. George's Hotel* has been erected in the settlement, and this pleasant little resort has ten bedrooms, with bath.

The inhabitants are an industrious people, descendants of hardy seafaring stock. They are also excellent farmers, and the Spanish Wellsians supply the Nassau market with fish and some of its best vegetables.

There are several privately owned islands where accommodation exists. One is *Cat Cay,* south of the Biminis which has been developed as a private club which offers fishing, sailing and golf. Another is *Walkers Cay Club* close to Grand Bahama.

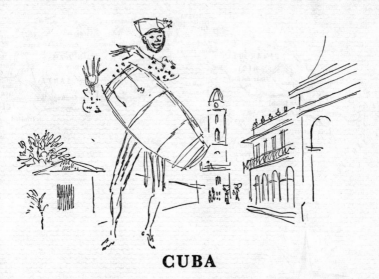

CUBA

Rum, Romance and Revolution

BY

DAVID A. PHILLIPS

(A former editor of Chile's "South Pacific Mail", Latin-America's oldest English-language newspaper, Mr. Phillips was a long-time resident of Havana where he worked as a lecturer and press correspondent.)

On the travel map of the Caribbean, Cuba is a tragic paradox. Rich in color, both human and geographical, and equipped with hotel facilities equal to any in the world, it has been all but wiped off the travel map. Only a few minutes by air from the mainland of the United States, it is now virtually as remote as the moon for Americans who, at the time of writing, are forbidden to travel to this island laden with political dynamite. While tourists of other nationalities are being sought eagerly by the government of Dr. Fidel Castro, self-appointed President of the Cuban Tourist Development Board, they are only a trickle compared to the American tidal wave of the past. Cuba's great tourist hotels and resorts are either empty ghosts or, in a few cases, the homes of new visitors from the other side of the Iron Curtain. In other words, this once-throbbing vacationland is now the furthest off the beaten path of any of the Caribbean islands despite such enticements as rebates to tourists on their flight costs, a reduction of hotel rates and a general ban against

241

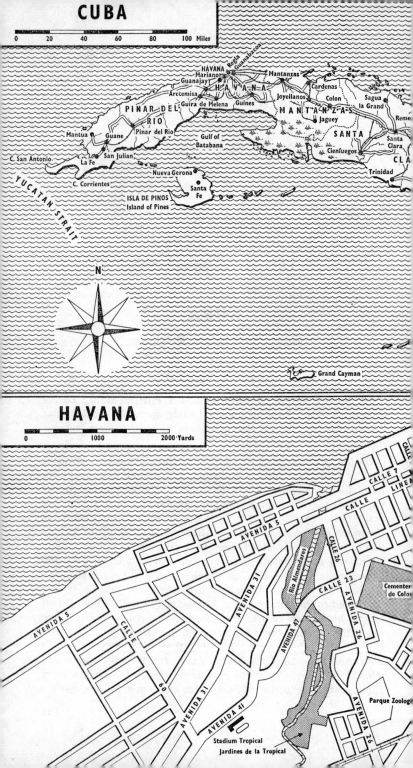

CUBA

0 20 40 60 80 100 Miles

HAVANA
Marianao
Guanajay
Aretemisa
Guira de Melena
Guines
H A V A N A
Regla
Guanabacoa
Mantanzas
Joyellanos
Cardenas
Colon
Sagua
la Grand
Reme

PINAR DEL
RIO
Pinar del Rio
Mantua
Guane
San Julian
La Fe
C. San Antonio
C. Corrientes

Gulf of
Batabana
M A N T A N Z A S
Jaguey

S A N T A
Cienfuegos
Santa
Clara
C L A
Trinidad

YUCATAN STRAIT

Nueva Gerona
Santa
Fe
ISLA DE PINOS
Island of Pines

N

Grand Cayman

HAVANA

0 1000 2000 Yards

CALLE 7
CALLE
LINEA
AVENIDA 5
CALLE 26
CALLE 23
AVENIDA 31
Rio Almendares
Cementer
de Colo
AVENIDA 5
CALLE
AVENIDA 47
AVENIDA 26
CALLE
60
AVENIDA 31
AVENIDA 41
AVENIDA 26
Parque Zoologi
Stadium Tropical
Jardines de la Tropical

CUBA

tipping. This is the situation as we go to press with the current edition of the Guide to the Caribbean, Bahamas and Bermuda. *We made all corrections and deletions that have come to our attention on the basis of meager available information, but it is quite probable conditions will continue to remain unstable. The Editor.)*

The first tourist to visit Cuba wrote in his journal: "This is the most beautiful land that eyes have ever seen". The traveler was Christopher Columbus and he had sailed into one of the many mangrove-fringed bays on the northern coast of Cuba. That was in 1492, soon after the discoverer of the New World had made his first landfall in the Bahamas. Of course he thought he had arrived in China or India—thus the Caribbean Islands are known today as Indies and the natives of America Indians. Columbus was the first but not the last visitor to be impressed to the point of poetry by the beauty of the "Pearl of the Antilles".

Cuba, less than a hundred miles from Key West, Florida, is the largest island in the West Indies group. Shaped like a long, head-heavy fish, its overall area is slightly less than England's but it spreads its length more than 700 miles—from the end of the curving chain of West Indian islands to a point halfway between Florida and Mexico's Yucatan Peninsula. Its width varies from 25 to 125 miles. A central highway which runs like a spine down the island is seldom more than 30 miles from the sea. The warm waters of the Gulf of Mexico run on its northern coast; on the southern shore the shallows and keys of the Caribbean proper.

Most of the land in Cuba consists of gentle slopes and rolling farmlands with occasional cameo valleys which give the country a postcard beauty. About a quarter of the island is mountainous. In the westernmost province of Pinar del Rio are found the low range of the Organos, in the easternmost province of Oriente the steep slopes of the majestic Sierra Maestra and Sagua Baracoa ranges. Cuba's highest peak, Turquino, juts 7,866 feet above sea level. Some 200 rivers lace the countryside, the largest being the Cauto. Around the island the coastline is indented by thousands of bays and inlets, once favored refuges for the buccaneers, today the ports and fishing grounds of the nation. The beaches are among the finest in the world; outstanding is the world-famous Varadero.

The Cuban landscape, so ardently sung by the poets, is covered with an extraordinary variety of trees and plants. So

CUBA

rich is the soil and so benign the climate that wooden fence-posts sprout like garden plants. Vast forests once mantled the island, but they have been ruthlessly leveled to make way for the sugar cane fields. But there still remain great groves of Spanish cedar, mahogany, pine, datepalm and black olive. The impressive royal palm, which seems to frame every view of the country, is one of over 30 varieties of palm trees.

Although Cuba is geographically tropical, soothing trade-winds temper the climate. The temperature fluctuates only slightly throughout the year; in Havana the average is a pleasant 72°. The rainy season extends from the middle of May through October. The island lies in the hurricane belt, with September through October the dangerous months; but most cyclones skirt the northern area.

You can find everything in Cuba, it has been said, except snowballs. Tobacco is a staple and a trademark. The Havana cigar owes its quality to peculiar qualities in the Cuban soil found nowhere else; indeed there are certain subtle strains which are grown only in limited areas—sometimes only a few acres—and used in the blending of the superior samples coveted by connoisseurs such as Winston Churchill. Visitors to Havana can visit the factories where the experts roll the cigars with nimble fingers. While they make up to 200 cigars a day the men listen to a professional reader seated on a raised platform, who recites the news of the day, mixed with political indoctrination. (Columbus discovered tobacco on his first voyage to Cuba; actually *tobacco* was the Indian name not for the weed, but the pipe used to smoke it. Cigar bands are said to have come in use because Cuban women used them to protect their dainty fingers while they smoked enormous stogies).

Rum is another name synonomous with Cuba. Few visitors fail to carry their quota of rum on the outward voyage after sampling the refreshing frozen *daiquiri.* (According to one of many stories, the first *daiquiri* was mixed in a moment of boredom by an American engineer in the mining town of Daiquiri). The *cuba libre,* rum with Coca Cola, was always more popular with visitors than Cubans.

Rum, of course, is a derivative from Cuba's principal product and export—sugar. The island produces a sizeable percentage of the total world crop. During the harvest long trains of cane converge on colorful mills throughout the country. National economy balances precariously on the world market price; the individual Cuban may enjoy a gay year or a dreary one depending on international sales. To lessen the dependence on a one-crop economy, Cubans are determinedly developing other resources. The island is an important producer of copper, chromium and manganese. In Nicaro is the Western Hemisphere's greatest nickel plant, and a petroleum industry is in its infancy. Marble is so common on the Isle of Pines that highways are paved with it. The country grows staples— coffee, corn, rice, fruits and summer vegetables—for its own use and export.

Schizophrenic Heritage

The strategic importance of Cuba, resting athwart sea lanes to the United States, Mexico and the Panama Canal, is emphasized by the U.S. naval base at Guantánamo. Its physical grandeur is a composite of natural harbors, shining beaches, undulating farmland, impressive mountain ranges and riotous foliage. Its personality is a marvel of adjustment to a schizophrenic heritage. The juxtaposition of old and new is found everywhere. Even the capital city of Havana is sharply divided into "Old" and "New" sections. There are constant signs of traditional Spain side-by-side with the later, fast-paced American influences and the socialism of the new regime: a television antenna sprouting atop a thatch-roofed hut; a bullock-powered wagon hauling sugar cane to a modern nationalized mill; a barge pushing its way through a bay where Cortés set sail for Mexico. In the clash of opposites, only the original Indian and his lazy civilization have disappeared. Today Cuba is a nation half-way between two worlds. Castro's series of revolutionary measures have already changed entirely the face of the country. Many tentative labels could be stuck on the new order of things, but it certainly cannot be called a "lazy civilization" any longer.

There are over six and a half million people in Cuba, a million or more in Havana, but not one of them is a prototype. The Indians that greeted Columbus and the colonizers who followed him were a happy lot, but of little use as laborers, and they soon perished as a race from the ravages of civilization. Mass importations of African slaves were necessary to the expanding agriculture of the Spanish settlers. (The annual carnival in Havana celebrates the traditional one day a year of freedom the slaves enjoyed.) The mixture of African and Indian was augmented by a swelling tide of European colonists and adventurers. Today the Negro composes about a quarter, possibly more, of the population, and is an active partner in the country's development. There is no obstacle to his participation in the cultural and political life of the country.

Guajiros, Caballeros, Habaneros

The Cuban *guajiro*, the rural farm worker, is easy-going, and has been one of the stalwart supporters of the new government and his rewards are becoming apparent. He is used to a sharecropper's existence, so the rewards have not needed to be spectacular. But nationalistic fervor sways him only briefly. The principal work is bringing in the sugar cane harvest, a few months out of each year. The rest of the time he and his wife do little, and in spite of months of inactivity, the *guajiro* shows little proclivity for handicrafts. Of all modern developments television has had the most impact on him. Often unable to read newspapers, he will sit for hours before the screen of a television receiver. In the country it is not unusual to see a small "theater" filled with farmers come to town on a Saturday night to watch favorite programs —and they pay 5 cents to the enterprising burgher who raised the capital necessary to buy a television set on the installment plan!

Whatever his lot, and however questionable his ambition, there is universal agreement that the Cuban *guajiro* is a thorough gentleman. *Un caballero.* At home he shares his meager lot with any visitor. When he comes to town for carnival (or is enticed in for a political rally) he is the perfect visitor, unobtrusive, courteous, sober, and touchingly appreciative of any little favor done for him.

Cuba had a fast-growing middle class in Havana and in the provincial cities and its members were among Castro's earliest supporters, though most are disillusioned today. They took their education seriously and they were active in social and cultural life. They worked hard and competently, even by non-Caribbean standards. Now they are faced with the tragic alternative of either submitting to totalitarian "Gleichschaltung" or fleeing home and country.

The wealthy in Cuba were the hardest hit by the last revolution. The first to go were, naturally, those who had struck gold in the incredible graft of previous political regimes. But later the old wealthy class, the landowners who once owned most of Cuba, were fleeing into exile as well. Agrarian land reforms took their properties away and they have lost even more. The old way of life enjoyed by heirs to immense sugar and tobacco fortunes became very much a thing of the past.

The visitors to Cuba will have little chance to know the

guajiro, but will almost certainly meet the typical *Habanero* (learn this word, the *Habanero* detests the name Havanian or Havanite). Here is a Latin who does not fit preconceived notions. The *Habanero* lives in a city of skycrapers, and has little time to act the part of a Hollywood version of the Latin you expect to meet. He works hard, staying in his office until the job is done. He is volatile. He will change an opinion or political party at the drop of a *sombrero* (a figure of speech since he never wears one). He is sentimental. Walk down a Havana street with a brace of blond children and they will be affectionately patted on the head half a dozen times. He is shrewd and businesslike. Many a fast-talking American who came to Cuba in the old, free-wheeling days, underestimated the acumen of Cuban businessmen and landed back in Toledo, working at his uncle's pickle factory. They are also touchy. It is not necessary to handle them with diplomatic kid gloves, but the pride of the *Habanero* is monumental.

The pride of the Cuban is an inherited Spanish trait, easily understood. Furthermore it is leavened with a lively sense of humor, even a sense of the ridiculous although the joke may involve self-ridicule based on a frank appraisal of faults. The visitor is not long in Havana before a Cuban will tell him this story, all the time chuckling with glee: "God decided that He would create a perfect spot on earth. He endowed it with the most desirable climate, the most beautiful mountains and valleys, and He planted it with the most breathtaking foliage. This island is a jewel on earth, God told Himself. But I must do at least one bad thing, God added, or I will have another Garden of Eden on My hands. So God filled the island of Cuba with Cubans."

The *Habanero* has a reputation for being a gay bird. He is. Office hours are interrupted so that he may join the cluster around the coffee stands a dozen times a day. (The coffee is inexpensive bitter and strong, and three cups will give the uninitiated a severe case of the shakes). In the evening the clubs catering for the working classes are vivid with the bright dresses of the women and the continual beat of the "cha-cha-cha." In the more affluent places the men wear their starched *guayaberas* or immaculate white suits with a flair, as they order a rationed dinner. The women are dressed carefully and provocatively, tightly cinctured (to be All Woman in Cuba it is necessary to display considerably more avoir-dupois in the broader aspects than is considered fashionable in other countries).

CUBA

It is only natural that the Cuban should be romantic. He is, after all, the product of an environment: moonlight shimmering on tropical water, soothing winds ruffling palm trees, the heady rhythms of aphrodisiac dance tunes. Sex is a fact of life, and there is no reason to evade the issue. What the foreigner finds difficult to understand is the Cuban's vacillating moral codes: even today chaperones often escort young girls on their dates, but the evening may be spent in a nightclub so dark the chaperone can't see across the table; a lady tourist wearing shorts on the streets of Havana shocks the passersby, but had the exhibitionist been a Cuban it would have been considered a national disgrace.

The Cuban is sensitive about his reputation as an ardent lover and man-about-town only because he fears that foreigners might regard this as an indication that he is not as civilized as they. Or that his conduct might possibly be regarded as sinful. Of course the Cuban is no more sinful than other peoples—he only releases his inhibitions in more attractive surroundings and in a more overt manner.

The sum total of Cuba, "the most beautiful land that eyes have ever seen", and its people, proud, gay and vivacious, means only one thing for the visitor. If he doesn't enjoy Cuba it's nobody's fault but his own—or the regime's.

Indians, Slaves and Spanish Kings

Although Columbus discovered Cuba in 1492 the actual conquest of the island was delayed until 1511, when Diego de Veláquez, commissioned by the son of Columbus, was given the job of securing the island for Spain. Resistance on the part of the gentle Indians was brief. The native chieftan Hatuey had proceeded Veláquez from what is now known as Santo Domingo to warn the Cuban Indians of the arrival of the Spanish. After two months of futile battle the fight was over. Veláquez condemned Hatuey to death by fire. There is a story that, as the flames began to rise, a Spanish priest attempted to convert Hatuey to the Christian faith by recounting to him the joy he would find in Paradise. Hatuey politely asked the cleric if the Spaniards, too, would be found in Paradise. On being told they would be, the Indian declined conversion, declaring that he had no desire to meet the Spanish again.

As the natives died from the diseases of the white man, the importation of Negro slaves steadily increased, until slavery was finally abolished in 1886. A stream of immigration from

Spain still continues today. The Spaniards founded the towns of Baracoa, Bayamo, Santiago de Cuba, Puerto Principe, San Juan de los Remedios, Sancti Spiritus and Trinidad. Veláquez made Santiago his capital. Havana was originally founded in 1514 on the southern coast of the island where the town of Batabanó is now located; later it was moved to the north coast and the more protective harbor.

Cuba under Spain was the hub of Spanish activity in the New World. From Cuban ports Cortés sailed for Mexico, De Soto and Ponce de Léon set out for the unknown lands of the north, and Balboa and Pizarro departed for their adventures in Central and South America. Pirates found that Cuba, with its thousands of hidden inlets, was an attractive base of operations. The Spanish settlers constantly scuttled into hiding, changed the sites of their cities, built fortresses such as the Morro Castles in both Havana and Santiago, to escape the sudden raids of the corsairs. Sir Henry Morgan and Sir Francis Drake attacked with impunity until the colonists became strong enough to defend themselves.

Dissatisfaction with the rule of a Spanish king thousands of miles away began early. A series of frustrated revolts marked Cuba's history until its final liberation. It is not generally known that Americans twice participated in the liberation of Cuba from Spain. For in 1762 a force of several thousand Americans (then British subjects) captured Havana; Cuba remained under British rule for one year, then was swapped to Spain for what is now the state of Florida.

Martí, Batista, Castro

The final phase of war was sparked by a brilliant Cuban writer and poet who had spent most of his life in exile and who planned the revolution in his apartment in New York. José Martí was a truly great man, and is Cuba's national hero. He was a scholar whose ideas on freedom rank with those of Paine and Jefferson, a poet still revered, and a hero—he died while charging the Spanish on horseback in the battle that was the beginning of the end. Everywhere today the visitor will see the gentle countenance of this man, who is the George Washington of his country. His bust stands in every Cuban schoolyard.

In February of 1898 the battleship *Maine* blew up in Havana harbor. It had been standing by to protect American citizens, according to the official story, and the circumstances of the explosion have never been clear. The U.S. congress declared

CUBA

war and Teddy Roosevelt and his Rough Riders defeated the Spaniards at San Juan Hill, while the U.S. navy won battles against the Spanish fleet in the Philippines. Spain renounced all her rights over Cuba on December 10, 1898. (A note for visitors: Cubans will be pleased if you refer to this conflict as *The War of Independence*; they feel "Spanish-American War" sounds as if the Cubans had nothing to do with it).

As provided by the treaty which ended the Span—oops— War of Independence the United States occupied and administratively controlled Cuba until the final abrogation of the Platt Amendment in 1934. Cuba's first president—Tomás Estrada Palma, who took office in 1902—was hardworking and honest. But he was followed by a succession of chief executives who systematically plundered the public coffers. In spite of this Cuba progressed as her sugar sold at sweet prices on the world market.

A new figure entered the political arena, "a sergeant named Batista". He dominated the country from 1933 to 1944, when free elections made Dr. Ramon Gran San Martin president, followed in 1948 by Dr. Carlos Prio. Dr. Prio was driven into exile in the last year of his term by a military complot which put Batista into power until the small hours of the morning of the first day of 1959. Fulgencio Batista's sudden flight into exile really began over two years before when a young revolutionary, Fidel Castro, arrived in a small boat from Mexico. With the support of a tiny band of dedicated followers, he began in the mountains of the Sierra Maestra the battle which ended when Batista flew to Santo Domingo.

We have already commented upon the collapse of tourism in Cuba since the present government has taken over, Castro's inducements notwithstanding. Since then, the Iron Curtain has come down with a loud clang over Cuba. Travel by Americans to the island is banned by the State Department and, considering Castro's policies, it is not likely that many would go to Cuba even if the ban were lifted. Many Latin American countries as well have grown wary of this impetuous neighbor and the Far Left course he is steering. But, no matter what their political regime, Cubans will never become a faceless regimented horde and Cuba itself will never lose its unique color to turn the dull gray of totalitarianism. Cuba has gone through many upheavals in her history and she will surely weather this one.

Even today, Cuba can be rewarding to the adventurous traveler who has the possibility of going there and seeing this sunny isle as it has remained behind its new window dressing. It is a

CUBA

pity for Cuba, and perhaps a greater pity for tourists who yearn to return there, that things are as they are now.

PRACTICAL INFORMATION FOR CUBA

SEASONS. Winter tourist season runs from December 14 through to April 1. The summer season is traditionally popular because of lower hotel rates.

VISAS. At the moment we have no information on visa regulations for American citizens, other than that they cannot travel to Cuba unless by special dispensation of the U.S. State Department, and that visas must be applied for at the Czechoslovakian Embassy in Washington D.C.

Visas are not required of United Kingdom and Canadian nationals for a stay not exceeding six months; nor for nationals of France, Netherlands, Norway, Sweden and Switzerland (three months). Latin American native citizens do not need a visa if traveling as tourists for up to 29 days.

Passports are required of all nationals except Canadians traveling direct to Cuba.

CUSTOMS REGULATIONS. On paper, these remain as before. However, the Cuban customs officials' attitude to incoming travelers depends on the passport the visitor holds.

MONEY. The peso, which is still officially pegged to the American dollar has fallen far below that on the world market. The amount of Cuban currency that can be brought into the country is strictly regulated. By all means abide by the rules.

TIPPING. Service charges are not added to hotel bills and restaurant checks. American tipping standards used to apply in Cuban hotels and restaurants and services. Recently, however, the government has announced an end to tipping. We have no information about the success of this campaign, but recollections from former days of the enthusiasm shown for tips by all and sundry make us wonder.

ELECTRIC CURRENT. 110 *A.C.*, in Havana hotels. Varies elsewhere.

POSTAL SERVICES. All types of correspondence must bear a special one cent Post Office Building stamp *plus:* Airmail to United States and possessions and Canada 12 cents for each half ounce; airmail to England and other European countries is 30 cents for the half ounce. Air rates to other areas vary by country, and should be checked with a hotel clerk. Ordinary mail in Cuba, all of North and Latin America, and Spain is 4 cents per half ounce and fraction thereof, with post cards at 3 cents. Ordinary mail to all other countries is 6 cents. Note: at time of writing no mail is delivered beween Cuba and the Dominican Republic.

DRINKING WATER. Everyone drinks mineral water, which will be served automatically in all restaurants. But do not hesitate to brush your teeth with tap water, or in emergencies, drink it. Chemists insist the local water is purer than New York's, if somewhat strong in mineral taste.

CUBA

HOURS. Shops are open from 9 to 12.30, then open again from 2.30 to 6 or 7 in the evening. Banks open at 9, close at 12, then reopen for one hour between 2 and 3. Major motion picture theaters do not open until late afternoon. You will be served as early as 6 or 7 p.m. at restaurants but you will probably be alone, as Cubans dine much later.

MOTORING. Cubans drive on the right side of the road, in theory at least. Foreign motorists must protect themselves either by driving very carefully or going all out as a form of self-defense. Whichever you choose keep a sharp eye, as the accident rate is high. Third party insurance is not compulsory, and all foreign driver's licenses are honored. Roads in Havana are generally good, and a central highway runs from one end of the country to the other. In the city do not make a left turn until both green and yellow lights are constant.

PRACTICAL INFORMATION FOR HAVANA

Havana is the capital of Cuba, and known as the fun capital of the Caribbean. The Cubans maintain a strict system of seasons (they stop swimming in September because it is "winter", though the water is still warm) but the tourist need only be influenced by the fact that everything is a bit cheaper in the summer.

HOTELS

There is a hotel in Havana for every taste and every pocketbook. All first-class hotels have facilities comparable with the best in any part of the world, including suites with stupendous views of a startlingly blue sea. Since July 30, 1960, prices and rates of all Cuban hotels have been set by official decree of Dr. Baudilio Castellanos, Director del Instituto Nacional de la Industria Turistica. Hotels are classified "A" (De Luxe), "B" (First Class), "C" (Moderate) and "D" (Inexpensive). All have minimum fixed rates, European Plan. For Class "A": $6 single, $8 double and $11 triple. For Class "B": $5 single, $7 double, and $9 triple. For Class "C": $4 single, $6 double and $7 triple. For Class "D": $2.80 single, $4 double and $5.60 triple. One must admit that these hotel prices represent one of the best bargains in the Caribbean.

DE LUXE (CLASS "A")

NACIONAL is the Grand Old Lady of Havana hotels. Superbly located on a verdant tropical plot overlooking the sea. Recently nationalized, it was closed at the time we went to press.

HABANA LIBRE is one of the three very new hotels in the luxury class in Havana, formerly known as the Hilton. Dramatic in design, it is the tallest hotel in Latin America. Rooms and suites are luxuriously furnished, and each offers a pano-

CUBA

ramic view of Havana. The *Sugar Bar*, on the topmost floor, is just right for an after-dark drink. Swimming pool, coffee shop and tourist shop arcade. A favorite spot for revolutionary leader Fidel Castro, who often holds levees in the kitchen. It is also a favorite of visiting Communist dignitaries.

THE THERESA is new and shiny, with a big city glitter. Slightly away from the center of town on the Malecon, the undulating drive which rims the Gulf. Large pool. Ocean-view rooms on both sides of the hotel.

CAPRI, last in the trio of new hotels, is somewhat smaller than the other luxury hotels. Roof-top swimming pool and patio. Lush appointments, gambling casino.

FIRST CLASS (CLASS "B")

ROSITA DE HORNEDO is a few minutes drive from downtown Havana and smack on the sea. Kitchenette apartments popular with those who plan an extended stay. Pools and sea-wall play areas make it a good place for children.

HOTEL COMODORO is a large attractive resort hotel with complete pool, beach and boating facilities. A fifteen minute car trip from Havana. Once quiet and exclusive, it is now almost impossible to obtain a room, as the hotel is used as living quarters for Soviet delegations.

VEDADO in the Vedado section (O St. No. 244) is small but excellent. Inexpensive food and central location.

MODERATE (CLASS "C")

Presidente (Calzada and G. Sts.), near town, an older but efficiently run hotel, and *Habana Deauville* (Malecon at Galiano St.) facing the sea in the old Havana section; both previously first class hotels, newly classified moderate. Smaller but acceptable hotels are *Lincoln* (Galiano and Virtudes Sts.), *St. John's* (O St. No. 208), *Bristol*.

INEXPENSIVE (CLASS "D")

Ambus Mundos (Obispo No. 153) was once a fashionable inn, but age is catching up with it. Still reeks with atmosphere as befits the place where Hemingway wrote "*A Farewell to Arms*". Others are: *Copacabana*, on the sea; *Hotel Sevilla Biltmore* on the Prado (also known as *Paseo de Marti*) a venerable establishment popular with travelers and businessmen who wish to be near the merchant houses. Gambling casino.

The following are recommended cautiously. Although prices are low, standards and sanitary conditions may not be what you want to write home about: *Caribbean, Colina, Dos Mares, Flamingo, Packard, Parkview, Plaza, Siboney, Surf, Victoria.*

FOOD AND DRINK

There are some 2,000 varieties of fish in the azure seas around Cuba so the visiting gourmet is offered a splendid array of sea foods. Most famous is the *moro* crab. This is a large-clawed rock-crab, and is found nowhere else. Many people claim it the finest delicacy the sea provides, preferring it served with a simple butter sauce. Popular choice of Cubans is *pargo* (snapper) served with fried bananas. The lobster (*langosta*) is the small non-claw type, somewhat stronger in taste than the big fellows.

The national dish is *arroz con pollo* (chicken and rice). A favorite of all classes is the intriguingly named *Moros y Cristianos* (Moors and Christians) which is a dish of white rice studded with black beans. Cuban meats are good, if sometimes poorly cut. Soups are excellent, especially *Caldo Gallego*, a broth filled with potatoes, onions, cabbage, ham, sausage and sometimes chicken. The staple vegetable broth is *ajiaco*—featuring, among other good things, the fruit of the *yucca* plant.

There are literally hundreds of exotic Cuban fruits, but their seasons are brief. For dessert ask for a mango in season, or mixed fruit any time—but beware of the smaller restaurants which will proudly serve canned fruit. Tiny *platanos manzanos* (apple bananas) are succulent but do not mix with alcohol, so avoid a severe tummy upset. Other Cuban desserts are cream cheese with guava, delicate combination that you will never forget, and *coco glacé*—ice cream made of coconut milk and served in the shell.

Cuban wines are not praiseworthy. French wines are available, as well as excellent Spanish vintages. Cuban beer is excellent.

Top the meal with Cuban coffee. It is delicious, but rough!

RESTAURANTS

The problem of food has become a difficult one under the present circumstances even for the visitor; while the great restaurants remain open they are permitted to serve only two choices on the menu: a minute portion of steak (at $6 per portion) and spaghetti. On the street the hamburger stands serve mostly thin bean soup.

The daily rations for citizens of Havana are meager indeed: 3 ounces of meat or fish a day, 3 ounces of rice, one-half ounce of cooking fat and 8 ounces of vegetables. But even this substandard ration is hard to get.

The situation is said to be slightly better in the provinces.

Such severe rationing of food stuffs make our references to gastronomy more than illusory of course. We nevertheless continue to give our readers information on the gastronomic front, as if everything were normal, hoping that Cuban restaurants will again revert to their former prowess in the culinary arts if and when conditions improve.

CUBA

THE VERY BEST

EL CARMELO. (Calzada and D sts.) has moved up lately into the front rank restaurants. The food is the best in town and the clientele consists of the last remnants of Havana's smart set. Prices are sky high.

The reason why the restaurant is exceptionally permitted to retain prerevolutionary culinary standards is that it has become Castro's favorite.

FLORIDITA, most famous restaurant in Havana, home of the frozen *daiquiri*.

Before dinner or lunch one of the delicious frozen rum drinks is in order. The *daiquiris* are the best in the world, and though the management is happy to provide guests with mixing instructions these *daiquiris* have never been duplicated elsewhere—even in Havana. For the really jaded visitor, there is always the *mulata*, made with several kinds of dark rum.

MONSEIGNEUR (in front of the Nacional) is very chic and very French. Strolling violinists circulate dramatically; candlelight is reflected in the gold plate. Naturally, you must pay for all this. Highly recommended to those with European tastes.

LA ROCA (21 St. near the *Capri*). A favorite for businessmen's luncheons (when the client is to be impressed). The best place for rare roast beef. Tourists with a yen for an American menu are happy in the evening.

LE VENDOME (Calzada St. No. 602) is a superb French restaurant specializing in escargots, frog legs, chateaubriand and coq au vin. French, Spanish and Cuban wines in the cellar.

TALLY-HO (23rd and J Sts.). An intimate spot very popular with Cubans. French specialties in an English decor. You will be very much alone before 10 in the evening.

OTHER TOP-NOTCH PLACES

EDEN ROC (23 and O Sts.) once popular for American steaks, is now known, in glowing neon, as *The Balalaika Russian Club*. The menu features crab cocktail Vladivostok, as well as Sputnik, Laika, Socialist, Molotov and Trip-to-the-Moon cocktails.

PRILLA'S (on the Malecon naer the *Riviera Hotel*) is a superior dining spot, very new but popular with Cuban society. Decor is modern and tasteful, if you don't mind seeing yourself reflected into infinity in the mirrored entrance.

LA RUE 19 (that street and H) is another European restaurant with candlelight dining and those ubiquitous violins. Most of the meals are served on a flaming sword.

MES AMIS in the Miramar residential section is rather quiet, except on Saturday nights. Just right for a drink, and there is no reason to go elsewhere when you become hungry.

EL PALACIO DE CRISTAL (San José and Consulado Sts.) is for serious businessmen and visiting firemen. Food is strictly continental.

SOME SPECIAL PLACES

As befits a city with a large Chinese population, Havana has several choice oriental restaurants.

THE MANDARIN has excellent Cantonese dishes, but unfortunately the decor is straight from a *Fu Man Chu* movie.

EL PACIFICO, in Chinatown (you'll never find it alone, so take a taxi). This is real. You enter an almost unmarked door in a grimy tenement and take a small elevator which jolts precariously to the top of the building. The trip is worth it. The food is exquisite and inexpensive.

CUBA

CUBAN COOKING

EL TEMPLETE (Avenida del Puerto No. 14) is the place for Cuban cuisine with a sidewalk view of the waterfront. A trio plays at lunch and dinner. Inexpensive.

LA ZARAGOZANA (Belgica No. 355) was established in 1830 and has been turning out excellent food ever since. Spanish in decor, specialties are Galician stew and any kinds of seafood. Rabbit is a standby. Prices are reasonable. (Note: check on this address, it is bruited that a change in location is being considered by the management).

LA BODEGUITA DEL MEDIO (just off Cathedral Square), if you can take it, is the most charming restaurant in Havana. This is the only truly bohemian spot in town and is located literally in the back of a grocery store. Patronized by artists and intellectuals and all the *avant guarde* crowd. The walls are covered with photographs of celebrities from all over the world. Food is very Cuban, and highly spiced. The waiter does not understand English, but he has dealt with tourists for years. Very inexpensive, but you should call ahead, as only a few tables fit in this tiny haven.

CENTRO VASCO (3 and 4 Sts. in Vedado) Spanish—Spain Spanish—cusine is found here and very good and inexpensive it is.

FOR A SNACK

There is a Chinese cafeteria called *Wakamba* (O near 23rd) where you can serve yourself to a good but cheap meal. At the counter, blue-plates from 70 cents. Coffee shops are good at all the big hotels. The dining room at the *Vedado* is inexpensive and has excellent pies. Sandwiches are tasty at *Sloppy Joe's* (Zulueta and Animas), once Havana's most famous bar. Near this can be found a small, unpretentious Chinese restaurant named *Canton,* a good place to eat until the remittance check arrives.

Out of town, on the road to Wajay, there are a number of Cuban countryside restaurants. You'll need a car to get there, and a driver who knows his way (although several of the tours stop for a meal). Best of these is *Rancho Luna.* Open dining under a tremendous thatched roof. All those people you see are Cubans who come here because the food is cheap and delicious. Highly spiced chicken and rice and fried bananas are the speciality of the house and you will never be able to eat it all.

Incidentally, connected with *Rancho Luna,* there is a tiny little scenic garden, with regular tours. Sort of fun while you're waiting to order. Among other things you see how Cubans climb those tall palms and a fight between two of the tiredest cocks you ever met. If you are in doubt as to whether you should tip the guide your indecision is solved for you: at the end of the tour there is a large sign: "Please Tip the Guide".

NIGHTLIFE

For many years Havana has been called the "Paris of the Caribbean". But the present revolutionary regime has let it be known that it disapproves of rampant gambling and prostitution and has taken steps to tone down the wide-open aspects of nightlife. Gambling is on and off again but only for foreigners, and nightclubs are having trouble meeting expenses with such thin attendance.

CUBA

NIGHTCLUBS. Some of the city's fabulous night clubs (Tropicana) are still open and offer two nightly shows to an over-filled house. The bars and cocktail lounges functioning as usual, except for the diluted scotch and the scarcity of beer, also attract many customers. If you are lucky, you can drink Russian champagne for only $7 a bottle, Albanian red wine, and of course, reasonable rum anytime at reasonable prices.

It is a good idea to check with the hotel clerk to see that the club still exists—*Montmartre* and *Sans Souci*, longtime favorites of New York visitors, have been closed.

Each of the luxury hotels has a nightclub. Recently they have featured Cuban talent instead of the imported stars, and the locally produced shows are fast in pace and brilliant in execution.

TROPICANA. The Cuban Government has taken over this club, long ballyhooed as Havana's most fabulous nightclub. This quite famous showplace is in suburban Havana, a Spanish mansion surrounded by nine acres of tropical gardens—onetime villa of a Cuban lady who was the widow of a U.S. senator. The reconstruction and decor are tastefully opulent. The gambling hall is inside the building proper and the shows are presented outside under a proscenium of magnificent palms. When it rains or the crowd is overflowing the show moves into a vast room of concrete and glass arches so adroitly designed that there is no feeling of being indoors.

STARLIGHT TERRACE, just between the Casino Parisien and the gambling lounge, is pleasant, with entertainment while you have a cocktail.

CARIBE ROOM (*Habana Libre*) has shows at 10:30 and 1 a.m. with colorful costumes, original music and long-limbed Cuban dancers.

COPA ROOM (*Riviera*) has also full productions at 10:15 and 12:30.

CASINO (*Capri*) has shows at 10:15 and 1:15.

If you want something Cuban try the smaller clubs. A typical place is the Bambú Club near the airport; the Night and Day is on the same highway.

In Miramar, near the dog track, is the Pennsylvania, where the crowd will be composed of Cubans of all classes.

Getting back to that highway to the airport, there's a place known as the Mambo. Here you will find dozens of unescorted women; young, beautiful, and attractively dressed. If you have the feeling they would retire with you to a back room you are quite right.

JUST FOR A DRINK. There are sidewalk cafés on the Prado in front of the National Capitol where you can watch the world stroll by.

There are several colorful—and just a little bit rough—bars on the waterfront which cater to seafarers and the braver tourists. A block off the Prado, the streets are lined with dubious bars which attempt to entice the lonely male travelers, and quite often succeed.

GAMBLING

During the Batista regime gambling of all sorts was wide open throughout Havana—casinos, cockfights, numbers games, national lottery, pin-ball machines and slot-machines. What gambling is left in Havana is largely for the tourist. Even the slot-machines have been banned.

The lottery vendors are still at work in Havana, but they have a hard time selling their wares. The lottery has been converted to an incomprehensible savings plan which returns your money with interest after umpteen years. Safe, but no fun.

SHOPPING

Shops catering exclusively to the tourist are found in hotel arcadas and all along the Prado, the main boulevard leading from the sea to the Central Plaza. The larger places have fixed prices, but there's no harm in haggling in the smaller ones. There is no central market of interest to the visitor, but scores of small stores offer a variety of merchandise and the two staples carried home by most tourists—rum and cigars. Except for a few decorative products, Cuba has little to please the traveler in search of native handicrafts. Imported goods have completely disappeared.

CIGARS. Havana cigars are known the world over and cost here about half what they do in the United States and Europe. They come in an amazing variety of shapes and sizes and blends, thus it is wise to investigate preferences before leaving home. If you are buying for a gentleman friend and don't have the vaguest idea what he smokes ask for *Monte Cristo* No. 4, a safe choice appreciated by almost any smoker. If the gift is extra-special cigar stores will arrange for personalized bands inscribed with name or initials.

Most Cuban cigars are absolutely topnotch, but the following brands are considered the best for foreign tastes: *H. Upmann, Romeo y Julieta, Hoyo de Monterrey, Larrañaga, and Partagás.*

RUM. It is not strange that Cuba, the world's greatest sugar producer, is known for its superior rums. Light and dark, they are as good as any in the world.

The best rum for the money is the light *Bacardi.* An excellent and inexpensive dark rum is *Matusalem* (sold in other parts of the world under the name *Matusa* because of copyright problems). The connoisseur will prefer the slightly more expensive *Bacardi añejo.* Travelers who fear overweight charges on air luggage have been known to buy their rum at the airport after checking in at the airline counter.

CORDIALS. Those who do not take their drinking seriously may desire to fill their liquid quota with cordials. Cuban brands are not the most subtle in the world, but they come in astounding tropical flavors at amazingly cheap prices. Coconut, cacao, banana, tangerine, coffee and dozens of exotic flavors.

WOMEN'S WEAR. Tobacco and rum as foremost attractions indicate that Cuba caters to the male visitor. Best bets for the distaff are in embroidered shawls and linen blouses and dresses of all kinds. Unfortunately styles tend toward the gaudy, but careful shopping will produce simple and attractive patterns. Cuban women do not wear hats except in social emergencies but in church they don delicate lace *mantillas*, often handkerchief size. These gossamer fabrics are popular as gifts for daughters and secretaries. Women also like the alligator bags, but do avoid the temptation to buy the ones with alligator head still attached unless you really know your woman.

MEN'S WEAR. The one male item which is absolutely *creole* and worn by Cubans in all walks of life is the *guayabera*. This is a shirt with a long tail worn outside the pants and traditionally white, although a few muted colors have been introduced in recent years. The finest are made of the best linen or sheer broadcloth. Usually worn with the collar open, this adaptable garment becomes socially acceptable with the addition of a bow-tie, and can be worn to all but the most exclusive functions. The pleats and pockets are a problem for laundries

outside Cuba and the *guayabera* has a sad tendency to wrinkle. But you should take at least one home as a souvenir. Available in junior sizes.

NATIVE GOODS. The tourist shops display a motley collection of leather goods, alligator shoes and bags and leather open-toed sandals. Much of this is junk, and should be carefully inspected. There are some interesting Cuban musical instruments, and the younger set is easily intrigued with a set of *bongo* drums. You will find bargains in native mahogany and other tropical woods, with durable salad bowls leading the list.

Generally it is a good idea to think carefully in the "native handicraft" shops. Be sure you can't get it cheaper at home.

SOMETHING SPECIAL. For the lover of art or the arcane, the cooperative Cuban Art Center in Cathedral Square offers a charming, often weird selection of voodoo charms and ornamental handmade jewelry. And some real bargains in colorful and really fine Cuban paintings and sculpture on permanent exhibition.

In this same square you can find intriguing hats woven of still-green fronds and colorful flowers. A great conversation-piece if you can get it home before the colors fade!

CALENDAR OF TRADITIONAL FIESTAS

When the Cuban decides it is time to celebrate, nothing stands in the way of a good time. The joyous Latin spirit spills into the streets in a riot of color and indigenous music. But the Cuban is orderly in his exuberance; and he is stimulated by the occasion rather than the bottle. Visitors are welcomed vociferously.

If you are in Cuba at the time of any of these celebrations don't hesitate to buy a supply of paper streamers and join the fun.

HAVANA. Carnival in Havana is held during the Lenten season on weekends over a period of three or four weeks. The weekdays are used to recuperate and prepare.

SANTIAGO DE CUBA. The founding of the city is celebrated with a three day donnybrook in which everyone takes part. Each year beginning July 24.

CAMAGUEY. Carnival from June 15 to June 30 annually.

TRINIDAD. The fiesta of *San Juan* and *San Pedro* June 24 to 30.

CIENFUEGOS. Fiestas during the four weeks following Easter.

CAIBARIEN. The *Parrandas de Noche Buena*, Christmas Eve and New Year's Day annually.

CUBA

The official holiday of the new revolutionary government is 26 July.

SPORTS

JAI ALAI. There are two *frontón* clubs in Havana, one of them known as "The Palace of Shouting". This ancient Basque game involves the use of three-walled courts, a hard, small ball and curved wicker baskets on the player's right hand. The fastest sport in the world, it demands incredible stamina—from player and wager— and is fascinating to watch. But since the government has seized the two *frontón* clubs, performances have not been resumed.

RACING. Oriental Park, Cuba's popular racetrack, has been banned by the government.

BOXING. There are regular Saturday night boxing matches, often with high caliber cards, at the Sport Stadium. This dramatic new arena—sometimes referred to as "the fried-egg buildinge"—is the unusual building you will pass coming into Havana from the airport. It seats 20,000 yet has no vertical supports.

SWIMMING. Finding a public beach in or near Havana is not easy, although the new government is opening several fine beaches east of the city in the near future. *La Concha* beach, in the Miramar residential section, can be reached easily by city bus from Havana proper.

GOLF. There are several top-notch golf courses in Havana that belonged to private clubs. But since the government has seized them, they have been left in a very poor condition, including the tennis courts, now property of the people.

COCKFIGHTING is a Cuban sport that commands a passion almost incomprehensible to foreigners. There are 800 cockfighting clubs in the country and the betting involves more money than any other sport. There are several arenas in Havana. Women are not usually welcome, except at the *Club Gallistico,* in the Vedado section.

USEFUL ADDRESSES. (All in Havana). *British Embassy,* Bolivar building, Cárcel and Morro Sts. *Canadian Embassy,* Infanta St. No. 16. *Cuban Tourist Commission,* Cárcel St. No. 109.

EXPLORING HAVANA

In spite of its brisk pace and imposing modern skyscrapers Havana is still a city marked with signs of the past and its Spanish heritage. Those who sample only its swimming pools, bars and gambling casinos will miss the opportunity to make a rewarding acquaintance with fascinating history. Even the most *blasé* traveler will admit that sometimes the best way to see a city is by guided tour. If time is short they are recommended, and can be arranged at any travel bureau or hotel desk. If you are on your own, inexpensive taxi rates allow individual forays. Unless you are guided by a local resident don't attempt the tours in your car because of parking problems. Guides will take groups of three or four at reasonable fees. If you do venture out alone and on foot, be sure you receive explicit directions—confusing at the very best, because many Havana streets have several different names!

Morro Castle

The battlement across the bay with the familiar lighthouse, Cuba's trademark. Can be reached by automobile through the new tunnel, but it's more fun to take the old route: board a small launch on the Havana side of the bay near the docks, take a puffing bus up the hill. Guided tours—you would be lost alone—leave the main entrance at regular intervals.

This splendid fortress was constructed by the Spaniards in 1597 against the threat of pirates and British attack after Sir Francis Drake sacked the town of Cartagena and sailed menacingly up and down in front of Havana. The Morro was designed after a famous Moorish fortress in Lisbon. Its walls soar a hundred feet above the Gulf of Mexico, which washes its base. Seventy-foot moats surround the building, many of them carved from solid rock.

The interior of the fortress is composed of central courts surrounded by storybook dungeons, casements, storerooms, magazines, kitchens, halls and crenelated walls. There is an ominous chute, once used for garbage and the bodies of executed prisoners, which spills into the water below. Even today the visitor can spot the sharks swimming in the water, waiting for a snack.

There are Morro castles in Cuba, Puerto Rico and many other islands. This is because the term *morro* (promontory or headland) was applied by the Spanish to any fort situated on jutting points of land.

La Cabaña Fortress

Situated just behind the Morro, this historic fort appears as a continuous wall along the bluff overlooking Havana bay. Also reached by the tunnel or motor launch. Completed about 1774 and known by its full title as *Castillo de San Carlos de la Cabaña*.

The history of La Cabaña is one of futility. Ten years in building, it cost the then fantastic sum of fourteen million dollars. When the Spanish King was told of this he gazed intently across the Atlantic, declaring that the walls must be high enough to be seen from Spain, or at least that's the way the story is told. In spite of the cost La Cabaña was useless as a fortress, and never a shot was fired in defense of Havana. And the convict workers imported to raise the battlement brought to Cuba with them a scourge of yellow fever which spread during the next century through America and Europe.

The only useful purpose the building served was as a prison and place of execution. In fact, Castro has made extensive use of it in the past few years.

El Templete

This ancient shrine commemorates the site of the first Mass said in Havana in 1517. The actual spot is marked by a giant ceiba tree, grown from an offshoot of an original which was cut down in 1828 and converted into relics. At one time the bones of Columbus were soberly inspected here by the citizenry. The chapel of Templete is open every day to tourists. It contains three paintings by the French artist Vermay. One pictures the meeting of the first municipal council, another the first Mass, with bewildered Indians as spectators. There is a bust of Columbus which is said to have provided a model for the features of Columbus in the painting now hanging in the rotunda of the capital in Washington.

A couple of minutes walk from Templete is La Fuerza Castle, the oldest fort in Cuba and second oldest in all the new world. Legend has it that De Soto departed from this building on the expedition that led to the discovery of the Mississippi river. And in one of the towers of the castle his wife waited in vain for his return, perishing from sorrow when she learned of his death.

Cathedral Square

Standing in the middle of this tiny plaza the visitor has his only really impressive view of the colonial facades of historic Havana. Even the commercial buildings retain the pattern of antiquity—by rigid construction law. One side of the square is dominated by the Havana Cathedral. The bones of Columbus, after a brief stay at Templete, were said to have rested here for over a hundred years. (Historians disagree on all the proudly proclaimed tombs where Columbus' bones are supposed to have reposed—there is no question that they certainly got around). Ponce de León, before he went to Florida to search for that elusive fountain, once lived in a house on this square. Behind the venerable walls are some decidedly up-to-date activities. Very modern and abstract paintings and sculpture are on exhibition in the Cuban Art Center opposite the cathedral. Next door a rum company provides free *daiquiris* in a building which is impressive in its colonial serenity. Gift shops, a bank, and a museum complete the square.

Plaza De Armas

The first public square in Havana dating back to 1519. For centuries the center of social and political life, it has been restored for modern visitors. Legend promises that De Soto's men, after harrowing adventures in Florida, fulfilled a vow by crawling on hands and knees to this spot all the way from the wharf.

Paseo De Marti

Better known as the *Prado*, this is Cuba's *Champs-Elysées*. It was designed by the French landscape artist Forestier to cut through Havana's most fashionable residential section and was paved and rebuilt in 1902 by Leonard Wood, then acting as governor of Cuba. Now beginning to assume a shabby Broadway appearance, it is still the heart of Havana.

Malecón Drive

The name means wall or embankment, and today's Malecón runs from the bay past the new section of Vedado until it is swallowed by the tunnel leading to the residential section of Miramar. Located on the Malecón, opposite Morro Castle, is La Punta fortress, destroyed by the guns of the Morro, briefly commandeered by the British in the siege of 1762.

Rum and Tobacco Factories

Nearly all rum and cigar companies have regular tours through their buildings. Many are located in Old Havana and provide a fascinating half-hour for the tourist. Most of the cigars are still made by hand, in spite of Rube Goldberg machines which turn them out much more quickly; the government regulates the output of the machines so the Cuban cigar-makers will not become jobless. In the rum houses you will be treated royally and plied with delicious *daiquiris*. They also sell their products. To be quite frank, rum costs more here than in stores, but after a few drinks you won't care.

Residential Sections

Every visitor should make one leisurely drive through the residential districts of Miramar, Biltmore and Country Club. Here are the homes built by sugar and tobacco fortunes. Their splendor represents a Cuba which is disappearing in the turmoil of social change. The palatial houses are set in forests of tropical fronds.

PROVINCE OF PINAR DEL RIO

A tour of the provinces with Havana as a starting point would logically lead the traveler to this western-most province of Cuba. There are comfortable buses, but the trip is short and a delightful drive by private automobile. The Central Highway is reached by following the Malecón through the Miramar residential section. On the way down take the highway through the interior. There are miles and miles where the road is entirely covered by arches of overhanging trees and the effect is that of driving through cool green tunnels. Along the highway the countryfolk stand by bright displays of tropical fruit. During the sugar harvest tiny trains and tractor-powered wagons will be bringing the sugar cane to the mills.

Mariel is the first town of any size. Here is located the Cuban Naval Academy, housed in an old fortress above a lovely bay which is delight to swimmers and skin-divers. Soon after leaving Mariel the motorist passes the second bay, Bahia Honda. From this point the terrain is mountainous—not very high mountains, but rising abruptly from the tropical valleys—and the scenery becomes more and more spectacular.

PINAR DEL RIO. The best place to stay in all Pinar del Rio province is at the *Hotel Rancho San Vicente,* nestled between some imposing mountains. It has a swimming pool, also some of the finest of Cuba's medicinal springs. Food is good in the modest restaurant, and fishing and hiking excursions are easily arranged.

There are also mineral springs in nearby San Diego de los Baños. The government has invested large sums here in improving the facilities of these excellent thermal springs.

S. Diego

Pinar del Rio (pine woods by the river) is the capital city of Pinar del Rio, the province. About 110 miles from Havana, some two and half hours along the Central Highway, or reached by bus or train. A pleasant unpretentious city, surrounded by some of the world's most fertile tobacco lands. The special leaf used to wrap the finest cigars comes only from this region.

A few minutes drive from Pinar del Rio is the lush, green valley of *Viñales*, named for a tiny hamlet nestling among the farmlands. The valley is walled by the Organo mountains and is a cameo of rich earth and tropical plants. This area is Cuba's hidden treasure, and the highlight of the excursion into Pinar del Rio province.

Returning to Havana the trip can be varied. At Mariel the motorist may choose the new, broad highway which follows the coast through Playa de Santa Fé and Playa Baracoa. There are dozens of inlets along this route to tempt the fisherman and the skin-diver.

S. DIEGO. Reservations should be made in advance at the hotels: *Julve, Cabarrouy, Mirador* and *Saratoga.* Altogether an ideal place for the visitor with flexible itinerary; Cuban spas are pleasant and very inexpensive.

PROVINCE OF HAVANA

This is the smallest province on the island, but it contains the capital, Havana, already covered. But there are interesting excursions from the city, now easily managed by the motorist due to the multi-million dollar tunnel under the bay. When the traveler emerges from the tunnel he is on a fine modern highway lined with futuristic lighting equipment that might have been designed by Calder. The road is wide and smooth through this new East Havana section to a series of quaint towns and beautiful beaches. Most of these were private property in exclusive housing developments until recently, but now have been made public. Ask to be directed to Veneciana, Hermosa, Cuba, or Santa María del Mar, all delightful beaches. Guanabo beach is known for its fishing, and boats can be rented for half the price charged in Havana.

Cojimar is a fishing village, once the home of Ernest Hemingway, and the scene of his *"The Old Man and the Sea"*. Small water-front cafés provide succulent seafood specialties with unpronounceable names.

The ancient city of Guanabacoa retains a colonial atmosphere which is quickly disappearing in nearby Havana. In years past wealthy families fled the capital to spend their summer months here, and some of the mansions are still standing.

An ambling drive through the city is of interest to those who wish to conjure up the past with the inspection of narrow streets, grilled windows and old churches. It is quite possible that Guanabacoa was a resort even before the arrival of the *conquistadores*, for the Indian name means "Place of Waters".

The Parochial Church at Guanabacoa is worth a stop and visitors in the area on 15 and 26 August each year should observe the religious procession honoring Our Lady of the Assumption. There is also an interesting church in nearby *Santa María del Rosario*.

Golfers will want to make at least one round at the very new *Villa Real* golf course, overlooking a beautiful valley to the south and forty miles of ocean to the north. This is a private course, but green privileges can be arranged at hotels —and it has been said that there's no harm in just showing up if you are serious. About twenty minutes from Havana, through the tunnel.

Speleologists will be in their element at the *Cuevas del Cura*. These caves are found about twenty miles from Havana at Tapaste, near San José de las Lajas, which is on the Central Highway. Interesting and well-lighted, so the whole family can go exploring.

Straight south from Havana about 36 miles—the width of the island—is the fishing center of Batabano. This is the center of Cuba's sponge industry and a favored sports fishing locale.

MATANZAS PROVINCE

Traveling east from Havana by road the motorist has a choice of two routes. Unless time is pressing, he should take one going and the other on the return trip. The Central Highway follows a languid course inland through storybook countryside, then doubles back to Matanzas, a trip of three or four hours. Until recently this was the only land-route but with the opening of a new sea-clinging superhighway the area can be reached in little more than an hour of driving past superlative beaches.

The city of Matanzas (the name means *slaughter*, it is sad to report, commemorating a massacre of Indians by Spanish troops) is a thriving commercial port on the north coast. A coral reef keeps smooth the waters of the broad bay, making Matanzas a shipping point for sugar and tobacco. Founded in 1692, the seaport city still offers signs of its antiquity, including cobbled streets and house numbers on sunken tiles in the walls. The citizens will proudly recite the city's qualifications as a cultural center—and they may remind you that it is known as the "Athens of Cuba".

Matanzas

There is an old cathedral to intrigue tourists on a history binge, with a Book of Baptisms which records births from the year 1693.

CUBA

Two of the principal tourist attractions of the province are close at hand. The *Yumuri* valley has been a favorite topic for Cuba's poets and writers, and is second only to *Viñales* in beauty. A postcard-size valley, it is surrounded by bluffs on three sides and by the Yumuri river.

About three miles from Matanzas and near the beach are the *Bellamar Caves*. These were discovered in 1861 when a Chinese workman digging limestone chopped through the rock into the roof of the cavern. The finest caves in Cuba, they have been compared to the Mammoth Caves of Kentucky. Visitors can follow miles of well-lighted tunnels and church-sized grottos. Guides are on hand from 7 in the morning to 8 p.m.

MATANZAS. There are several clean but small hotels, including the *Gran Paris* and the *Velasco,* but most visitors are heading for the luxury spots in nearby *Varadero.*

Varadero

Varadero is a few minutes drive from Matanzas, east and ten miles out on a long key which juts out from the mainland. Many veteran travelers consider this the best beach in the world. It certainly has the finest sand, the most impossibly blue waters and the best reputation in the Caribbean, reached from Havana in twenty minutes by air, or by bus or automobile. On weekends the roads are jammed with *Habaneros* who maintain beautiful homes there, or stay at the many hotels and boarding houses. In the first part of August each year Varadero draws enthusiastic crowds to the annual boat races, and skin-divers have found the clear waters just right.

The beach itself is not long, but the sand gleams like powdered silver, the water is delightful and the accommodations are plentiful. The only flaw in this perfect spot is the prevalence of mosquitoes after dark, so it is a good idea to come armed with a good repellent. The town and beaches are crowded during summer (and during Holy Week) by Cubans, but foreign visitors come during the entire year. There are excellent facilities for yachtsmen and the fishing is good.

HOTELS. There are a score of hotels on the beach, and some are very good.

Most spectacular is the *Varadero Internacional,* a traditional resort hotel with all the trimmings, including large pool, nightclubs, and tourist shops.

There is a new motel-hotel which is swank in every way, the *Oasis.*

CUBA

Rates are high here, but service is excellent and the place has a pleasant sense of intimacy...

At the end of the beach is the unusual *Kawama Club*. There are delightful thatched-roofed bungalows among the palm trees and only a quick skip to the water's edge. A perfect place for a quiet holiday. A reservation needed here.

There are many smaller places, some of them expertly managed.

The *Casa La Rosa* and the *Casa Happiness* are pleasant and informal but sufficiently modern. Others tend to the old-fashioned—with large airy rooms. Travelers have reported agreeable stays at *Hotel Astoria Inn*, *Leon* and *Imperial*.

RESTAURANTS. *The Red Coach Inn* is located at the International Yacht Basin and overlooks the water.

Most of the best food in Varadero, however, is at the hotels. The *Kawama* gets top billing, for food and for relaxing atmosphere. The buffets are fine. Also the *Oasis* and the *Varadero International*, for more formal dining. The sea food is excellent and very inexpensive anywhere you see a thatched roof and a tablecloth.

San Miguel de los Banos

A few miles south of Cardenas is the famous resort, which boasts five carbonated springs. Located in beautiful surroundings, it has long been known as the Vichy of the Americas. The affectionate couples you see are probably newly-weds; this is a favorite spot for Cuban honeymoons.

This spa was supposedly discovered by a Negro slave; after drinking the magic waters his ulcerated leg was completely healed. That's the story, anyway. It is true that Cuban doctors recommend the healing waters for internal and external use, but the tourist can settle for the delightful countryside and restful atmosphere.

San Miguel is a quaint city known for the noted religious shrine high on a nearby hilltop, visited by thousands of Cubans during Holy Week.

S. MIGUEL. Hotels are the *Cuba*, *San Miguel*, *Villa Verde* and *Gran Hotel del Balneario*.

LAS VILLAS PROVINCE

Next in the eastward tour is the province of Las Villas, with the capital city of Santa Clara. At last, a capital city without the exact name of the province it governs. But this is not really the case, as this area is often called "Santa Clara province".

Santa Clara, on the familiar Central Highway, is a progressive city with new buildings still scarred by the battle which was the turning point in the recent revolution. There was heavy bomb damage in some sections of the town, now largely repaired.

At night there are band concerts from the stand in the center of the plaza. The visitor soon realizes that this is the principal diversion of the townspeople, in spite of the new nightclub. Here the traditional Latin promenade takes place: the boys and girls circle the plaza—in separate groups unless engaged—and exchange flirtatious pleasantries as they pass.

S. CLARA. There is a new hotel, the *Gran,* rising rather incongruously in the middle of town, which features a rooftop bar and restaurant. Other hotels are the *Central* and the *Santa Clara.* A touch of city life has been brought to the capital with the new *Venecia* nightclub, near the airport.

Cienfuegos

This old city (of "hundred fires") was founded in 1514 and is known as "The Pearl of the South"—which makes it the "pearl" of the "Pearl of the Antilles". You seldom hear an auto horn here, as the local Rotary club accomplished the seemingly impossible job of campaigning successfully against traffic noise.

The entrance to the city of Cienfuegos by water is guarded by the old Spanish fortress Castillo de Jagua which overlooks the bay. Visitors are welcome here and can inspect the ramparts from which the city was defended many times from pirates.

Within short distances of Cienfuegos are found two prized attractions of the area. The Hanabanilla Falls are worth a side trip, and also the Botanical Gardens, the largest center of its kind in the western hemiphere. The Botanical Gardens are open to visitors.

CIENFUEGOS. The recently completed *Hotel-Motel International Jagua,* is a quite modern resort, housed in a reconstructed mansion. Other hotels are the *Bahia,* the *Bristol,* and the highly recommended *Pasacaballos Club.* Speciality of the restaurants is sea food, with tiny oysters from the bay as the first choice.

Caibarién, famous for its fishing, lies on the northern coast of Las Villas province.

Hotels are the *Gran Hotel Sagua* and the *Comercio.*

Sancti Spiritus is an old town distinguished by Moorish influences. The cathedral was constructed in the 16th century, and the first sermons demanding freedom for Cuba's slaves were delivered from its pulpit. Probably the oldest building in the town is the theater, built on the banks of the river. The town is located at a point near the exact geographical center of Cuba.

Hotel is the *Perla de Cuba* with American plan rates.

CAMAGÜEY PROVINCE

The province has been called "the Texas of Cuba". For the first time the Central Highway leaves the meandering route through mountains and enters rolling flatlands much like the *pampas* of Argentina or the plains of the American southwest. Here are seen the Cuban cowboys—the *vaqueros*—who dress in the best Western tradition. A fancy handtooled saddle, boots and whips, spurs and a ten-gallon hat set him apart from other Cubans. In the fields there are herds of humped-backed cattle, the result of inbreeding the native stock with the hot-weather species developed in Texas and Florida.

The capital city of Camagüey is—you might have guessed it—Camagüey. The city was originally on the north coast and was known to Columbus as *Puerto Principe*. But the constant danger of pirate invasion forced a move to the present site. Despite the precaution, Henry Morgan once sacked the town and locked the leading citizens in a church while he plundered their homes.

The colonial atmosphere still clings to the city, known for its churches and beautiful women. Except for the gilded interior of *Nuestra Señora de la Merced*, however, the churches are more in quantity than quality. As for the women, a Cuban only has to say "she is from Camagüey" to bestow a pretty compliment.

Camagüey is on the rail and bus lines to Havana, the trip usually taking about 10 hours, and a stop on Cubana Airline's interior flights. Most visitors are curious about the huge, gracefully-designed earthenware jugs, some six or seven feet tall, which are seen all over the town. These are *tinajones*, used to catch rain water in the days before central water supply, and today bright and interesting lawn decorations.

There are few noteworthy attractions for the tourist, other than really fine hunting—pigeon, quail, guinea hen—and excellent fishing on both coasts. In Camagüey province, as well as in Las Villas, motorists are often startled by highways covered with land crabs, millions of them. The only thing to do is to drive ahead unmercifully.

CUBA

Hotels are the *Colón*, the *Plaza*, the *Residencial* and the *Gran*. This last is one of the strangest hotels in Cuba—it is spread over three acres of ground, looks like a feudal castle, and was once a barracks for Spanish cavalry. There is also a motel, *Santa Lucia* about 50 miles from the city.

Trinidad

This quaint sleepy little town is Cuba's most authentic historical center. The third town settled by the Spaniards in 1514, is was here that Hernán Cortés prepared the expedition with which he conquered Mexico. One of the first settlers was William Becker of Philadelphia; his descendants, with the new name of *Bécquer* are still living in the town.

Once the richest and most opulent town in Cuba, Trinidad has fallen on sad days. For more than a century it was forgotten and rarely visited, even though historians class it with Toledo in Spain and Taxco in Mexico as an example of Hispanic architecture. The town came to life briefly when the Cuban government declared the entire town a national monument, and placed it under the control of the Cuban Tourist Commission. Unfortunately very little has been done to follow up this move. In many sections of the town priceless colonial houses and roads are deteriorating. Nevertheless there are many fascinating points of interest to be seen today. The old Serrano Square is the actual spot where Cortés recruited his men; in the tiny plaza called *Jique* is the old residence where the first Catholic service was held; and just in front of this house, the ruins of the old city hall. The barracks of the Spanish soldiers is now a public school. There is the house where Alexander Humboldt, the famous German naturalist lived for two years, and many other residences with the grilled windows and studded doors of colonial architecture.

The streets of Trinidad are narrow and twisting and for the most part cobbled with tiny round stones laid a century ago by slaves and political prisoners. Today there are "pro-cobble" and "anti-cobble" factions in Trinidad. The first is composed of those who wish to retain the historical pattern of the town, the second who insist the cobble-stoned streets are uncomfortable and useless. Recently the two groups clashed so violently that only a stern word from Prime Minister Fidel Castro stopped the quarrel.

Townspeople love to recite to visitors the story of the Trinidad man, many decades ago, who began to decorate the floors of his mansion with mosaics from Europe. It was whispered in Trinidad that he did not have enough money to complete the work. This so offended his dignity that he paved the floors of his home with $17 gold pieces. But the governor reminded him that it was illegal to "tread on the King". So the eccentric millionaire removed all the gold coins, replacing them edges up! Unfortunately neither house nor gold pieces remain to verify the story.

In the nearby *San Luis* valley there is still standing a strange tower of unknown function nearly seven stories high. The explanation of this one is that the man who built it was weary of hearing the boasts of a neighbor who had the deepest well in Trinidad. In the early 17th century church, *Santisima Trinidad*, visitors can see the famous crucifix, *Christ of Vera Cruz*. The ship carrying this relic had tried unsuccessfully to leave the harbor on two occasions. The captain decided that this was an omen that the crucifix was meant to remain in Trinidad—and there it has been since 1713.

Three miles from Trinidad is the best beach on the Caribbean side of Cuba, Ancon Beach. Several hotels and restaurants are being constructed here to meet an expected tourist demand.

TRINIDAD. There are two small, old-fashioned hotels in the town, the *Canada* and the *La Ronda*. But high on a mountainside on the edge of Trinidad is a fine new motel, *Las Cuevas*. There is a good restaurant and bedrooms look out over a panorama of hills and sea and the red tile roofs of Trinidad. The motel is perched over the mouth of *La Maravillosa*, an intriguing cave converted into a nightclub. Here the tourist may enjoy the rather weird ritual of drinking rum among the stalactites and stalagmites.

ORIENTE PROVINCE

This is the easternmost province in Cuba. The decisive battles in the Cuban War of Independence were fought here, and the revolutionary movement of Fidel Castro was spawned in the rugged *Sierra Maestra* mountains.

Santiago de Cuba

The capital of the province, once capital of the country, is one of the oldest cities in the Americas. It was founded in 1514 and moved across the bay to the present site in 1522. Hernán Cortés was the first mayor of Santiago, and enchanting traces of the colonial epoch are still evident everywhere. But Santiago also bears the imprint of French influences. In 1776 a revolt of the slaves in Haiti sent thousands of French colonists in flight to Santiago; the stamp of French customs, culture and surnames was impressed permanently on the city.

Santiago is not on the regular tour for travelers. As a result there is more color and fewer tourist traps, the pace is relaxed,

CUBA

and travelers who do not speak Spanish will have to make signs to the waitress. The city is reached by only one major airline, the country's own *Cubana*. There is train service, and Santiago is the terminal point on the Central Highway; the drive from the west over the mountains is spectacular.

The heart of the city is the *Parque de Céspedes*, unusual for Cuba in that it contains no bandstand, monuments or statues. But after sunset the promenades are filled with laughing, talking townspeople and strolling musicians. This is a good vantage point for visitors who wish to observe the traditional carnival held each year in July. This is a popular party, designed for the people and not the tourists; the streets are lavishly decorated and business comes to a standstill so that everyone can shuffle through the town to the beat of incessant drums.

 HOTELS. None of the hotels in Santiago are comparable with the modern facilities in Havana. In the city itself *The Versailles* is probably the best for creature comforts, and is usually favored by foreigners, along with the older *Casa Grande*. The *Imperial* is not quite up to the *Casa Grande*, but the restaurant is better. It is not unknown for a tourist to stay at the latter, but to take his meals at the *Imperial*. The *Venus* is recommended for budget-minded travelers.

If you are traveling by private automobile you will prefer to stay at the fine *Rancho Club Motel*, a few minutes drive from the center of town. Restaurant, air-conditioned rooms and a wonderful view of the city of Santiago and its harbor below.

RESTAURANTS. The above mentioned *Rancho Club* is slightly expensive by *Santiago standards*, but you pay for the view when you settle the bill. *The Lido Club* is in the *Vista Alegre* residential section; a good spot for a drink and a chance to observe the town's younger set, although the place is dark as a stack of black cats.

The *Club 300* is a popular luncheon spot. An interesting place for a full evening is the *Club San Pedro del Mar*, practically in the shadow of Morro Castle. Excellent sea food. Dancing, and a show on Saturday nights. At the airport a restaurant features native dishes under the thatched roof of a Cuban *bohío*. *Lechón asado* is particularly good; those with a yen for the unusual may order the fried fruit of the *yucca*.

Bacardí Municipal Museum. There is no admission charge to this interesting museum, open daily from 8 to 11 a.m. and 2 to 4 p.m. (but closed on Saturdays and national holidays). Endowed by the *Bacardí* family, of rum fame. Collections of Indian relics, historical momentos and a large display of art objects and paintings.

San Juan Hill. About two miles from the city, this is the site of the decisive battle of the Cuban War of Independence, where the Rough Riders won the day on July 1, 1898. At that time an old Spanish fort stood near the hill. Today the area consists of gardens laid over the original trenches and memorials to the heros of the battle. There is a stone tower from which the visitor can see the surrounding country across which the Americans advanced to the attack on Santiago after landings in Siboney and Daiquiri.

Morro Castle. High above the bay, this fortress, older than Havana's *Morro*, is somewhat smaller but more accessible than its namesake in Havana. Practically carved from the rock on which it stands, this fort was the key to Spain's defense of Cuba in the early 1900s. On the land side it is approached by crossing a 30-foot moat. Visitors are free to explore in the crumbling ruins, and they may see the dungeons where Hobson and his comrades were held prisoner after the sinking of the *Merrimac*. There is a marvelous view of the harbor and of Santiago resting against the mountains—this landmark of the Spanish Main is Cuba's "land's end".

Santiago Cathedral. This ancient building is unusual in that it is some 18 feet above street level, with the ground floor being occupied with shops and offices. One of the oldest of the Spanish cathedrals, this was the center of the second diocese established in the New World—it once held ecclesiastical jurisdiction over Florida and Louisiana.

The Cemetery. In this case at least, an interesting place to visit. Many of Cuba's most illustrious citizens are buried here. The tomb of José Martí is encircled with a lovely garden bright with the white roses he wrote of so often. Here too is the tomb of Estrada Palma, Cuba's first president. It is the custom to spend large sums on the burial places of loved ones in Cuba, and the cemetery is a small city of the dead.

Turquino Peak. Cuba's tallest mountain. Very popular with climbers. No water but there is a wild grapevine from which refreshing liquid can be extracted. Jamaica, almost a hundred miles away, can be seen on a clear day. Best reached from Santiago by boat.

El Cobre Sanctuary. About a dozen miles from Santiago, out the Central Highway and up into the mountains. This religious shrine is dedicated to the *"Virgen de la Caridad del Cobre"*, Cuba's patron saint. The altars are inlaid with exotic tropical woods and the stained-glass windows are the best in the area. Visited every day by the devoted, and once a year the end of a long pilgrimage in which thousands take part.

ISLE OF PINES

A possession proudly held by Cuba—but only since 1925, when a treaty transferred the title from the United States. A fabled island from the time Columbus discovered it in 1494 (he was once stranded there) until Robert Louis Stevenson used it as the model for his classic *"Treasure Island"*. About the size of the state of Rhode Island, *Isla de Pinos*, was for many years almost unknown except to occasional sportsmen who pulled fantastic catches from its sea-shore perimeter. In 1955 an American capitalist, Arthur Vining Davis, purchased a large share of the island for tourist and business development, sparking a temporary boom. The island also attracted numerous visitors due to its status as a free port. But this privilege has been suspended and the development of the island has slowed.

CUBA

The *Isle of Pines* is just below the Cuban mainland. There is regular ferry service from *Batabanó*, an overnight trip, or frequent flights on "Q" Airlines, a flight of just over half an hour. The capital and principal city is Nueva Gerona, and the island is under the administration of Havana province.

Visitors are surprised to see marble used everywhere in the island as common building material; even streets and sidewalks are sometimes paved with it. There's marble in them thar hills.

For the tourist the lure of the Isle of Pines is found in its scenic beauty, and the magnificent beaches and fishing grounds. At Bibijagua, on the north coast, is one of the world's best black beaches. If you prefer your sand in conventional colors, the entire island is rimmed with miles of white sand beaches.

At this writing, Isle of Pines is out of bounds for tourists. It is the site of the country's biggest concentration camp and compound for political prisoners.

SPAS. There are mineral springs at Santa Fé and Santa Barbara.

JAMAICA

Fivefold Riviera

BY

WILLIAM W. DAVENPORT

(Mr. Davenport is also the author of subsequent sections on Haiti, Exploring Puerto Rico, The Virgin Islands, Leeward Islands, French West Indies, Windward Islands, Trinidad & Tobago and the Dutch West Indies.)

"Xamayca," the gentle Arawaks called it, "a land of streams and forests." Historian Andres Bernaldez, a shipmate of Columbus, pronounced it "the fairest isle that eyes have seen," adding in the next breath (or was it a printer's error?) a startling bit of misinformation: "It is not mountainous." Columbus was more accurate. Asked by Queen Isabella to describe Jamaica, he crumpled a piece of paper and tossed it onto a table. "It looks like this, Your Majesty," he said.

This magnificent scrap of deep green crumpled paper floats in the blue Caribbean 90 miles south of Cuba, 500 air miles from Florida. The island capital, Kingston, with more than 350,000 inhabitants, is the largest English-speaking city south of Miami. Behind it lie the folded mountains. Four of the island's peaks rise to heights of more than 6,000 feet, the highest, Blue Mountain, soaring to 7,402. This, within the confines of a country no longer than 144 miles, no wider than 49, gives the island the grandeur of a continent in microcosm.

There are continental variations in the climate too. On the

sun-drenched, palm-shaded beaches you are most definitely in the tropics. Climb a thousand feet or so to one of the typical "hill stations" and you're suddenly in England on a balmy night in spring. Another thousand feet will have you reaching for a cashmere sweater or sitting happily by an English fire. The highest peaks occasionally know the sting of sleet, the swirl of snow.

In spite of these tonic changes, Jamaica remains the tropical island "par excellence" with all that this term evokes of exotic splendor. The vegetation, indescribably lush and green, is laced by hundreds of cascades, spilling down from the well-watered mountain heights and rushing to the coast in a series of arrowy rivers. At the mouths of these rivers lie the tranquil harbors of Jamaica with beach after splendid beach sweeping along the coast.

Jamaica has not one but five goldcoasts: Kingston, Montego Bay, Ocho Rios, Port Antonio, Mandeville. They are among the most developed in the Caribbean. Only Bermuda, Nassau and Puerto Rico can rival them from the point of view of tourist luxury, and none of these has the wild beauty of Jamaica's interior. The routes to the goldcoasts, good roads though narrow, lead through the tropical rain forests, deep gorges, and lush planted valleys of this interior; you won't see more spectacular scenery in all the West Indies.

British Accent

But scenery is not all. What will enchant you as much if not more about this island is its British accent. In spite of bumptious Bustamante, "Operation Shoulderstrap", and burning problems of its new independence Jamaica remains outwardly as British as Buckingham Palace, with all the delightful pageantry, pomp and peculiar circumstance that that implies. Handsome British Army officers, hand-picked and happy to be assigned to this fashionable station, set the tone, impeccable in shorts, imperious with swagger sticks. Native police, in pith helmets and fetching whites, are as big and bland as any London bobby. Even the little black schoolgirls, incongruously prim in their colorful uniforms, remain unmistakably British.

If you think Old England's slipping you'll change your mind when you participate in the elaborate tea rituals of the golf clubs or attend one of the garden parties at King's House. The clipped U-accent of the colonial whites, the lilting "broad a" diction of the colored natives: everything conspires to impart an enchanting British flavor to Jamaica, even Calypso verses when purveyed by masters with such fine old Anglo-Saxon names as *Sugar Belly, Pork Chop* and *Lord Fly*.

Away from the chink of the teacup, behind the bone china facade, Jamaica wrestles with the socio-economic problems of a semi-literate colonial people rising awkwardly but inevitably to political power and its attendant responsibilities. The seething political life of the island revolves around two cousins, bitter rivals, who have led Jamaica's million and a half descendants of African slaves in the struggle for self government. One is Sir Alexander Bustamante, a fast-talking, dynamic leader who made political hay of the aspirations of thousands of unskilled laborers whom he organized into an omnibus union, known as the Bustamante Union, and eventually into the Jamaica Labor Party. Known as Busta throughout the Caribbean political world this man, for better or for worse, is a power to be reckoned with in the fast-moving political evolution of the Caribbean. Once a hothead with a magnetic platform manner, he's a towering figure in Jamaican and British Commonwealth politics.

His rival, Norman Washington Manley, is the voice of moderation. A former Rhodes scholar and respected Kingston lawyer, he is the leader of the People's National Party and now Premier of Jamaica. The two men, both colored, symbolize the split personality of Jamaica. Bustamente represents the same sort of resentful, intuitive, exacerbated sensibility that caused the natives to stone the coffin of Governor Sir Edward Denham two decades ago because he had left orders to be buried at sea, thus, the mob insisted, "scorning to lie in Jamaican ground." Manley, a socialist, cultivated, reasonable, urbane, is the spirit of British gradualism in politics.

Secession from the West Indies Federation

Jamaica was the most reluctant of the ten scattered islands which became full members of the Federation of the West Indies in 1958. Six hundred miles removed from any Federation member, and the richest member after Trinidad, Jamaica feared she was destined to lose rather than gain economically by her membership in the Federation. Right from the beginning, Jamaicans were dissatisfied with their representation in the Federal government. It was felt that Jamaica, with her population of 1,700,000 (about half of the population of the Federation) was entitled to more than her allocated 17 seats in the Federal House of Representatives, which had 45 members in all. Already a heavy contributor of grants to the Federal government, Jamaican opposition mounted when the govern-

CAYMAN ISLANDS

Little Cayman

Cayman Brac

Boatswain Pt.

GRAND CAYMAN

Bodden

Georgetown

CARIBBEAN

SEA

Long Bay

Montego Bay

Montego Bay

Falmouth

Rio Bueno

Clark's Town

Brown's Town

Lucea

Green Island

N. Negril Pt.

C O R N W A L L

S. Negril Pt.

Negril

M I D

Savanna La Mar

Frankfield

Bluefields Bay

Bluefields

Mocho

Crab Pond Pt.

Santa Cruz

Luana Pt.

Black River

Mandeville

Por

Parottee Pt.

Gt. Pedro Bluff

JAMAICA

0   10   20 Miles

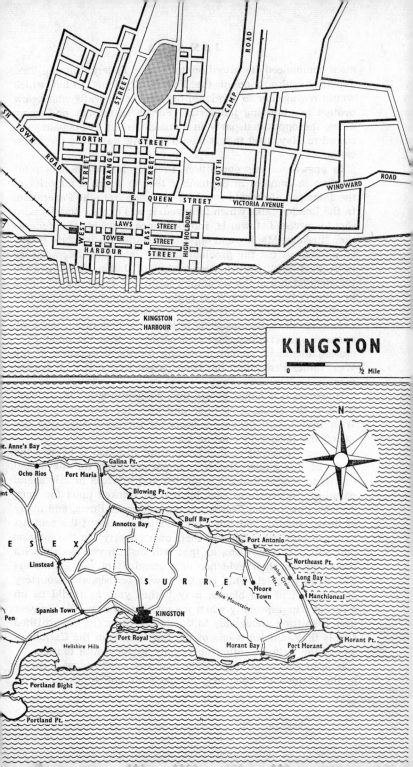

KINGSTON

0   ½ Mile

KINGSTON HARBOUR

NORTH STREET
ORANGE STREET
STREET
E. QUEEN STREET
LAWS STREET
TOWER STREET
WEST STREET
EAST STREET
HARBOUR STREET
HIGH HOLBORN
VICTORIA AVENUE
WINDWARD ROAD
CAMP ROAD
SOUTH
SPANISH TOWN ROAD

N

St. Anne's Bay
Ocho Rios
Port Maria
Galina Pt.
Blowing Pt.
Buff Bay
Annotto Bay
Port Antonio
Northeast Pt.
Long Bay
Moore Town
Manchioneal
John Crow Mts.
Blue Mountains
MIDDLESEX
SURREY
Linstead
Spanish Town
KINGSTON
Port Royal
Hellshire Hills
Pen
Portland Bight
Portland Pt.
Morant Bay
Port Morant
Morant Pt.

JAMAICA

ment announced its intention to levy a Federal Income Tax. Jamaicans also opposed the Federal Customs Union which would require her to eliminate the high tariff walls which now protect her budding industries. For these reasons and many more, the opposition party in Jamaica led by Bustamante declared in May, 1960 that it would no longer support the Federation.

In answer to this opposition, Premier Manley held a referendum in Jamaica in September 1961 in which a majority of the Jamaican electorate voted for secession from the Federation. In the London talks which followed, it was agreed that Jamaica should proceed towards independence outside the federation. Premier Manley and opposition leader Bustamante reached agreement on: the proclamation of Jamaican independence in August 1962; British sponsorship of Jamaica's application for membership in the Commonwealth; and Jamaica's readiness to support the existing West Indian Common Services pending permanent arrangements for their future.

As a result of the decisions to leave the Federation taken by Jamaica and Trinidad, and in accordance with the other Federation members, an act providing for the dissolution of the West Indies Federation has been passed by the British Parliament.

However, it is hoped by all, that the continuation of, at least, some of the common services and also, the University of the West Indies, will provide a basis for further cooperation between the former Federation members.

A deeper analysis of this fascinating situation is beyond the scope of this guide. But it is important even for the casual tourist to realize that all is not tea and hibiscus in this island paradise. Native Jamaicans have been worked upon for some decades now by the fire-eating magnetism of Busta, and many of them, equating tourism with colonialism, resent the contrast between tourist wealth and their own poverty. In the interior you will pass native shacks that will disturb you deeply with their squalor, their evidence of a standard of life almost inconceivably abject. This, combined with occasional discourtesy on the part of the blacks, may bother you, as it did us on a recent trip, especially when we reflected that political power here is shifting ineluctably to the darker race. The unvarnished fact is that Jamaica is one of the few islands in the Caribbean where the native is often unfriendly to the white tourist.

It is of course quite possible that any evidence of serpents in the Garden of Eden may escape your notice. Certainly in the hotels of Jamaica you will find the exemplary courtesy and superb service which are the hallmark of British-trained personnel. The tourist enclaves of Jamaica are far from the madding crowd's ignoble gripe.

Many tourists will find, however, that the political ferment of Jamaica adds a certain dimension to travel experience beyond the conventional formula of sun, fun and rum. Intelligent Jamaicans of both colors are aware of the island's vicious circle problem of overpopulation and underemployment. To cope with it, the government has launched an ambitious economic development program similar to Puerto Rico's famed "Operation Bootstrap." Designed to attract Canadian and American capital investment in island industry, the Jamaican program has been nicknamed "Operation Shoulderstrap" because one of the new industries brought in is the manufacture of brassières. When you see the mountains of this merchandise in the shops of Jamaica, you may be tempted to rename the project "Operation Uplift"; that's what it is in more ways than one.

There was a time when Jamaica needed only moral uplift. The island's history is the familiar Caribbean saga of human adventure and greed. Colonized by Columbus' son Diego as a kind of private fief under the Spanish crown, the island suffered the usual horrors of Spanish inefficiency and cruelty. When the Spaniards built their first settlement, New Seville, in 1509, there were about 60,000 native Arawaks on the island. In 1655 when the English seized Jamaica there were none of these gentle Indians left.

"Babylon of the West"

Under British rule, Jamaica became the greatest base for pirate fleets roving the Caribbean. Leader of the pirates was that famous British buccaneer, Henry Morgan. He had excellent connections; his uncle was the Governor of Jamaica, and the freebooters operated under the official protection of His Majesty's Government. They made their headquarters a town called Port Royal on a spit of land across from present-day Kingston. This place became a bazaar where British merchants could buy pirate loot at bargain prices. The waterfront was like a giant flea market, teeming with pirates and their wealthy customers. With the contempt of the glutted, the buccaneers lost fortunes in gambling; it was always easy enough to recoup. Rum flowed freely, golden green, "a hot, hellish and terrible liquor" so strong that the Spanish marvelled at the British capacity to consume it. Prostitution flourished, and the first recorded strip tease in the New World was performed without benefit of G string. Port Royal was the "Babylon of the West," "a Hades where Mammon holds sway," in short "the wickedest city in Christendom."

Less than 30 years old, Henry Morgan was the cock of this gilded walk. When tried on charges of piracy, he contended that he was not a pirate at all, but a respectable privateer, since England had been at war with Spain during most of his career. The jury agreed. He was acquitted, knighted, and appointed Lieutenant Governor of Jamaica! Sir Henry Morgan died in bed in 1688 and had a state funeral in Port Royal. Four years later, on June 7, 1692, an earthquake tilted two thirds of the city into the sea. Two thousand citizens perished; 6,000 houses collapsed, all the shops crumbled and sank with a million pounds sterling worth of pirate treasure irretrievably into mud. A tidal wave finished the job. Many called it the judgment of God. In any event, now it was Kingston's turn.

Sugar with its attendant prosperity and misery dominated island life throughout the 18th century with close to a million slaves passing through the slave market of Jamaica. By 1785 the island population numbered 250,000 black slaves, 25 for every one white inhabitant. In addition there were 10,000 vari-colored freedmen, most of them the manumitted offspring of white masters and black slaves. The Jamaica slave trade was abolished in 1807; slavery itself in 1833. The stage was set for the problems that face Jamaica today.

Most important factors in the island economy, in addition to the new industries of Operation Shoulderstrap, are sugar, bananas, coffee, and you. There were more than 225,000 visitors last year in this "fairest isle that eyes have seen," and Jamaica, whatever its local problems, remains a favorite of tourists with a taste for the social whirl. The roster of distinguished visitors over the last few years is headed by the Queen of England, includes such notables as her sister, Margaret Rose, Winston Churchill, Adlai Stevenson, Noel Coward, Alicia Markova, Kirk Douglas, Cleveland Amory, Laurence Olivier, Gene Kelly, the Oscar Hammersteins, Francis, Cardinal Spellmann, and Hedy Lamarr. You can get into the swim here without getting your feet wet.

PRACTICAL INFORMATION FOR JAMAICA

HOW TO GET THERE. *By Air.* Pan American has daily flights from New York and Miami to both Kingston and Montego Bay. Both Avianca and British Overseas Airways have direct service non-stop from New York to Kingston. British West Indies Airways, KLM and BOAC also provide regular service from Miami. Aerovias Panama Airways provides 30 day Caribbean triangle excusions from Miami to Kingston and Panama City at the special low price of $112.50. There are scheduled flights from Montreal by Trans Canada Airlines and BOAC; daily flights from New Orleans on Delta.

From Great Britain BOAC has regular daily flights from London to Kingston and Montego Bay, via New York.

By ship: Eastern Shipping Corporation offers regular sailings from Miami. United Fruit Line (New York) has accommodations for passengers on some of its cargo vessels. Innumerable cruise ships call at Kingston in winter season.

From Great Britain: Fyffes Line, Jamaica Banana Producers Line, Pacific Steam Navigation Co. and Royal Mail Lines. Also the French Line from Southampton and the Continent.

PASSPORTS. None are required of British subjects or citizens of Canada or the U.S.A. entering Jamaica as tourists for any period up to six months. You may occasionally be asked to show your return ticket as evidence that you are not settling down here permanently. British subjects require passports to re-enter their own country and to return home by way of the U.S. You will be given a tourist card on your arrival in Jamaica, which should be presented to the Immigration Officer on arrival and must be returned to immigration authorities on your departure.

CUSTOMS. You must make a customs declaration on arrival, but it's very simple. Most of the formalities take place painlessly while you're having that first rum punch. Personal belongings, including cameras and films, are admitted duty free if for traveler's own use.

CURRENCY. Jamaica is in the pound sterling area, so the official money is English pounds, shillings and pence. The Jamaican pound is worth $2.80 in U.S. dollars, $2.75 in Canadian dollars, subject to minor fluctuations, quoted in the daily press. The U.S. dollar is negotiated at seven shillings. Dollar conversion tables are furnished at all points of entry by the Jamaica Tourist Board. West Indian dollars (valued at four shillings, two pence) are also legal tender here.

FOR WOULD BE SETTLERS. The local labor market is saturated, except for highly-qualified professional and technical personnel. One of Jamaica's problems is lack of employment for the native population. Prospective settlers wishing to invest or engage in business, should write to the Government's Industrial Development Corporation, 4 Winchester Road, Kingston. British subjects seeking employment in Jamaica should write to the Ministry of Labour, 110 East Street, Kingston. Income taxes must be paid by all residents on the British graduated scale, and by non-residents on income from Jamaica. The Industrial Incentives Law provides freedom of income tax for up to seven years for new industries in the Island; other laws provide for duty-free import of raw materials and machinery, and 100 per cent freedom from income tax in perpetuity for international service companies. Excellent opportunities exist for enterprise capital

JAMAICA

in the tourist industry, and the Hotels Aid Law gives builders excise duty and income tax relief. Residential business and agricultural properties may be bought from £3,000 up. The Jamaica Tourist Board, 80 Harbour St., Kingston, will furnish a list of real estate agencies on request. Cost of living for a middle class family of four in Kingston is estimated at £2,000 ($5,600) per year, basic minimum to cover house rental, food, servants, schooling, clothing, and maintenance of a motor car. Domestic help in Jamaica is relatively cheap. Wages range from 50 shillings ($7) a week, without food or quarters.

 HOW TO GET ABOUT? If you arrive at Kingston, chances are that your ultimate resort goal will be on the other end of the island. If you come in at Mo' Bay, as the habitués call Montego Bay, you will still have to cross the island to see the sights. These excursions by car can be murderous both figuratively and literally. They are expensive, and you should find fellow tourists to share the costs with you; otherwise it may be prohibitive. If you want to drive yourself, be on guard; Jamaican native drivers are more than reckless, they are downright bloodthirsty. Night driving is definitely not recommended, as the narrow roads are full of drivers whose normal width and depth perception, none too accurate to begin with, may have been considerably dulled or distorted by rum. With a little prudence, you'll be all right driving in the daytime.

Best bet for a U-drive or chauffeur-driven car is *Martin's Tours*, affiliated with the Hertz Car Rental System. This outstanding organization operates from Kingston at the corner of East and Harbor Streets, and at 45 St. James Street in Montego Bay. They will rent you a private limousine and chauffeur from $18 per day with 60 miles allowed between 8 a.m. and 6 p.m. Rates for extra mileage are 20 cents per mile, for additional night driving (between 6 p.m. and 8 a.m.) $1.65 to $2 per hour. In the U-drive department (winter season) you have a wide choice of English cars from a Ford Anglia sedan at $45 a week to a Jaguar Sports Convertible at $110, mileage unlimited. In the summer season (April 16 to Dec. 15), these rates range from $40 to $85. Daily rates are from $8 plus 5 cents per mile to $14 plus 9 cents per mile, depending on model. Full third party insurance is included, and cars will be delivered to you free in the Kingston, Ocho Rios or Montego Bay area. You can have them waiting for you on your arrival at Kingston or Montego Bay airport if you want to.

The local office of the Hertz-Rent-A-car System is in Kingston, on Harbor Street. There are also offices in Ocho Rios, Montego Bay and at the Palisados Airport Terminal Building.

Your local driver's license from home is all you need to drive in Jamaica. Make sure you have it; otherwise you will have to apply for the license in person at the local tax office, take a driving test, and pay a fee of $3, all three of which steps are unmitigated bores. British rules govern traffic here, and you drive *on the left hand side of the road*.

There are buses and taxis in Kingston. The taxi drivers have a tendency to ask tourists more than the legal fare. Ask at your hotel what the fare should be, and pay that amount. The 8 mile run from Palisadoes airport to Kingston is $1 per seat in a taxi; $4.50 if you take the whole cab by yourself. Bus terminal is Victoria Park at the top of King Street; service to the suburbs and suburban hotels is good.

We do not recommend travel by bus in the interior of the island. The local color is apt to be a little on the ripe side in these crowded, antiquated vehicles; the service is desultory, and this is one place where you might very well meet up with native sullenness and hostility.

There is a train service between Montego Bay and Kingston and Port Antonio every day. Fare to Montego Bay is $3; to Port Antonio 88 cents. Kingston to Montego Bay or vice versa by train will give you a long, 4½ hour kaleidoscope of the life and scenery of the Jamaican interior.

You can also fly between Kingston and Montego Bay. BWIA has a local service daily and the cost is about $10 for the flight. Pan Am makes the flight daily, but only for passengers holding international tickets.

Martin's Tours operates a regularly-scheduled transfer service between Kingston, Ocho Rios, Port Antonio and the North Coast Area.

Martin's also offers a number of excellent sightseeing tours originating in Kingston, Ocho Rios and Montego Bay. These include an all-day trans-island tour from Kingston to Montego Bay ($13.50); a four hour High Mountain tour ($7.50), a North Coast tour, a Night Life Tour ($10 including cocktails and dinner), and an all day tour for $12 which includes the Jamaican specialty of rafting on the Rio Grande. The company also features comprehensive sightseeing tours of longer duration: Jamaica Jaunt (3 days and 2 nights, $75 winter); A Week in Jamaica ($160); Ten-Day Economy Tour ($225) and Ten-Day Deluxe Tour ($295).

HOTELS

Jamaican hotels often reflect the social aspirations of their guests. The range of accommodations is one of the widest in the Caribbean: from ultra-modern deluxe hotels to pleasant family guest houses. More exclusive are the distinguished converted plantation "great houses" which are operated along the lines of elegant private clubs. The "hill station" type of hotel is seldom frequented by foreign tourists, but offers some amusing insights into the old folkways of British colonial life. *Special note for low-budget travelers:* Accommodation is non-existent outside the resort areas. Don't hope to penetrate the countryside expecting cheap accommodation. There is an almost total lack of amenities for visitors.

KINGSTON AND VICINITY

COURTLEIGH MANOR, set in a tropical garden in Half Way Tree, one of Kingston's exclusive residential sections, adjacent to the Liguanea Country Club where guests may play tennis and golf. Swimming pool on the premises, and hotel guests have free use of Morgan's Harbour Beach Club for swimming and fishing. Has 64 rooms, all with bath and radio and free air-conditioning, restaurant with good food and cellar, bar, cocktail lounge and

dancing. Rates, Full American Plan, are $20 to $22 per day single, $36 to $38 double, $48 triple from Dec. 16 through April 15. Summer rates run from $16 tot $18 single, Modified American Plan, $26 double, $36 triple. Joe Tschaler is the manager of this spacious, well run establishment, operated by Federal Catering Services. Tel. Kingston 68174. Cable: Courtleigh, Jamaica.

FLAMINGO HOTEL in suburban Cross Roads, two miles from Kingston, 13 from the airport, has 30 rooms, all with bath. It's a charming place with friendly, smiling service. Large filtered pool in the garden with circular poolside bar built around a shady tree. Food: fair. Rates are moderate, especially for Jamaica, and Mr. "Bamah" Nunes, the manager, further palliates the pain by adding 10 per cent to the bill to cover all tips if you so desire: a great convenience, and an economy. Modified American Plan. Rates (Dec. 16-April 15): $15 per day single, $24 double, $36 triple. Summer rates: $12 single, $20 double, $30 triple. Half rate for children under 12 if in same room as parents. Tel. Kingston 67652 and 67618. Cable: Flamingo, Jamaica.

MANOR HOUSE is a delightful, old style sort of place in the foothills of the Blue Mountains, six miles from Kingston and about 600 feet above it, thus about 10 degrees cooler than the humid capital. Thirty-six rooms, all but four with bath, have verandahs overlooking mountains, sea and 40 acres of beautifully-landscaped grounds.
There is a swimming pool, also tennis. Guests may play at the 18-hole Constant Spring golf course nearby and have membership privileges at Morgan's Harbour Beach Club. Manager Derrick Franklin provides free transportation for shopping sprees to Kingston, and he will also arrange for you to go rafting on the Rio Grande (see sports). Manor House has good food, operates on Full American Plan. Winter rates (Dec. 16-April 15) are $14 daily single with bath, $28 double, $39 triple. Summer rates: $10, $20, $30 for same accommodations. Tel. Kingston 61161. Cable: "Rutty"Jamaica, but don't let that give you ideas about this pleasant family hotel.

MELROSE HOTEL, right in Kingston, simple, homey, comfortable and reasonable. In spite of its unpretentiousness, it does have such amenities as cocktail lounge, ca-

lypso music, and a large swimming pool. Mrs. Florence Fraser is the manager. Her guests have privileges at Morgan's Harbour Beach Club, and she can arrange such diversions as golf, tennis and fishing trips on request. Good home-style cooking. Full American Plan only. There are 24 rooms, 18 with bath. Winter rates: $9 and $13 per day single with bath ($7 and $8 without); $18 and $26 double with bath ($14 and $16 without); $27 and $39 triple with bath ($21 and $24 without). Summer rates from $7 single with bath, $14 double, $21 triple. Tel. Kingston 3102 and 4788. Cable: Melrosetel, Jamaica.

MYRTLE BANK HOTEL, in Kingston overlooking the harbor, is a famous landmark of Jamaica, the capital's largest and best known hotel. It belongs to the Hon. Abe Issa, dynamic leader of the Jamaican tourist industry. Catering to both a resort and commercial clientele, it offers its guests a spacious, tiled, salt water pool, two dining rooms, three cocktail lounges, native floor shows, dancing to Calypso music, a free port shopping arcade and post office right on the grounds, and the sensation of being right in the middle of the social life of Kingston. There's always something going on here: a big ball, a military band concert, a local committee meeting. Delicious buffet lunches are served every day but Sunday, and the air conditioned cocktail bar is a popular rendezvous, an oasis in humid Kingston. The cuisine is competent. Full American Plan winter rates are $22 and $24 single with bath; $34 and $38 double with bath; $51 and $57 triple with bath. Summer rates range from $6 single, $12 double, $27 triple. Amiable manager Jim Hooks will have your room air conditioned at an additional cost of $2 or $3 per day, depending on its size, and you can stay in this celebrated hostelry on the European Plan during the summer season (April 16-Dec. 15) at $5 per person less than the American Plan tariff. Tel. Kingston 4681. Cable: Myrtlebank, Jamaica.

SOUTH CAMP HOTEL in a large tropical garden about a mile from Kingston combines the traditional charm of one of the capital's oldest hotels with such modern amenities as swimming pool and cocktail bars. It has a 50-year-old reputation for hospitality and personal attention, which explains the fidelity of most of its clients. Both bars are popular with locals. The cuisine is only fair: American and Continental with some Jamaican additions, but the Manager, Mr. David Gonsalves, lends a sympathetic ear to such problems as special diets and children's meals. He'll also arrange for nursemaids and baby sitters for the small fry. There are 35 rooms, only 6 without bath. Full American Plan. Winter Rates are $24 single with bath, $20 without; $38 double with bath, $32 without. In summer deduct $1 per person. Tel. Kingston 81341. Cable: Jomin, Jamaica.

Children from 3 to 12 half rate if they share parents' room.

ABBEY COURT HOTEL is a guest house with the charm of an old family mansion, which is precisely what it was before conversion. Surrounded by garden and spacious lawn, it's in the residential suburb of Half Way Tree, close to two golf courses and swimming pool. Tennis court and bar on the premises. Full American Plan (including afternoon tea) May 1 through Nov. 30: $6 per day single without bath; $15 per day double with bath. From Dec. 1 through April 30 it's $8 for single without bath and $10 for single with bath; $20 for double with bath.

BAMBOO LODGE BLUE MOUNTAIN CHALETS are nicely-appointed cottages with a glorious view and bracing climate 2400 feet up in Jamaica's Blue Mountains. There are ten housekeeping cottages with double bedrooms, dinette, living room, patio, bath and kitchenette, fully equipped to accommadate 2, 3 or 4 persons. You do your own cooking, also marketing. The Chalet Home Store has meat, vegetables, fish, native fruit, everything you need. There's a swimming pool in the chalet gardens. It's blissfully cool up here (average temperatures: 72 in winter, 76 in summer), just half an hour from Kingston. Mr. and Mrs. Alan Stokes are the owner-managers, and can be addressed at Irish Town P.O., Jamaica, W.I. Cable: Bluechalets, Kingstonja. Year round rates per cottage per week are $60 for 2 persons, $70 for 3, $80 for 4 in the "standard" cottages; $80 for 2, $90 for 3, $100 for 4 in the "superior" chalets. The price includes maid service, gas, hot water and light.

GREEN GABLES is a small hotel of the guest house type with accommodations for 26 people in residential Half Way Tree, about 3 miles north of downtown Kingston. Bus service is just half a block away. Tennis club and golf course nearby. Full American Plan. All season rates: Single without bath $7, with bath $8; double without bath $14; with bath $16 and $18.

LIGUANEA TERRACE HOTEL is in the foothills of the Blue Mountains about four miles north of Kingston. It can accommodate 46 guests in modern apartments and bungalows. Atmosphere is easy, relaxed, do-as-you-please. There is a swimming pool, also badminton court, open air dining room and amusing Bamboo Bar. Guests enjoy golf privileges at nearby course. Full American Plan winter rates: single room with bath $12 and $14; double with bath $24 and $28. Summer rates Continental Plan, range from $6 to $17 per day. Selfcontained housekeeping suites are available from $60 weekly, winter season; $50 summer. You do your own cooking in these.

MIMOSA LODGE HOTEL can accommodate 35 guests in 23 airy bedrooms, each with private bath or shower. The hotel is set amidst spacious grounds in residential Half Way Tree just north of Kingston. The hotel has a big fresh water swimming pool, cocktail bar, dance floor and roof garden, minutes from downtown Kingston by public bus which stops right at the entrance. Mostly commercial and local clientele. Full American Plan Winter rates: $10 single, $20 double per day. Summer (April 16-Dec. 15): $8 single, $15 double.

SHERATON-KINGSTON HOTEL is Jamaica's largest luxury hotel. Recently completed, the 200-room air-conditioned hotel is a complex of eight buildings of a tropical design surrounding a swimming pool. In addition, the hotel has a large ballroom which will accommodate 800 persons, a speciality restaurant and a large outdoor terrace to serve the hotel guests and local residents.

Architects for the hotel are Charles Griller Assocs. Rates on application.

STRAWBERRY HILL, 2800 feet above sea level in Irish Town, 14 miles from Kingston, is deliciously cool and calm. Mrs. Harold da Costa, the owner-manager, runs it in the tradition of the West Indies small guest house. All rooms have private bath, and there's a swimming pool in the garden. Continental Plan year round rates (breakfast only) are $7 per person daily. Other meals served on request. Mrs. da Costa will arrange transportation from airport and Kingston.

THE STONY HILL is a cottage type hillside hotel accommodating 40 guests. It has swimming pool, riding facilities plus a magnificent view. Rates: Winter, Continental Plan, single $20, double $30. Summer, American Plan, double occupancy only, $30 to $40.

PORT ANTONIO

This section of the northeast coast of Jamaica, 60 miles from Kingston was Jamaica's first tourist resort and is still redolent of the "roaring twenties." The area, now in the throes of a new boom, lies between superb beaches and the Blue Mountains. The town of Port Antonio is a center for deep sea fishing and that unique Jamaican sport: rafting on the Rio Grande.

THE JAMAICA REEF, formerly the *Titchfield,* is the outstanding hotel here with its own beach, twin swimming pools, tennis and badminton courts and saddle horses for exploring mountain trails. The late Errol Flynn once owned this place. Many famous deep-sea fishermen have stayed and do stay here, tempted by the game fish 100 fathoms deep just half a mile off shore. Mr. Ben Atherton, the manager, arranges expeditions in fully-equipped twinscrew cabin cruisers. The hotel can accommodate 68 guests. Full American Plan Only. Winter rates (Dec. 16 through April 15) are $14 to $18 a day single, $28 and $36 double with bath. In summer they are $14 single, $28

double. The management will air-condition your room on request at $1 per person per day extra.

The **BONNIE VIEW HOTEL** could not be more appropriately named; it sits on top of a 600 foot hill half a mile from Port Antonio, looks north over the Caribbean, south to the Blue Mountains. Taking advantage of this, most of the hotel's 18 rooms have private verandahs. Private beach, cocktail terrace, calypso music, and proximity to rafting on the Rio Grande make this hostelry a popular north-shore rendezvous. Good food. American plan rates are $14 single, $28 double with bath, winter season; $12 single, $22 double, summer.

JAMAICA

FRENCHMAN'S COVE is the latest addition to this resort area, owned by Garfield Weston, multi-millionaire manufacturer and financier. It's the last word in luxury, "brand new and fabulously attractive" to quote our correspondent. There are rooms with bath for 80 guests in 18 cottages and main building. The grounds are so spacious that you will be assigned a golf buggy on arrival for your personal use in traveling about these acres. Rates: $2,500 for two persons for two weeks including literally everything—meals, liquor, accommodation, transportation, a private car and,—well everything.

OCHO RIOS

This is the name of a town and a whole 42-mile-long resort area in the middle of the north coast of Jamaica. It is one of the prodigies of modern tourism, a younger sister to Montego Bay which may end up by surpassing the older girl.

TOWER ISLE HOTEL is the big favorite of Ocho Rios, and the one that started the boom. Abe Issa's creation, it is a complete, self-contained resort right smack on a private, palm-lined beach. It offers its 216 guests everything from archery to free movies with resort and free port shop thrown in. The hotel is under same owner-management as the Myrtle Bank in Kingston and the Montego Inn in Montego Bay, and it's an experienced, smooth operation. Nicky Brimo is the resident manager. All 118 rooms have private bath, balcony or patio with view toward mountains or overlooking the sea and Tower Isle. There's dancing every night under the stars; there are native floor shows, Calypso music, and such diversions as soldier-crab races. The management provides facilities for boating, sailing and spear fishing and can arrange golf privileges at Upton Country Club and deepsea fishing at moderate rates. Winter rates, full American Plan are $35 per day single for east wing oceanview room with shower; $45 double hillview room; $54 double oceanfront room. Garden villas, each containing two double rooms with baths and accommodating up to four persons, are $112 per day per villa. You can get a single cabana type room with private shower and patio facing the pool for $22. Summer rates (April 16 through Dec. 15 are $17 single; $30 double (hillview); $34 double (oceanfront); $14 single cabana. Tel. Ocho Rios 271. Cable: Towerisle Jamaica.

ARAWAK HOTEL, 176 rooms, one of the largest hotel in Jamaica. Ultramodern and luxurious, has a commanding beach front situation five miles west of Ocho Rios. The entire hotel is air conditioned. You'll have your choice of swimming from the private white sand beach or in the freeform fresh water pool. Managing Director Ken Rogers offers his guests all the pleasures of a waterside resort: sailing, fishing, boating, spear fishing, and a private yacht anchorage. The service is as stream-lined as the architecture; in other words, the last word. Full American Plan only. Winter rates (Dec. 16 through April 15) per day: $48 single for oceanfront room; $40 and $42 on mountainview side; $63 double (oceanfront), $53 and $58 mountainview. Oceanfront rooms in summer rent at $23 per day single; $35 double. Mountainview rooms from $18 single $30 double. There's dancing every night in open-air patio or in the Arawak's air-conditioned nightclub. Buffet luncheon served daily on pool patio. Tel. St. Ann's Bay 333. Cable: Arawak, Jamaica.

EATON HALL is an old Great House,

built on 300-year-old Spanish foundations. It has its own sand beach on Runaway Bay 72 miles from Kingston. A perfect place if you're looking for something small, intimate and relaxed. There are only ten rooms. There's no swimming pool (it's almost a relief!), but there is excellent beach and rock swimming with diving board for those who like their sea without sand. Good food, a well-stocked bar, a shady garden are the simple attractions of this comfortable hostelry managed by Captain A. M. Hetherington. Good horseback riding here-abouts too. Full American Plan. Winter rates are $12 per day single without bath, $14 single with bath; $24 double without bath; $28 double with bath. Summer rates range from $9 per day single to $20 double. Tel. Runaway Bay 204. Cable: Eatonhall, Jamaica.

THE FALCONDIP, brand new in 1959, is right next to Tower Isle, features a spectacular cliffside swimming pool, a private beach with all amenities for fishing, sailing, water-skiing, skin diving, and a concept of "guest interest" which provides opportunities to see and share in local life. The hotel owns a nearby estate to which guests are taken on "Plantation Picnics," which feature barbecue lunches. "Get-acquainted" moonlight parties are another facet of the program. The hotel has 53 rooms all with private bath and balcony. Full American Plan only. Daily winter rates are $25 single (hill view), $30 single (ocean front), $35 single, (de luxe "skyline" ocean front). Doubles are $40, $45 and $50 respectively. Off season rates (April 16 through Dec. 15) range from $13 single to $26 de luxe "skyline" double. The Falcondip also has a very ultra ocean front penthouse with two double rooms, two baths, living room, kitchenette, tropical sun and promenade deck. This rents for $150 per day (accommodating up to four persons) in winter; $96 a day in summer. The new manager is Stu Sharpe.

JAMAICA INN overlooks its own beautiful, palm-studded beach just a mile and a half east of Ocho Rios. This intimate hotel has 40 airy rooms each with private bath and patio facing the beach. A long, single story, gallery-like structure, it has a kind of tranquil Colonial charm which the stream-lined skyscrapers don't achieve. The food and service are just about perfect. The managing Director is another hotelier who has adopted the commendable policy of adding a service charge (it's only ten per cent) to the bill to relieve the guest of the inconvenience of constant tipping. Tipping is not allowed at Jamaica Inn during the winter season. In addition to swimming, skin diving and fishing, the hotel can arrange for you to play golf, tennis or ride horseback at Upton Country Club a couple of miles away, tennis at Plantation Inn just next door. This is an expensive place, but its clients are so happy with it that you must reserve early. Winter rates are $30 a day single occupancy; $60 double; $90 triple, Full American Plan. Summer rates: $17 single, $32 double, $45 triple. The management does not take children in the winter season. Kids are welcome in summer at half rates if they are under eight years of age. Tel. Ocho Rios 516. Cable: Jamaicainn, Jamaica.

MARRAKESH BEACH HOTEL, opened 1960, is the largest and most luxurious of Jamaica's resort hotels with room for 400 guests. There are 204 air-conditioned rooms, each with terrace. Luxury suites are complete with step-down living rooms and sunken Grecian baths. The hotel is built on a slope above the ocean with gardens leading down to a cabana rimmed private beach. The usual resort diversions available including tennis, golf, horseback riding, water skiing and fishing. Its Spanish Galleon Room is billed as the largest air-conditioned night club in the Caribbean. Manager: Harry Snow. Rates: A. P. Winter $40 to $52 single, $50 to $67 double; Summer $18 to $25 single, $30 to $37 double.

PLANTATION INN is a new resort estate, next door to Jamaica Inn, under the same management and providing the same luxurious amenities and tranquil atmosphere at exactly the same rates. About the only difference is in the architecture. Here you are higher up and have a different and slightly more dramatic perspective on the sea from your balcony. There are 46 rooms, all with private bath and verandah. Rates: Winter season Full American Plan single $30 to $45, double $45 to $65; Summer season single $17, double $15 to $16.

Three miles east of Ocho Rios in a lovely, eight-acre terraced garden, **SANS SOUCI** offers its clients 25 rooms with private bath overlooking a protected private beach. A unique feature is the circular radio active mineral water pool constantly replenished by a natural spring high in the cliff gardens. Spear fishing is wonderful here. If you want golf, tennis or horseback riding, the management will arrange it at Upton Country Club two miles away. *Sans Souci* has the usual cocktail bar and lounge, dancing and native floorshows. Full American Plan rates (winter) are $35 single, $50 double, $65 triple. In summer, they are $20, $30 and $40 for same accommodations. You can have Modified American Plan in the winter season if you prefer (room, breakfast and lunch; no dinner) for $28 single, $42 double. European Plan is optional in summer season at $6 single, $12 double. No tipping allowed. A service charge of 10 per cent will be added to your bill to cover this item. Tel. Ocho Rios 225. Cable: Sansouci, Jamaica.

CASA MARIA. A new beach hotel with impressive hillside location overlooking Caribbean at Port Maria. Accommodates 60 guests. American Plan Winter $28 single; $38 to $54 double, cottage $150 per week; Summer $18 single, $22 to $44 double.

CARIB-OCHO RIOS, something new and different in Jamaica resort developments is this cooperative apartment-hotel now completed and opened on the central north shore. The vast project aims at establishing 500 cooperative apartment units and cabanas on the ocean property of historic Sylvia Lawn Estate. When fully completed there will be room for 2,000 guests, making the project the island's largest to date. In addition to the housing units, sport, recreation and shopping areas are planned as well as a guest apartment-hotel. An exclusive feature of the resort will be a sulphur spa bathhouse fed by curative mineral waters and springs, among the most potent in the Caribbean. Don Bardowell is Vice-President and resident manager. New York offices are at 745 5th Ave. N.Y. 22, N.Y.

SILVER SEAS, an eighth of a mile from Ocho Rios and equidistant (60 miles) from Montego Bay and Kingston, is an ocean-front, palm-cooled resort dream. The private beach has an 80-foot pier, which doubles as a sun lounge, and the hotel has a 42-foot cabin cruiser, the *Skylee* for deep-sea fishing and "pirate cruises" of exploration along this splendid northern coast. Skin diving, water skiing and other liquid pleasures are practised here along with more sedentary ones at the well-stocked bar. There's a Marine Garden 200 yards from the hotel which was made for gogglers like us. The food at the Silver Seas is excellent: Continental plus Jamaican with a nice emphasis on imaginative presentation. Try the coconut ice cream, for example, served in the scooped-out shell: the essence of the tropics. The

293

wine cellar is almost Parisian in its pretensions. The accent here is on gaiety with dancing nightly to the Silver Seas Calypso Band. The service is smooth, and the friendly waiters remarkably efficient even when called upon to balance a gastronomic ship on the head. In short, Manager Don Sutton-Brown can be very proud of this operation holiday. Full American Plan. Winter rates: $30 to $35 single; $50 to $54 double. From April 16 through December 15 they drop to $14 and $15 single; $24 to $26 double. The Modified American Plan applies in summer. All 54 rooms have private baths; majority face the ocean and capture the trade winds by means of cross ventilation. Tel. Ocho Rios 556. Cable: Silverseas, Jamaica.

HIBISCUS LODGE is a guest house next door to the Silver Seas Hotel. It's an old world cottage with annex on a bluff 30 feet above the sea, accessible by terraced path. All bedrooms have private bath or shower. Moderate American plan rates, including afternoon tea. Winter season singles are $14; doubles $28 daily. Summer rates are $12 single; $24 double. Capacity of Hibiscus Lodge is 20 guests.

GOLDEN HEAD BEACH HOTEL, newly opened at Oracabessa accommodates 128 guests in 17 cottage units and in a single-level main building. Forty-four miles from Kingston, the 250 acre resort is on a triangular piece of land, bounded on one side by Jacks River and on the other by the Caribbean. Mr. Gerald Ames is the new manager.

Rates for double rooms are $30 to $34 from Nov. 12 to Dec. 15; from $50 to $60 from Dec. 16 to April 15.

SHAW PARK BEACH CLUB is an informal, intimate hotel situated right on the beach. There are 46 air-conditioned rooms. All-year-round sports program, complimentary golf (summer-autumn). Summer rates are $14 to $16 per day single; doubles from $40 to $45. Mr. Paul Davis is the manager.

WINDSOR HOTEL on St. Ann's Bay is five miles west of Ocho Rios, one mile west of the Arawak Hotel. Once a Plantation Great House, the Windsor has been modernized without losing any of its gracious charm. Its homelike atmosphere is typical of Jamaica's guest houses. There are accommodations for 36. You can swim from the beach or in the new 80,000-gallon swimming pool, but many clients prefer the swimming at Dunn's River Beach to which the management provides transporation free of charge. They will also make arrangements for horseback riding, cycling, boating and fishing. American Plan rates (December 16 through April 15): $18 single with bath; $15 to $20 double with bath. Summer rates: $12 single; $10 to $12 double, rates for Modified American Plan (no lunch) are slightly less. Harry Bentley is the new manager.

MONTEGO BAY

Capital of Jamaican tourism, this is Queen Bee of the Caribbean. To call this celebrated resort area the "Riviera of the West Indies" is to mislead the reader. There are great differences. First of all, the weather here is far superior to anything on the Cote d'Azur, especially in winter. The water temperature doesn't drop below 78 degrees in the winter season, and you can bathe every day. Try the Mediterranean at Cannes in February, and you'll come down with pneumonia. Secondly, there are no gambling casinos here; the pleasures of this riviera are less artificial and frenetic. Finally, despite the imposing

JAMAICA

concentration of luxury hotels in the Montego Bay area, there is nothing comparable to the jam-packed, house on house, traffic-snarled resorts of Southern France here. It is still possible to walk for miles on great stretches of strand without meeting another person, and the hotels are set, not on bustling esplanades but in the midst of tranquil beach front estates and tropical gardens. And what hotels! Here's a rundown:

BAY ROC, less than a mile from Montego Bay international airport, is an architectural marvel of open construction with deep eaves, louvred walls, and striking modern design. Fashionable, deluxe, it offers its guests a lovely private beach, an Olympic size swimming pool, delicious cuisine punctuated by tempting Jamaican dishes, and 72 luxuriously-appointed rooms with private bath. Most of them face the beach; all are air conditioned. In addition to sailing, fishing and boating, guests enjoy membership privileges of Montego Bay Country Club (five miles away) where they can ride horses, play golf or tennis. Harold DeLisser manages this smart resort hotel. Winter rates in the main building for de luxe room with private bath and verandah, facing the sea are $35 single, $50 double, $75 triple per day, Full American Plan. Villas with private patio facing the sea are $37 single, $54 double, $81 triple. From April 16 through December 15 rates drop to $18 single, $30 double, $45 triple. Dancing nightly to calypso band and orchestra. Tel. Montego Bay 2181. Cable: Bayroc Jamaica.

THE CASA BLANCA hotel looks as though it were growing in the sea. It is the first resort hotel ever built in Montego Bay, and it conserves its venerable charm in spite of recent redecoration. It overhangs the Caribbean just a step from the famous Doctor's Cave Beach Club, which started the Montego boom in 1906, and guests have club privileges at this beach, which many travelers insist is the most beautiful in the world. Wonderful views from the private balconies and terraces of this gracious old lady. Guests automatically become temporary members of Montego Bay Country Club three miles away. Don Knight is the manager, and there are 46 rooms, all but four with baths. Winter rates in effect from Jan. 17 through Mar. 27 are $25 to $35 single, $40 to $45 double, Full American Plan. Summer rates in effect from April 17 through Dec. 19 are $18 single, $28 to $32 double. M.A.P.; add $2 for lunch per person. Tel. Montego Bay 2393. Cable: Casablanca Jamaica.

CASA MONTEGO under same owner-management as the Casa Blanca is the much younger sister hotel, a striking eight-story, elevator building whose terraces and perforated walls give it the look of a cube of filigreed ivory. A few steps from Doctor's Cave Beach, the hotel has a large salt water pool, shops, airlines offices, banking facilities, two bars and a delightful roof garden. There are a hundred bedrooms; all have private bath and terrace, cross ventilation, and, as if that were not sufficient, air conditioning. Jim Tapson is the manager; his guests are automatically temporary members of Montego Bay Country Club and Doctor's Cave Bathing Club. Daily winter rates (Dec. 20 through April 14, Full American Plan): $32 single, $48 to $52 double. Off season these tariffs drop to $16 to $20 single; $30 to $32 double. You can stay here on the Modified American Plan (room, breakfast and dinner) during the Summer Season for $15 single; $26, $28, $30 double.

GLOUCESTER HOUSE is opposite Doctor's Cave Beach and has its own private entrance to that celebrated strand. Ruby Harvey manages this fine resort hotel, justly famous for its food, wine cellar and excellent service. There are 52 rooms with bath and private porch, cool, screened, tastefully appointed. Modified American Plan: room, breakfast and dinner. Winter rates per day are $27 single; $38 to $44 double. Luxurious penthouse apartments with roof garden and sun deck from $45. Summer rates, also Modified American Plan, are $14 to $18 single; $24 to $28 double. Tel. Montego Bay 2372. Cable: Gloucester Jamaica.

MONTEGO BAY RACQUET CLUB, formerly the **CLARAGE'S** brand new cottage-type hillside hotel which has room for 30 guests with a cozy, comfortable and casual atmosphere. Kidney shaped pool is the dominant feature of the hotel's decor. The club has three flood-lit tennis courts and an air-conditioned clubhouse and locker rooms. Dining beside the pool is a real pleasure. The new manager is the Marquis Enzo Coscia. M.A.P.
Summer rates $18 single, $25 double.

THE COLONY. Charming new cottage hotel built right on the beach. Luxury suites are available with bedrooms, bath, kitchen, private patio and veranda. Maids and cooks available on the hotel staff cater to your every need. Golf course, tennis courts, croquet courts and shuffleboard for the athletic minded. Rates: Continental Plan Winter bedroom (1 or 2 persons) $30, studio-Living room (1 or 2 persons) $40, entire suite (up to 4 persons) $70; Summer bedroom (1 person) $20, (2 persons) $20, studio-living room (2 persons) $30, suite $50.

GOOD HOPE is something different: a small, exclusive hotel on its own 2,000 acre cattle and coconut plantation, 28 miles from Montego Bay, and 500 cool feet above sea level. If you like to ride, this is Nirvana. The rates include the use of a horse which is personally assigned to each guest upon arrival, and there are more than 200 miles of trails on the estate. In addition the hotel has a swimming pool and lawn tennis courts on the premises. Sea bathing is done from a private beach nine miles distant; the hotel provides transportation. Ask the manager, Patrick J. Tenison, about arranging excursions to Windsor Caves, the Phosphorescent Lagoon, and the nearby Maroon Country, still inhabited by the descendants of escaped and unsubdued slaves. Good Hope is only open during the Winter Season, Dec. 16 through April 15. All 24 of its rooms have baths. There is dancing, cocktailing, native entertainment, but the dominant atmosphere recalls the leisure and tranquility of an older day. Rates are $28 to $33 per day single; $46 to $50 double. Full American Plan.

HALF MOON is located on a wonderful white sand beach, seven miles east of Montego Bay, four east of the airport. Its 42-acre estate was once part of historic Rose Hall, a great plantation of early colonial days. The new Managing Director is Curt Peyer—a top name in the international hotel field. His competence and urbanity is proverbial. The result is highly successful. The keynote is at once smart and casual in the intimate bar, in the dining room, and during the charming buffet lunches served daily on the terrace. "Get acquainted" cocktail parties, beach bonfire picnics are characteristic of the club-like atmosphere. The rooms (there are 88 of them) are attractive duplex suites, all with bath. Rates, Full American Plan, Winter Season are from $40 single, $55 double, $70 triple. Summer rates are from $18 single, $32 double, $42 triple.

MONTEGO BEACH HOTEL, a mile west of the airport, a mile east of Montego Bay, is a large, modern, superlatively-appointed resort hotel. You don't have to choose here between sea or mountain view; every balcony is right on the Caribbean. The food, a combination of Continental and native cuisine, is absolutely tops and so is the service. M. P. Archibald and Charlie Morrow are the managers of this smooth operation, and they offer you sailboating, fishing, water skiing, spear fishing, dancing to Calypso music and other diversions in addition to guest privileges at nearby Montego Bay Country Club where you can indulge in golf, tennis and horseback riding. The management requests no children under 12. Full American Plan only. Winter rates: $34 single; $50 to $60 double per diem. In summer the tariffs are $18 and $20 single; $30 to $36 double; $44 to $50 triple. Tel. Montego Bay 2101. Cable: Mobehotel, Jamaica.

MONTEGO INN is a smart, modern hotel, towny and toney, overlooking the harbor on the road between the airport and Montego Bay. It's under the same ownership as the Tower Isle and the Myrtle Bank, and it's next door to all the blandishments of Issa's, the biggest free port shop in Jamaica. You can enjoy sea bathing at nearby Doctor's Cave Beach. Montego Inn operates on the European Plan only. Its 26 rooms all have baths and individual air-conditioning units, which guests can adjust to suit themselves. Coffee shop and cocktail lounge are also air conditioned. Winter Rates: $14 a day single; $20 double. Summer rates: (April 16-Dec. 15) $7 single; $10 double.

ROUND HILL may not be the last word in luxury resorts, but it's a close contender. A favorite with international society it's on a 98-acre peninsula that juts out into the Caribbean eight miles west of Montego Bay. Surrounded by gardens, the hotel overlooks its own private beach and a stunning view of the north shore of Jamaica. You can

have your choice here between a hotel suite with private balcony a step or so from the beach, or a de luxe cottage with private entrance and verandah on the hill above the beach. The cuisine is French and so are the chefs, and the daily luncheon buffet is a work of art. They don't disdain Jamaican dishes either, and they have a penchant for cool rum concoctions served up in pineapples or coconuts. Calypso music at night and dining by candlelight; civilized and beautiful. There are 32 suites in the hotel plus 25 cottages. Winter season only. Full American Plan. Rates per day are $40 single for deluxe suite in the hotel; $60 in the cottages; $60 double in the hotel; $62 in the cottages. De luxe cottages are available for double occupancy from $65 to $100 daily. Double $60 to $75 from Jan. 18 to April 1, no single accommodation during this period. Children's rates on application. Water sports here run the gamut: canoeing and sailing to water skiing.

ROYAL CARIBBEAN is right on the Caribbean at Mahoe Bay about four miles east of Montego Bay, two from the airport. The architecture is Jamaican colonial with eight buildings arranged in a semi-circle to capture every breath of the Trade Winds. Center of interest is the attractive freeform swimming pool, equipped with tables and chaises longues for perfect relaxation. Private beach is over 500 feet long. Facilities for water sports, water skiing and deep sea fishing are excellent. First class cuisine: French, American and native. There's dancing nightly to Calypso music, and it's rather dressy after the sun goes down. Modified American Plan (breakfast and dinner only). Winter rates are $34 per day single, $45 double, $78 triple in luxurious Royal Suites; $41 single, $50 double, and $72 triple in Caribbean Suites; $35 single, $44 double, and $66 triple in Caribbean rooms. All 80 rooms have private bath; most are air conditioned. From April to Dec. 20 the singles run $20, $18, and $16 per day; doubles $32, $30 and $28; triples $46, $44 and $42. The management is requesting no children under 12 in the winter season, none under 6 in summer. Tel. Montego Bay 2146. Cable: Royalcarib, Jamaica.

SILVER SANDS BEACH CLUB, half way between Montego Bay and Ocho Rios has a commanding situation on its 1800 foot beachfront of white sand. It has 27 rooms all with bath in a number of attractive self-contained cottages. The atmosphere is definitely Jamaican until you get to the Jolly Friar Tavern, which is even older England in spirit. Cuisine is very good; accent is on informal vacation leisure. Full American Plan. Rates from Jan. 15 to Mar. 31 are $25 single; $35 for single occupancy of a cottage; $45 for two persons; $60 for three. April 1 to April 30 and Dec. 15 to Jan. 14 singles are $15; single occupancy of cottage is $20; two persons $38; three, $46. The rest of the year it's $12 per person Modified American Plan. No tipping is permitted. Ten per cent service charge is added to hotel bill instead, to the great credit of the enlightened managers, M. P. Archibald and Charles Morrow. Tel. Duncans 282. Cable: Silversands Jamaica.

SUNSET LODGE HOTEL is smart, exclusive, expensive with 40 rooms and bath directly on the sea 1½ miles from Montego Bay. Guests have membership privileges at Montego Bay Country Club three miles away, and Manager Nelson Vickers will arrange such diversions as deep sea fishing, alligator hunting and polo for his guests. Golf and tennis at country club. The hotel has a free port shop and features a delicious buffet lunch every day. There's dancing at night to orchestra and Calypso band. Sunset Lodge is open only in the winter season from Dec. 16 through April 15. Attractively furnished bedroom suites with verandah facing the sea are $35 single, $50 double, $70 triple, Full American Plan. The management does not want child guests under 6 years of age.

BLAIRGOWRIE HOTEL, four miles west of Montego Bay, overlooks the town from a 300-foot-high hilltop garden. This is another of those small Jamaican guest houses, accommodating 32. The hotel has its own swimming pool with poolside terrace, also private beach. Free transportation provided by car or speedboat to Doctor's Cave Bathing Club where guests enjoy honorary membership. Guest privileges at Montego Bay Country Club for golf, tennis, horseback riding. Full American Plan rates December 20 through April 15: Singles $19 to $26 daily; doubles $36 to $42. Summer rates: $15 single; $25 double. You can also take your accommodations on the Continental Plan at about $5 less per day per person.

This list by no means exhausts the number of hotels and guest houses with excellent accommodations in the capital of Jamaican tourism. The following hostelries are highly spoken of by their guests, though not yet personally checked by us:

Hacton House with 21 rooms and baths adjoining the grounds of Hotel Casa Blanca, a minute's walk from Doctor's Cave Beach; *Miranda Lodge* on main road above Montego Bay is small (20 guests) but has excellent reputation for food, service, and Free Port and dress shop; *Tro-pical Terrace Hotel:* smart, modern, new with screened bedrooms, all with private patio, freeform swimming pool, lovely view from hillside near Doctor's Cave where guests have membership privileges.

Chatham Hotel on the north edge of Montego Bay has its own beach and pool, 64 rooms, and, we are told, fine cuisine with winter American Plan rates starting at $25 double; the *Coral Cliff* overlooks Montego Bay, is next door to and under same management as Casa Blanca where guests take their meals. Rates are lower, however. There are 18 rooms, many with sea view balconies; *Ridgeley's*, on the sea half way between town and Montego Bay airport, is highly spoken of by its clientele; has 20 rooms with oceanview terraces, and winter rates, American Plan double as low as $26.

The *Tryall* is situated in its own garden on a hill 12 miles west of Montego Bay, has its own five-hole golf course and private beach on Sandy Bay; American Plan winter rates from $30 daily, double; *Richmond Hill Inn* overlooks town of Montego Bay from a hillside, has relatively reasonable rates from $28 double per day, American plan, winter season.

MANDEVILLE AREA

About 60 miles northwest of Kingston, and roughly in the middle of Jamaica, is the village of Mandeville, something quite different from the sun-burnished fleshpots of Montego Bay. Here in the rolling uplands, 2,000 feet high, you will find the typical atmosphere of the British colonial "hill station", cool, self-contained, as English as a novel by E. M. Forster. This, if you like, is the most "unspoiled" of Jamaica's tourist resorts, and we are happy to report that its provincial charm has not been damaged by the incursions of a new mining operation which is making Jamaica one of the world's chief suppliers of bauxite. Enjoying a temperature which seldom exceeds 78 degrees, this "summer capital" attracts an older, staider and stuffier type of tourist than other areas, but it merits the attention of anyone in search of cool tranquillity and the heart of Colonial Jamaica. It isn't all tea and crumpets either; there's plenty of opportunity for sports here at the Manchester Country Club where the Mid-Island Golf Championships and All-Jamaica Hard Court Tennis Championship are played each summer with many visitors taking part. Although chiefly favored by the British, more and more Americans are discovering the refreshing climate and refreshingly lower rates of Mandeville. It's the best corner of this tropic field to meet the true-born Englishman, and many an Anglo-American friendship has blossomed on the Manchester golf course. Hands across the tee! There is daily train service between Kingston and Williamsfield, about six miles from Madeville.

MANCHESTER HOTEL, half a mile from the center of Mandeville, is the leading hotel of the area. A two-storied structure with big comfortable porches, it caters frankly to the retiring and the retired. We have seen more than one charming young English thing there, however, enjoying the facilities of tennis court, bar and cocktail lounge. Managing Director Captain R. A. Adamson will arrange temporary membership in the nearby Country Club for guests who want to play golf and ride horseback. There is sea bathing about half an hour away by car, and there's lots of activity for the bridge and canasta set. In addition to the dining room, (British cuisine with colonial overtones) there's a short-order Snack Bar where you can get a good steak. There are 23 rooms, comfortably old-fashioned, all with bath. Full American Plan Winter rates (from November 16 through April 14) are $12 to $14 per day, single; $22 to $26 double. Daily summer rates are from $10 single to $20 double. Lest

you think that Captain Adamson ignores the aspiring in favor of the retiring, he welcomes children up to 10 years of age at half rates.

THE MANDEVILLE HOTEL is Victorian England plunked down in a spacious tropical garden. Its 19th-century charm is not vitiated by such additions as a contemporary cocktail lounge. This venerable resort hotel has 16 rooms and can accommodate 25 guests, all of whom enjoy country club privileges at the Manchester Club nearby, which has a nine-hole golf course and tennis courts. Year round rates $10 per day single, $20 to $22 double winter; summer rates are $8 to $10 single and $16 to $20 double; all American Plan. Room for additional guests in bungalow suites.

There are smaller hotels and guest houses in the Mandeville and South Shore areas at even lower rates. Among the hotels:

Manchester Inn and *Villa Bella* in Christiana; the latter has American Plan rates as low as $8 per person per day. Among the guest houses: *Milk River Mineral Bath* (daily rates from $3.50); *Wickham House*,

Mandeville, Mrs. Maynair's *Wales*, Newport (from $7), and *Treasure Beach*, a gem of a guest house at the edge of Mandeville, overlooking the beach. Rates seem to be reasonably low.

JAMAICAN FOOD

To masquerade the taste of brines and other preservatives used to keep food from spoiling, the Jamaicans like other residents of the tropics have always made liberal use of pungent spices and peppers.

Some typical Jamaican dishes are *Rice and Peas,* a tasty dish with no peas at all, but rather kidney beans, white rice, coconut milk, scallions and coconut oil. *Salt Fish and Ackee* is delicious; it's made of dried codfish and the cooked fruit of the ackee, an exotic vegetable that grows on the tree. Jamaican curries are hot and good; *Curried goat and rice* is an island favorite. *Mackerel and Bananas* combines the leading island fruit with imported salt fish. The famous Jamaican *Pepperpot Soup* is made of salt pork, salt beef, okra, and Indian kale, the island variety known as Calaloo. It's greener than the sea and a million times as thick. Jamaica-style *Chicken Fricassee* is quite different from anything you've ever had at home. It's a thick, rich chicken stew with carrots, scallions, yams, onions, tomatoes and peppers all prepared in unrefined coconut oil.

JAMAICA

The *ne plus ultra* of the Jamaican cuisine is a *roast suckling pig*. It should be a three month old piglet, boned, stuffed with rice, peppers, diced yam, and thyme, mixed together with shredded coconut and corn meal, then roasted whole to a crisp golden brown. It is a dish fit for a king.

Jamaican fruits are exotic and delicious, especially the mango, which is the favorite of most tourists. But try also the delicious sweetsop, and passion fruit. Other fresh island fruits are the rose apple, rare and crisp; guineps, custard apples, pineapple, and, of course, the fruit that made Jamaica famous: the banana. If you see *Matrimony* on the menu, it's a marriage of star apples and oranges in a unique fruit salad. Slices of Bombay mango in coconut cream make another exotic dessert, and a wonderful melange of Jamaica and France is mangoes sliced and served in dry champagne.

RESTAURANTS

The Full American Plan, accent on *full,* is the order of the day in the vast majority of Jamaica's resorts and the average tourist happily consumes his customary three squares, augmented by high English teas and cocktail snacks in his own hotel. During the last few years a handful of good new restaurants in Kingston and suburbs have helped to change the old pattern of local citizens' and tourists' alike eating exclusively in hotel dining rooms. Some of the more successful ones:

Morgan's Harbor at Port Royal, a good, moderately-priced place for seafood, accessible by car or across the bay by launch from Kingston. Good dining is available also at the *Stony Hill Hotel* and the *Casa Monte* in the hills near Kingston, and at the *Terra Nova Hotel,* a few minutes' drive from downtown Kingston.

Blue Mountain Inn, pleasant manor house type place in a lovely natural setting with a mountain cascade, excellent grilled meats and wine cellar—better reserve; *Dairy Products Limited* on Half Way Tree Road is a super-duper sandwich and short order place, open from breakfast until midnight, features milk drinks and other wholesome concoctions at low prices; *Balcony Inn,* cheek by jowl with the Myrtle Bank Hotel, is air-conditioned, has a nice chop house atmosphere and features, among other items, Dover sole, which presumably does not swim to Jamaica under its own power.

All the latter restaurants are very moderately-priced, especially by American standards.

The big ne-plus-ultra dinner in Kingston's Myrtle Bank Hotel, for example, is $3.

Jamaica Arms, featuring a wide variety of local and exotic dishes, served up in posh, sophisticated, air-conditioned atmosphere.

Bird-In-Hand on Half Way Tree Road, brand new and very smart; *Continental,* at Half Way Tree, air conditioned and run with typical thoroughness by two Swiss chefs who know their business. *Cathay Club,* 80 Princess Street, has the best Chinese food in town.

JAMAICA

NIGHT CLUBS

Night life, which rocks and rolls on the terraces and in the bars of the big resort hotels, is practically nil elsewhere. Typical is the dancing on the pier of *The Myrtle Bank Hotel*, which is the center of Kingston night life. But the Calypso music stops here nightly at 11:30.

The *Glass Bucket Club* jumping till dawn on Saturday nights, out at Half Way Tree to the music of two bands; the floor show may remind you of Major Bowes' Amateur Hour, but it's more colorful and less self-conscious.

Club Havana at Rockfort has good down-to-earth Jamaican music and entertainment and food. Patronized by the local guys and dolls, it can be colorful and amusing, but not for the conservative and fastidious.

Rainbow Club, Half Way Tree, a rock and roll center for local teenagers, will make you feel at least a hundred years old.

If you're addicted to pub crawling, you'll find a bar on almost every corner in Kingston. The rum is strong and prices are low in these places where the average Jamaican enjoys himself. But these haunts were not designed for tourists. Better leave the girls at home and go in pairs, if at all.

For sophisticated sipping of that golden Jamaican rum, try *Jamaica Arms* on Port Royal Street, Kingston's new contribution to the never never world of air-conditioned cocktail lounges. Very comfortable and attractively decorated, not the least element in the décor being the girls girls girls.

Tourist favorites for after dark dancing and entertainment on the fabulous north shore are *The Tower Isle Hotel* at Ocho Rios, featuring nightly dancing and native floor shows on Wednesdays and Saturdays.

The nearby *Galleon Club*, is a new entry, a smart, posh, luxurious night club which is enjoying a fashionable success.

Silver Seas Hotel near Ocho Rios, with dancing and Calypso music every night, has native floor shows on Tuesday and Saturday.

Jamaica Reef Hotel at Port Antonio, an increasingly popular Saturday night rendezvous.

The Reef Club, just opened by Neil Brown, features recorded music for dining, dancing and cabaret shows. Just outside Montego Bay, a good new spot.

SHOPPING

Free Port shopping is one of the big attractions of Jamaica. Only visitors are permitted to take advantage of the duty-free, "cost" prices on such luxury imports as French perfumes, Swiss watches, Danish silver, German cameras, British woolens, cashmeres, linens, fine china, crystal and the whole dazzling gamut of the world's best consumer products. Prices are 30 to 60 per cent less than those for the same items in Canada or the United States. Because local residents are not entitled to these bargains, you will select your merchandise at the Free Port Shops, get a receipt for them, and have them de-

JAMAICA

livered to you either at dockside or airport in the presence of a Customs representative. In effect the Free Port Shops are sample rooms where you order the merchandise you want. Both the Palisadoes (Kingston) and Montego Bay airports have a wide range of items for sale, and here of course you buy over the counter, taking your purchases with you. There are 72 Free Port Shops in Jamaica.

We had my wife, who knows stores all over the world, case the dress shops on our most recent trip and she noted a few of the outstanding bargains: cotton native hand-embroidered blouses at $3.45; hand-embroidered linen blouses, $12.90 and $17.95; tie shoulder cotton blouses, $3.45; beautiful Moygashel linen hand-embroidered dresses, $35; Liberty cotton dresses, $15.75; native embroidered dresses of spun linen, $12.90; African print sequin dresses, $14.95; native designed appliqued skirts, $12.90 to $21.45; straw linen Jamaica length shorts, $4.90; white cotton peasant blouses, $5.

Her tip: don't buy anything without trying it on first. The British, who tailor anything in the trouser department to perfection, can go way off on dresses, even and especially when they are thought to be fit for a queen.

Of course there can be no quarrel with the English cashmeres; all the great names are available in Jamaica's Free Port Shops: Ballantyne, Braemar, Lyle and Scott, and Turner Rutherford, Bernhard Altmann, Bryants, and Pringles.

Issa's arcade of specialty shops in the Myrtle Bank Hotel in Kingston, and *Issa's Montego Shop* at Montego Inn, are the biggest of all. Issa's Myrtle Bank Shop is actually a multiple operation including a gift shop (jewelry Swiss watches such as Ulysse Nardin, perfume, cameras, glassware, and Spode, Royal Worcester, Minton, Crown Staffordshire china; a Liquor Shop, a Men's shop, (specializing in imported fashions), a "Midget" Shop (textiles, imported knickknacks), a

Souvenir Shop, and the Tropical Dress Shop, featuring ladies' embroidered and appliqued dresses, blouses and sportswear. Also recommended: *Bardowell's* and *L.A. Henriques Ltd.*, both on King Street in Kingston.

IN KINGSTON. *The French Doll,* 81 Harbour Street in Kingston, is a good free port bet for Swiss watches, French perfumes, Danish silver, cashmere sweaters, jewelry, cameras and binoculars.

Jamaica Arms, in addition to providing an air-conditioned oasis for cocktails on Port Royal Street, is one of the most mouth-watering liquor stores you've ever seen. They have a wonderful selection of local rums, French liqueurs, imported whisky, including Scotch at a sensational free-port price: $2 a fifth; it's positively demoralizing.

The *English Shop* at 12½ King Street has enough imported men's and women's clothing and accessories to keep you happily broke, even at free-port prices for the rest of your trip.

At the *Swiss Stores* in Kingston, Montego Bay and Ocho Rios you'll find a good selection of Swiss watches, including the well-known productions of the International Watch Co., Piaget and Zodiac.

A great many Hindus, sharp merchants all, have gotten into the free port act in Jamaica, and you'll find bargains in jewelry, perfumes, textiles and souvenirs, as well as saris and other exotic Indian imports at *Bombay Bazaar, Chandiram Ltd., Dadlani's* and *Hindu Bazaar* all within a dhoti's throw of each other on King Street, the main shopping drag of Kingston. Most

303

of these have branch bazaars in Montego Bay on St. James Street.

Jamaican handicrafts? You'll find them everywhere, but the greatest concentration is in the big, bazaar-like *Victoria Crafts Market* at the foot of King Street in downtown Kingston. Don't miss this. It's the biggest straw market in the Caribbean, and the range of items for sale is practically limitless. You'll see hand-woven sisal rugs, beautiful bamboo baskets, raffia-decorated bags, purses and hats of long-wearing, washable jippi jappa, a Jamaican specialty.

There are some charming necklaces made from colorful island seeds, mahogany wood carvings, paintings of the Jamaican scene by well known artists like Albert Huie and Karl Parboo Singh as well as by lesser-known painters whom you may discover for yourself. You'll find a raft of hand-embroidered skirts and dresses, appliqued blouses and skirts, boldly designed and executed in splashy tropical colors. To complement the local color,

you'll hear Jamaican folk songs and Calypsos in the market.

IN MONTEGO BAY. *Issa's Shop* on Fort Street has a choice of cameras, watches, perfumes, jewelry, silver, textiles and men's and ladies' wear —all beautifully displayed. For women's wear, sports or formal try *Dorothy McNab* at 5 Market Street. *Calypso* in the Casa Montego Arcade specializes in Polly Hornburg originals—both sportswear and evening separates. The *English Shop* at 39 St. James Street, a free port shop, has men's and ladies' imported clothing and beautiful textiles as does the *Hindu Bazaar,* its neighbor at 36 St. James Street.

IN PORT ANTONIO, try *Johnston & Co.* for a fascinating melange of ironmongery, hardware, groceries and liquor at free port prices; also *Sang Hing Co.* with tempting imported perfumes, liquors and curios at big savings.

IN OCHO RIOS there are free port shops at *Tower Isle, Silver Seas* and *Plantation Inn* hotels.

SPORTS. *Swimming* practically everywhere. *Rafting* at Port Antonio on the Rio Grande. It's fun and perfectly safe. You ride on a two passenger bamboo raft, poled by a native raftsman. A seven mile trip on the fairly swift river costs about $4 for the raft; $2 for a driver to take your car downstream to meet you at the end. Call the management at the Bonnie View Hotel (Tel. 752) or arrange this excursion through your hotel. *Alligator Hunting* is a special island thrill; there are plenty of these scaly creatures in the swamps along the south coast. They are actually crocodiles, not alligators, but the natives insist on the misnomer. They can be shot (by night) or captured alive (by day), and they make beautiful shoes and belts. Bernard Cridland in Aguilar's Fishing Shop, 93 Harbor St. Kingston, is one guide; Dennis Cooke (Montego Beach Hotel) is another. All equipment is supplied. There are eight *golf courses* in Jamaica; you can arrange to play through your hotel. *Tennis* is popular here; there are many courts including seven beautiful grass ones at the Montego Bay Country Club. Port Antonio is the center for *deep sea fishing,* and all hotels can make arrangements for this and island river fishing; no fishing license is required. Kingston is one of the great centers for Caribbean *yachting;* the Royal Jamaica Yacht Club is headquarters, or contact Sir Anthony Jenkinson at Morgan's Harbor, Port Royal, for charter. The 300-mile cruise around the island is one of the most beautiful in the West Indies. *Water skiing* at Ocho Rios and Mo' Bay. As for the national sport; matches every Saturday afternoon in Kingston from spectator sports, they are principally *polo* (there are 6 clubs) and *cricket,* January through April.

JAMAICA

EXPLORING JAMAICA

KINGSTON AND ENVIRONS. The tourist possibilities of Kingston are soon exhausted, and so is the tourist, especially if he hits the capital during a humid spell, in which case his one thought will probably be to escape to the cool uplands or the beaches of the north coast. The Victoria Crafts Market, described above, is certainly one of the sights of this busy town, a kind of bright pendant to the somewhat tarnished chain of shops which is King Street.

That famous colonial caravansary, The Myrtle Bank Hotel, should certainly be seen, an oasis on the waterfront, but no one but a social worker or a sailor thoroughly sick of the sea will enjoy the adjacent squalor of Negro shacks and dives of doubtful repute where the local color isn't deep enough to compensate for the wretchedness of poverty. Since you can't do anything but deplore the situation, our advice is to escape as soon as possible into the past by taking the Myrtle Bank motor launch across the harbor to Port Royal at the tip of the Palisadoes, that long spit of land on which so many tourists first touch down on this island.

The harbor itself, seventh largest in the world, has all the attractions of a bustling, present-day port.

Port Royal has the special fascination of time past, of a silent monument to the vanity of this world. A sleepy fishing village now stands where buccaneers once wenched, swilled rum, and gambled in the richest and bawdiest city of the New World. Port Royal's wealth and sin and glory have departed, but a romantic aura still emanates from the site of this town, whose sudden destruction seemed to survivors like something from the Book of Revelation. A few oldsters still claim that, when the wind and tide are right, you can still hear the bells of engulfed Christ Church, tolling in the fathoms of the sea. In any event, the proud merchant houses still stand on the ocean floor, and the romantically and athletically-inclined may dive for buried treasure or explore the sunken forts and silent streets of the ghostly underwater city. *Sic transit gloria mundi.*

Far above this watery grave, the popular *Morgan's Harbour Beach Club,* assists snorkel-explorers and other vacationers with its excellent equipment for yachting, water-skiing, skindiving, spear and deepsea fishing.

Outstanding among the landlubberly sights of Port Royal is

JAMAICA

Fort Charles, which the English erected in 1656 to guard the entrance to Kingston Harbor just in case the disgruntled Spaniards should take it into their heads to reclaim their stolen property. Named after that profligate Charles II, who never saw the place but would doubtless have enjoyed the diversions of Port Royal, the fort became the most important bastion of island defense. Horatio Nelson paced the ramparts here as a young lieutenant of the Royal Navy on the lookout for hostile French ships. You'll see a plaque commemorating his presence here, embedded in the wall of the King's Battery, still bristling with two tiers of guns, recalling the days when Britannia ruled the waves of the Caribbean.

Enough of Port Royal has survived the great earthquake and subsequent tremors and fires to keep the place historically alive. You will enjoy walking down the narrow streets, flanked by ancient houses. St. Peter's Church, built in 1725 to replace Christ Church, which slid into the sea in the cataclysm of 1692, is one of the famous landmarks of the Kingston area. Its sun-bleached walls bear the unmistakable patina of time. They enclose some interesting treasures: early 18th-century candelabra and altar railings, and an extraordinary organ loft, spectacular testimony to the craftsmanship of 18th-century Jamaican artisans. There are many monuments to distinguished early citizens of Jamaica, not the least of whom was Lewis Galdy, a French emigré who was responsible as churchwarden for the rebuilding of St. Peter's. He had a very personal stake in the enterprise, according to his tombstone in the churchyard. He was flung into the sea during the earthquake of '92, kept himself alive by swimming, was rescued and returned to the devastated city by boat. St. Peter's proudest possession? The silver Communion Plate, gift of Henry Morgan, the notorious buccaneer who became Lieutenant Governor of Jamaica and died in the odor of sanctity. Were these handsome pieces of silver part of his pirate loot? Dead men tell no tales.

If Port Royal and its vestiges of glory have whetted your appetite for island history, don't fail to visit the Institute of Jamaica back in Kingston. In this museum-library the island story is unfolded in a series of graphic exhibits ranging from Arawak Indian carvings to living examples of Jamaican fauna. There are some fascinating old charts and almanacs here; some stranger-than-fiction documents like the Shark Papers, damaging evidence tossed overboard by a guilty captain and found years later in the belly of a shark; a number of paintings and prints of more historical than artistic interest, and an outstanding library on the West Indies.

Parade Gardens, the civic center of Kingston, is handsome and dull in the worst tradition of the official mall, but it will almost certainly be surpassed by George VI Park, about a mile farther north, where Queen Elizabeth has already planted a tree and new official buildings are to be erected. Very dull is King's House, official residence of the Governor. Presumably earthquake-proof, it has been built with concrete flying buttresses that any medieval architect could have designed with more flair. More inspired is the functional modern architecture of the University College of the West Indies. This institution, organized by the various West Indian governments after World War II, is a symbolic achievement of the West Indian Federation, holding much promise for the future scientific and cultural progress of the British West Indies. A stroll through the campus, once a sugar plantation, and a glimpse of the 500 or so native university students in or between classes will give you an insight into the progressive tenor of life in Jamaica today.

The most widely-visited sight of Kingston is actually five miles out of town: the famous Hope Botanical Gardens. Given to Jamaica by the Hope family after slavery was abolished, the gardens are part of an agricultural center and have about 200 acres of beautifully-landscaped tropical trees, plants and flowers. They are all clearly identified. You've never seen such orchids unless you've been to Hawaii, and if you are a fancier of these exotic, wicked looking perennial epiphytics, you will have reached the pearly gates when you come to the Hope Gardens orchid house. The gardens are handsomely maintained by the Jamaica Department of Agriculture; highly qualified guides are on hand to escort visitors through the grounds, and the whole operation is a tremendous success. If you want more of the same, there are the Castleton Gardens, also maintained by the Department of Agriculture, at a height of 2,000 feet 19 miles from Kingston. Here in the cool uplands you will find an impressive ensemble of native trees and plants along with various shrubs, flowers and other plants that have been imported into Jamaica and have flourished in this soil. Excellent guides are also available here, and the charms of the visit are further enhanced by picnic facilities and invitations to swim in a refreshing mountain stream near the gardens.

At Castleton Gardens you are already far from the heat and hustle of Kingston and well on the road to Port Antonio and Ocho Rios.

JAMAICA

PORT ANTONIO. Following route A3 from Castleton, turn right (east) at Annotto Bay and follow A4 31 miles along the coast to Port Antonio. This northeast coastal corner is the cradle of Jamaican tourism, for it was here, half a century ago, that the United Fruit Company built the old *Titchfield Hotel* and started that migration to the north beaches. Port Antonio was the holiday capital of Jamaica before Montego Bay and Ocho Rios were generally heard of, and it still holds its own with the newer resorts. In fact it is enjoying a boom of its own with the late Errol Flynn's second Titchfield Hotel, now under new ownership, completely renovated and renamed *The Jamaica Reef*; with Canadian Millionaire Garfield Weston's luxurious new hotelry at *Frenchman's Cove*, and with club-type hotels planned for Folly and Boston Beach.

Port Antonio, which American poetess Ella Wheeler Wilcox called "the most exquisite harbor on earth", is the chief banana port of Jamaica, a land-locked bay behind which rise the majestic Blue Mountains. The picturesque islet in the center of the harbor is Navy Island, a favorite spot for swimming and picnics. The harbor is just about perfect for sailing, and all the necessities are immediately at hand including an almost constant breeze.

Twice Your Weight in Dolphins

Port Antonio is especially noted as a Caribbean center for deepsea fishing. Some anglers pronounce it the best in the West Indies. The 100 fathom-line is just half a mile from shore, so there is no long and boring trip to the fishing area. Marlin, tuna, kingfish, wahoo, yellowtail and bonefish swim these waters. Even nearer at hand are tarpon and snook. Port Antonio bills itself as the place where "the big ones don't get away", and visitors have been known to pull in twice their weight in dolphins in the course of an hour's fishing, an achievement any fisherman should be satisfied with.

Port Antonio's picture book charm is accentuated by Folly, the romantic ruins of a palatial mansion, whose crumbling walls and yawning windows produce a surrealist effect that will have you reaching for your light meter.

But the chief "sight" of Port Antonio lies seven miles to the east along the coastal highway. It is the justly famous Blue Hole, more elegantly known as the Blue Lagoon, which is precisely what it is, though much deeper than the average lagoon. In fact it appears to be fathomless, a phenomenon which accounts for the unusual fact that its water, though crystal clear, is the deepest ultramarine in tone. Far bluer than any blue grotto of Capri, it has to be seen to be fully apprehended. We've tried shooting it in color, but have never quite succeeded in capturing the incredible depth of pigment. The surrounding scenery makes a striking contrast to the Blue Hole; there's an adjacent white sand beach and a background of lush, brilliant green tropical jungle. This combination is characteristic of the scenic bays along this coast: San San Bay, Priestman's River, Boston Beach, and Frenchman's Cove. In the waters off shore, the "aerobatic" fighting tarpon average about 60 pounds.

Rafting on the Rio Grande

Port Antonio is headquarters for rafting on the Rio Grande, a unique Jamaican pleasure—it is not, strictly-speaking, a thrill—which you ought to enjoy while here. The Rio Grande is one of those swift Jamaican rivers, fed by the torrents and cascades of the Blue Mountains, and becoming navigable only as they approach the sea. Your trip will be made from a rafting base on the river near Berrydale downstream to the fishing port of Burlington where the river flows into the Caribbean at St. Margaret's Bay. The rafts, made of bamboo, are 25 feet long, 4 feet wide, and accommodate two passengers and a native raftsman who stands amidships or near the bow to guide this craft with a long pole. It is a pleasant three hour ride, mostly a glide through tropical scenery, occasionally accelerated by "rapids" which only a tourist folder could call exciting. This is not to minimize the pleasures of rafting. They can be varied by fishing and bathing from the raft when it pauses in some tranquil pool, and you can take a picnic lunch and eat it on the raft or river bank. Some rafters have been known to augment such lunches by fish and lobsters caught en route. At all events, the trip, through a jungle of ferns, palms, and feathery bamboos is a delightful experience, fit for a princess; at least it was for Margaret Rose.

Eastward and southward beyond Boston Bay, Jamaica is little-known, little-visited by tourists. This is enough to tempt the adventurous, but the lack of resort facilities in eastern Jamaica will discourage the average tourist. There is a government-sponsored resort at Bath where there are hot mineral springs, but this is practically back to Methusaleh.

The big attraction of the eastern section is Blue Mountain Peak, the highest point in Jamaica, 7,400 feet above sea level. This affords one of the more energetic diversions of the island to those who are athletically inclined. The trip to the summit can be made on foot or by mule. From Cedar Valley, a village in the Blue Mountains 30 miles east of Kingston, you drive north until reaching Whitfield Hall, which will be your base of operations. Here you set out, usually at night, with guides, mules and food on the ascent to the peak, 3,400 feet higher. Your arrival at the top is planned to coincide with dawn, and the experience is both physically exhilarating and soul-filling. The climb can also be made from Mavis Bank, but it's farther that way. Climbing Blue Mountain Peak is no more perilous than rafting on the Rio Grande. But take a couple of warm sweaters; it's cold in them thar' hills.

OCHO RIOS, center of another of Jamaica's five resort areas, can be reached in a number of ways. You can continue on route A3, following it as it turns northwest at Annotto Bay. But most tourists, coming from Kingston, take A1 west through Spanish Town, through the spectacular gorge of Bog Walk (a grunting Anglo-Saxon equivalent of the original Spanish *Boca de Agua*), over Mount Diablo, turning right at Moneague and proceeding by way of Fern Gully, a beautiful gorge, shaded by giant tropical ferns, to Ocho Rios (Eight Rivers). Fern Gully itself is a travel experience: three miles "meandering in a mazy motion" of green shade and dappled light in a deep defile at the base of fern-clad cliffs, twisting and turning through an eroded stone pass until the deep blue of Ocho Rios Bay bursts on the vision with an impact that familiarity never dulls.

The 60 mile stretch between Discovery Bay and Annotto Bay, included in the area of Ocho Rios, is one of the most scenic coastal areas in the world, and one of the places most touched by the tides of New World history. At Discovery Bay, you can tread where Columbus trod when he landed here in 1494. Sixteen miles east at St. Ann's Bay, you will be standing on that part of Jamaican soil first settled by the white man. Nearby is the site of Sevilla Nueva, which the Spaniards founded in 1509; its last vestiges now marked by a sign amidst the shimmering plumes of sugar cane, and a monument dedicated to Christopher Columbus' memory.

About four miles east of St. Ann's Bay, you should visit one of the Island's most delightful scenic spots: Dunn's River Falls and beach. At this point the clear waters of a mountain stream, rushing down through a wooded gorge, suddenly widen and fall in a transparent film over a natural stone stairway before meeting the warm Caribbean. The cascades and pools of Dunn's

River can be explored from a trail that flanks the stream, but the best thing by far is to put on trunks or bikini and get into the swim. Of all the countless hours of blissful basking and immersion in the West Indies, none are more memorable than the ones spent here, alternating a warm, lazy swim in the Caribbean surf with a cool plunge in this mountain stream. And just to sit on this stone and liquid stairway, legs dangling in the cool cascade, eyes gazing out from the shade to the dazzling Caribbean, is a tropical dream come true. Indeed, all of Ocho Rios, with its beaches, sugar plantations, coconut and banana groves seems to be conspiring to realize this dream.

At least part of your exploring of the Ocho Rios area should be done under water or with benefit of a glass bottom boat. For Jamaica's marine gardens begin just a hundred yards off shore in front of the *Silver Seas Hotel*. The hotels, of course, are the final, man-added touch to this tropical reverie. Their many facilities for relaxation and enjoyment have been noted above. Some of them, like *Tower Isle, Arawak* and the new *Marrakesh,* are showplaces in their own right. Many of them are following a delightful custom that originated here in Ocho Rios. This is "exchange visiting", a system by which guests at one luxury hotel may enjoy guest privileges, including dining, at others. Guests at *Tower Isle, Plantation Inn* and *Jamaica Inn* are already enjoying the variety that derives from these privileges, and it is expected that the practice will be extended in this and subsequent seasons.

MONTEGO BAY, usually called Mo' Bay by anybody who's been in Jamaica more than 24 hours, is, to put it conservatively, the greatest and the most. It has its own international airport, and there are innumerable gilded beachcombers of the International Set who have never set foot on any other part of Jamaica. Why should they? They've found what they wanted here.

It all began back at the turn of the century. People didn't swim in those days; they bathed. And only a few hardy souls did that. Men wore bathing costumes to the knee; women were encased from head to foot and from wrist to wrist in what looked like mourning weeds. They also wore hats and shoes. Thus protected from sun and surf, bathing was said by certain advanced thinkers to have a certain therapeutic value, providing of course that it wasn't overdone. One of these innovators was Doctor McCatty, a physician of Jamaica, who indulged in bathing with other daring medical spirits at a beach he happened to own in Montego Bay, a shining, white, unpopulated strand, which was entered through a cave. Residents who saw these physicians carrying on in this odd way, called the beach "The Doctor's Cave." In 1906 Dr. McCatty and his friends, convinced of the tonic effect of bathing on the nervous system, decided to form a club. Dr. McCatty donated the beach, and *The Doctor's Cave Bathing Club* was established. The rest is resort history: the development of one of the most extraordinary gold coasts in the Western Hemisphere.

The Montego Bay area stretches 50 miles from the *Silver Sands Beach Club* in the east to *Round Hill Hotel* in the west. It is symbolic that the sector should be confined by two such splendid caravansaries. For luxury is the be-all and the end-all of this resort. One could limit one's explorations to dining room and bar interiors, one's investigations to a comparative study of the virtues of freeform, kidney-shaped, and circular pools. (A few hotels even have old-fashioned rectangular ones.) Some tourists have seen the Caribbean sky and sea merely as a crescent above the rim of a cocktail glass. For this is a self-sufficient world of cabanas and Calypso, yacht clubs and country clubs, seaside and poolside, beach mats, straw hats, black waiters in white coats, and rum drinks, tall and cold to relieve the tedium of a sun-drenched Shangri-la.

Land of Look Behind

Behind this golden curtain is one of the most primitive sections of the whole West Indies, that wild and violent area known as the Cockpit Country with its strange pitfalls and potholes carved by some primitive geological force into the limestone. It was here that the fugitive slaves of the Spanish took refuge from the conquering English in 1665. From hideouts in these impregnable hills they waged such relentless guerrilla warfare against the new invaders that the English called for a cease fire on the ex-slaves' terms. The descendants of these unsubdued slaves, known as Maroons, live to this day in the Cockpit, free of taxation and other government interference in their affairs, their rights guaranteed by treaty. Only in the event of a capital crime can they be called to account by the government. Just 15 miles from Montego Bay, this is the historic "Land of Look Behind" where British colonials rode back to back on a single horse to avoid being ambushed by these fierce fighters for freedom. The Maroons—there are about 2,000 of them—are ruled by one of their number known as "the colonel", and you must receive his permission before entering their country. The country can be explored on horse-back, and some adventurous tourists have been known to do it from Good Hope. Incidentally, the natives who live just outside the borders of Maroon Town and the Maroon country are not at all happy about their neighbors' tax exemption.

For less strenuous sightseeing, drive ten miles east of Montego Bay along the coast road to the majestic ruins of romantic Rose Hall, still standing on the sugar estate of which it was once the "great house." And a great house it was with more than 50 doors, 365 windows, a dozen stairways, perhaps the grandest 18th-century plantation house in the whole West Indies. The second mistress of Rose Hall was Annie Palmer, a sort of female Bluebeard. She is credited by local history with having murdered two husbands and a plantation overseer who was her lover. She herself was done in by another lover who added insult to injury by dismembering her fair white body. Annie's violent amours and amorous violence have been duly recorded in a novel called The White Witch of Rose Hall. Negroes in the vicinity of this fascinating old house swear that Rose Hall is still haunted, as why should it not be after such a history.

On the sea in front of Rose Hall Plantation you may see a herd of cattle being driven into the sea with the help of small native boys and plantation horses and mules. This is a weekly delousing project, designed to remove ticks and other parasites from the cattle. The Montego Bay Hotel Association once got a striking color photograph of the cattle coming out of the water, and ran it in a tourist brochure with the following caption: "So wonderful is the bathing in Montego Bay that even cattle, horses and mules come down to bathe at sunset on the deserted beaches on the outskirts of town." Fie, gentlemen; you'll have the cattle stampeding onto the cruise ships in New York in their mad desire for a swim at Montego Bay!

Another of Jamaica's picturesque harbors is Falmouth, 12 miles east of Rose Hall on an estuary looking out to sea and back inland to the Cockpit Country. Note the courthouse. It's a faithful copy of an early 19th-century structure that was destroyed by fire in 1926. Originally built before the abolition of slavery at the height of Jamaica's sugar-cured opulence, it is considered one of the most beautiful buildings in the island.

You can fly from Montego Bay to Kingston, and enjoy a graphic geology lesson looking down on Jamaica from the air. You can take the long and magnificent drive around the eastern end of the island, one of the scenic splendors of the world. Or you can take a train. The third is the cheapest and in many ways the most interesting way. You'll be pulled by a small diesel, and slowly. It will take you 4½ hours to cover the hundred miles between Montego Bay and the capital. There will be stops and station waits, long enough for you to get out, stretch your legs, and look over the local scene. In the course of this leisurely ride, you will pass rivers, mountains, valleys, virgin forests, coffee and banana plantations, mahogany groves, sugar cane, native huts, native men tilling their fields, native women pounding corn, tending pigs, suckling babies. In short, you will pass through the heart of Jamaica.

MANDEVILLE, the cool "summer capital" of Jamaica is 65 miles west of Kingston. Take route A1 past 900-year-old Tom Crindle's Cotton Tree to Spanish Town, once the Spanish capital of Jamaica. Don't expect any touches of old Castile, however; the place is as English as Trafalgar Square. But Admiral Rodney, not Lord Nelson, stands in Government Square to greet you, flanked by two cannons he captured from the French in 1782. Don't let his Roman costume fool you; he's as English as the Union Jack. So is King's House, so is the old House of Assembly, and so is the nearby Cathedral of St. James, oldest Anglican church in the West Indies. The impression of Englishness grows as you drive west to Old Harbour where a slight detour will take you past the Little Ascot Race Course to Colbeck Castle. This monumental ruin with its four square towers was built in the 17th century by Colonel John Colbeck of His Majesty's Army. Its main facade, over a hundred feet in length, and its symmetrical proportions will remind you of the great country houses of England. The fortress-like construction of the towers, 40 feet high with walls nearly three feet thick, show that Colbeck Castle was more than a residence; it was a sentinel and bastion against the fierce Maroons.

If you're in the mood for exploring you can turn south at Freetown onto secondary road B 12 and make a big loop to The Alley, an important sugar town where the big *Monymusk Refinery*, one of the most modern in the world, will show you and the kids how the raw cane is processed into sugar. The village of The Alley itself is charming with its little English church of St. Peter's surveying the cane fields. This is a corner of Jamaica seldom seen by tourists.

A ten mile drive north and west of The Alley will bring you to *Milk River* on the stream of the same name, which flows south to empty into the sea at Farquhars Beach. South of the village on the west bank of the stream is *Milk River Bath,* a government owned and operated spa, capitalizing on a hot mineral spring which Jamaicans claim is the most radio-active in the world. Fifty-four times more radio-active than the waters of Baden Baden, Milk River Bath is reputed to cure or ameliorate a host of ills from arthritis to zymosis. Suffering only from a slight case of prickly heat, we preferred the bracing 80 degree waters of the nearby Caribbean to the 92 degrees of radioactivity at Milk River. This is not to minimize the therapeutic value of the baths. They are not imaginary; there's too much grateful evidence to the contrary. Reasonable rooms are available for those who want to take the cure. The main road north to Mandeville follows the Milk River a good part of the way. As you approach this corner of a foreign field that is forever England, you may be reminded of the rolling hills and valleys of Devonshire. The illusion is quickly spiked by the sharp, fan-like outlines of palm fronds, the red flame of poinciana blossoms, the golden forms of orange and grapefruit in the splendid citrus groves. But Mandeville itself does seem English with its village green, its Georgian courthouse, its neat cottages and gardens, and above all its parish church whose tall steeple would be perfectly at home in the Midlands. The climate is crisper here too and so are the accents, rather more consciously U as befits this elevated hill station. The social atmosphere of Mandeville is frankly stuffy. Outsiders may be tempted to laugh. But the Mandevilleans just look down their noses at such unseemly levity as they look down from their cool mountain height at the vulgar fleshpots of Kingston and Montego Bay.

For the tourist interested in Jamaica's agricultural and industrial life, Mandeville will have special charms. This is the center of the island's citrus industry; in season the oranges and grapefruits are miracles of size and flavor. The colorful native market in the town square overflows with the fruits and flowers of the tropic soil. The excursion to the Monymusk sugar plantation and refinery, mentioned above, is usually made from here. And the installations of Alumina Jamaica Limited and the Kaiser Bauxite Company may be visited on the outskirts of the city.

Croquet and Crocodiles

Less "touristed" and therefore much less expensive than the better known Jamaican resorts, Mandeville has its quiet provincial charm, far removed in spirit and price from the activities or passivities of the international set. Horseback riding, cycling, croquet, hiking, tennis and golf are the diversions here, and you feel more like engaging in them in the cool climate. If you want something more active, you need only descend to the coast for two more strenuous specialties of the Mandeville-South Shore area: deepsea fishing and crocodile hunting.

Headquarters for the former is the Blue Water Fishing Club at Whitehouse. Prize catches of marlin, tarpon, kingfish and wahoo have been made here in these waters which rival those off Port Antonio for game fish. Center for crocodile hunting is Black River, the town at the mouth of its namesake stream, the largest navigable river in Jamaica. The humid marshy banks of Black River are home sweet home for those thick-skinned aquatic reptiles that make such handsome belts, shoes and other accessories dear to the tourist heart. The natives and even the tourist office call these creatures alligators, but if you catch one you will see that their snouts are longer and narrower than an alligator's and (look out!) their lower teeth clamp shut into marginal notches, not into pits as does an alligator's. After which biological instruction, you are at liberty to bag your own crocodile bag. It's easily arranged (see Sports), and a native will skin your catch before you can say *crocodilus Jamaicensus*.

Even if you are the conventional type of tourist who prefers to do his crocodile hunting in a shop, you should take the drive from Mandeville to Black River, for it passes through one of the great scenic wonders of Jamaica. Just west of West Lacovia the road enters a grove of giant bamboos which meet overhead. This is the famous Bamboo Avenue, a cool, airy Gothic nave of light and shade extending for a mile and a half. Tourists almost instinctively descend from their cars here to walk under this lovely archway of feathery trees. Take your camera; the chiaroscuro effects of shadow splashed by filtered sunlight are extraordinary. Bamboo Avenue is one of the most photographed sights of Jamaica. You probably will enhance its reputation with at least one more shot of its dappled beauty.

East Lacovia, a few miles back on route A2 toward Mandeville, is the junction from which the adventurous drive north through such English place names as Newton and Maggotty into the Land of Look Behind. From Maggotty you can take route B6 for 36 twisting scenic miles through the western reaches of the Cockpit Country to Montego Bay. One un-numbered road leads from Maggotty north to the Maroon capital of Accompong (which must be a Maroon corruption of "accompany"); another leads to Quick Step. To visit either of these Maroon villages, you must have permission from the "colonel", the village chief who still exercises his autonomous rights in Jamaica. Getting permission involves advance dickering through your hotel manager or Kingston tourist office. Furthermore the roads to these settlements are imposible at best, impassable at worst. Sorry to dampen your enthusiasm. Better go back to Mandeville for a spot of tea, or, if you really crave excitement, a perfectly ripping game of English billiards. That's the thing about Mandeville. As the contented residents will tell you, they have all this tropical trumpery—and England too.

CAYMAN ISLANDS

The Cayman (or Alligator) Islands, which the natives proudly refer to as the islands that time forgot, lie about two hundred miles northwest of Jamaica. Politically speaking, they are part and parcel of Jamaica; geographically they could just as easily belong to Cuba. Ethnically, they are unique, an anomaly in the British West Indies. The whites outnumber the blacks, and are descended from buccaneers, shipwrecked sailors, and Scottish farmers. The women are very pretty and outnumber the men, many of whom are away at sea. If this whets your appetite for tropical romance, it should be added that Scotch Presbyterianism has triumphed over the pirate strains in Cayman blood. You've never seen so many church-going people in so small an area. Drinking is frowned upon from the pulpit, but the per capita consumption of "ardent spirits" remains very high. Church or no church, sailors will be sailors, Scots remain Scots.

PRACTICAL INFORMATION FOR THE CAYMANS

HOW TO GET THERE. Flight time from Miami has been reduced to only two hours with several flights offered weekly by British Overseas "BWIA" Airlines and Pan American "LACSA" Airlines. You can also fly in from Kingston or Montego Bay.

CUSTOMS AND CURRENCY. Same as Jamaica.

HOTELS

SEAVIEW HOTEL (20 double rooms with twin beds) on the ocean just outside Georgetown is new, modern, comfortable, has a pool and excellent dining room with tasty American and native dishes. It provides its guests with free island tours and transportation to and from the airport. Winter rates are $10 per person with private bath, $8 with semi-private bath per day American Plan. Summer rates are $6 per person.

THE PAGEANT BEACH HOTEL, new and up-to-date, has no beach but a pool fed directly by the sea. Winter rates: single $15, double $25 to $32.50; summer single $10 to $14, double $14.50 to $22.50. All rooms with bath; American Plan.

THE GALLEON BEACH is the old standby. Good location on superb beach, good food and service. Rates slightly higher than those at the Seaview.

THE TURTLE INN is a pleasant six-room guest house where you can stay for as little as $6 a day dining on turtle soup and steaks.

EMERALD BEACH COTTAGES are found on the southern coast of Grand Cayman. You can still see the wrecks of ships on the reef in the harbour there. Cottages are especially designed for honeymooners, retired couples or the tired mother and father who want to escape from humdrum life. Only 10 minutes drive from the airport, you still have a shopping center in Georgetown only 2½ miles away by car. Cottages are equipped with modern gas stoves, refrigerators, linens and utensils, with showers and screens. For rates write manager, James McMurry or New York office, 64 LaSalle Drive, Yonkers, N.Y., Tel. SPencer 9-4327.

SUNSET HOUSE south of Georgetown is in easy reach of all the amenities of the town. Snorkle and skindiving are specialties at the edge of the garden. Rates: Winter American Plan $12 single, $20 dou-

ble; Summer $8 single, $14 double.

GLEN AND SANDY, Cayman's newest guest cottages are located on the beautiful West Bay Beach only 50 feet from the shore. Rates: (maid included) $12 per day, $75 per week, $290 per month. A cook can be obtained if you wish.

NEW BAY VIEW HOTEL, brand new two story hostelry in Georgetown with screen-glass front dining room with harbor view. The beach and port are within walking distance. Beach cabanas have been built comprising 7 new rooms. Apartments with kitchinettes are also available. Rates: Winter American Plan, $10 to $12.50 single, $16 to $25 double. European Plan $7 single, $10 to $15 double. Weekly rates from $40 to $85. Manager-owners Caroline and Orrie Merren; Representatives in New York, Frances Junge, 64 LaSalle Drive, Yonkers Tel. 9-4327.

BUCCANEER'S INN located on Cayman Brac, south of Cuba and easily reached from Grand Cayman, has the distinction of a view of the Caribbean in three directions. Lovers of solitude will like this spot where time stands still. Only opened in 1956 when the airstrip was completed, modern civilization has really by-passed this island. The Inn is extremely modern, excels in seafood cuisine and native fruit and home-baked bread. Excellent fishing, skindiving and beach areas. Rates: Winter single $12 to $17.50, double $18 to $25. Summer single $9 to $11, double $14 to $16.

For more information about this relatively little-known vacation spot, write to Mr. Andrew Morris Gerard, Commisioner of Cayman Islands, Grand Cayman, B.W.I.

EXPLORING THE CAYMANS

There are three Cayman Islands: Grand, Little and Cayman Brac. They are comparatively flat, but you've never seen such beaches. One of them, West Beach on Grand Cayman, sweeps along for six miles. It makes Mo' Bay look like a kiddie pool.

JAMAICA

The Caymanians follow the sea and follow the turtles. Hunting these green monsters has always been a specialty of the Caymans. There were so many of these toothless, toothsome reptiles here when Columbus hove in that he called the islands Las Tortugas. The stock is depleted in the immediate vicinity of the Caymans, but they still hunt and capture the big fellows in Nicaraguan waters. You'll see the giant turtles being fattened up in pens, with owners' initials carved in the lower shell. The turtle steaks are unsurpassed here. You'll also find a variety of tortoise shell souvenirs carved by the natives.

Grand Cayman, largest of the three islands, is best equipped to accommodate tourists. It is only relatively grand: 20 miles long, six wide. Its green mantle of tropic vegetation is streaked with orchids, flowering trees and the flashing forms of wild canaries and parrots. Capital of Grand Cayman is Georgetown. It has an ice cream parlor, a dry cleaner, two bakeries, two laundries, many many churches, and movies in the town hall. The houses and gardens have that neat, well-tended English cottage look.

Cayman Brac's limestone bluff is a spelunker's paradise and the fishing is fabulous, both inshore and deep sea.

The winter season, mid-November to March, is a tropical heaven. The weather then is cool, clear and dry, the ardor of the sun tempered by the constant air conditioning of north east trade winds. Summer can be a tropical hell with torrential downpours and swarms of mosquitoes who attack with the organized fury of Stuka dive bombers.

The important point is that The Caymans are still offbeat enough so that you can have a West Indian winter vacation here at summer prices, real relaxation far from the ritual conventions of more travelled places. Swimming, sailing, snorkeling and other briny pleasures are the pastimes, plus fishing, lobster progging, wild duck hunting and the fun of searching for pirate treasure with the aid of a mine detector. This last can be borrowed or rented here. If you're planning on serious fishing, better bring your own equipment. There are good instructors now for spear-fishing, and the water is absolutely perfect for this sport. One of the specialties, lobster progging, is done with a guide. The expedition reaches a climax when the catch is cooked for lunch right on the beach. Best lobster we ever ate south of Cape God.

HAITI

Rhapsody in Jet

Of all the countries of the Caribbean, Haiti exerts the strongest fascination with its exotic flavor and its strange harmony of contrasts. Its people come from Senegal, from Sudan, the Gold Coast, Dahomey—and from France. The folkways of half the tribes of Africa have been transplanted to a tropical island along with the culture of Europe's most civilized country. In the 18th century Saint Domingue, as Haiti was called then, knew the mincing tempo of the minuet, the classic cadences of Corneille, the brilliance and wit of salon conversation, the luxury of Paris fashion. Life, for the upper classes at least, was as gay and glittering as a ball in the Faubourg St. Germain, if anything more sensuous, thanks to the combination of slave-supported indolence and the climate of the tropics. In the background, scarcely heard, like a muffled menace in the jungle, was the beat of Voodoo drums, drums of the kidnapped Quimas, the Bambaras, the vigorous Mandigues, the melancholy, homesick Ilos who were to rise in revenge against their masters and forge a new destiny from the broken chains of slavery. The violent, dramatic story of that rebellion, ending with the establishment of the first and

HAITI

only Black Republic in the New World, is the history of Haiti. Add to the mixture of African primitivism and French sophistication the spirit of a proudly independent people, and you have the key to the special atmosphere of Haiti.

The republic occupies the western third of that land which Columbus discovered on December 6, 1492 and named La Isla Española or Hispaniola, The Spanish Island. The native Arawaks called their island *Hayti*, "the mountainous country". This is most accurate; four-fifths of Haiti is mountainous, with peaks soaring as high as 9,000 feet. The Arawaks, who referred to themselves, again with accuracy as *Tainos*, "the good people", made the mistake of greeting Columbus with gifts of gold. Subsequent Spanish colonists "fell upon their knees, then fell upon the natives", exploiting, enslaving and slaughtering them in their frantic search for gold so that within 50 years all but a few hundred of the original million Arawaks were dead. Somebody had to do the dirty work; the importation of African slaves began. French buccaneers got into the act in the 17th century, founded the city of Cap Français (now Cap-Haitien) in 1670 and had this land grab officially recognized in 1697 by the Treaty of Ryswick, which gave them Haiti and left the eastern two thirds of the island, now the Dominican Republic, under Spanish control.

On the map Haiti has been compared to the yawning mouth of a crocodile, its upper lip in the Atlantic, its lower jaw in the Caribbean, getting ready to make a pass at Cuba about 50 miles to the northeast. Port-au-Prince, 655 miles southeast of Miami, is the crocodile's gullet, to pursue the metaphor, but when you see this most backward of West Indian capitals with its open sewers and squalid, malodorous slums, you'll be tempted to call it the cloaca maxima of the Caribbean.

A Country on the March

This is, fortunately, neither the first nor the dominant impression of Haiti. The first visual impact after the familiar sight of green mountains and blue water, is one of people. Haiti, with a population of nearly 4,000,000 squeezed into a mountainous terrain no larger than Maryland (10,700 square miles), teems with humanity like a technicolor India. The green mountains are like ant hills, but in Haitian society, the female of the species is sturdier than the male, and it is the women who are on the march both day and night. The Haitian farmer-smallholder is the backbone of the country, tilling his own soil. But most of the work and all of the "merchandising" are done by women, who are often the only beast of burden he has. It may take the farmer's wife turned *marchande* a hike of several days and nights to bring a basketful of produce to market, but when you see her en route, back erect, gaudily dressed, balancing the basket on her head, you'll agree she looks more like a gypsy princess than a beast of burden.

This strong and graceful silhouette strikes the dominant note in the Haitian scene: color. The color of Haiti with its gardens, flowers and flaming trees, above all with these dusky women in reds, blues and yellows against a background of forest green mountainside, azure sky and turquoise sea, strikes even the visitor who is normally indifferent to variations in the spectrum. One tourist, who had felt that the colors were exaggerated in the work of Haitian primitive artists he had seen in New York, changed his mind upon arrival in Port-au-Prince. His revised opinion: "They were only painting what they saw!"

The Creole Elite

The country is ruled by a mulatto aristocracy which prefers to call itself "creole". These "gens de couleur", descendants of French colonials and African slaves, are extremely interesting people. They are, almost without exception, very good looking, combining café au lait complexions and African warmth with a Gallic refinement of feature. Many of the women are great beauties. The creoles are amateurs of literature and art. Many are Paris-educated and have the intellectual complexity and vivacity of the French. Their manner in general is polished, worldly, cultivated and suave. If you are the kind of Anglo-Saxon who has innate feelings of superiority, especially vis a vis a darker skin, you will be astounded to discover that the Haitian creole feels smugly superior to both Americans and English, who, after all, have never had the cultural advantages of a French academic education. This attitude, so exasperating to Americans when they meet it in Paris, becomes almost insupportable when they find it encased in a Manila envelope. To make matters more complicated, the creole, with the sensitivity of the cross-breed and the pre-conceived notion that the average American tourist is probably Governor Faubus in disguise, is apt to be defensively upstage with foreign whites.

Do not make the mistake of thinking that the current elite is affected or that they are the *nouveaux riches* of Haiti. Remember that the mulattoes had a privileged position in plantation days, that they too had slaves. The creoles' interest

Even buses are colorful in Haiti

in books, in art and music is not factitious. Their witty, easy conversation in soft but perfect French would make the discussions in a Jamaica club sound puerile by comparison. Their attitude toward women is especially interesting, a curious mixture of Gallic sophistication and African sensuality. The gallant conversation of men with women has an undertone of French mockery touched with a darker note of disdain as if to remind the ladies that women do belong to the inferior sex, that their function is to please and work for the male. They are past masters on the dance floor. All Western veneer dissolves at the call of the tam-tam, and they let themselves go with atavistic abandon and supreme animal grace and skill to the beat of the music.

This light-skinned elite class—the lighter the better from their point of view, though they draw the color line at pure white, the mark of the foreigner and outsider—is subdivided into closely-knit clans, which alternate in political power. But the creoles, for all their education and for all their charm, are not a good ruling class by any standards. A sort of coffee-colored *herrenvolk*, they feel entitled to ownership of the country by virtue of superior birth, education and worldly wealth. They seem perfectly content to let the rest of the nation exist in "have-not" status in tumbledown country shacks or city slums that are a disgraceful blight on the face of what otherwise seems a tropical Eden. When you see naked black children and black pigs foraging and wallowing in the filth of that eastern Port-au-Prince shantytown en route to Pétion-ville, you'll be tempted to wonder if their slave forebears were any worse off; if the ruling elite is any less callous and indifferent than the plantation aristocracy of old.

A Good-natured People

It must be added, to relieve this dark picture, that the average run of Haitians, even the poor ones, seem to have a childlike capacity for the simple enjoyment of life. They are good natured and affable; you will not sense any of the hostility toward white foreigners here that is so evident in Jamaica. If you speak French to them, they will try very hard to understand, and sometimes they will. If they don't, they are apt to laugh appreciatively as though you have just told them the funniest joke they ever heard. One thing is certain; you will not understand *their* French, which isn't French at all, but an unwritten Afro-French dialect known as "creole". Exceptions: two universal Haitian phrases: "pa conay" and "pa capab",

Packaged idyll in the Dominican Republic

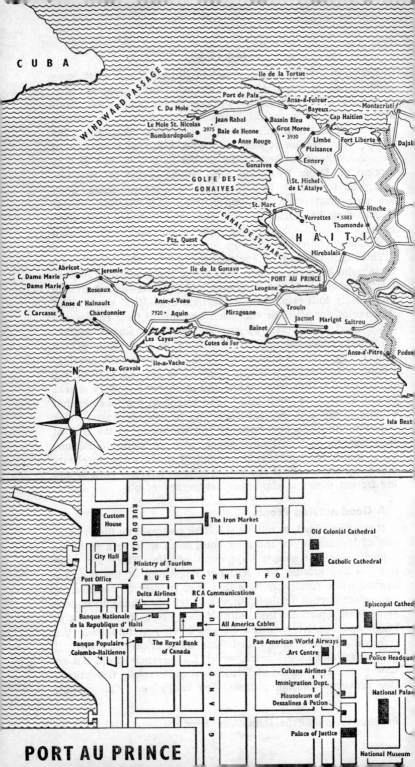

CUBA

WINDWARD PASSAGE

Ile de la Tortue

Port de Paix — Anse-à-Foleur
C. Du Mole — Bayeux — Montecristi
Le Mole St. Nicolas — Jean Rabal — Bassin Bleu — Cap Haitien
Bombardopolis — 2975 — Baie de Henne — Gros Morne — Fort Liberte — Dajabo
Anse Rouge — 3930 — Limbe — Plaisance — Ennery — Fort Liberte — Dajabo

Gonaives

GOLFE DES GONAIVES

St. Michel de L' Atalye

St. Marc — Hinche
CANAL DE ST. MARC — Verrettes — 5883 — Thomonde
Pta. Quest — HAITI
Mirebalais

Abricot — Jeremie — Ile de la Gonave
C. Dame Marie — PORT AU PRINCE
Dame Marie — Roseaux — Leogane
Anse d' Hainault — Anse-à-Yeau — Trouin
C. Carcasse — Chardonnier — 7920 — Aquin — Miragoane — Jacmel — Marigot — Saltrou
Les Cayes — Bainet
Cotes de Fer — Anse-à-Pitre — Pede
Ile-a-Vache
Pta. Gravois — Isla Beat

N

PORT AU PRINCE

Custom House
RUE DU QUAI
The Iron Market
Old Colonial Cathedral
City Hall
Catholic Cathedral
Ministry of Tourism
Post Office
RUE BONNE FOI
Delta Airlines
RCA Communications
Episcopal Cathed
Banque Nationale
de la Republique d' Haiti
All America Cables
Banque Populaire
Colombo-Haitienne
The Royal Bank
of Canada
Pan American World Airways
Art Centre
Police Headqua
GRAND RUE
Cubana Airlines
Immigration Dept.
Mausoleum of
Dessalines & Petion
National Pala
Palace of Justice
National Museum

HAITI
DOMINICAN REPUBLIC
(HISPANIOLA)

0   10   20   30   40   50   Miles

C. Isabela
Luperon
Puerto Plata   C. Macoris
            Sosua
        Sabaneta
4003   Gaspar Hernandez
Santiago   Moca
                Mantanzas
San Jose   S. Francisco
de las Matas   de Macoris   Sanchez   C. Samana
202   La Vega   Samana
        Jarabocoa
D O M I N I C A N   C. San Rafael
                        Miches
San Juan   Constanza   1742   Monte Plata
R E P U B L I C   Hato Mayor
                Bayaguana   El Macao
    San Jose de Ocoa   Higuey
    9200   San Pedro   C. Engano
                de Macoris   San Rafael
    Azua   La Romana
4199   San Cristobal
BAY   Bani   SANTO DOMINGO
DE OCOA
rahona   Pta. Salinas   Isla Saona
6348   MONA PASSAGE
so
Enriquille
El Can

AVENUE MARTIN
Airport

OZAMA RIVER

Columbus Ceiba

BENITO GONZALEZ STREET   National Museum   Columbus Castle

VICINI STREET   AVENUE

St. Francis Monastery

The Modern Market   ISABELA LA CATOLICA ST.

Sun Dial

MELLA   Senate Palace

DELGADO   MERCEDES   CONDE STREET   Tower of Homage
        STREET
SANTOME STREET
IEL   STREET
AVENUE   National Shrine   BILLINI   STREET

BOLIVAR   PADRE
STREET
INDEPENDENCIA AVENUE   GEORGE WASHINGTON AVE.

SANTO DOMINGO

meaning "I don't know" and "No can do" respectively. The affinity with *"Je ne connais pas"* and *"Pas capable"* is obvious enough.

Although this creole patois is being taught in adult schools, French remains the official language of Haiti. If you know a little French, don't hesitate to use it. The natives will appreciate it as a sign of courtesy, and your efforts will not be rewarded with the blank uncomprehending stares they might be greeted with in Paris. Your hotel manager and anyone else having anything to do with the travel business will speak English. English is taught in Haiti's schools as a compulsory subject.

Young Haitians are avid for education, regarding it as one way to pull themselves up from the slough of poverty. If you pass through the Exhibition Grounds of Port-au-Prince in the evening, you'll see dozens of students doing their homework under the city's street lights. They are not going to let a little thing like lack of electricity at home slow them down. We heard one college student reciting Cicero in impeccable Latin. The students memorize their lessons out loud by sound and rhythm. At exam time the city streets hum with their last minute cramming. It sounds like a jungle chant, but it's just the rhythmic recitation of Molière, Shakespeare or the quantum theory. This passion for self-improvement is strong in the national consciousness of the Black Republic.

Four National Heroes

In order to understand that consciousness, you should share the Haitian's awareness of his country's four great national heroes: Toussaint l'Ouverture, Henri Christophe, Jean Jacques Dessalines, Alexandre Pétion.

In 1791 voodoo drums of Saint Domingue (as Haiti was then called) beat out a tattoo of freedom and revenge. The black slaves, inflamed by the libertarian ideals of the French Revolution and enraged beyond endurance at the cruelty of their masters, rose in revolt against the French plantisocracy. With proud plantation houses going up in flames, their occupants massacred, the slaves running amok, and the Spanish and English moving in to occupy Saint Domingue, the French were juggling a hornet's nest. The French Civil Commissioner, Sothonax, seeking to win over the rampaging blacks, proclaimed the slaves of the North free in 1793. French General Leveaux then summoned an ex-slave, François Toussaint, a leader of his people, to restore order. Toussaint arrived with a small Negro army from neighboring Hispaniola, drove out the Spanish and English and liberated Leveaux himself, who had been held prisoner by the British at Cap Français. So swift and manouverable was Toussaint on the battlefield that a French general remarked, "Cet homme fait ouverture partout" (This man makes openings everywhere). The name stuck. Henceforth and forever in history, the "first of the blacks" was to be known as Toussaint l'Ouverture. Toussaint became commander-in-chief of the French Colonial Army. Order was restored. A constitution was promulgated giving the black Haitians the rights of man which the French Revolution had proclaimed, and Toussaint was Governor General, in control of Haiti. This did not set too well with that defender of the Revolution and lover of freedom across the seas, into whose hands the destiny of France and Europe had now passed: Napoleon Bonaparte. He sent 70 warships and 45,000 men under the command of his brother-in-law General Leclerc to seize "this gilded African", bring him and his leading generals, Christophe and Dessalines to Paris, then re-enslave the blacks for the greater glory of France. When Leclerc and his formidable forces arrived at Cap Français, General Christophe in command of the city, refused them permission to land. Leclerc attacked. Christophe, an originator of the "scorched earth policy", burned the city to the ground. The dogs of war were unleashed. Toussaint came close to winning the war; the French with their superior forces were baffled by the quick-striking Ouverture. But some of Toussaint's generals, including Christophe, surrendered. Toussaint, under a guarantee of security from Leclerc, went to French headquarters to discuss an armistice. There the black patriot was immediately seized, bound, thrown into the hold of a ship and sent to France. He died less than a year later, this black hero of tropical Haiti, of starvation and cold in the glacial dungeon of a prison in the Jura.

Independence

With this example of treachery before their eyes and the sudden disclosure of Napoleon's intent to restore slavery in Saint Domingue, Generals Christophe, Dessalines and Pétion resumed the war against the French. It was now a war of independence. The French, decimated by yellow fever, which killed off Leclerc, capitulated in November 1803 with Dessalines in the role of George Washington, General Rochambeau as Lord Cornwallis. France had lost her richest colony and a crucial staging area for Napoleon's grandiose designs on North America. One result: the vast Louisiana territory was sold to the United States for a paltry $15,000,000.

On January 1, 1804, the second Declaration of Independence in the New World was promulgated; Saint Domingue resumed its old Indian name of Haiti; an independent country had been born, different from any other; it was black.

Dessalines, imitating his little white brother overseas, was crowned Emperor of Haiti as Jacques I in a ceremony rivalling Napoleon's coronation in pomp, if not circumstance. He didn't last long. The brutal, ferocious side of his nature that had served him well as a general, served him badly as a king. He was assassinated in 1806, probably by mulattoes who were terrified by the emergence of a black autocracy. Haiti now became a republic with Henri Christophe as its first president, but a power struggle ensued between this colorful character and light-skinned, French-educated Alexandre Pétion, whom the southern mulattoes preferred as a ruler. The ensuing civil war ended in a stalemate. Pétion ruled in the southwest of the island, a quiet, cultured statesman. A pioneer exponent of the ideal of Pan-Americanism, he supplied Simon Bolivar with funds and arms for his heroic struggle on the Spanish Main leading to the independence of Venezuela and Bolivia. Pétion also founded the first high school in Haiti, which still bears his name, the Lycée Pétion in Port-au-Prince.

A blacker and stormier brew of coffee was Henri Christophe. Proclaiming himself King of the North, the North West and the Artibonite, he surrounded himself with a self-appointed nobility and embarked on a megalomaniac building career that constructed eight châteaux and nine royal palaces in less than 14 years. Two hundred thousand men performed the labors of Hercules in erecting Sans-Souci Palace and the fabulous Citadelle Laferrière, eighth wonder of the world, as grandiose a testimony to the vanity of man as all the pyramids of Egypt. The Citadelle is certainly the most impressive architectural monument in the New World, with the possible exception of certain New York skyscrapers, and it's one of the "musts" of the Caribbean (See below: Exploring Haiti). King Henri I, growing more and more tyrannical, less and less popular with his hard-worked subjects, committed suicide in 1820, with a silver bullet, say legend and Eugene O'Neill, and he was buried in the Citadelle.

HAITI

Modern Haiti

The bizarre days of Haitian royalty were over. History became more commonplace with such mundane events as establishment of banks and postal services, concordats with the Holy See, a graduated income tax. Governments rose and fell in the best French style at the beginning of the present century. Financial chaos and unrest were an excuse for the landing of U.S. troops in 1915. Real reason: to protect the Panama Canal from German U-boats. The occupation lasted until 1934 during which time the economy of the Black Republic was bolstered by U.S. loans and the first trickles of tourists discovering Haiti. From 1946 to 1950 President Dumarsais Estimé was in office, and a road-building, civic-beautification program was pushed, culminating in the Bi-Centennial Exposition at Port-au-Prince. The shiny new buildings were never kept up. Plaster cracked, stucco peeled; though still in use, they now look as though they were suffering from scurvy. Estimé ended up *désestimé*, and was forced out of office by political opponents and the army. A military junta took over, and in the new elections one of its members, Colonel Paul Magloire was elected president, the first chief executive to be chosen by direct popular vote. His popularity lasted for a while. He initiated a five-year plan of industrialization, workers' housing and tourist development. One result: the waterfront highways leading out of Port-au-Prince. But graft raised its ugly head; there were cracks in the new roads and buildings. Haiti's economy was also cracking. The hurricane that slammed into Haiti in 1954 and the floods of 1956 could hardly be blamed on Magloire, but they added to the rip tide of opposition. In December 1956, Magloire revealed an Emperor Jones complex by resigning as constitutional president and immediately succeeding himself as de facto Chief Executive, apparently appointed by some obscure Voodoo *loa*. Haiti's answer to this *coup d'état* was a national sit-down strike whose battle cry was "Chita la caille", "Stay in your hut." Not since Mahatma Gandhi has passive resistance worked so well. Magloire, after a few vain flourishes with machine guns, was forced to resign and leave the country.

You will find Haiti today a land of constant, striking contrast between the old and the new, the African and the French; the Christian and the pagan, the ultra-sophisticated and the primitive: gingerbread colonial houses cheek by jowl with modern, air-conditioned villas; burro carts and Cadillacs tangling in the bustling traffic of Port-au-Prince; the latest in "little black dresses" from Paris passing the gaudy native costume replete with a basket of fruit on the head; the latest French movies and plays not far from the febrile excitement of a cockfight; Roman Catholicism, the official religion, side by side with the primitive rites of Voodoo. All these combine to make Haiti a unique travel experience, not only in the Caribbean but in the world.

Voodoo

Voodooism, a barbaric African Negro religion, is now found almost exclusively in Haiti where, in spite of the official strictures against it by the Catholic Church, it flourishes, apparently in response to some deep, primitive need in the Haitian soul. It is a living religious practice with its liturgy established in a series of complex ritual drawings, songs and dances, accompanied by the rhythm of sacred drums. The symbolic significance of the drawings is not perfectly clear, even to the practitioners of voodoo; their origin probably goes back to a superstititous priesthood which drew them as magic signs to supplicate or propitiate some god, and did not feel called upon to explain the mystery to the communicants. The drums need no explanation. Even on white neophytes, the percussion produced by expert Haitian drummers on these instruments exerts a strange compulsive effect. It is difficult not to be "carried away" by the relentlessly-accelerating rhythms of Voodoo drums. It is this quality of being carried away, "possessed", "out of this world" which probably accounts for the persistence of Voodoo in Haiti. The ability to lose oneself in a religious ceremony must have been consoling to the hundreds of thousands of transplanted slaves for whom Voodoo offered at the same time an opportunity to remember and forget. To remember the very pulse beat of the tribal life from which they had been so cruelly and irrevocably cut off. To forget, momentarily, the dawn-to-dark labor, the whippings, the chains, the rack and the other afflictions of their slave lot. It was the sound of Voodoo drums beating in the jungles of Haiti that was the first tocsin of the revolution that created The Black Republic. The blood of Black Africa, though many miles and generations removed from its tribal roots, responded to that tocsin. And it responds today.

So much for Voodoo's persistence. But what is it? It has been called "a set of beliefs and practices that have been passed down among the peasants from ancient times, claiming to deal with the spirits of the universe and keep the individual in harmonious relationship with them." You yourself will be able to see practitioners of Voodoo "transported", "elevated", in a state of religious ecstasy, which is the essence of mystic religious experience and no doubt puts them in a "harmonious relationship with the spirits". But how it happens and just what the mysterious signs and chants employed in the process mean, will not and probably cannot be explained.

Saturday night is Voodoo night in Haiti (see Night Life below), and you should arrange your trip so as to be able to see these unique ceremonies. The version you will see may be shorter and more "touristy" than the exhausting all-night ordeals that go on among the natives all over the country. Nevertheless, it will be authentic Voodoo, conducted by an authentic Voodoo *houngan* (priest) or *mambo* (priestess) in a charm-bedecked *hounfour* or neighborhood Voodoo temple. The last will very likely be decorated with primitive Haitian art, representing various Voodoo gods or *loa*, of which there are many. One, *Damballa Wedo*, a rain god important to any peasant, is symbolized by a snake. The persistence of the snake motif has led some people to believe that Voodooism is "snake worship", but this is as simple-minded and innacurate as to describe Christianity as "cross worship". There will be all sorts of charms, trinkets, gourds, colored paper, bottles and other incongruous objects hanging from the ceiling of the temple. There will be a pole, like a painted maypole in the center of the temple, and there will be *rada*, the sacred Voodoo drums, so taut and resonant that to touch them sets off a throbbing vibration. When the Haitian drummers start in on these; when the initiated come in singing; above all when the dancers start whirling about the center pole, you'll be caught up irresistibly in a furious percussive rhythm that will make the hot nightclub drummers back home seem like the ghost of Yankee Doodle. The participants in the Voodoo ceremony dance with an abandon which is enough to make the senses reel and which often reaches a climax with the dancer going into a trance. This trance-like, "out-of-this-world" state means the dancer is "possessed" by the *loa*; the god has actually entered into his body and soul.

It may sound corny. It may be scientifically explained simply as nervous exhaustion. Nevertheless, it is impressive, and probably the nearest thing you will ever know, even vicariously, to a basic, primitive religious experience. During the ceremony, *veveys*, mysterious, cabalistic designs are drawn on the floor in a white chalky wash. Sometimes they are very beautiful, but their meaning is not interpreted. That, of course, is the baffling thing about Voodooism. It is not explained. Perhaps it is wisest to accept it without questioning too far into its mystery; Voodoo, like a poem, should not mean, but *be*. You may scoff at it; you may share the church's disapproval of this pagan African ritual. But one thing is certain: Voodoo is deeply ingrained in the soul of the Haitians, and it probably will be for a long time to come.

By far the best description of Voodoo for Western readers is to be found in an account of an all night session in Hugh B. Cave's excellent book, *Haiti, Highroad to Adventure*. Mr. Cave lived in Haiti for some years, learned creole, and made friends with Haitians who took him to a *hounfour* where no tourist had ever set foot. At the end of a 12 hour ceremony, he saw neophytes dipping their hands into boiling oil, passing their bare feet through fire without a murmur of pain. His conclusion about Voodoo, and even about Zombiism: "The skeptic may consider it nonsense, but the longer one lives in the land of Voodoo the less one is inclined to scoff." You will probably not have the good fortune to stay in this exotic land as long as Mr. Cave. You will have to be content with the Voodoo Ceremony arranged by your travel agent or hotel manager (see below), but, even on the basis of a limited experience with Voodoo, you probably won't feel like scoffing.

Haitian Painting and Folk Art

The celebrated renaissance in Haitian painting began in 1944 when an American artist and school teacher DeWitt Peters opened the *Centre d'Art* in Port-au-Prince. Three years later Haitian painting caused a sensation at the UNESCO international exhibition in Paris. In 1948-49 Haitian "primitives" were shown and bought in New York and all over America. The same year the American poet and art critic, Selden Rodman, launched the mural movement in painting. Thirteen tempera murals were painted by native Haitian artists the following year in the Episcopal Cathedral of the Holy Trinity (see Exploring Haiti), and the walls of hotels, airport and Exposition buildings began to glow with the rich colors of these self-taught primitive artists. Many of the painters are now widely known wherever pictures are exhibited and bought: the late Hector Hyppolite, who was a Voodoo priest; Wilson Bigaud, the first Haitian to exhibit at the Carnegie International; Philomé Obin and Enguerrand Courques, whose pictures are in the permanent collection of New York's

HAITI

Museum of Modern Art. In recent years the movement has grown more diverse. The Centre d'Art continues to support the work of primitive painters. The rival *Foyer des Arts Plastiques*, dominated by Max Pinchinat, who studied abroad on a fellowship and became a friend of Picasso, emphasizes the less parochial, more international work of New York and Paris-trained artists of the contemporary school. The most recent splinter is the La Brochette Group, which struck out under the leadership of Paris-trained Luckner Lazare to establish a contemporary style of national Haitian art. The work of many Haitian painters is still colorful, original, imaginative and inexpensive, providing the tourist with an unusual chance to acquire good originals for enjoyment and as an investment. Among the scores of artists to look for are Rigaud Benoit, Castera Bazile, Luze Turnier, Antonio Joseph, Toussaint Auguste, Adam Léontus, Préfète Duffault, Dieudonné Cedor, Jasmin Joseph, René Exumé, Max Arnoux, Daniel and Emile Lafontant. The most interesting approach is to visit the three art centers mentioned and make your own choices on the basis of which style appeals to you most. You are certain to find something among the hundreds of pictures available that has your name on it as well as the artist's. There is no better souvenir of exotic Haiti than the record of it conceived and executed by a native painter.

Haiti's sculptors of importance are Jasmin Joseph, Odilon Duperrier, André Dimanche and Georges Liotaud.

Haitian folklore, the richest in the Caribbean, reaches the apogee of its expression in music and the dance. The folk music throbs with all the heat and color of Africa. If you have a chance to hear the magnificent Déjean Male Choir, don't miss it; it's a revelation in the tonal color possibilities of massed male voices. The drumming, as in the Voodoo ceremonies, is extraordinary. As for the dancing, it is self expression par excellence, full of overt suggestion and no more restrained by sexual inhibition than the Haitian peasant. Some tourists are shocked by these "sex-crazed" exhibitions, but they are quite possibly the ones with the dirtiest minds. It has been pointed out, and should be reiterated, that, no matter how abandoned the dancing, it never has the cheek to cheek, navel to navel intimacy of social dancing in a New York night club.

The *Meringue* is the popular ballroom dance, as proper and discreet as anything at a debutante party. *Ra-Ra*, which sounds like an American cheering section, looks like one that had left the stands for a triumphal snake dance. Its singing, tapping and stamping is rather like a secular version of Voodoo, and is most often seen at the pre-Lenten Carnival. A bunch of Haitians indulging in Ra-Ra make Katherine Dunham's troupe look like the ladies' sewing circle.

PRACTICAL INFORMATION FOR HAITI

 HOW TO GET THERE. *By Air.* Pan American has non-stop flights from Miami to Port-au-Prince and service from New York via Santo Domingo, San Juan, Puerto Rico or Kingston, Jamaica. There are direct inter-island connections between Haiti and Jamaica, Puerto Rico, the Dominican Republic, and Caracas, Venezuela via Pan American World Airways. Most other islands are connected by air with Haiti by Pan Am.

By Sea. You can sail weekly from New York on the Grace Line, 3½ days to Port-au-Prince on air conditioned boats. Royal Netherlands Steamship Company has accommodations for passengers on its cargo ships between New York and Haiti. From Miami it's the Eastern Shipping Corporation. You can also sail from Canada (Montreal) on Saguenay Terminals S.S. Line. The French Line's Transatlantic service includes Port-au-Prince among its ports of call.

 PASSPORTS, VISAS. American and Canadian citizens are not required to have passports or visas for visits of 30 days or less, but Canadians passing through the U.S. en route to Haiti must have passports. British subjects should have passports. All tourists are required to have proof of citizenship, valid smallpox vaccination certificate, and a ticket out of Haiti. You are required to buy a tourist card (cost $2) on arrival. This card is good for two years.

 CURRENCY. The unit of Haitian money is the *gourde,* divided into 100 centimes. The gourde is worth 20 cents in U.S. money, and is issued in notes of 1, 2, 5, 10, 20, 50 and 100. There are 5, 10, 20 and 50 centime coins. American money is acceptable throughout Haiti at even exchange value, as are travelers checks. You can bring in any amount of foreign currency but it can't be in denominations of more than $20.

CLOTHING. Light summer weight clothes for both sexes. Shorts and slacks okay for women, but not on the streets of Port-au-Prince. Slacks or riding pants are a must for the excursion to the Citadelle. (See below: Exploring Haiti). The accent is generally on informality, though men are expected to wear jackets and ties at dinner. Formal clothing only required if you expect to be entertained at official functions or at the exclusive clubs. Temperature range is 70 to 85 degrees, but bring stole, sweater or light topcoat for the mountains.

HAITI

HOW TO GET ABOUT. There is a public bus system, which, like everything else in Haiti, is colorful. You are not likely to use it. Some of the buses are gaily-painted wooden superstructures, superimposed on modern truck chassis and given such names as *Toujours Immaculée*. Station wagons connect Port-au-Prince with Pétionville. Fare is 10 cents. There is a red flag taxi service which amounts almost to a random shuttle; the taxis have a red flag waving from the radiator cap, and take people at 10 cents a person wherever they want to go in town. You may have to wait for previous passengers to disembark, and may be taken out of your way while they are taken to their destination. Other taxis are hired individually, and legally are not supposed to charge more than $1 per person for any trip within the limits of Port-au-Prince. But look out. Although the Haitian taxi drivers were once on the verge of being the Caribbean's most successful racketeers, new government laws now protect tourists for the most part from the piratical and dictatorial tendencies which have governed their business acumen for years. Rates are now fixed, and taxis carrying the letter L on license plates are driven by English speaking chauffeurs and covered by passenger accident insurance. Taxi fare is displayed on back of driver's seat. If not displayed, ask for it. Never allow a taxi driver to influence you in your choice of hotel, shop or restaurant. Choose the place you want from the Fodor list or through a reputable travel agent and insist upon being taken there and nowhere else. Always make sure to fix the price of the taxi ride in advance.

There are many car hire places, including a branch of Hertz Drive Yourself in Port Au Prince. Haitian Travel Service can also rent you a car. Cost is about $10 a day. Reliable sightseeing tour operators, many of whom have limousine service with chauffeur, are Agence Citadelle, Heraux Tours, Caribtours, Southerland Tours, Haiti Tours, Pierre Tours and Magic Island Tours.

The 200-mile trip from Port-au-Prince to Cap Haitien, which used to take 7 hours over horrendous roads, is now reduced to about 4½ thanks to a new highway. For $16 you can fly there in only 40 minutes on scheduled flights of the Haitian Air Force. The air view of Haiti and the Citadelle is stunning. You can also charter planes from the Haitian Air Corps. Prices start at $30 an hour for a three-passenger job with reliable pilot included.

HOTELS

Of all the Caribbean islands, Haiti has the most individual hotels by virtue of their local color and flavor and their frequently magnificent sites. Port-au-Prince is like a grandiose theatre with its hotels built in tiers on three levels. In the "orchestra" are those like the *Beau Rivage*, immediately adjacent to downtown shopping, sightseeing and entertainment. Higher up, hotels like the *Castelhaiti* and the *Oloffson* sit like debutantes or dowagers in the diamond horseshoe of the "mezzanine". Still higher, the tier of Pétionville hotels form the first row of the balcony overlooking that magnificent

HAITI

spectacle. Many of these are real gems of imaginative taste (the *Ibo Lele*, for example) and a far cry from the conventional "modern" monstrosities. The Haitian touch that will make the strongest impact on the visitor is the generous use of local art, easel paintings but particularly murals with which the hotel premises are brightened up and personalized. There are some hotels in which the walls of every room are covered with murals painted in joyous mood and riotous colors by some of Haiti's best artists. Here the government and tourist industry are to be congratulated in creating what amounts to a unique style in hotel decoration. It is a happy departure from the chrome and chartreuse routine, and so successful that many visitors associate the vivid color of Haiti with the decor of their hotel, and remember the latter even after other impressions have faded.

(Note: Such luxuries as swimming pools and air conditioning are almost necessities in downtown hotels).

The local color permeates the service and the kitchen too. Most hotels have had the happy inspiration of always including at least one Haitian dish on the menu (See below: Food and Restaurants), and these hotels will be remembered for their cuisine long after you've forgotten the food in other Caribbean hostelries.

PORT-AU-PRINCE

BEAU RIVAGE. Managed by M. Raymond Roy, and, forgive the personal observation, his beautiful wife. The Beau Rivage has 40-air conditioned rooms, delightful public rooms, garden and pool. There's open air dancing in the gardens. A favorite of visiting businessmen, this attractive hostelry is on ocean-front Truman Boulevard, convenient to shops, offices and the International Casino. American Plan winter rates: $18 single per day; $30 double. The Roys, among Haiti's most gracious hosts, will also receive guests on the European plan, and can arrange to accommodate you in suites if you wish.

CASTELHAITI. One of Haiti's newest. Its ultra-modern skyscraper pretensions are not necessarily in harmony with Haitian individuality, but it has much to recommend it: magnificent views (every one of

the 65 rooms has a large private balcony); and all the de luxe amenities, swimming pool, air conditioning etc. The standard of cuisine is just as high as the building, which is to say tops. Modified American Plan winter rates: Singles, $16 to $18; doubles, $28 to $34, all with private bath.

EXCELSIOR. Small hotel (13 rooms), inexpensive, and conveniently located near the city shops and sights. No pool. Food can only be termed fair, but it seems captious to complain when Manager DuVall's American plan winter rates are only $5.70 to $7 a day single, $10 to $12 double.

MAJESTIC. Small (15 rooms) with comfortable, homelike atmosphere. In the heart of the city. (Don't confuse it with the *Majestic* at Pétionville). No pool. Good food. Inexpensive American Plan rates:

When you patronize our advertisers, please refer to this guide as your source of information. You will thus be assured of preferential treatment.

HAITI

$7.50 to $10 single, $12 to $18 double. Mrs. Zamor is the name of the manager.

MON RÊVE. A dream for anyone who's looking for a small, reasonable hotel with local atmosphere. There are nine rooms in an old mansion in an old garden. Plain, comfortable, but can be a little warm. Chief attraction is the collection of Haitian paintings on the walls which makes the place seem like an annex of the Art Center. They're for sale, and you can live with them in your own room before deciding to buy. J. S. Kenter is the manager. He and his wife know all about Haiti and are happy to share their knowledge with guests. American Plan rates: $7.50 per day single; $15 double.

OLOFFSON. This is a Haitian landmark, a most delightful, old-fashioned hotel on the "mezzanine", but within the city area. It's a French colonial-style house with lovely gardens and swimming pool. Its owners were among the first patrons of Haiti's famed art movement, and the hotel's collection of paintings is first rate. So is the food. This is a preferred meeting place of local and visiting intelligentsia and "Bohemians". Mr. A. Seitz is the owner-manager's name. The winter rates: $14 single, $24 to $30 double per day, American Plan with bath.

PARK. Small (16 rooms), conveniently located, no pool, fair food, inexpensive. Rates: $6 to $8 daily single, $12 to $15 double, American Plan with private bath. Miss Clerie is the manager.

PLAZA. Has 26 rooms in town. American Plan rates are $8 to $10 single, $15 to $18 double per day. Manager is M. Pierre Louis.

SANS SOUCI. One of the oldest hotels in Haiti, has very comfortable air conditioned rooms, a pretty tropical garden, swimming pool, a charming bar which is popular with the local elite, and a dining room where the food is so good that it's patronized by non-residents as well as hotel guests. G. Heraux is the manager. American rates are $15 daily single, $28 double.

CARIB HAITI. Very attractive, facing the bay, has lovely gardens, a swimming pool, and air conditioned rooms. The rates, American plan, are $13 to $20 a day single, $26 to $34 double. 32 rooms.

SPLENDID. Started life as a private mansion and keeps the charming, old-fashioned atmosphere of a former day. In addition it has a swimming pool. Close to downtown, patronized by businessmen, a sure sign that the food, if not gourmet fare, is substantial. A. Mans is the manager. There are 40 rooms. American Plan rates: $8 to $15 per day single, $15 to $25 double.

CACIQUE ISLAND. The newest development in Haitian resorts, Cacique is unique from several points of view. Instead of the usual posh glass and steel hotel or the very sleek cabanas, Cacique offers native huts in such peaceful surroundings that you'd think they were the real McCoy. Even though the banana-thatched living quarters may look like something straight out of a native village, the intrepid Haitian architect who designed the entire project, Robert Baussan, student of Corbusier, has thought of 20th century comfort, too. The walls are slatted like the native type, but so cleverly constructed and designed that you need not fear wind and rain on those occasions when they come along. The huts are single, double and cottage style family size. They are fully equipped for housekeeping, (in 20th century manner and not native style). Now open with thirty huts, extensive additions are planned for the very near future. Facilities for tennis, golf and boating and a fresh water pool are under construction. This is no spot for the fidgety, but ideal for those who seek sun, swimming and

337

solitude with some degree of comfort. M. Baussan says the island is shark-proof because it is ringed by a reef. The color of the water itself is a delight, from jade green to eggplant purple. New developments are on the planning boards for a hotel and restaurant on Cacique for those who want something a little more ordinary. Present rates are $6 a day single and $12 double, European Plan. Port-au-Prince is only a little over half an hour by car and five minutes by boat distant. Postal address for Cacique is P.O. Box 1096, Port-au-Prince Haiti. Transportation to the resort is still troublesome, but plans are afoot to provide free trips for guests.

PETIONVILLE

Note. This suburb in the hills above Port-au-Prince is the resort area of the capital. None of the Pétionville hotels is more than 15 or 20 minutes by car from the city, but transportation can be very expensive (See above: How to Get About). Never use "free lance" taxis if you can help it. Ask your hotel manager to arrange transportation and let him do the haggling for you.)

CHOUCOUNE. One of Haiti's finest, has 35 air conditioned rooms, swimming pool, roof garden for dining and dancing, and delicious food, as good as you'll find west of Paris. Its *Cabane Choucoune,* built in the authentic style of an African tribal hut, is *the* place to sample Haitian night life in the company of Haiti's creole elite. R. Marini is the manager of this smoothly-run hotel. American Plan rates: $20 to $25 single per day; $35 to $45 double.

DAMBALA. In lonely splendor 2,000 feet up. Comfortable rooms, tennis, swimming pool, good food, and views that make you catch your breath. 32 rooms. Manager is W. Francis. Rates, American Plan: $15 to $20 single per day; $26 to $40 double.

EL RANCHO. De luxe plus. A jewel operated by Mr. Ben Shindler of N.Y. and managed by Thomas M. Dell, this hotel has 55 rooms in its beautiful main buildings and bungalows, handsomely decorated with Haitian murals and artifacts. Swimming pool, air conditioning, splendid gardens, views and service. The food is a gastronomic experience. American Plan Rates: Winter single $30 to $35, double $45 to $60, summer single $18 to $24, double $30 to $40. Children welcome, sitters available.

IBO LELE. 60 Rooms. This romantically named (after a Voodoo god) hostelry is a special favorite of ours. It embodies all the charms and attractions of Haiti. Public rooms glow and blaze with Haitian painting. Lovely rooms and suites with hundred-mile view. Swimming pool and terrace-bar. The food is Franco-Haitian at its best; it's the kind of place where you anticipate the delights of the next meal. The hotel's *Shango* nightclub, open nightly during season, has authentic Haitian music and voodoo dances. André Roosevelt is the manager. American Plan winter rates are from $18 to $30 a day single; $30 to $60 double and worth it.

MAJESTIC. On Pétionville Square. Has 18 rooms, pool, friendly atmosphere, *Bacoulou night club,* very good food at very attractive prices. American Plan rates: $10 to $15 per day single; $18 to $25 double. Mrs. Gerald Wiener is the manager, and she knows the magic formula of getting guests to return.

MARABOU. Also on Pétionville Square. Another small (16 rooms) and congenial hotel. Swimming pool. The Marabou operates on the Continental Plan with winter rates at $8 per day single, $14 double. They can give you lunch and dinner, however, in a very good, inexpensive restaurant specializing in unadulterated Haitian food.

MONTANA. A delightful mountain hotel with panoramic view, nice gardens, swimming pool, air conditioning. Excellent service and food. 36 rooms. American Plan winter rates: $20 to $29 per day single; $35 to $55 double. Frank Cardozo is the manager.

VILLA CREOLE. Pleasant, modern, 39-room hotel with large swimming pool. Good French cuisine plus charming creole buffet lunches in informal surroundings. **Dr. Assad** is the manager. American Plan winter rates are $15 to $18 per day single, $30 to $35 and $40 double.

VILLA QUISQEYA. A charming small hotel (7 rooms) with pool and old-fashioned, truly Haitian atmosphere. Mme. Carmelle Heraux manages this place, which may remind you of a French pension, especially at meal times. The food is excellent. Inexpensive. American Plan winter rates: Single, $10 per day; double, $18.

CAP-HAITIEN

This town, once the fabulous Cap Français of French Saint Domingue, is the jumping-off point for exploring the famous Sans Souci Palace and Citadelle of Henri Christophe. Two hundred miles from Port-au-Prince, Cap Haitien is fast developing as a tourist center in its own right. The pick of current hotels follows:

ROI CHRISTOPHE. A 20 room hotel with swimming pool, tennis and use of private beach. Lovely old garden. Comfortable, hospitable ambiance, excellent Franco-Haitian cuisine. The manager is Mrs. Castalogne. American Plan rates are $14 per day single, $25 double.

MONT JOLI. Recently opened. Beautiful view from hillside setting. Has swimming pool, beach, cocktail lounge, and an excellent cuisine, featuring both creole and French dishes. Manager of this 18-room hostelry is Mrs. Busenius. American Plan. Rates are $10 to $14 single, $18 to $25 double.

BECK. Also new and modern. Fine view over town, mountains and sea. Private beach, resort facilities, good cuisine. Mr. Beck is the owner-manager of this 12-room hostelry. Rates are $13-$15 daily single; $20-$26 double, American Plan.

PENSION ANDRÉ. Eight rooms, $4 single, $8 double per day American Plan, a windfall for the budget-conscious tourist.

PENSION MARTIN. Ten rooms, simple but clean. American Plan. Same rates as the André.

FOOD AND RESTAURANTS

Haiti is about the only Caribbean island, with the exception of the French ones, that can legitimately claim to be remembered for its contribution to the fine art of gastronomy. The French cuisine is authentic. The creole specialties, combining French, tropical and African elements, are delicious. Here are some of the special dishes worth tasting: *guinea hen with sour orange sauce; tassot de dinde,* dried turkey; *grillot,* fried island pork; *diri et djondjon,* rice and black mushrooms. *Riz et pois* is rice and kidney beans (this is not a mistranslation; it's a Caribbean idiosyncrasy). *Langouste flambée* is flaming lobster; *ti malice,* a delicious sauce of onions and herbs; *piment oiseau,* a hot sauce that will make you feel like a fire-breathing dragon. A native favorite is *grillot et banane pese*, pork chops and island bananas. If you have a sweet tooth, you'll love *pain patate*, the famous sweet potato pudding, and mango pie. The *haute cuisine française* has all the great specialties: onion soup, snails, and a superb *bouillon de crabe*. Fresh coconut ice cream is an island specialty; cashew nuts are another, and there's a full array of avocadoes, mangoes and other tropical vegetables and fruits.

You'll find plenty of French wine and champagne at bargain prices with which to wash all this down, and a whole gamut of French liqueurs plus local cordials. But the island drink of Haiti is rum, and the best rum you ever tasted is probably *Barbancourt*. Island-made, it's distilled like a cognac. It's smooth and mellow and available in about 70 different island cocktails and punches from a morning Eye Opener to a Shady Lady late at night. Don't try them all in a single day. There's a charming rural tour from Port-au-Prince to Damiens where you can see the sugar-cane fields, the clay peasant houses with thatched straw roofs, and tour one of the local distilleries, sampling their celebrated rum on the house. If you wish to taste what the poor natives take to solace themselves and toughen their stomachs, go into a bar and drink some *clairin*. It's the cheapest local rum and very raw. No one but a fire eater could remain indifferent to its special quality.

Hotel restaurants have the best reputations in Haiti; those with exceptional cuisine have already been noted in our hotel list. There are some outstanding restaurants, however, where dining out will be a rewarding adventure. The following are all in or near Port-au-Prince. All are moderate in cost, especially as compared to comparable eating places in New York.

Le Perchoir. Three thousand feet up, this unique restaurant is suspended in mid-air from a cliff, and you dine in the clouds on such French-creole delicacies as *escargots*, curry of chicken, and *soufflé au rhum*. A high gastronomic experience; in fact it's vertiginous.

Picardie. Charming French restaurant in Pétionville. Among its specialties are tiny Haitian *escargots* and flaming lobster. Fine wines in the best French tradition.

Aux Cosaques. Why this misleading name was selected for the best Port-au-Prince restaurant specializing in genuine Haitian food is beyond comprehension. Cossack or Turkoman, it is *the* place for local gastronomy: *tassot de dinde, diri et djondjon* and other creole concoctions mentioned above. The *langouste flambée*, lobster going up in a blaze of cognac is a thing of beauty and a joy for dinner. The murals on the walls were done by Haitian "cossacks".

Nobbe et Bondel. *Sauerbraten, Wiener Schnitzel*, Hungarian Goulash and other *gemütlich* dishes in an indifferent setting across from the International Casino in the Exposition Grounds.

Buteau's Rond Point. More flaming lobster, served up with a flourish on a pleasant terrace. Order the *coq au vin* with a not-too-heavy Bordeaux, close your eyes, and you're on the Rond Point des Champs Elysées.

La Belle Créole. A soda fountain in the Belle Créole department store, featuring sandwiches, malted milk etc. At lunch time it's as busy as Times Square.

SUNSET LODGE. Haitian-American cuisine at its best. Coffee served on the garden terrace.

AU RESERVOIR. Restaurant at Bourdon. Every Monday evening there is a Rotary dinner, and Mr. and Mrs. Hollant are the hosts.

NIGHT LIFE

There's plenty to do after dark in Haiti, and most of it is done to the beat of those African drums. Almost all floorshows feature folklore dances, and there are special shows and dances every single night at different hotels and night clubs. Gambling is the chief amusement at the government-sponsored International Casino, but many non gamblers go there to gambol. There's dinner dancing nightly. The music starts at 9 p.m., the floor show at 12:15 in the morning.

Saturday night is the night for Voodoo. You can arrange to see a ceremony through your hotel or travel agent. Maybe it won't have all the "possessions" and animal sacrifices, but it will give you a good idea of Voodoo all the same. Some adventurous souls prefer to play it by ear, wandering about Port-au-Prince and environs, listening for the throb of Voodoo drums, then following that magnetic sound to its source, which is often a neighborhood *hounfour* in a shack half open to the night air. Some guide books advise "slipping in unobtrusively", but, unless you're black, you'll be about as unobtrusive as Paul Robeson at a D.A.R. tea. It's best to ask permission, which will probably be granted as long as your demeanor is appropriately modest and respectful. Remember Voodoo is a religion. Don't try to take pictures of the ceremony; that will surely be resented and with a violence that may leave your Leica in small fragments. Once the natives get caught up in the ceremony, they will pay no further attention to you. Try free lancing if you like, but your chances of success are indifferent.

Similar to voodoo in dance pattern, though without the religious significance, is *bamboche,* a sort of peasant hoedown in which the natives really jump to the music of drums and bamboo pipes. Saturday night is usually the night for bamboche too, but these neighborhood parties are not regularly scheduled. This Haitian version of the square dance usually takes place in an open air community dance hall covered by a thatched roof. Why these places remain standing is one of the mysteries of the world. If they're bamboche-proof, they must be earthquake and hurricane-proof as well. You've never seen such rhythmic stomping, such hip swinging, such shoulder turning, such sheer animal vibration. It must have been this sort of thing that tumbled the walls of Jericho. Try to see *bamboche*. Any good local tourist outfit, including your own agent's correspondent, will know when and where one of these shindigs is scheduled. Few things are more typical of Haiti.

Plays are given periodically (in French) by the *Comédie de Paris Troupe,* and there are regular native dancing and drumming exhibitions on Thursday and Sunday nights at 9 : 30 by the *Troupe Folklorique d'Haïti* in the open-air Théâtre de Verdure. These cannot be too highly recommended. The dances, stemming from Voodoo and African folklore, are unforgettable. Ti-Roro, is quite probably the best you'll ever hear. The very popular Bacoulou Dance Troupe, is another outstanding group that should not be missed.

The big Haitian hotels have adopted a sensible policy of alternating their floor show evenings so that there is something on at least every night in the week at one of the major hotels.

Castelhaiti has its show on Sunday, for example; *El Rancho* and *Oloffson* schedule floorshows on Monday night; *Ibo Lele,* Tuesday; *Montana,* and *Bacoulou,* Wednesday; *El Rancho,* and *Villa Creole,* Thursday; *Choucoune, Ibo Lele,* Friday.

Saturday, of course, is the big night everywhere, and if you're not going to see Voodoo, we suggest you head for *Cabane Choucoune* for dining and dancing to two superb orchestras with the local elite and some of the prettiest creole girls you ever laid eyes on. The setting (see Hotels above) is unforgettable. Dancing starts at

9:30. Floor show is at midnight.

International Casino on the bay is a modern air-conditioned night club with nightly folklore and continental floor shows and enchanting open air dancing.

What about little unpretentious places, far from the flesh pots of tourism? You'll find a few little bars and bistros in Carrefour, the Montparnasse of Port-au-Prince.

On your way out Avenue Roosevelt toward Carrefour you'll see a lot of houses strung with colored lights. They keep those colored lights going till dawn. You see, Aunt Matilda, a girl has to make a living somehow.

SHOPPING

Old shoppers never die; they just go to Haiti. With the Virgin Islands and Curaçao, the Black Republic is one of the big three of Caribbean shopping. Port-au-Prince is a free port, so you'll find the expected array of duty-free imported bargains. In addition there are Haitian handicrafts, perhaps the most original and striking in the West Indies. In this department, you will find paintings of the vigorous Haitian primitive school; beautiful mahogany sculpture in *objets d'art* and more utilitarian things like salad bowls; the celebrated copper jewelry of voodoo-inspired Winifred Chenet; Haitian blouses and embroidered shirts; beautiful hand-loomed and hand-spun cottons; hand-woven and hand-dyed rugs; René Armand's striking textiles; and voodoo drums, so handsomely-decorated that you may want to own one even if you can't beat out shave-and-a-haircut-bay rum. There are, of course, many many items in sisal and straw.

Imported goods in order of best buys are watches, china, Irish linens, gloves, sweaters, French perfumes and liqueurs. The last are special bargains thanks to preferential trade agreements between Haiti and her *ex-mère* across the sea. Whisky is no great bargain here, but cognac and the like are. You may be tempted to take back your entire liquor allowance in that mellow, aged-like-cognac Barbancourt rum.

Shopping centers are conveniently located in the Exposition Grounds and around the dock, but you'll find shops scattered all around the city from the sea wall to the residential section and up to the surrounding mountain spots. There are also some nice shops in Pétionville if you're staying up there.

CENTRE D'ART is one of the galleries where Haitian paintings and artifacts may be sampled. This original fountainhead of native art, located on the Rue de la Révolution, still sells about a thousand paintings annually at prices that range from $1 to $1,000. You can meet artists there and get to know them and their work.

FOYER DES ARTS PLASTIQUES, on the Exposition Grounds, is headquarters of a dissident group. It also has a wide selection of excellent work for sale.

LA BROCHETTE, operated by outstanding Haitian painter Luckner Lazare, displays some of the best painters of the Haitian school, many Paris or New York trained.

RED CARPET, facing El Rancho hotel, has a wide selection of mahogony, sisal goods, also original sculptures.

CENTRE DE CÉRAMIQUE, on Rue Bonne Foi, is also worth trying.

LA BELLE CRÉOLE in the center of the shopping district on Rue Bonne Foi, is a department store with exclusives on such items as Wedgwood, Spode, Royal Worcester, Rosenthal and Royal Copenhagen china; Georg Jensen silver; Kislav gloves; Lalique and Baccarat crystal, and the big names in cashmere sweaters. Their price for a Patek Philippe watch is $305 as opposed to $525 in New York; Omega Lady-matic in 18K gold is $113 here instead of $245 in the States; Ulysse Nardin watches and chronometers are also good buys. Kislav gloves, $4.90 as compared with $9.50. Their branch shop up at *Le Perchoir* carries similar merchandise. A special service here allows you to pay for liquor shipped to your home address duty free.

FISHER'S ART AND CURIO SHOP has great bargains in French perfumes and liquors; Danish silver; porcelain, crystal, Swiss watches, English woolens, Liberty prints, Haitian hand-embroidered dresses, and hand-loomed cotton fabrics and rugs. Their Haitian book and record section, is a delightful place to browse. A branch of Fisher's shop located on *Bonne Foi* Street, has a wonderful show room full of mahogany works made in his own factory and sold at factory prices for shipments to all four corners of the world. Liquor can be shipped custom free to you.

CARLOS, on Avenue Pie XII, is an ultra-modern shop where you will find Swiss watches, imported gift items from Germany, France and Denmark, and French perfumes and liqueurs in addition to a complete line of Haitian handicrafts and Haitian rum.

FOUAD A. MOURRA, in the Grand' Rue, is an ultra-modern shop where you will find Swiss watches. Exclusive agent of Zodiac.

LITTLE EUROPE, corner of Rue Bonne Foi, has fine Swiss watches shown to you by sari-clad Mme. Dadlani, owner.

THE GIFT FAIR, is now on the Exposition Grounds behind the Post Office. They have ready-to-wear clothes and will whip you up a custom-made dress with impressive speed. Hand-embroidered blouses and skirts in this shop are beautiful.

RUSSO FRÈRES is good for imported gift items and local Haitian wares.

LA PERLE DES ANTILLES has a similar range of attractive articles.

PAUL ANSON, in the Grand' Rue, is a good place for recorded Haitian music. (You're allowed to take ten disks back home duty free.) Ask for drum records of the famed Ti-Roro, a souvenir that will always bring Haiti back to you with its compelling Voodoo rhythm.

SILA on the Rue du Quai, is outstanding for sisal.

RENÉ ARMAND is best known for his hand-woven carpets.

MADAME PAQUIN'S SOUVENIR SHOP is still going strong after two decades of operation at the same address on the Rue du Quai. You may come here for Haitian embroidered skirts, Haitian mahogany and sisal mats, noted for quality and for Mme. Paquin's discriminating taste.

There's been a renaissance in Haitian couture with clothing designed by "those little dressmakers trained in Paris". Here you'll have to look closely and check fittings carefully.

Current purveyors of these styles include *Jacqueline's*, in the Place d'Italie; *Mme. Alexandre Celestin*, 124 Avenue John Brown; *Ouvoir National* in the Exposition Grounds; and *Carlos.*

If you want to visit and buy directly from handicraft factories, here are four that will be glad to let you stop and look even if you don't purchase: *Caribcraft Mahogany Mfg. Co.*, 63 Rue Martinière, Bois Verna; *Meinberg,* Grand'Rue; *Fritz Mevs Mahogany Factory*, Avenue José Marti, and the *Cardozo Factory*, Rue du Quai.

Finally, you'll go to the picturesque, twin-turreted Iron Market, at its colorful best on Saturdays. Loads of fun, and there are some good souvenir buys, mostly in the straw and sisal department. Most popular are the baskets. Just for fun, get a *tête gridape*, amusing conversation piece and souvenir of your visit. But don't do any serious buying here; the specialties are refurbished rejects and other items that aren't going to last very long.

SPECIAL EVENTS. *Carnival,* replete with the usual parades, floats, kings, queens, disguises and prizes is a touch madder here than anywhere else, thanks to those African overtones. It occupies the three days before Ash Wednesday. *RaRa* is another carnival, held from Good Friday to Easter in Leogane, 22 miles from Port-au-Prince. Features African dancing and such Afro-additions to the Christian story as the burning of Judas Iscariot.

HAITI

SPORTS AND OTHER AMUSEMENTS. Haiti is not famous for its beaches, though they are being developed and made more accessible as in the case of Kyona Beach. Best bet for swimming, snorkeling, spear fishing, sailing and "boomba" racing in native dugout canoes is at Kyona and Port-au-Prince. Most swimming is done at hotel and beach club pools.

Fishing boats and equipment for *spear fishing* are available for hire at Port-au-Prince pier.

Water skiing is becoming a popular Haiti pastime.

Hunting is a notable all-year-round Haitian diversion but the best season is from October to April, especially for duck shooting. It is no exaggeration to say that in the various lakes and Etangs of Haiti, there are at least 63 different varieties of duck during the hunting season. The most important lakes for this are located in central Haiti, in the south and in the west. All these points can be reached by car from Port-au-Prince. Alligator can also be hunted in the lakes and the area around abounds in wild pigeon and guinea fowl. The season for pigeon, guinea fowl and quail is August to January. Permission to bring gun and ammunition into Haiti is required: it can by obtained by writing to the Chief of Army, Grand Quartier General, Port-au-Prince, Haiti. More esoteric hunting is for wild boars and goats on nearby islands of Tortuga, Conave and Il-à-Vache, for crocodiles in rivers and swamps. All local travel bureaus can arrange hunting trips.

There's a 9-hole *golf* course at the Pétionville Club.

Tennis may be played at Pétionville Club, Cercle Belle Vue Club, Tennis Club of Turgeau.

Glass-bottom boat trips to Sand Cay leave the International Casino pier daily at 9:30 a.m. You'll see a wonderful panorama of submarine life over this reef, one of the most spectacular in the Caribbean. You transfer to an inflated tube, wear a mask and are taken over the marine gardens where the fish will eat out of your hand. Take camera and bathing suit. The cruise lasts three hours, returning to pier at 12:30 p.m. Cost: $5.

Cockfighting is the national passion of Haiti: what baseball is to America, bullfighting to Spain. There are fights every Saturday and Sunday in the circular *Gaguere,* the open-walled cockfight stadium on the Exposition Grounds in Port-au-Prince. There are also many informal fights all over the island, but the Gaguere is the easiest place to see this "spectator sport". Here you'll see the Haitian in his habitat as he lives. This sport is not for the tourist but for the Haitian himself, and he knows the pedigrees, past performances and proclivities of these birds the way a bookie knows horses. The owners of these rigorously-trained cocks carry them under their arms, arrange fights with other owners right there in the cockpit. If a deal seems promising, they place the two cocks on the ground, each one held by a cord around its ankle. If the cocks attack each other, the owners notify the referee. The arena is cleared, the betting begins. Officials examine the fighting cocks and smell them to make sure no artificial stimulants have been given. The owners whip out pen-knives and give a last minute honing to the birds' talons. (Artificial spurs are not used.) When the whistle blows, the birds leap into the air and so does the crowd. It's mayhem, a fight to the death, with the frenzied spectators providing a greater show than the spectacle.

HAITI

EXPLORING HAITI

Port-au-Prince, with a population of 200,000, is the capital of Haiti, full of color, full of incongruities, full of squalor. Among the city's landmarks is the National Palace, the gleaming white residence of the President of the Black Republic. You may visit the Hall of Busts, marble sculptures of all of Haiti's heads of state. The Place des Héros de L'Indépendance, more popularly known as the Champs de Mars, spreads out before the palace. This handsomely-landscaped park contains monumental statues of Jean Jacques Dessalines, father of his country, Henri Christophe and Alexandre Pétion. Adjoining the Champs de Mars is the Place Toussaint l'Ouverture in whose center stands a statue of the hero, executed by Haitian sculptor Normil Ulysse Charles. Government buildings surround the Champs de Mars; the Dessalines Barracks, the General Hospital, Headquarters of the Haiti National Guard, a new U.S. Embassy building located on the Exposition Ground, a number of hotels and restaurants. The National museum now occupies the former residential palace of ex-President Magloire in Turgeau. There you will find interesting exhibits of Haitian history including one most impressive relic: the anchor of Columbus' flagship, the *Santa Maria*, which broke up on a reef in Haiti and furnished salvage for the construction of the island's first white settlement. On one side of the National Palace in Pétion Square, Dessalines and Pétion lie in a dignified mausoleum, closer together in eternal death than they ever were in life. On another side, the twin-towered, pink and white Catholic Cathedral rises in unreal ethereal grandeur against the tropic sky, its Romanesque cupolas recalling those of Sacré Coeur in Paris, though there is no central dome. The rosace, highly regarded, will not overwhelm you if you've seen the cathedrals of Europe. Finished in 1915, this is the official religious center of Haiti, just as the Champ de Mars is the official center of Port-au-Prince. Less grand, but architecturally more appealing, is the Old Church, built in 1720 and recently restored. One of the few genuine relics of French colonial days, it lies just northwest of the cathedral.

Of more general tourist interest is the Episcopal Cathedral of the Holy Trinity (Sainte Trinité) a couple of blocks north of the Champs de Mars. The apse of this church with its celebrated murals constitutes the most important single monument of that Haitian primitive art renaissance which took the art world by storm in 1947. The depiction of Biblical events in the

346

A corner of Puerto Rico untouched by "Bootstrap"

brilliant colors of contemporary Haiti never fails to touch the visitor with its naive, direct charm. These murals are your best introduction to Haitian painting. If you like it, you must visit the Centre d'Art where it all first came to public attention and where you can see not only a dazzling collection of paintings, but the students and teachers of this fecund movement at work. Now, with your appetite thoroughly whetted, go on to the Foyer des Arts Plastiques and to the other galleries mentioned above under Shopping.

Speaking of which, a visit to the old Iron Market is practically obligatory. You can't miss it. Its two iron warehouses linked by a gate with two vaguely Moroccan looking minarets, is one of the landmarks of Port-au-Prince. There are hundreds of stalls clustered about; it's a sort of cross between the Caledonia Market, the Paris Marché aux Puces, and an Oriental bazaar. Bargaining and haggling are the order of the day in this miniature city of barter, teeming with humanity and local color, to say nothing of local smells. You'll be fascinated by the *marchandise* and especially by the *marchandes*.

One of the many sharp contrasts so characteristic of Port-au-Prince is provided about a hundred yards west of this native bazaar by the International Exposition Grounds, centuries removed in atmosphere and architecture from the Iron Market. The Exposition Grounds are on the waterfront, bordered by Truman Boulevard, a wide thoroughfare built in the best spirit of Western city planning. The buildings of Haiti's bicentennial International Exposition, modern in design but a bit seedy after ten years of desultory upkeep, are now used as shops, government buildings, theatres. This is now the tourist center of Port-au-Prince, especially since the opening of the International Casino and the Beau Rivage Hotel, two handsome modern additions to the local scene. The charming illuminated fountain provides a focal point for the Exhibition Grounds, and there are a number of pleasant sidewalk cafes and restaurants in the immediate vicinity. (See above: Restaurants). Also important in this area: The open-air Théâtre de Verdure; the Museum of Fine Arts, the Museum of the Haitian People, and, cheek by jowl with these in typical Port-au-Prince contrast, the circular Gaguere cockpit. At night, with the fountain illuminated and people strolling through the landscaped plaza of the Exposition Grounds, the place still has the atmosphere of a World's Fair.

Up to the Flowering Alps

The attractions of Port-au-Prince are debatable, some tour-

Bliss in the sun of the Virgin Islands

ists going so far as to say that they like the capital more the farther they are away from it. But there is unanimous agreement on the charms of *Pétionville*, the mountain village resort 2,000 feet above the capital; on those of *Kenscoff*, 4,000 feet higher, and of those of *Furcy*, still higher at an altitude of 7,000 feet. A motor trip into these Haitian "Alps" is most rewarding. The road winds through forests and trees supporting vines of crimson blossoms, past modern villas, vintage Victorian mansions, humble thatched *cailles* or peasant huts, each form emphasized by contrast with the other. Always and always one passes the figures of the *marchandes*, the seemingly endless line of strong, graceful women making their way to market with their headbaskets full of the fruits and vegetables of their gardens. Pétionville, with its luxury view hotels and famous Cabane Choucoune night club, is the home and the playground of Haiti's well-to-do creole elite.

The road continues through fields of flaming poinsettias, that Christmas flower we are accustomed to seeing singly in pots, to Kenscoff. The native market at Kenscoff is a sight you'll never forget; the farmers and the *marchandes* display their colorful wares on the mountain slopes; barter and good-natured haggling are the order of the day. Take your camera for this and plenty of color film for another sight too. This is the *Châtelet des Fleurs* with its acres and acres of sweet peas and other flowers grown for air shipment to the U.S. market. In its spectacular green mountain setting, this floral display surpasses anything we've seen on the French Riviera.

The road, narrow, twisting and full of switchbacks beyond Kenscoff, ends a thousand feet farther up at *Furcy*. The view from here, beyond description and beyond praise, is worth the climb. That majestic peak you see from here is La Selle (the Saddle), Haiti's highest, soaring to nearly 9,000 feet, and robed in a mantle of dark green pines. This unique pine forest, in whose density escaping slaves once took refuge, can be reached by a long trek from Port-au-Prince. The road is terrible, but the exotic spell of the Virgin forest and the crocodile-filled waters of Etang Saumâtre on the border of the Dominican Republic more than compensate hunters and explorers for their spine-shattering ordeal.

On the southern extremity of Haiti's lower jaw, Jacmel is a delightful, unspoiled little hill town overlooking the bay of the same name. Ten miles east is Carrefour Raymond with the most beautiful white sand strand in Haiti, the obvious answer to that line of rocks and shale so euphemistically described as a "beach" in Port-au-Prince.

The old port of Saint-Marc; the romantic buccaneer island of Gonâve, home of primitive fishermen and the giant iguana; Jérémie with another unspoiled beach; Gonaives, where Dessalines proclaimed his country free: these are a few of the places off the beaten track and difficult of access that will appeal to those who want something different.

Climax of Haitian Tourism

Easier to reach, though it still takes a little doing, is the grand climax of Haitian tourism, *Cap-Haïtien* with its twin wonders of Sans Souci and La Citadelle La Ferrière. Cap-Haïtien, called Le Cap by local residents, is Haiti's most historic and most beautiful town. Once known as the Paris of Saint Domingue, it was the richest colonial capital in the world, supporting its local gentry in such style as to furnish a new simile for the salons of Europe: "rich as a creole."

The city itself, with its multi-colored houses trimmed with Victorian gingerbread, exhales an aura of history, palpable as a scent. This, in spite of the fact that only a few of Le Cap's colonial monuments have survived the fires of revolution, civil war and earthquake. The Centennial Cathedral still stands, the Justinien Hospital, sections of the historic bulwarks, and some lovely old French fountains. In the suburb of Carenage you can visit the ruins of the palace where Napoleon's sister, Pauline Bonaparte held court. This property, acquired by the famous dancer Katherine Dunham, has been given by her to Haitian Government, and has been restored as a botanical and historical show place.

In 1951 Cap-Haïtien underwent an $8,000,000 renovation program. Such improvements as the new waterfront boulevard, paved streets, a new water system, underground sewers and an enlarged airport were effected without sacrificing any part of the old city's French-Creole charm. Accessible by a 40 minute air trip or a 4½ hour drive over the reconstructed highway from Port-au-Prince, Cap-Haïtien is developing beach and hotel facilities.

It is, of course, already a Mecca for the brief visitor, thanks to the two major attractions of the area, Sans Souci and the great Citadelle of Henri Christophe. To reach these you drive 20 miles south to the village of Milot, which the Black Emperor wished to develop as a kind of New World Versailles, though his royal palace was to be an imitation of King Frederick's

Sans Souci at Potsdam. No camera has yet been able to capture the grandiose effect of "the most regal structure ever raised in the New World", rising in ruined splendor against the deep green of tropical mountains. The superb double staircase like a dramatic stage against the facade of time-worn brick, sets the proportion of this incongruous palace. You will walk through the reception rooms, the ballrooms, the banquet halls, roofless now and bare, romantically exposed to the tropic sky. You will see the remains of the conduits which brought the waters of a mountain stream under the main floor to cool the palace. You will see the private quarters of the royal family, the waiting rooms where courtiers with such absurd names as the Duke of Marmelade danced attendance on this resplendent black despot. Try to imagine it as it was, panelled with mahogany, hung with imported Gobelins tapestries, ablaze with crystal chandeliers. Reflected in the golden mirrors, a black queen moved, a black Prince Royal, two dusky princesses and an ebony emperor, dressed to their gleaming teeth in satin and brocade, bizarre carbon copies of the royal pomp of Europe.

Eighth Wonder of the World

If this was vanity, wait until you see the Citadelle. You approach this "eighth wonder of the world" with the indispensable assistance of horse or mule and guide, all of which are for rent at Milot. The ascent takes about two hours up a steep trail through mahogany and palm groves, banana and pomegranate trees, past native *cailles,* redolent of good strong Haitian coffee. If you tire of the journey, solace yourself with the thought that you are not on foot and dragging the tons of masonry, cannon and iron that were brought up this tortuous trail to build the Citadelle. Two hundred thousand former slaves were conscripted by Henri for the work; 20,000 of them lost their lives. They must have wondered at times if emancipation had bettered their lot. The evidence is that they adored this mad King Christophe. And they shared their monarch's haunting anxiety: the citadelle must be finished as an impregnable defense against any future invasion by the hated French. In 1817, after 13 years, the last stone was fitted into place.

On the final lap of the trail you are 3,000 feet high in the shadow of the Citadelle, soaring upward from its rocky base like the prow of a great stone ship. The walls, 140 feet high, are 12 feet thick at the base, six at the parapet. More than a masterpiece of architectural engineering, they are a symbol of unconquerable human will.

HAITI

You enter the precincts of the Citadelle through an iron-studded gate, and find yourself, as though back in the middle ages, in a world of battlements and terraced stonework. The lower reaches of the fortress are a labyrinth of storehouses, cisterns, dungeons, built on a scale to accommodate a garrison of 15,000 men. Christophe actually stocked the place with enough provisions to enable such a garrison to withstand a year's siege. A stone staircase will lead you to the gallery of the cannon, a vast esplanade, 30 feet wide and 150 feet long, bristling with cannons, 365 of them cast in England, France, and Spain, each one dragged up here by Henri's men. There are four such cannon galleries, each with round ports for firing on the invader that never came.

The guide will show you the suite of 40 rooms which King Christophe modestly assigned himself, and the royal billiard room with an open fireplace worthy of a feudal lord. Climax of the Citadelle is the upper court, opened to the sun and the trade winds, providing an unsurpassed panoramic view of mountains, valleys and the sea. It was on these rarified heights that Christophe is said to have given the order to a troop of soldiers to march off the parapet into space in a demonstration of their loyalty for the benefit of an English visitor. Whether this is apocryphal or not, it must have been similar excesses of cruelty and vanity which provoked the revolt of Christophe's own palace guard in 1820.

After that, the final mad touch of vanity, a silver bullet in the brain, and Henry's body was brought here to the upper court and buried in quick lime to save it from the fury of the mob. So the Citadelle became King Henry's tomb. His epitaph here on the ramparts, ends with the motto he invented for his made-up coat of arms: "I shall rise from my ashes." Beyond the ramparts, serenely unconcerned by such pretensions, the green mountains of Haiti plunge down to the sea and the blue Atlantic stretches northward farther than the human eye can reach.

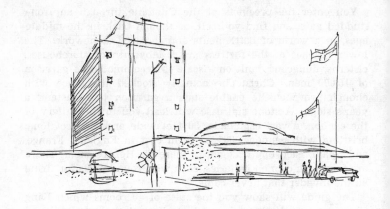

DOMINICAN REPUBLIC

The Land Columbus Loved

Second largest of the Greater Antilles (after Cuba), the Dominican Republic occupies the eastern two-thirds of the island which Columbus called La Española or Hispaniola. He discovered it on December 5, 1492 and was ecstatic over the beauty of its majestic mountains, rising 10,000 feet and more (the highest in the Antilles) from the cobalt Caribbean.

In 1496 Columbus's brother Bartolomé, governor of the new colony, founded the city of Santo Domingo. Capital of the country, it is the oldest city of the New World—and the newest, having risen from the rubble of a hurricane in 1930 to become one of the handsomest modern capitals of the West Indies.

Santo Domingo (or the Dominican Republic) has had two periods of flourishing growth: the first half of the 16th century and the present. In 1509 Columbus's son, Diego Colón, came to Santo Domingo as viceroy, bringing with him as his wife and first lady of the colony, Doña Maria de Toledo y Rojas, high-born niece of Ferdinand of Aragon, King of Spain. Santo Domingo became the hub of Spanish commerce and culture in America. A Gothic-Renaissance cathedral was built and a Renaissance palace worthy of the viceregal couple. In the great reception rooms and galleries of this splendid alcazar, the conquistadores of Spain's golden age were entertained: Diego Velásquez de León, who settled Cuba; Hernando Cortés, conqueror of Mexico; Ponce de Léon on his way to colonize Puerto Rico and discover Florida; Alonzo de Ojeda, explorer of the Spanish Main; Vasco Nuñez de Balboa, discoverer of the Pacific, and Francisco Pizarro, who stopped en route to Panama and the conquest of Peru.

Ironically, the flourishing colony, center of New World civilization, fell victim to the success of these distinguished guests. For richer lands were conquered, and Santo Domingo declined in importance as the gold of the Aztecs and the Incas dazzled the eyes of the world. In 1586, England having already challenged Spain's monopoly on the New World, Sir Francis Drake attacked and plundered Santo Domingo, putting it to the torch while he waited for a ransom the town was too poor to pay. Blackened by fire, the Renaissance monuments crumbled. The proudest Spanish city of America became a ghost of its former glory.

This was just the beginning of nearly four centuries of misfortune. French buccaneers, operating from Tortuga, seized the western third of Hispaniola, and this land grab was legalized by the Treaty of Ryswick in 1697. The French soon extended their sway over the whole island, but concentrated on the fertile western third which became their prize colony of Saint Domingue, growing rich beyond belief on sugar and slaves until its whole brilliant structure toppled in the fires of the French Revolution and the slave revolt that established the Black Republic of Haiti.

In 1809 the Dominicans revolted with British help, and Spanish rule was reestablished until 1821 when the Dominicans revolted again and proclaimed themselves independent from *España Boba*, Silly Spain as they called the mother country. In 1822 the Haitians invaded the new country and occupied it for 22 years, leaving its inhabitants a shade or two darker than those in other Latin American countries. An underground movement developed, led by a secret society called La Trinitaria (because each resistance cell was composed of three men). In 1844 another revolution resulted in independence and the establishment of the Dominican Republic.

56 Revolutions

In the following century the Dominican Republic became a kind of comic opera prototype of Caribbean instability. From

1844 to 1930 there were 43 presidents and 56 revolutions! In 1904 the Dominican Republic proposed that the United States take the country over as a protectorate. The U.S. Congress vetoed the idea. But by 1916 the Dominican situation was so chaotic that Uncle Sam stepped in to restore order, protect American interests, and bolster the sagging economy of the Dominican Republic with multi-million dollar loans.

The U.S. Marines got out in 1924, leaving the local population a shade or two lighter. Six years later on May 16, 1930 Generalissimo Rafael Leonidas Trujillo Molina was elected president. As an unexpected inauguration gift, his capital city was struck by one of the worst hurricanes in Caribbean history and literally levelled to the ground. Trujillo at once began its reconstruction along with a vast program of economic and educational reform, including a drive on illiteracy. Within a decade the handsomest new capital of the Caribbean had risen like a phoenix from the rubble. The Dominican National Congress renamed it Ciudad Trujillo in honor of its renovator, whose despotic figure became the center of a personality cult. The adulation reached a peak when Dr. Hector A. Cabral Ortega, editor of *Seguridad Social,* rewrote the Twenty-third Psalm to read, "Trujillo es mi pastor; nada me faltará. Trujillo is my shepherd; I shall not want."

This may have been overdoing it a little, and it did not represent a unanimous sentiment. But three decades of the Trujillo era produced a good measure of material renaissance particularly for the supporters of his regime, even if at the expense of suppression of individual liberty.

The violent death of "El Benefactor" together with the joint actions of the American States precipitated a change over into a more liberal and democratic form of transient government. Things are gradually settling down and the democratic elements are gaining in strength after some three decades of political hibernation. Still suffering from the uncertainties of the immediate post-Trujillo era, the tourist industry in the Dominican Republic is gradually returning to normal.

The tourist facilities in the attractive modern capital of Santo Domingo are not yet running at full capacity—the country's second largest hotel, the Jaragua is still closed as we go to press—but it looks as if the tourist business will soon be in full swing again.

DOMINICAN REPUBLIC

PRACTICAL INFORMATION FOR THE DOMINICAN REPUBLIC

 HOW TO GET THERE. Santo Domingo is one of the air hubs of the Caribbean. You can fly direct from New York by Pan American World Airways, "Varig" Brazilian Airlines, Eastern Airlines (via Puerto Rico), and charter flights of Resort Airlines. The republic's own airline, Compañía Dominicana de Aviación will fly you in from Miami, and so will Pan Am and Resort Airlines. Delta Airlines are among the biggest carriers in the Dominican Republic tourist service; they have regularly-scheduled flights to Santo Domingo from New Orleans, Chicago, Houston and Havana. Pan American links the Dominican Republic with San Juan, Puerto Rico; Port-au-Prince, Haiti; Jamaica, Curaçao and Venezuela. Compañía Dominicana links Puerto Rico and Haiti with home base.

You can reach the Dominican Republic by sea from New York on ships of the Dominican Republic Steamship Company, Bull Lines and Royal Netherlands Steamship Company. Eastern Shipping Company will bring you in from Miami while Alcoa maintains regular passenger and freight service between Santo Domingo and New Orleans.

 PASSPORTS, VISAS. Tourist cards (most recent cost $2.24) are issued by your carrier to citizens of the United States, United Kingdom and Canada. These are valid for visits of from 15 to 60 days and eliminate all passport and visa requirements. You will be required to have a return trip ticket and to fill out an information form upon arrival. Vaccination certificate is required by all travelers except those in transit who do not leave the airport. When you arrive, you will be photographed and X-rayed; they're looking for concealed weapons and other contraband from Cuba.

CURRENCY. The Dominican peso, divided into 100 centavos, is at par with the American dollar. There are no restrictions on import and export of currency.

 HOW TO GET ABOUT. Public transportation in Santo Domingo is excellent and cheap. Double decker buses are only a dime a ride. Taxi rates are fixed at 50 cents a ride within city limits, $3 an hour for the whole cab. There are still a few horse-drawn carriages for hire at $2 an hour; these provide a delightful way to explore the city. Hertz Drive-Yourself cars are available. The taxis in front of the major hotels usually have well-indoctrinated English-speaking guides, and they are the ones who can arrange to get the required police permission for you to visit places outside the capital.

HOTELS

Santo Domingo is one of the best-equipped of Caribbean capitals in the luxury hotel field. If the general tourist policy of the country were on a par with the accommodations and services provided by its hotels, there would be no complaint from anybody, and the Dominican Republic would resume its rightful place as a Caribbean tourist mecca.

355

DOMINICAN REPUBLIC

EL EMBAJADOR. Intercontinental's handsome, ultra-modern 310 room hostelry is the Ritz of the Caribbean. Entirely air-conditioned, it offers its guests every facility for a complete vacation. Luxuriously-appointed rooms (in French provincial style), smart Embassy Night Club, tremendous swimming pool, 18-hole golf course, gambling casino, riding horses, even a polo field is adjacent. The food is top notch too. But all this, splendid as it is, would not make a good hotel without that essential ingredient, top flight management. This was the case until Curt Peyer left for Jamaica. The new manager will no doubt continue in the Peyer tradition. Rates (winter season) are $10 to $12 single, $14 to $17 double European Plan. Add $10 per day per person for full American Plan price. Off season rates (April 16 to December 15) are from $10 minimum single to $17 double, European Plan.

JARAGUA. For the time being, the luxurious Jaragua is closed due to the sudden fall off in tourism in the Dominican Republic; there is a good chance that it may re-open when and if tourism picks up once again.

EUROPA. Well situated in downtown Santo Domingo, the Europa is handy for businessmen. There are 32 rooms.

FAUSTO. The 25 room Fausto is located in a quiet residential district. It is a little far from the center of town, but good if you like to sleep in quiet, relatively peaceful surroundings.

HOTEL PAZ. Near the fair grounds, facing the sea, this is the third of Santo Domingo's luxury quartet. Social life revolves around its charming swimming pool patio, and guests enjoy access to the recreational facilities of El Embajador. There are 150 rooms. Rates are from $5 single, from $8 double, European Plan, winter season. Add $10 a day for American Plan.

COMERCIAL. As its name indicates, this is a hotel for businessmen, but comfortable and modern all the same with 75 air-conditioned rooms with bath, bar, cafeteria, barber shop. All rooms have radio and telephone. Year round rates are $5 single, $8 double, European Plan.

GAZCUE. A most pleasant family-type hotel with a private sports club known as *The Golfito Club.* It is very reasonable, popular with Dominicans, and managed with that personal touch by a German woman, Mrs. Maloch, whose cuisine is highly appreciated by her guests. Rates are as low as $4 single, $6 double, European Plan the whole year round. Add $4 a day for three squares and you have a bargain. Mrs. Maloch gives discounts up to 25 per cent for guests who want a monthly rate.

AMERICA. Conveniently located near all the public buildings and historic monuments of Santo Domingo, this hotel on the Ozama River also has convenient rates: $6 single, $10 double, full American Plan.

COLON. Good food, Dominican atmosphere, and bargain rates in the heart of historic Santo Domingo. There are 33 rooms, and the service is fine. $3 a day single, European Plan. Only $7.50 single, $14 double with three meals thrown in, and very copious ones too.

HOTELS OUTSIDE SANTO DOMINGO

NUEVA SUIZA. A Swiss chalet type of hotel at Constanza, 4,000 feet high with average temperature at 75 degrees. The Dominicans themselves are fond of this 66 room resort hotel, especially in summer. The setting is lovely (pine forests, roses and other untropical surprises) and the place is a center for hunting and horseback riding. The

DOMINICAN REPUBLIC

hotel arranges tours to nearby hydro-electric dam, waterfalls, and other wonder of nature and man's handiwork. Rates are $7.50 single, $14 double American Plan.

HOTEL HAMACA. Outstanding hostelry on a lovely lagoon at the celebrated resort of Boca Chica. Hotel has its own beach club which furnishes guests with equipment for water skiing, boating, fishing and other aquatic diversions. The manager, Dr. Brea Messina, will arrange for you to see a cockfight if you want to. Pleasant atmosphere here and very good food. Rates (November to April) are $9 single, $17 double, full American Plan. Off season they are reduced.

SAN CRISTOBAL. Modern hotel with swimming pool, cocktail lounge and other amenities in the town where El Benefactor first saw the light of day. Rates are $4 single, $7 double, European Plan. Full American Plan: $7 single, $14 double.

HOTEL SAN JUAN. At San Juan de la Meguana, a hunter's paradise. Swimming pool and bargain rates: $5 a day per person with meals.

HOTEL MONTANA. A favorite mountain resort with swimming pool, horseback riding, good cuisine. A self-sufficient sort of place, it has TV and movies, also a children's playground. Good family place. Rates are $5 single, $7 double, American Plan.

FOOD AND RESTAURANTS. The food is American-International in the big hotels. There are many restaurants in old Santo Domingo's which have *arroz con pollo a la Valenciana*, *pastelitos* and other gastronomic echoes of old Spain. The food, generally speaking, is not as good as what you will find in Cuba, Puerto Rico or neighboring Haiti. Among Santo Domingo's better restaurants are *Vesuvio* (Italian), *Roxi*, *Lina*, *Agua Luz El Conde*, *Cremita*, *Dragon*, the *Pan American*, and *Mario's* (Chinese and Dominican).

Locally-distilled rum and ditto-brewed beer are not exactly world famous, but they'll wet your whistle, and they are very cheap.

NIGHT LIFE. *The Embassy Club* of the Embajador Hotel is smart for dinner dancing, and there is also a gambling casino. A *Southerland Nightlife Tour*, leaving your hotel at 8:30 will take you to the spectacular theater of Water and Light (Aqua Luz) with its half hour show, a Caribbean version of a modernistic Versailles.

SHOPPING. Outstanding local buys are carved mahogany figurines and bowls, embroidery and straw work. You should visit the *Mercado Modelo*, Santo Domingo's highly antiseptic, ultra-modern, spotless model market with attractive displays of fruits, vegetables, mahogany ware, baskets, hats, sandals, tortoise shell work and other island souvenirs. There's a good craft shop in the El Embajador, and *Timi's Studio Gift Shop*, opposite the old cathedral, is outstanding for original tortoise shell designs. Prices are high, and the chances are you will not be tempted to shop in Santo Domingo, especially if Haiti, St. Thomas, Jamaica, or Curaçao are on your itinerary. There is, however, a free port shop in the permanent fair grounds where you will find a selection of Swiss watches, French perfumes and other imports at low prices.

DOMINICAN REPUBLIC

SPORTS AND OTHER ACTIVITIES. Swimming and all aquatic sports are popular, especially at Boca Chica where you can rent water skis, spear fishing equipment and other gear through the Hamaca Hotel. Deep sea fishing is excellent; you can rent fishing cruisers, accommodating six, for the amount of $60 a day. Tourists can play golf on the excellent course (18 holes) of the El Embajador Hotel, one of the finest in the Caribbean. Popular spectator sports are polo and cockfighting. January through April is the season for the former, and one of the star players is apt to be Porfirio Rubirosa. Best way to see a cockfight is to check with the manager of the Hamaca Hotel at Boca Chica; the feathers fly frequently nearby. Year round horseracing at Perla de las Antilles track features some of the finest horseflesh in the West Indies, and the track itself, like so many other things in Santo Domingo, is the last word in modernity and efficiency. The same thing applies to the Stadium, a favorite spot for exhibition games and workouts by big league American baseball teams which choose the Dominican Republic for winter practice.

EXPLORING THE DOMINICAN REPUBLIC

Despite the fires of Drake and the destruction of the 1930 hurricane, there are enough relics of 16th-century Spain in Santo Domingo to make it one of the most fascinating of Caribbean capitals from the historic point of view. Among the many churches, the greatest is the Cathedral of Santa Maria La Menor with its splendid Renaissance facade and its vaulted Gothic interior. Begun as early as 1523, it took two decades to complete. In the nave, guarded by four baroque columns carved to resemble royal palms, the mortal remains of Christopher Columbus lie in a marble sarcophagus, in the spiritual heart of Hispaniola where the discoverer wanted to be buried. The cathedral is a treasure house of Colonial Spain. Notice its high altar, a masterpiece of carving, faced with the silver of Santo Domingo's mines. A Madonna by Murillo, a silver carillon by Benvenuto Cellini, and a king's ransom in splendid jewels are among the riches that make America's first cathedral the rival of many in Europe.

If the cathedral is the greatest religious sight of Santo Domingo, the most imposing secular monument is The Alcazar of Diego Columbus, built in 1510 and restored in 1957. The restoration, which involved the painstaking reassembling of authentic Columbus relics from the museums of Spain, is a marvel of sensitive reconstruction. Nowhere else in the Caribbean will you have so vivid an impression of the brilliant material civilization which Spain brought to the New World. Sumptuosly furnished with beautiful paintings, statues, tapestries of the epoch, the palace is equipped as it was when the viceroy held court here, even down to the dishes, the salt cellars and the viceregal shaving mug! Whatever else you miss in Santo Domingo, don't miss the Alcazar; it's one of the big experiences of the Caribbean.

While the palace was being built, Diego Columbus lived in The House of the Cord (opposite the Post Office on Calle Isabela Católica). Built in 1502, this is the oldest house still standing in the Western Hemisphere, miraculously spared by both hurricane and Drake. The latter, burning Santo Domingo block by block, finally desisted when he received his ransom money here in this very house. Not far away is another historic memento: the Columbus Ceiba, the stump of the big silk cotton tree to which Columbus is said to have tied his ship when it was moored in the Ozama River.

The National Museum of the Dominican Republic is a splendid place to see a good pre-Columbian collection of the arts and artifacts which were already flourishing here when the explorer arrived. The museum's exhibits, all handsomely displayed, provide an excellent historic perspective on the Dominican Republic. This can be supplemented by a visit to the National Museum of Fine Arts, which features the work of latter day painters and sculptors.

Gleaming New Capital

The new Santo Domingo is in its way as impressive as the old. Its tone is set by Avenida George Washington, a magnificent palm-lined boulevard, punctuated by the white obelisk that reminds every visitor of the Washington Monument in the U.S. capital. Between this handsome street and the Avenida Independencia, the 125-acre tract of the International Peace and Progress Fair of 1956 has now become a permanent civic center, replete with mammoth outdoor theater, casino, and important public buildings. Among the many beautiful parks which grace the capital is Parque Ramfis, designed for children and providing them with wading pool, playground, nursery, story-reading room, and even a nurse and doctor to watch them while mama and papa have a daiquiri or a beer in the adult enclave which has also been provided. Children are also enchanted by the Zoo and its miniature electric train, a gift to the kids from El Benefactor. The adjacent Botanical Gardens provide a top flight tropical garden plus caves with pre-Columbian petroglyphs, a pleasure for those who like exploring without tears.

Other points of interest in this gleaming modern capital are The National Palace, a pink marble edifice of imposing design which ranks with the best public buildings in the West Indies; University City, a most impressive ensemble of modern functional architecture and campus landscaping, and the Columbus Memorial Lighthouse. This immense memorial in the form of a recumbent cross 3/4 of a mile long is an international project, approved by the United Nations, and will eventually house a Columbus museum and the remains of the discoverer, which are to be transferred from the cathedral.

Excursions outside of Santo Domingo are currently somewhat circumscribed by the government's security program. It was still a simple matter on our last visit to take the 19 mile drive east of Santo Domingo, by a superb modern highway, incidentally, to the popular resort of Boca Chica with its lovely mile-long lagoon offering perfect conditions for swimming, snorkeling and other aquatic pleasures. Your driver will procure the necessary police pass to take you on this trip.

Southerland Tours, with offices in the El Embajador Hotels, has two regularly-scheduled half day tours to Boca Chica at 9:30 a.m. and 2:15 p.m. They also have tours departing at the same hours daily for San Cristobal, El Benefactor's birthplace, now a model industrial town. When you drive through the lush countryside en route, passing luxuriant fields and mountains clothed with mahogany groves, crossing the lovely Haina River (and, incidentally, passing the world's largest sugar mill), you'll begin to understand why this was the land that Columbus loved best.

The dances and voodoo drums of Haiti (above) were still in Africa when Diego Columbus ruled Hispaniola from the splendid Alcazar. The palace, restored with its original furniture, is in Ciudad Trujillo.

The pace-setting Caribe Hilton Hotel and its new wing are among the modern landmarks of Puerto Rico's capital, expanding ever eastward from venerable El Morro and Spanish-flavored Old San Juan.

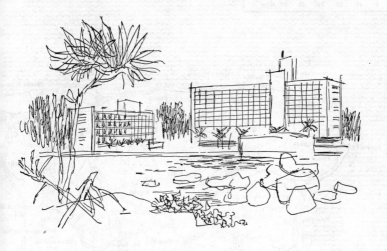

PUERTO RICO

Destination: El Dorado

BY

WILLIAM J. KENNEDY

*(Mr. Kennedy has been writing about the Puerto-Rican scene
since 1956. He is a Time-Life correspondent and managing
editor of the "San Juan Star", an English-language daily.
The sections on Practical Information and Exploring Puerto
Rico were written by William W. Davenport.)*

From the time he steps from the airplane and sloshes around
in the depths of a cool daiquiri thrust at him by the promoters
of local rum, to the time he heads homeward, sunburned,
debilitated and with luggage bulging with souvenirs, the tourist
sees in Puerto Rico the brightest side of a once-poor, now
bright and booming island in the throes of what the government sloganeers call "a cultural and economic renaissance."

The tourist's lot is luxury hotels, fancy restaurants, govern-
ment-supervised gambling casinos (blackjack, craps, roulette),
sun, sand, surf, steel bands, palm trees, balmy breezes and a
communion with a culture dating back to the conquistadors.

The tourist should expect to be bombarded with superlatives
about the island's progress, its graces, its beauty. He will find

361

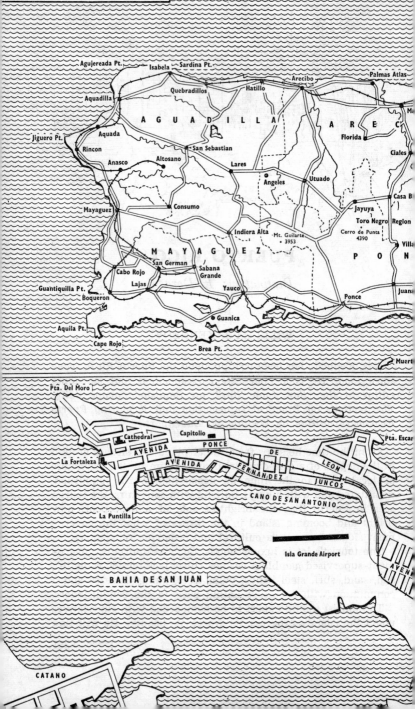

PUERTO RICO

0 10 20 30 40 50 Miles

Agujereada Pt.
Isabela • Sardina Pt.
Arecibo
Palmas Atlas
Quebradillos
Hatillo
Aquadilla
A G U A D I L L A
A R E C
Jiguero Pt.
Aquada
Florida
Rincon
Ciales
Anasco
Altosano
San Sebastian
Lares
Mayaguez
Consumo
Angeles
Utuado
Casa B
Jayuya
Toro Negro Region
Cerro de Punta
4390
Indiera Alta
Mt. Guilarte
• 3953
M A Y A G U E Z
P O N
Villa
Cabo Rojo
San German
Sabana
Grande
Yauco
Ponce
Juana
Guantiquilla Pt.
Lajas
Boqueron
Guanica
Aquila Pt.
Cape Rojo
Brea Pt.
Muert

Pta. Del Moro
Cathedral
Capitolio
Pta. Escar
La Fortaleza
A V E N I D A
P O N C E
D E
L E O N
A V E N I D A
F E R N A N D E Z
J U N C O S
La Puntilla
C A N O   D E   S A N   A N T O N I O
Isla Grande Airport
A V E
B A H I A   D E   S A N   J U A N

CATANO

that even the most rational residents behave like public relations counselors, become self-declared experts on the beanstalk growth of the island, once a newcomer's ear has been wangled. This particularly applies to continentals (i.e. stateside residents; remember that Puerto Ricans are also Americans) who somewhere along the line discovered Puerto Rico for themselves and are as smug in their discovery as Columbus must have been when he first found the island in 1493. These pop-offs are not blind to the island's shortcomings and troubles, the slums and shacktowns which still blot the cityscape. But they see the good, and the progress toward greater good, and that is their story.

The master of this more-than-twice-told tale of progress is Puerto Rico's first elected (and thrice reelected) Governor Luis Muñoz Marín. As the architect of "Operation Bootstrap," the code word for this economic mushroom, he is continually besieged by visiting journalists to retell the modern Puerto Rican story. One of his methods is to begin by describing Puerto Rico as "a group of islands—the main one being Puerto Rico, the others being the offshore islands of Vieques, Culebra, Manhattan, Brooklyn, Staten Island."

The joke is no joke. New York City, with its 720,000 Puerto Rican residents, is a larger Puerto Rican city than San Juan, the island capital, which with all its sprawling suburbs can count only 650,000.

The influence of Puerto Rico on the United States, on Latin America, on many others areas of the world is indeed unusual when the size of the island (population: 2.4 million) is considered. One hundred miles long by 35 miles wide, it is in area 30 per cent smaller than Connecticut. Yet, through a politico-economic formula which has spawned success like eggs from a fertile salmon, this spit of land washed by both the Atlantic and the Caribbean, has become an international showcase of economic and social accomplishment.

Among the visitors who come to stare at the showcase are thousands of technical experts and administrators from underdeveloped countries of Africa, Asia and the Middle East, invited by the U.S. State Department as part of America's technical assistance program. The example of "Bootstrap" in operation never fails to instruct and inspire these visitors. Would that all of Uncle Sam's propaganda efforts were as subtle and successful as this one!

The showcase also attracts industrialists who come in increasing numbers to an economic utopia of no taxes, high profits, relatively cheap and productive labor, and an ideal climate in which to enjoy the fruits thereof.

Success Beyond Capacity

Purely as a tourist area, Puerto Rico is successful beyond its capacities. Tourists have been jamming all available facilities on the island since the Caribe Hilton kicked off the industry in 1949.

The stateside advertising campaign had invented the line: "Suddenly everybody's going to Puerto Rico." After the rush the government wrote an apology to disgruntled vacationers explaining: "Suddenly everybody *did* go to Puerto Rico."

Despite the biggest hotel building boom in the hemisphere, Puerto Rico still needs more hotels. This is complicated by detail but not by want of projects. The Department of Tourism is generally considering, at all times, more than 100 projects of various types—major tourist hotels, commercial hotels, guest houses, restaurants, amusements parks, boating services and boardwalks.

Unaffected by all this unregenerately "square" planning is the newest group of Puerto Rico's tourists, those pseudo-expatriates, who can leave home without really leaving home, who can brush elbows with the artists, writers and free spirits of another culture, another language.

Nightlife is fundamentally Latin American but is rather tame and slick, and seekers after the uninhibited cabaret performances of Havana will be disappointed. The plush clubs are mainly in the hotels, with a few exceptions, and during the season attract such performers as Maurice Chevalier, Nat King Cole, Eartha Kitt, José Greco, Belafonte and so on. Now more than a dozen small late spots with pianos, guitars and combos have sprouted in the last year. There are a few places of lesser repute with a different form of diversion but you have to follow your nose (or ask your hotel porter) to find them. They aren't heralded in the tourist guides.

If, in spite of all the rapid and recent development in Puerto Rico, certain gaps in the island's tourism program are still evident, this can be explained simply by the fact that tourism in Puerto Rico is little more than a decade old. True, tourists have been coming to Puerto Rico for several decades, but they were a small group of loyalists of the type that attends class reunions. It is only in 1949 that the current tourist boom began, and then is was as a by-product of another need. At any rate, the accelerated rhythm of building should soon produce complete and competent tourist facilities.

Some fine hotels had been in existence for years in San Juan, but when industrialization began to catch on in the mid-1940s, the traffic of businessmen picked up. The government often found itself about to clinch a Very Big Deal with a Very Big Wheel, only to learn that all first class hotel facilities were full. Rather than put him in second-rate accomodations, officials often rolled the wheel home and put him up until the deal was clinched. This, obviously, had its limitations.

The government's answer was to build a luxury hotel and lease it to an operator on a two-thirds (for the government) and one-third (for the operator) profit-sharing basis. The word went out to four major hotel chains. Only Conrad Hilton answered. Up went the *Caribe Hilton* at a cost of $7,500,000. Its first season was a banner one and it has been deep in the black ever since. Architecturally (designed by local architects Toro, Ferrer and Torregrosa) it drew international attention and imitation. Financially it proved to Hilton the obvious worth of the lease arrangement and thus prompted the creation of *Hilton International*.

The government has built one other hotel since then, *La Concha* (the seashell), which opened in December, 1958. It cost $8,000,000 and has been leased on the same two-thirds, one-third arrangement, to *Associated Federal Hotels*.

Probably the government's last venture into hotel construction will be the new Hilton in Mayaguez. Hotels are eligible for tax exemption if they conform to regulations, and with tourism growing the way it is there is no longer any need for official impetus. Hotel promotors know a good deal when they see it.

What the government is doing now is watching development carefully, trying to avoid what one official termed "the Chinese wall of Miami Beach, where the ocean isn't even visible." Regulations now demand open space, greenery and plenty of parking area around the new hotels. "The main idea," the official said, "is to keep it exotic. We want the hotels to be built for Puerto Ricans and then they will be liked by all tourists. If we lose our identity, why should the tourists come? They could then get the same thing in Atlantic City."

Land of Two Cultures

Loss of identity is a recurring argument heard in Puerto

Rico since the success of the industrialization program prompted a reverse migration. The government has happily resolved the influx of Americano influence by describing the island as "a land of two cultures." What those two cultures are is a matter of constantly changing opinion, just as the cultures themselves are chameleonic. But basically one is home-grown under centuries of Spanish domination and residual influence, and the other—strongly felt after only a half-century of development—stems from the association, and free interchange through common citizenship, with the United States.

The Spanish culture dates to 1508 when Juan Ponce de León (whose remains are entombed in the San Juan Cathedral) established the first settlement. For three centuries thereafter an international rivalry flared for possession of the island. Sir Francis Drake tried for it in 1595, but was whomped. Peace reigned in the 19th century. Luis Muñoz Rivera, the George Washington of Puerto Rico, won from Spain in 1897 the Charter of Autonomy which gave the island dominion status. But the autonomy was short lived. The Spanish-American War erupted and U.S. forces landed on the south coast July 25, 1898. Under the Treaty of Paris, proclaimed April 11, 1899, Puerto Rico passed from Spanish to U.S. sovereignty.

Military government prevailed until the Foraker Act of 1900 was passed, reestablishing civil government, but a colonial one under the thumb of Washington. The islanders were Puerto Rican citizens, ruled by a foreign power, an abuse perpetuated until 1917 when the U.S. Congress made them American citizens and yielded up a smidgen more of autonomy. Very little changed, except for the poor classes. For them, things got worse.

In 1926 under the sugar barons, cane cutters were getting ten cents an hour and eagerly selling their vote for $2 to elect company lawyers to the island legislature. Needlewomen, for hemming a dozen handkerchiefs, earned three cents.

Governor Muñoz, then a hotblood agitating for independence, described his island in 1929 as "a land of beggars and millionaires, of flattering statistics and distressing realities. More and more it becomes a factory worked by peons, fought over by lawyers, bossed by absent industrialists, and clerked by politicians..."

Puerto Rico was called a lot of things. One writer called it "A cherished slum." Another: "The poorhouse of the Caribbean."

Rexford Tugwell, a Franklin Roosevelt aide and later Puerto

Rican governor, titled a book about the island "The Stricken Land."

A U.S. Senate subcommittee as late as 1943 termed the island "an insolvable problem."

By 1938 Muñoz had satisfied himself that independence was not feasible and that fighting for or against it was a sterile battle that availed nothing. In groping for something more practical he formed the Popular Democratic Party and following a hill-country, plain-talking, shirtsleeve campaign in which he promised land reform and labor laws instead of independence. He was elected to the island Senate.

Experience had shown that Puerto Rico could not survive on agriculture and so the Popular Party set in motion a plan to industrialize the island. "Operation Bootstrap" was underway.

By 1942 the agency which evolved into the present Economic Development Administration (known as Fomento—the Spanish word for development) had been set up. During its first eight years of operation 86 new manufacturing plants were established. By 1955 manufacturing was contributing more than agriculture to the island's net income. In 1961 there were 700 Bootstrap factories in operation among almost 2,400 that had opened since the program began. New factories were establishing at the rate of two a week. And the per capita income, which was $121 in 1940, went over the $600 mark, the second highest in Latin America.

The drive toward the abolition of poverty was effected by two instruments: ten years of tax exemption for manufacturing and tourism ventures which met certain requirements; and the use of government capital as a catalyst for promoting private investment.

Tax exemption has been possible because the island, during its time as an unincorporated territory, could not be taxed by the Federal government without representation in Congress. In 1952 Munoz & Co. achieved something new under the sun with the creation of the present Commonwealth status, a highly controversial arrangement without constitutional precedent in the U.S. which granted Puerto Rico the right to write its own constitution providing local self-government but maintaining the U.S.-Puerto Rico association. The tax exemption remains.

Maidenform and B.V.D.

The private investment catalyzed by the Commonwealth cash has come almost totally from the States, and with it, naturally, the Americanos. The influx has wrought some dramatic changes in the island. Supermarkets, unheard of six years ago, now dominate the food distribution picture. Such stateside names as General Electric, Sunbeam, B.V.D., Sperry Rand, Thom McAn, Grand Union, Lerner Shops, Firestone, Maidenform, Woolworth, Star-Kist, many others—all with either factories or commercial outlets here—are now household words. Also heard around the house, as you might expect: AFL-CIO, ILGWU, SIU, ILA, and, of course, Teamsters.

The argument that this influx of Americans and their mores is corrupting the native culture is an egghead one, bandied about generally in university salons or over rum drinks in the local equivalent of the Greenwich Village squirrel cages. But it has also been the longtime rallying cry for the diehard Independence adherent (whose party lost its place on the ballot in the 1960 election), and in particular, members of the movement's lunatic fringe, who used to whip out the "Yankee Go Home" placards and wave them at visiting conventioneers. (Snapped a recent visitor from Dixie: "What riles my blood is being called a Yankee.")

As the independence movement wanes, the Statehood movement grows new muscles. This is attributable to a number of factors.

Among them: the continuing warm relationship with the U.S. The fact that through migration an enormous number of Puerto Rican families now have ties in the states. The fear that the independence movement may at some future date recoup its losses, get the independence which has been promised by the U.S. (if the Puerto Rican people ask for it), and thus do away with all the advantages accruing to a land in the U.S. family. The fear that Muñoz, in asking for more and more autonomy for the Commonwealth, is not, as he professes, seeking merely to perpetuate the Commonwealth, but rather is edging surreptitiously toward independence.

The last item is the one which has given the movement an inspiring shot in the hind quarters. For the first time in the history of Puerto Rican statehood stumping, the cause is not only unlost but seems distantly achievable. Plebiscites are being talked up, politically non-partisan statehood groups are being formed. As a practical matter, however, even the statehood politicians don't want, and well know that they won't get, statehood immediately. The island is still in the midst of an essential development period and if statehood were granted now economists are of the common belief that the Federal tax burden (and the resulting elimination of tax exemption as an attraction to industry) would be a severe and perhaps killing blow to the economy as it now exists. But the politicians keep stumping, as they've stumped for years. It keeps the cause in the newspapers.

Like Angels and the Devil

Despite all the clamor for statehood and independence, Governor Muñoz, his Popular Democratic Party and Commonwealth status contine to dominate the scene. Muñoz has the people in his back pocket. He swept every town but one during the 1960 election. In the name of "Operation Serenity" he has been able to ram culture down the public throat and make it palatable, has imposed high excise taxes on cars and other items to finance further cultural ventures and to keep down conspicuous consumption. Muñoz explains his tactics succinctly: "We must live like angels and produce like the devil."

The basic aim of this is not to develop a new culture, but rather forestall a cultural decline in a period when economic success might, with a villainous smirk, turn the heads of people too long benumbed by poverty and wretchedness. The threat of a newborn middle class plagued by acquisitiveness and throttled by unpaid bills prompted "Serenity's" creation.

This emphasis dates only to 1955 when "Serenity" became an official aim of the Commonwealth. But for centuries Puerto Rico had developed artists, musicians, writers whose work had transcended coastlines and brought them international acclaim. The work of painter Francisco Oller hangs in the Louvre. Puerto Rican writers offer a continuing enrichment to Spanish language literature. Followers of fine music will recognize the names of pianist Jesus María Sanromá, singer Graciela Rivera. The names and faces of Jose Ferrer and Juano Hernandez are familiar to moviegoers.

"Operation Serenity" can not create these talents but what it can do is create a climate in which talent can grow and flourish. To this end the Puerto Rico Symphony Orchestra, a conservatory and a music school have been created by direct subsidy. The orchestra has as its leader Pablo Casals, the famed cellist who has adopted Puerto Rico, the birthplace of his mother, as his permanent home. Also government-sponsored is the Casals Festival, a highly successful annual series of concerts by the great names in music, organized by Casals.

"Serenity" has also prompted the establishment of the Institute of Puerto Rican Culture, which is successfully effecting a renaissance of appreciation of the island's creations in folklore, music, sculpture, painting, theater—the last through an annual theater festival. The Institute is also busy bringing back the past—refurbishing old churches, historic landmarks, building museums and supervising the slow (but quickening) restoration of a sizeable chunk of the old quarter of San Juan.

Another manifestation of "Serenity" is formal education, to which 30 per cent of the Commonwealth budget is devoted.

But while serenity is an official aim, the word is hardly an apt one to describe the Puerto Rican people. Indeed the only people it would adequately describe would be a tribe of emotionless glunks content to lie beneath a shady palm tree sipping coconut milk and collectively contemplating their navels.

Puerto Ricans are busier than that.

In some ways they are still staunchly and sensibly resisting the souped-up life of the American. But progress, and all the parking lots that go with it, is a fact of life now, pressing in heavily on siesta time and on the old lackadaisical ways out of a past era when hurrying was unimportant because there was no place to go. Now everyone has a destination.

The slum dweller is anxious to leave his shanty. Once on higher ground (perhaps in a government housing project where the rent ranges from $3 to $35 monthly, or in a $350 self-help home built with government supplied materials, communal effort) he is after the next jump to the middle class.

On the higher economic levels of society almost everyone is scurrying (but not at the expense of politeness and generosity), and big deals of assorted sizes are in almost everyone's future. An idealistic young expatriate from Manhattan, sour on "the rotarian democracy in the U.S.," recently made a discovery (à la Columbus and all the rest) that the Puerto Rican people are fired with enthusiasm and hope, qualities he says are in short supply on the mainland.

Perhaps it is just that they are more visible on an island where the focus is microscopic, but there is no denying their presence. Enthusiasm is here, abundantly. And hope is spilling out of everybody's pockets.

A local newspaper writer recently noted an itinerant gardener whose tools for years had been a machete and a green thumb. "Now," the writer said, "he owns his own lawnmower."

It's a sign of the times.

PRACTICAL INFORMATION FOR PUERTO RICO

HOW TO GET THERE. *By Air.* Possibly the biggest air travel bargain in the world is the $94.30 round trip economy fare from New York to San Juan. The average mile cost is less than a ride on the New York subway system. Round trip economy fare from Miami is $77.90. Round trip tourist fare from New York on 600 mph jets is $110, from Miami $95.70, and the Delta Airline jets from New Orleans $101.60, from Los Angeles $192.95. First class on the jets costs $108.65 from New York, $70.30 from Miami with a 10 % discount on round trips. Chief air carriers from New York and Miami are Pan American, Eastern and Trans Caribbean Airways, from New Orleans and Los Angeles on Delta Air Lines. You can fly from Chicago by Delta Air Lines (via Miami) and by Eastern Air Lines (via Atlanta, Tampa, Miami). Pan American has non-stop service from Washington, Philadelphia and Boston, and direct service from Chicago, Cleveland, Detroit, Houston and the West Coast. Direct inter-island connections are provided by Caribbean Atlantic Airlines between San Juan and St. Thomas, St. Croix, Dominican Republic, Haiti, and St. Maarten. Pan American links San Juan with the Dominican Republic, Haiti, Jamaica, Trinidad, Guadeloupe, St. Croix, Barbados, Martinique, Antigua and major South American cities. Trans Caribbean runs a $25 scheduled flight to Aruba. British West Indian Airways also link Puerto Rico with the major islands of the Caribbean. Iberia Airlines flies to Europe.

By Sea. Alcoa Steamship Company takes passengers from New York, Baltimore, New Orleans and Montreal to San Juan. The Bull Lines link New York and Baltimore with Puerto Rico. You can travel from New Orleans, San Francisco or Los Angeles to San Juan on ships of Waterman Lines, from Galveston via Lykes Lines. San Juan is also a cruiseship port.

PASSPORTS, VISAS. None are required for U.S. citizens arriving from the United States or the Virgin Islands. Re-entry regulations must be complied with by those coming from foreign ports. Non-U.S. citizens must have passports and clear Immigration when coming from their own country or from the U.S. or Virgin Islands.

CURRENCY. The Yankee dollar is the only legal tender here.

CLOTHING. Summer clothing and sports clothes, but there are enough vestiges of old world Spanish modesty here so that women should not wear shorts in the city streets. Evening clothes are optional in the fancy resort hotels. Bring along a sweater or light wrap if you're going to the mountains.

HOW TO GET ABOUT. Transportation by buses or *guaguas* in San Juan and vicinity is excellent. Fare is 10 cents. There are loads of taxis, metered at 25 cents for the first quarter mile, 5 cents each additional quarter. If a taxi doesn't have a meter, don't get aboard without making precise arrangements as to price and destination. For public transportation outside of San Juan, it's the famous *públicos*. They are seven or five-passenger cars of various vintages, and they run all over the country on more-or-less scheduled runs. If you want to see the island cheaply as the Puerto Ricans see it, take a público. There are plenty of them and you'll find them along the waterfront of the Old Town in San Juan, or at the Rio Piedras Plaza, ready to take you, bag and baggage, practically anywhere in Puerto Rico. Or call 2-3747 to have a público pick you up at your hotel. Fare from San Juan to Ponce, for example, is $2.50. The Puerto Rico Motor Coach Co. has daily scheduled service in fast air-conditioned coaches between San Juan and Mayagüez.

There are loads of Drive-yourself cars available in San Juan and at the airport. Olin, Hertz, Avis, Caribe and Continental have cars for hire at rates from $7 daily, $35 weekly plus 8 cents a mile. A car with chauffeur will run you about $25 per day. There are a number of sight-seeing tour operators who cover the chief sights of the islands in comfortable buses or limousines. Try Southerland Tours, Puerto Rico Tours Inc., Jibaro Tours, Inc., all in San Juan; Turismo Internacional and Independent Tourist Service in Santurce; Agencias Soler in Mayagüez; Gonzalez & Co. Inc. in Ponce; Jorge Bird Travel Service Inc. at Rio Piedras. The last is not for the birds; it's for tourists.

Caribair and several other small airlines have daily flights from San Juan to Ponce, Mayagüez and other towns around the island. Round trips cost about $11. Puerto Rico Helicopters offer interesting aerial tours of the island for $15. The Tourism Department has an information booth at the Airport and in Santurce. If you're ever lost, call Tourist Information Service at 3-8576 in San Juan.

HOTELS

Ever since 1949 when Puerto Rico put up the famed *Caribe Hilton Hotel,* this island has been setting a fast pace in hotel development. The Hilton remains a smart center of society activity, but already has three spectacular rivals: *El San Juan Hotel,* which with its superb beach and matchless facilities has become the focal point of the fast-growing Isla Verde section; *La Concha,* a masterpiece of modern abstract design, both inside and out; and the *Dorado Beach,* fabulous new resort with 18-hole golf course on the Atlantic. Things move so fast here that the *Dorado Beach* has already added an entire new building and is starting on a third one. More than $68,000,000 worth of new Puerto Rican hotels are in the blue-print or building stages at this writing, including some new budget rate hotels spotted around the island's south, west and east coasts. An island just off the eastern coast, Vieques, is the scene of a new $16,000,000 resort development by Fred and Norman Woolworth. All the resort buildings, private houses, and cabanas have been planned in the Spanish style that belongs by tradition to this island. When completed the resort will have full installations for golf, tennis and bathing, a shopping area and a riding stable. Members will be those constructing houses according to club specifications. Other members may be proposed by owners and approved by the Board of Governors.

Guest privileges will also be available for limited periods. Address inquiries to Vieques Island Development Corp., 4 West 58 St., N.Y., 19, N.Y.

New hotels are constantly opening in Puerto Rico, and those under construction as we go to press include the 421-room *Sheraton* in San Juan; the 280-rooms *Holiday Inn* and 398-room *Americana* in Isla Verde; the *Dorado Riviera* and *Cayo Lobos* in Fajardo.

The winter season in Puerto-Rico extends from December 15 to April 30. There used to be no seasonal variation in hotel rates, but this situation has changed with the announcement of reductions from 20 to 45 per cent from May 1 to December in many of San Juan's major hotels. *Dorado Beach* will reduce their rates by 40 per cent below their winter figures. *La Rada* is paring its single rates from $16 to $10 minimum, doubles from $18 down to $14. *La Concha* has reduced its single rates for off season to $12 up single and $16 up double, the *Condado Beach Hotel* from $13 single, $16 double. *The Normandie* and *Escambrón Beach Hotel* are offering their accommodations at 20 to 40 per cent less than winter season prices. Since this is the most enterprising hotel industry in the Caribbean, you may expect most of the other hotels to follow suit. All rates quoted below are for winter season European Plan unless otherwise noted.

SAN JUAN

CARIBE HILTON. *Fomento* put up this pace-setting resort caravansary with $7,500,000 of its own money in 1949, imported Conrad Hilton to run it. Hilton made $1,000,000 the first year and set out from Puerto Rico to conquer the world. The *Caribe Hilton* remains a top favorite. It's on the ocean front near old Fort San Gerónimo, has 435 air-conditioned rooms and suites all with private bath, sea view. Dancing and entertainment in the *Club Caribe*. Cabañas, beach, swimming pool, tennis courts, smart shops, casino, the works. Mr. Alphonse Salomone, Jr. is the manager and the service is just about flawless. Rates are from $20 to $30 single per day; $25 to $35 double.

EL CONVENTO. The $3,000,000, 107 rooms resort recently opened in Old San Juan, was financed mainly by Dime-Store Heir Robert Frederic Woolworth, and built from the shell of an abandoned 315-year-old Roman Catholic convent. It combines superb modern conveniences (air conditioning, a swimming pool) with colonial charm and old-world elegance (tapestried rugs, four-poster bed). Mr. A. A. Stutzer is the manager. Rates are from $16 to $25 single per day; $20 to $30 double.

LA CONCHA. On the ocean front in the Condado section of San Juan, a new eight million dollar baby with 252 air-conditioned rooms and suites with private bath. Beach and cabaña club, swimming pool, tennis courts, shuffle board, restaurants, coffee shops, bars, and casino. Frank Vidal is managing this shiny new enterprise. Singles from

$22 to $30, doubles from $26 to $37.

EL SAN JUAN HOTEL. Sorry to be so mercenary; this one only cost $7,500,000 to put up. Opened in 1958, it stands in its own 15-acre tropic estate on 1500 feet of private beach near the International Airport. Everything is ultra-modern; their Tropicoro Night club, for example, has a parabolic ceiling. The food, French and American, maintains the exalted standards of the Intercontinental Chain. There are 303 attractively-appointed air-conditioned rooms with balconies facing the sea and plans for an additional 200 rooms and 50 sleeping cabanas, will make this hotel the largest so far in the Caribbean. The expansion program includes *Le Pavillon*, the hotel's gourmet dining room. There's an Olympic size free-form pool, where skindiving is taught, a wading pool for the kids, a Cabaña Club, sailboats and pedalboats on the beach and a smart casino where you can play roulette, black jack (twenty-one) and craps. Rates are $18 to $28 single, $23 to $33 double. Alan Mald is the general manager and operational head of the hotel.

LA RADA. In the Condado section of San Juan on the Lagoon has 100 air-conditioned rooms or suites with private bath, some with kitchenette, all with pleasant modern décor. Their *Hapsburg Rendezvous* restaurant (Austro-Hungarian dishes) is esteemed throughout the West Indies, as are the drinks in the Chanteclec Bar, which overlooks the garden and swimming pool. This is a good center for boating and water skiing on the Condado Lagoon. President and general manager of La Rada is José Alegría, and his guests are *muy alegre*. Single rates, $20 to $35; double from $24 to $40.

CONDADO BEACH HOTEL. Still a gay favorite despite the competition from some of the *nouveaux riches*, this ocean-front hostelry has 180 air-conditioned rooms with bath, (expanding: 161 rooms more),

Cabaña Club, private beach, swimming pool and tennis court. The food and entertainment in the Fiesta Room are A-1. There's an art gallery in the mezzanine. Several bars, shops, coffee shop and an air of general contentment which only satisfied returning clients can supply. Fred E. Dieterle is the manager. Rates: $15 to $25 single, $18 to $28 double.

ATLANTIC BEACH HOTEL. On the oceanfront in the Condado section, has 42 air-conditioned rooms, half with sea view, all with private bath. Rooftop cocktail lounge features nightly entertainment and roast beef dinners, magnificent view. Coffee shop a step from the beach. Hugo Durán is now the manager. Singles from $12 to $17; doubles from $15 to $22.

MIRAMAR CHARTERHOUSE HOTEL. Smart new tourist hotel in Miramar section. 205 air-conditioned rooms and suites with a rooftop lounge, supper and night club and swimming pool. Rates are $10 to $17 for singles, $14 to $30 for doubles. Operated by Hotel Corporation of America.

ESCAMBRÓN BEACH HOTEL. On its own beach at Punta Escambrón, has 58 rooms and beach cabañas with bath. Swimming is good at the private beach club, and Manager William C. Otero has Riviera water bicycles, a fishing pier and most of the necessary equipment for a happy watery holiday. Tennis courts for landlubbers. The Lira Room features big floor-shows and Latin American dance music nightly (See below: Night Life). Rates: Single, from $9; double, from $14.

NORMANDIE. Also managed by William Otero. Shaped like a ship and in ship shape now that it's been renovated. Center of attraction is the big indoor swimming pool. There's also a private beach with cabañas. The 165 rooms are actually "junior" suites with private bath. Air conditioning available. Much gaiety at night with good dancing, Voodoo Room bar and casino. Rates: $9 to $14 single; $14 to $18 double.

INTERNATIONAL AIRPORT HOTEL. Provides 55 sound-proof, air-conditioned rooms with twin beds and private bath on the third floor of San Juan's modern International Airport Terminal Building. Singles are $11 a day; doubles, $15. If you want to rest in air-cooled comfort between planes, ask the manager, Señor Catalino de Jesús, about his special day rates. Note: In spite of the soundproofing, we put Flents in our ears to further muffle the tones of the public address system. Better check on your own decibility-tolerance.

CAPITOL. On Avenue Ponce de Leon on the new Miramar business section, has 100 rooms with or without bath; some are air-conditioned. Popular with mainland businessmen. There's a restaurant, the Flaming Pit, which attracts a local and international clientele in search of good Italian food. Manager of the Capitol is Julio Encarnacion. Rates are $5 to $7 single; $9 to $12 double.

CENTRAL. Managed by the owner, Tomas Gonzalez, this hotel is on San José Street in Old San Juan. There are 63 rooms, with and without bath; some have balconies. There's a cafeteria where you can get breakfast and lunch. Rates are the lowest of any hotel we recommend in San Juan: $2.50 to $5 a day single; $5 to $8 double.

COLUMBUS. Near the shops in the Miramar Section, caters to mainland businessmen. Some of the 57 rooms have kitchenettes to accommodate those who want to settle in for a longer stay. Dining facilities nearby. José Colón is the manager. Rates are $7 to $10 single; $12 to $15 double.

THE PALACE. In old San Juan, has 67 rooms with private bath, some with balconies and a glimpse of the bay. Far from the smart resort hotels, this old timer has a certain

local Puerto Rican charm to recommend it along with the cheaper rates: $4 to $9 single; $7 to $14 double. Miguel Angel Jimenez is the manager. There's no dining room.

SAN LUIS HOTEL. On Muñoz Rivera Avenue in the San Gerónimo section, just across from the Supreme Court Building. There are 34 rooms, 6 suites, all comfortably air-conditioned, some with kitchenettes. Singles $10 to $12 a day, doubles, $14 to $16. Mrs. Felicita Morales is the manager.

GALLARDO APARTMENT HOTEL. On Avenue Magdalena (1102) in the Condado Section, has 62 rooms with bath and kitchenette in housekeeping suites with maid, linen and telephone service. Convenient for long stays. Rates are $6 and $9 single, $13 and $15 double. Manager is Rubén Aponte.

VILLA FIRENZE GUEST HOUSE. 655 Miramar Ave. Italian-type pension, run by Mrs. Lily Leget Burzio in the house where José Ferrer was born. Rates from $4 and $8 single, $6 to $11 double. Meals served.

MIRAMAR. 609 Olimpo Ave. 19 rooms, some air-conditioned. Owned and managed by Edith Morales. Singles $3.50 to $7. Doubles $6 to $9.

OLIMPO COURT. Another apartment hotel on Miramar Avenue with 116 rooms and kitchenette apartments, 45 of which are air conditioned. Complete hotel service with restaurant. Rates are $5 to $15 single, $6 to $17 double. For weekly rates for longer term stays, consult the owner-manager, Charles Axtmayer.

THE Y.M.C.A. at Stop 1, Ponce de Leon Avenue, welcomes transient students and other male guests in addition to Y.M.C.A. members at $2.50 per day single, $3 and $4 double. Weekly and monthly rates can be arranged. The Y.W.C.A., down the street at Stop 14, has comparable budget rates for the girls.

PUERTO RICO

ANTILLES. 804 Ponce de Leon, in the heart of town. 8 air-conditioned rooms. Manager is Mrs. Lucila A. Vega. Single $8 to $12, double $10 to $15.

DUFFY'S BY THE SEA. 9 Isla Verde Road. Charming 9-room beach villa with private bar and patio. Single $10, double $12 to $15, with breakfast. Owner is Bill Hirst.

LA POSADA. On Isla Verde Road near the San Juan Intercontinental Hotel. 10 air-conditioned rooms with private patios, and a swimming pool. Half-block from public beach. Owner-manager is Mrs. Josefina Arana. Rates: $9 single, $10-$14 double.

TRADE WINDS. Centrally located at 614 Olimpo Ave. 12 rooms, breakfast and dinner served. Rates are $6 to $13 single, $8 to $15 double, European plan. Mrs. Tommie Rosen is the manager.

COLONIAL. 606 Olimpo Ave. in Miramar section. Centrally located. 21 rooms managed by Mrs. Edward M. Cruthards. Rates are $6 to $10 single, $8 to $20 double.

HILS BEACH HOUSE. 1850 Atlantic Street. 16 rooms overlooking beach. Singles $6 to $10. Doubles $8 to $18. Manager is Mrs. Hil Cushing-Murray.

ISLAND HOUSE. 1017 Ashford Ave. On beach with own natural rockbound pool. Manager is Mrs. Binnie Borden. Seven air-conditioned double rooms. Rates include breakfast: $20 to $24.

LA CASA ROSA. 2071 Cacique St. in residential Santa Teresita section, block from beach. 9 air-conditioned rooms plus furnished suite. Singles $8 to $10. Doubles $10 to $18. Mrs. Zayda Cuebas de Steffens, manager.

HOTEL PIERRE. Centrally located in Santurce. 132 delightfully furnished rooms all with private baths. Wall to wall carpeting and air conditioned throughout. Restaurant, cocktail lounge, bar, swimming pool, shopping arcades, beauty parlor, car rental and complete sightseeing services. Continental atmosphere and true Swiss hospitality. Mr. Guido Gnocchi is the manager. Rates range from $12 to $16 single, and $17 to $24 double (European Plan).

LA PROVIDENCIA. 153 Calle Parque, convenient downtown location. 9 air-conditioned rooms. Rates: Singles, $7, doubles, $9 to $12. Manager, Clodoaldo Queipo.

SAN ANTONIO. 1 Tapia Street. 7 air-conditioned rooms overlooking beach, private patio, kitchen privileges. Singles $10, doubles $16. L. Catinchi is owner.

THE OWL. 151 Tetuan St. in Old San Juan, has 12 rooms, with rates, including breakfast, at $10 single and $20 double. Facilities include a sunroof and bar.

WASHINGTON GUEST HOUSE. 67 Washington Ave. in the Condado section, offers 7 rooms at $9 to $12 for singles and $14 to $20 for doubles. Manager is Mrs. Marinette Nelson.

OUTSIDE SAN JUAN

COPAMARINA BEACH HOTEL, near Guánica on the south coast, has 24 air-conditioned rooms; swimming pool, cocktail lounge, restaurant, sailing boats and private beach. Rates are $16 single, $26 double, M.A.P.

DORADO BEACH HOTEL. Twenty miles west of San Juan on the Atlantic Coast, one of the latest and rarest blooms on the Puerto Rican vine. Laurence Rockefeller went all out to the tune of $10,000,000 to create an ideal resort hotel, and he's come about as close as you can. The *Dorado Beach* is situated on a private estate of 1,500 acres with beach, pool, wading pool, tennis courts, facilities for all the recreation and sports in the book.

PUERTO RICO

Biggest feature is the beautiful 27-hole golf course laid out by the celebrated Robert Trent Jones. Smart shops, excellent entertainment program for guests, top flight cuisine. There are 236 air-conditioned rooms and suites all with private bath. G. Bland Hoke is the manager. Daily Modified American Plan (breakfast and dinner) rates are $40 to $55 single, $50 to $65 double. Off season, they drop to $22 to $34 single, $30 to $42 double.

EL BARRANQUITAS. A de luxe resort hotel in the mountains, 2,300 feet above sea level. It has 42 rooms with bath and offers a swimming pool, tennis courts, a children's playground with kiddie pool, horseback riding, a five-hole pitch and putt golf course, lake fishing and boating. Near historical town of Barranquitas. No need for air conditioning here on the cool heights; in fact all the lounges have wood-burning fire places. Nicholas Albors is the resident manager of this attractive resort. Transportation is provided daily at 9 a.m. and 3 p.m. from the Condado Beach Hotel in San Juan. Daily rates: $15 to $18 single; $18 to $21 double.

HACIENDA ROSES. A small new hotel with comfortable facilities on a giant coffee plantation near the mountain town of Florida in Puerto Rico's northwest corner. Swimming pool, horses, lake fishing and boating, ancient Indian caves to explore. The ride to and from the hacienda offers a breathtaking view of the island's lush landscape. Minnie Roses is the young manager of her father's estate here. Daily rates, including meals, sightseeing and transportation to and from San Juan, are $15 single, $22 double. Very calm and restful.

HOTEL MONTEMAR. This comfortable resort hotel dominates the western coast of the Island at Aguadilla. The views of the sea, especially from restaurant and bar, are wonderful. There's a pool and

arrangements can be made for golf and riding. All 40 rooms have private bath. Rates are $7 and $10 single, $10 to $14 double.

HOTEL MIR. Commercial type with 25 rooms and bath on the Main Plaza of Arecibo, port about an hour from San Juan. Businessmen who come here to negotiate with the Ron Rico distillery speak well of the food and service. Warren James is the manager. Rates are from $4 to $8 single, from $5 to $9 double.

TREASURE ISLAND. High up in the mountains on Lake Cidra, this is a grand place for family vacations. There are 20 cabañas, cottages and family cabins and a swimming pool. Horseback riding, fishing and rowing are the chief diversions. American Plan Rates are $10 a day single, $20 double, and Mrs. María Luisa Marín, the owner manager, will make even more attractive arrangements for families.

ROSARIO MOUNTAIN RESORT. At Rosario on Route No. 348 near Mayagüez. 24 rooms with private bath. Swimming pool, horseback riding, restaurant, bar and fresh mountain air. Luz P. Fernandez is the manager. American Plan Rates are $11.50 single, $18.50 to $20 double. European Plan Rates: $6 single, $9 double.

FRENCHMAN'S HOUSE. An elegant 18th-century sugar plantation hacienda converted into a 12-room hotel as the first step of the Vieques resort project. Horses, boating, swimming pool, restaurant and cocktail lounge. Modified American Plan (breakfast, dinner included) $20 single, $30 double.

VILLA PARGUERA HOTEL. Overlooking Phosphorescent Bay in the little south shore fishing village of La Parguera. This is a popular guest house type of place, informal, comfortable and home-like. Puerto-Rican-American cuisine. There's a swimming pool. Also boats and facilities for deep sea fishing, exploring and sailing. Owner-manager is Carlos Quiñones. There are 40 rooms with private or semi-private bath; most are air conditioned. Rates are from $5 to $10 single, $7 to $14 double.

EL OASIS. Ten rooms in a modernized old Spanish house in the center of historic San Germán. Patio dining room with good Puerto Rican food. Rates: $6 per room, $7 for air-conditioned rooms. Nicolas Torres is the manager.

COSTELLO HALL GUEST HOUSE. Also at San Germán, is on the campus of the Inter American University, where the International Music Institute now meets for classes and concerts. There are 11 rooms, $4 to $5 single; $7 to $8 double. Mrs. Gladys Fisher is the hostess. Three meals served daily.

EL CONQUISTADOR. Built on an east coast hilltop with a spectacular view, this hotel offers 80 air-conditioned rooms, a tiled swimming pool, an 18-hole putting course, a tennis court, two English bowling greens, facilities for sailing, fishing, and skin diving. It operates a funicular to bring the guests down to the private ocean beach. Full American Plan summer rates start at $22 single, and $35 double; from Dec. 14; through April 14, rates begin at $35 single and $56 double. Manager is George Cummings.

CARIBE HOTEL. Not to be confused with the Caribe in San Juan, this small Spanish-type hotel does well with Puerto Rican dishes. Primarily for visiting businessmen in Guayama, the largest town on Puerto Rico's southeast coast, it has 24 rooms, some with private bath, on the plaza. Well-managed by Luis Delgado Navas. Singles are $2 to $5, doubles $4 and $7.

LA SIERRA. 19 rooms, some with private baths, and a restaurant in the mountain town of San Sebastian where Irish settlers brought the green eyes and blond hair that everyone in town seems to have. Rates are $2.50 to $5 for singles, $4 to $7 for doubles. Manager is Mrs. Carmen C. de Acosta.

LA CASA ROIG. Charming 8-room Spanish Colonial guest house in Yauco, the heart of the coffee country near the south corner of the island. Complete meals served home-style. Rates are $3 to $6 single, $6 to $8 double.

HOTEL CARMEN. On the offshore island of Vieques. A quiet 16 room commercial hotel that will soon see business pick up when Woolnor Corp. starts its multi-million dollar resort project. Inocencia de Morales is the manager. Rates are $3 for singles, $5 for doubles.

PONCE AND VICINITY

Fomento has all sorts of things, on the drawing board for Ponce, Puerto Rico's second city, on the south shore, 74 miles from San Juan. In the meantime, here are the best bets for this fast-developing southern port:

HOTEL MELIA. A good, up-to-date city type hotel on Calle Cristina near the center of town. All 64 rooms have baths, many are air conditioned. Now expanding. Smart cocktail lounge, patio restaurant, and cafeteria. Juan Melia is the manager. Rates are $5 to $10 single; $8 to $15 double.

EL CASTILLO. Comfortable and modern. 11 rooms, all with bath, some with balconies, some with air conditioning. There's a cocktail lounge and a patio restaurant, locally admired for its good Puerto Rican food. Ramón Fernandez is the manager. Rates are $5 to $8 single; $6 to $10 double.

SAN JOSÉ GUEST HOUSE. Two blocks from the Plaza. Eleven air-conditioned rooms plus the charm of a Spanish colonial setting. Owner is José Méndez, Jr. Rates: Single, $6; double, $10 to $12. No meals are served here.

PUERTO RICO

EL PONCE INTERCONTINENTAL. On a hilltop overlooking Ponce, this new and already popular resort offers a night club, restaurant, circular cocktail lounge, casino, swimming pool magnificent view of the most Spanish of Puerto Rico's cities. 170 air-conditioned rooms, each with bath and private balcony. Guests can use golf courses, sailing and boating facilities of Ponce's private clubs. Tours leave daily for the city where horse-drawn carriages wait at the plaza to take you through the reminders of old Spain. Singles are from $12 to $20, doubles from $16 to $24 on European plan. Leo Riordan is the genial manager.

FOOD AND RESTAURANTS

The local cuisine, as might be expected, has a strong Spanish accent. Among the favorite dishes is good old *arroz con pollo,* chicken with rice, and the Puerto Ricans do it well. But you'll want to sample some less familiar native specialties. One of these should not be missed; it's *Arroz Gallego,* a tempting concoction of diced beef filet and mushrooms, fried eggs, onions, olives, cooked beans and dry wine, all soaked up in that saffron-colored Spanish rice. Try also the celebrated *Asopao,* as Spanish and as thick as its name. The basis of asopao is usually chicken or seafood cooked with rice in a wine sauce. After that, it's garnished with peas, pimentos, asparagus and hard-boiled eggs. *Habichuelas* are red beans; *gandules* are pigeon peas with pork. Try *Tostones*; they're the big island plantains (bananas) fried in deep fat. *Lechón Asado* is suckling pig roasted on a spit. You'll find this crisp and succulent specialty at *lechoneras* all over the island; they're as popular as barbecue joints at home. Some Puerto Rican creations like *hallacas* and *pasteles* will remind you of *tamales,* but they're not half as fiery as their counterparts north of the border up Mexico way. *Paellas,* savory rice with saffron, chicken or seafood, are delicious. *Pescao* is the name for any fish caught, but if you get it fresh out of the Caribbean in the little fishing village of Parguera on the south coast, you'll ask the cook for more. Sea-food around the island is generally excellent, especially the lobsters. The latter have a terrestrial relative: *jueyes* or land crabs. Try these at one of the native specialty houses. The national drink of Puerto Rico is rum, and it is available in a staggering variety of combinations. Some excellent island rums—Barrilito, for one—are made in such small quantities that they never reach the mainland.

Most of the major hotels have fine restaurants, and it usually is necessary for non-guests to reserve.

380

PUERTO RICO

OLD SAN JUAN

LA MALLORQUINA. Typical Spanish and Puerto Rican dishes are served here in a Spanish colonial atmosphere worthy of Puerto Rico's oldest restaurant. Their *asopao* is the best in Puerto Rico. If you see, *Calamares en su tinto* on the menu, it means squid in its own ink. Go ahead; don't be a sissy. If you're not the adventurous type, the steaks and seafood have been appreciated here since 1848.

EL BURRITO. A very good restaurant with the charm of a 17th-century colonial house and garden patio. The cooking is good home-style American. The great specialty of the house is home-made pies; we found them better than mother used to make, and mother was no slouch. Prices are most reasonable.

MAGO' SAXONY. A beef-eater's paradise with thick prime steaks charcoal-broiled to your individual order. The restaurant is air conditioned.

LA BOTELLA. A recommended place in the Old Town for good American food. The place, open until 2 a.m., is in a remodelled old Spanish house, and the atmosphere, with bar and tinkling piano, will remind you of little places you know in the East Fifties in New York.

EL MEDITERRANEO. Despite the air conditioning, the atmosphere here is *muy* Old Spain and so is the cuisine with a few Puerto Rican specialties thrown in for good measure. On Calle San Justo in Old San Juan it prides itself on being "*el mas autentico restaurant español de todo el Caribe.*"

LA ZARAGOZANA. Newest and most exclusive Spanish eatery in historic Old San Juan colonial house. The setting will whisk you to old Spain. Latin cuisine, prepared by experts, is tops. Comparsa (miastrel) entertainment every night.

MEXICO IN PUERTO RICO. Some like it hot, and this is the place for the hottest tamales in the island. Every Mexican dish you can think of with a few Puerto Rican side dishes to cool the palate. The atmosphere is Mexican plus air conditioning, and there's a Puerto Rican jam session Thursday through Sunday nights. On Cristo Street in the Old Town.

LA DANZA. Near the Governor's mansion, this delightful air-conditioned restaurant has an all-Puerto Rican menu. (English translations on the back.) Atmosphere is decidedly Spanish and a piano plays island folk tunes. Service is good, prices low.

EL MORRO. Spanish and Puerto Rican dishes in a replica of one of the rooms of a 16th Century Spanish fortress. No trouble getting through the guards, but you may not want to leave. The food's that good. 203 Tanca Street midway between Old San Juan's two plazas.

RED ROOSTER. Two resaurants serving American dishes at moderate prices; one located on the corner of Muños Rivera Avenue and the road leading to the Caribe Hilton Hotel; the other on Ashford Avenue across the street from the Condado Beach Hotel.

TRADER VIC'S. The famous restaurant specializing in Indonesian food. Located in the Garden Wing of the Caribe Hilton Hotel.

MIRAMAR AND SANTURCE

SWISS CHALET. The perfect blend of the Swiss tradition and history. *Fondu* and other Swiss delicacies served up in a mountain chalet out on Avenida de Diego. Designed by Claudio Vital, one of Switzerland's leading architects. There are several dining rooms, a pastry shop, a sidewalk café, a delicatessen. You can dine and dance here to the music of one of Puerto Rico's best combos, but better reserve (Phone 724-0120) as the place is very popular with the local gentry and may be crowded. Air conditioned and moderately expensive.

EL NILO. At Stop 22 on Ponce de León Avenue, this is a modern, air-conditioned cafeteria, gaily decorated with scenes of the Mardi Gras, and featuring Spanish, Puerto Rican and American dishes. The chicken *asopao* is very good here, and so is the seafood. Excellent place for informal lunch, dinner and snacks, early and late.

CATHAY. The best Chinese restaurant in town, opposite the Naval Base on Avenida Fernández Juncos. Cuisine and decor are San Francisco oriental, but there are also steaks and chops if anyone in your party is allergic to exotic food.

LA RONDE. A four-way operation on Ponce de León Avenue. First, at Stop 11, there's the La Ronde self service cafeteria, serving American and Puerto Rican food from 6:30 a.m. to 10 at night. Right next door

is La Ronde Seafood, featuring blue point oysters, cherrystone clams, broiled lobsters, island parguera and other denizens of the deep. At Stop 22, another cafeteria and an excellent Steak House. All four restaurants are air-conditioned.

EL CENTAURO. Italian specialties in a roomy and tastefully decorated touch of Venice on Ashford Avenue. Also Puerto Rican dishes and a guitarist that roams the tables to sing for your supper.

COTILLON ROOM. Opposite the Caribe Hilton, serves excellent steaks and chops, cooked or broiled to your liking.

TOP OF THE FIRST. Magnificent view from the top of San Juan's new skyscraper, the highest spot in Puerto Rico except for the Cordillera Central Mountains. Run by the successful Swiss Chalet owners, it is an exclusive membership club till 6 p.m., when it opens to the public. International cuisine. First Federal Savings Bank Building. Stop 23. Closed on Sunday.

ISLA VERDE

BIRD'S SALON RUISEÑOR. In the International Airport. You can watch birds taking off outside and listen to small ones singing inside the restaurant. The décor is striking and the food is excellent. This is a good place to sample the Arroz Gallego, mentioned above. If you're in a hurry between planes, there's a separate coffee shop and a cafeteria where you can be served with jet age speed.

CECILIA'S PLACE. On Boca de Cangrejos Road, this is the oldest seafood restaurant in Puerto Rico, and *the* place, as far as we're concerned, to sample Puerto Rican cooking. The *Jueyes,* milk-fed landcrabs, are delicious whether you have them *al carapacho* (in the shell), *empanadilla* (in a crust), *en asopao, con arroz frito* (with fried rice), or in a salad or *tortilla* (omelet). All the

traditional dishes are on Cecilia's menu, and her *amarillos al horno* (baked ripe plantains) are without peer. If you have a sweet tooth, order *Biscocho con Bienmesabe* for dessert, a cake with thick coconut syrup. Too heavy? Try a papaya stuffed with fresh pineapple. Cecilia's *Sopa de Pollo Criolla* (native chicken soup) is a masterpiece, and so is the fresh fish soup, *Caldo de Pescado Fresco.* If you're afraid to go native, order something called *Enlatadas Americanas.* Know what it is? Good old Campbell's canned soup. The wine cellar has everything from Spanish cider to French champagne. Prices are reasonable; most expensive item on the menu is *Langosta a la Parrilla,* a broiled lobster at $2.40.

MARIO'S RESTAURANT. Near the airport on the Isla Verde Road, is a big air-conditioned place with good food, seafood and Puerto Rican specialties, and the best turtle steaks we've eaten east of Grand Cayman Island. Owner-Manager Mario Mercantoni has a way with fried chicken too, and a well-stocked bar. Open from noon until one in the morning. Moderate prices.

ON THE FRINGES OF TOWN

LA CUEVA. 507 Avenue Muñoz Rivera at Stop 33½, a moderately-priced air-conditioned restaurant with gypsy paintings and cave decor. Specialties include chicken in the basket and a big choice of Italian pizzas. Open from noon until 2 a.m. There's a bar where you can drink to the sound of accordion music. The more you listen, the more you drink; the more you drink, the better it sounds.

ZIPPERLE'S. On Roosevelt Avenue in Hato Rey, a moderately-priced, comfortable, modern, air-conditioned dining room where you can get *sauerbraten* and other German specialties in addition to Puerto Rican food.

OUT ON THE ISLAND

In addition to the dining rooms already listed in our hotel list, the following eating places can be recommended:

ARECIBO. The *Arecibo Country Club* welcomes visitors; the cuisine is on the hearty side and strictly native. *El Aquarium* is an air-conditioned restaurant-soda fountain-coffee shop with good Puerto Rican and Continental food. *El Gran Café* on highway no. 2 is a fully air-conditioned fountain type place with both American and island food on the menu.

CAGUAS. The *Roosevelt Inn* on the Main Square is an ultra-modern air-conditioned restaurant and pastry shop, specializing in American and Italian food.

GUAYNABO (route 20 out of San Juan). *La Rosaleda* offers outdoor dining on the terrace of a luxurious Spanish town house. Puerto Rican cuisine and fresh sea food.

LAS CROABAS (on Route 987 near Fajardo). *Rayito de Sol* is one of those little Puerto Rican restaurants in a fishing village, specializing in lobster and other gastronomic temptations direct from the sea. This is the northeastern counterpart of those *pescao* places you'll find in Paguera on the southwestern coast.

LUQUILLO. The *Ocean View Club* overlooks the Atlantic and provides good down-to-the-sea Puerto Rican cooking.

MAYAGÜEZ. *Bolo's Place* on Guanajibo Playa features fresh lobster and other seafood brought in daily from Cabo Rojo, well cooked and served in air-conditioned comfort.

PONCE. *Jack's Rendezvous* has accordions and excellent French and American cuisine. *Main's Restaurant* in the fashionable La Rambla section is a top-notch steak house.

SALINAS (near Ponce). *Ladi's* specializes in fish and *tostones* (fried plantains) so effectively that they drew special kudos from famed expert Clementine Paddleford.

SANTA ISABEL. *El Aquarium* is beautifully situated on the Caribbean from which comes a daily catch of lobster and other denizens of the deep which the chef prepares in various ways including an authentic Marseillaise *Bouillabaisse*.

EL YUNQUE. Over 3,000 feet up in the Caribbean National Forest, you'll have an appetite for *asopao, paella a la Valenciana* and other sturdy and savory native specialties provided by the *El Yunque Resort* along with Spanish *vino tinto* to wash it down. The low prices are almost as refreshing as the high mountain air.

PUERTO RICO

Puerto Rico's $50,000,000 plus annual tourist industry is not built on sea, sun and sand alone. When the sun goes down, the bright lights go up in the big hotels and out comes the brightest galaxy of stars this side of the Gay White Way. Eartha Kitt was raising temperatures at the Caribe Hilton when we were last there; Yma Sumac was raising the parabolic roof at the El San Juan Hotel's Tropicoro Club, and Cab Calloway was raising Ole Man Mose at the Flamboyan. Other top international stars to appear recently in San Juan are Nat King Cole, Maurice Chevalier, Gloria de Haven, Carmen Cavallero, Jose Greco, Lisa Kirk, Vic Damone, Andy Russell, Carmen Amaya, and Roberto Iglesias and his Spanish dancers. This will give you an idea of the type of performers you can expect to see at La Concha, the Condado Beach, the San Juan International and the other smart hotels of Puerto Rico. In other words you can count on the New York-Hollywood-Las Vegas routine without dipping into your pocket for luxury, amusement and old age taxes. The leading night spots in this international circuit all feature dinner dancing and nightly floor shows.

In addition to the pleasures of dining, dancing and floor show, most of these hotels offer their guests the chance to play roulette and lose money in other exciting ways at government-sponsored gambling casinos. The newest and most posh is the one at the El San Juan Hotel, but you can drop from a quarter to $100 just as fast at any of the others.

Outstanding are *Club Caribe* in the Caribe Hilton Hotel; the *La Concha Supper Club* in La Concha Hotel; *Tropicoro Night Club* in the El San Juan hotel; *Les Chandeliers* at Escambron Beach Hotel; the *Voodoo Room* of the Hotel Normandie. The *Fiesta Room* of the Condado Beach Hotel; the *Flamboyan Club* at 886 Ashford Avenue for topflight dance bands.

You can find plenty of good Latin American dance music and Puerto Rican entertainment away from the big hotels.

There's dancing nightly at the *Swiss Chalet,* highly regarded as a supper club as well as a restaurant by local Sanjuaneros.

For good mainland jazz stop by the *Ocho Puertas, The Red Door,* or the *Owl* in old San Juan. *La Carreta* on De Diego Ave. has a Spanish guitar and piano.

Increasing in popularity are the smaller places where you can eat and drink in a dim East 52nd Street blur to the "stylings" of various vocalists and pianists.

Stateside jazz players are piano stylists at *La Botella,* one of the more popular of these places.

If you like this sort of thing, duck into the *Verney's Uptown* at stop 19 or at *Al's Little Club,* Stop 23 on on Ponce de Leon.

La Ronde Cocktail Lounge at

384

Balconies overlook the Danish roofs of Christiansted, St. Croix while the hills of St. Thomas look down on Magens Bay, whose protected strand is the Virgin Islands candidate for the title of "World's Most Beautiful Beach".

In the tranquil Leewards, Sint Maarten's quaint Dutch capital of Phillipsburg is only two streets wide; English Harbor, Antigua's shrine of British history, is so tightly land-locked that you need a chart to find its entrance.

Stop 11 has more of the same, only the piano is an organ and may remind you of intermission at Loew's Valencia Theatre.

The real *aficionados* of steel bands, mambo, cha cha cha and other rhythmic delights congregate at *El Afro*, Stop 10 or at *El Calypso*, Stop 22. The clubs open at 9 and stay open until 5 a.m. Dancing from 10 on.

Other late spots include *The Gallery* near the El San Juan Hotel for a night of escape from the big hotel going-ons; and *The Stage Door* at 56 San José Street where during the small hours local musicians and visitors from the hotels join in lively jazz sessions.

SHOPPING

If you are looking for bargains in imported perfumes, porcelain, glassware, watches and the like, you should go to St. Thomas (half an hour away by air), Haiti, Curaçao; Puerto Rico is not a free port. If you want standard American stuff, San Juan has it all in its well-stocked department stores: *Padin, International Department Store, New York Department Store* and even *Sears Roebuck* and *Woolworth's*. But you probably didn't come to Puerto Rico to buy Grand Rapids Furniture or New England percale sheets. The fun of shopping in Puerto Rico is in looking for unusual buys in local handicrafts: hand-embroidered clothing, hand-carved wood and tortoise shell, hand-woven straw, hand-painted fabrics, hand-designed ceramics. If you want to see what local artists are up to, go to the *Galeria Campeche*, recently opened at 153 San Sebastián in old San Juan. There are four salons devoted to exhibitions of painting, sculpture and books by Puerto Rican artists, and the artists themselves run the place. Other art galleries in the old city: *Caribbean* at 105 Fortaleza, *San Juan* at 257 Cruz and *Medina* at 200 Cristo Street.

DON ROBERTO'S, at Calle Cristo 205 in Old San Juan, is another place to browse among the creations of local artists. The copper jewelry here was designed by the proprietor, and you'll find enough variety in the local carvings and paintings to suggest many gift possibilities.

CASA CAVANAGH. San Juan branch of this well-known St. Thomas shop has original dynastry fashions for women and men and Puerto Rican dolls, hats and handicrafts. Ask to see their Siamese silks and water buffalo sandals for an unusual gift. On Cristo Street.

DOLPHIN COURT. Another Cristo Street shop, this one is near the chapel in a restored Spanish building. Table mats, drapes, lamp shades and hand-embroidered slip covers with gay Puerto Rican designs. Ask Emilia de San Juan (an immigrant from Boston) to show you how the looms work.

TIMI'S. His Tortoise-shell originals at 200 Tetuan should not be missed. These are the best tortoiseshell creations we came across in the Caribbean. The artist is John Timiriasieff, a Californian transplanted to Puerto Rico, and the range of objects he has designed and executed in tortoise shell shows a lively imagination and skill. Timi has a branch shop at the International Airport as well.

MARTHA SLEEPER'S SHOP, 106 Fortaleza in the Old Town, features originally-designed tropical wear, hand-screened fabrics, "voodoo" women's and men's shirts mostly designed by the very charming Martha herself once a Broadway and Hollywood actress, plus a good selection of native handicrafts and Spanish antiques. The shop is as enchanting as the merchandise; it's in a three-centuries-old building with a patio and bar. The drinks are on Martha.

GALERÍA DE LA ANTILLAS, in the guest house of the Caribe Hilton Hotel, is one of those shops you'll want to come back to, to see if you've missed anything. Good selection of sculpture, painting, hand-woven fabrics and ceramics by talented Angel Botello Barros, co-owner of the gallery with Lorraine Dora. Her contribution is hand-painted and hand-embroidered clothing, original and imaginative.

GIUSTI CARIBBEAN SHOP is just across from the Caribe Hilton; they also have hand-painted dresses and fabrics along with an exotic selection of stuff from India and Siam.

THE WEST INDIES MAHOGANY AND NOVELTY GIFT SHOP and **ROSITA'S GIFT SHOP** are two other places worth a look in the vicinity of the Caribe Hilton.

PUERTO RICAN POTTERY, on the Paseo Cavadonga opposite the Y.M.C.A. is headquarters for local ceramics and china. This is a good place for those well known Puerto Rican jugs. They will make things to your personal order here, and you can watch the process or even do it yourself.

INDIA HOUSE, 101 Fortaleza has imported Indian and oriental jewelry, trinkets, clothing.

Puerto Rican straw work, known as *sabutan,* is among the best in the West Indies, made from a reed which is both strong and pliable. You'll find it in almost every handicraft store we've mentioned and under various forms: place mats, screens, bags, lampshades; one of the buys of Puerto Rico.

NOTRE DAME INDUSTRIAL SCHOOL at 256 Ponce de Leon Avenue at the Puerta de Tierra is the oldest handicraft school and shop in the island. Here you will see that lovely Puerto Rican drawn work and hand embroidery in handsome lunch and dinner linens and charming handmade dresses for little girls.

NANCY NANCE, 650 José Marti Street, has more of the same for sale.

THE EVERGLADE SHOP at 205 Fortaleza is another store of similar type.

FERIA DE LOS JUGUETES at 318 Avenida de Diego is worth trying if you are looking for an unusual toy. Hand-painted Miguel, in wood, not plastic, will be happy in the arms of any child, and there are plenty of other imaginative things to appeal to kids and their parents. Better save the Swiss music boxes for St. Thomas, however; they're cheaper in the free port shops.

PUERTO RICO

SPORTS AND OTHER ATTRACTIONS. *Swimming* at island beaches and in hotel pools leads the long list of aquatic sports.

Next comes *deep sea fishing*, which has undergone a boom in Puerto Rico as the waters off Florida have been depleted. You can make arrangements to fish for marlin, albacore, bonito, tarpon, sailfish and other through your hotel.

Or you can write to Captain Art Wills, c/o Caribe Anglers, P.O. Box 1133, San Juan. He has boats for charter, fully equipped for as low as $60 per day, and he will give lessons to neophytes at no increase in charge. *Fresh water fishing* is also popular in the well-stocked mountain streams and lakes of Puerto Rico. Bigmouth bass and catfish abound.

Boating and sailing activities have their headquarters in the yacht clubs of San Juan, Ponce and Mayaguez. Fishing boats and other pleasure craft are available through Cangrejos Yacht Club, La Parguera, Caribe Anglers and Captain Wills. Island sloops can be rented for sailing at Las Croabas on the east coast. Sailing boats also leave the San Juan Intercontinental beach and La Parguera for cruises around the island. *Sail-a-Day* calls for you at your hotel for a day's sail to a deserted island off the east coast.

Water skiing attracts more devotees each year. Luquillo Beach and La Rada Hotel are the best places for this; the latter has a school for beginners.

Tennis may be played at hotel and club courts and on the public courts of Rio Piedras. Most impressive are the cork-turf ones at the Caribe Hilton.

There are two nine-hole *golf* courses, one at El Morro, right in San Juan, one at the Berwind Country Club in Rio Piedras. The latest, and one of the most beautiful in the world, is the 27-hole course at the Dorado Beach Hotel. Guest privileges are extended.

There's *skeet and trap shooting* at the Club Metropolitano de Tiro in Rio Piedras. In the mountains, it's El Rancho and Barranguitas Hotels for horses and trails.

Rio Piedras is also the best center for *horseback riding*; see the Sabana Line Stables.

Spectator sports include *horse racing* all year round on Wednesdays, Saturdays, Sundays and holidays at El Commandente in Rio Piedras.

Cockfighting on Saturdays and Sundays throughout the year in the many *galleras* throughout the island. The most convenient cockpit for tourists is the Canta Gallo in the Santurce suburb of San Juan.

Carnival season is in February in the towns around the island, but San Juan waits for June to celebrate carnival with parades, street dancing, public masquerades and general merry-making lasting for about 2 weeks.

The most popular spectator sport is *baseball*. The Puerto Ricans are wild for it. Games are played at night in the ball park near the Hotel Normandie, and the rivalry between San Juan, Santurce, Ponce, Caguas and Mayagüez is fiercer than anything in the U.S.A. The season starts in September and lasts five months, at the end of which the Puerto Rican pennant winner plays the champs of Cuba, Venezuela and Panama in a four-way Caribbean world series. Sightseeing by air is a specialty of Coastal Airways at the Isla Grande Airport.

CULTURAL EVENTS

There are many of these in Puerto Rico, the greatest being the annual *Casals Festival*. This is a three week series of concerts, organized around the great cellist Pablo Casals, now a resident of Puerto Rico. The appearance of this master musician here has made Puerto Rico as famous in the musical world as Prades, the little French town where Casals has played for many years, refusing to return to his native Spain as long as Franco is in power. Casals, who celebrated his 86th birthday on December 29, 1962, had a heart attack just before the '57 Festival, but recovered completely. Among the artists who have appeared at the Casals Festivals are Yehudi Menuhin and Jascha Heifetz, violinists; Victoria de Los Angeles, soprano; Rudolf Serkin, pianist, and the renowned Budapest String Quartet. The Festival is usually held the first three weeks in June. Announcements of soloists and programs emanate from The Casals Festival Office at 666 Fifth Avenue, New York, where tickets for the series may be bought. They are also sold through Mayfair Travel Service, 119 West 57 Street, New York. These offices will also have information on the Opera season, and the San Juan Drama Festival which brings Broadway stars and hit shows to San Juan during the summer. A new addition is the International Music Institute which has its headquarters in San Germán and roams the island giving recitals and concerts throughout the summer; also active around the island are the Puerto Rico Symphony Orchestra and Teatro del Pueblo.

EXPLORING PUERTO RICO

When you see San Juan from the air: the moss-covered battlements of El Morro, the shadowy precincts of the Old Town, the tides of ultra-modern concrete and glass streaming east and south into the green countryside, you already begin to sense the special charm of Puerto Rico and its capital. Nowhere in the Caribbean does the old meet the new with such dramatic impact. When you land at International Airport at Isla Verde, you may even be a bit disappointed. It's almost too new, too shiny. You might as well be in Chicago or Miami, except that this bustling major terminal outshines everything on the mainland but Idlewild, which was still on the drawing boards when Isla Verde opened for business. Perhaps you were trying to escape from glass and gloss and the relentless efficiency of public address systems? Even so, you cannot walk down the immense hall of this terminal without responding to its grand, aspiring proportions and what they symbolize: the aspirations of Operation Bootstrap, the renaissance of "the stricken land."

PUERTO RICO

Unregenerate antiquarians, be patient. In a matter of minutes you can be away from this lofty temple of our times, exploring the shrines of an earlier day. The place to do that is in the old town of San Juan, and as you descend from the bus at the Plaza de Colón, the pearly gates are nigh. You will be glad to know that the buses or *guagas* are not allowed to penetrate beyond this point into the narrow streets of the Old Town. So, having cast an eye at the statue of Columbus, which was erected in the Plaza in 1893 to commemorate the 400th anniversary of his discovery of Puerto Rico, you can step into the past with the risk of mayhem reduced. There are some cars in Old San Juan, but not enough to spoil the charm of the old streets, some of which are still paved with blue stone, brought to Puerto Rico as ballast in the galleons of Spain.

Actually situated on an islet just off shore from the "mainland" of Puerto Rico, Old San Juan was founded in 1521. It has not remained untouched by subsequent centuries. You'll find old Spanish buildings juxtaposed with modern houses, office buildings, smart shops, but somehow the old town, still partially encircled by its walls begun in 1630, preserves the atmosphere of 16th and 17th-century Spain. In this respect it is more attractive even than the old parts of Havana. The best way to savor the atmosphere is simply to wander through the seven square blocks of cobbled streets, noting the wrought-iron balconies, the blue-tiled patios, the little details of sight, sound and smell that remind you everywhere: this is still a Spanish city.

The chief tourist attraction of Old San Juan is El Morro, the great fortress which the Spanish constructed at the northwest tip of the city from 1533 to 1586. Covering more than 200 acres, rising 145 feet above the Atlantic, this great bastion of colonial Spain remained impregnable from the sea even when attacked in 1595 by such doughty foes as Drake and Hawkins. It was taken by the English from the land side and held briefly in 1598. The Spanish continued to improve the fortifications, and it wasn't until 1783 that El Morro was completed. It is still in active use as a fort, garrisoned by soldiers of the Antilles Forces of the United States Army. A national historic site, it may be visited on scheduled guided tours which leave the main entrance of El Morro four times daily: at 9:30 and 11:30 a.m., 2 and 2:30 p.m. There's a splendid view from the ramparts, of course, and the exploration of the labyrinthine tunnels of the fort is fascinating. *Not recommended, however, for anyone with a heart condition or an allergy to climbing.* The guides, employees of the National Park Service, are highly qualified and will trace the history of the fortress for you. During the tour you will notice that the precincts of El Morro shelter a most unusual golf course, ingeniously laid out with fairways replacing the ancient moat, flanked by the castle walls. The nine-hole course is reserved for military personnel and their guests, but may also be used by the public. Ask your hotel manager about this, especially if you are anxious to twist your wrist on the celebrated Hole in the Moat.

Near the main entrance of El Morro is San José Church, the oldest Christian place of worship still in use in the Western Hemisphere. Started by the Dominicans in 1523, the church preserves its vaulted Gothic ceilings, a rare survival of authentic medieval architecture in the New World. Ponce de León lay buried here for three and a half centuries before his mortal remains were transferred to the Cathedral. His family coat of arms still hangs beneath the ceiling of the main altar. Outside on the plaza Ponce himself stands in brazen glory, his statue fashioned from bronze cannons captured from the British in 1797. Next to the church is the old Santo Domingo Convent, built by the Dominican Friars at the same time as San José Church. A handsome example of 16th-century Spanish colonial architecture, it was taken over by the government in 1810 when the Dominican order was dissolved. The friars who inhabited this monastery would doubtless be astonished to know that their rooms were being occupied by personnel of the United States Army.

Casa Blanca or the Ponce House at the foot of Calle San Sebastian near the ramparts of El Morro, was built in 1523 as a residence for Ponce de León while the governor was away looking for the Fountain of Youth in Florida. He found not the fountain, but presumably the secret of eternal life. In any event Ponce de León did not live to move into this beautiful house. His descendants lived here for two centuries until 1773 when the Ponce family sold the house to the Spanish Government. It became the home of the Spanish military commander, and is now the official residence of the commander of the Antilles Forces of the United States Army, attached to the army post of Fort Brooke. As loyal American tourists, we cannot refrain from hoping that other quarters for the general will some day be found so that the public will be permitted more than just a peek at the gardens of this splendid house, which as a part of Puerto Rico's rich heritage, should be a national monument open to all.

La Fortaleza, the official residence of the Governor of Puerto Rico, is open to the public, and well worth a visit. It's just a short two block walk to the left of Casa Blanca as you face the bay. En route you will pass San Juan Gate, completed in 1641 and once the main entrance to the walled city of San Juan. The view of the bay, of Casa Blanca, and the massive ramparts of the town is most impressive from here, and it is not hard to imagine the colonial governor arriving in his official barge, bowing his head in prayer like everyone else who entered the city by this gate, crowned by an oratory, and proceeding a short distance left of the gate to La Fortaleza.

Begun in 1533 as a fort to protect the city, this remarkable building, half-palace, half-fortress, was burned by the Dutch in 1625, rebuilt in 1640, enlarged and restored to its present state in 1847. Oldest executive mansion in the Western hemisphere, it has been the residence of 170 governors and the seat of Puerto Rico's government for more than four centuries. Its two 16th-century towers are among the oldest military constructions in the New World. Sitting down to a state dinner in La Fortaleza's splendid candlelit dining room in June 1958, American Vice-President Nixon said, "I couldn't think of a better place to be." His host, dynamic Puerto Rican Governor Luis Muñoz Marin, replied with that age-old expression of Spanish hospitality, enduring heritage of Puerto Rico: "*Está en su casa* (you are in your own house)."

You will probably not see the dining room, but you can pass the wrought-iron gates, see the lovely terraced gardens, the magnificent mahogany stairway, the marble floors of the reception rooms, the mosaic-studded chapel, the room once used by the Puerto Rican treasury for the storage of gold, and other rooms of this fine executive mansion. The public may visit La Fortaleza from 8 a.m. to noon and from 1 to 5 p.m. Monday through Friday. Tours are conducted by special aides.

Catholic Shrine

Proceed, still on foot, down Calle del Cristo with its blue ballast stones, past the Cathedral to which you'll return later, to the Santo Cristo Chapel at the bottom of the street. This chapel was built to mark the spot where a horse and rider in 1753 leaped over the 70 foot bluff on which it is built. Since the rider wasn't killed, it was obvious that there must have been divine intervention; hence the chapel. Now back up Calle del Cristo to the corner of Calle de la Luna and the great Catholic shrine of Puerto Rico, the Cathedral of San Juan Bautista. Begun as early as 1519, the Cathedral has risen several times like a phoenix from its ashes. The present building dates from 1802 but conserves Gothic details dating from 1540. In it you will find the tomb of Juan Ponce de León, numerous mementoes of *los reyes Catolicos,* Ferdinand and Isabella, and, in a glass case opposite Ponce's tomb, the body of a converted and martyred Roman centurion, St. Pio, once buried in the catacombs of Rome, now seen in the light of the New World. Ask to see the Renaissance madonna and the 16th-century chalices, part of the cathedral treasure which is shown to visitors on request.

You will have noticed by this time that following the streets of the Old Town as they wind up and down hills is good for the ankles and the stomach muscles. Half way between the Cathedral and San Juan Gate, you will find one of the original staircase streets which has not succumbed to exigencies of automotive traffic. This is the Callejon Las Monjas, and you'll be grateful as generations have been before you for the help of the stairs in negotiating this steep ascent.

There are one or two more sights which you should see before abandoning the Old Town for the refreshing attractions of your hotel bar and beach. La Casa Del Libro at 255 Cristo Street is a superb museum of rare books in an 18th-century house, so beautifully restored and furnished that you should see it even if you never learned to read. It's open to the public from 11 a.m. to 5 p.m. every day but Sunday. The Alcaldia, north of the Plaza de Armas, may look familiar to you if you've travelled in Spain. It's an exact reproduction of the municipal building in Madrid, built here in the 18th century. It houses a small museum of San Juan's history. The patio is lovely and the whole building, with flower vendors selling their wares in the Spanish arcade, is a delightful example of traditional Spanish architecture and color.

If you are an addict of military architecture, you will want to visit the Castillo de San Cristóbal, built in the 17th century to protect San Juan from any land attack from the east. It has gun emplacements, ramparts, and a courtyard similar to those of El Morro. The average tourist, having seen the latter, will probably be content with a glance at San Cristóbal's massive exterior before continuing back to the Plaza del Colón. Here the city walls of Old San Juan terminated in a gate which no longer exists. Just south of the Plaza are the harbor piers and the colorful waterfront of Old San Juan. From here you can take a ferry boat ride to Cataño across the bay, an excursion whose chief rewards are refreshing breezes and a splendid view of El Morro and the Old Town. (The 10¢ ferry ride, a 15¢ ride from Catano to the University of Puerto Rico, and another dime for a *guagua* to your hotel makes up the popular 35¢ tour of a section of San Juan's suburbs.) To the east of Plaza del Colón the island becomes an isthmus with three major thoroughfares, Avenida Ponce de León, Avenida Muñoz Rivera and Avenida Fernandez Juncos leading out of the Old Town to the booming business and tourist sections of Miramar, Condado and fashionable Santurce. Muñoz Rivera Park, the Escambrón, Normandie and Caribe Hilton Hotels, though geographically at the eastern end of San Juan Island and less than two miles from the Plaza Colón are already centuries removed from Old San Juan in appearance and in spirit. As far as San Juan is concerned, Operation Bootstrap is the Drang nach Osten.

East of Old San Juan

Once east of Plaza del Colón, distances are too great and sights too decentralized to warrant further exploration afoot. You can go by bus, taxi, or *publico* to places of interest along Ponce de Leon Avenue. They include the stately Institute of Puerto Rican Culture with its exhibits and fine art collection and El Capitolio, Puerto Rico's imposing white Georgia marble capitol, a neo-Renaissance building, whose interior, housing the Senate and the House of Representatives, is lavishly adorned with Italian marble and travertine. Just west of El Capitolio is another copy of a renaissance building, this one more painstakingly authentic, the Casa de España. This is an exclusive private club, but you can get permission to see the patio and gardens, decorated with ceramic work and tiles imported from Spain and decked out with a copy of the celebrated Fountain of the Lions in the Alhambra at Granada. The royal coat-of-arms which you will see on the exterior wall to the right of the porte-cochère once crowned one of the gates of the old city. East of the YMCA on Ponce de León Avenue, the Ateneo Puertorriqueño is a cultural center with an interesting small collection of old paintings, prints and books. The famous School of Tropical Medicine, long operated jointly by Columbia University and the University of Puerto Rico, is east of the Capitol. It is now a part of the University of Puerto Rico whose main campus (see below) is at Rio Piedras, south of San Juan. You will probably be tempted to photograph the old walls of

Fort San Gerónimo, whose crumbling, sun-mellowed texture provides such a striking contrast with the spit-and-polish facade of the Caribe Hilton Hotel immediately to the west. Built in 1771, San Gerónimo staved off a major English attack in 1797. It has been restored and now houses a museum of Spanish military armor and weapons. A pleasant place to stroll far from the madding traffic (no cars allowed) is Muñoz Rivera Park with its tropical flowers, shrubs and trees. Near the entrance you'll see the old Powder House (Polvorín), now the Museum of Natural History, containing stuffed and live specimens of Puerto Rican fauna in addition to minerals and archeological exhibits. Opposite the park on Muñoz Rivera Avenue is the Sixto Escobar Stadium, named in honor of Puerto Rico's bantam weight boxing champion of the world. This is the scene of those fabulous night baseball games. The place only seats 15,000 but it makes more noise than the Yankee Stadium and Polo Grounds combined. If you want to see the Puerto Ricans at a fever pitch, go to one of these fierce contests of *beisbol*. If you want to see them in a quieter mood, cross the bridge to Cabras Island where you will find a popular picnic area with swings and thatched huts, a 17th century Spanish fort, El Cañuelo, in picturesque ruins, lovely views of the bay and the Old City, and local inhabitants enjoying the great outdoors. You'll probably be the only tourist there.

More frequented by travelers is Boca de Cangrejos, a beach and picnic resort east of booming Santurce near the spectacular International Airport. Beautifully situated on lagoon and sea, Boca de Cangrejos offers excellent bathing and fishing and a chance to explore the beautiful Submarine Gardens through whose coral caves and mountains swim schools of brilliant tropical fish. Glass bottom boats leave twice a day from the pier, but only between May and September. Center of activity in Boca is the Cangrejos Yacht Club whose members keep power boats moored in the lagoon near the clubhouse. A public bus passes the lockers, showers and fine restaurant of the new public beach in the area.

If you're looking for those technicolor local markets, shining with mangoes, avocadoes, passion fruit, peppers, mountain apples and all the rich produce of the tropics, you'll find two that will keep your shutters fluttering in Santurce and Rio Piedras. The first district with its shiny shops and office buildings you will already have passed through, driving down the main drag, Avenida de Ponce de León. Santurce is new, gleaming, fashionable. Its "progress" from tranquil suburb to booming metropolitan hub is the story of 20th-century San Juan. Away from the traffic of Ponce de León Avenue, you'll still find a few old Spanish estates, vestiges of a quieter day, but most of them have been subdivided. Smart modern houses are the mark of residential Santurce today. One local problem is thievery. Puerto Rican second story men are apparently among the most agile in the world; the walls of exclusive Santurce villas do not exclude them. Puerto Rican friends of ours who live on the "best street" of Santurce had been robbed twice in five months, once in broad daylight with the lady of the house at home. In the meantime, Bootstrap is licking the problem with huge low-income housing complexes like the great project at *Las Casas,* southeast of Santurce; with new employment opportunities; with new efforts to elevate a standard of living already doubled in the past 15 years.

Sparkling Rio Piedras

The accomplishments of Bootstrap are probably nowhere more manifest than they are in *Rio Piedras,* once a quiet town, now a southern suburb of San Juan, a bustling center of new industry, surrounded by the most modern factories. No smog-filled depressed conditions here. Rio Piedras is sparkling clean. One of the big low income residence developments is here: the San José Housing Project. The University of Puerto Rico is here with its attractive campus and museum, offering guided tours to visitors. Founded in 1903, it has more than 17,000 students enrolled, making it eighth in size among U.S. land grant colleges. Among its schools and facilities: an important Agricultural Experiment Station which anyone interested in the flowers, trees, crops and agricultural economy of Puerto Rico will want to visit, as well as a new atomic research center. For the industrial equivalent of the experimentation section, visit the School of Industrial Arts, a splendid craft and trade school where young Puerto Ricans can learn to be mechanics, printers, butchers, bakers and candlestick makers, the last in one of the best wood turning shops we've seen in years. The bakery and printing shop are also worth a visit; the machine shop rivals those of America's best technical high schools. This is no minor manual training outfit; it's the biggest school of industrial arts in the world. As one university wit put it, "A little isle shall lead them."

Before extending your explorations "out on the island", as the Puerto Ricans say, perhaps you will want to see another industrial process in action, the distillation of rum. If you are planning to go to Arecibo or Ponce, you can save this experience for the Ron Rico or Don Q Rum distilleries which operate respectively in those two towns. Otherwise drive to the little town of Palo Seco (Pale Dry!) on the northwestern shore of the Bay of San Juan where the Carioca and Bacardi people will show you how sugar is transformed into rum and ply you with copious draughts of same, after which the view across the bay to El Morro and San Juan seems even more romantic than usual, shimmering, as it were, in a golden, rum-colored haze.

Out on the Island

Puerto Rico has about 4,000 miles of good roads, and you could spend weeks exploring the island. Most tourists will not have that much time, so we suggest the following short tours which you can drive yourself, arrange through one of the agencies indicated in How to Get About, or take with your own group in a publico. First tour, and an absolute must, is to El Yunque, "The Anvil", in the northeastern corner of the island. You can do it easily in a half day, but the superb tropical rain forest which clothes the slopes of El Yunque is so beautiful that you may want to be more leisurely about it. You take Route 3 from San Juan via Carolina, Loíza and Rio Grande to Palmer, then Route 191 to the top of El Yunque, 3,496 feet high. As you drive you ascend into a cool magical world of giant ferns, exotic trees, wild orchids, green vines, brilliantly-colored parrots, splashing mountain waterfalls. You are in the Caribbean National Forest, one of the most luxuriant in the world thanks to 200 inches of rainfall per year. When you look down from the observation tower on the sea and palmy plains of Puerto Rico, you'll be astonished that two such different worlds can exist within so small a compass. There's a restaurant here, whose terrace affords a splendid panorama, and there are cabins for those who want to stay overnight. More than one tourist has altered his plans here in this lush rain forest, staying to ride horseback on the mountain trails and swim in the cold mountain pool.

Returning to San Juan take the same route as far as Rio Grande. At this point, if you want to swim at one of the most beautiful beaches in the whole Caribbean area, turn right to Luquillo Beach, a palm-shaded, gently-sloping, sweeping crescent of sand without peer in Puerto Rico and with few peers anywhere else.

PUERTO RICO

At Rio Grande, the scenic way back to San Juan is Route 187, following the coast to Loíza Aldea, a charming colonial village whose church of St. Patrick was the first in the western hemisphere to be dedicated to Ireland's patron saint. Take the old hand-poled ferry across the Loíza River and follow the coastal road. The spectacular ocean views, the rural communities, as primitive as the hand-poled ferry, make this a delightful drive. San Juan is just a few miles—and several centuries—away.

Rum and Pineapple Route

Our second tour, an all day affair, could be termed the rum and pineapple route, since it will permit you to visit both a distillery and a pineapple cannery. Take Route 2 west out of San Juan through Bayamón, Vega Baja and Manatí. Branch right on Route 681 beyond Manatí and follow the coastal road to *Arecibo*. Settled in 1556, Arecibo is one of Puerto Rico's oldest towns. Four miles east of the town you can visit an Indian cave, used as a place of worship before the Spaniards came, its walls decorated with pre-Columbian drawings and carvings in low relief. There's a splendid white sand beach near the old Spanish lighthouse if you want to swim, but you'll have to change behind a tree; there are no bath houses. Arecibo is a center for deep-sea fishermen; boats may be chartered in town. Fresh-water fishermen also like to try their luck near here in the lakes made by Dos Bocas and Caonillas dams, two of the largest in Puerto Rico. There are also dozens of mountain caves and ruined Spanish sugar mills to explore. But the chief tourist magnet is the Ron Rico Rum Distillery, Puerto Rico's biggest, which welcomes visitors with open vats. After a few *aperitifs* here, you can lunch at the Hotel Mir, El Gran Café, or the Arecibo Country Club (see above: Hotels and Restaurants), take a quick glance at a sugar mill, and be off in a cloud of granules on Route 2 back to Manatí, the heart of the pineapple country. Here you take Route 670 toward Vega Baja, stopping at the Silver River Pineapple Company whose cannery will show you the works and regale you with chilled juice. If you want a swim after all this heavy sightseeing, *Vega Baja* is deservedly proud of its wonderful beach with the quaintest dressing rooms you've ever seen. They're made of palm thatch and can be rented from one of the local *cantinas* which will also provide you with liquid and solid refreshment. So, pined, wined and dined, back to San Juan on Route 2.

PUERTO RICO

These are but two possibilities among scores of possible tours which can be arranged for you. The most fun, of course, is to get a road map, plan your own tour, hire a car or publico and be off. In organizing such a tour, here are some places of more than ordinary tourist interest which you won't want to overlook as you explore Puerto Rico: *Aguada* on the northwest coast was founded in 1506, claims to be the place where Columbus first set foot on Puerto Rican soil and marks the spot at the foot of Calle Colón where the Admiral's foot presumably stepped. *Aguadilla*, a few miles to the north, disputes the foregoing claim, has its own monument to tell you that it was Aguadillan soil that first received the celebrated footprint. Aguadilla is a center of the island's thriving straw hat industry, also a beach resort highly regarded by the Puerto Ricans themselves. The Montemar (see Hotels) with its ocean-view terrace is the best place for a stopover here. Excellent swimming beach. The town is just a few miles south of Ramey Air Base, one of Uncle Sam's bastions of defense in the Caribbean.

Aguas Buenas. Half an hour from San Juan up into the cool mountains. Good hiking trails and bridal paths leading to mountain caves. Unless you are equipped for camping, you had better not plan to spend the night here.

Barranquitas. A charming mountain town almost in the center of Puerto Rico between San Juan and Ponce, this is a popular year-round resort because of its cool climate. Birth and burial place of the great statesman Luis Muñoz Rivera (1859-1916), father of the present governor, the town has the aspect of a national shrine. Muñoz Rivera's home is now a library and museum, open to the public. If the door is locked, ask anyone to direct you to the curator. The El Barranquitas hotel (see above) is a famous resort hostelry, center of local tourist activity.

Cabo Rojo, once the lair of the pirate Roberto Cofresí, is a quiet town on the dry southwestern coast, known by the Puerto Ricans as the "desert" country. About eight miles south of Cabo Rojo are the marine salt beds with a commercial production of some 12,000 tons of salt annually. The salt, washed up by the sea and drying in the blazing sun, looks like fields of glistening snow. You'll want your dark glasses.

Caparra, just a few minutes south of San Juan, is historically interesting as the site of the first settlement in Puerto Rico. You can still see the foundations of Ponce de León's first house, built in 1509.

Dorado Beach, 20 miles west of San Juan, site of the splendid resort project constructed by Laurance Rockefeller in cooperation with Puerto Rico's tourist expansion program. (See above: Hotels).

Fajardo. On the northeast coast of the island, this fishing and sailing center changed hands three times during the Spanish-American War. Nearby is Los Croabas with crystal clear skin diving waters.

Sugar and Sharks

Guánica was the site of the American landing on the south coast in 1898. Good beach with dressing rooms and *cantinas*. Picturesque old Spanish lighthouse. There's a sugar central here which saw stormy labor troubles back in the thirties. One lawyer, imported by the company from America, went swimming and was promptly dispatched by a shark, giving rise almost immediately to one of those newsy *plenas* or popular songs which ends with the refrain:

Tintorera del mar, tintorera del mar, tintorera del mar,
Se ha comido al abogado de la Guanica Central.
The shark of the sea, the shark of the sea
Ate up the lawyer of the sugar companee.

Hormigueros. A southwestern village a few miles south of Mayagüez, it is famous for its Shrine of Our Lady of Monserrate, who, in the 17th century responded to a peasant's call for help and saved him from the charge of a mad bull. An annual pilgrimage takes place every September 8 with the faithful climbing the church steps on their knees to solicit the Virgin's favor.

Humacao is a bustling industrial town near the eastern coast of the island. It's like Operation Bootstrap in microcosm, gleaming with fresh paint and new buildings, producing tons of sugar in the most up-to-date refineries, and providing a dramatic contrast to sleepier, undeveloped villages in the neighborhood.

Jájome, the attractive summer residence of the Governor of Puerto Rico is located on the Jájome Highway between Cayey and Guayama, an old south coast Puerto Rican city, founded in 1790. The 16-mile highway crosses Jájome Alto, the northern range of the Cordillera Central in superbly-graded serpentine style with more than 250 curves and switchbacks winding through marvelous tropical flowers and flowering shrubs. The road itself is universally admired by engineers, and the scenery makes it a top flight favorite with tourists. Opposite the

Governor's beautifully-landscaped summer residence is a replica of the celebrated Grotto of Lourdes.

Mayagüez, with a population pushing 100,000 is the third city
of Puerto Rico, smack in the center of the western coast. It
is the needlework center of the island, a good place to pick up
some of that lovely embroidery and drawn work. Just north
of town is the Federal Agricultural Experiment Station with
the largest collection of tropical plants in the New World and
the West Coast campus of the University of Puerto Rico. The
splendidly-landscaped grounds are full of exotic trees: ilang
ilang, cacao, cinnamon, green and yellow bamboo, and wonderful tropical lilies and orchids. If you like flowers, shrubs and
exotic plants, this will be one of your chief memories of the
Caribbean.

Phosphorus and Fish

Parguera is a delightful fishing village on the southwestern
coast, popular with visitors, but still "unspoiled". You can rent
fishing boats and tackle here, eat wonderful fresh seafood at
the Villa Parguera Hotel or in a number of unpretentious little
shacks where they know how to grill lobsters and fry *pescao.*
The great attraction here is Phosphorescent Bay, glimmering
and flashing mysteriously in the night. The slightest agitation
sets off a shower of greenish phosphorescent sparks. Draw
your arm through the water and you describe an arc of darting
quicksilver flame. Impressive on any night, the phosphorescent
effects are most striking during the dark of the moon. You
can arrange for a motor boat tour of the bay at the Villa
Parguera.

Forever Spain

Ponce, the "Pearl of the South", is the second city of Puerto
Rico, and its nacreous luster has now been doubled with the
opening of the $3,500,000 Ponce Intercontinental Hotel and the
construction of an 18-hole golf course by the Ponce Country
Club with the assistance of PRIDCO, the Puerto Rico Industrial
Development Company. With a population nearing 150,000,
Ponce is already an important port and tourist center. Bring
your color film to this handsome Spanish city. You'll want to
shoot the two lovely plazas, each one dominated by the graceful
form of Our Lady of Guadalupe Cathedral which rises between
them. The Parque de Bombas, Ponce's ancient firehouse is the
most-photographed single object in Puerto Rico. When you see
its red and black stripes, punctuated by green and yellow orna-

ments, you'll add to its reputation. Those one hoss shays at the side of the plaza are for rent, and you'll enjoy riding through this charming provincial capital in the Spanish style and pomp which suit its colonial atmosphere. Note the *rejos*, balconies and other wrought iron details on the old Spanish houses. The local market and waterfront are exceptionally colorful, and the Playa de Ponce, about three miles south of the city, will be developed as a first rate beach by the time your guide goes to press. If you still haven't seen the process which turns sugar cane into demon rum, here's another chance, free samples and all, at Ponce's Don Q Rum Distillery.

San Germán in the southwest sector of the island is one of the most attractive towns in Puerto Rico and in the West Indies. Founded on its present site in 1570, it keeps the look of a little Spanish town, the special ambiance of Mediterranean civilization. Although its population is under 10,000, San Germán was once the rival of San Juan, a sort of second capital of Puerto Rico. But while San Juan is pulling hard on its bootstraps, San Germán remains relatively untouched by the innovations of a newer time. When you visit the lovely Porta Cocli (Gate of Heaven) Church, you are back at the dawn of the Renaissance. Built in 1606, it is the oldest church in the territorial U.S.A. to remain intact, its altar, its carved wooden pillars, its heavy entrance doors just as they were nearly five centuries ago. It now houses a museum of colonial religious art. You will enjoy rambling about among the old buildings, one of which on the Calle Luna, now houses the pleasant El Oasis Hotel. When evening falls, the plaza in front of the church becomes a *paseo* in the old Spanish style. Watch the animated communal strolling here and you are suddenly transported to the *ramblas* of Gerona, Barcelona and Castile. Here, more than anywhere else in this thriving Latin-American island community, you will realize that, bootstrap or no bootstrap, there are parts of Puerto Rico that remain forever Spain.

THE VIRGIN ISLANDS

Shopping Lanes in Shangri-La

Pastel-colored, old world Danish towns rise incongruously from blue Caribbean bays; stream-lined modern buildings gleam amidst a thousand tropic blooms: these are the U.S. Virgin Islands.

You may have heard them described in such provocative terms as "Left Bank of the Caribbean," "St. Germain des Prés of the New World," "West Indies Greenwich Village." The point was well made—some years ago. But the new order changeth, yielding place to the old.

In the great urge toward the sun that followed World War II, the Virgins were rediscovered by as motley a crew as ever sailed the Caribbean. Pre-beatniks arrived on these silver shores, followed by exurbanite ulcer cases, refugees from New England country clubs, and a liberal sprinkling of the inter-mediate sex. The last group has already migrated, with en-couragement from the wise Virgin Islanders, to fruit-laden Capri, gay, gay St. Tropez and the Greek isle of Mykonos. The

402

ulcer-country club set has stayed on, content with their idyllic combination of slowed-down activity and stepped up American plumbing. As why should they not be? They have the exoticism of the tropics, all the comforts of home, and free port liquor prices to palliate the high cost of living. Rum is one dollar a fifth; you've never been to such parties!

As for the beatniks, you'd never recognize them. They are keeping shops, running hotels, discovering the charms of double entry bookkeeping, and behaving like perfect squares. The philistines have won the battle for normalcy, hands down. And the Virgins have emerged in this year of grace as very respectable Danish-American girls, immaculate, well-groomed, addicted to comfort, and highly-efficient at getting it. The price is high, but as one ex-New Englander told us, "It's wuth it to get away from the Boston and Maine."

The Three Saints

There are three principal Virgin Islands, St. Thomas, St. Croix and St. John (strange names for Virgins!) plus about 37 lesser isles and cays. The three main islands are delightfully different from each other. Quiet, agricultural, exclusive St. Croix is as different from cosmopolitan St. Thomas as Westchester County is from Manhattan. St. John again is utterly different: a splendid tropic wilderness with a handful of resorts at its fringes. They lie 40 miles east of Puerto Rico like jewels on the hilt of that Antillean scimitar curving southward to the Spanish Main.

Columbus first sighted these sand-fringed volcanic cones in 1493 and named them in memory of St. Ursula's 11,000 virgins who died in an epic defense of their chastity. A less pious admiral, Sir Francis Drake, rebaptised the islands a century later in honor of a more worldly virgin, Elizabeth the First of England.

The Virgins have always been more accessible than their 11,001 prototypes. In the course of five centuries they have been ravished by the Spanish, the French, the English, the Dutch, the Knights of Malta, the Danes, and most recently by the Americans.

The Americans were the only ones who paid for the privilege. The Danes offered the islands to the United States in 1869 for $7,500,000. In 1917, with Kaiser Wilhelm making googoo eyes at the Panama Canal, Uncle Sam finally bought them for $25,000,000. The price, about $300 an acre, was considered scandalously high at the time. With Virgin Islands land now bringing as much as $10,000 an acre, that opinion has been revised.

As elsewhere in the Caribbean, the impingement of several national traditions on a chain of tropical islands has enriched the fabric of life. In 1832 the bustling port of St. Thomas included men of more than 140 different nationalities. Vestiges of this cosmopolitan background strike the visitor today, especially in Virgin Islands architecture. The dominant note is Danish with 17th and 18th-century houses suggesting the charm of a pastel-painted stage set. In addition there are Spanish patios, French ornamental grille work, Dutch doorways, and sloping northern roofs, which, of course, have never been called upon to shed the snows of winter. American contributions are evident in clean-cut new construction which blends admirably with the old, and in the conservation and sensitive remodeling of such landmarks as the magnificent old warehouses of St. Thomas. There is a current building boom, reflecting the prosperity of the tourist trade as the 18th-century boom reflected that of the slave trade. Alexander Hamilton, who grew up on St. Croix, remembered seeing the merchants of St. Thomas carting their money to the bank in wheel barrows. That was in those wild roistering days before the advent of the armored car.

The People

More than 80 per cent of the Virgin Islands' 30,000 inhabitants are colored. They run a gamut of hues from light walnut to deep ebony. They tend to be very tall, long-limbed, and lanky rather like the rangy cowboys of the American southwest. The majority are descendants of kidnapped African slaves who worked the Danish sugar plantations until the emancipation of 1848. They are affable and hospitable. You will sense in them a certain proud consciousness of a new destiny. They are realizing that destiny in an atmosphere which has not been poisoned by the usual long cleavage between whites and blacks. The Americans were welcomed in 1917 and were not equated with the former Danish colonials.

An enlightened American policy has not hesitated to appoint Negroes to important civil service posts from the governor on down. The current governor, from St. Thomas, is the second white local boy to make good. The Virgin Islanders elect their own legislature without benefit of poll taxes and other Dixieland diversions. There is no overt color discrimination, no segregation except for that proceeding from a tacit prejudice which

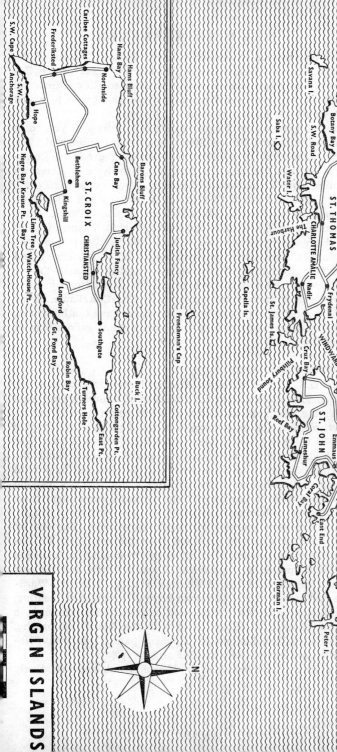

VIRGIN ISLANDS

would be ashamed to announce itself. To the Negroes of the West Indies, the Virgin Islander is the aristocrat of the Caribbean, enjoying American wages, working conditions, material standards, and even relief payments in a Shangri-la to which they would all like to migrate.

Anyone born in the Virgin Islands is a Native. If you come from the mainland United States, you are a Continental. The white population, in addition to a growing group of Continental settlers, includes a few old Danish and American families, some Portuguese and Spanish Jews, numerous Puerto Ricans, and an interesting group known as the Cha-Chas, descendants of French refugees from St. Barthélemy. They settled on a strip of land at the west end of St. Thomas Harbor and have always remained separate from the rest of the community, completely unassimilated. Truck gardeners and fishermen by choice, they speak a curious Norman-French patois, wear straw hats much prized by tourists, and keep to themselves in their picturesquely ratty Cha-Cha Town. Some of them are strikingly handsome, but many have the big-eared, loose-jawed degenerate look that comes from generations of inbreeding.

Settling Permanently

The U.S. Virgins combine American standards of comfort, efficiency, sanitation with the exoticism of a foreign land. Add to this the shopping advantages of a free port (the only one on American soil) and an average year round temperature ranging from 77 to 82 degrees. Subtract such *bêtes noires* as hay fever and high humidity, and you will begin to understand the growing popularity of these American Virgins, not only with tourists but with that ever-increasing army who are looking for a new way of life away from subways, commuter trains and bumper-to-bumper traffic.

Here are some pointers for would-be settlers. The cost of food, most of which is imported from the mainland U.S., is high. This can be somewhat offset by revamping one's diet to include lowpriced local products. Rents are high, and the cost of land is skyrocketing. A housing shortage persists. Wardrobe costs are low, and you don't have to worry about heating. Island standards are simple and unpretentious; there is a notable absence of "Keeping up with the Jones" philosophy. Nevertheless, the famous St. Thomian paradox is true: "Necessities are expensive; luxuries are cheap."

Real estate subdivisions in the Virgin Islands are a relatively new idea. But the idea is catching on at the rate of about a million dollars of annual turnover. Best sources of information on renting or purchasing of houses are the Chambers of Commerce at St. Thomas or St. Croix. Ask about club community projects through which you can buy a lot and build a cottage either for self-occupancy or rental purposes. A useful booklet called *Pertinent Facts* is available from The Department of Commerce, St. Thomas.

Modern health and sanitary facilities are available in all towns. So are electric power, telephone, public libraries, schools and other amenities.

St. Thomas has a serious water problem, however, one which they have still to lick. The catchments and cisterns which somewhat mar the romantic disorder of Charlotte Amalie's hillside scenery are not adequate to supply the needs of this rain-starved community. One resident told us it cost him 35 cents every time he flushed his toilet. Distilled sea water is a solution, but the cost is prohibitive. However, a 250,000-gallon-a-day desalting plant has been installed in St. Thomas.

There are few opportunities for salaried jobs; preference is naturally given to Natives. Business opportunities are many, but must be financed by mainland capital. Local banks do make loans for expansion and improvement of concerns already operating.

Federal income tax obligations are the same here as they are on the mainland, but there is a local tax exemption program to stimulate new industries. For information, write to Tax Exemption Board at St. Thomas or St. Croix, Virgin Islands. For detailed information on business, write to Government Secretary of the Virgin Islands, St. Thomas.

Boating

For settlers and tourists alike, one of the prime attractions of the Virgin Islands, is its unrivalled opportunity for sailing and water sports in general. East of St. Thomas lies Tortola, a completely relaxing if slightly seedy British island, and more than a score of lesser Virgins, owned by the U.S. and Britain. Here it is possible to cruise for days in a small boat under idyllic circumstances, never venturing into the open sea. Tortola has primitive accommodations without electricity and hot water at the Hotel Fort Burt, but lack of comfort is compensated for by miles of unsullied beach which you can reach only by boat. Many of the islands and cays, unchanged since Columbus first saw them, are virgin in fact as well as name, and they beckon irresistibly to certain 20th-century explorers. Best people we know to supply you with the necessities for this and all other forms of watery pleasure are Commander and Mrs. Harry Harman of St. Thomas, whose facilities are indicated below under Sports.

Carnival

The winter season of the Virgin Islands comes to a febrile climax in the last week of April with a popular festival that used to celebrate the spring sugar harvest. This is the justly-celebrated St. Thomas Carnival. See it if you can, but make your plans early. More and more visitors join in the annual fun, and the hotels of St. Thomas are apt to be full.

Certain folklore specialties of the Virgin Islands are featured at this time. Watch for Africanized quadrilles and Irish jigs, relics of plantation days, danced with trap drum and flute accompaniment that is unique in the West Indies.

Carnival finds the streets of Charlotte Amalie a riot of color. Pennants, streamers, palm fronds flutter in the tropic breeze, Native faces are wreathed in smiles under carnival hats, and you'll wear one yourself or be asked to pay a fine for outrageous negligence and non-conformity. The early days of Carnival are marked by the coronation of the Queen, surrounded by her ladies in waiting, as pretty a selection of *café au lait* as you'll ever lay eyes on. There are boat races, Calypso contests, more or less spontaneous jam sessions, and the opening of Carnival Village with rows of decorated booths selling stewed conch, fried fish, a whole gamut of island delicacies and souvenirs.

The whole city throbs to the rhythm of steel bands, those inspired ensembles of instruments made from huge oil drums. This music is the heart-beat of Carnival, and you'll find your feet responding involuntarily to the tempo. The entire populace participates. Like the enchanted rats after the Pied Piper, they follow the bands on nightly "tramps" through the city. Nothing is easier than to join one of these tramps or shuffles. The rhythm is infectious; you can't help keeping step as the good-nature crowd sweeps you along, as though borne aloft by an irresistible tide. When you get tired, you can drop out and have a drink at one of the many small bars where Calypso singers carry on the spirit of the Carnival. Here you'll probably resume dancing, indoors or al fresco; it makes no difference on a balmy night like this.

Climax of Carnival is a huge Saturday costume parade.

1·2·3 GO! TO THE VIRGIN ISLANDS, U.S.A.
ST. CROIX * ST. JOHN * ST. THOMAS

Island-hop to three kinds of paradise . . . each golden beach whispering a charm all its own . . . laced by fragrant breezes never below 70 degrees. There are shimmering waters to swim, sail, water-ski, fish, snorkel or just plain dream by . . . flowers overhead . . . calypso underfoot . . . intriguing personalities . . . rum and gourmet magic on the table. Just a half-hour from San Juan. No visas, passports or shots necessary. And you enjoy $200 worth of duty-free shopping at amazing savings. Come laze with us any time of year . . . or all the year. The U. S. Virgin Islands are a good place to do business, too.

For full information, write or phone: Virgin Islands Gov't. Information Center, 16 West 49th St., New York 20, N.Y., JU 2-4520.

THE VIRGIN ISLANDS

Presided over by a character called Mocko Jumbi on 10-foot stilts, this fabulous procession winds for five miles through the city with the participation of thousands of onlookers, active or passive, depending on their mood. The parade ends at the ball field where judges announce all sort of awards for best costumes, best floats, best steel bands. Then all the bands unite in a final grand tramp leading the shuffling multitude back to Carnival Village. At the stroke of midnight, the revelers head for home like Cinderella leaving the ball. But the memory of Carnival lingers on, one of the vivid recollections of a Caribbean holiday.

PRACTICAL INFORMATION FOR THE U.S. VIRGIN ISLANDS

WHEN TO COME? All year round since there's only a five degree fluctuation (from 77 to 82 degrees) between average winter and summer temperatures. The "winter season", December through April, is smarter but it's just as pleasant in summer. Depends on whether you are more anxious to escape the rigors of winter or the horrors of summer in the so-called north temperate zone. Winter rates are about 30 % higher than summer rates. See Hotels.

Special events that might influence choice of dates are the St. Thomas *Carnival* the last week of April, featuring parades, street dancing, calypso singers, scratchy bands, carnival village; St. Croix *Christmas Festival* December 26 with decorated floats, calypso singers and natives acting out Bible stories; hilarious St. Croix *Donkey Races* at Christiansted February 22.

HOW TO GET THERE. By Air: from New York, Pan American World Airways direct to St. Croix; Pan Am, Delta and Eastern Airlines to San Juan, Puerto Rico, connecting with Caribbean Atlantic Airlines to St. Croix and St. Thomas. From Miami, Pan American and Eastern Airlines via San Juan to St. Thomas and St. Croix. From New Orleans, Delta Airlines via San Juan. From Great Britain: BOAC flies thrice weekly from London to Trinidad, from which island there are Monday, Friday and Saturday flights by Pan Am to St. Croix.

From other Islands: Pan American and Eastern connect Virgin Islands with Jamaica, Haiti, Dominican Republic and Puerto Rico.

By Sea: From New York, Alcoa Steamship Company to St. Thomas. From New Orleans and Gulf Ports, Alcoa (via San Juan), Delta Line, Lykes Brothers (via San Juan), Waterman Steamship Co. (via San Juan).

HOW TO GET ABOUT. They drive on the left hand side in the Virgin Islands, a hangover from Danish days, apparently. When the Americans tried to normalize this situation there were so many accidents caused by recalcitrant Virgin Islands donkeys that the authorities had to give in. So you drive left. Bring your license, by showing it and paying $1.00, you will get a Virgin Island license. When you are sightseeing on foot, remember to look right as well as left before stepping off that curb. Best way to see St. Thomas and St. Croix is by taxi. Rates are relatively reasonable. Current examples, always subject to inflationary changes: 25 cents per passenger within town limits. Most of the drivers are courteous and qualified to act as guides. A 5-passenger taxi and driver can be hired for $4 per hour, and you will find it easy to arrange sightseeing tours with friends, paying $3 to $4 per passenger for the whole tour. Taxi tariffs are fixed for most itineraries at reasonable rates: it's 60 cents between the St. Thomas airport and any hotel within the city limits of Charlotte Amalie. 50 cents for each additional passenger; 35 cents for one passenger from Charlotte Amalie to Bluebeard's Castle Hotel, 30 cents for each additional passenger. The driver will tell you the rate in advance. U-Drive cars may be rented on St. Thomas at Lindquist, Maguire, Hertz, or Tropical Motors; advance registration possible. On St. Croix there is the Hertz Drive-U-Self System, Hamilton, Erikson and Southerland Tours. Private cars are also available through taxi operators or hotels. Donkeys, horses and jeeps may be hired on St. John, but the usual transportation there is by boat. Harbor Cruises and Glassbottom boat trips are offered by V.I.P. Boats and Nautilus Yacht Facilities, Charlotte Amalie.

BOAT HIRE AND CHARTER. It is possible to charter various craft from a 75-ft yawl to a 45-ft twin screw fully equipped fishing cruiser. Plenty of sloops, snipes and outboard motor boats too. Contact V.I.P. Boats, Nautilus Yacht Facilities, St. Thomas Yacht Haven, all on St. Thomas. On St. Croix it's the St. Croix Yacht Club or the Department of Tourism at Christiansted. Prices range from $10 a day for a 10-ft. sail boat to $900 a week for a big schooner. Figure about $75 a day with food for a boat that sleeps four.

SPORTS. *Swimming* at Morningstar Beach, Lindbergh Beach, Magens Bay, Sapphire Bay, Water Island, Bluebeard's Beach (St. Thomas); Cramer's Park east of Christiansted and Sandy Point at Frederiksted (St. Croix); St. John has the best beaches of all, marvelous crescents of white powder sand rimming the many bays; Caneel Plantation has no less than ten of them. *Skin Diving* *water skiing*, and *snorkeling*, especially on St. Croix and St. John. The celebrated *Virgin Islands Spearfishing School* for beginners and experts is on St. Thomas. (Phone 932). One of the great attractions of St. John for skin divers and underwater photographers is exploring the wreckage of the French luxury liner Rhône which sank a few miles south of Salt Island a hundred years ago in a hurricane. The Barrier Reef along the north shore of St. Croix is also souvenir-hunting ground among the many wrecked ships there. *Boating* is excellent and facilitated by Virgin Isle Tours, Tony Daniels Tours, Harman Boats, and Yacht Haven with many small boats for hire at St. Thomas. *Fishing* of all types—deep sea, net, seine, line, spear fishing, and even catching lobsters with a gloved hand. Equipment and boats supplied through hotels or from natives who will take you out from St. Croix or the Anglers' Club at Maho Bay, St. John. *Tennis* on municipal courts of St. Thomas and St. Croix and at various hotels. There's the 9-hole Herman E. Moore Municipal *Golf* course on St. Thomas; Green fee $1 and the 9-hole course at Estate Carleton, St. Croix. *Hunting* season (non-resident license costs $15) is July 15 to September 30 on St. Thomas; October 1 to December 31 (for white-tailed deer) on St. Croix. There are good trails and bridle paths for *Horseback riding* on St. Croix and St. John; the latter also features donkey riding out of Cruz or Caneel Bay; guides accompany you. As for spectator sports, there's *Baseball* every Sunday and *cockfighting*, also on the Sabbath, thus reflecting the mixed national personality of the Virgin Islands.

THE VIRGIN ISLANDS

HOTELS

The Virgin Islands offer a variety of accommodations ranging from the luxurious ($30 to $50 per day for a double room with breakfast and dinner) to basic comfort ($5 per day European plan in an ordinary commercial hotel.) The Virgin Islanders are striving to keep up with the demand for accommodations which their booming tourist popularity has produced. In the meantime, it is wise to reserve early, especially if you want rooms in the winter season.

ST. THOMAS

ADAMS 1799 GUEST HOUSE. Accommodations for ten guests in old colonial mansion five minutes' walk from center of town. Manager Alton Adams, a native of St. Thomas and former U.S. Navy bandmaster presides. Excellent view of harbor and city. Few facilities, no private baths. Creole and American cooking. Rates are $5 for single, $9 double, Continental Plan. Good place for students, teachers, musicians. Tel. 235.

BLUEBEARD'S CASTLE & BEACH CLUB. Bluebeard's, a famous landmark high above Charlotte Amalie, five minutes by taxi from town, has 99 rooms, well appointed restaurant, lounge. Recently remodeled gardens, terrace, romantic Bluebeard's Tower, splendid views from all rooms, and swimming pool. Winter rates (Modified American Plan) from $23 single, $40 double. Summer from $20 single, $27 double. Tennis, golf privileges, dancing on terrace. The Beach Club, about 30 minutes from hotel by car (free transportation), has modern cabana accommodations on beautifully-landscaped private beach. Singles (European Plan) from $15 (summer) $22 (winter); doubles from $20 (summer). Tel. 750,751,752. Cable: Bluebeards. Milan V. Glumidge is the general manager.

DOROTHEA BEACH CLUB. New beachfront resort with 5 cabins, accommodations for 15. E. P. $35 daily, winter M.A.P. $45.

CARIBBEAN HOTEL. Delightful place on own private beach with unobstructed view across Lindbergh Bay. One of coolest spots on the island, only five minutes from town. Charming decorations: Danish colonial plus some ingenious native touches. Cocktail lounge, tropical gardens, dancing to native orchestra. Food is very good; wear a jacket and tie at dinner. Snorkeling equipment available. 50 rooms. Doubles $34 to $43 per day; Singles $23 to $28 (Dec. 15 to April 30). Summer rates from $24 double; $15 single. Modified American Plan. Guests are met at the airport. Manager, William C. Dowling. Tel. 860. Cable: Cariban.

ESTATE CONTANT between airport and town has 12 rooms for 24 guests, restaurant, garden, library, station wagon service to beach, airport, town etc. High and cool. Rather expensive. Rates M.A.P. winter $30 single, $40 to $50 double; summer $17 single, $24 to $26 double, cottage $150. Tel. 137. Cable: Contant.

GALLEON HOUSE. High on a hillside two minutes' walk from town, this is a six room guest house managed by Ben and Jinny Yates. Terrace bar and restaurant with view. Rates, Continental plan, are $9 per person per day with bath, $8 without. No seasonal price change. Tel. 445. Cable: Galleonhouse.

GRAMBOKO INN has 40 rooms on a promontory overlooking the Caribbean between Charlotte Amalie and airport. Seafront cocktail lounge, sidewalk cafe, scheduled transportation to airport, town and beaches. Manager, Eleanor Clinton. Rates: (May 1 to Nov. 30) from $12 a day (single without bath) to $26 (double with bath). Winter rates from $14 single to $26 double. Modified American Plan with full breakfast. Tel. 575. Cable: Gromboko.

GRAND HOTEL on the main square overlooking King Christian Fort. The hotel itself is a century-old landmark and can accommodate 40 guests in its 18 rooms. Singles without bath from $8 per person per day; with bath, from $10. Doubles without bath from $10, with bath from $10 to $14. European plan. Restaurant, bar, terrace, sample rooms for salesmen. Golf privileges at Herman E. Moore Course. Guests make own arrangements for swimming. Manager is Mrs. Hein Christensen. Tel. 35. Cable: Grand.

HARBOR VIEW MANOR. Ten rooms high above the city with panoramic view over harbor and Charlotte Amalie. Continental plan. Rates per person: $10 single, $28 double (winter), $9 single, $18 double (summer). Restaurant, bar, outdoor terrace, guest privileges at beaches. Tel. 55. Cable: Harborview.

HOTEL 1829. This delightful guesthouse (14 rooms) has been host to such luminaries as King Carol of Rumania and Lupescu, Alec Waugh, Suzy Parker and our friend Sydney Clark, and it's loaded with charm. Original century-old beams, old rooms with colonial furniture and big terraces. The old kitchen with its Dutch oven has been converted into an enchanting bar. Beautiful Spanish staircase. Good food from the outdoor charcoal kitchen. Mrs. Walter J. Maguire manages this jewel. Rates (May 1-Nov. 30) are from $10 single (without bath), to $28 double (with bath). Modified American Plan. From Dec. 1 to April 30, they jump to $12 and $36 for same accommodations. Hotel

is five minute climb from shopping district. Transportation arranged for swimming. Box lunches available, $1. Tel. 313. Cable: Maguire.

ISLAND BEACHCOMBER. (Studio Apartment Hotel). Twelve studio apartments for 24 people and 12 hotel rooms on white sandy beach on Lindbergh Bay. You do your own cooking in these attractive units, but a maid comes in daily to do the dirty work. Each apartment has kitchenette, breakfast bar bath, dressing room, patio. Popular with the young crowd. Rates (Dec. 16 to April 30): $18 single, $25 double; (May 1 to Nov. 30) $14 single, $20 double. Managers Michael and Lorette Resch supply beach and snorkeling equipment, arrange sailing and boating parties, furnish transportation in private car to airport and town. Tel. 416. Cable: Beachisle.

MAFOLIE is an apartment hotel 800 feet above St. Thomas Harbor on Mafolie Hill. View and cool climate are unsurpassed. You can even see Puerto Rico. Twelve double rooms, two one room apartments. European plan. Breakfast available. Summer rates (May 1 to Dec. 15) run from $6 to $12 single; $10 to $16 double. Singles in winter range, from $8 to $20, doubles from $12 to $26. The apartments are $20 to $35 in the summer season; $30 to $40 in winter. Tel. 1081. Cable: Mafolie.

MIDTOWN GUEST HOUSE. Twelve quiet rooms with private baths, centrally located near post office. Singles $7 per person. Doubles $10 to $12 European plan.

MILLER MANOR has 20 rooms three minutes from town high up on Frenchman's Hill. Continental plan rates (including full breakfast) rate from $7 per day (single without bath) to $18 (double with bath) from Dec. 15 through March 15. During rest of the year this range drops to $5 minimum single, $12 double. Beach transportation, beach parties, sightseeing and fishing trips can be arranged through the manager, Mrs. Aida Miller. Tel. 535. Cable: Millermanor.

MORNINGSTAR (Beach Club and Cabanas) has 25 luxurious rooms. Beautiful location on Morningstar Beach, gentle surf. Masks, snorkels and fins available. European plan, but you can get breakfast and lunch on the shaded terrace. Single rooms are $20, double $25 from Dec. 1 to April 30. From May 1 to November 30 they are $10 and $15 respectively. Suite $33. There's a bar. Manager is G. Malling Holm. Tel. 412. Cable: Mornstar.

MOUNTAIN TOP HOTEL dominates Signal Mountain 1500 feet above Charlotte Amalie with a stunning panorama over Magens Bay. Home of the famous Banana Daiquiri it's a modern hostelry in the midst of a big estate. All of the rooms have twin beds and private bath. Modified American Plan Rates are $25 single, $40 double (December 1 to April 30); $18 single, $30 double (May 1 to Nov. 30). The food is excellent in the handsome, glass-enclosed terrace restaurant, surrounded by a magnificent tropical garden. Free transportation is provided to and from beach and airport and to a small private island reserved for guests' picnics and fishing expeditions. Quiet luxury is the keynote at the Mountain Top. Bring a light wrap for walks in the cool of the evening through the hotel's 22 acres of tropical gardens. Tel. 200. Cable: Mountop.

NEW ISLANDER, a small guest house with a magnificent view. Comfortable and friendly, it is run by a brother and sister team, David and Sharon Elledge. Accommodation for 15 guests. At the small bar, you can fix yourself a drink for 50 cents. Summer rates are $10 double; winter, $12 to $16, European plan. Cable: Newisle.

SAPPHIRE BAY BEACH CLUB, owned by David E. Maas is expanding its facilities on Pillsbury Sound at the eastern end of St. Thomas.

This is an ideal spot with a palm-lined beach 15 minutes by car from Charlotte Amalie. Rates European Plan, winter $18 to $22 single, apartments $45, summer $10 single, apartments $28. Write P.O.-Box 509, Sapphire Bay, St. Thomas.

SEA HORSE INN is a plantation-style guest house, run with good taste and simplicity by Marion Weber for those who want quiet surroundings. Free taxi service is provided to Lindbergh Beach and from airport, five minutes away. Accommodations for 14 guests. Continental Plan. Double room with private bath $16, Dec. 1 to May 1; May 1 to Dec. 1 $12.

SURFSIDE, managed by the ubiquitous Marion Weber, offers six rooms directly on the beach at Lindbergh Bay. Continental Plan. Other meals by reservation in the restaurant. Rates (Dec. 1 to April 30) range from $17.50 to $21. Off season rates are lowered to $12 to $16. Tel. 1560. Cable: Surfside.

THATCH FARM, facing golf course has a secluded setting in the old Botanical Gardens, but is within walking distance of beach and night clubs. There are four housekeeping cottages with private gardens and maid service. Rates are $20 per day for single, double or triple occupancy. Manager: Joseph P. Maronna.

"THE GATE", managed by Herb Martin, is one of St. Thomas's best known guest houses. Right in town, many of its 16 rooms have old-fashioned private verandahs. There are a restaurant, patio bar, library, record player with good selection of disks, most of the comforts of home. Swimming at Morning Star Beach with free station wagon service provided. Accommodations: single rooms with bath, $10 winter season, $8.50 from May 16 to Dec. 14; 14 doubles with bath, $19 to $21 winter; $17 in summer. Tel. 236. Cable: Thegate.

THE NEW FLAMBOYANT HOTEL is both new and flamboyant, beautifully situated at East Point, overlooking the harbor and Morningstar Beach. Accent is on gaiety. Life centers around the pool and on the Pool Terrace, a grand place to dance at night. Accommodations for 110 guests. All rooms have private bath. Daily rates, modified American plan: $40 double, $25 single (Dec. 1-April 30); $25 double, $15 single, off season. Attractive villas for one or two persons are available at $45 (winter), $30 (summer). The efficient manager is an old hand at arranging fishing, sailing, golf and yachting parties.

TRADE WINDS HOTEL on Brewer's Bay Beach is within a five minute walk of the golf course. Managed by E. C. Jennen it's a good example of the way Virgin Islanders are meeting the hotel challenge. This one is a converted Marine Barracks, providing 40 rooms, 11 of which open onto a sun deck. Restaurant, lounge, garden and terrace are among the amenities, and they are planning further renovation and the addition of a swimming pool, Modified American Plan rates range from $12 for a single to $36 for a double in the winter season, depending on the room. Rates are cheaper in summer: doubles running from $11 to $24, singles as low as $9 a day. European plan also available. Also (summer only) weekly and monthly rates. Tel. Bourne Field 1521. Cable: Tradewinds.

TROPIC ISLE HOTEL is located on a hillside above its own beach on Lindbergh Bay. No restaurant, but breakfast is served, and other meals available nearby. There are 12 rooms, three apartments, all with private bath. Daily trips to town in private cars. European Plan. Double rooms are $15 and up, single $10 and up, Apartments $25 and up from Dec. 1 to April 30. Off season rates are $10 and up double, $6 and up single, $12 and up for an apartment. Tel. 716. Cable: Tropicile.

VILLA SANTANA. On Denmark Hill, overlooking the city and harbor and only two blocks from the center of town, this 10 room guest house was once the estate of General Santa Ana. The charming manager specializes in personal attention and keeping guests informed on island activities. Continental Plan. Single room $10, double $15, Dec. 15 to April 30. From May 1 to Nov. 30 the range is from $7 to $17.50. Tel. 810. Cable: Vilsan.

VIRGIN ISLE HILTON which has now added a new 40 room wing, is the largest and most luxurious here and one of the leaders of the whole Caribbean area. It may remind you of some of the Florida palaces, but its setting on a mountain top with sweeping view of sea and mountains is pure Caribbean. Never a dull moment seems to be the motto of the management. There is nightly entertainment including everything from bingo to turtle races in the kidney-shaped Tropicabana Pool. Fiestas, fashion shows, Calypso costume parties, moonlight swimming parties; the list is endless. Sailing, water skiing, yachting and kindred water sports are available at the hotel's private Beach Club, to which free transportation is provided. Dancing in the Frangi-Pani dining room and in the Pavilion Under the Stars.

Has 200 rooms; all have private bath and terrace. From December 1 to April 30, Modified American Plan rates range from $27 single to $55 a day double. There are double penthouses $65-$78 per day, the Presidential Suite at $115. Off season you can have a single from $16, a double from $27, apartments for $420 per month and stretch out in the Presidential Suite for only $75 per diem. Golf, tennis, masseur, gift shops, transatlantic phone in rooms; you name it, the Virgin Isle has it.

WATER ISLE HOTEL AND BEACH CLUB has 31 rooms, two cottages, 12 efficiency apartments on a private island in St. Thomas Harbor, a five-minute boat trip from the Submarine Base. Fine sand beach and facilities for sailing, snorkeling, spear fishing etc. for free use of guests. Water Isle Hotel is a great favorite with honeymooners. Rates (Modified American Plan) run from $22 (single) to $36 (double) per day from Dec. 1 to April 30. Off season range is from $14 to $24. Efficiency apartments are $145 a week winter season, $110 in summer. All rooms have twin beds, private bath, and terrace on the sea. Calypso singing and dancing to native orchestra. Walter H. Phillips manages this attractive enterprise. Tel. M-20. Cable: Waterisle.

YACHT HAVEN COTTAGE RESORT has 40 apartments in a coconut grove on the Yacht Basin. Charming restaurant overlooks St. Thomas Harbor. Jacket and tie obligatory for dinner. Meals are also served at the side of the kidney-shaped (what else?) pool. Accommodations are complete suites with living room, bedroom, efficiency kitchen, bathroom, terrace. All units are air-conditioned. European plan rates (December 15 to April 30) from $25-$35 single, from $32 to $42 double per day. Modified American Plan will cost $30 to $40 and $42 to $52 for the same accommodations. Off season prices M.A.P. single $17 to $27, double $26 to $36. Monthly rates upon request to manager, Harry B. Howe, Tel. 903, 904, 905, 906.

PINEAPPLE BEACH CLUB. An unique design of "bubble" form cement makes this new St. Thomas resort a real eye catcher. Owner Herb Baltic operates the club himself and does a real first class job with meals and cocktails served beachside. Located about 20 minutes drive from the center of Charlotte Amalie with a perfect beach at your doorstep. Rates are $24 double on the European Plan (if you want to do your own cooking), and $35 on a modified American Plan.

RESTAURANTS

Virgin Island cuisine is basically American with emphasis on charcoal-broiled steaks and lobsters. In addition there are some mouth-watering West Indian creole dishes and some reasonable facsimiles of Danish and French cuisine. The local *Cruzan* rum from St. Croix is excellent and very cheap (less than a dollar a fifth), the basis for a great variety of punches. Local seafood is recommended, especially lobsters and the turtle steaks. Another specialty is pigeon pea soup; if they serve you a plate of that, it's a compliment; it means they want you to come back. Nearly all the hotels in our list have restaurants ranging from adequate to excellent, and they are generally open to the public. But reserve in advance, as guests naturally have priority. In some of the flossier hotels like the Virgin Isle, it has become the fashion to dress for dinner in the winter season. But in most hotels and restaurants in the Virgin Islands, dressing for dinner just means wearing a sports jacket and tie.

THE VIRGIN ISLANDS

ST. THOMAS

Bluebeard's Castle offers a tempting buffet lunch from 12:30 to 2 p.m. daily ($2); dinner ($5.50) 7:30 to 9:30, followed by dancing on fascinating tombstone terrace to the music of various bands, typical of the Virgin Island group. Breathtaking view. Reservations obligatory. Jacket and tie required.

Caribbean Hotel and Beach Club. Lunch from 12 to 1:30, 75¢ sandwich and up. *Luaus* Tuesday and Thursday; steel band. Dinner from 7:30 to 8:45, $5.50. Dinner dancing. Reserve.

Chateau Chinon. Finest and most elegant of St. Thomas restaurants. Cuisine française, serving until midnight. Reservation obligatory, and so are jacket and tie for dinner. The manager has described this eatery as "fairly expensive, but damn good." We concur.

Coffee House open from 8 a.m. to 7:30 p.m. Good place for breakfast, brunch or sandwich lunch. Good pastries and coffee. Serves continuously.

New Flamboyant Hotel serves lunch from 12:30 to 2, dinner from 7 to 9, $4.50. Dancing every night. Reservations, jackets and ties not required except on Saturday night. Patrons of restaurant enjoy free use of Flamboyant pool.

Galleon House. No lunch. Dinner is served at 8, from $3 up. Try their curry, a Tuesday night specialty. Reservations are necessary here, but jacket and tie are not.

Seven Queens Quarter for breakfast, lunch or dinner in air-conditioned comfort.

Gramboko Sidewalk Cafe has substantial dinners from $2.75 to $4.50. Curry is the specialty on Saturday night; an Italian dinner is the feature Sunday evening. Free *fondu* with cocktails from 6 p.m. and Calypso music nightly.

Grand Gallery serves lunch and snacks from 11 until 3:30 p.m. and cocktails until 7. Try their special drink, a His Nibs Collins, and guess what's in it beside rum.

Hotel 1829 serves dinner (no lunch) from 7 to 8, $3.50. They have a special five dollar dinner, featuring lamb chops, steak, or lobster from the charcoal grill; deservedly famous. Reservations are required, and so are jackets.

L'Escale at the airport serves continuously from 8 a.m. and puts on a good international dinner from $3.75 including liqueur. Excellent prime meats served here. House specialty: fried chicken dinner for $1.95. Atmosphere is informal; no jacket, tie, or reservation required. Air conditioned.

Mountaintop Hotel. Good food with stunning view. Lunch is from 12:30 to 2:30, dinner from 7 to 9:30. Steak nights Weds., Sats., buffet Sunday night. Better reserve for dinner, and wear a jacket.

Left Bank. Culinary art from Haiti has created one of St. Thomas' most attractive restaurants, featuring Haitian and French cuisine. In the back room hangs Coster's collection of Haitian primitive art, known as one of the finest anywhere. No jacket required.

Petite Pump Room. In the luxuriously planted Palm Passage, the island's newest shopping center. The owner is Camille Dupleix, for many years associated with the famous Pump Room in Chicago. Beautifully arched restaurant and bar. Menu features native dishes daily. Jacket and tie not necessary.

Sebastian's on the Waterfront. Increasingly popular. Lunch from 12 to 4 p.m. from 65 cents up. Dinner from 7 to 11, $2.75 and up. You can forget about ties, jackets, reservations.

Virgin Isle Hilton. Excellent lunch in patio or at poolside from noon to 5 p.m. Dinner from 7:30 to 9:30 starts at $4.50. Better reserve, and wear jacket and tie except for informal barbecue on Thursday nights. A lot of people wear evening dress here on Saturday. Dancing to two bands; recording star Bill Fleming with terrific calypso and ballads. Also entertainment in the posh Foolish Virgin Bar from cocktail time on.

Water Isle Hotel. Beach lunch and dinner from 8:30 to 9, $4. Reservation required, but not jacket and tie. Entertainment is good here, but unscheduled. Check before going.

Tony Quetel's Delicatessen and Normandie Bar is a picturesque sailors' bistro at the base of Gallows Hill. Proprietor Tony is the mayor of Cha-Cha Town, or was when this edition went to press.

NIGHT LIFE

Greatest variety is on *St. Thomas,* and the big leader is the *Virgin Isle* where big name bands play nightly for dancing. A favorite with the locals is *Pilgrim's Terrace,* featuring cool breezes and ditto music. *The Trade Winds* is currently tops for Calypso singers, and *The Gate* is a great favorite for dancing to the best steel bands on Sunday, Wednesday, Friday and Saturday nights. *Bruno's Black Patch* has Latin combo and songs. Also popular are *Sebastian's,* as well as the *Mahogany Club.* Most bars stay open until you feel like leaving; many have steel bands or juke boxes, and sometimes the dancing overflows into the streets.

SHOPPING

As the only free port on American soil, the Virgin Islands offer the advantages of merchandise from all over the world at duty-free prices and purchasable in U.S. dollars. In addition, the merchants are Americans with an innate knowledge of what Americans want. They know better than anyone else in the Caribbean how to cater to the American buyer, and they are better stocked with items tailored to American taste and size than any other shopkeepers we have come across in our Caribbean travels. In other words, you are going to have a field day, browsing and buying in attractive shops which are loaded with imported silver, china, leather, jewelry, linens, woolens, perfumes, wines and liquors at from 20 to 50 per cent less than they cost at home. Your U.S. customs allowance is $200 after an absence of 48 hours from the U.S. instead of the normal $100. But a minimum $100 worth of purchases must be from the U.S. Virgin Islands, which makes this an exceptional position; especially as Customs evaluates goods on wholesale prices, thus giving your allowance a possible $300 value. Your only problem is choosing among the Swiss watches, English woolens, Danish silverware, Royal Copenhagen porcelain, Italian silks and linens, modern Scandinavian ceramics and jewelry, Peruvian silverwork, Florentine leather, and the countless products in mahogany, sisal, tortoise-shell, glass, coral and leather from Mexico, Haiti, Guatemala, Puerto Rico and places close to home. Here's a rundown on all the shops, what they have to offer, and what prices you can expect to pay. Incidentally, we have yet to come across a dishonest Virgin Islands shopkeeper. Prices are fixed, and the savings really are staggering: $15.75 for four ounces of Revillon's *Carnet de Bal* as opposed to $70 on the mainland; Bing and Grondahl white porcelain sea cherubs at $5.50 compared with $10.50 stateside; Exakta Camera with Biotar F-2 lens, $249.50 instead of $399 in New York. This will give you some idea. Happy hunting!

ST. THOMAS

AMERINDIES SHOP has half the desires of a woman's heart, including Amalfi shoes from Italy, made on American lasts, at half the backhome price; Pringle cashmere sweaters ($20 for the classic cardigan which costs $32 on the mainland); lingerie, bathing suits, shorts, French skirts and matching bags, blouses, and a big collection of U.S. designer clothes in cottons and silks from $19.95 to $49.

THE BAMBOULA stocks everything from Austrian petit point bags to voodoo and steel band drums. You'll love their sandals from India (from $2.50) and their selection of straw hats and bags from the Virgin Islands, Haiti, and Jamaica from 40 cents up. You'll find all the perfumes of France in this emporium; men's and women's Swiss watches; Thailand silk stoles and scarves; French mantillas as low as $1.98; Madras shirts, shorts, swim trunks; handsome costume jewelry from France, Portugal and India; Danish silver, German clocks, Italian leather.

G. BERETTA specializes in Italian imports: Florentine and Venetian tooled leather, an extensive line of the celebrated Motta candy, and Murano glass. We saw a pair of Murano figurines for $42 which sells for $85 at home. Beretta also has Italian original oil paintings, rosaries, enamelled copperware, and alabaster figurines. There's an excellent selection of Italian and native dolls for any little girl on your list. For a bigger girl, yourself for example, the beaded bags from France and Belgium start at $12.50.

THE BOLERO SHOPS (one on Main Street, one in the Virgin Isle Hotel) has an exclusive on Ballantyne cashmere sweaters for men and women. (The $29.95 classic cardigan is only $18.95 here.) There's a wide selection of linens (Swiss place mats from $1; they start at $3 stateside) and there are beautiful organdy and linen cloths and napkins from Madeira. Look at their hand-crafted Norwegian sterling silver tableware, $10 less per 6-piece place setting than you will pay at home. The china department features Royal Crown Derby and Tuscan (English); Haviland and Limoges from France, and good old U.S. Lennox. Many lines of crystal, including the famous Val St. Lambert from Belgium, Harbridge (English), Daum (French), and Murano Venetian glass. There's a tempting selection of English antiques, and you'll find enough jewelry for a queen; the Danish enamelled sterling stuff starts as low as $1.50. The wood department has an excellent selection of Haitian mahogany: serving pieces from $1.25 are a bargain, and so is the large salad bowl at $8.95.

THE BOMBAY BAZAAR presents all the riches of the East plus such items as Taunton & Thorne English doeskin gloves (an exclusive) at one-third of what they cost in the continental U.S.A. Their jewelry covers a wide range of items in

A composite of unspoiled Leeward Island forms

Siamese etched silver, jade, cultured pearls, and Indian silver and crystal. If you have a yen for ivory elephants, Bombay has them and other figurines in a price range from 75 cents to $125. A favorite item here, and a wonderful gift, is the scarf. They have those gauzy Indian ones with gold threading at $3 and $4; Italian silk scarves start at $5.95. Hand-loomed silk saris, shot through with 24 karat gold threads run from $30 to $125, and there are Indian cashmere embroidered skirt and dress lengths beginning as low as $16. Madras is only a dollar a yard; the colors are wonderful. Italian straw shoes (at $5.95) are a good buy here, and so are the Italian and Indian leather sandals, at $6.95 and $4.95 respectively. A specialty of the house: Irish linens, hand-embroidered in Hong Kong, with handkerchieves from $1.25, table cloths from $30 up. There is a good selection of handbags; French beaded ones are from $10 to $30; Zari bags from India, $2.95. If you go for carved screens, inlaid tables and the like, Bombay Bazaar has them for about one half of the price in your own home town.

BOUTIQUE FANTASIA specializes in Italian imports, and they are simply scrumptious with all their handstitching and embroidery. One luxurious bargain is a printed silk foulard blouse at $30, one dollar more than what it costs in Rome, $22 less than the continental U.S. price. Plain and decorated Barra gloves start at $6.25; Italian leather handbags from $40. You'll find a tempting selection of linens here, all with that fine Italian handdetailing, and Italian silk ties in wonderful profusion. Among the gift items: Franceschi leather and ceramic ashtrays, bowls and vases, individually-designed-from $3.25 to $30.

C. W. L. CALLWOOD specializes exclusively in fine hand-made jewelry, designed and executed right here in the shop's studio. Among favorite souvenir items are the hand-made 14 karat gold charms in exclusive designs at $15 and up. "The Smiling Virgin Islands Sun" and "Foolish Mermaid" are two of the most popular. Another Callwood specialty is unusual wedding rings studded with oriental pearls and precious stones. You can buy diamonds, rubies, sapphires and many other precious and semi-precious stones here, mounted or unmounted. Prices are from 35 to 50 per cent lower than those for comparable items back home, and jewelry made in Callwood's studio may be taken into the U.S. duty free.

THE CARIB SHOP specializes in imported and island-designed clothes for the entire family. Their bathing suits are wonderful, and great bargains to boot. The imported ones such as Slix suits (British) and Mayogaine (French) sell at about half the U.S. price. The locally-designed ones in Madras and other imported fabrics are well-conceived and executed, and Carib will make you a suit to order if you like from a wide selection of fabrics. Madras is one of the big shop specialties, made up into smart shorts, blouses, shirts etc. for men, women and children. Dresses, designed and executed in the Carib's workrooms, start at $14.95. They also have an exclusive on those well-tailored Daks skirts and shorts for women. If you have a little boy or girl you want to dress, you'll find a grand range of styles, sizes and fabrics here. Straw hats and bags for women and children? Carib has them from Italy, Jamaica and the Virgin Islands. Other notable items in this attractive store: Fownes gloves from Great Britain (from $2.75); belts and ties for men, and enough toys from England and Germany to delight the heart of any budding engineer.

C. & M. CARON (Leslie Caron's

419

The lure of the French West Indies

parents) has a complete line of French perfumes and a dazzling array of costume jewelry: Mexican, Danish, French and Italian. See the French gold-aluminum necklaces, starting as low as $1.25, and the hand-made enamelled French enamelled pieces, all signed, from $5.50 up. There are some lovely items in wood: Florentine boxes and trays; Haitian Mahogany bowls; pepper mills, religious figurines, hand-carved in Italy and Germany. You'll find a wonderful collection of time pieces in this shop too, including cuckoo clocks from the Black Forest. One item calculated to charm old ears as well as young: Swiss music boxes that play Calypso tunes. Caron's line of Swiss watches includes those of Piaget, Mido, Girard Perregaux and Zodiac. Variety in wrist, stop and coin watches is almost endless. If you've got a young man on your list who's always hankered for a Swiss watch, they have a line of boy's watches here for less than $10. This is a great shop for swimming and fishing equipment; they stock everything from rods and reels to underwater guns and water skis. If you are not the active type, take a look at their "passive" sports equipment, including such inviting items as rubber rafts and mattresses. Caron also has a raft of souvenirs: Island dolls, Haitian drums, straw hats and bags from St. Thomas and Haiti, and they have an exclusive on that French oven proof Porcelain de Paris, to say nothing of a big line of small Limoges coffee cups and miniature china.

CAVANAGH'S is another shop specializing in clothes designed and made on the premises. Cotton dresses start as low as $9.95 here, hand-detailed blouses from $5.95. Siamese hand-loomed silk scarves sell at $2.95, stoles at $7.95, and those marvelous Pakamas (extra-large stoles) or dress lengths at $19.95. The last cost $55 in your home town. Here's a shop that doesn't neglect the male; there's a grand selection of Thai silk ties, cummerbunds and shirts, Madras walking shorts, Chinese silk robes (only $7.95!) and pajamas. You'll probably want to stock up on ties (Madras, Swiss silk, Chinese brocades) from $1.95 up, and you're sure to like the sport shirts and matching swim trunks designed and executed by Cavanagh's for tropical smartness and comfort. For the kids on your shopping list, there's a variety of stuffed animals from 60 cents, amusing raffia creatures from 75 cents, and native dolls at $2.95. Other gift items: hand-blown Venetian glass necklaces from $1.25 (earrings from 75 cents); beaded bags from Hong Kong ($4.95; $6.95 with matching belt); hand-embroidered linens from Italy and Hong Kong; straw luggage from Hong Kong (starting at $2.95); straw hats and bags from Italy and the West Indies. There are also a number of decorator items: Korean teak chests, Chinese vases, brass cocktail tables, cheaper than they are in New York, but you have to like this sort of thing a lot to lug it home from The Virgin Islands.

THE COMPASS ROSE is a corner of old and new Nippon set down in the Virgin Islands. Among the popular items imported from Japan, "Happy Coats" and kimonos from $3.95 up. There are some bargains here in pongee and raw silk shirts for men, blouses for women, and long reversible evening coats of silk brocade at $87 and $98. Cultured pearl jewelry starts at $11; pearls and workmanship are Japanese. Canon and Nikon cameras are a specialty of the Compass Rose. The Model S-2 Nikon sells here for $175; it's $197 in other Caribbean free ports and $354 in the U.S. Binoculars start at $8.50; telescopes at $15.50; transistor radios at $39.50. There is a big selection of oriental furniture. Among the many impressive bargains: a lacquer chest with brass fittings for $285; you pay $800 in the continental U.S.A.

THE CONTINENTAL is a great store with just about the widest selection of goods in the Virgin Islands. They've gone to the ends of the earth to offer you a staggering variety of china, perfume, crystal, glass, clothing, fabrics, gloves, bags, jewelry, linens, furniture, woolens, silver, luggage, watches and gift items. They have the exclusive on Certina and Orator Swiss watches for men and women. Among the outstanding things: Danish sterling flatware and hollowware by Hans Hansen, Cohr, Morgensen, Andersen and Holger Rassmussen, all beautifully designed. While you're at it, look at the various lines of imported stainless steel flatware. In the sweater department, you'll find Braemer cashmeres (the classic cardigan is $19.95) and great names like Bernhard Altman and Luisa Spagnoli in addition to a tempting array of French, Danish and Norwegian knits. Wedgwood, Limoges and Schumann dinnerware as low as $2.50 for a five-piece place setting. There's a glittering selection of French, Swedish and Danish crystal and glass, and an almost infinite variety of dresses and fabrics from all over the world. Danish sterling silver jewelry starts at $1, and there is a wide selection of handsomely-designed Danish furniture, rugs and cooking utensils. Men's wear is not neglected here; you'll find some nifty jackets in cashmere, linen, Madras, tweed, and Viyella at a fraction of their mainland cost. The variety of gift items, covering the world from Guatemala to Hong Kong, is unsurpassed. You name it; we'll be surprised if The Continental doesn't have it. One of the best shopping centers in the entire Caribbean.

COQUINA COURT specializes in clothes designed and made in St. Thomas. Dresses executed in a variety of foreign fabrics start at $18.95. Hand-embroidered and appliqued dresses of Irish linen are among the bargains at $29.95 to $39.95. There is a selection of hand-embroidered silk and linen blouses and skirts, original hand-painted skirts, and skirts of hand-loomed cloth from the Caribbean, South America, Italy and India. Custom-made Benares Sari dresses are outstanding here, and the shop will make almost any item of ladies' clothing to order. Sports clothes for the whole family are sold here; hand-embroidered Kashmir stoles and capes; hand-made German jewelry; ready-made and custom-made bathing suits, and an excellent selection of straw hats and bags from most of the seven seas including the surrounding Caribbean.

FRAN DEPINA also specializes in clothes designed and made here in St. Thomas, in Madras, Moygashel linen, Liberty prints and many other fabrics. Very popular is their travelling dress in Liberty cotton, with wrap-around skirt and matching shorts, $24.90. Beautiful dresses made from Indian saris start at $80, and the shop has a complete line of "Island Calico" fashions. Cotton challis, hand-sequinned skirts with matching blouses sell for $79, the retail price here being exactly the same as the wholesale price to mainland shops. Another specialty of Fran DePina is a great variety of mother-and-daughter, father-and-son outfits. Little girls love these dresses in Liberty cotton, and so do their parents. You'll be interested in the silver jewelry from Peru, and in the precious and semi-precious stone jewelry from Brazil here. This is a good place for Caribbean straw hats and bags and assorted souvenirs of St. Thomas.

ELVERHOJ is a celebrated name in the Caribbean for imaginative island-designed clothes. They are made here in the shop's workrooms. Price range is from $19.95 to $95. Customers may choose their own fabrics from a wide selection to be

THE VIRGIN ISLANDS

made up from a choice of a dozen or more original designs. The shop is a marvel of speed and efficiency, usually able to fill an order on the day it is made. There's a large stock of ready-made skirts, blouses, shorts and swim suits. Men will have a field day here too with English linen jackets at $29.95; Italian silk jackets at $49.95, and English Daks linen slacks at $16.95 (they're $22.50 at home). You can get English shorts too in addition to some smartly-tailored ones made on the premises from $8.95 up. Take a look too at the sweaters from Italy and Germany ($6.95 to $25) and at the Christian Dior gloves, starting at $3.95 a pair.

L'ESCALE in the St. Thomas airport offers several lines of Swiss watches at half the U.S. price (see the assortment of women's dress-watches from $12.95 to $19.95); a complete line of French perfumes; a large selection of costume jewelry from Mexico, Denmark, Spain; stuffed toys and cuckoo clocks from Germany; Italian dolls and toys, and a raft of straw stuff from Italy and the Virgin Islands including highly-useful tote bags in which to stash some of your last-minute loot.

THE FRENCH SHOPPE, which used to evoke a lot of sub-conscious sympathy by being known as Madame Souffrant's, is a small shop with some very big bargains. First of all, the shop specializes in perfumes, and has the distinction of being the only authorized importer of products by one of the greatest of French parfumeurs, Guerlain. Here you will find the largest line of Guerlain perfumes in the Western hemisphere, and there are even some which we haven't seen in the Guerlain shop on the Champs Elysees. Altogether there are about 55 different marks of perfume on sale here, about 300 different scents with low prices that may make the whole operation go to your head. Other luxury items from la belle

France include Kislav gloves from $5.95 to $13.50 (about half what they cost in the U.S.); beaded bags from $15 to $150; St. Louis crystal in 50 different patterns; Haviland china in 40, from the least to the most formal; and French silk ties, pipes, Kislav gloves and belts for men. All is not French in the French Shoppe, however; there are some magnificent sweaters, hand-knit by Swedish fisherfolk: $60.

GAVE HUS is the place to go to buy or rent books. There's a good selection, many on the Caribbean and Virgin Islands. For flat, packable gifts and souvenirs of your trip, we recommend the water colors and prints of local Virgin Islands scenes as well as various maps of the West Indies. You'll find a selection of Christmas and other greeting cards by island artists here too. You'll find handbags, mats and luggage from the Virgin Islands, Jamaica, the Philippines and other stops on the straw and raffia circuit, including those famous St. Thomas Cha-Cha hats with their fanciful decorations, from $1.95 up.

GRAND GIFT SHOP is just that, offering enough linens, mahogany bowls, gloves, perfumes, jewelry, bags, and sterling silver to supply most of the people on your list. Among their special temptations are Madeira linen bridge sets from $10 to $20, sumptuous banquet cloths with 12 napkins from $85 up. They have an exclusive on the celebrated Frigast sterling flatware from Denmark. Lovely petit point bags from France and Austria start at $38; beaded ones from Belgium at $15. There's a nice selection of gold jewelry, including charms, from Germany and Italy, and of silver jewelry from Mexico and Denmark. Spanish and French mantillas are a specialty here, starting as low as $1.25.

HIBISCUS SHOPS (one in Beretta Center, one on Main Street) have charming dresses, designed and made in the shop's Workrooms of

Indian, African and Italian printed fabrics. These start at $18.95. Custom-made dresses of Swiss cotton, madras, batik, linen and other imported fabrics can be delivered within 24 hours. Nothing slow about these Virgin Islanders! You can buy saris, uncut, from $35. Made up into dresses, they start at $60. There are cotton blouses here to suit every taste and purse (Mexican embroidered ones are $5.95) and they'll make one up for you at the drop of a tape measure. There are hand-embroidered grass cloth skirts from Italy, a large selection of hand-painted and printed cottons, Madras swim suits from England, and yards and yards of wonderful Madras and African batik at prices that will tempt you to buy by the rod. Pappagallo shoes are cheaper here than they are at home. There's a good selection of straw bags and hats from Italy, Japan, St. Thomas, right down to the last straw. You'll find most of your favorite Calypso and Steel Band records here too.

THE LITTLE SHOP has a big selection of silver, porcelain, crystal, jewelry, linens, perfume, men's and women's wear, and—you guessed it—straw. Sterling flatware and hollowware by outstanding Danish designers is side by side with traditionel Gorham silver. There are some beautiful Sheffield carving sets, steak knives and coffee services, and a good selection of that handsome Danish stainless steel flatware. In the porcelain department, there are Dahl-Jensen figurines, vases, and craqueleware from Denmark; Nymølle earthenware, Wedgwood pottery. The Little Shop has shining Lalique and Baccarat crystal from France; Swedish crystal by famed Stromberg Hytten, and Kastrup Danish glassware. You'll find good inexpensive gift items among the tie clasps, cuff links and money clips of Danish sterling silver, and there's a pleasing variety of Siamese etched silver and Danish enamelled silver jewelry. Dents English gloves are another notable item here—for both men and women, and there's a nice choice of Argyle socks, Liberty ties and linen handkerchiefs for men. Women will find it hard to resist some of the Scotch mohair stoles, scarves and throws, and may be tempted by the colorful Guatemalan skirts and jackets.

LITTLE SWITZERLAND GIFT SHOP. If you're looking for toys and gifts for children, you'll be delighted by this important store. It's a children's and an adults' paradise of Swiss music boxes, cuckoo clocks (many designed especially for children), mechanical toys from Germany, dolls and stuffed animals from Sweden, Switzerland, France, Italy and Germany. Swiss watches for children and adults start as low as $6. There are German binoculars from $2.95, German cameras from $11.95. The German chrome-plated tool sets from Germany will make many a male eye shine, and we can't think off hand of a better present for a boy than one of those superb Swiss army knives, the perfect companion on a hiking trip. Swiss children's and infants' wear is a specialty here. And you're a stronger character than we are if you can resist the English Glen Cree mohair scarves and throws from $1.50; the blankets are $25.

THE LITTLE SWITZERLAND JEWELRY STORE has more of the same, but the accent is not so much on youth. This is the place for big name Swiss watches at relatively small prices: Piaget, Mido, International Watch Co., Eterna, Vacheron & Constantin, Girard-Perregaux, to name a few. Gubelin's rainbow watch for ladies with four bezels and four matching straps sells here for $59.50; it's $89.95 in the U.S. Ernest Borel's cocktail watch, $71.50 on the mainland, is only $35 here. Similar bargains exist in the crystal department, which has an exclusive on Irish

Waterford stemware in 11 different patterns. A goblet in the Lismore pattern is $3.50 here, $7 in the continental United States. You've never seen so many clocks, from little travel alarms all the way up to the venerable Mauthe Grandfather with its Westminster chimes. Kern-Beck, Zeiss and Japanese binoculars are on sale from $12.50 up, and you'll find most of the cameras you ever heard of from Agfa to Zeiss. In addition there is a galaxy of fine and costume jewelry from France, Germany, Italy, and, of course, Switzerland.

MAISON DANOISE would dazzle a color-blind bull with its array of Spode, Wedgwood, Royal Doulton, Royal Copenhagen and Bing and Grondahl dinnerware. Except for Wedgwood, all these marks are exclusive in the Virgin Islands with this house. Savings are sensational, about 50 per cent on prices back home. The famous George Jensen sterling flatware and hollowware are another major attraction here, with six-piece place settings starting at $35.75. We found the handsome and much-admired Acorn pattern cost $56.50 for the place setting here. In New York it's $78. Savings up to 50 per cent are frequent in Orreforrs Swedish crystal, and in decanters and other crystal by Holmegard of Denmark. There is a good selection of sterling silver jewelry here by George Jensen and other modern Danish designers.

MONIQUE DE PARIS, another enterprising designer of Island clothes for women, has ready-to-wear as well as custom-made dresses from $15 up. She has some smart two-piece silk dresses at $29.95; two-piece, hand-embroidered linen dresses at $24.50. Her shorts for men as well as women are reasonably priced from $4.95. She's done some imaginative dresses and skirts in Madagascar straw cloth, and has an exclusive on beautifully hand-detailed blouses and table linens from Morocco. Blouses are $24.50

for women, $7.15 for children. The Gallic touch of Monique is evident in her Bikinis, very French and very brief. Washable French handbags are $14.95. There are some interesting shop-designed feather earrings at $10, and a collection of French costume jewelry that will make you think you've wandered into a shop on the Rue de Rivoli.

THE PARAKEET has shell jewelry from $1.25 up, designed and made in the shop's workrooms. There is also a variety of jewelry from Austria, Italy, Holland and Israel, and a collection of ivory miniatures from China and India as low as a dollar. Shell collections and native dolls are also priced from a dollar, and there are lots of native Christmas and greeting cards available. In addition to these low-priced souvenirs, The Parakeet has men's sport shirts of Madras and African batik at $5.95 and $6.95 made in the shop's workrooms. There are Madras skirts, cotton Indian skirts from Ecuador, and skirts with Virgin Islands designs. They also sell Madras and African batik by the yard from $1 to $1.65.

THE PATIO, which does double duty as a night club, is a haven for men and for women who are looking for men's gifts. Among their imported specialties are Church shoes from England: $22.50 a pair here, $35 in the U.S.A. Gino Paoli Italian sweaters are another trade windfall; they sell for $65 on the mainland, for only $32.50 here in The Patio. You'll also find some good looking Cox-Moore and Drumlanning cashmere sweaters from England. The famous English Kent brushes are about half what they cost at home. Viyella robes and shirts are 40 per cent under U.S. prices, and there's a bargain selection of English Aertex shirts from $5.50 to $6.50. Comoy pipes and other male miscellany are correspondingly priced. Our own buyer was personally delighted with his Madras jacket at $19.95, and if you've ever had a hankering for luxurious English doeskin, here it is from $4.75 to $12.50 a yard.

A. H. RIISE GIFT SHOP. You'll be lucky if you get out of here without countersigning your last traveler's check. The lure here includes Royal Vienna Augarten porcelain; Royal Crown Derby, Rosenthal, Royal Delft, and Dresden figurines at about one-third less than stateside prices. French beaded bags from $19 and Imperial Madeira linens at half the U.S. price will tempt you, and so will the H. Stern jewelry from Brazil and the Tostrup enamelled sterling from Norway. Exclusive designs of the Riise shop are the 18 karat gold charms, "Blackbeard," "Bluebeard," and "The Little Mermaid". They are $25 each. Ask to see the unmounted amethyst and topaze from Brazil. There's a lot of that Venetian glass in comical designs, which we can personally forego, but it will be hard to resist the Sorensen-designed Danish sterling flatware, and the high shine of silver plate from Denmark, Germany, Holland, Sweden and France. Take a good look at the hand-made Mexican silver hollowware by Codan too. The sweater department features Lyle & Scott cashmeres for men and women; Luisa Spangolis from Italy, and some smart, rugged hand-knits from Scotland, Holland and Norway. Swiss watches start at $7.95, and you'll find enough of these and German clocks to keep time from now till kingdom come.

THE SCANDINAVIAN SILVER CENTER is as smart and stream-lined a shop as you'll find in New York, San Francisco or even Dallas. It specializes in Scandinavian and English imports in silver, dinnerware, crystal, pottery, and jewelry with a few Zeiss and Leica German cameras thrown in, not to mention Zeiss and Hensoldt binoculars and telescopes. If you're a Royal Worcester fan, you'll be walking on air here among the large selection of this superb English bone china at 40 per cent less than mainland prices. There's some Swedish china that's worth looking at while you're at it, and some handsome earthenware patterns with complementary serving dishes and oven-proof casseroles. Sterling flatware and hollowware by Hingelberg starts as slow as $38 for a six-piece place setting. Their other favorite designer is Michelsen. Our bet is that you will be sorely tempted by the collection of sterling candelabra, some of it unusually well-designed. There's a lot of stainless steel flatware here: Danish, Swedish and German; it's interesting to compare them. Two lines of crystal, Kosta (from Sweden) and Stuart (English) are available in a variety of stemware, vases, decanters and other objects that ring out clearly to the thump of a finger nail. There is some good-looking hand-made Danish sterling silver jewelry, and a large line of David Andersen Norwegian enamel, not only in jewelry, but in flatware such as demi-tasse and dessert spoons and forks.

ALICE SHELDON has charming straw hats, bags, mats, scuffs and other useful items, designed and decorated in the shop's workrooms here in St. Thomas. Hats and bags start at $2.50. Cotton dresses range from $10.95 to $100. This is a good place for Island-designed swim togs, shirts, blouses, skirts, suits and dresses for kids of both sexes. There's a good selection of typical island dolls and souvenirs that shout West Indies. If you take a growing boy into Alice Sheldon's don't expect to get out without at least one stuffed alligator, or some other memento of your voyage such as a turtle, a bamboo flute, a voodoo drum, a pair of maracas, or a wooden knife. A full-grown man with rhythm in his soul may not be able to get past the full-grown ceremonial drums just sitting there begging to be beaten.

THE SPANISH MAIN has a wide selection of its own original designs in dresses, skirts, blouses, shorts and swim suits, plus such high fashion imports as the creations of Contessa Bernardini. Cocktail dresses from France, Germany and Austria round out a rather catholic collection. Prices run from $18.95 to $125. There are over 300 models of straw hats and bags, mostly imported from Italy and Spain. A feature in the sweater department are jewelled cardigans from Mallorca, $39.95 here, $85 at home. Luisa Spagnoli decorated sweaters are from $10 to $20 under their New York prices. There are many gifts for men. Our choice is the Italian sport shirts at $8.95 (they're $15 to $20 in mainland stores). You can also get shirts of exclusive prints made in The Spanish Main's workrooms. In the jewelry department, there's a perfect hailstorm of Austrian rhinestones and some interesting costume creations from West Germany, Italy, Egypt, and of course France.

SPARKY'S BOUTIQUE looks like a conquistador's dream of South American treasure, glittering with gold, amethyst, acquamarines and topaze. Unmounted, these semi-precious stones range from $25 up. Gold Calypso charms, typical of the islands. are priced from $22 to $39. The collection of precious and semi-precious jewelry from Brazil is guaranteed by the management to be exactly half the price that it is in the U.S.A. Added to the glitter of South American gold is the nacreous sheen of cultured pearl jewelry from Japan (from $15) and a number of more or less precious gold-mounted jewels from Italy. Swiss watches for women (Longines, Carlbro and Fabri) start at $67.50; for men (Longines, Invicta, Record Geneva) at $29.95 up. The automatic watch at $29.95 is $65 in the U.S.A. plus tax. Beaded and petit point bags from France, ranging from $8.95 to $50, and a full gamut of French perfumes.

STEELE'S GIFT AND GADGET SHOP. A typical bargain is a Japanese Canon camera VT de luxe model with 1.2 lens; it's $297 in this seventh heaven for males; $458 back in the states. Many other Japanese-made cameras at large savings over prices on the mainland. This applies to the large selection of Japanese binoculars. Photographers using black and white films can now have them developed and printed within a couple of hours in a brand new laboratory. In the toy department, you'll find all kinds of German mechanical wonders, assembly and tool sets; English dinkey toys and regimental soldiers. There's some wonderful cutlery here: pen knives, hunting knives, skin divers' knives, carving knives. German pocket flashlights sell at $4.95; binoculars start at $42, and there's a German transistor portable tape recorder for $219, which we have never seen in the U.S. for less than $345. Among the amusing souvenirs: those big musical postcards which play steel band music. Half a dollar.

STONERS OF ST. THOMAS have antique and modern precious and semi-precious stones, unset. An army of charms in Italian 18 karat gold include two island-inspired ones, "Long John Silver" and "The Steel Bandsman", $19.50 a piece, and exclusive with this shop. You'll save about 35 per cent on Italian leather goods, many of which are Stoner exclusives. They also have an exclusive on Dunhill smoking accesories, Royal Belvedere figurines and hand painted bronze birds from Austria, and some handsome English pewter tankards, made from original molds two centuries old.

TROPICANA has enough loot to tempt a pirate: French perfumes; Swiss watches; Danish sterling flatware; French, Italian and Madeira linens; jewelry from the world over, and French beaded bags as low as $10. But the big magnet here for some women will be Minton bone china, a Tropicana exclusive, which sells for $13.50 a place setting instead of $22.50 in the U.S.A. Crown Staffordshire birds and flowers are another specialty of this little treasure trove.

CASA VENEGAS has Rosenthal china dinnerware and figurines (exclusive) and the famous Hummel figurines (also exclusive). These, at prices from $2.50 to $13 are at least one-third less than they are at home. Swedish ceramics and Cacciapuoti figurines from Italy are other specialties. Venegas has a number of exclusive lines in cameras which reads like a roll call of the aristocracy: Minox, Contax, Rolliflex, Rollicord, and Edixa. A Leica camera body at $199 here costs $297 in the U.S., and lenses which sell here for $65 cost $105 in the stores back home.

SMALL WORLD. This is St. Thomas' most complete children's shop, and it is located in picturesque Palm Passage. You will find Swiss infant wear, Madeira blouses, lederhosen, hand-made embroidery, appliqué and smocking, Italian sweaters, girls' sandals, Swiss velvets, English and West German toys. There are also Calypso fashions for boys and girls, as well as straw goods, Caribbean toys, dolls and bongo drums. If you are visiting the Islands with children, don't miss this shop.

Many of these shops sell liquor by bottle and case at prices that could turn you into an alcoholic if it weren't for Uncle Sam's one-gallon-per-person duty-free limit on "spirits." A. H. Riise has a good liquor department; so do *Sparky's, A. H. Lockhart and Co., Bolero, Stoner's, George Levi & Sons,* and *Liquer Locker.*

For Calypso fanciers, there's an *RCA-Victor Shop* on Dronningens Gade, and a place appropriately-called *Calypso* at 12 Noregarde.

EXPLORING ST. THOMAS

Thirteen miles long, less than three miles wide, the island of St. Thomas rises abruptly from the sea to an altitude of 1500 feet. The Atlantic cuts its sprawling shores on the north, the Caribbean indents it on the south into a series of jagged, spectacular bays. One of these forms the deep water harbor of the Virgin Islands' superbly-situated capital, Charlotte Amalie.

This historic port, more commonly known as St. Thomas Harbor, reminds many tourists of Hong Kong. St. Thomas has been host to as many kinds of ship and mariner as ever plowed the waters of this world. It was the nearest thing to a home port for such notorious cutthroats as Captain Kidd and Edward Teach, better known as Blackbeard the Pirate. For Sir Francis Drake it was a lair from which to strike like lightning at Spanish galleons laden with New World gold, lumbering through the Anegada passage on their way back home to Spain.

Today the harbor bustles with ships on more peaceful missions, bringing meat, vegetables, fish, bauxite, and, above all, tourists to St. Thomas. At the height of the season you will see as many as three major cruise ships tied up in a row at the main wharf of Charlotte Amalie.

The colorful capital, Charlotte Amalie, climbs as high as it can with benefit of terraces, dominating the harbor with its pastel-colored houses from Denmark, Synagogue and Government Hills, which sailors still compare to the foretop, main and mizzenmast of a ship. The Danes, who moved quietly into St. Thomas in the 17th century amidst the colonial squabbles of England, Spain and France, built this town and named it after the consort of King Christian V. The governor divided the island into plantations and rented them out at a cost of one turkey a year per 125 acres. Soon there were over 170 thriving sugar plantations. The governor dined well. So did the planters. So, above all, did the slave traders. St. Thomas, supplying the plantations of America, became the biggest slave market in the world.

Waxing prosperous, Charlotte Amalie, already famous as a free port, welcomed all comers: New England sea captains, Civil War blockade runners, religious refugees from Europe, even pirates who came to buy supplies and sell their loot in this busy trading post with no holds barred, no questions asked. On two occasions the pirates actually captured the place. On two others the British seized St. Thomas in protest against the toleration of so much illegal piracy. St. Thomas, accustomed to receiving visitors of every stamp, took everything in its stride. The visitors in their turn stamped the port of Charlotte Amalie indelibly with all the color and excitement of a busy waterfront town.

The color and excitement are still there. And, despite the ravages of time and termites, fires and hurricanes, the city, with its narrow streets, ancient warehouses and old walls, remains redolent of colonizing, buccaneering Europe. It is a town to be explored on foot, and with sensible shoes to negotiate the cobbled streets, winding lanes, and time-worn stone stairways that struggle up to the heights of the city.

Starting at the top, the vista from the Skyline Drive, overlooking the town and harbor of Charlotte Amalie, is one of the most memorable views of the Caribbean. Beginning at the bottom, no tourist worthy of the name will miss the splendid old terra cotta warehouses which run from Dronningens Gade (Main Street) to the harbor. These have been transformed into a score or more of shops, cut by narrow Orchid Row, Hibiscus Alley, Jasmine Lane. The whole ensemble, known as Beretta Center, is one of the most attractive shopping districts in the Caribbean, or for that matter anywhere. Even if you have left your travelers checks with the purser, you will love ambling through the alleys of this area, fascinated by the display of merchandise and the color that meets the eye at every turn—in native bandanas, flaming bougainvillea cascading over ochre walls, glimpses of the tourquoise Caribbean, more intense for being held within a frame of island architecture.

Here in the heart of the shopping center, most visitors are surprised to learn that the great impressionist painter Camille Pissaro was born upstairs over what is now the local branch of Sears Roebuck; his parents are buried in the Jewish Cemetery of St. Thomas. Note: Even if you can resist a solid gold Brazilian charm for your bracelet at only $2.95, don't finish your exploring of the Beretta Center without ducking into A. H. Riise's Gift Shop to see an ancient Danish fireplace they'd be proud to have in Denmark. By the same token, even if you can withstand the temptation of a madras swimsuit at $3.50, don't miss the beautiful arches and stonework of The Carib.

A twice-daily pageant of local color is provided by the inter-island boats coming in at dusk or in the early morning and unloading their bright, beautifully-woven baskets of produce on the waterfront sea wall. Best of all is the weekly Saturday market with natives unloading their donkeys and setting up stalls of gleaming tropical fish, brilliant fruits and vegetables in a maze of color and sound.

Venerable Buildings

Over half the buildings of St. Thomas are more than a century old, something of a record for an American community. Most venerable of all is Old Fort Christian, built by the first Danish settlers nearly 300 years ago and named for King Christian V. A striking example of 17th-century military architecture, this fort served as jail, church, vicarage, courthouse and governor's residence all rolled into one massive pile of masonry. Numerous pirates, including one of the meanest of them, the notorious Fawcett, were hanged at Fort Christian. It is still used as a jail and police station.

Also dating from the 17th century are the Nisky Moravian Mission and the tower of Bluebeard's Castle, now part of a hotel. Two old churches are worth a visit: the Dutch Reformed Church, one of the first of this faith in the New World outside of New Amsterdam-New York, and the 18th-century Lutheran Church, second oldest in the Western Hemisphere and still using its two-centuries-old ecclesiastical silver.

The Jewish Synagogue, the second oldest under the U.S. flag, long thought to be the first is the only one on American soil to maintain the old tradition of keeping clean sand on its floor to commemorate the flight of the Jews from Egypt through the desert. This place of worship and the interesting Jewish cemetery are another reminder of the rich cultural heritage and the tradition of tolerance which have shaped the Virgin Islands, one of whose 17th-century governors was a Jew.

Charlotte Amalie's Grand Hotel, which opened in 1841, is a fascinating relic of 19th-century luxury. Its original third story was blown off in a hurricane. Other buildings of more than usual interest include the handsome Government House with its beautiful wrought iron balcony, near the top of the much-photographed Street of the 99 Steps; Hotel 1829, a patrician residence of that date, whose thick walls and splendid patio reflect the opulence of plantation days; the Lutheran Parsonage and the Danish Consulate, dominating the whole bay from Denmark Hill, both typical of 19th-century Danish architecture; and "Quarters B," once the German consulate, now a government office building famous for its unusual staircase, transplanted from a ship. The character of the whole municipal area of Charlotte Amalie is protected by a watchful government commission which checks all construction plans before issuing building permits.

If you have prowled around the waterfront and the Beretta Center, climbed the 99 Steps, and seen more than one of these historic buildings, you will be ready for some refreshment. Take a cab to Bluebeard's and try their buffet luncheon served up with a wonderful view; or go up to the Mountain Top Hotel and sample their celebrated Banana Daiquiri. The food is good there too, and so is the panorama. If you're not ready for lunch, the Coffee House downtown can offer you almost every kind of coffee you ever heard of, hot or iced, plus some homebaked pastries to refresh and sustain you. If you're allergic to coffee, order a Virgin Daiquiri at Sebastian's or Hagen House on the waterfront. It will take your mind off your feet and fortify you for further sightseeing.

There is still the post office with murals painted by Stephen Dohanos under WPA auspices before he struck it rich with The Saturday Evening Post. There is Cha-Cha town, the French village at the west end of the harbor, a fascinating ethnic enclave well worth a ramble. There is the Virgin Islands Museum, depleted of its greatest treasures by the Smithsonian

Institution, but still conserving enough mementoes of island history to warrant a visit. Oil and watercolor paintings by local artists? You'll find these at the Grand Gallery, mostly island scenes, at $15 and up.

Having explored Charlotte Amalie, it is time to cross the mountain range that cuts St. Thomas in two and visit the north side of the island, far more beautiful, the northsiders will tell you, than anything on the Caribbean side. Here are the splendid panoramic views over the Atlantic, Magens Bay which many call the most beautiful beach in the world, and the whole panoramic eastern sweep of American and British Virgins, green in the opalescent sea. The north side has more rain, lusher vegetation, more tranquillity, better beaches. Best way to see it all is to take the standard island tour in a taxi. It takes about two hours, costs four dollars a head, and can be easily arranged through Virgin Island Tours or Silver Streak Taxi Company.

The drivers, excellent guides, will point out all the points of interest: Drake's Seat, where that old sea dog surely never sat, but from which you will have a grand view of the waters in which he operated and which are now named in his honor; Venus Pillar, the astronomical obelisk on Magnolia Hill; Mafolie, the quaint French refugee settlement with its pretty little church, and the Estate Dorothea, agricultural experiment station, a must for students of tropical fauna. When you return to Charlotte Amalie, don't miss seeing it at night with its twinkling lights like stars reflected in the harbor.

If you are planning to stay in St. Thomas longer than a day, you should see the Marine Gardens by glass bottom boat and take the sunset harbor cruise. The Marine Gardens, surpassing those of Nassau and Catalina, are the most interesting this side of Australia. The tour takes about an hour, costs $2.50, and leaves five times daily from the V.I.P. boat dock next to the submarine base. You can also take the Water Isle hotel ferry from the submarine base dock for a day at Water Island outside St. Thomas Harbor. A station wagon will meet you and take you to the Water Isle Hotel and Beach Club on Honeymoon Bay. You're welcome to use the small boats and beach equipment; a barbecue lunch is served, and you can have a day of complete relaxation for about $3.50. A more ambitious nautical affair is the *Slingarin* (from an old West Indian word, meaning to have fun). This includes "glass bottoming," snorkeling, spear-fishing, sailing, charcoal-broiled lunch on the beach and an afternoon of deep sea fishing in calm waters. Price for the Slingarin is $12.50 per person, all inclusive. The boat leaves the V.I.P. dock at 10 a.m., returns to St. Thomas at 5 in the afternoon.

PRACTICAL INFORMATION FOR ST. CROIX

HOTELS

THE BUCCANEER, which overlooks Christiansted harbor and its own three beaches, has 39 rooms, eight suites, accommodations for 75 guests. Latest additions are the Doubloon cottages along the beach, same size and price as the hotel's suites with one extra—a Jeep Gala thrown in for cottagers. It's a modern resort hotel, well run by Mrs. John Colby. You can go spear fishing or rod fishing from the hotel grounds, but bring own equipment. Rowboats and beach house for the use of guests. Good restaurant, bar, snack bar on beach, tennis court and golf privileges. Saturday night buffets with steel bands are fun. Rates, Modified American Plan, run from $22 a day single to $42 double; suites $52 from Jan. 15 to April 1. Summer rates (May 1 to Dec. 20) are from $16 single to $30 double; suites $34. Mrs. Colby also has some tempting "between season" rates in effect from Dec. 20 to Jan. 15 and from April 1 to May 1. They start at $18 single and offer doubles at $38; suites $48. All rooms have private bath. Tel. 400. Cable: Buccaneer St. Croix.

CANE BAY PLANTATION offers six completely furnished housekeeping cottages with private baths on the north shore drive between Christiansted and Frederiksted. There's a private, tree-shaded beach at the foot of the driveway. Manager Dorothy Colby provides a dinghy for fishing with glass spotting box for the wonderful undersea gardens just off shore. Snorkeling equipment is available. The cottages are set in a 40-acre Shore Estate, a good

center for hiking over mountain trails. Cottages are for two, but ample enough to accommodate a third person. The Studio, Fruit Hus, Terrace and Stoney Hus rent for $65 a week in winter (Dec. 1-Apr. 30), $45 a week in summer. Long Hus, with a 30 foot screened gallery and view of mountains and sea will cost you $85 a week in the winter season, $60 in summer. Extra occupant pays $21 per week. Trip by car to the airport is $4. Mrs. Colby also provides her guests with a good library and can arrange for car rental.

CLOVER CREST HOTEL, three miles from Frederiksted, 10 from the airport, has spacious private wooded grounds, large salt water pool. Luncheon is served at the tropical bar beside the pool. Mrs. Beulah Hinkson operates this comfortable establishment on the Modified American Plan. The cuisine, American and Cruzan, is recommended. Beulah's buffets are something special and her "fantail" cocktail is served at the poolside and upper level bars. Recreation includes snorkeling, fishing, lobstering, horseback riding and dancing to the steel band. From Dec. 1-Apr. 30 single rooms are $22-$24 per day; doubles $34-$38, and suites $45. Singles in the summer season are $14-$16; doubles $26-$28; suites $40. All rooms have private bath.

CLUB COMANCHE, owned and managed by Edward C. Dale Jr. and Guy O. Reynolds, is a most attractive resort hotel in the center of Christiansted overlooking that picture postcard harbor. The facilities include Mainhouse, an old Danish residence; Bridgehouse, a cottage near the pool; Staghouse, which offers reasonable accommodation for men (without private baths); and Sugar Mill, a cottage on the water designed for honeymooners. In addition, the Club Comanche hotel provides a salt water pool, two bars, sailboats, rowboats, canoe and a 72-foot yawl, the Comanche, for its guests. Good meals are served on the Pavilion Terrace. Continental Plan rates (Dec. 15-Apr. 15) are $11 to $13.50 single; $18 to $30 double. Off season the rates are $7 to $11.50 single; $15 to $26 double. Tel. 24. Cable: St. Croix.

COTTAGES-BY-THE-SEA are just south of Frederiksted on a beach of fine white sand near Sandy Point Lagoon, a pleasant situation ameliorated by shade trees. There are two cottages for two persons, one for four, all furnished for housekeeping with electricity, hot and cold water. Winter rates for the smaller cottages are $85 to $115 weekly, $300 a month. $2 per day for third person in small cottages. Summer rates (May 1 to Nov. 30) are about 35 per cent less. Harold J. Benedict, owner.

THE CRUZANA, just outside Christiansted, has the ample graciousness of a former plantation great house and a spacious view over the harbor and the Caribbean. Its 12 guests are generally in a state of euphoria thanks to the personal attention of the owner-managers, T. Holland and Elinor C. Hunter, who provide them with good food, island tours, frequent trips to town and beach, box lunches, and plenty of opportunities for sailing, spearfishing, lobster hunting and other Cruzan delights. Rates (Dec. 16 to April 15) are $19 to $22 in doubles with connecting bath. Singles pay from $16. Rates from April 16 to Dec. 14 are $16-$23 per couple par day (a bargain, especially if you draw a suite), $12 single. Conti-

nental Plan. Tel. 246. Cable: Cruzana.

ESTATE CARLTON is a top flight luxury hotel on a 325 acre 18th-century sugar plantation just 2½ miles from the airport. Set in a grove of tamarind trees, this sumptuous establishment has 60 rooms, each with private bath and gallery, facing well landscaped grounds. It offers its lucky guests a private beach, a tennis court, a nine-hole golf course, a swimming pool, and a first class American cuisine spiced with Cruzan and European delicacies. George Papadam is the manager of this highly successful enterprise, and he will arrange to have you met at the airport if you give him advance notice. You can also arrange for car-hire at the hotel. The Estate Carlton is on the expensive side, especially in the winter season, but worth it. Rates, Modified American Plan. Summer rates (April 1 to Dec. 30) are $15 to $20 per day single, $20 to $35 per day double. At time of publication the winter rates had not yet been set. Tel. Frederiksted 30J and 135J. Cable: Carlton St. Croix.

ESTATE GOOD HOPE HOTEL, was purchased in the fall of 1959 by Laurance Rockefeller. It offers its clients the privacy of a large pool and its own crescentshaped beach, proximity to golf course, good fishing and snorkeling. Excellent food in the dining terrace overlooking the sea. With an 8-room addition it can accommodate 44 guests, two to a suite, or 88 four to a suite. Good Hope is open all year round, while more than a quarter of a million dollars has been spent on new additions, enlarging the pool area and installing the air conditioned rooms. American Plan rates from Dec. 20-Apr. 15 are $38 single, $55 double and $65 for the suites. A third person in a suite is $16 per day. Last summer's rates were $35 per day double, American Plan. Tel 170. Cable: Goodhope.

THE VIRGIN ISLANDS

GRAPETREE BAY HOTEL AND COTTAGES, seven miles from Christiansted, is directly on the water with a backdrop of hills separating it from the north shore and the extreme east end. New in 1959, it has 32 private cottages which provide 57 bedrooms, 25 studio bedrooms, 14 suites, all in the midst of a 750-acre resort estate. The main building has two dining areas, the formal dining room and the snack luncheon tables around the salt water pool on the ground level. There is an open-to-the-sky lounge for cocktailing aand dancing. Shops attracts the guests from the lobby. There are tennis courts and arrangements can be made for golf, sailing, snorkeling and fishing. The cuisine is first-rate, American with a few Cruzan specialties. Modified American Plan. Daily rates from Dec. 1-May 1 single $30-$38, double $42-$54, cottages $130-$150 with a third person in room $14 per day. Off-season rates $11-$13 single, $21-$25 double Modified American Plan. Tel. 385-J. Cable: Grapetree.

HOTEL-ON-THE-CAY on private Protestant Cay in Christiansted Harbor is the first resort hotel established on St. Croix fourteen years ago. You reach it in a boat (the distance is only 150 yards) rowed by a native boatman. When you disembark you'll find a wonderful old 18th-century house in the midst of a mahogany grove. This used to be the official summer residence of the Danish governor. On hand to greet you will be Mr. and Mrs. Paul Gilles, the managers, as nice a couple as you'll find in the hotel business. They're very proud of the place, as well they might be, and they want you to enjoy yourself. To help you do so, they provide first rate meals and all sorts of water sport equipment. Luncheon is served every day of the year buffet style under the trees at the water's edge. Rates, Modified American Plan range from $20-$28

single, $30-$38 double, 3rd person in room $14 per day for the winter season from Dec. 15-May 1. For an unusual travel experience, evocative of old world charm, ask for the Governor's Master Bedroom. There's a Honeymoon Cottage Suite that is a "honey". Off season rates, both American and European plan, run 20 to 30 per cent lower. Tel. 264. Cable: Gillesisle St. Croix. The Gilles' also run the *Pink Fancy* apartments (see below).

KING CHRISTIAN APARTMENTS on the second floor of one of Christiansted's fine old buildings on the wharf facing the harbor, where yachts are moored and schooners from neighboring islands tie up at the dock to discharge and load cargo as they have been doing for over two hundred years, are completely furnished for housekeeping. There are six apartments of 1½ or 3½ rooms, each. Rates, European Plan, from Dec. 20 to May 1 are $25 daily and $150 weekly, with a $5 a day extra charge for third person in the apartment. During the summer the apartments rent from $72-$90 a week. On the ground floor is a restaurant and cocktail lounge in a lovely setting overlooking the harbor. Open to the public. Dancing in a garden patio most evenings. Tel. 373W. Cable: Hilty St. Croix.

LA GRANGE HOUSE is five minutes from Frederiksted and has its own beach where luncheon is served in great comfort at the beach house. Dining in the former great house of the estate, with its Danish furnishings, with the superlative Danish-American Cruzan cooking of the owner, Mrs. Asta Fleming, is reminiscent of the days of the prosperous sugar plantations. At La Grange the Fleming family, who have lived on St. Croix for generations, provide authentic island atmosphere of a bygone era. There are accommodations for 36 guests in double rooms, waterfront beach cottages and a waterfront suite. Rates Modified American Plan are

THE VIRGIN ISLANDS

$28 single; $40-$50 double, third person $10 per day from Dec. 1 to Apr. 15. All rooms have private bath or shower. Summer rates with only a double rate: $14. Tel. 66. Cable: LaGrange.

PELICAN COVE COTTAGES, two efficiency units, are located on a white sand beach under the shade of coconut palms three miles from Christiansted. Each apartment is for two persons and each has a private patio facing the sea. There is a small beach club on the property with a snack bar. Guests may use the club and meet residents of the island who are members. Dinner is usually served Saturday nights and on some special occasions.
European Plan rates are $20 daily and $100 weekly from Dec. 1 to May 1. Off-season $65 weekly. Phone 173W2. Cable: Pelicove.

PINK FANCY APARTMENTS are attractively furnished, fully equipped apartments grouped around a private fresh water swimming pool in the heart of Christiansted, five minutes' walk from the Hotel-on-the Cay dock. Since Pink Fancy is owned by Paul Gilles of Hotel on the Cay located on Protestant Cay in Christiansted Harbor, guests enjoy all the privileges of the Cay (see listing under hotels), including morning coffee and afternoon tea served free on the beach to Pink Fancy guests. There's a supermarket in Christiansted if you want to do your own cooking. You'll get warm welcome. Modified American Plan rates are $25 single and $32 to $34 double from Dec. 15 to Apr. 15; off season $13 single and $25 double. The apartments, actually most are separate cottages, accommodate from one to four persons. European Plan rates range from $85 to $175 weekly from Dec. 1 to May 1 and from $55 to $75 off season. These rates include daily maid service. Tel. 159. Cable: Gillesisle, St. Croix.

RICHMOND PLANTATION HOUSE, half a mile from Cristiansted, overlooks the harbor, offers excellent Danish and Cruzan cuisine, use of two private beaches, golf privileges, its own car rental system. Six rooms, all with gallery and private bath. Once the Plantation's great house, this small, intimate place is highly regarded by all who have stayed here. Owner-Manager Balifour Fleming. Tel. 316. Cable: Richill.

ST. CROIX BY THE SEA welcomes its guests in their spacious lounge with its Danish furniture, old street lamps from Copenhagen and tropical planting below the window-wall beyond which the surf breaks on the beach. Their freeform swimming pool is constantly replenished with salt water pumped in from the sea. This comfortable, relaxing hotel is owned by Erik Lawaetz, a member of one of the old Danish families of St. Croix. He recently added a wing of 25 air-conditioned rooms and a large night club, the *Obia* (Black Magic), with dancing and entertainment. Although the hotel is operated on the Modified American Plan there is always available at noon time a buffet luncheon in the main patio dining room or snacks at the poolside. From Dec. 16 to Apr. 16 the rates are Modified American Plan $26 to $34 single and $34 to $44 double. Mr. Lawaetz has no objection to children; he'll put a crib in the room for $2.50 a day extra, a third bed for $12. Off season rates are $16 to $22 per day single, and $26 to $31 double with $10 per day for third person in room. Tel. 208. Cable: Cruztel.

SPRAT HALL is an attractive, beautifully-furnished guest house on a 200-acre shore estate with private white sand beaches just a mile and a half out of Frederiksted. Accommodations for 20 guests in 12 rooms, all with private bath and such luxury touches as beautyrest beds. Among the attractions are free horseback riding, fishing boat for charter, a 90 foot steel-dock for boating and swimming, water ski-

435

ing, aquaplaning, outboard motor boat and sail boat. Dining room was recommended by Duncan Hines; lunch is served on the beach, and of course there's a bar. Joyce and Jim Hurd manage this appealing place. Rates, American Plan are $22 single, $40 double and $10 for a third in the room from Dec. 16 to April 30. Off season rates are $14 single, $26 double American Plan. Sprat Hall is closed in May. Tel. Frederiksted 145. Cable: Sprathall.

MAHOGANY INN. Built in 1750, the Mahogany Inn, as it is known now, must be considered as one of the finest examples of Danish West Indian architecture and personifies the luxury under which the people of that era lived. A large stone walled enclosed courtyard, shaded by century-old mahogany trees, can accommodate up to 100 luncheon and dinner guests. Mohogany Inn serves cocktail and dinners by candlelight and specializes in exotic dishes. The building itself has 8 accommodations with air conditioning optional. Manager-owners are Virginia and Rutherford Eakin. Winter rates are $24 and up, double; summer rates $14 and up, double. Rates include a Continental breakfast (no single rooms during the season).

BELVEDERE ESTATE, Box 6, King's Hill, St. Croix; R. L. Weser, owner-manager. Tel. 249W1. Cable: Belvedere. On picturesque north shore 25 minutes from Christiansted and Frederiksted. One 2-bedroom house sleeps 6, two 1-bedroom cottages, sleep 2 to 4 each, one efficiency, single occupancy only. All accommodations with private bath, electric kitchens, galleries and/or terraces. Large fresh water swimming pool, private beach, automobile available. Free transportation to and from airport; first breakfast and dinner supplied by management. Summer weekly rates for two bed-room house $100, cottages $65, efficiencies $50. Extra person

$25. Children under 6 no charge. From Dec. 15 to Apr. 15 the rates run from $85 to $120.

TRANQUILITY COTTAGES, Box 388, Estate Northside, Frederiksted. Tel. 139J2. Seven cottages on hill sites overlooking the sea. Each completely furnished for housekeeping, 2 bedrooms, bath, kitchen, roofed patio. Sleep up to 5. 600 ft. beach below. Rates on request.

IRVIN APARTMENTS in Frederiksted, near center of town. Mrs. Rea Irvin, owner. Tel. 125W or 199. Two housekeeping residences with 2 double bedrooms, large living room, kitchen, bath, gallery, private tropical walled garden with each. Rates, $85 each per week summer; from Dec. 1 to May 1, $150 week. Beach facilities available. West Indian type restaurant serving excellent food for lunch and dinner on premises.

ST. CROIX BEACH APARTMENTS, Estate Turner Hole. About 10 miles from Christiansted on the south shore of St. Croix. Thirty-eight modern, furnished housekeeping apartments, each with its own lanai facing a 60 ft. wide sandy beach. Sea bathing and a swimming pool. Small commissary for that forgotten grocery item. Guests may enjoy free use of boats, fishing pier, bicycles, beach umbrellas and shuffle board. Lon Southerland, manager. Summer rates Modified American Plan, from $28 per day double, $14 per day single.

VILLAGE AT CANE BAY, Box 677, Christiansted. Cable Village. Mr. and Mrs. John Blair, owners. On the north shore road between Christiansted and Frederiksted just above private beach. Five cottages for 2 or more guests each. Unusually well and tastefully furnished. Radio in each unit. Boat and motors. Fishing. Well stocked commissary. Cars for rent. No charge for transportation to or from airport. Maid service available. Rates, Dec. 15 to Apr. 15, $85 to $140 weekly, third person $15 weekly.

THE VIRGIN ISLANDS

SUNSET BEACH APARTMENTS. Located on their own white sand beach, these new apartments provide the utmost in comfort. Six of the ten apartments have two bedrooms with connecting baths, a galley kitchen, and a large living room with magnificent view of the setting sun over your own beach.

The other four apartments are one bedroom arrangements with the same galley kitchen, living room, bath, and beach. Ably operated by a young couple, John and Jan Petersen. Rates, on a European Plan, are $125 per week for larger apartments.

RESTAURANTS

Rasmussen's Coffee Shop and Soda Fountain, Christiansted, despite that wonderful Danish name, is about as American as you can get, a real lunch counter with pie, doughnuts, double rich malteds, and coffee brewing away in glass pots. You can dine at a table if you prefer and have cocktails in the Rasmussen's small modern restaurant, which, if memory serves, is called The Elbow Room. Good American dishes, occasionally with native Cruzan overtones, and the prices are moderate.

Prosperity Plantation Club is a popular restaurant just out of Frederiksted, and doubles as a night club. Big and gay; dancing under the stars, Wednesdays and Saturdays to an orchestra. Other nights it's apt to be to the dulcet strains of a juke box. For good local entertainment try to go when they are having a community benefit on the terrace.

King Christian Restaurant is one of the most attractive on St. Croix. meals and drinks are served in the indoor cocktail lounge, in the garden and on the large outdoor patio facing Christiansted Harbor. The new manager, Charlie Lebano, of Juan les Pins, promises an even more attractive spot for the winter season. Local bands for dancing play every night except Sunday.

La Piazza Restaurant is one of the most delightful in Christiansted. This is not a fancy name for a fancy place; it is literally "on the cobblestones", with nothing above you but the blue sky. There is an awning over the bar, however, to insure against watered-down martinis just in case it does rain, which is rare. *La Piazza* is under the able ownership and management of Nicole and Verne Wyss. Verne is cook and bartender as well, and does a magnificent job with Swiss and French specialities, all served *al fresco,* of course.

Other well patronized restaurants in Christiansted are *Mahogany Inn,* food and drink served on the ground floor of a splendid, centturies'-old building, facing the garden patio. Everything cooked to order and best quality; *Hamilton House* on the second floor of the building where Alexander Hamilton clerked in his youth, serving very good American and West Indian food—Aubrey Saunders, a dashing Englishman, entertains at the piano for after dinner customers. *Friday's* is unique—small, in a garden patio, serving only breakfast, luncheon and drinks. If you wish to go farther afield, just outside of town is the *Pelican Cove Club* where you may order a hamburger and a drink at lunch time.

Cocktail spots in town are the *Stone Balloon* and the *Comanche bars,* among others.

Frederiksted boasts two very superior eateries. *McConnell's* is the sort of place you expect to find on the second floor of an old West Indian building. The food is imaginative and very good. One of those spots where local characters, nice ones (Barbara McConnell is something of a character herself) other residents and visitors gather to compare notes and enjoy each other's company.

Hotels and guests houses welcome other than their own guests for meals but appreciate reservations.

NIGHT LIFE

On St. Croix it's the attractive *Morningstar Club* on a hilltop about five miles outside of Christiansted. Jackets for men, please, after 7. Or the large *Obia Club* at the St. Croix By The Sea hotel. In Frederiksted you'll enjoy dancing outdoors on the Rainbow Terrace of *Prosperity Plantation* (see under St. Croix Restaurants). There are some attractive little bars where informal dancing is the order of the night on this relatively sedate and subdued island. You'll have no trouble finding them; just follow your ears.

Most hotels offer nightly entertainments, and your hotel manager will be glad to advise you about them.

SHOPPING

Although not the merchandise mart that St. Thomas is, at the rate it is growing, St. Croix will eventually catch up with it. Already there are branches of some of St. Thomas' leading shops, the *Continental, Little Switzerland, Compass Rose, Casa Venegas* and *Cavanagh's*. The latter has two shops on St. Croix —in Christiansted and Frederiksted Unique any place would be *The Little Guardhouse* which features antiques related to the Caribbean area and Soch Svender's extraordinary wood sculptures and water colors. Just to browse around this shop is a treat. *Jeltrup's* is a professional bookshop where you will find most of the books available on the Virgin Islands and the Caribbean. *Danish House*, with a branch in Frederiksted, is one of the larger shops carrying predominantly Danish goods, with a fine assortment of china dinnerware and porcelain figurines. *William Baar's International Shop* is outstanding for its island-made ceramics and hand illustrated cards. They have created island dolls. In addition they carry a wide assortment of imported merchandise.

Island Imports represent *Maison Danoise* with their fine line of china, glass and silver and in addition have a fine stock of English leather goods, framed old prints and maps, straw hats and bags.

The Island Sport Shop outfits milady with dresses, skirts and blouses, as well as sportswear from Italy, France and other centers of style and fine fabrics. To adorn her further there is a lovely collection of costume jewelry, purses and scarfs. The men aren't overlooked —they will be attracted to the practical sports shirts, shorts and shoes.

Two men's outfitters in the sporty madras jackets and shorts, tropical ties and all the adornments male vacationers like are *Behr's* and the *For Him Shop*.

There are many other small shops and the liquor merchants—*Rassmussen's, Dam's, The Gallery, Alexander Moorhead's, Andrews* and *Carib Cellars*—all of whom will pack your five duty-free bottles in a safe carrying carton.

Danish furniture is available in a wide selection at *Copenhagen, Ltd.* and at the *Continental*. They'll take your order and have it delivered to the States from Denmark duty-free. Just declare the purchase on your customs return.

Snorkeling is a great sport in the Virgin Islands and *Bill Miller's, Dick Newick* and the *Island Marine Shop* have good stocks of fishing and snorkeling gear.

THE VIRGIN ISLANDS
EXPLORING ST. CROIX

Seven national flags have floated over St. Croix since Columbus was met by a shower of Carib arrows when he landed at Salt River in 1493. The island, called St. Croy by the Natives, is the largest of the Virgins: 28 miles long, up to 10 miles wide, and encompassing 84 square miles of rolling, cultivated land. The ruins of great plantation houses recall the days when St. Croix rivalled Barbados as the greatest producer of sugar in the West Indies. Acres of nodding silver plumes are a reminder that sugar still looms large in the island economy, now under the auspices of the U.S. government.

St. Croix is 40 miles southwest of St. Thomas, 25 minutes away by Caribair, a world apart in atmosphere. When you set foot on St. Croix you have stepped back briefly into the past, from a century of neon, as one traveler put it, to a century of candlelight. While this may not be literally true, it does express the strange sensation of time receding that is common among so many travelers with the leisure and good fortune to visit this "Garden of the West Indies."

The impression is especially striking in the island's tiny capital, Christiansted, whose population barely exceeds 4,000 souls. More than one visitor has described it simply as the loveliest town in the West Indies. In any event we have yet to meet a traveler who has not been enchanted by this beautifully-preserved old Danish port, rimming the crystal-clear water of a coral-bound bay on the north eastern shore of St. Croix. The red-roofed, 18th-century buildings are pale blue, yellow, pink and ochre with that subtle pastel combination of high brilliance and low saturation that produces a wonderful patina in the tropic sun. As if this were not enough, the pastel colors are punctuated everywhere by a blaze of bougainvillaea or hibiscus, usually glimpsed through the wrought-iron gates of some patio or garden. And then the scene will be animated by some graceful Cruzan woman, her head bound in an orange kerchief; or a donkey cart will pass, loaded with avocadoes.

At first glance it all looks like a perfect setting for an operetta. But then you make the tactile discovery that Christiansted is quite real. The houses are solid stone, their thick walls still performing miracles of 18th-century air conditioning. Arcades have transformed sidewalks into the coolest of colonnades, a European touch that makes shopping and sightseeing in this miniature free port a pleasure.

The town square and waterfront area at the foot of King

Street have, since 1952, been officially classified as a National Historic Site. This is the best place to begin your exploration of Christiansted. Outstanding in this remarkable ensemble of history preserved in stone are the 17th-century Dutch Fort Christiansvaern, the Danish Post Office, the Public Library, the original Customs House, the old church known as The Steeple Building, and Government House.

The Public Library houses the St. Croix Museum, not the big, exhausting type, but a fine small collection of pre-Columbian artifacts plus a number of historically interesting relics of Danish plantation days. It is open from 10 to noon and from 3 to 5 daily, Sundays from 3 to 5; highly recommended.

Alexander Hamilton Worked Here

The lovely ball room of Government House, original capitol of the Danish West Indies, is decorated with replicas of the original Danish furnishings, a gift from Denmark to the United States. Across from Government House is a celebrated hardware store, still in operation, of special sentimental interest to Americans; it was here that Alexander Hamilton worked at the age of 13. The quondam clerk would probably have been astonished to know that this emporium would one day be known as Alexander Hamilton's Store.

The shopping center of Christiansted is cheek by jowl with the National Historic Site. Centering on Company Street and King Street, it's smaller than the one at Charlotte Amalie, but has the same free port advantages and offers similar temptations.

Fifteen miles from Christiansted (you can go by bus or taxi) is the almost equally appealing port of Frederiksted, harboring assorted ships and a population of some 2,000 at the western end of the island. The town was ravaged by a fire in 1878. When the houses were rebuilt, Victorian architecture was the rage. So you have the pastel-colored Danish-type houses plus lacy galleries of iron and wood, cupolas, curlicues and enough gingerbread details to illustrate all the fairy tales of Hans Christian Andersen. The pretty little Old Fort, built in 1760, looks positively stark by comparison. It was here that the proclamation abolishing slavery in the Virgin Islands was read in 1848.

Frederiksted is headquarters for the St. Croix Landmarks League, an excellent organization which arranges "Open House Tours" of some of the most interesting homes on the island.

The tours, scheduled two days a week in the winter season, are an outstanding bargain at $3 per person. Among the houses, graciously opened to the public by their owners, is *Annaly*, a typical round stone sugar mill, transformed by Ward Canaday into the kind of residence you would like to move into. Two other outstanding places included in the tours are *La Grange*, lovely old Danish manor house and garden, and *Butler Bay*, a beautifully restored and furnished plantation house, as gracious as a quadrille by candlelight.

Between the towns of Frederiksted and Christiansted are the old plantations, some in picturesque ruins, some still in use, some restored as guest houses. Their names are haunting, often redolent of the pangs of misprised love: Anna's Hope, Peter's Rest, Upper Love, Jealousy, Lower Love, Sally's Fancy. They are fascinating with their round sugar mills, their noble double stairways, their mute, melancholy testimony to past grandeur. Among the most interesting is Estate Bulow Minde. Built in 1838, this was the home of the Danish Governor Peter von Scholten, who freed the slaves a decade later. It has everything to appeal to a romantic temperament: a secret staircase, a chapel, associations with the passion for human liberty, and an octagonal watchtower with not one but eight magnificent views.

One off-shore aspect of St. Croix which should not be missed is *Buck Island National Monument*. Plan to devote a full day to this adventure, with a leisurely morning sail (cold beer provided on board, but better ask your hotel to pack a picnic lunch). Buck Island itself has a glorious border of beach, but its principal attraction is the underwater snorkeling trail. Swimmers are able to follow a sequence of labels that identify the different types of coral, underwater growth and brightly-hued tropical fish. A late-afternoon sail back to Christiansted Harbor completes the day. Ask at your hotel about chartering one of the many sailboats available for this short haul.

Whim, three miles from Christiansted, near the airport, is a French chateau which was spared during the slave uprisings, the French chatelaine having had the decency to be kind to her servants. It has been restored to serve as a museum. *Judith's Fancy*, modelled after a French palace, was once the residence of the Governor of the Knights of Malta. It is a romantic, picturesque ruin set in the midst of an estate of several hundred scenic acres, now being promoted as a real estate development for home sites.

If you are interested in the process of producing sugar, the

THE VIRGIN ISLANDS

still flowing life blood of St. Croix, the Bethlehem Sugar Factory is most hospitable to visitors. The botanically-minded will gravitate to the U.S. Agricultural Experiment Station. And no one with the slightest feeling for history can remain insensible to the experience of seeing where Columbus anchored at Salt River in 1493. Columbus called it El Cabo de las Flechas, or Cape of the Arrows in memory of the reception he got. You may anticipate a warmer welcome today.

ST. JOHN

Three miles east of St. Thomas across Pillsbury Sound lies the island of St. John. It's about half an hour by boat from St. Thomas Harbor, and it comes close to realizing that travel folder dream, "an unspoiled tropical paradise." In addition to its scenic and climatic advantages, it is said to be one of two places in the world where the common cold does not exist. Three-fourths of St. John's 21 square miles officially became The Virgin Islands National Park in 1956, the 29th American area to receive this guarantee of national protection. St. John's restrained and tasteful development to date and its presentation to the American people are the work of Laurance S. Rockefeller, who has contributed largely to the historic Caneel Bay Plantation, one of the most attractive small resort developments anywhere.

Beautiful and seemingly undisturbed St. John is covered with a lush mantle of tropical vegetation including a bay-tree forest whose leaves supply St. Thomas with the raw material of its fragrant bay rum. Clean, gleaming white sand beaches fringe the many bays that are scalloped out along the northern shore, and the iridescent water is just about perfect for swimming, fishing, snorkeling and underwater photography.

Historically, St. John followed the path of its larger sisters, up to a point. It has known the tread of Dutch, English, Spanish, French and Danish adventurers. The Danes, who first came to the Virgin Islands in 1670, didn't settle on St. John until 1717. By 1726 all available land was taken over by plantations, and sugar was king. The slaves, ill-treated by their Danish masters, revolted in 1733 at which time many of the planters took refuge at Caneel Bay Plantation. It took French soldiers imported from Martinique to quell the rebellion. Many of the slaves threw themselves off the cliff at Mary's point in preference to capture and its consequences. The Natives insist that the ghosts of these ancestors still haunt this lofty promontory. The abolition of slavery in 1848 dealt

442

The placid platinum coast of Barbados

a death blow to the sugar economy of St. John. The planters left. The tropical jungle took over, and the island returned in an incredibly short time to bush.

Today there are only 750 Natives on St. John and about a hundred Continentals. The Continentals are in the tourist business or permanent residents who have found their ideal place to retire. The Natives do a little fishing and farming, and they weave some of the most beautiful baskets you ever saw from the black wist vine. Aside from these sturdy items, plan to do your Virgin Island shopping on St. Thomas or St. Croix.

St. John is for the traveler who wants to escape from the pressures of 20th-century life for a day, a week, perhaps forever. Sightseeing is done on horse or donkeyback, or by jeep. All three means of transport can be hired on the island. Guides are useful, sometimes indispensable in exploring the scenic mountain trails and the sobering bush-covered ruins of old forts and palatial plantation houses. You can take a trail once used by the Indians from Cruz to Coral Bay long before Columbus stumbled on these islands. Another trail will lead you to ancient, still undeciphered Indian inscriptions on the rocks above Reef Bay. The warlike Caribs were here and the peaceful Arawaks, whose language survives them in two of our adopted words, a reflection of amenities bequeathed to the white man: tobacco, hammock. Both tribes are gone. The land remains, the beaches, the forests, the mountains, the lagoons, and the ambient sea.

HOTELS ON ST. JOHN

CANEEL BAY PLANTATION is a dreamy tropical beach resort adjoining the new Virgin Islands National Park. There are 64 beachfront rooms, 12 beachfront suites, and 33 double rooms in nine cottages. Modern Danish decor predominates, and the entire ensemble of luxurious cottages, open dining pavilion and cocktail terrace deserves its world fame. The setting is superlative. The property has no less than ten beautiful beaches, fringing superb bays. The plantation cruiser meets hotel guests at Red Hook landing on St. Thomas, and a municipal cruiser also operates between Red Hook and Cruz Bay. Diesel powered boats, native sloops, sail boats, snorkeling equipment are all available at hotel. American plan rates (Dec. 1 to May 1) are $28 to $53 single, $60 double for beachfront rooms, from $40 to $45 for double cottage rooms. Off season about 25 per cent less. Day guests from St. Thomas, limited to 15 persons per day, may enjoy a day at this unique resort for $12.50, lunch, transportation, towels and beach gear included. Accommodations are also provided in nearby Turtle Bay Estate Guest House. Managed by Leslie H. Moore, Jr., Caneel Bay Plantation is a million dollar beachcomber's paradise, back to nature with

443

Steel-bandsmen are the kings of Trinidad

all the advantages of modern plumbing, innerspring comfort, and a nice cool daiquiri close at hand. Write Box 1091, St. Thomas, Virgin Islands. Cable: Caneelbay.

GALLOWS POINT, managed by Richard Ellington, is a colony of seven housekeeping cottages on a private peninsula in Cruz Bay with superb private beaches on both sides. Designed to accommodate two to four persons each, these cottages are tastefully furnished and efficiently organized. No food is served, but native maid-cooks are available at 50 cents an hour. Winter season rates (December 1 to May 1) are $125 weekly for the smaller cottages, $175 for the larger. Off season they rent for $75 and $125 a week. Mr. Ellington will furnish more information about these away-from-it-all digs if you write to him at Cruz Bay Post Office, St. John, Virgin Islands, U.S.A. Cable: Gallowspoint.

LITTLE MAHO, operated by well-known Erva Boulon Thorp—of Trunk Bay fame—and her husband, Bill. Located at Maho Bay and reached by boat after a short drive from Cruz Bay, St. John. The apartments are perfect for a brief respite from city life. Bill's addiction to chess makes him a willing partner if the snorkeling, swimming and boating are not to your liking. Dinner is served at the Thorp's house, family style, and you may cook your own breakfast and lunch in your St. John "home". Rates are $15 single and $20 double on the American plan.

RESTAURANTS ON ST. JOHN

If you aren't cooking up a ragout in your efficiency kitchen on this primitive island, you can make reservations in advance for meals at *Caneel Bay Plantation*, or *Mrs. Keating's Boarding House* in Cruz Bay. If you see two Mrs. Keatings, you haven't had one too many; she has a twin sister. The great culinary specialty of St. John, incidentally, is turtle steak. There are only two bars on St. John: *Mooie's Bar and Pool Room* in Cruz Bay and the cocktail lounge at *Caneel Bay Plantation*.

THE BRITISH VIRGIN ISLANDS

North, east and within sight of St. John lie the British Virgin Islands. There are about three dozen of them, eleven of which are inhabited. The principal British Virgins are Tortola, the largest with 21 square miles; Virgin Gorda ("The Fat Virgin"), Anegada and Jost Van Dyke. Tortola, flanked by a cluster of smaller islands, is the center of one of the world's choicest yachting areas. The British Virgins, commanding the Anegada Passage, were a favorite rendezvous for pirates lying in wait for the treasure-laden ships which passed between the New World and the Old. If your childhood was haunted by "Fifteen men on a dead man's chest," that overcrowded vision will now be modified by the knowledge that Deadman Chest, to which the old buccaneer ditty refers, is one of the British Virgins. Another, Norman Island, is said to be the prototype of Robert Louis Stevenson's *Treasure Island*.

The English first settled in Tortola in 1666. The islands were granted a charter in 1773 and have been British ever since.

The climate is unusually healthful. Temperatures range from 71 to 82 degrees in winter; from 78 to 88 in summer. Add forested green hills, a string of lovely beaches, the ideal cruising waters mentioned above, and you have an interesting tourist potential.

Only very recently have the islanders begun to take advantage of their potential. Road Town, capital of Tortola, and about 1,000 in number, now has three small but comfortable hotels, and more are in the plans. With an airstrip completed on Beef Island (Leeward Islands Air Transport flies in every Wednesday from Antigua and St. Kitts) and a regular ferry service between St. Thomas and Road Town, more visitors will certainly be tempted to these islands, virtually inaccessible heretofore save by private yacht.

HOTELS ON TORTOLA

Road Town's hotels are the *Fort Burt* built on the ruins of an old fort that dates from pirate days and affords an excellent view. Room for 10 to 12 guests. Single room with bath, $10 a day American Plan, $25 double. A new salt water pool has recently been added. Manager Owner, C. R. Hammersley. *Treasure Isle Hotel* is an attractive new hotel at the opposite end of town from the *Fort Burt*. Here they hold occasional dances to steel band music. Daily rates American Plan $11. Manager C. S. Roy. The *Lagoon Plaza* is the other newly opened hotel in Road Town. It is built on a lagoon in the heart of the town. Rates: $6 a day Continental Plan. Manager, Mrs. E. N. Osborne.

There are also two Guest houses providing unpretentious accommodations. They are run by H. R. Penn and Mrs. A. Jennings. Furnished hillside cottages are occasionally available. Write J. R. Roy for information. For those visitors to St. Thomas who would like a day's excursion on Tortola, Alexander, Parish Ltd., Travel Agents in Road Town have a number of fascinating day tours by launch from St. Thomas to tour Tortola. One is on horseback.

Food and other necessities of life are cheap on Tortola. American currency is used, even though this is a British island. The reason: so many Tortolians go to St. Thomas to work for the Yankee dollar that this is the chief currency on the home island. It is said that many of these enterprising, island-hopping laborers have St. Thomas "wives" as well as Tortola "wives", both without benefit of clerical interference. This is a luxury that few tourists can afford.

Escapists who want to fish, sail and comb beaches far from the tourist track are naturally attracted to the British Virgins. If St. John is far out, the British Virgins are at the end of the line. One way of having your cay and eating it too is to apply to the *Guana Club,* Charlotte Amalie, St. Thomas, U.S.

Virgin Islands, for accommodations on Guana Island, which is privately owned by a group of Americans who bought the island as an exclusive sportsmen's paradise. The Guana Club consists of a main lodge, excellent dining room, and a score of houses. When space is available, paying guests are welcome, but applications should be made long in advance if you want to rough it in comfort in this private Eden. The Guana Club maintains motor cruiser service for members, members' guests, and paying guests between St. Thomas and Guana.

A delightful club on Beef Island is the Trellis Bay Club, a relatively recent development built on a bay recognised in pirate days as a dandy and completely safe anchorage, and more recently by yachtsmen exploring the Caribbean for its natural rugged beauty. Cottages have been built around the sandy crescent, and a club house complete with bedrooms, restaurant and bar have been built on a tiny island, Bellamy Cay, in the center of the bay. There is a fully equipped Marine Slipway and boatyard for the repair, servicing and overhaul of yachts (up to 100 tons). Yachts and boats of all kinds are for hire. Rates for rooms in winter, American Plan, $20 single, $30 double, summer $15 single, $23 double. Beach cottages for 1 to 4 people range from $125 to $175 weekly, with lower rates for longer stays. Meals at the club house are from $2 to $3 each.

Marina Cay is a tiny island with guest cottages, boating, snorkelling and skin diving amenities. British ex-Naval Commandar Allan Batham is the owner—the man who crossed the Atlantic with his wife and son in a 36 ft. ketch. Rates are from $12.50 single to $25 double, all meals included.

Other developments seem in the wind for these charming and unspoiled areas in the Caribbean. Mr. L. S. Rockefeller is now in the process of constructing a 1½ million dollar resort on Virgin Gorda. Beef Island now has an airstrip with regular service from other islands. A new resort has opened up on Little Thatch Island, ten minutes by motor launch from West End, Tortola. Islanders gossip about the international gamblers who are behind these schemes.

There are hotelmen and other developers with their eyes on the unspoiled hills and beaches. It probably won't be long before the British Virgins are as decked out in hotels, restaurants, nightclubs and other worldly finery as their matronly American cousins to the south. In the interim, if you are looking for a real escapist's haven, here's one of the few remaining places.

BRITISH LEEWARD ISLANDS

Bits and Pieces of Paradise

From the hilt of Puerto Rico and the Virgin Islands, the Lesser Antilles swing east and south like a saber pointed at the Spanish Main. The northwestern islands making up the shank of this scimitar are known as the Leewards. The curving blade of southeastern islands are called the Windwards. The terminology is confusing, especially since the trade winds, blowing steadily from the northeast, strike the whole scimitar with equal force on its convex cutting edge so that no part of the archipelago can be said to be in the lee of the wind. "Leewards" is used none the less for the British islands of Antigua, Montserrat, Barbuda, Redonda, St. Kitts, Nevis, Anguilla and the English Virgins. To compound the confusion, Saba, St. Martin, and St. Eustatius, geographically part of this same archipelago and with exactly the same orientation to the northeast trades, are known as the Dutch Windward Islands. The designation of Leewards and Windwards must be taken on nautical terms. The buccaneers who plowed these waters didn't give a damn for metaphors—a saber was something to cut human flesh with—and since the northwestern islands were the farthest from the point from which the wind blew, they called them the leewards. It may help to clear up the semantic confusion by pointing out that the Windward Islands, south and slightly east of the Leewards, do get the trade winds first so that the Leewards are *to* the lee but not *in* the lee of the Windwards. Get it? At this point we're not sure which way the wind is blowing, and find ourselves overcome with admiration for one of our favorite travel writers, Sylvia Martin, who dismissed the whole problem with superb female good sense merely by saying, "Please don't ask why they're called Leeward. It has something to do with the wind." Blow us down if a truer word was ever spoke.

ANTIGUA

Antigua, discovered by Columbus in 1493, was named after Santa Maria la Antigua of Seville, but don't give it a Spanish accent. Antéega will do, thank you veddy much. It was first colonized by the English in 1632. After a brief period of French occupation, it was formally given to England by the Treaty of Breda in 1667, and it has remained as British as Devonshire cream ever since. Even the rolling hills of Antigua are reminiscent of England, except that they are covered with sugarcane and dotted with perfectly-preserved sugarmill towers as far as the eye can reach. Capital of the British Leeward Isles and the only one of the group with any serious tourist pretensions, Antigua will remind you of another Little England, Barbados. It is smaller (108 square miles to Barbados' 166), but its natural assets are similar and even superior to those of Barbados. The coastline is peerless for its rugged indentations and superb beaches. The climate is dry and sunny with temperatures fluctuating between 75 and 85 degrees. Summer heat, happily free of humidity, is tempered by the trade winds. The health record of Antigua is tops: malaria and other tropical diseases don't exist.

Given all these natural advantages, it is not surprising that Antigua caught the fancy of a group of American millionaires who were looking for a haven to recuperate from the ignoble strife of this world. They cased the Caribbean, looking for gilt-edge security in a paradisiac setting. Antigua was their choice. The result is the Mill Reef Club. It consists of a large estate with a number of elaborate residences, each securely secluded within its own private acreage. Social center of the estate is the elegant clubhouse overlooking beautiful Exchange

BRITISH LEEWARD ISLANDS

Bay, the most attractive setup we have come across in our West Indian travels. Originally built to accommodate guests of colony members, the clubhouse now accepts outside guests at a price (see below: Hotels.) Owners of some of the residences come periodically to the island for vacations; others live there all year round in exclusive retirement. Among the 30 odd members of this pluto-Shangri-la are John Cowles, Dean Acheson, and Archibald Macleish, whose presence here may inspire more than one poet to telephone a stock broker.

Many of the club members participate actively in the civic and social life of their adopted island, and they have set up a trust fund which contributes to social welfare and educational programs. The friendly Antiguans—in our opinion the friendliest natives in the whole Caribbean—have nothing but praise for the individual millionaires whose exclusive club actually launched Antigua as a resort. But there is some bad feeling on the part of both white and native British against this millionaire's enclave, especially since it is protected by gate keepers in fancy uniforms who are often tactless and over-energetic in keeping out unauthorized visitors. There's no point mincing words about it: some Antiguans and their neighbors somewhat resent the intrusion of a foreign colony with police-enforced segregation measures in the midst of their own island.

Heirs of Nelson

One of the chief attractions of Antigua (see below) is English Harbor, redolent of Nelson and the great days of the British navy and still an international meeting place of yachtsmen from all over the world. A 20th-century counterpart of Nelson came to this anchorage one day in the form of ex-Royal Navy Commander V.E.B. Nicholson, on a round-the-world trip on his own yacht with his two strapping sons as crew. A wealthy American asked to charter the boat for a few days' cruise. Commander Nicholson consented. He now operates 18 ketches, sloops and schooners including the magnificent 134-foot Te Vega, in one of the smoothest, most reliable yacht charter services in the world. Nicholson and Sons have hired a number of outstanding yachtsmen who take paying guests on wonderful cruises as far as Trinidad. Their chartering program has been developed to such a fine point that many crew members are trained musicians providing the diversion of having a Calypso or steel band aboard. Stewards serve

449

lunch on deck, dinner below, and cocktails *in the water* if you happen to be swimming; all this in some of the most beautiful and isolated sailing spots in the world. The cruising ground is generally between Antigua and Grenada with the trade winds blowing across the line of advance, providing calm water sailing in the lee of the islands. Charter prices range from $40 per day for a two-berth yacht, up to $1,500 per week for the larger yachts and up to $2,500 per week for more luxurious yachts. Overall costs run from $30 to $45 per person per day, including charter fee, food, fuel and running expenses. Commander Nicholson is a born teacher as well as a yachtsman, glad to share his knowledge with even the rankest beginner. His address is Box 103, St. John's, Antigua, B.W.I. Most popular are the two week cruises from Antigua to Guadeloupe, Dominica, Martinique, St. Lucia, St. Vincent and through the dazzling Grenadines to the landlocked harbor of Grenada.

Beside these outstanding yachting facilities and a climate and topography which made the Mill Reefers decide that this was "the place", Antigua has less to offer in the way of organized tourist recreation and facilities than Barbados, Jamaica and other more highly-developed resorts. This, in our opinion, is a temporary state of affairs. Various factors are already operating to change it. First is Coolidge Airfield, built in World War II, one of the best in the Caribbean, already in regular commercial use by Pan American, British West Indian Airways and other airlines. Second is Antigua's position as one of the important links in the chain of Caribbean missile-tracking stations. The Antigua Beach Hotel, as a result, has the look of a glorified "special service club", and more and more Americans are hearing about the beauties of Antigua in enthusiastic letters home from service personnel. Third are the natural resources of Antigua and its satellite islands.

Barbuda, to the north for example, has some of the best beaches in the West Indies, and some of the best hunting and fishing. On the south-eastern tip of the island is newly opened *Coco Point Lodge,* with sporting facilities for all guests, financed and built by the Barbuda Development Co. Ltd. Finally, even though there's an implicit color bar in Antigua, the Negroes, who are always referred to as Natives here, are the friendliest and most welcoming in the Caribbean. If you are looking for the less sophisticated, les luxurious charms of the less developed places, Antigua is for you.

Note: Antigua is intensely British, and any criticism or mockery of British customs is deeply resented. Ladies are

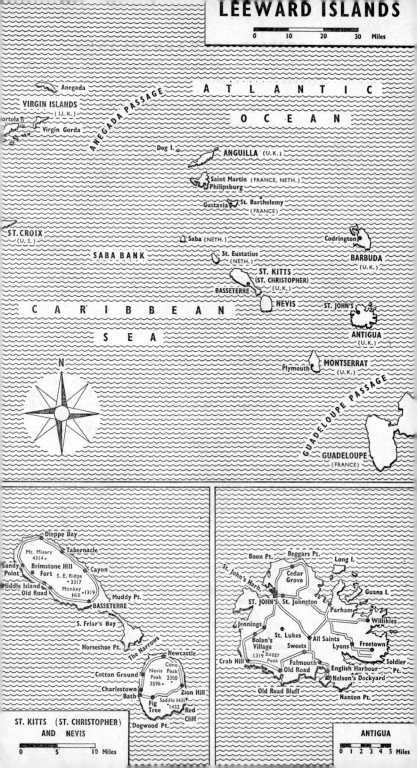

LEEWARD ISLANDS

0   10   20   30   Miles

Anegada

VIRGIN ISLANDS (U. K.)

Tortola

Virgin Gorda

A T L A N T I C

O C E A N

ANEGADA PASSAGE

Dog I.

ANGUILLA (U. K.)

Saint Martin (FRANCE, NETH.)
Philipsburg

Gustavia **St. Barthelemy** (FRANCE)

ST. CROIX (U. S.)

Saba (NETH.)

SABA BANK

St. Eustatius (NETH.)

ST. KITTS (ST. CHRISTOPHER) (U. K.)

BASSETERRE

Codrington

BARBUDA (U. K.)

NEVIS

ST. JOHN'S

ANTIGUA (U. K.)

C A R I B B E A N

S E A

N

Plymouth **MONTSERRAT** (U. K.)

GUADELOUPE PASSAGE

GUADELOUPE (FRANCE)

ST. KITTS (ST. CHRISTOPHER) AND NEVIS

0   5   10   Miles

Dieppe Bay

Tabernacle

Mt. Misery 4314

Sandy Point

Brimstone Hill Fort

S. E. Ridge 3317

Cayon

Middle Island
Old Road

Monkey Hill 1319

Muddy Pt.

BASSETERRE

S. Friar's Bay

Horseshoe Pt.

The Narrows

Newcastle

Cotton Ground

Cone Peak 2350

Nevis Peak 3596

Charlestown
Bath

Zion Hill

Saddle Hill 1432

Fig Tree

Red Cliff

Dogwood Pt.

ANTIGUA

0 1 2 3 4 5   Miles

Boon Pt.   Beggars Pt.   Long I.

St. John's Harb.

Cedar Grove

ST. JOHN'S   St. Johnston

Guana I.

Parham

Willikies

Jennings

St. Lukes

Bolan's Village

Sweets

All Saints

Lyons

Freetown

Crab Hill

1319 Boggy Peak

Falmouth
Old Road

English Harbour

Soldier Pt.

Old Road Bluff

Nelson's Dockyard

Nanton Pt.

BRITISH LEEWARD ISLANDS

advised not to wear shorts while shopping in the capital, St. John. Men are asked to wear coats and ties at dinner.

PRACTICAL INFORMATION FOR ANTIGUA

HOW TO GET THERE. *By Air.* Pan American World Airways and British West Indian Airways have non-stop jet flights from New York. You can also take Eastern Airlines to San Juan, flying to Antigua from there by BWIA or PAA. Pan Am round trip fare San Juan-Antigua is $68 by prop plane; $72 by jet. Trans Canada Air Lines has weekly flights from Montreal and Toronto. *By Sea.* Booth American Shipping Corp. freighters call at Antigua twice a month.

PASSPORTS, VISAS. Not required for Americans, Canadians or citizens of the United Kingdom for stays up to six months. You must have some proof of citizenship, however (birth certificate, naturalization papers, or passport) plus a transit ticket from Antigua to somewhere else.

CURRENCY. The British West Indian dollar is legal tender at about $1.69 to the U.S. dollar. American and Canadian dollars and travelers checks are accepted.

CLOTHING. Informal, wash and wear is best. Men and women wear slacks and Bermuda shorts.

HOW TO GET ABOUT. There are more taxis than the place needs, hence much competitive offering of services; you can make your own terms for any short ride. Here are the fixed rates for longer hauls, approved by the Antigua Taxi Association. Rates are for the entire taxi, given in British West Indies and American dollars:

Trip	$ Bee wee	$ U.S.
St. John's to Beach Hotel and Return	4.00	2.50
„ „ to Fort James and Return	2.00	1.25
„ „ to Anchorage and Return	2.00	1.25
„ „ to Trade Winds and Return	2.00	1.25
„ „ to White Sands and Return	4.00	2.50
„ „ to Airport and Return	4.00	2.50
„ „ to Nelson's Dockyard and Return	10.00	6.00
„ „ to Long Bay and Return	12.00	7.50
„ „ to Morris Bay and Return	12.00	7.50
„ „ to Half Moon Bay and Return	13.00	8.00
„ „ to Mill Reef and Return	15.00	9.00
„ „ to Nelson's Dockyard including Clarence House (if open)	12.00	7.50
„ „ as in 12 above, including Shirley Heights and Block House	15.00	9.00
„ „ Around the Valley and Fig Tree Hill	12.00	7.50
„ „ to Dockyard and Return via Coolidge & Beach Hotel	16.00	10.00
„ „ to Dockyard and Return via Valley and Fig Tree Hill	20.00	12.00
Airport to St. John's	4.00	2.50
Airport to Beach Hotel, or White Sands	2.00	1.25

452

Airport to Trade Winds or Anchorage	6.00	4.00
Airport to Dockyard	14.00	8.50
Airport to Mill Reef	15.00	9.00
Airport to Long Bay	12.00	7.50
Airport to Morris Bay	15.00	9.00
Anchorage to Coolidge, Beach Hotel or White Sands	6.00	4.00
Fort James to White Sands, Beach Hotel or Coolidge	6.00	4.00
Town Service per hour	5.00	3.00
St. John's to Gambles Golf Club	1.00	0.75
Charge for waiting per hour	3.00	2.00

There are some good roads, though many are one car wide and full of bumps, but the coastal scenery is worth the shaking up. There are no buses on Antigua. Leading tour operator in St. John's is *Alexander, Parrish Ltd.* They provide cars with or without chauffeur, sightseeing excursions, island tours, inter-island tours, and even fishing boats. U-Drive cars are now renting at $9 per day including insurance. L.I.A.T. (Leeward Islands Air Transport) operates a scheduled inter-island air service to Barbuda, Montserrat, Nevis, St. Kitts, St. Eustatius, St. Martin, Anguilla, Tortola in the British Virgins, Barbados and San Juan, Puerto Rico.

HOTELS

The tourist boom is evident in the recent opening of several new resort-hotels, with more on the way. The newest, *Jolly Hill Beach,* is the largest to date with 80 rooms. Others include the *Antigua Horizons, Curtain Bluff, Blue Waters,* and the *Kensington,* now under reconstruction. All rates quoted below are in United States currency. Add 10% service charge.

ANTIGUA BEACH HOTEL. At Hodges Bay on the northern coast, 6 miles from St. John's, 2½ miles from the airport, has 20 double rooms and 10 single rooms with bath, plus 10 cottage rooms about 200 yards from main hotel. Excellent sea bathing right near the premises; recently added is the *Jabberwock* beach-bar which features weekly steel band music. Dining room, cocktail lounge, and that indispensable British institution: afternoon tea. The service is good, the food has improved. The place as indicated above, is popular with American missile-tracking personnel, and reservations for the winter season should be made far in advance. American Plan Rates are $13.50 to $21.50 single, $24 to $35 double, winter season. In summer these drop to $9 to $12.50 single; $15.50 to $21.50 double.

TRADE WINDS HOTEL. Trade Winds Hotel is situated on a hill overlooking beautiful Dickinson Bay.

It has 25 cottage units with a lounge, cocktail bar and dining room forming the main unit. Situated about 5 minutes walk from the beach. It has a swimming pool as well. Facilities are available for sailing, fishing, water ski-ing, horseback riding and golf. Food and service are good. It is managed by Gordon Crowe. Dancing 2 nights weekly. Rates are $15 single, $28 double, in summer.

ANCHORAGE HOTEL. This is a beach bungalow resort, one of the most unusual we've seen anywhere. The cottages have been constructed in the style of South African native Zulu *kraal* huts, a style which transplants most successfully to the Caribbean. The bungalows are round with conical palmthatched roof and are gaily painted light blue. High-ceilinged interiors are both airy and spacious. There are twenty-five of these units for two set in a coconut grove on a wonderful beach, and a recent addition provides a total of 70 air-conditioned rooms. There's also a swimming pool, a wonderful bar on the terrace. We paid a visit to the kitchen here and found it spotless and ultra modern with a deepfreeze to accommodate steaks and other imported foods from the U.S. American Plan winter rates are $22 to $32 a day single, $35 to $48 double. Summer rates are $15 to $23 single, $24 to $35 double.

THE ADMIRAL'S INN. This small but enchanting establishment, newly opened under the aegis of Desmond Nicholson (son of the Commander), is set within the walls of Nelson's Dockyard at English Harbour. Food is excellent, and is served at tables right by the water's edge. Among the activities listed are yacht watching, sitting, and goat watching! (Plus, of course, beachcombing, sailing, fishing, snorkeling, water skiing and swimming.) Rates are $24 to $32, double; $18 to $26 single. Summer rates are $19 to $23 double; $12 to $16. All Modified American Plan.

CARIBBEAN BEACH CLUB. One of the newest and most delightful, this hotel has 32 rooms in thatched roof units right on the beach. For the active, there are facilities for skin diving, snorkeling, water skiing, sailing and deep sea fishing from the hotel's own 40-foot boat. Dining, wining and steel banding all take place on the hill above the beach, reached by a tram complete with red and white striped surrey top. Rates are $19 double beach room, $24 double beach suite, and $29 for a single beach room. In summer they drop to $12, $16 and $18 respectively. Breakfast is included in the above; for full American Plan add $6 per person per day.

GALLEY BAY. Another newcomer, it has 12 rooms with sunken baths. Right on the sea, there are frequent beach barbecues. Winter rates are $40 double, $24 single. Summer

rates ars slashed neatly to $21 and $11.50.

HAWKSBILL. Newly built and furnished with Antigua's native furniture, this hotel gets its name from the island just off its main beach, which looks like a turtle—with a hawk's bill. The rooms open on the beach and there are "couple-size", "family-size" or "party-size" cottages. Rates run from $26 single to $88 with a family cottage. In the summer rates range from $16 to $68 M.A.P.

HALF MOON BAY HOTEL. Managed with competence, this is one of the nicest hotels in Antigua. It's on the eastern shore of the island at Half Moon Bay, 16 miles from St. John's, 17 from the airport. All 16 rooms have private baths and porches facing the sea. In addition to the white sand beach of Half Moon Bay, there's a large swimming pool. Dancing twice a week on outdoor patio. Good bar and excellent cuisine. Winter rates, American Plan, are $30 single, $42 double. Off season rates: $18 single, $28 double.

MILL REEF CLUB. An absolute gem of a small hotel with everything one could ask for a luxurious tropical holiday. Twenty rooms with bath. Reservations must be accompanied by a deposit of 50 per cent of the total charge for the reserved period. The food is wonderful. Daily rates, American Plan from December 16 to April 15 are $38 single, $46 double; cottages from $75. Summer rates drop to $18 single, $32 double, $40 and up for a cottage. Atmosphere is pleasantly informal; the price is not out of line for what you get.

LONG BAY HOTEL. A new cottage colony on Dian Point, you'll find here accommodations for 30 or more guests in 20 comfortable rooms, all with private bath. Every cottage has its individual waterfront terrace and two private beaches provide ample privacy for sailing, fishing and swimming.

Under the management of Mr. C. Grunlund. Winter rates are $25 single and $40 double American Plan. Summer rates are about $10 cheaper per person.

FOOD AND RESTAURANTS

The big specialty of the island is lobster and other denizens of the surrounding deep, and you can't go wrong when you have these grilled fresh from the sea. The ordinary British cuisine is pepped up with creole additions, and we found it generally better than the food on other British islands. One welcome adjunct to the diet is lots of fresh fruit and vegetables, most of them brought in daily from Dominica and Montserrat. Try Barbados Cherries; a single one could supply you with your minimum daily requirement of Vitamin C. The island drink is rum. The *Admiral's Inn* is extremely pleasant for lunch if you are in the vicinity.

NIGHTLIFE. Nearest thing to a night club is the *Pelican Club* at Hodges Bay, which has dancing to steel band on Wednesday and Saturday nights. Most of the hotels have steel bands for weekend dancing. *Michael's Mount*, overlooking the city, and the *Jabberwock* are added attractions to night life; if you are feeling brave, go to the *Strip* for real native night life.

SHOPPING

If you descend from a cruise ship you'll be mobbed by chattering natives using a bulldozer technique to sell their wares. Don't be bulldozed! High Street in St. John's is the shopping street with additional shops on St. Mary's Street and side streets in the central area. Local products worth considering are the cleverly hand-woven bags, hats, slippers, place mats etc. of native sisal, date palm fronds, coconut, palmetto and banana leaves.

A popular local item with tourists is the "Mary hat" of madras-lined linen, which folds absolutely flat for packing. Tortoise-shell jewelry and souvenirs are locally made, but it will take some discrimination to find the good from the bad. Local seed and shell beads are cheap and surprisingly effective. Imported English woolens and linens are very good buys, and there's lots of cashmere and madras to choose from. English tobacco and pipes are offered at tempting prices, and so of course is West Indian rum. Locally made ceramics and furniture are both unusual and inexpensive.

There are "Federation skirts", wrap-around jobs embroidered with island names, and $10 silk scarves graced with maps of

Antigua, both of which we found rather ghastly, but they are popular souvenir numbers, the stock being constantly replenished.

COCO SHOP, in the Brown House on St. Mary's Street, is our favorite emporium here. We found a grand choice of Madras, Sea Island cottons, and Batiks in items for men, women, and children, in this outstanding shop. There is also a good selection of Irish linen, British tweeds and leather goods. The shop's hand-screened prints on Sea Island cotton were above the ordinary run of this sort of stuff, and so were their hand-embroidered fabrics. They also have some stunning Siamese silks and a very wide selection of native crafts, especially Antigua pottery.

HANDICRAFT WORKSHOP now on High Street has pottery, handmade by Antiguan craftsmen, an interesting local product. There are lots of local arts and crafts in this shop, sponsored by the government.

SHOUL'S CHIEF STORE, St. Mary's Street, where you may purchase genuine West Indian Sea Island Cotton, Irish and English linens, cashmere sweaters, Madras swimsuits, English suitings and tropical wear.

O'NEAL'S CURIO SHOP at the corner of High and Thames Streets has a good selection of local stuff plus British imports at prices way below those in the States.

JOHN AND FRANCIS ANJO at 54 High Street where you can find some bargains in tobacco, Swiss watches, Danish ware and, to leap from the ridiculous to the sublime or vice versa depending on your point of view, the best fishing tackle in Antigua.

MR. PIGGOTT, the barber in High Street has a 48 hour developing service, apparently spending his time between clients and the dark room.

SPORTS AND OTHER ATTRACTIONS. Best beaches for *swimming* are at Hodges Bay, Fort James and Corbizon Point.

Boating and *yachting* are unsurpassed; boats are for hire at all hotels, yachts by day and week through Commander Nicholson at English Harbor (see above.) Equipment is also available for *deep-sea and spear fishing.*

Hunting for deer, ducks, pigeon and guinea fowl on nearby Barbuda; you can go there by chartered boat, making arrangements through Parrish Travel Agency.

Tennis may be played at the Antigua Beach Hotel, the Antigua Lawn Tennis Club, and the Antigua Bowling and Tennis Club. There are two nine-hole golf courses at Gambles Golf Club and Antigua Beach Hotel.

Horseback riding is rewarding here; horses are for rent at Antigua Beach Hotel and Mill Reef Club. Chief spectator sport in this microcosm of England is *cricket,* played at various clubs, also football, rugger to you.

Two of Antigua's *Steel Bands* are famous throughout the West Indies. They are the Brute Force and Hell's Gate Bands, much in demand for weddings, funerals, parties, festivals, and appearing on special nights at various clubs when nobody is getting married, dying or otherwise occupied.

There are *amateur theatricals* at Princess Elizabeth Community Hall, sometimes very amusing.

Local *art exhibits* are held in the Council of St. John's Court House.

EXPLORING ANTIGUA

St. John's, the capital of Antigua and the Leewards, has a population of 21,000, mostly black and smiling, and usually milling about in what seems to be an aimless way. Chief center of the milling is the open-air native market and the pier at the foot of High Street. Here at the edge of the picture-book harbor is the center of St. John's popular and commercial life. A new market is situated in the South end of the city. Schooners come and go, island produce is unloaded and loaded, stuff is bought and sold; it's the history of merchandising in miniature, fun to watch, easy to grasp. The narrow side streets of the town are a little sad. Local authorities are proud of the dull new Administration Building, and of the interesting old Court House. The latter is a venerable relic of Antigua's colonial glory, and you should see its Council Room where, incidentally, there's a revolving exhibition of local pictures. St. John's Cathedral (Anglican, of course) and the 300-year-old military barracks complete the roster of public buildings worth a gander. At the northwest tip of the harbor, on your right as you gaze out from the pier, is old Fort James, which guarded St. John's in the days of derring do. Built in 1703, its ruined ramparts overlook small islands in the bay; its cannons still point out to sea, no longer shooting but shot at. They are a favorite photographers' target. The big attraction is the *Fort James Beach Club*. Steel bands, occasionally, and a juke box, usually, provide music for dancing. You can get a drink here, have a snack and a swim at a beach that's small but one of the island's best.

The sight of sights in Antigua is Nelson's Dockyard in English Harbor. Seeing it involves a 30-mile round trip from St. John's on roads that will loosen your plate. One lady said the trip took more pounds off than two sessions of Slenderella. In any event, you should do it. You'll pass some small villages with one-room thatched huts falling apart at the seams. The piles of stones at the side of each hut are used for stretching out the wash, and you'll see native women in water-poor Antigua doing their wash in basins far from home near one of the public pumps, after which they lug it back in a basket to dry it on the rocks. You'll also see a lot of sugar cane and stone sugar mills, then, suddenly, some of the most magnificent coastal scenery in the Caribbean.

English Harbor

Nelson's Dockyard was built in 1784 in land-locked English Harbor, so protected from the open sea that approaching yachtsmen rush to their charts, wondering if they've somehow missed the place. Horatio Nelson first came here in 1784, senior captain of the station at the not-so-tender age of 25. He became Commander-in-Chief of the Leeward Islands Squadron. Under his command was the Captain of *H.M.S. Pegasus,* Prince William Henry, Duke of Clarence, who was to ascend the throne of England as William IV, the "sailor king". He was Nelson's close friend and best man at his wedding to the young Widow Nisbet which took place on the island of Nevis in 1787. You will see Clarence House, the handsome stone residence built for the prince on the heights opposite the Dockyard. Now the summer home of the Governor, it should be visited as well as the old Block House and the fortifications on Shirley Heights. "Crowned with grey ruins crumbling in decay", they cannot fail to touch the heart of anyone with a feeling for history. The view from Shirley Heights, sweeping all the way to Guadeloupe, surpasses description and is beyond praise.

The whole of Shirley Heights and English Harbor are fascinating, their buildings now being reclaimed from time by the Dockyard and Shirley Heights Restoration Fund and the Society of Friends of English Harbor, which have been doing noble work in preserving a noble area. The Dockyard, with its Museum in Admiral's House, with a display of Nelson mementoes, Porter's Lodge, Guard House, Engineer's Workshop and surrounding wall, carved with hundreds of names of 18th-century sailors, their ships, their hometowns and their dates of service, is a vivid reminder of history, a living monument to the men and their commanders: Nelson, Rodney, Hood.

If there's time and your back will stand Antigua's primitive roads, take an all day round-the-island tour. You'll have your fill of beaches and bays like Half Moon Bay on the Atlantic Coast and Falmouth Bay with Black Point where the bewildered ancestors of the present natives were landed. You'll drive through idyllic tropical scenery: lush foliage, cane fields, coconut groves with the sea and the spectacular coastline re-emerging time and again, never staled by familiarity. The villages are a fascinating combination of the Caribbean and old England. One of the nicest English touches are the gardens, which surround even the humblest houses. The natives have adopted the English love of gardening, and annual horticultural competitions among the villages are very keen. The results are delightful with some of the settlements looking like tropical versions of Shottery. Antigua, as much as Barbados

and Bermuda, remains a "corner of a foreign field that is forever England."

ST. KITTS AND NEVIS

These islands, 50 miles west of Antigua and separated from
each other by a two mile strait, go together like Rosencrantz
and Guildenstern. You reach St. Kitts by inter-island air connections provided by British West Indian Airways, KLM Royal
Dutch Airlines, Pan American World Airways or Leeward Islands Air Transport Services Ltd. LIAT has scheduled flights
from Antigua, Montserrat and St. Eustatius to St. Kitts and
Nevis. You can fly (ten minutes) from St. Kitts to Nevis daily
except Saturday and Sunday, or go by boat. There's an all-day
pleasure excursion from Antigua to Nevis, conducted by Alexander, Parrish Ltd. in Antigua (all inclusive cost about $48 per
person), and a weekend trip offered by the same company,
covering both Nevis and St. Kitts, (all inclusive cost for three
full days, about $100).

Nevis, incidentally is pronounced with a long e, "Neevis".
Just one more example of the kind of English orthography
that drives foreigners batty when they try to learn the
language.

ST. KITTS

St. Kitt's official name is St. Christopher, but to call it that
would be like calling Babe Ruth, George Herman, or Ike
Eisenhower, Dwight. Columbus discovered the island in 1493
and named it after his own patron saint. The English anglicised
that almost as soon as they arrived, "determined to found a
little bit of England overseas", which they most emphatically
did in 1623. Oldest of the British West Indian settlements, St.
Kitts is proud of its title, "Mother Colony of the West Indies",
which it earned by sending out colonizing parties to other
islands.

The French and the British battled over St. Kitts for a
century and a half, a fact which is reflected in the name of the
capital, Basseterre on the southwest coast. The English, who
got full title to the island by the 1783 Treaty of Versailles,
could have changed the name, but they prefer to get their
revenge by pronouncing it as though they were calling somebody a dirty name. Another relic of the Anglo-French
squabbles is in the name of the lovely village of Half-Way
Tree where a big tamarind tree still marks the point of demarcation which once separated French from English natives. This

segregation, of course, is a thing of the past; St. Kitts today is as English as St. Ives.

There are about 38,000 people on St. Kitts' 68 square miles, busy raising cane and sea island cotton, and smuggling in French liquor and other Gallic refinements from St. Barthélemy, mostly for their own consumption. The villagers are very skillful at this and also at distilling their own rum. The police used to get a bonus for cracking down on illicit stills. The reward incentive was removed in 1952 by one S. A. Hammond, commissioner for the suppression of alcoholism. With the profit motive gone, the police relaxed. No smash, more mash. Home distilling flourished. The grateful "distillers" call their harsh, raw, highly potent product *Hammond Report* to this day in fond memory of their benefactor.

PRACTICAL INFORMATION FOR ST. KITTS

HOTELS. St. Kitt's is a sleepy little island which only recently has begun to equip itself to receive tourists. There are now four small hotels in Basseterre equipped to receive about one hundred guests in total. Commercial travelers still make up the more regular year-round customers. The *New Royal Hotel* has 26 rooms with rates at $10 single, $20 double, American Plan. Mrs. R. de Freitas is the manager. The other principal hotel is *The Palms* which was formerly called *Shorty's Hotel* and is still so called by the local gentry whose favorite pastime is sitting on the porch and chatting with everyone who passes by, native or tourist. *The Palms* charges $9 a day single, $18 to $24 double, also American Plan. Other Hotels to be noted are the following: *Hotel Seaside* with 10 rooms and the *Blakeney* with 16 rooms. The last two named are most recent and more expensive hostelries with singles $10 and up and doubles running as high as $28.

St. Kitts also has a few guest and boarding houses if you're looking for low-budget, off-beat, go-native accommodations. The best of the lot is kutely kalled *Kool Korner*.

SHOPPING. There are more shops than you might expect in this little capital of 11,000 souls. They're all in the main part of Basseterre from the Circus up Fort Street and on little side streets with big urban English names: Liverpool Row, Bank Street, Princes Street and the like. English imports and local handicrafts are the chief stocks in trade. Best selections of native and local articles our buyer saw were at the *Curio Shop* and *La Tropical,* both on Fort Street. Embroidery and tortoise-shell stuff were cheaper here than in Antigua.

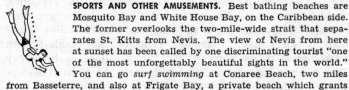

SPORTS AND OTHER AMUSEMENTS. Best bathing beaches are Mosquito Bay and White House Bay, on the Caribbean side. The former overlooks the two-mile-wide strait that separates St. Kitts from Nevis. The view of Nevis from here at sunset has been called by one discriminating tourist "one of the most unforgettably beautiful sights in the world." You can go *surf swimming* at Conaree Beach, two miles from Basseterre, and also at Frigate Bay, a private beach which grants permission to use its premises. *Hunting* of migratory birds is popular here between June and September, pigeon shooting between October and December. You pay $1.20 for a license for your gun. You can play *tennis* and also *croquet* at St. Kitts Lawn Tennis Club.

The volcanic topography of St. Kitts lends itself to *hiking* and *mountain climbing,* and the big climb is to the top of 3792 foot Mount Misery, the pride of St. Kitts despite a name that would be enough to daunt Sherpa Tenzing.

The only sign of *nightlife* we saw in Basseterre was some dancing to canned music at The Palm's Hotel. And you'll get a pretty good idea of the culinary thrills of St. Kitts when we tell you that one of the recommended restaurants is a Milk Bar on Church Street.

EXPLORING ST. KITTS

The harbor of Basseterre has that old-print look and the charm of the pier where inter-island boats discharge their cargoes and products are sold right on the dock. The "Circus" with its gingerbread fountain clock tower is on the Grimm side. Government House is a nice example of the old colonial style and so is the Old Court House on Pall Mall Square. This spot, flanked by the Catholic Church and some fine private houses, is another of those incongruous examples of Georgian England in the tropics. The public library on the second floor of the courthouse contains some interesting historical exhibits, including pre-Columbian relics of the indigenous Carib Indians.

You can rent a drive-yourself car at *Felton's Garage* in Basseterre to take the 30-mile tour around the island, or you can go in a taxi at a fixed fee of $7. A good road follows the coast and girdles the island completely except for that strange spit of land in the south which thrusts out towards Nevis. On your tour, you will see Brimstone Hill, "The Gibraltar of the West Indies", ten miles from Basseterre. It is impressive with its frowning ramparts rising 700 feet straight up from the sea. In spite of its look of impregnability from the ocean, you can drive up easily from the land side where you can look down on that historic sea where the British defeated De Grasse in an empire-saving struggle. The view, encompassing the Dutch islands of St. Eustatius and Saba, St. Martin and St. Bartholomew on the west and Nevis to the southeast, is the high point of this tour. The rest is the sea on one side, the monotony of sugar cane on the other, punctuated by places of historic interest: Old Road Village where Thomas Warner and his intrepid colonists first stepped ashore in 1623; Sandy Point, their first settlement; Middle Island Village with St. Thomas Church and tomb of Sir Thomas Warner who "gave forth large narratives of military worth written with his sword's poynt." Many ruined forts and battlegrounds bear mute testimony to the ancient enmity between England and France, and one place, Bloody Point, marks the spot where they combined forces in 1629 to repel with great slaughter a mass attack by the original owners of this island, the Carib Indians.

NEVIS

Two miles south of St. Kitts, Nevis is a dramatic 50-square-mile volcanic island, its forest-clad slopes rising from the sea to Nevis Peak, 3,596 feet high in the island's center. This mountain is joined by a saddle to two lesser peaks, Hurricane Hill (1,192 feet) in the north and Saddle Hill (1,432 feet) in the south. Reminded of a snow-covered range in the Pyrenees, Columbus called the island Las Nievas. The "snow" is a halo of white cloud which usually crowns the crest of this beautiful island. Most of Nevis is surrounded by coral reefs, and there are miles of palm-tree studded beaches, waiting to be developed.

PRACTICAL INFORMATION FOR NEVIS

Some travelers come to Nevis from St. Kitts by air (see above), but many prefer the 12-mile, hour-and-a-half trip by boat from Basseterre to Charlestown. These boats leave Basseterre every day but Sunday at 2.30 p.m., arriving in Nevis in time for a sightseeing drive around the island before night falls. You can spend a night in Nevis, returning with the boat on the next day. Wednesday there is a morning boat from St. Kitts to Nevis, returning that same afternoon. The round trip boat fare is just under one and a half Beewee dollars. That's a bargain in any currency.

HOTELS. Two very small but very charming beginnings have been made in the direction of tourism.

The *Golden Rock Estate* at the base of Nevis Peak has been developed with typical American ingenuity from an old sugar estate by Mr. and Mrs. Frank Galey, who began by converting the sugar tower into an attractive apartment, then turned the estate's animal watering plant into a large swimming pool. The Galeys now offer six attractive rooms with bath, two sparkling white beaches, a 33-foot cruiser for charter and all you need for a vacation of swimming, boating, snorkeling and fishing. Their rates are $20 single with bath; $34 double, American Plan in winter. Summer rates are $12 single, $22 double.

On the windward coast, 8 miles north of Charlestown and 2 miles east of the airport, Mrs. Mary Pomeroy is developing the plantation house of the old Nisbett Estate into an attractive beach resort, the *Nisbett Plantation.* The setting is lovely: 64 acres of coconut grove with a private beach. At present there are five rooms with bath available in this pleasant, unpretentious guest house. Mrs. Pomeroy's year round rates are $25 to $35 a day for two, American Plan, *and* including liquor.

In Charlestown, the tiny capital, there are the 6-room *Parmenter's Guest House* and the 7-room *Hamilton Bicentennial Hotel,* both charging $6 a day single, American Plan.

Aside from these, there are no hotel accommodations on this superb island which has all the natural facilities necessary to make it a tourist haven. Certain outside interests are casting covetous glances in the direction of Nevis, and the local authorities are anxious to develop tourism. But they do not want any tourist "compounds" on their tight little island with the resultant segregation. It was here, among the mild and hospitable natives who are looked down upon as "country yokels" by their patronizing big-island cousins on Trinidad and Barbados, that we heard the most bitter comments about the Mill Reef Club in Antigua. And it was interesting to note that these negroes, relatively shy and unaggressive, had very positive views on politics and are strong partisans of complete independence from the white man and from the British Commonwealth. This attitude, it must be added, does not imply any hostility toward visitors. On the contrary. As in St. Kitts, cordial "Good mornings" and "Good afternoons" are the order of the day, even between strangers. But it's a matter of island government policy and "national pride" that will not permit the establishment of hotels or resorts on Nevis and St. Kitts unless there are guarantees that no color barriers will be established between the project and the island people, who are almost all negroes except for a handful of white government officials and businessmen.

Nevis is no place for shopping, nightclubbing and big resort swank. It is even more somnolent than St. Kitts, a state of affairs that is reflected in agricultural statistics: St. Kitts grows 26 to 28 tons of sugar cane per acre, Nevis produces from 6 to 8. The pace is leisurely. There's no shopping to speak of, and any sounds of revelry you hear by night are made by the whistling frogs. Nevis is the place for relaxation in a nearly perfect climate (the average temperature is 79 degrees); for swimming in the crystal water of Pinney's Beach and other white sand havens where you have the whole place practically to yourself; for picnics and fishing and exploring for Carib Indian relics, and for a leisurely browse through the leaves of 18th-century colonial history.

The most romantic of those leaves concerns the rich young widow Fanny Nisbett whom Nelson wooed and won here. You will see the Fig Tree Church where the official record of the marriage is on the register, a charming Anglo-Gallic church of cool, crumbling stone, pure in style, looking as though it had been transported by some miracle straight from a Breton or a Cornish village. Beneath the memorial plaque you may read the tattered register with the signatures of the newly-weds, wed two centuries ago. Nelson's, with a fine 18th-century flourish, betrays a bridegroom's impatience or perhaps a nervous tremor such as he never experienced at Trafalgar.

Americans are always moved by the sight of the staircase and the foundations of the house where Alexander Hamilton was born in Charlestown in 1757, though members of the D.A.R. may wince at local reminders that he was the illegitimate son of James Hamilton, a Scotsman, and Rachael Lavien, a resident of Nevis. An orphan at the age of 11, Alexander went to Christiansted in the Virgin Islands to live with a favorite aunt, worked there as a general clerk in Cruger's Store. At the age of 13 he was running the Frederiksted branch of the business. In August 1772, an account of a hurricane in St. Croix written by Alexander was published anonymously in a St. Kitts newspaper. Its literary style was so high that the Governor of St. Croix, discovering its author, persuaded a relative to send the boy to college. At 15 Alexander Hamilton was on his way to Boston and to immortality. In 1957 Nevis celebrated the bicentennial of this distinguished son's birth and issued a special stamp to commemorate the anniversary.

These historic places may be visited on a four hour circular tour of Nevis, which also includes a sampling of the 200-year-old thermal baths at Bath House, an 18th-century luxury hotel which is due for renovation and a comeback; a look-in at St. Thomas' church, oldest on the island, and its ancient tombstones; and a half hour or more of sightseeing in Charlestown with its carved Chinese Chippendale galleries, its venerable courthouse and its pretty waterfront.

ANGUILLA

We often wonder if the Mill Reefers were tempted by this lovely 16-mile sliver of land about 60 miles northwest of St. Kitts.

Called the "Snake Island" because of its shape (never more than three miles wide), this coral island is on the Monday, Tuesday, Thursday, Friday schedule of LIAT planes from St. Kitts, which come down at the U.S.-constructed World War II landing field. You can also reach Anguilla by boat from St. Martin (daily) and from St. Kitts by government coastal steamer, which makes regular calls. Rain is almost unknown here. The beaches and the fishing are A-1. Boats can be rented, but bring your own fishing tackle.

BRITISH LEEWARD ISLANDS

Principal port of entry is Road Bay, a lovely little town. Industry is salt; the government-owned ponds cover 50 acres and are exploited commercially by private industry. The 5,000 natives of Anguilla grow pigeon peas, sweet potatoes, Indian corn, beans and sea island cotton on small farms.

There is one hotel at present, the *Anguillan* with five rooms, charging $6 single, $12 double per day, American Plan. It's not exactly the Waldorf, but then neither are the prices.

Anguilla is looking for investment capital to start a tourist resort. The island is *entirely* surrounded by white sand virgin beaches. Anybody wanna beat a track?

Anguilla, northernmost isle of the Leewards, is a part of the colony known officially as St. Christopher, Nevis and Anguilla. The hospitable natives are always glad to rent a room to an overnight visitor if the hotel is full, and you can arrange through Alexander Parrish at St. Kitts to rent a house on Anguilla if you want to.

BARBUDA

Even less well-known than Anguilla, this 70-square-mile island was once the private preserve of a Colonel Codrington, who used it as a stud farm to develop strong specimens of African slaves. Upon hearing this, one lady tourist with strong, retroactive abolitionist sentiments, said, "Well, at least they had *some* fun." The stud-farm story may be apocryphal, but the natives of Barbuda are notable for their fine physiques and proud carriage, and are said by some authorities to be descendants of slaves of superior intelligence and physical development who were used as plantation overseers. The coral island, 68 square miles in area, is a hunting preserve, stocked with birds, guinea fowl, fallow deer. The *Coco Point Lodge* offers a complete package deal that is a sure lure: room, meals, liquor, use of small fishing boats, water skiing, snorkel equipment, guides, hunting and fishing licenses, ammunition, and all air and land transportation from Antigua and return— all for $90 a day double, reduced after the third day to $70. There are twenty double rooms along with a cottage colony. Complete information is available from The Barbuda Development Co., Ltd., P.O. Box 45, St. John's, Antigua. Barbuda is on the Saturday morning schedule of that ubiquitous LIAT outfit, leaving Antigua at 9:30, arriving Barbuda, after various stops, at 11:15. If you don't go by air, you sail in by sloop, and that's a special thrill as the skipper has to wait for the opportune moment before negotiating a narrow passage through the reef.

REDONDA

A stepping stone between Nevis and Montserrat to the south, Redonda is a mile long, half a mile wide, and was once claimed by a mad Irishman, Matthew Shiel, as a private fief for his son and heir whom he pleased to call King Felipe I. There are no little Shiels there, and no subsequent heirs are apparent. In fact there are no human beings. Redonda is for the birds.

MONTSERRAT

Montserrat, "the saw-toothed mountain", was named by Columbus in honor of that more famous mountain in Spain where Ignatius Loyola dreamed up the Society of Jesus. This Montserrat is 27 miles southwest of Antigua, has 32 square miles of exceedingly rugged terrain and a smouldering sulphurous volcano named Soufriere to which nobody pays much attention. The Irish, in their perpetual desire to get away from the English, colonized this island from St. Kitts in 1632, having stood their Anglo-Saxon brethren on "the Mother of the Antilles" for eight long years. Today's result: you have the astonishing and completely charming experience of hearing the natives speak English with a sort of Afro-Irish brogue. Montserrat, with its rugged scenery and golden beaches, has not been accessible until very recently. Now the Leeward Islands Air Transport Service has a regular air shuttle service between Antigua and Montserrat (15 minutes).

Plymouth, the capital of Montserrat, has one hotel, the *Crescent Hill* where you can stay with all meals for as little as $4 a day. Boarding houses are even less.

If it's beginning to sound like a budget-sized paradise, there are also wonderful mangoes, avocado pears, breadnuts and good rum punches, made with home-grown limes. The natives also raise cotton, tomatoes, carrots, pumpkins, cabbages and peanuts. There were some bad crop failures as recently as 1956 due to soil erosion and various blights. One result was considerable migration to Curaçao and Aruba. The government has undertaken modern crop-conservation projects with striking results in increased quality and yields.

Best way we know of exploring Montserrat, unless you have your own boat, is to take the all day tour conducted by Alexander Parrish from Antigua. This leaves at 8:30 a.m. by twin-engine Piper Apache plane, is met by car and driver at

Blackburne Airfield and whisked across the 1200-foot central island pass to Plymouth where you can buy craft stuff and sample Montserrat's wonderful fruit. You then drive along the rugged northwest road through luxuriant tropical growth to Woodlands Estate, a Planter's mansion where you stop for morning tea and pick up your picnic lunch. There follows a hair-raising descent into the steep valley of charmingly-named Soldier's Gut where the English and the French almost annihilated each other two centuries ago in a fight for the island. You end up at the African hut or "shimbeck" on lovely Car's Bay where you can swim and enjoy your West Indian lunch of River Prawn salad, mountain chicken, souse (there's a good old West Indian word!) and iced tea. Another pleasant touch: free rum punch on the house. You leave at three, have tea at Woodlands, and are air-borne for Antigua at 5 p.m. All inclusive price of this outing is about $42. It's an on-beat offbeat trip to a little known, wildly beautiful place, and you meet the Black Irish into the bargain.

FRENCH WEST INDIES

Gallic Holiday à la Créole

France's holdings in the Caribbean are the large islands of Martinique and Guadeloupe, the latter accompanied by its tiny satellites: St. Martin, St. Barthélemy, Marie-Galante, Désirade and Les Saintes. Guadeloupe is near the southern end of the Leeward Islands; Martinique is the northernmost of the Windwards. Sail south from Guadeloupe for about 30 miles and you reach British-owned but French-in-spirit Dominica. Thirty miles southeast of this limey interloper is Martinique.

Both Guadeloupe and Martinique are Departments of France. Their half million inhabitants are full French citizens, and they think of themselves first and foremost as French. Considerations of race, pigmentation and previous conditions of servitude are secondary. There is no color bar; there are no "natives". Everyone here is a *citoyen de la République Française*, and proud to be so. Despite this, the islands are cinderellas of Caribbean tourism. Far more beautiful than many of their sisters, they have been kept in rags by *La Belle France*, who, dressing herself fit to kill for tourists, has let her West Indian daughters languish like stepchildren. Good hotels

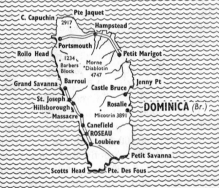

and other tourist amenities are conspicuous by their absence on Martinique and Guadeloupe. In the midst of a general Caribbean boom, they have remained tourist backwaters.

There are encouraging signs that France has now been awakened, possibly by the sound of hard Yankee and Canadian cash dropping into the tills of Puerto Rico and Jamaica, and that her twin cinderellas may soon be properly dressed for the big West Indian ball. A crash program envisages at least three new hotels for each of the islands. Plans include for Martinique a first rate hotel with 100 rooms on the outskirts of Fort de France on the *Batelière Estate*; a cottage hotel of smaller capacity near *Sainte Luce*; possibly a hotel in the region of *Tartane* on the Caravelle Peninsula, another cottage type 30-room hotel already under construction at "La Prairie" on the coast between François and Vauclin, and the conversion of Martinique's picturesque old Fort Saint Louis into a 250-room luxury hotel in the manner of the Intercontinental at Willemstad. In Guadeloupe at least two hotels should begin construction aiming at a total of 160 rooms. *La Vielle Tour* an 18-room tourist hotel has opened recently near Point à Pitre. The rooms are equipped with showers and there is a pool for the guests. The French part of St. Martin has not been forgotten. At the time of printing there are five different plans under consideration which would mean 550 hotel rooms for this territory. It is hoped that with a government outlay of about $3,000,000, tripled by private investors, there will be an annual income of $7,000,000 from the tourist trade throughout the decade of the 1960's. Among the many private investment groups eyeing Fort de France and the splendid empty beaches of Guadeloupe and Saint Barthélemy is one headed by Edmond de Rothschild. The name of David Rockefeller has also been heard in connection with tourist projects. These wand-wielders have turned more than one pumpkin into a coach, and their interest augurs well for the future of the overpopulated, under-developed French West Indies.

Up to now the islands have been subsisting on sugar and its byproducts, including blackstrap molasses. But man cannot live by rum alone. Tourism is an obvious solution, especially when Nature has been so prodigal with the necessary raw materials: lush tropical scenery, spectacular mountains, virgin beaches, and the loveliest girls in the Caribbean.

These spice-colored creole beauties are walking arguments against race prejudice. The mingling of African and French blood has produced a kind of classic cinnamon beauty. French coquetry and the languour of the islands have combined to achieve a very special type of personality: soft, gracious, provocative, utterly feminine. You may find it disturbing. You'll still see a few *Martiniquaises* in their striking *madras et foulard* costumes. The colorful madras is tied onto the head with a flair that suggests the little milliners of the Faubourg St. Honoré. In a few cases, the "point" system is still used, a girl's amatory status being indicated by the number of points exposed in her headdress. If one point is exposed, the wearer's heart is free and unattached: green light. Two points exposed: she's lovely, she's engaged: red light.

Three: I'm happily married, so be on your way. *Feu rouge*.

Four: I have a husband, but I still like to play. You can interpret that as green or orange, depending on the kind of driver you are.

Most of the girls you see in the tourist centers of the French West Indies are not going to have their pretty heads done up in these madras squares. When you come into the French line pier at Fort de France, you'll think you've hit a tropical version of the Rue de la Paix. Never in all our travels have we seen a more attractive crowd greeting a ship. The girls, almost without exception, had what the French call *un chic fou,* beautifully turned out in summer cottons and prints that could have come from the salons of Dior and Balmain. Don't be too sad at the gradual disappearance of the madras. It had its points, to be sure, but a girl doesn't have to wear her heart on her head.

Tip: The French are the hand-shakingest people in the world, and the habit has been taken over here. You shake hands on all meetings, not just the first, and upon all arrivals and departures. When in doubt, shake.

GUADELOUPE

It was Sydney Clark who first said this "Emerald of the Caribbean" looked like a pair of inflated water wings, a comparison whose force may be lost on the tube and kickboard generation. Guadeloupe is actually two islands, separated by a hundred-yard-wide channel of the Caribbean called the *Rivière Salée*. The northeastern section, flat and agricultural, is called Grande Terre. Pointe à Pitre, a city of 60,000, is here, right on the Rivière Salée. Across a drawbridge is the other island, called Basse-Terre (Low Land), despite the fact that it is crowned by towering volcanic mountains: La Soufrière

FRENCH WEST INDIES

(4,870 feet), Sans Toucher (4,855) and other peaks whose cascading mountain torrents feed half a dozen rivers of Guadeloupe. The town of Basse Terre on the southwestern coast of Basse-Terre is the capital of Guadeloupe. Its population is only 16,000. The drive from Pointe à Pitre, where the planes land, to Basse Terre is the "compulsory excursion" of Guadeloupe, through some of the most spectacular scenery in the Caribbean.

It was on November 7, 1493 that Columbus discovered Guadeloupe. On the preceding Sunday he had sited Dominica, which he named in honor of the day. He went ashore at Marie Galante, named the island for his flagship, the *Maria Galanda*, and proclaimed it and the whole archipelago to be the property of their Catholic Majesties, Ferdinand and Isabella of Spain. The luxuriant and majestic island which appeared shortly afterward on the port side was Guadeloupe. In giving this name to a tropical island, Columbus kept a promise made to the monks of the monastery of Guadeloupe in Estremadura. Ponce de León and other Spanish soldiers of fortune never succeeded in colonizing the island. The Spaniards abandoned it in 1604. The French moved in in 1635, and played musical chairs for the place with the English until it was finally restored to France by the Congress of Vienna in 1815. It has been a full-fledged department of France since 1946.

PRACTICAL INFORMATION FOR GUADELOUPE

WHEN TO COME. November through July. August through October is the rainy season.

HOW TO GET THERE. *By air.* Raizet airfield, two miles from Pointe-à-Pitre is served by regular flights from New York and Miami by jets of Pan American World Airways, BWIA and Caribair.

Air France has daily flights between Guadeloupe and Martinique, and twice weekly flights linking the island with Puerto Rico, Antigua, St. Martin, Barbados, Surinam, Trinidad and French Guiana. This inter-island service has bi-weekly connections with Caracas, Bogota, Quito, Lima, Santiago, Lisbon and Paris.

Antilles Air Service links Guadeloupe to its dependencies: Marie Galante, Desirade, St. Martin and St. Barthèlemy.

Pan Am links it with Trinidad and Puerto Rico.

By sea, the French Line (Compagnie Transatlantique) links Guadeloupe with Martinique, Barbados, Trinidad, La Guaira, Curaçao, Cartagena, Jamaica and Haiti. An Italian company, Grimaldi Siosa, effects once a month the circuit; Palerma, Naples, Genoa, Cannes, Barcelona, Teneriffe-, Pointe-à-Pitre, Fort de France, La Guyana, Trinidad, and back.

PASSPORTS, VISAS. A passport, a vaccination certificate, and a ticket

472

FRENCH WEST INDIES

out of the country are required. If you are island hopping and have not provided yourself with a passport, some other documentary evidence of your citizenship will be accepted, providing you are not going to spend more than 8 days in the country.

 CURRENCY. The new franc, currently computed at 4,83 to the dollar, is legal tender. Both, old and new currency will be accepted, with prices quoted in both old and new francs. Paper money issued on Guadeloupe and Martinique is *only* good on these islands; do not expect to reconvert it outside. Money issued by the Banque de France is convertible. There is no limit to the amount of money you may bring in. U.S. and Canadian dollars are accepted in most places; dollar travelers checks everywhere.

 HOW TO GET ABOUT. The manager of Grand Hôtel at Pointe-à-Pitre provides four sightseeing tours and a number of 5-passenger self-drive cars. Another tour operator is Guadeloupe Voyages also at Point-à-Pitre. There are taxis, government-regulated. Also *transports en commun*, buses. They are of a certain vintage. The creoles call the bus *la voi*, short for *la voiture*. They careen around the country, and will stop anywhere at the wave of a hand. This is the cheapest and "most island" way to get about; the fare for the spectacular two-and-a-half-hour ride from Pointe-à-Pitre to Basse Terre is under 400 francs, less than a dollar. It can have its uncomfortable and even harrowing moments however. The drivers of Guadeloupe are as speedy and highstrung as the French, and the accident rate is high. If you're driving, be careful. Pay special attention to the picturesque traffic hazard of the two-wheeled bullock-drawn carts (straight out of the Dordogne) and even more attention to the drivers of sugar-cane trucks. *Caribcars*, a Hertz licensee, just opened a car rental system in Pointe-à-Pitre.

 HOTELS. The island, at this writing, is just beginning to show the results of its "crash program" of hotel development, and is slowly becoming equipped to cater to the tourist trade. In addition to the hostelries listed below, the *Fort Royal* will open during the winter of 1962/63. Its rates will be the same as for *La Caravelle*, which is described below. The dependent island of St. Barthelemy is also on the threshold of new realizations. A luxurious club colony is being planned. At Dole-les-Bains, 6 miles from Basse-Terre, there are therapeutic mineral waters and baths. You can stay in the small hotel—16 rooms with bath—for $10, American Plan. There is also an excellent restaurant with French and Creole cuisine.

LA CARAVELLE. This new and important hotel, with its own private beach, opened in the fall of 1962. La Caravelle has 20 acres of ground with 100 rooms and a swimming pool to size; also, the beach is protected by coral reefs. Cuisine is French, *naturellement*, and the wine cellar has the making of one of the best in the Caribbean. An outdoor dining terrace adds to the enjoyment of these gastronomic pleasures. All rooms are air conditioned. The project is financed by an important French hotel chain and a metropolitan French banking group. It is eventually planned to have 250 rooms and bungalow accommodations. Modified American Plan rates (Dec. 16-April 15) are: $35 per day single; $42 double. Off-season rates (April 16-Dec. 15) are:

473

$20 single, $32 double. 10% tip included.

GRAND HOTEL. Second largest (65 rooms) in Point-à-Pitre. Every room has a bath and a bidet, but the plumbing is more French than functional. Sometimes the water just stops flowing altogether. About sixty rooms are air-conditioned; 15 are more-or-less permanently reserved for Air France personnel. Definitely not a tourist hotel, but, this being French soil, it does have a good restaurant. M. Diligenti is the proprietor. Manager is Mr. Saizeau. His European Plan rates are $5 to $7 single, $9 to $11 double per day.

LA VIEILLE TOUR (The Old Sugar Mill) has just opened for business. Located on a private estate covering 15 acres about 5 miles from the Guadeloupe International Airport, this being French soil, it does have rooms and a suite, all with showers, hot and cold water, and air-conditioning. There is a private beach as well as a swimming pool with a snack bar nearby. Between Dec. 15 and Apr. 30 you pay $24 for a single, $36 for a double; from May 1 until Dec. 14 it is only $18 for a single and $30 for a double. These prices include three meals a day, wines, taxes and tips. There are two restaurants and a night club.

PERGOLA. At Le Gosier, about four miles from Pointe-à-Pitre, this is a charming group of cottages (the owner, M. Petrelluzzi calls them "Pergolettes"), facing a white sand beach and wonderful view. Beach and pergolettes are in the shade of an almond grove. The crowning glory of La Pergola du Gosier is its restaurant, with terrace looking out over the towering silhouette of La Soufrière. Whoever said you can't transplant the *haute cuisine française* has obviously not had a meal at this exceptional restaurant. Among the specialties are red fish *au court bouillon*, Chicken Petroluzzi, Oysters en Brochette. Try also the *Langouste au Vin* and the delicious local land crabs *farcies*. No matter what the dish or what French wine you choose to go with it, the fare at the Pergola will stand comparison with the best that France can provide. The waitresses in foularde and madras are as appetizing as the food. A lunch or dinner here is enough in itself to warrant a trip to Guadeloupe. European plan rates are $8 a day single, $10 double. American Plan: $18 a day single, $29 double. There are only ten bungalows available at the moment, and they're always filled. Thirty more are planned; they will be too. Reserve early.

ROCROI BEACH. Ten bungalows on the sea at Vieux-Habitants. Manager is Mr. Salmon. Rates are $6 per day single, $8 double, European Plan.

ROYAL. Basse-Terre's only hotel worth mentioning, and not worth a very loud mention at that. Twenty rooms. European Plan rates $3 single, $4 double. Meals in the hotel restaurant are good and cheap.

 FOOD AND RESTAURANTS. French imagination and taste are happily apparent throughout island cuisine. The sea supplies wonderful raw material: lobsters, turtle, red fish. So does the land. Among the island specialties are stuffed crab with rice, stewed conch and octopus, roast wild goat, jugged rabbit, fricassee of raccoon, ragout of water fowl. Broiled dove and skewered larks are a delicacy, as highly regarded here as they are in France. There are plenty of highly-spiced creole dishes to vary the French diet. To complement the cuisine, there is a great supply of French wines, champagne, liqueurs at the lowest prices in the Western Hemisphere, plus the excellent local rum, which is even cheaper.

FRENCH WEST INDIES

In addition to *La Pergola* and the hotels mentioned above, try *Le Grand Large* at Ste. Anne; *Le Robinson,* manager-owner Mr. D. Michaux, in Basse-Terre.

Two important new developments on Guadeloupe's gastronomic front are worth remembering. The well-known Lacascade brothers opened not one, but two restaurants at Raizet airport. These twin establishments, *l'Oiseau des Iles* and *le Madras* boast two chefs from Maxim's (Paris)—no less. The Lacascades have also raided Maxim's legendary wine cellars and thus succeeded in transplanting a truly Parisian gastronomic outpost into the Caribees.

The new *l'Eldorado* at Pointe-à-Pitre is another addition to this encouraging situation.

SHOPPING. Rue Frébault and Schoelcher in Pointe-à-Pitre are the shopping centers. It's not the Rue Saint-Honoré, but the shops have enough of that wonderful French lingerie and perfume on hand to make any woman happy, and at prices which will gladden the heart of most husbands. The perfumes are actually less than they cost in France. In addition to these French luxury products, there is a grand selection of wines and liqueurs. Native rum of very good quality is as low as 60 cents a bottle. Native objects of straw and wood are good local buys, including the Chinese looking bamboo hats or *selacas,* worn by the fishing folk of Les Iles des Saintes. Native doudou dolls, baskets and objects of aromatic vetivert wood are good souvenirs. Discount of 20 % if you pay with travelers checks.

Among the shops you'll enjoy browsing through, half a dozen are outstanding: *Echanges Commerciaux, Galeries Parisiennes, Week-End, A. Kattar, Selection,* the *Quimbois, Camps-Elysées* and *Réalités.* Remember you are in a department of France; the stores close for a long lunch and siesta from noon until 2:30. They also close on Saturday afternoons and Sundays, unless there's a cruise ship in, in which case your time is their time.

SPORTS AND OTHER ACTIVITIES. *Swimming* is good at a number of beaches. Best facilities are at Le Gosier where you can rent dressing room, shower, beach chairs and other equipment from La Pergola. For refreshing and invigorating sea bathing as well as pleasant sun bathing, the beaches at Ste. Anne (about 14 miles east of Pointe-à-Pitre) and at St. François, ten miles farther east, are among the finest in the Caribbean. Completely undeveloped, they are usually empty. Moule, on the northeast coast of Grande-Terre, is another splendid strand, waiting to be developed.

Headquarters for *sailing* are the Yacht Clubs of Pointe-à-Pitre and Basse-Terre where both sailboats and motorboats may be hired.

Hiking and *mountain climbing* activities center in the Mountain Club in Basse-Terre, which has all necessary information and equipment, and maintains a mountain hut on the way to the spectacular Chutes de Carbet (Carbet Waterfalls), a two day climb from Basse-Terre. You can arrange through the club for automobiles and guides for the trip to the summit of La Soufrière. Go early in the morning to insure the best atmospheric conditions for the beautiful views of Dominica and Montserrat from the volcano summit. Tip: Stick close to the guide, especially in the final stages of the ascent, fraught with treacherous hot lava bogs which look firm but aren't.

Bicycling is just as popular here as it is in France; there are races every Sunday. The roads on flat Grande-Terre lend themselves admirably to this form of locomotion.

For *fishing, spear-fishing, lobster-progging,* make your arrangements through hotel or directly with local fishermen at Ste. Anne, St. François or some other fishing village.

Chief *spectator sport* is cockfighting every Sunday at the Pointe-à-Pitre cockpit and St. Anne.

As for *nightlife* on Guadeloupe, it is currently restricted to Saturday night dancing at *Ma Bretagne* and *La Vieille Tour* at Gosier, *Le Grand Large* at Plage Sainte-Anne, and once-a-month Saturday night fling at the *Grand Hotel* in Pointe-a-Pitre.

Carnival (see below: Martinique) goes on intermittently from New Year's Day to Ash Wednesday with attendant singing, dancing, parades and masquerades.

EXPLORING GUADELOUPE

Grande-Terre, flatter and less interesting than Basse-Terre, is a mass of green and silver sugar cane. The roads are good; the beaches wonderful. Driving east from Pointe-à-Pitre, a jaunt of five miles will take you to Le Gosier and the delights of La Pergola, already noted under Hotels. Ten miles farther east on the same road is Ste. Anne, a little sugar town, neat and prosperous, boasting an unsurpassed stretch of magnificent beach. The route continues, often shaded by flowering pepper trees, to St. François and the Pointe des Chateaux at the extreme eastern point of the island. Lonely and unspoiled, here is a place to remember. The sea flings itself against huge rocks, which seem to have been thrown down by some giant hand.

Six miles to the northeast is the isle of Désirade; formerly a leper colony, now an extremely picturesque place well worth exploring; the isles of Petite Terre are on your right to the southeast. The jagged cliffs of Pointe des Chateaux suggest the majestic headlands of Brittany. On one of them stands an impressive cross, dominating this spectacular scene; it is the only sign of man's handiwork here.

Le Moule, not far from here on the northeast coast, is another one of those superb beaches, waiting to be developed, but which may be enjoyed in almost solitary splendor in the meantime. This one is shaped like a horseshoe. Despite its peaceful aspect, it has been a battleground. Carib warriors, French and English soldiers fought here, and an old cemetery nearby commemorates their ancient conflict with petrified skulls, unearthed by the final victor, the sea. Swimming in these crystal waters, basking on this unspoiled beach, you may come across an unexpected souvenir, a sun-bleached human relic of Caribbean history.

The 40-mile drive from Pointe-à-Pitre to the capital city of Basse-Terre is much more interesting than the Grande-Terre tour. Almost as soon as you cross the drawbridge over the Rivière Salée, the scenery becomes spectacular. Sugar cane alternates here with banana trees, their great shredded fronds rustling in the breeze. Watered by more than 70 streams, the lush green of the tropics becomes almost stagey, vivid with every hue of hibiscus. Brooding backdrop is the cloud-capped peaks of Soufrière and Sans Toucher. You'll see the weasel-like forms of mongooses scurrying across the road. Since there have never been any snakes on Guadeloupe, it is to be wondered why they were ever imported there. Now, to the great annoyance of Guadeloupe's farmers, they have developed a taste for chicken.

You will drive through Goyave, a fine village which lives up to the Guadeloupe ideal of being *rangé et propre*, clean and orderly. Despite the poverty of Guadeloupe, you will not be depressed. There's too much good old-fashioned self respect to let things slide.

The road surface deteriorates around Ste. Marie, where Columbus landed in a flurry of Carib arrows and proceeded to chastise the natives for this unfriendly reception. You'll notice a lot of ochre-faced East Indians in this vicinity. They are the descendants of laborers who were brought in at coolie wages to work the sugar plantations, replacing negro slaves who had revolted and who were emancipated in 1848. On the slopes of Mt. Soufrière, 1800 feet up, you may visit a typical East Indian village, Matouba, where ancient rites, including the sacrifice of animals, are still practised by survivors of this transplanted nation.

Trois Rivières is the jumping-off place for a fascinating excursion to the Iles des Saintes (see below). You may also want to stop here for a visit to the "Valley of the Ancient Caribs" whose sculptured rocks, heavily incised with Indian inscriptions, are among the most impressive of the few relics left by the fierce race which once dominated the Caribbean.

After Trois Rivières, the road cuts inland, past Dole-les-Bains with its therapeutic mineral baths. There is a charming, if somewhat antiquated resort hotel here, a favorite of the locals for its restaurant, good wines and, particularly its pool. You drive through the village of Gourbevre, shortly after which the silhouette of Fort Richpance guards the approaches to Basse-Terre. It's a post-card capital, with well-laid-out parks, handsome administrative buildings, a 17th-century cathedral, all in a dramatic setting between the sea and Mt. Soufrière. Take the steep and narrow road inland to St. Claude, a suburb four miles from Basse-Terre. Here, amidst the lushest of tropical trees and gardens, live the wealthy owners of banana plantations and, more modestly, the higher echelon of that eternal army of *fonctionnaires*, the civil servants of France. At St. Claude, you are already on your way up the slopes of majestic Soufrière. You can drive past Rivière Noire and Rivière Rouge to Matouba, the East Indian village mentioned above, and on into the marvelous tropical rain forest of giant trees and ferns, a cool and sunless world whose unearthly, primordial hush is broken only by the splash of waterfalls. This is one of the unforgettable high points of Guadeloupe.

The highest point, of course, is the 4,900-foot summit of the Sulphurous One itself. You cannot reach it by road. The peak is a good two-hour hike and climb after you leave your car. It isn't the Matterhorn or the Jungfrau, but it's enough to tucker the amateur. Don't attempt it without a guide (see above: Sports and Other Activities) unless you are quite experienced. In any event wear stout shoes, the kind that keep shale and pebbles out, a raincoat and a hat. The climb to the resthouse is relatively easy along a well-marked trail that ascends through the superb forest of huge ferns and giant, vine-clad acoma trees. There are usually guides at the resthouse (even if you have not arranged for one in Basse-Terre) and they are a necessity for the final surge. Their fee? A bottle of native rum (make sure you have an extra one in your pack or pocket). Incidentally, don't get any gourmet ideas about that rest house. Lunch is not served; you bring your own. The reward for all this effort, especially if you have had the foresight to check on weather conditions in advance, is a magnificent view, a sense of accomplishment, and that special heady feeling that comes from being at least temporarily on top of the world.

ILES DES SAINTES

Les Saintes are a cluster of five islands off the southern coast of Guadeloupe, accessible by boat, leaving daily from either Basse-Terre or Trois Rivières. The trip, apt to be rough, takes anywhere from two to five hours, depending on the conditions of weather and sea. The two main Saintes, Terre de Haute and Terre de Bas, attract many Guadeloupians as weekend resorts. The first and more interesting to visit, has about 1,000 inhabitants, of which about 300 are the descendants of Breton and Norman sailors. They look like a bunch of blue-eyed Vikings with those apple-cheeks that come from salt air, Calvados and cider. Many of these whites have preferred inbreeding to intermarriage. *Les Saintois* as they are called, are said to be the best seamen in the West Indies. Certainly they are the most picturesque, thanks to the fetchingly-curved straw hats they wear. A touch of the Orient in the Caribbean, these *salacos* as they are called, look like inverted saucers. They were originally imported by the French from Indo-China. They are locally made with strips of split bamboo acting as ribs over which, parasol-like, a piece of white cotton is tightly stretched. They are extremely chic, and much appreciated as souvenirs.

The ability of the *saintois* as seamen is equalled only by their prowess as smugglers. They are very busy "importing" such items as cigarettes, whisky and Maracaibo textiles, which are very popular with the belles of Guadeloupe. There is said to be a regular smugglers' shuttle service between those two terminals of holy name: Les Saintes and Dominica.

The chief settlement of Terre de Haut is Bourg, a single paved street, following the curve of the fishing harbor. The white houses lining this main drag are painted with blue and red trim and occasionally sport a carved balcony or some other quaint touch of Victorian gingerbread. A local curiosity, often photographed, is a house built in the form of a steamship, decks, stack, anchor, portholes and all. It seems to be emerging, bow first, from a cliff.

Bourg abounds in local color, little French bistros and bars, and a sort of timeless primitive charm. Donkeys are the local beasts of burden. Fishnets are drying all over the island on racks. Children without benefit of bikinis enjoy the beaches and water in a state of pristine innocence such as must have preceded the fall of Man.

There is a fascinating ruin, Fort Napoléon, which you can explore to your heart's content. But all of Terre de Haut was made for exploring, for ambling, rambling, meandering, alternating with swimming and sunbathing on the lovely leeward beaches.

There is a six-room *pension de famille* where you can eat with wine for less than $5 a day, and les Saintois could not be more friendly when it comes to renting rooms to strangers. Far from the toot of any cruise ship's whistle, Terre de Haut does have electricity, running water, and a couple of jeeps and cars. Otherwise the clock stopped here before the atom age began.

SAINT BARTHELEMY

More popularly known as St. Barts, this island dependency of Guadeloupe, lies 100 miles to the north of its mother, near the top of the Lesser Antilles. Forty miles north of St. Kitts, 15 south of St. Martin, it is accessible to those islands by intermittent schooner service and is linked to Guadeloupe by Antilles Air Service which flies between the two islands at least once a week.

The island has an interesting past and an even more promising future. The latter is predicated on an ideal beach. The beach, three miles long, protected by both cliff and reef, is one of the best in the world. It awaits development, and has in fact already caught the eye of investors who are looking for another and a better Mill Reef. St. Barts was made to be a superlative beach resort. Ground work has already been done by Conseiller Général Remy de Haenen, who lives on the beach, has been flying visitors in on charter planes, and who has built the beach hotel of his dreams on St. Barts. It is the *Eden Roc Guest House* at St. Jean. There are four "ordinary" rooms with cold running water and one "chambre de luxe". The former cost $15 single or $25 double; the luxury comes to $25 single or $35 double. This includes all your meals, the use of a private garden and a very nice beach near by. Although he only plans to rent his rooms between December 15 and April 15, is it possible to arrange something with Monsieur de Haenen for a date outside that period.

Pending future developments, St. Barts remains an interesting backwater, a strange and striking white enclave in the coffee-colored Caribbean. The 3500 people on St. Barts are of French and Swedish background, the French having sold the island to the Swedes in 1784. In 1878 a plebiscite resulted in its becoming French again. The capital, Gustavia, is situated on a superb, circular, landlocked hurricane proof harbor, perhaps the most perfect in the West Indies.

The people of St. Barts speak old Norman French and wear the provincial costumes of Normandy. The old ladies, sporting starched white caps, look like the women who are chasing dirt in the Old Dutch Cleanser ad. They do chase dirt too. Though poor, these people are immaculate. The girls are blonde, blue-eyed, long-limbed and attractive. The men are excellent seamen, like their cousins on Les Saintes. Like the Saintois, they are old hands at smuggling, doing a rushing rum-running business between St. Barts, Anguilla, Barbuda and other British islands.

Once headquarters for a less surreptitious type of buccaneering, St. Barts is said to have more than its share of buried pirate treasure. Whether it has or not, there's tourist gold in them thar hills, and it's just a matter of time before it's mined.

MARIE GALANTE

Twenty-five miles, two hours by launch from Basse-Terre, this is a sugar island with a population of some 26,000. If you want to see colorful foulard-et-madras costumes, come here on a Sunday. The women are dressed to the nines in turbans and long dresses, rakishly kilted up to show a dazzling array of subversive slips. The capital is Grand Bourg with a population of about 8,000 and a protected beach. There's the *Hotel de la Concorde* where you can get a lunch or dinner worthy of the French provinces, but you won't be staying overnight unless you miss the boat back to Basse-Terre.

SAINT MARTIN

This is the French half of that Dutch Windward island you read about under The Netherlands Antilles. The Dutch side has the best hotel accommodations and the airport, served by both Air France and KLM. Marigot is the French capital. The chief industries are lobster fishing and the breeding of fine horses. This suggests two corollary tourist activities. In addition to riding, fishing, and eating good French food, you can spend your time swimming, sailing and going to cock fights. Though the official currency of St. Martin is francs, guilders and the Yankee dollar are equally acceptable in return for the bargain perfumes, lingerie, and French liquor with which the shops of Marigot are amply stocked. A brand-new shop, the *Europa* has fine china and glassware from Europe at freeport prices. There is a hotel on the French side too, the *Beau Séjour*. We don't know how long or how beau a sejour you are expecting, but you can count on one thing: good meals. Rates are about $10 per person per day, full American Plan.

With all these assets, it is no wonder that St. Martin, the French side of the island gradually is gaining in prominence.

MARTINIQUE

"Queen of the Antilles", Martinique is the largest and northernmost of the Windward Islands. It is 50 miles long, 19 wide and has a population of 250,000. When Columbus landed at Carbet on the western coast in 1502, he got such a hot and arrowy reception from the Caribs that he had to beat a hasty retreat without even naming his latest discovery. The Carib name, Madinina, meaning Island of Flowers, thus remained, eventually to be gallicised as Martinique. It could not be more appropriate; Martinique is a bower of hibiscus, anthurium, bougainvillea, wild orchids and other exotic blooms. A lush land of year-round summer, the island's average temperature varies between 75 and 80 degrees. There's a cool and dry season from November to April, the best time to come; a warm and dry season from April to July. From July to November, the weather is warm and rainy with more than a hint of cyclone in the air. That's the time to stay away from the moody Queen of the Antilles.

French colonization of Martinique dates from 1635. From that time on, this mountainous island shared the turbulent history of the mother country, knowing revolts, insurrections, foreign occupation and all the hazards of colonial competition, but it has remained French in language, manners, morals and spirit. Since 1948, it has been a *department* of France with a Prefect and all the rights and privileges of the 83 departments of metropolitan France.

The variety of terrain in Martinique's 425 square miles is remarkable, ranging from the salt fields and barren rock of the arid south to the verdure-clad slopes and luxuriant rain forest of the north. Fort-de-France, with a population of more than 66,000, is the capital of Martinique and a popular port of call for cruise ships.

Across the bay is the village of Les Trois Ilets. This is historic ground, the birthplace of the creole beauty, Josephine Rose Tascher de la Pagerie, who was to captivate the heart of Napoleon Bonaparte and reign for five years as Empress of the French. Something in the soil or air of Martinique seems to have produced women of irresistible fascination. Madame de Maintenon, first the mistress and finally the morganatic wife of Louis XIV, was raised in Martinique. These were two white women of the island, but the alchemy operates regardless of pigmentation; cinnamon-colored *Martiniquaises* are world famous for their beauty and grace. The most striking scenery of this scenic island moves about on two feet.

Martinique's other crops sound like a description of the local color gamut: rum, vanilla, coffee, cocoa, cinnamon, mahogany. The greatest of these is rum. *It* comes in a variety of colors, and could fool experts on the matter with its special flavor. It has the quality of a good Cognac. There is "Vieil Acajou" (Old Mahogany) and "Jeune Acajou" (Young Mahogany), a poetic way of saying dark and white. There is also double-distilled "Coeur de Chauffe", a poetic way of saying light, strong, and hot as the tropic sun.

The hottest thing in Martinique, however, is neither rum nor sun. It's the *biguine*. Contrary to popular superstition, Cole Porter did not begin it. He patterned his great song after Martinique's *danse du pays*. The native version of it makes Cole Porter's look like the scarf dance of Cecile Chaminade. The place to see it is at the *Plantation* a night spot in Fort de France. You can watch the torrid proceedings on the dance-floor from the vantage point of a cool balcony. The *biguine* is more than a dance. Its suggestive movement of the hips exceeds mere symbolism. Its rhythms, voluptuous at first, soon become lascivious. The net result is sensational. "Never had so much fun with my clothes on," was the reaction of one tourist. The *Plantation* is for narrow hips and broad minds. The club itself is new and located in an old colonial house about three miles from the center of town. It has proved to be popular with such well-known writers on the Caribbean as Horace Sutton.

Les Diablesses

A session at this uninhibited palace of the danse will give you a taste of what Carnival or *Vaval* is like in Martinique. It's the event of the year. It gets underway right after the New Year hangover and builds up a head of steam which finally explodes on Monday and Tuesday before Lent. Masquerades and singing and dancing in the streets are the normal order of events for three months, the celebrations growing more gay and elaborate as Mardi Gras approaches. There is a great parade and ball on that night, but the best is yet to come. On Ash Wednesday, when the exhausted celebrants of more effete lands are having their fevered foreheads blackened with cinders, nearly 30,000 masked *Martiniquais* jam the streets of Fort de France. These are *les diablesses* (literally, the female devils, but both sexes participate à la Martiniquaise). All are grotesquely masked and costumed. Anything goes as long as one principal rule is adhered to: the costumes must be in two colors only, black and white. Clarinets and trumpets announce the fête; the chachas start the rhythm. The parades of this protracted wake in honor of *Bois Bois*, king of the carnival, start early in the morning. By noon, much rum has gone down the hatch and many a *diablesse* is drunk. Luncheon has a sobering and strengthening effect, fortifying the devils for the really strenuous work of the afternoon and evening. By afternoon, Bois Bois's funeral corteges are jumping. The whole town is like some wild, grotesque ballet. The funeral pyre of Bois Bois is built on the savannah of Fort de France. The street dancing grows more febrile. When dusk falls, the pyre is lighted. The *diablesses* dance around it in a frenzy compared to which Walpurgisnacht is a meeting of the vestry. Shrieks, screams, unearthly wails, all the hysteria of mock grief greet the effigy of Bois Bois which is now consigned to the flames. The frenzy is at its apogee; the *diablesses* are possessed, wild, grotesque shadows dancing in the flickering flames. "Au 'voir Bois Bois, adieu Vaval!" Soon Bois Bois is consumed. The flames subside. Think it's over? Man, it's only 9 o'clock! This is Martinique! There'll be dancing until midnight at every hotel and ballroom of Fort de France, then the final funeral cortege as Bois Bois' coffin is buried at last with everyone weeping, singing, waving torches. Carnival is over until next January.

So much for La Fête de la Diablesse, a rare spectacle, in fact unique. If you can arrange your itinerary to coincide with this climactic event, do it. In the name of all the black and white devils of Martinique, we promise you an Ash Wednesday you'll never forget.

The Biguine and La Diablesse indicate only one facet of the character of Martinique. There is the grace and charm of the Mazurka, reminiscent of Josephine's day, with the lovely creole girls in empire gowns stepping and gliding in a dance which ends as they fall limply into their partner's arms. There are the vigorous folklore dances of the sugar cane harvest, done to the rhythm of swinging machete and beating drum. There are country dances as old as Africa or Auvergne. Above all, there is the sweet side, the sentimental aspect of Martinique, best expressed in the famous song, *Adieu Foulard, Adieu Madras,* retelling the simple story of a creole beauty's hopeless love for her *Doudou*, her naval officer lover whom orders compel to sail with the tide. It sounds positively corny in print, but when you hear this haunting *chanson doudou*, you will probably know the same misty-eyed response that it has produced in thousands of visitors before you.

It's a heartbreaking lament, pathetic with the pathos of the transient state of human affairs. The sadness of departure expressed in the song becomes equated with one's sorrow at leaving this lovely island, although with the tourist it need not be, "*hélas, c'est pour toujou'*". *Adieu Foulard, Adieu Madras* has the simple, direct appeal of the creole; when you hear it, you are close to the languorous heart of Martinique.

PRACTICAL INFORMATION FOR MARTINIQUE

HOW TO GET THERE. Fort-de-France's up-to-date Lareinty airdrome, at Le Lamentin about nine miles from the capital, is linked with New York by Pan American World Airways via Puerto Rico, and British West Indian Airways via Antigua.

Air France has twice weekly service between Paris, Lisbon and Martinique as well as a regular service to the three Guianas. You can also fly from Miami to Fort-de-France by Pan American. Air France has nine flights a week between Martinique and Guadeloupe, also provides direct inter-island connections with Puerto Rico, Trinidad and Barbados.

PAA links Martinique with Trinidad and Puerto Rico.

BWIA with Trinidad, St. Kitts, Antigua, Barbados and the rest of the British islands.

Alcoa Steamship Company has passenger freighters out of Halifax which stop at Fort-de-France. Booth American Shipping has monthly freighter sailings from New York. There is weekly boat service between Martinique and Guadeloupe by way of Dominica.

PASSPORTS, VISAS, CURRENCY. Same as for Guadeloupe.

HOTELS

Pending completion of Fort St. Louis, the Batelière and the Hotel de la Prairie, Martinique's newest hotels, there are projects for other hotels, such as the 112-room resort on the beach of Sainte Anne. Our list is alphabetical. All rates are for full American Plan.

AUBERGE ANSE MITAN. Four miles (20 minutes by launch) across the bay from the capital, L'Anse Mitan is an unspoiled fishing and sailing village, and a snorkeler's dream of heaven. Recently refurnished, the Auberge, run by M. Rapricault and family, is a typical French inn with 17 comfortable rooms and baths and with three delicious meals a day. In addition to a regular local boat service, guests of the Auberge make use of the hotel's private launch, which shuttles between L'Anse Mitan and the capital. The beauty of this place is in its peace and tranquility (no cars) in spite of proximity to bustling Fort-de-France. Very few North Americans or Europeans have discovered this haven to date. Our room had a balcony overlooking bay and beach, and it was ideal for a simple, pleasant holiday of swimming and sailing. Rates are $10 and $12 a day single, $16 and $18 double.

AUBERGE VIEUX CHALET. A six-room inn, high and cool in the mountains at Morne-Rouge. Nearby is the *Rivière des Ecrevisses, Crayfish River*, which supplies the manager, Mme. Duplan, with one of the bases for her cuisine. Rates are only $6 a day single, $12 double.

LA BATELIERE. Located just 2 miles from Fort-de-France, this new hotel will have 120 rooms and all modern recreational facilities, including a casino. It was built by the Martinique Hotel and Touristic society. Rates on request.

BERKELEY. Most modern of the island's hostelries to date with 30 attractive rooms with baths and air conditioning. It's 10 minutes from Fort-de-France on the road to Schoelcher, not an ideal location by any means. M. Parfait, a gracious and competent *hotelier*, is the manager; the meals are French; the rates are about $17 per day single; about $30 double.

BRISTOL. In Fort-de-France with a good view over the bay. Small, a bit on the gone-to-seed side, but with French meals at provincial French prices: $8 single, $14 double. M. Carrère is the manager.

IMPERATRICE. On the Place de la Savane in the heart of town, a modern 30-room hostelry with private baths and air conditioning. It's named in honor of that local girl who made good. M. Charles Glaudon is the manager; his kitchen is recommended. His rates: $13 to $16 single, $22 to $25 double.

LIDO. This is the best resort hotel currently operating in Martinique.

It has been completely rebuilt and offers another 32 air-conditioned rooms. It's at Schoelcher on Anse Colas (about 20 minutes from Fort-de-France) in a lovely garden setting above the sea. Below, way below, is a good little black sand beach, with new docks, cabins. The hotel's new bungalows offer the most modern accommodations available at the current writing. The Lido is a multi-level affair, with swimming pool, bungalows and main building all constructed on a steep hillside. The resultant stairs may be too much for the aged or the ailing, but once you have climbed to the bar and terraces, the view is splendid. So is the food, and so are the accompanying French wines. It's all very pleasant and gay. Rates are winter $24, summer $18 single per day; winter $30 double.

MADIANA-PLAGE. A ten-room hostelry with air conditioning available, at Fonds Nigauds, a 15 minute drive from Fort-de-France. M. Lelièvre is the manager. Rates are $10 to $12 single; $20 to $22 double. We don't know this place personally, but guest reports on food and accommodations are okay.

HOTEL DE LA PRAIRIE. A new hotel on the east coast of Martinique in Vauclin. Situated on a promontory, the hotel offers two beautiful white sand beaches. Thirty rooms with rates on request.

VIEUX MOULIN. At Didier, about 4 kilometers from Fort-de-France, this is a converted sugar mill on top of a hill with a good view. The place has a private zoo (we saw two ocelots) and more than a soupçon of antique if somewhat decrepit charm. Madame de Montfleur is in charge. She has 20 rooms with bath, and first rate food. Rates are $10 and $11 per day single, $18 and $19 double.

FRENCH WEST INDIES

FOOD, DRINK AND RESTAURANTS. To the many dishes described under Guadeloupe, add *colombo*, an Indian stew of seeds and beef or pork cooked with rice. The stuffed crabs are delicious here, and the French cooks do wonderful things with the local fresh water crayfish (*écrevisses*), which incidentally are bigger than the ones in la Belle France, approaching the size of a small lobster. Try *calalou*, a subtle and savory French-Creole herb soup. Other local specialties are heart-of-palm salad, roasted wild goat (a little strong and gamey for some tastes), raccoon, tortoise and a big variety of seafood. The French cuisine can stand comparison with Parisian standards, and the local cellars are full of excellent French wines. The big island speciality in the drink department is *Le Punch Martiniquais*, Martinique Punch, about as good a tropical rum punch as you'll find in your travels.

As for restaurants, the dining rooms of the *Lido, Vieux Moulin* and *Hotel Europe* are the leaders.

L'Auberge du Manoir, on a hilltop overlooking Fort-de-France, is a great favorite with local people. Their two specialties are *escargots* and *écrevisses*. There's a good bar here, also dancing.

Chez Etienne is the best moderate priced French restaurant in Fort-de-France.

You can also find good food without frills at the *Hotel Bristol* and the *Restaurant A & L Gelin*, which are like low-priced French neighborhood eateries, and *Le Calaloo* serving only local dishes.

Roger Albert's *Beach House* at Anse D'Arlet for those who want to spend a day on one of the best beaches in the Caribbean; only 1½ hours from town by car. Arrangements can be made at Roger Albert Voyages in town.

A visit to the picturesque village of *Sainte Anne* can be further enhanced by a meal at the little creole inn and restaurant *La Dunette*.

You should visit *Robert*, and include a meal at the miniature restaurant *Fruit de mer*. They only serve sea food dishes which are excellent.

Our own long-cherished respect for *la cuisine martiniquaise* was reinforced on our last trip by an unexpected gastronomic experience. We had been swimming at *Diamant Plage* (attention: the undertow is strong), after which we repaired to *Madame Lucienne's*, a hotel and terrace restaurant straight out of Maugham if not Michener. Mme. Lucienne received us, a majestic 300-pound Martiniquaise, her natural grace unconstrained by such "civilized" devices as girdle and shoes. In a dress of formidable decolletage, she invited us to change in one of the hotel rooms. The room did not inspire us with any desire to settle down in it, nor did our confidence soar when we were ushered within sight of an indescribably sloppy kitchen to the terrace. We sat down to lunch with a certain trepidation. It quickly vanished with the arrival of a fish soup, one which we venture to say could not be surpassed by *Prunier* or the *Mediterranée* in Paris. Then, as though to show that this was no flash in the pan, Mme. Lucienne brought on a simple but exquisitely-prepared *court-bouillon* of fish, garnished with boiled breadfruit and a *maçedoine* of other tropical vegetables. Dessert was a whole fresh pineapple. After this memorable meal, we have two suggestions. First, to our readers, arrange your exploration of Martinique to include at least one meal chez Mme. Lucienne. Second, to all cordon-bleu chefs of the Caribbean de luxe hotels: take a refresher course at Mme. Lucienne's culinary finishing school.

FRENCH WEST INDIES

NIGHTLIFE. *Plantation* (see introduction) is the hottest, jumpingest place in town on Saturday night. They serve drinks and you'll have fun, whether you look upon the *biguine* as a spectator or participant sport. Don't take grandma unless she's very progressive.

There's dinner and after-dinner dancing quite often at the *Lido*, smart weekend social center. If you want to hear the old songs and see the old dances of Martinique, see Roger Albert at 7 Rue Victor Hugo. He runs a famous Free Port Shop (listed below). M. Albert has done more than any other single person to revive and perpetuate the colorful folklore of the island. Many cruise passengers have seen his programs aboard ship, and he can arrange them on land as well.

SHOPPING. Fort-de-France is the place to buy all French luxury imports. The chief shopping streets are Rue St. Louis, Rue Victor Hugo, and Rue Schoelcher. If you buy perfumes, china, crystal, lingerie and other French items, pay with travelers' checks. This establishes your tourist status, and whatever excise taxes are involved are immediately deducted from your bill. The deduction, for all practical purposes, puts Fort-de-France in the free port category as far as French products are concerned.

Outstanding values in the shops are French perfumes, china, porcelain, crystal, lingeries and liquor. You'll also find plenty of silver, straw, jewelry, local ceramics, Oriental curios, and island souvenirs, including Martiniquais dolls in native costume. The world-famous rum is also a good buy. It is among the best of its kind in the West Indies.

Leading emporium is *Roger Albert's* on Rue Victor Hugo, has doubled in size. His is the most famous perfume shop in the Caribbean. He has the best scents of 50 French parfumeurs, including the great names like Guerlain and Lanvin plus some lesser known ones like Sauzé and Molinard, which are definitely worth trying. So far as we know, nobody in the New World undersells Roger in this department. He gives you a substantial discount if you pay with U.S. or Canadian travellers checks, and returns the change in your own currency. He also has a good selection of Swiss watches, French Baccarat and Daum crystal, Limoges (including popular pattern with effigy of the Empress Josephine), scarves, silver spoons and local souvenir items.

For the latest Paris fashions in the Antilles, look in at *Marsan* on the Rue Lamartine. They have millinery, fabrics, shoes and ready-to-wear clothes for men, women and children.

For dolls and souvenirs of Martinique, an outstanding West Indian novelty shop is *Au Printemps*; they also have a good selection of Baccarat crystal and Limoges china.

Mad, across from Roger Albert is the best shop for madras, souvenirs and all native basketry, woodwork and handcrafts in general. Mad, incidentally, is a specialist at tying the madras and will demonstrate it on your own head if you like.

For local and imported jewelry, best shops are *Cadet-Daniel* and *Derogatis*.

488

FRENCH WEST INDIES

SPORTS AND OTHER ACTIVITIES. There's *swimming* at many black sand and white sand beaches. The black one at the Lido Hotel is the nearest to Fort-de-France. The one at L'Anse Mitan is white, tightly-packed, but varies dramatically in width with the tide. One of the most beautiful beaches we ever saw is undeveloped 6-mile-long plage, *Le Diamant,* the Diamond, about six miles out of Fort-de-France on the southwestern coast. If you want to swim in a pool, the Lido and the Vieux Moulin are your best bets.

Your hotel can make arrangements for you to *sail* from Fort-de-France Yacht Club, and will also indicate best places for both sea and river fishing.

You can play *tennis,* if it's not too warm, at the Vieux Moulin hotel and on the courts of the tennis club in Fort-de-France.

There are bicycles for rent everywhere; the local passion for cycling exceeds even that of the mother country.

Mountain climbing and hiking are also popular.

There are a number of private clubs open to visitors. They have bars, billiard rooms, social programs and provide an opportunity to meet businessmen and community leaders. It's a help if you speak French in these places. Hotel managers will help with entrée to these clubs as well as to the *Yacht Club, Club Nautique, Maison du Sport* and the *Aero Club des Antilles.*

You'll find books in both French and English at the Public Library and the local office of the United States Information Service.

EXPLORING MARTINIQUE

Fort-de France, capital of Martinique and the French West Indies, is a bustling port of 60,000 people, most of whom fit Lafcadio Hearn's description of a population "straight as palms, supple and tall, colored women and men (who) impress one powerfully by their dignified carriage and easy elegance of movement." If you see them on Saturday night, possessed by the ecstasy of the *Biguine,* you may not recognize them as they go to mass on Sunday morning. The latter time is suggested by the tourist office for photographing the local belles, some of whom still dress for the Sabbath in their bright-colored costumes, foulards, and intricately-tied madras headdresses. They are extremely gracious about posing. There are two favorite places for photographing them: outside the cathedral with its wrought-iron steeple, and in the Savane, the centrally-located park which serves as a fashionable promenade for the capital. It is dominated by Vital Debray's realistic white marble effigy of the Empress Josephine in the high-waisted flowing robe of the first Empire. A short trip by cab or bus will take you to the village of Trois Ilets and Josephine's childhood home where, in her own words, she breathed the perfumes wafted by the zephyr's breezes, delighted to hide in the verdant woods that surrounded her dwelling.

489

FRENCH WEST INDIES

If Napoleon's romantic creole empress is the national heroine of Martinique, the hero is a more democratic type. He is Victor Schoelcher, Alsatian deputy and leading French abolitionist, whose efforts were instrumental in freeing the slaves of the French West Indies in 1848. On the Savane, the Schoelcher Library honors his memory. His statue stands in front of the *Cour de Justice* building. One of the shopping streets of Fort-de-France is named after him, and so is the first west coast town you come to after driving out of Fort-de-France.

Fort-de-France reminds American visitors of New Orleans, and there is a vintage resemblance especially in the houses with their French iron grillework. But once you have explored the Savane and its side streets and taken in the waterfront with the lovely view of the Bay of Fort de France, you will be ready for those untrammeled views of nature which led Paul Gauguin to greater heights of enthusiasm than even Tahiti could evoke.

There are 175 miles of well-surfaced road on Martinique, but don't expect to get around in a hurry on this mountainous terrain. Some of the hairpin curves are enough to put a couple of waves in your own hair. If you want to explore the island thoroughly, buy the excellent *carte routière et touristique*, which shows every nook, cranny and knoll.

You can rent a drive-yourself car at the *Garage Americain, Voitures Location,* or through *Roger Albert* in Fort-de-France. You can also travel high and wide, but not handsomely, in the local buses. If they're a bit on the dirty side, they're also dirt cheap. In addition, there are coastal motor boats that run from Fort-de-France to such points of interest as Trois Ilets and Anse d'Arlets. If you want to climb Mount Pélée, the 4,500 foot volcanic giant which obliterated the latter city in 1902, you can hire guides and cars at Morne Rouge. The ascent involves an hour's hike. There is no danger at the moment; fire-breathing Mount Pelée apparently let off enough steam in 1902 to keep here quiet for centuries to come.

The coastal drive from Fort-de-France to St. Pierre is the classic tourist promenade of Martinique, a magnificent 30 mile drive which can be, and usually is, taken even by tourists from briefly-pausing cruise ships. Exploring the ruins of St. Pierre is at once a fascinating and sobering experience. The city, gay prosperous, and cultivated, was once known as the "little Paris of the West Indies". Its 40,000 citizens were puzzled but not unduly alarmed early in May 1902 when the volcano spread a dark cloud of smoke over the sky and scattered ashes and soot about. The mayor was reassuring, and on the morning of May 8, his confidence seemed justified in the dawn of a brilliant sunny day which dispelled clouds, smoke and ashes like some golden broom sweeping the sky clean. The citizens sighed with relief to see the sun. Normalcy had returned, and they went about their business in the normal way. Suddenly there were two explosions, which literally rocked the island. One whole side of Mount Pelée burst apart in a gigantic convulsion. Less than a minute later, St. Pierre was buried under an avalanche of fire and lava. Twenty-eight thousand people were dead. The incredible news was flashed to every corner of the civilized world: the city of St. Pierre exists no more.

Pompeii of the New World

No longer Paris, but Pompeii, St. Pierre will give you an eerie feeling as you explore its ruins, its broken statues toppled from the villa gardens, its boulevards vanishing beneath a tangle of tropical growth. Some new houses have risen from the ashes of the old; some streets have grown back, like pale ghosts rising from the grave. But St. Pierre has never recovered and probably never will. For a graphic documentation of the disaster, visit the *Dr. Frank Perret Musée Volcanologique*. It's open from 9:30 to 12 and from 2 to 5 daily, except Tuesday when, like all the museums in France, it shuts down. Pictures of the ruined city and relics dug from the debris complete the story of St. Pierre, indelibly fixed in the mind as a nightmare passage from the Book of Revelation.

Less spectacular, less overpowering both scenically and philosophically, but certainly gayer is the excursion south of Fort-de-France to Le Diamant and the *Rocher du Diamant*, known to the English as HMS Diamond Rock. This rock, off the southern coast, was actually commissioned as a sloop of war in the British Navy. A British garrison of 120 manned it in 1800, and held it for 18 months in the face of the most devastating bombardment by French coastal artillery. HMS Diamond Rock seemed to be as impregnable as it was unsinkable. The French thought up a Gallic ruse, a 19th-century version of the Trojan horse. Aware of a certain British weakness, they sent rum-laden galleys drifting against the Rocher du Diamant. When the ships broke up on the shore, the floating rum barrels were eagerly collected by the thirsty men of HMS Diamond Rock, who promptly rolled them "aboard ship". History does not record how many Englishmen were sober when the French finally took over Diamond Rock a short time later. France had won another skirmish in the long struggle for Martinique. And the W.C.T.U. and *Santé Sobriété* had a sufficiently horrendous example of the effects of demon rum to supply them with propaganda forever more.

Mementoes of Josephine de Beauharnais make Les Trois Ilets a must for any tourist who is interested in history. The ruins of her childhood home, the church in which she was christened in 1765 and where her mother is buried, and the little Beauharnais Museum all combine to make this picturesque corner of Martinique as touching as Malmaison. You can visit it all while your ship is tied up in Fort-de-France, then echo the sentiment of Napoleon: "I hold Martinique dear for more reasons than one."

THE BRITISH WINDWARDS

Sleeping Beauties of the Antilles

With the exception of Martinique, all the Windward Islands are British-owned, but a strong French flavor persists as it does in Canada and other places which were Anglo-Gallic battlegrounds. Some of these islands changed hands as many as 15 times; hence the persistence of French habits, French place names, and creole patois. Northernmost of the British Windwards is Dominica, not to be confused with the late Generalissimo Trujillo's "republic". Place the accent on the penultimate syllable in the best British manner, and you have Do-mi-*nee*-ca, after which there can be no confusion with anything Spanish. About equidistant between Guadeloupe and Martinique, Dominica is the northernmost of the British Windwards. Extending south from Martinique are St. Lucia, St. Vincent, the scattered diamond dust of The Grenadines, and Grenada. Georgetown, capital of this southernmost island, is also the colonial capital for the entire group.

493

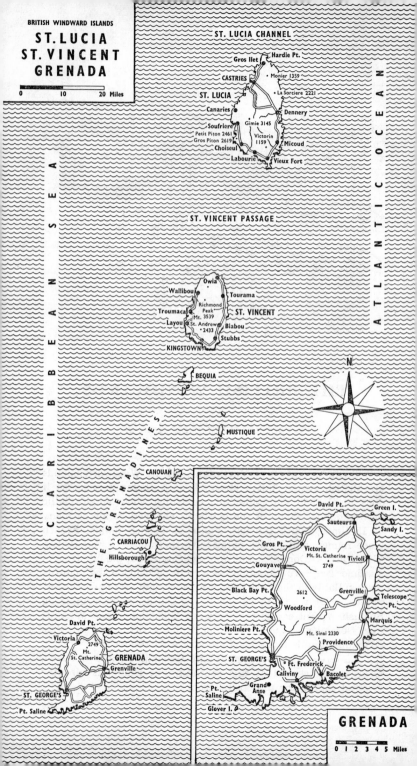

BRITISH WINDWARD ISLANDS
ST. LUCIA
ST. VINCENT
GRENADA

0   10   20 Miles

ST. LUCIA CHANNEL

Gros Ilet   Hardie Pt.

CASTRIES
· Monier 1359
ST. LUCIA   · La Sorciere 2221

Canaries   Dennery

Soufriere   Gimie 3145
Petit Piton 2461   Victorin
Gros Piton 2619   1159   Micoud
Choiseul
Labourie   Vieux Fort

ATLANTIC OCEAN

ST. VINCENT PASSAGE

CARIBBEAN SEA

Owia
Wallibou   Tourama
Richmond
Troumaca   Peak
Mt. 3539   ST. VINCENT
Layou   St. Andrew   Biabou
· 2433   Stubbs
KINGSTOWN

N

BEQUIA

MUSTIQUE

CANOUAN

THE GRENADINES

CARRIACOU
Hillsborough

David Pt.   Green I.
Sauteurs
Gros Pt.   Victoria   Sandy I.
Mt. St. Catherine   Tivioli
Gouyave   2749

David Pt.   Black Bay Pt.   2612   Grenville
Victoria   Woodford   Telescope
2749   Pt.
Mt.   Moliniere Pt.   Mt. Sinai 2330   Marquis
St. Catherine   GRENADA   Providence
Grenville   ST. GEORGE'S   · Ft. Frederick
ST. GEORGE'S   Caliviny   Bacolet
Pt. Saline   Pt.   Grand
Saline   Anse
Glover I.

GRENADA

0 1 2 3 4 5 Miles

These islands, all discovered by Columbus, have much in common. Their language is English; their government the West India Federation, their currency the W.I. dollar. They are laved by the same seas, cooled by the same trade winds. In addition, they are relatively "backward", which is to say undeveloped from the tourist point of view. These poor relatives of the Caribbean care less about modern "progress" than their Greater Antilles. They remain untouched by crash programs, casinos, cabarets, "unspoiled" by luxury resorts. The natives themselves are slower on the uptake, shyer and less aggressive than their brown brothers on the bigger islands. Barbadians, Jamaicans, Trinidadians, more self-possessed, now compatriots, look down their broad noses at these simple Small Islanders. "When dey gone wake up," one Bajan said patronizingly, "it gone be already de day aftah tomorrow. Mahn, dat gone be too late."

Meanwhile they seem content to drowse in their sunlit seas, and it is still the day before yesterday in the Windward Islands. Lack of progress has its compensations. If the level of tourist amenities is lower here than elsewhere, so are the prices. If the assets of progress are missing, so are the liabilities. If the plumbing is slow, so is the pace. The old-fashioned virtue of hospitality is much in evidence.

It is the Windward Islands that flash into the mind when one hears a phrase like Bradley Smith's "Escape to the West Indies." Collectively, they are among the loveliest in existence, "like green jewels embedded in a sea of stained glass". With all this in common, the Windwards offer enough differences to whet the appetite of the traveler with that variety which, even for the escapist, is the spice of tourism.

DOMINICA

Twenty-nine miles long by 16 broad, this island at the top of the British Windwards was discovered by Columbus on a Sunday morning in 1493, and named Dominica in honor of the Sabbath day. It is the most ruggedly beautiful island in the West Indies, a distinction that has been a drawback, for the rugged terrain, towering mountains and forests so thick that you can't see the trees, have made Dominica almost inaccessible. Morne Diablotin (4,747 feet) is the highest peak. The island is laced with rivers, fed by an annual rainfall of 300 inches in the interior, and these have a way of washing out roads and other man-made improvements. The dry season is from February to May. *Après ça le déluge.*

THE BRITISH WINDWARDS

There are 59,479 people on Dominica, cultivating bananas and the biggest, most beautiful limes you ever saw. Rose's Lime Juice is made here. Other crops are oranges, copra, cocoa and vanilla. Some of the plantations are cultivated by American, British and Canadian expatriates who wanted to "get away from it all". They came to the right place. Smuggling is rampant; there's more than a trickle of French perfume and liquor flowing in from Martinique without payment of duty.

Capital of Dominica is Roseau (population 14,000). The little port with the good harbor is Portsmouth (pop. 2,000). After decades of construction, punctuated by washouts, a road finally connects these two towns.

Though English is the official language, most of the people speak a French patois. The French hated to give the place up. After several exchanges, the island was officially given to the British in 1783. But the French tried to invade it in 1795, burnt Roseau in 1805, and finally had to be bribed to leave the island to the tune of 12,000 pounds sterling. It's the sort of place you get attached to.

Pure Carib Settlement

One of the few things the French and English had in common was enmity with the Caribs. On Dominica these Indians fought with such fury that in 1748 both the French and the British agreed to call the island no man's land and let the Caribs have it temporarily while they turned their attention elsewhere.

As a result of this neutralization policy, Dominica has the last settlement of pure Carib Indians in the Caribbean. You can visit their villages high in the hills above Prince Rupert Bay. There are about 100 pure-blooded "red" Caribs left on the reservation, but the offspring of mixed marriages are hard to distinguish. Carib skin is actually yellow, not red; the Caribs have wide, prominent cheekbones, black straight hair, small slanted eyes as shiny as black beads. They look like tropical Eskimos. They live in neat thatched huts just as they did before the white man came. They make dugout canoes, beautiful sleek craft, each one contrived from a single gommier tree. They also make handsome sturdy baskets. They have not exhibited cannibalistic tendencies since the 18th century so you can visit them without fear of being eaten. If they seem a little dour and silent when you enter their domain, produce a bottle of rum and there will be smiles all around. The money they make from their baskets is used to buy this

THE BRITISH WINDWARDS

fire water, which they dearly love. Add tobacco to an original gift of rum, and they'll start loading you with baskets. It was this sort of thing that led to the purchase of Manhattan Island for $24.

PRACTICAL INFORMATION FOR DOMINICA

HOW TO GET THERE. To vary the Cunard Line ad, getting to Dominica used to be half the trouble. Times have changed, however, and now Dominica boasts three flights a week by *Leeward Islands Air Transport* (Agents, B.W.I.A.) on Tuesdays, Wednesdays and Fridays from Antigua and Barbados. There are also Saturday LIAT flights to St. Lucia and Martinique. Planes land at Melville Hall Air Field and are met by an airline company bus for the thirty mile trip to Roseau. By sea, there are fortnightly visits headed north and south by the *Hermann Langreder*, a ship operated by the Federal Government Shipping Service. The *M.V. Moby Dick* comes to Dominica from Martinique usually on Mondays, and from Guadeloupe Fridays. Agents: P. Porry in Martinique, and M. Melon in Guadeloupe. In addition the *M.V. Ripon* operates between St. Kitts, Nevis, Antigua, Montserrat, Dominica and Barbados.

HOW TO GET ABOUT. Buses, taxis at fixed rates, U-Drive cars for rent.

HOTELS. Accommodations are improving with better transportation to and from the island.

Hotel rooms have recently doubled in Dominica but the total is still under 50. They are reasonably clean and comfortable and fairly expensive. The largest is the *Normandie*, 13 miles from Roseau, recently built, with 10 double rooms at $20 per day winter rate and $10 summer rate. Others are *Cherry Lodge* $7 per day single, twelve rooms. *Sutton* is $8 per person per day and *Rest Inn* $6 per person per day. For those who favor plantation life, there are accommodations for visitors in plantation houses by Archbold Plantations Ltd., Box 41, Roseau. Single per day is about $9, double $15 on the American Plan.

FOOD AND RESTAURANTS. There is plenty of the former, but you'll eat in your hotel or with friends. Local culinary specialties include "mountain chicken", which are succulent giant frog legs; stuffed land crab; local crayfish; fried titiri (a tiny local fish that may remind you of English whitebait), and heart of palm salad. The Dominican version of *callaloo*, a West Indian crab stew, is wonderful. So are the local citrus fruits and bananas.

SHOPPING. The grass rugs woven by native girls are famous beyond the shores of Dominica; they are very beautiful and very cheap. Carib baskets, some of them ingeniously waterproofed, are also celebrated; they come in many shapes and sizes up to suitcase proportions. Local shell work is also good. See and buy these items in Roseau at The *Convent Industrial School* (where the fibre rugs are made); the *Handicraft Shop* on Cork Street, and the Saturday morning *Native Market*, occasionally attended by Carib Indians. Best shop in Portsmouth for souvenirs and Carib handicrafts is *Jessie Garroway's*.

497

SPORTS AND OTHER ACTIVITIES. *Swimming* conditions are not ideal, especially around Roseau where rocky, pebbly conditions prevail. There are beautiful sandy beaches in the northern district, completely undeveloped. Good beaches on windward coast. There's also plenty of opportunity for fresh water swimming in the 30 or more rivers of Dominica.

Deep sea fishing is limited; *lake and river fishing* fine.

You can play *tennis* at the Dominica and Union Clubs in Roseau. The rugged terrain of Dominica appeals to *hikers*. Among the destinations are the Carib Reservation, Boiling Lake, Fresh Water Lake and Boeri Lake.

Mountain climbing enthusiasts will find the four-hour ascent of Mount Diablotin a sufficient challenge; others stay away.

There's some rather specialized *hunting* for crayfish in the rivers and for the giant frogs known locally as mountain chicken. There is also pigeon, dove and partridge shooting.

The *Aquatic Club* in Roseau is open to tourists. Motor launches can be rented. If you want to sail in a Carib dugout canoe, inquire at Portsmouth or at the Dominica Tourist Association in Roseau.

EXPLORING DOMINICA

This can be a delight for the adventurous, for this rugged, forest-clad rock is still not completely explored. You've never seen such a tangle of bamboo, mahogany, cedar, mango and palm in your life. The road from Roseau to Portsmouth, finished after years of struggle to dominate an almost vertical landscape, provides some of the most staggering, not to say vertiginous, scenery in the West Indies. If heights, curves and potholes give you the whim whams, you can take this same trip by government launch. The government highway cuts across the northern end of the island to Petit Marigot on the northeast coast. Any exploring you want to do on the eastern shore or in the interior, must be done on horseback or on foot. Scott's Head and Soufriere Bay on the southern tip of the island can be approached only by sea.

The Carib Indian Reservation is reached from Portsmouth. It's an all day excursion involving a two hour climb by shank's mare or the four-legged kind. If you aren't a good horseman, better trust to your own feet; the going is rough and often slippery. You really should have a guide for this interesting trip. Make arrangements through the Dominica Tourist Association in Roseau, Mrs. J. Osborne, Secretary, and don't forget to bring gifts to the Caribs. Otherwise this vanishing race will vanish even faster right before your eyes.

This is the most rewarding expedition which Dominica offers. Less ambitious and strenuous are trips in the vicinity of Roseau. The Botanical Garden just outside the town should on no account be missed; it is one of the most beautiful in the West Indies. The twin waterfalls of Layou and Pagoua in

Roseau Valley (about four miles from town) provide an ideal picnic spot in a wild romantic setting. Rose's Lime Juice Company welcomes visitors to its lime plantation in Morne Valley, just a few miles from the capital. From the company's hilltop headquarters, the view of valley and mist-shrouded mountains will confirm the impression that Dominica is the most ruggedly beautiful of West Indian islands.

SAINT LUCIA

Second largest of the British Windwards (after Dominica), Saint Lucia (the English pronounce it Loó-sha) is 25 miles south of Martinique, 20 north of Saint Vincent. It is 27 miles long, 14 wide, and its 233 square miles are distributed over a mountainous landscape cut with deep valleys full of hibiscus, oleander, bougainvillaea, flamboyant trees, orchids, roses, lilies and other exotic blooms. There are 95,000 Saint Looshans, of which 25,000 live in the Capital, Castries, a picturesque town with beautiful, land-locked harbor. Twice destroyed by fire within a single generation, Castries does not have the late Georgian or Victorian-Colonial look that is the hallmark of so many British West Indies towns, though you'll find plenty of Victorian bric-a-brac stuck onto the modern façades.

Columbus discovered the island on St. Lucia's day, June 15, 1502 during the course of his fourth voyage; however, some say the first visitors were unknown Spaniards later in 1605. The Caribs held the island until the middle of the 17th century. When the English established a colony in 1639, the Caribs murdered every one of them. The French, who claimed Saint Lucia in 1642, also had a hard time with the original owners, and were finally compelled to make a treaty of peace with them in 1660. From that time and for nearly a century and a half, the English and the French battled over the island, which changed hands no less than 14 times. This accounts for its split Anglo-Gallic personality today. Although the British have been in the cat bird seat officially since the Treaty of Amiens in 1802, the Saint Lucians are jealously attached to their French heritage. They are constantly referring to their "French ancestry", and they are most condescending to their neighbors of Saint Vincent, accusing them of a puritanical lack of *joie de vivre,* and regarding them as heretics, since they are mostly Anglican, not good French Catholics.

Aside from its beautiful scenery, Saint Lucia has a number of unique features. Vigie Airport, just outside Castries, is the only one in the Caribbean, and possibly in the world, with its own private beach. You can actually swim while waiting to meet a plane! Sulphurous Mount Soufriere is the only active "drive in" volcano in the world; you can drive to the lip of its smouldering crater. Nearby are sulphur springs and baths, established for soldiers of Louis XVI and still offering their therapeutic waters to sufferers from arthritis, rheumatism, or just plain tourist fatigue. Most famous landmark of all and the most photographed mountains in the whole Caribbean are the Pitons, twin conical peaks, half a mile high, rising in majesty from the sea at the west coast town of Soufriere. Petit Piton is 2,461 feet high; Gros Piton, 2,619. These photogenic volcanic plugs are a continuing challenge to climbers. They are said to be a favorite haunt of the deadly fer-de-lance snake which exists only on this island and on Martinique. A whole party of British seamen are said to have been killed by these poisonous serpents while attempting the ascent. But that was in the P.M. days, Pre-Mongoose. No snakes have been encountered here in recent years. If you should see one, run, do not walk to the nearest exit.

PRACTICAL INFORMATION FOR SAINT LUCIA

 HOW TO GET THERE. British West Indian Airways flies in twice daily from Trinidad, and makes connections with the major Caribbean islands. Steamship Lines calling at St. Lucia are the Booth American Line, the French Line, the Royal Netherlands Steamship Co., and Saguenay Shipping Ltd. The Federal Government Shipping Service has two ships based in Trinidad which link all the islands as far north as Jamaica twice a month (the first-class, one-way fare from Jamaica is $112; cabin class, $82). There are also schooners and small motor vessels connecting Saint Lucia with nearby islands. As a haven for yachts St. Lucia stands second only to English Harbour, Antigua, in the Caribbean. Hundreds of yachts come to Castries annually where safe anchorage and fresh supplies are easily available.

 HOW TO GET ABOUT. Island buses are colorful, cheap, open and hard of seat. A sign exhorts passengers to kindly ride inside the bus! There is adequate taxi service with fixed rates for certain established excursions. You can hire cars with or without driver from *Bridge Street Garage, The St. Lucia Motor Garage, Cresta Garage, Roxy, Freddy's Garage* and *Self-Help Garage,* all in Castries. There are regularly-scheduled round-the-island services by launch, and you can hire a motor launch for your private use if you want to.

 HOTELS. Pending a new hotel development at the former U.S. Naval Base at Gros Ilet, the construction of a new luxury hotel at Reduit Beach (opening before 1963) under ownership of the Hon. A. E. Issa, and the new *Marigot Bay Yacht Haven,* Saint Lucia's hotel offerings are limited to about nine hostelries. They are generally clean and simple. Their cuisine, expect for broiled lobsters and seafood, is uninspired. Local meat isn't very good, and there's a dearth of fresh vegetables, a result of soil erosion and native disinclination to tend gardens.

BLUE WATERS. Bills itself with some inaccuracy as the only Beach Hotel in Saint Lucia. It is situated on Vigie Beach just outside of Castries and has 12 reasonably comfortable rooms. The hotel is adding 7 luxury cabanas on the beach and a new 10-bedroom wing. Mrs. I. Ford is the manager, and her hospitality is proverbial in Saint Lucia. Her rates are $15 and up single per day; $28 and up double, about the most expensive in the island.

CLOUD'S NEST. In the village of Vieux Fort near the southern tip of the island. There are 11 rooms in a wooden building with partitions doing duty as walls. Perfectly okay for one night, not for a prolonged stay. The view is lovely. Miss Williams is the manager. Her rates are $12 and $13 a day single, $17 to $20 double.

MARIGOT BAY YACHT HAVEN. Recently opened, yacht marina, restaurant, and six luxury cabanas 8 miles from Castries. In a deep and almost land-locked inner harbor, it is a favorite spot for yachtsmen. Plans to increase living accommodations. Rates up to $25 a day. Capt. Boudreau is the manager.

MISS EUDOXIE'S BOARDING HOUSE. Behind the town of Castries in a site that was not designed to capture island charm, but when you hear Miss Mabel Eudoxie's rates, you won't carp: $6 single, $12 double for room and all meals. There are only four rooms, so reserve in advance if you're planning to retire on $100 a month.

MISS JAMES' GUEST HOUSE. Also in Castries, has eleven rooms. Her rates are $6 to $8 single, $12 to $13 double, and quite a bargain.

ST. ANN'S GUEST HOUSE. Faces the main square of Castries, has a commercial clientele, but tourists find it comfortable enough. Mrs. E. F. Auguste manages. Her rates are $8 per day single, $16 double. There are six rooms.

ST. ANTOINE. Fifteen rooms on Morne Fortuné overlooking Castries and the Caribbean. View from the terrace is superb. Mrs. S. H. Friend is the manager, and the name is most appropriate for this helpful hostess. Her kitchen rates an honorable mention. Rates are $17 and up single. $34 and up double.

VILLA HOTEL. With its new modern wing and bar, now has 26 rooms, biggest hotel in Saint Lucia. It's in Castries on the slopes of Morne Fortuné with splendid Caribbean view. Miss Salmon is the manager. Food has the reputation of being the best hereabouts. Rates are $9 to $15 per day single; $20 to $30 double. This is the only hotel with private bath for each room and available air conditioning.

VILLA HOTEL BEACH CLUB. On Palm Beach, 4 miles from Castries, 3 from Vigie Airport. Wonderful location but only 4 rooms so far. Rates are $25 single, $34 double.

In addition to these hotels there are two small ones on the island, *Allain's Guest House* at Soufrière where a single can be had for $8 and a double room for $14, and the Pigeon Island enterprise of Mrs. Josette Legh Snowball, an absolutely unique place described below under Exploring St. Lucia.

FOOD AND RESTAURANTS. St. Lucia's lobsters are so famous that planes are always dropping by just to pick up shipments. The predominantly Creole cuisine has just enough French finesse to give it a certain quality. Barbados rum is the local drink. Few gastronomic experiences can beat the beach picnics of St. Lucia with daiquiris or gin and coconut water preceding grilled lobster that you've progged yourself.

THE BRITISH WINDWARDS

The Blue Danube is Castries' gayest and most modern restaurant, open from 9 in the morning till the last person leaves. Good place for lunch, tea, dinner or just drinks and snacks. There's a dance floor with radio, occasionally orchestra, supplying the music for dinner dancing.

The *Gaiety Club,* just opened, and *Billy's* provide more of the same. *The Havana Club,* "owned and managed by a seaman for the comfort and enjoyment of seamen", offers food, drink, dancing and hostesses long after the rest of Castries has pulled in the sidewalks and gone to bed.

NIGHT LIFE. See above. Also try the *Star Club* if you want to watch uninhibited Saint Lucians dancing to juke box.

 SHOPPING. Best local buys are imported British woolens, doeskins and linens. The last, in 27 inch width, are less than $2 a yard. Doeskin, 57 inches wide, is about $7 a yard; woolens start at $8.40. Native straw work is excellent. Scotch, gin and Barbados rum are the leading liquor bargains. Most Castries stores are on Bridge or Jeremy Street. They are open from 8:30 to 12:30 and 1:30 to 4. Closed on Wednesday afternoons and Sundays.

For English imports, including fabrics by the yard, you'll find the best selection at *Clinton Evans* and *Minivielle & Chastanet Ltd.* on Bridge Street. See also these three shops on Jeremy Street: *George G. Cox Company, J. Q. Charles Ltd., Balboa Edwards & Company.* Clinton Evans, incidentally, makes a specialty of English shoes; they have a good selection at prices far below those in the U.S. or in England.

All of these stores carry local handicrafts as well. But in this department, you'll want to look over the crop at *The Home Industries* on Bridge Street; they have straw hats, bags, sandals, place mats, everything at low prices.

Minivielle & Chastanet's ultra-modern operation includes a first rate liquor department. Other leading wine and spirit merchants are *Peter & Company Ltd.,* and the *Lafayette Fruit and Produce Company.*

Books? Stationery? *The Voice Publishing Company,* who get out the local daily paper, can supply most of your needs, and exhibit an admirable tendency to increase the number of British and American titles in their book collection.

 SPORTS AND OTHER ACTIVITIES. The *swimming* is excellent. Vigie Beach just outside Castries is popular. Reduit Beach, facing Pigeon Island, is about the best in St. Lucia. You can also swim at Pigeon Island (accessible by rowboat or launch) and at Rat Island (ditto). Choc Beach, just north of Vigie, is another good one.

The *fishing* is reputed to be great, but we had only 5 bites in two hours of trying about two miles off the coast. Dolphin, mackerel, tarpon, kingfish, tuna and marlin are the babies you'll be after. Boats and some equipment may be rented, but you'll want your own tackle if you're a serious fisherman. Canoes, motorboats, rowboats, even whalers are for hire for the *boating* set.

Yachting facilities are good in Castries Harbor, and there are good anchorages along the coast. The New Marigot Bay Yacht Haven has excellent yachting facilities. They have two yachts for charter, the 110-foot luxury yacht, *Le Voyageur,* and the *Lady Phyllis.* Information and details from Captain G. W. Boudrau, P.O. Box 260, Castries, St. Lucia.

You can play *tennis* on the public courts of Castries in George V Park or at the Palm Beach Aquatic Club. There are good mounts for hire and excellent trails for both *horseback riding* and *hiking*.

EXPLORING SAINT LUCIA

Visitors arriving by cruise ship in Castries come directly into the harbor, thanks to the docks that have been built out into the deep blue water. A steelband greets you from the wharf, and the Tourist Bureau offers you your choice of three island specialties: rum punch, lime juice or coconut water. There are more than 200 cars available for sightseeing in addition to the gay buses that link the towns of this gay island.

Castries itself has the look of a modern suburb, having been largely rebuilt after a disastrous fire in 1948. The modern garden villa look with wide spaces between the houses results in part from rebuilding along the sides of ruined structures instead of on top of them. Two hills rise behind the town and its blue protected harbor, La Morne Fortuné and La Vigie. Drive to the top of the former to see Fort Charlotte, a well-preserved example of the 18th-century fortifications which figured in the 150-year tug of war between France and England for this pretty prize. It was Queen Victoria's father, the Duke of Kent, who captured it for the British in 1794 for keeps. The view of the harbor from here is one of the thrills of the island, especially in that brief tropical sunset that turns the deep blue harbor wine dark.

Despite its recent renascence from the ashes, Castries is not lacking in local color. There are still enough old French stone houses, old English ones of brick, to lend the place an old-world Anglo-Gallic flavor. Save some color film for the native women. Many of them wear the madras and foulard of their cousins on French Martinique and Guadeloupe. Notice the banana fibre rings, or *colta,* which they wear on their heads. They are used to balance baskets and will help explain the prodigious grace and ease with which these women carry such huge burdens with such a wonderful air of jaunty carelessness. You'll notice that the local girls are great smokers too; a pipe seems to be as indispensable as the colta.

There are two classic excursions, one minor and one major which you should try to take to appreciate what Saint Lucia has to offer. The minor attraction is Pigeon Island, the major, one of the highlights of the Caribbean, is the active volcano of Soufriere.

Getting to Pigeon Island is a simple matter. You drive north out of Castries just ten miles to the sleepy little fishing village of Gros Ilet near the northern end of St. Lucia. About a mile off shore you will see Pigeon Island, so called because the famous British Admiral Rodney once kept pigeons here. There is usually a rowboat or launch ready to take you to the island. If none is in sight, blow the horn of your car and wave until someone takes off from the Pigeon Island pier to get you in a rowboat or dugout canoe. In a very short time you will land at that small and rugged pier before an open tropical pavilion with a steeply pitched thatch roof into which two big shuttered dormer windows have been cut. Right on a pretty white sand beach, this is the domain of one of the most colorful characters of the Caribbean, the owner of Pigeon Island. She is an Englishwoman, Mrs. Josette Legh Snowball, and she's just as much of an odd ball as her name suggests. Once a member of the chorus in the famed Doyly Carte Gilbert and Sullivan troupe, she gave up singing years ago to become a sort of female Robinson Crusoe in this beachcomber's paradise. She and her mother built the hut, replete with staircase from attic to ground floor to enable them to make a grand entrance before their guests. The aura of the theatre clings to Mrs. Snowball and to her beach restaurant, an internationally known rendezvous for yachtsmen.

Josette's mother, who died not long ago, once distinguished herself by swimming safely home at the age of 80 after her canoe capsized half a mile from shore.

Mrs. Snowball now carries on alone. She announces the serving of lunch or dinner by blowing on a conch shell, as stirring as all the trumpets of Iolanthe. She usually wades out to assist at your landing, and she has not one, but several, Men Fridays about, who capture lobsters and other marine delicacies with which Mrs. Snowball supplies her larder. The atmosphere on Pigeon Island couldn't be more informal. You can rent rooms or a Crusoe cottage. You drink and dine in the main lodge. The food isn't cordon bleu, but the drinks are first rate, and so is the entertainment provided by your hostess. The only thing that flows more easily than the whisky and rum punch is the stream of reminiscences. There's nothing to do on the island but swim, sunbathe and stroll around, far from the smell of carbon monoxide and the jangle of 20th-century noise. A more relaxed and relaxing place we've never seen. If you're coming for lunch or plan to stay overnight, try to give advance notice so that Men Friday can catch a few more fish, puff up the pillow on the bed, and—maybe—give the place

Fishing villages on the coast of Martinique captivated Paul Gauguin before he ever saw Tahiti, and so did the merchandise and merchants of native markets like this one at Pointe-à-Pitre on Guadeloupe.

Typical of government attempts to improve West Indian crops is this careful checking of pods on a cocoa tree by an expert from an agricultural experiment station on the "Spice Island" of Grenada.

a good cleaning. Address Mrs. Snowball at the Pigeon Island Club, St. Lucia, BW. Although the island is her property, she's perfectly relaxed about letting people bathe and picnic.

To The Volcano

There are three ways of reaching the major attraction of Saint Lucia, the volcano of Soufriere. Two are by land, the other by sea. Soufriere is only about 12 miles south of Castries. There is a direct road passing through the valleys of Cul-de-Sac and Rosseau, through the villages of Anse-la-Raye and Canaries and then on to Soufriere. It is an extremely fascinating and scenic road and the drive by car takes one and one-half hours.

Because of the rugged topography, Soufrière can only be reached on the other road by a 60 mile drive clear across the island, south along the east coast, then looping northward to your destination. Scenically, it's all magnificent. But don't count on doing it in less than six hours. Frankly, it's a horrendous road, steep, narrow, full of dizzying curves: a kind of mountain roller coaster.

Going by sea is shorter and easier on the nerves. The daily government mail launch takes passengers from Castries and deposits them after a pleasant scenic voyage of two hours at the beautiful little town of Soufriere right at the base of those two celebrated Pitons. The town itself is a picture post card of pastel houses, golden beach, limpid water, fishermen going out in native dugout canoes, children basking in the sun and plunging into the sea. You can't walk more than a few steps in its streets without bumping into a guide whose business and pleasure it is to escort you to the volcano. There are plenty of cars for rent, and the ascent, like Vergil's descent into hell, is easy. The experience, as you walk from the parked car, over the lip and down into the crater of Soufriere, *is* like some descent into a classic version of the nether regions. You are actually inside the volcano, surrounded by jets of sulphurous steam, seemingly as isolated as Brunhilde behind her curtain of magic fire. There's no need to be anxious. Volcanologists keep a sharp eye on La Soufriere, and it is precisely these jets of steam that keep her from building up the uncontainable pressure that would cause her to blow her top.

After you have explored this boiling cauldron to your heart's content, ask the guide to show you the nearby sulphur baths. They have been in use since 1785 when Louis XVI had the water channeled for the benefit of his colonial troops. The hot baths have been compared with those of Aix-les-Bains for their healing powers. Whether you suffer from rheumatism, arthritis or not, here is your chance to have a private bath in the same tubs that once comforted the weary limbs of French soldiers. It's a restorative experience, productive of pure euphoria. The hot baths are really invigorating. Nature has thought of everything on Saint Lucia.

ST. VINCENT

This delightful volcanic island lies just 21 miles south of St. Lucia and about 95 due west of Barbados. South of St. Vincent are the Grenadine Islands, sparkling in the sea like a string of precious stones. Their names sound like exotic jewels: Bequia, Mustique, Mayreau, Canouan, Union Island, Carriacou. St. Vincent is 18 miles long, 11 wide, and has a population of 80,000. The people are an interesting mixture of various elements, reflecting a history that is unusual, even for a West Indian island.

Discovered by Columbus on St. Vincent's Day in 1498, the island remained under the undisputed control of the Carib Indians until 1627. The fierce, war-loving Caribs had been here for several generations before Columbus, having arrived from the South American mainland and exterminated the gentle, indigenous Arawaks. The Caribs fought off all would-be colonists with such fury that St. Vincent was declared a neutral island by French and British agreement in 1748. Ceded to the British in 1763, it was captured by the French in 1779, restored to the British by the Treaty of Versailles in 1783. A century earlier a cargo of negro slaves had been shipwrecked on the coast of St. Vincent, and the Caribs, however inhospitable they may have been to white callers, received these dark visitors without reservation. In fact the welcome was so cordial and cosy that a new race sprang up, the Black Caribs. The Black Caribs soon outnumbered and dominated the original Red Caribs, and in 1795 they made common cause with the French against the English colonists, slaughtering them right and left, burning their cane fields and pillaging their houses.

The English, however, turned out to be tougher and more obstinate than Black Caribs and French combined. With the arrival of reinforcements in June 1796, they defeated the black and white coalition and shipped 5,080 of the Black Caribs to Honduras. A number of them hid out in the hills to avoid deportation; however, you'll see plenty of Black Caribs on St. Vincent today.

The Negro slaves were emancipated on St. Vincent as early as 1838. Eight years later, more than 2,000 Portuguese immigrants had come in to work on the plantations. East Indians arrived as coolie laborers in 1861. Most of these eventually returned to India, but enough remained to leave its mark on the fascinating polyglot population which inhabits St. Vincent today.

Sometimes called the "Breadfruit Isle" because Captain Bligh first introduced the tree here from Tahiti, St. Vincent produces this plus sugar, coconuts and bananas. But something has been added: arrowroot, that highly nutritive and digestible starch that is the basis for half the food consumed by American infants. St. Vincent's volcanic soil is admirably suited to the production of this valuable food. The island has what amounts almost to a world monopoly, and exports millions of tons of arrowroot annually, mostly to the U.S.A. This crop, plus St. Vincent's superior grade of sea-island cotton, has helped to raise the island's economy several notches above that of its neighbors. One result is an impression of greater optimism and bounce among the people than is registered in many of the West Indian Islands. The Saint Vincentians seem gayer and more energetic than many of their Caribbean cousins.

Best place to savor this gaiety and energy is at the Saturday morning native market in Kingstown, St. Vincent's miniature (pop. about 15,000) capital. Small boats, loaded to the gunwhales with all the fruits and spices of the tropics, are moored at the quayside. Other produce is brought in from the country by bus. The rich color of both merchants and merchandise would be hard to match anywhere. It has its aural equivalent in the cadences of island speech, the thick-tongued French patois which they themselves would call "cweole".

The French influence persists, even though St. Vincent is the most English of the Windward Isles. You need only glance at your map: Chateaubelair, Grand Bonhomme, Petit Bonhomme, to see that the island has the usual dual personality. Of course there is Mt. Soufrière. So many volcanic mountains in the West Indies have this name that some travelers have been misled into believing that this is the French word for Volcano. (Actually, it means sulphur mine.) St. Vincent's Soufrière has been a bad actor. On May 6, 1902, she put the island on the map by killing 2,000 of its inhabitants in a major eruption. It was world news, but only for two days. On May

8, Martinique's Mt. Pelée blew *her* top, wiping out the whole town of St. Pierre and its 28,000 people, relegating St. Vincent's tragedy to the inside pages. Soufrière, now officially classified as "semi-dormant", hasn't been heard from since. You can walk all over her. It's one of the favorite tourist pastimes on St. Vincent and as safe as a stroll in a park, despite its former bad manners.

PRACTICAL INFORMATION FOR ST. VINCENT

HOW TO GET THERE. St. Vincent now has a new 4,800 foot airstrip which can handle planes of the DC 3 type. That has made possible services by BWIA and Leeward Islands Air Lines with flights which connect with service to other major Caribbean islands. A new low fare from Trinidad to St. Vincent via the Leewards costs $24 one way or $43 round-trip. Charter service with Piper Apache four-seaters and 6 seater Beachcraft based on St. Vincent is available for local flights to neighboring islands.

By sea, St. Vincent can be reached from Canada by ships of the Canadian National Steamship Company and Alcoa Steamship Company. There are weekly auxiliary sailing ships (sail plus motor) linking St. Vincent with Trinidad, Grenada, St. Lucia, Aruba and Barbados. In addition, there are weekly connections by auxiliary schooner between Trinidad, Barbados and St. Vincent, and scheduled voyages by Motor Vessel between St. Vincent and Aruba, Trinidad, Grenada, St. Lucia and Barbados.

HOW TO GET ABOUT. Public buses run from Kingstown along the coastal roads, providing bargain transportation. Cars, with or without chauffeur, are also available at bargain prices (under $5 a day). You can hire them at any of the following garages in Kingstown: Colony, Choice, De Luxe, Empire, Olive's, Star. There is also a motor launch service between Kingstown and Chateaubelair on the western coast. The St. Vincent Tourist Board in Kingstown is most helpful about suggesting and arranging sightseeing tours of the island.

HOTELS. There are 12 hostelries on the "Breadfruit Isle", providing less than 100 rooms among them. Aside from the *Sugar Mill Inn*, *Blue Lagoon Guest House*, *Heron Hotel* and the *Blue Caribbean*, these have no pretensions whatsoever to being luxury vacation resorts. Their accommodations are adequate, however, and their prices so low as to make St. Vincent one of the bargain places for the budgetminded traveler. Our list is alphabetical. All rates quoted are for American Plan accommodations.

BLUE CARIBBEAN. In Kingstown right on the bay, this is the largest of St. Vincent's hotels. Its clientele is chiefly commercial. There are 20 rooms, 11 with bath. Mrs. Layne is the manager. Very good French-Creole cooking. The rates are $13 to $17 a day per person.

BLUE LAGOON GUEST HOUSE. About 5 miles out of Kingstown, on beach next to golf course, this is an attractive 10-room guest house has private baths and other amenities above the average St. Vincent level. Prices are higher too: Winter rates are $17 to $25 per day; summer are $12 to $18. The manager is Mr. Errol Rooks.

HADDON HOTEL. Near Kingstown, this is a cozy 12-room hotel managed by Mrs. Sylvia DaSilva. Rates range from $8 to $14 per day.

HERON HOTEL. Just across the street from the Blue Caribbean, this is a 11-room establishment managed by friendly Mrs. D. Mc Kenzie. Room and board comes to a modest $12 per day.

KINGSTOWN PARK GUEST HOUSE. Ten clean rooms at dirt cheap rates: $8 per person per day. Miss Paynter is the manager.

OLIVE'S HOTEL. Also in Kingstown, provides 8 rooms at low rates: $8 to $10 single. S. Ballantyne is the manager.

SEA VIEW. Prices at this 10-room inn at Edinboro soar to $8 and $12 per person per day. A bargain.

SOUTH BRIDGE. This is a guest house with 6 rooms, small and neat, managed by Miss Agnes Grant. Another Kingstown bargain with rates at $8 to $10 a day per person.

SUGAR MILL INN. Managed by Mrs. Palmer, an excellent hostess, this is the nicest place on the island. Four miles from Kingstown, it's on a cliff overlooking the Grenadines, one of the loveliest of all Caribbean views. Excellent swimming and snorkeling at Aquatic Club below the hotel, also in hotel pool. This is St. Vincent's nearest approach to a luxury beach resort, a most attractive and restful place for a holiday. Rates are from $20 to $25 a day per person less 20% after April.

NEW HAVEN HOTEL. This eight room hostelry has the advantage of being only 10 minutes drive from the airport, opposite the pier and overlooking the sea. Proprietor is Mr. J. Baynes. Rates are $12 per day per person.

VILLA LODGE HOTEL. A charming 6-room villa overlooking the beach. Manager is Mrs. Rosie Brisbane. Winter rates are $16 per day; summer are $12 per day.

WINDEMERE GUEST HOUSE. Another small hotel in Kingstown with that astonishingly low rate which seems to be the popular prix fixe of St. Vincent: $8 per person per day. Miss Paynter, who also runs the Kingstown Park Guest House, is the manager here.

FOOD AND RESTAURANTS. The former is plentiful, the latter not so save for a neat little cafe called the *Beachcomber* in the center of town where everyone meets for snacks and tea. The St. Vincent cuisine is creole cum seafood. The tropical fruits are wonderful: mangoes, bananas, cassavas, avocadoes. The local rum is fine. The local drink specialty is a rum punch made with a *gru gru swizzle stick*, a favorite island drink. We found it less inviting than the natives apparently do.

NIGHT LIFE. Saturday night dancing at the Sugar Mill Inn and Seaview's Idle Hour. At least on one other night there is dancing on the terrace of the Blue Lagoon. Otherwise you can hear a breadfruit drop anywhere in the island after 9 p.m.

SHOPPING. Native handicrafts and imported English woolens and other fabrics are for sale in Kingstown. Most shops are on or near Halifax Street. You can browse through the lot of them in an hour. Best place for local straw and shell work is the *Education Department Shop*, which encourages native craftsmen. *J. E. Trotman's* and *Mrs. Abbott's* shops also have a good selection of island handicrafts. There are three photo supply shops, locally known as Photo Studios. They are *Charles'*, *Alleyne's*, and *Miss Paynter's Studio*; they have the raw materials and can develop the finished product.

THE BRITISH WINDWARDS

SPORTS AND OTHER ACTIVITIES. The *swimming* is especially good at Tyrell Bay (where Aquatic Club and Sugar Mill Inn are.) and also at the Coronation Club at Indian Bay. Crystal clear water also good for snorkeling, skin diving and other subaqueous exercise.

Sailing and boating conditions are perfect; you're just an hour or two away from the lovely Grenadine Islands (see below: The Grenadines).

Fishing is generally good; the unique St. Vincent thrill is going out with the natives to catch blackfish, a kind of whale. It's very exiting, the nearest thing to chasing Moby Dick. Arrangements for doing this can be made at the Aquatic Club or through the St. Vincent Tourist Board in Kingstown.

Tennis is played on the excellent turf courts of the Kingstown Lawn Tennis Club and Kingstown Youth Club.

There's a 9-hole *golf* course at Ratho Mill. Mount Soufriere is the magnet for *mountain climbers*.

Victoria Park for those who want to watch or play *cricket*.

The Aquatic Club and the Coronation Club are social centers, gay, friendly, informal, hospitable. They often have dances and other social programs to which visitors are welcome.

EXPLORING ST. VINCENT

Aside from the vivid and vibrant Saturday native market, Kingstown's foremost sight is its Botanical Garden, the oldest in the West Indies. Its chief ornament is a breadfruit tree grown from the original seed brought here from Tahiti by Captain Bligh of the mutinous *Bounty*. The town of Kingstown itself is as English in character and spirit as its name. Some of the 19th-century houses will remind you of places you've seen in the quiet streets of Mayfair or Chelsea. St. George's Cathedral, St. Mary's and the Methodist Church are symbols of Anglican and dissenting England, transported bell, book and candle to the tropics. Don't miss the view from Fort Charlotte, 600 feet above the capital: wonderful panorama over city, harbor, the Caribbean and the Grenadines.

Of St. Vincent's 400 miles of road, only about 80 are paved, and these stick to the edges of the island. A trip north of Kingstown up the leeward coast is notable for splendid scenery and lovely little fishing ports like Layou and Barrouallie. The latter is headquarters for local whaling. You can join one of these expeditions and give chase to the blackfish. It's usually a two day affair. When the fishing parties return, the whole village rejoices in a grand outburst of singing and dancing.

A drive through the Mesopotamia Valley takes you to the agricultural heart of this beautiful island: 28 miles of rural beauty. Equally interesting is the trip to Sandy Bay, 30 miles from Kingstown; here you will see the descendants of the Carib Indians.

There are three popular St. Vincent rendezvous for those who like to climb. Easiest is Dorsetshire Hill, about three miles from Kingstown, with a sweeping view of the capital and its harbor. Mount St. Andrew, on the outskirts of Kingstown, involves a pleasant climb on well-marked trail through a rain forest. Mount Soufriere is for the young in heart if not in body. Getting to the base is a project in itself. First you go to Chateaubelair by car or by launch. Then you must proceed by canoe or rowboat to the mouth of the Wallibou River. Here the trail begins winding up to the summit, more than 4,000 feet high. It takes about three hours to the mouth of the crater, swept by such stiff trade breezes that you have to lean into the wind to maintain your stance. The view, with all St. Vincent and the Caribbean at your feet, is worth the effort of the climb. The trip can be made by car along the Windward coast, crossing the famed *Rabacca Dry River* on the way and continuing up to the *Bamboos*. From there on, you have to hoof it, and its all uphill. It takes about two hours to reach the summit, some 4,800 feet up.

One of the delights of exploring St. Vincent is that so much of it can be done by coastal boat. That is the only way, for example, to see the beautiful 60-foot cascade, the Falls of Baleine, at the northern end of the island. There is daily service between Kingstown and Chateaubelair. A government auxiliary schooner leaves Kingstown three times a week for the island of Bequia and the Grenadines, and there are daily sailing ships that make the same run. One of the chief attractions of St. Vincent, especially for yachtsmen and off-beat island hoppers, is its proximity to the Grenadines; that lovely fleet of islands anchored in the Caribbean between St. Vincent and Grenada.

THE GRENADINES

There are at least a score of these islands, some of them no more than specks on the map. The chief ones, north to south, are Bequia, Mustique, Canouan, Mayreau, Union Island, and Carriacou. The first five are dependencies of St. Vincent. Carriacou is a dependency of Grenada, the southernmost of the British Windwards.

If you think the Windwards in general are off the beaten path and away from it all, you haven't seen the Grenadines. Many of them are uninhabited. There may even be some where a human footprint would be rarer than on Crusoe's island. Most of them remain uncorrupted by such products of the industrial revolution as electricity and the automobile. Movies and television? No. Radios? Yes, but they run on batteries.

All the Grenadines are famous for their beautiful beaches, crystal clear water, superlative sailing and fishing conditions. They are a favorite haunt of yachtsmen sailing south from Antigua. You don't have to be a millionaire to explore these islands, however, though you do need time to adapt your schedule to the mail boats and inter-island schooners that ply between Grenada and St. Vincent. You can go from Grenada to Carriacou for as little as $1.32. From St. Vincent to Bequia, the fare is less than half a dollar.

There's nothing to *do* on these islands, except bathe, fish, sail and read. That is their beauty for some, their horror for others.

There are accommodations, at prices which are as far removed from the high cost of living as the Grenadines are off the beaten track of tourism.

On Bequia, the *Sunny Caribee Hotel* has 9 rooms, one bath, your great grandfather's pitcher and basin, oil lamps, and good West Indian cooking. You have the whole beach and Caribbean at your doorstep and utter peace and quiet. The rate, including meals, is about $10 a day. Gladys and Tom Johnston are the managers and they help make it a haven of refuge from the age of anxiety.

On Union Island, you can stay at the 6-room *Adams Guest House.* Your host, Conrad Adams, supplies the basic necessities of life including three meals a day for $2.40. You could stay there as a permanent guest writing a book called, *How I Retired on $75 a Month!*

On Carriacou, largest of the Grenadines, lying just north of Grenada, has an 8-room hotel, just opened in 1959, by *Joe Daniel,* secretary of the Carriacou Tourist Committee. Deeply grateful to the American Navy for sending in supplies after everything on the island was flattened by Hurricane Janet in 1955, Joe Daniel now aims to make this beautiful phoenix known to tourists. It shouldn't take long. His hotel charges about $3.50 a day for room and board. He's getting out a travel folder. And there's a new sound in the island in addition to the rustling of trees and lapping of waves: the vibrant throbbing of Carriacou's first steel band.

At least one taxi is already available to take you sightseeing on this scenic island. Its 13 square miles are laced with roads built by the French so they could move their caissons about quickly to bombard English ships at sea. The English got back by murdering the French language. One of France's Grenadine bastions, *Quai Qui Gêne* is now officially known as Kick-Em-Jenny.

For further information on Carriacou, write to Joe Daniel, Carriacou, Grenada, BWI. For information about the rest of the idyllic Grenadines, communicate with the ever-helpful St. Vincent Tourist Board in Kingstown.

GRENADA

Most southerly island of the Windward Group, Grenada is 68 miles southwest of St. Vincent, about 90 north of Trinidad. Its 120 square miles of area encompass volcanic mountains, lush valleys, lovely beaches and every feature of an ideal tropical landscape. It is a leading contender for the honor of being the most beautiful of West Indian islands. Its capital, St. George's, wins hands down as the prettiest port in the Caribbean.

Columbus laid eyes but not hands on the island in 1498, naming it Concepcion, never dreaming that it would one day be owned by the English and mispronounced Gre-nay-da. The British first tried to colonize the island in 1609, but abandoned their efforts in the face of a most unsportsmanlike attitude on the part of the Carib Indians. The French tried a mercenary approach. In 1650, they bought the island for a handful of hatchets, knives, beads and two bottles of brandy. When the chief sobered up, he realized he had sold his birthright for a hangover. Hostilities began. Carib savagery was no match for the ferocity of the French, especially when they were defending an investment. Nor were Indian flint hatchets a match for more civilized weapons. The French pushed the Caribs north to Le Morne des Sauteurs (Jumpers' Bluff) where most of the Indians leapt off the cliff into the sea rather than be captured. Those who didn't probably wished they had. The French hacked them down, irrespective of sex or age. This was just the first of many blood baths. The French and the English fought over Grenada for a century. The British had no sooner taken official possession of it in 1783 than there was a slave uprising in which the Lieutenant Governor and 47 of His Majesty's subjects were massacred. This rebellion was put down with proper reprisals, but trouble persisted until the abolition of slavery.

It's hard to imagine such bloodshed in this idyllic, almost dreamlike setting, just as it is difficult to visualize the violence of Hurricane Janet which swept over Grenada in 1955, de-molishing trees and houses in its wake. The tropics bruise easy and heal quick. Nature creates more than she destroys. Bathed in a golden green light, enveloped in an aura of aromatic spices, Grenada today is like some pristine Eden or prophecy of that golden age when dust shall be the serpent's meat. "Spice Island of the West," she is called, "Island in the Sun", "Jewel of the Caribbean". Such phrases are enough to make the traveler wary. In Grenada's case they are well applied.

All the natural advantages for a superior tourist resort exist, then, in Grenada. But tourist development lags here as it does in the rest of the Windward Islands. Hotel accomodations (see below) cannot meet tourist demand, and a tropical lethargy seems to affect many whose business it is, or should be, to bolster Grenada's nutmeg economy with tourist dollars.

True Blue

There is one striking exception to this *dolce far niente*, one which merits the attention of all who long to visit or live on an island in the sun. This is the *True Blue* development. True Blue was started by a group of far-sighted business men from Caracas, Venezuela, and Grenada. After a long search for the ideal setting, they bought a 250 acre peninsula at the southern end of Grenada, and are now developing it into a residential resort with large private lots, roads, electricity, water, telephone, all the basic amenities. The celebrated Brazilian landscape architect, Roberto Burle Marx, is one of many specialists whose talents are being utilised in realizing the project. Four beautiful reef-protected bays and three superb white sand beaches are among the natural assets of True Blue. Another is "Uncle Johnny's" farm, property of an island-born-and-bred octogenarian, the grand old man of Grenada. A new farm will supply True Blue with a recreation area for children, mounts for horseback riders, and milk, eggs, meat, chicken and fresh vegetables for the community. A golf course is already under construction, and a hotel-restaurant is on the boards. One hundred and fifty residential lots of 25,000 square feet have already been put on the market, of which more than half are sold. True Blue's architects are available to assist you in constructing your permanent home or vacation bungalow, and their real estate consultants will help you rent your bungalow during periods when you do not plan to use it yourself. This intelligently-planned project is worth watching. For brochures and other information on True Blue, write to The Caribbean Development Company C.A. Edif. Capri, Plaza Altamira Sur-Oficina 3, Caracas, Venezuela.

A Similar development is underway on 150 acres at Wester-hall Point sponsored by Beresford Wilcox. Information can be obtained by writing direct to Westerhall Point, Carenage, St. George's Grenada. Another development will shortly be under-way, the brainchild of two Americans, Mr. and Mrs. James

THE BRITISH WINDWARDS

Needham. They have planned 15 small housekeeping cottages overlooking the southern end of Grand Anse Beach. The Needhams can be reached at Albany House in St. George's.

PRACTICAL INFORMATION FOR GRENADA

HOW TO GET THERE. Access is easy by air, but involves a transfer in Barbados or Trinidad to British West Indian Airways. Trans Canada Airlines will fly you from Canada to Barbados and Trinidad. From New York, it's Pan American World Airways, BWIA. From London, fly by the reliable British Overseas Airways Co. (BOAC). From Paris, Air France will fly you to Martinique, from which BWIA will bring you to Grenada. BWIA has direct weekly service between Grenada and Caracas. From Central and South America you can fly in by KLM Royal Dutch Airlines, Linea Aeropostal Venezolana, Aerolineas Argentinas, Pan American, BOAC and BWIA.

Although at least 25 cruise ships stop at Grenada each season, there is no regularly scheduled boat service to St. George's. If a sea voyage is what you want, take a ship to Trinidad (see below: Trinidad: How To Get There) and then hop over to Grenada by BWIA.

HOW TO GET ABOUT. Local buses are cheap, but more picturesque than comfortable. Plank seats. Take a taxi. Fares are fixed: 60 cents for the first mile, 30 cents for each additional mile. Fare from the airport to your hotel (a 45 minute drive, by the way) is $1.80 ($3 W.I.) per seat; the whole car rents at $7.20 ($12 W.I.). Self-drive cars are available at rental of $8 to $10 per day. See McIntyre Brothers or Ferguson's, two of St. George's most reliable garages. They also arrange round-the-island trips and shorter sightseeing excursions.

HOTELS. After a three year lag in hotel development, Grenada is taking steps to catch up. The *Silver Sands Hotel*, opened in 1960, was one of the island's largest. Two other new luxury hotels are the *Spice Island Inn* and, the largest of the new beach facilities, the *Grenada Beach Hotel*, a 120-room project operated by Abe Issa, scheduled to open as we go to press. You should reserve in advance for the winter season: December through April. All hotels operate on American Plan.

SANTA MARIA. This hotel has an extraordinary location and splendid views over St. George's, the harbor and the lagoon. Crowning a hill, it dominates the port like a fortress. It's almost as big and bleak as a fortress, too, but it's one of the best places on the island even so. There are 35 rooms, spacious and cool, with private baths. The food is good, the bar well-stocked. The hotel supplies free transportation to town and beach. Rates are $13 to $20 per day single; $25 to $27 double.

SEAVIEW GUEST HOUSE. In St. George's, overlooking town and harbor, this is a delightful family *pension*-type place. The atmosphere is intimate, and the food is top flight, the best we had in Grenada. Mr. Curtis Hughes, a retired civil servant, runs this guest house. It's hard to get in because the food is so good and accommodations are limited to 8 beds. Reservations should be made in advance. Rates are $6 a day single, $12 double for room with bath; $4.80 single, $9.60 double without private bath.

515

THE BRITISH WINDWARDS

SILVER SANDS HOTEL. Good beach and resort hotel operated by Eversley Gitens. A combination of cottages and hotel area, it can accommodate more than 60 guests. There is an outdoor restaurant where the food is good, a barbecue area and a bar, all located right on Anse Beach. Rates on application.

SPICE ISLAND INN. Recently opened, the inn has 10 double-unit cottages that border the Grand Anse beach. There is a dining room, dancing terrace, and gift shops. In season rates range from $26 single to $44 double.

ST. JAMES. Another hillside hostelry in St. George's with fine views to north, east and south. There are 21 rooms, the majority with private bath. This is a comfortable, informal place with good bar, good simple fare, and fair rates. W. E. Julien is the manager. He charges $6 a day single, $14 double. (It's the double rooms that have the private baths).

GREEN GABLES GUEST HOUSE. Just outside of St. George's with nice view of the town to the west and harbor to the south. Mrs. Renwick, the manageress, has 13 comfortable rooms at comfortable rates: $4.50 single, $9 double. There's a small bar.

ROSS'POINT INN. A pleasant small hotel (19 beds) at Belmont, two miles from St. George's, overlooking the sea and a small beach. The food is good, atmosphere informal and friendly. All rooms have hot and cold running water, most have private baths. Curtis Hopkins is the manager. Rates are $7.25 a day single, $14.50 double.

Note: The True Blue Development is preparing to offer some furnished houses to visitors who plan longer vacations on the island. Furnished cabins are also available at L'Ance Aux Epines, a secluded peninsula with good beaches; direct inquiries to Mrs. Brathwaite, P.O. Box 187, St. George's.

FOOD AND RESTAURANTS. There's a lot of small truck farming in Grenada with the happy result that this island has more fresh fruit and vegetables than its neighbors. Bananas, mangoes, oranges, grapefruit, mandarines, tangerines, sapodillas, guavas, paw paws, water melon, sugar apples, sweet potatoes, breadfruit, yams, cush-cush, tannia, avocado pears, peas, plaintain: the list is endless. There are lots of good fish in the sea too: rock lobster, conch, sea egg (sea urchins), turtle, whelks, oysters and all the finny tribe.

Note: The hotels have a general tendency to ignore these gifts of nature in favor of a more conventional English meat and potatoes diet. It isn't mean-spiritedness, however, just lack of imagination. They are very nice about acceding to requests, and you can help the cause of Grenadian tourism by asking for some of the items suggested above if you don't find them on your hotel menu.

Grenadian rum punches, made with lime juice, syrup, Angostura bitters, grated nutmeg and either Barbados or local rum, are among the delights of the island. Gin and coconut water is another popular local mix.

There are only five restaurants in St. George's beside the hotel dining rooms. Try *Nick's* on the main street; it's an air-conditioned up-to-the-moment place with an excellent bar and quite satisfactory meals. *Harbour Lounge* on the Carenage has a good bar, wonderful harbor view, acceptable short order meals at any hour. *Cactus*, also on the Carenage, serves good food and good drinks amidst cool and pleasant surroundings. Latest in restaurants is the *Rock 'n Roll*, specializing in, of all things, Chinese food. West Indian dishes are provided by the *Carib Restaurant*.

THE BRITISH WINDWARDS

NIGHT LIFE. Night clubs are non-existent in Grenada. There is the *Morne Rouge Beach Club*, however, with a juke box and, occasionally, steel band if you want to get some exercise on a Saturday night. There are some social clubs in St. George's where bingo, canasta, bridge and other wild things go on, sometimes even dances. Up-to-the-minute movies are released in the town's two modern cinemas.

 SHOPPING. Legislation is under consideration to make Grenada a "token tax port" with duties scaled down to 3½ to 5 per cent. Such action would bring Grenada into line with such places as Curaçao and Aruba, and probably cheaper for certain things than the U.S. Virgin Islands. Grenada's chief contribution to the souvenir trade is the spice basket, hand woven panniers of palm-leaf or straw, filled with cinnamon, nutmeg, ginger, vanilla, bayleaf, cloves and all the pungent aromatic spices for which the isle is famous. Straw and sisal products from Dominica also abound. Straw mats and carpets woven in attractive patterns are an excellent buy.

You'll find these along with other straw goods at the *Grenada Manufacturing Company* in Granby Street. There are loads of imported English woolens and other British goods at prices which are downright anti-American.

Try *Granby Stores, R.M.D. Charles & Co., Everybody's Stores Ltd., Supply Stores, George Joseph*, or *T. E. Noble Smith & Co.* These should take care of all of your needs in the textile, jewelry, perfume, cosmetic and spice line.

The tradition of the general store obtains in Grenada; hardware and liquor go hand in hand.

If you're looking for the latest in imported ladies' dresses, costume, jewelry, etc., *Mrs. Alan Evison* and *Mrs. W. E. Julien* in Church Street have about the best selection in town.

For unusual gift items and curios from all over the world, visit *Tikal* on Young Street run by Jean Fisher and Vera Craig of Caracas.

 SPORTS AND OTHER ACTIVITIES. *Swimming* is just about perfect at Grand Anse, a long white sand beach with crystal water, and at Levera and other beaches around the island.

Spear fishing is popular among the coral reefs and along the rocky coastline.

Deep sea fishing is excellent in the Grenadines. Boats may be chartered for $4.25 and $4.80 an hour; $39 to $51 a day (food and drink not included.) Rods, reels and lures can be rented, but tackle on charter boats is definitely limited. Yacht cruises along western and southern coasts of Grenada are a delight; your hotel can arrange them, but better plan to make it a full day's outing.

If you want to play *tennis*, you're limited to two concrete courts at the Richmond Hill Tennis Club. One is flood-lighted for night playing. Contact the secretary. *Golf.* The Grenada Club has a nine-hole course and new club house where you can play for a fortnightly green fee of $3. Local mad dogs and Englishmen do not go out in the midday sun; the club doesn't come alive until four in the afternoon. You can play in the morning, however; see the caddie master.

Spectator sports include cricket (from January to May), football (from July to December), and horse racing.

517

There are four annual race meetings, each meeting being a two day affair. The Easter and August meetings are at Queen's Park, St. George's. The New Year's and Whitsuntide meetings are at Telescope, St. Andrews. It isn't as colorful and exciting as on Barbados, but fun all the same.

Grenada's *Carnival* takes place each year on the Monday and Tuesday before Ash Wednesday. There are pageants, steel band processions, floats, beautiful girls, coronations, street parades and the like. Climax is the mass band parade from 4 to 7 p.m. on Mardi Gras at which time the local frenzy is at its height. Anti-climax comes with the Tuesday night dances when, according to our Grenadian correspondent, "not many people attend because they are too exhausted to continue and so retire in preparation for the next day's work."

EXPLORING GRENADA

St. George's on its protected harbor and blue inner lagoon is the most delightful little city in the Caribbean; Willemstad can compare with it in European atmosphere and color, but St. George's has the advantage of being even smaller, quainter and more "unspoiled" than the Dutch capital of Curaçao. Pastel warehouses cling to the curving shore of the Carenage; gabled houses, red, white and rainbow, rise above it, a kaleidoscope of cubist form and primary color against the green golden slopes of verdant hills. One of these is so steep that it cuts the capital in half. But old world charm can hide marvels of engineering; there's a tunnel connecting the two sections. A stroll through the town with its neat houses, gardens, flamboyant and frangipani trees, is a walker's delight. You'll want to explore the Carenage, both the inner and outer harbors, old Fort George (built by the French, now used as Police Headquarters), the Market Place, and the stores, many of which are housed in old buildings of the Victorian epoch. You can "do" St. George's on foot in about two hours. Before you start, drop in at the office of the Grenada Tourist Trade and Development Board on the Carenage.

Among the most popular tours are an afternoon tour of St. George's and environs, including Grand Anse beach, and an all day round-the-island trip, which hits all the high spots. Whether you go by tour, island bus (the cheapest, most colorful and most uncomfortable way) or drive-yourself, here are some of the treats in store for you:

Grand Anse Beach, a two-mile stretch of gleaming sand and transparent water just south of St. George's. Its claim (one of at least 10,000) to be the most beautiful beach in the world is not without foundation. You can get bathhouse, drinks, snacks at the Morne Rouge Beach Club here, but bring your own towel. The view of St. George's from Grand Anse is one more argument in favor of scenic Grenada.

Grand Etang Lake. A marvelous glass-like sheet (13 acres) of cobalt water 1800 feet high in the crater of an extinct volcano. The drive to the lake is through magnificent tropical jungle and giant tree ferns. The lake is in the midst of a bird sanctuary and forest reserve. Take a sweater or light wrap; it's cool up there.

Annandale Falls. A mountain stream cascades from a height of 50 feet into a pool, surrounded by liana vines, elephant ears and other exotic tropical flora. This is a wonderful place for picnicking and swimming in clear fresh water.

Pointe Saline. The southwestern tip of Grenada. Just 150 yards apart on either side of the point are two beaches, one of dazzling white sand, the other jet black. The contrast is stunning. The views from the Pointe Saline lighthouse are without compare, even in the Caribbean. You're just a step here from True Blue, and when you see the deep brilliant blue of the Caribbean at this point, this rather trite name will take on a new dimension.

Gouyave, a colorful market town on the coastal road north of St. George's, one of the centers of the nutmeg industry. There's a factory where the nutmeg and mace are processed. But you'll get a better idea of the manufacture at Grenville (see below).

Sauteurs. This is Grenada's third largest town with the great cliff from which the Caribs leapt rather than be captured by the French. A church and cemetery nearby seem entirely appropriate in this dramatically morbid setting. Looking down from the forbidding height of Le Morne des Sauteurs, you can imagine the ferocity of the French to whose tender mercies the Indians preferred death on the jagged rocks below.

Levera Beach. An idyll of sand, water, palm trees and sea grape at the northeast corner of Grenada where the Atlantic meets the Caribbean and the Grenadines start curving north to St. Vincent. More beautiful than Grand Anse, Levera has few equals in the Caribbean. The two offshore islets are Levera and Green Island.

Grenville. The second city of Grenada, it's on the east coast. There is a waterfront fish market. The fruit and vegetable market (Saturday mornings) a block inland from the bay is without peer in the Caribbean for local color and animation. Grenville is still recovering from 1955 Hurricane Janet which destroyed 90 per cent of the nutmeg crop. The nutmeg factory welcomes visitors, and you can watch the whole process of making nutmeg and mace. If you're used to nutmeg in small cans or sprinkled on top of an eggnogg, you'll be impressed by the huge sacks and crates of shredded mace and nutmeg here.

The nutmeg itself (Mysterica fragrans) grows on trees in shady groves. You can see it on the tree or being sorted by colorfully-dressed native women at the lovely spice farm of St. David's. On such a farm you can sense the economic heartbeat of the Spice Island. On the cocoa plantations, with their trays of chocolate-colored pods drying in the sun, you can watch men polishing the cocoa by treading on it in vats with their bare brown feet. The Grenadians many of them with small farms of their own, have a green thumb, a knack for cultivating the fruits and spices of their native soil. This knack, plus a certain independence of spirit, has raised them above the level of other small farmers in the Caribbean. If the energy and imagination that have gone into island agriculture are applied to the development of tourism, Grenada may one day be among the leaders of the West Indies.

BARBADOS

Platinum Coast in the Golden Caribbees

Easternmost of all the Caribbees, Barbados swims aloof from the rest of the Lesser Antilles. Keeping them at a proper 90-mile distance, she looks toward England. This is symbolic. Barbados is the tropics anglicised. Except for her Iberian name, Barbados ("the bearded ones", said to have been given her by her Portuguese discoverer because of the beard-like vines on the island's fig trees), she is English to the core. Under the Union Jack without interruption since 1625, she is more British than Britain herself, and proud of the distinction.

Barbados even looks like "England's green and pleasant land". Almost every inch of the island's 166 square miles of fertile soil is under cultivation. The placid countryside, rolling as the hills of Devon, is a tidy patchwork of square fields, flecked with tiny houses, bright with orchards and gardens which remain essentially English despite exotic notes of purple moonflower, red hibiscus. An 18th-century visitor, George Washington (father of American tourism!) described himself as "perfectly enraptured with the beautiful prospects... on every side, the fields of cane, corn, fruit trees in a delightful green setting."

BARBADOS

English place names—Yorkshire, Windsor, and Hastings—strengthen the English illusion, as do the gray village churches, to whose Anglican services the populace dutifully flocks every Sunday, tubbed and scrubbed, prayer books clutched in pink-palmed hands, black faces and black shoes shining in the not-so-English tropic sun.

Tree-lined roads of crushed coral wind from village to village, narrow and meandering as English lanes. You drive a right-hand British car, and you drive left. The traffic policemen are London bobbies in photographic negative: dusky faces, white helmets and jackets. The regimental bandsmen are technicolor carbon copies of Her Majesty's Cold Stream Guards.

The ritual of high tea takes place every afternoon at half after five. The ritual—nay the national cult—of cricket is widely practiced. During international and inter-island matches, business comes to a standstill; half the population watches, the rest huddles around radios. If Barbados beats the visitors, island joy is unconfined. If the local side loses, the general gloom is so profound that one might think the sugar crop had failed. Through prosperity, through adversity, the devotion to cricket persists, uniting all Barbadians, regardless of race, creed or color in a bond that only true-born Englishmen can understand.

Bridgetown, the island capital, has 30,000 inhabitants, quaint, narrow streets, modern avenues, some smart shops. The chief place is Trafalgar Square, dominated by a statue of Lord Nelson, 27 years older than the one in London. The planters of Barbados put it up in 1813 in grateful recognition of the hero who saved their sugar profits from the French. You'll see other reminders of Nelson. The harbor police wear the Jack Tar uniforms of his sailors: white middies, bell-bottom trousers and those flat, round, wide-brimmed straw boaters, everything but the pigtails. Barbados is more than "Little England"; it's Old England, cherishing its British past, clinging to it with an insular tenacity, preserving its old world charm in a modern sea of troubles.

Barbados' chief trouble is over-population. With nearly 250,000 inhabitants, it is one of the most densely-populated islands in the world. Oxford-educated Sir Grantley Adams, founder of the Barbados Labor Party and first Prime Minister of the West Indies Federation, has fought this problem for years, advocating planned parenthood, trying to persuade America to lift the restrictions of the McCarran Act, under which no more than 100 immigrants from each West Indian

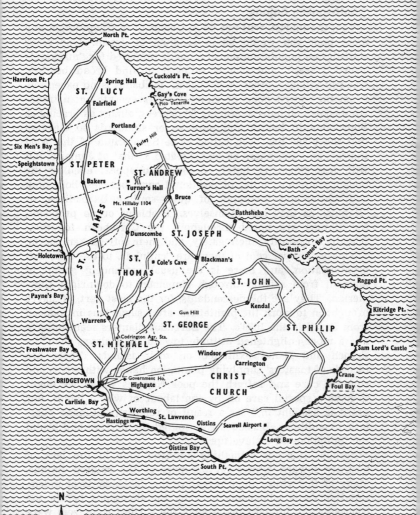

BARBADOS

0 1 2 3 Miles

ATLANTIC OCEAN

North Pt.

Harrison Pt.

Cuckold's Pt.

Spring Hall
ST. LUCY
Fairfield

Gay's Cove
Pico Teneriffe

Portland

Six Men's Bay

Farley Hill

Speightstown

ST. PETER

ST. ANDREW

Bakers

Turner's Hall

Bruce

Mt. Hillaby 1104

Bathsheba

ST. JAMES

Dunscombe

ST. JOSEPH

Bath   Conset Bay

Holetown

ST.
THOMAS

Cole's Cave

Blackman's

Ragged Pt.

Payne's Bay

ST. JOHN

Kendal

Kitridge Pt.

Warrens

Gun Hill

ST. GEORGE

ST. PHILIP

Codrington Agr. Sta.

Freshwater Bay

ST. MICHAEL

Windsor

Sam Lord's Castle

Carrington

Crane

BRIDGETOWN

Government Ho.
Highgate

CHRIST

Foul Bay

Carlisle Bay

CHURCH

Worthing

St. Lawrence

Hastings

Oistins

Seawell Airport

Long Bay

Oistins Bay

South Pt.

N

island can be admitted to the United States per year. In the meantime, the island tries to support more than 1300 people to the square mile on its traditional crop of sugar, rum and molasses, to which has been added another sweetening for the island economy: tourism.

Soft-spoken Bajuns

You, the tourist, will not be conscious of overpopulation any more than you would be in Belgium or Japan. One reads statistics on population density, one is prepared for "mackerel-crowded seas", and one is relieved to find broad beaches, tranquil villages, great open spaces. Barbados is no exception. From the tourist point of view, it offers everything: a trade-wind cooled climate, averaging 80 degrees, almost as bracing as Bournemouth; health and pure water standards so elevated that the place has been called "The Sanatorium of the West Indies"; an atmosphere as sophisticated as that of Jamaica, but with less expensive hotels, designed to appeal even to the budget conscious; miles of powdered coral beaches, both pink and white, and thousands of quick-smiling Barbadians, or "Bajuns" as they call themselves. Problems or no problems, the Bajuns are noted throughout the Caribbean for their friendly hospitality, their gaiety, and their soft-spoken charm.

Ninety-five per cent of them are "culluhd", to use their soft pronunciation, and there is the usual entrancing gamut of pigment from saffron through cinnamon to downright Cimmerian. They are the descendants, for the most part, of slaves brought in to work the plantations after sugar was introduced from Brazil in the 1630's. The Barbados planters seem to have had a more enlightened attitude toward their slaves than the French and Danes exhibited on their islands. There are records of masters' supplying plantation hands with wives and rum "to cure and refresh the poor Negroes whom we ought to have a special care of, by the labour of whose hands, our profit is brought in." As a result of relatively humane plantation conditions, Barbados was spared the horrors and brutal recriminations of a slave uprising.

Perhaps there is something atavistic then in the lack of hostility toward whites on the part of the colored Bajuns. Many of the whites themselves are the descendants of indentured servants who came here by the thousands before the Negroes were brought in. Among the earliest colonizers were inmates of English prisons transported overseas to do forced labor on the plantations. Their number was augmented by

Royalist captives of Cromwell and indentured political prisoners who supported the bastard Duke of Monmouth's abortive rebellion against James II. Barbados, in short, became a 17th-century dustbin in which the rulers of England summarily dumped thieves and desperate men, unruly Scots and Irishmen, Presbyterians, Quakers and other dangerous dissenters and free thinkers. It made for a strange and interesting assortment of first families.

Many of the descendants of these involuntary immigrants live in St. Andrew's parish and in the northeast corner of Little England, known consistently enough as Scotland. They are called "Redlegs", an old English term for a bare-shanked kilted Scotsman. Though the application is indiscriminate and inexact, it sticks. At one time, the Redlegs had the reputation of keeping to themselves, equally removed from the Bajuns, the white plantation managers and the rich British and Americans, both winter residents and retired yearrounders who kept to *them*selves in the exclusive precincts of St. James and Hastings.

Freedom from Tension

All this business of people keeping to themselves suggests the crucial question: Is there a color bar in Barbados? There is, but it seems almost more economic than racial, the result of three centuries of white ownership-management of the island. Paradoxically the Bajuns are the best-educated and the most politically-literate Negroes in the West Indies, natural leaders in the evolution toward self government symbolized by the West Indian Federation. Sir Grantley Adams, a Bajun so English in temperament that he lists his hobbies in Who's Who as gardening and cricket, typifies this natural leadership. He is admired by colored and white alike; certainly he is socially accepted by the latter, and this is significant for the future. What is significant for the present is the freedom from tension, despite the persistence of the color bar. Barbados may have its clubs exclusively for whites, but the Bajuns look upon this with an equanimity amounting almost to indifference. In their eyes such things are vestigal relics of colonial days. They know that history is moving inexorably to redress whatever real wrongs persist. They are aware that Britain is muddling through to a solution, and they have reason to be convinced of her good faith. They can afford to be patient, having already won a notable victory of the spirit over economic facts of life.

BARBADOS

You will find whites and colored people keeping to themselves in many hotel, restaurant and social situations. But you will not find the ugly tensions of Little Rock or Harlem. Barbados is too sophisticated for that. Remember that the tradition of British tolerance is already in its fourth century of evolution on this bright little island.

Most tourists, both the gregarious and hermit types, respond to this atmosphere of real sophistication. There's lots to do on Barbados, but one is under no compulsion to do anything. Even if you are one of those queer blighters who are immune to the charms of tea and cricket, you are not obliged to participate in these long established religious practices. For the rest, Barbados offers you wonderful swimming and fishing, polo, horse racing, golf, tennis, a yacht club, a splendid climate, a little theatre group, British tailoring at bargain prices, and a world-famous golden light rum, available at night clubs from 25 cents per Cuba Libra. That price, incidentally, is indicative of the general low costs which combine with all the other attractions to make Barbados the most popular resort in the Lesser Antilles.

PRACTICAL INFORMATION FOR BARBADOS

 HOW TO GET THERE. Few islands are better served by air. British West Indian Airways (BWIA) will fly you direct from New York. They also have an excellent New York-Barbados flight by way of Bermuda. Pan American World Airways has flights from New York via Puerto Rico, Antigua or Trinidad. Delta Airlines links New York and Barbados via Jamaica, Puerto Rico and Caracas. You can fly via Eastern Airlines to Puerto Rico, and hop over to Barbados by BWIA.

From Miami by air, take BWIA via Jamaica; KLM Royal Dutch Airlines via Trinidad; Pan American World Airways via Puerto Rico and Trinidad, or Eastern Airlines to Puerto Rico with BWIA connection for Barbados.

From Montreal and Toronto you have a choice between BOAC via New York and Trans-Canada Airlines, flying to Barbados twice a week with Bermuda stopover. During the winter season, Trans-Canada adds 2 weekly services from Toronto to Barbados and Trinidad, via Bermuda.

From London there is weekly service by BOAC Britannias which links the British capital with Bermuda, Barbados and Trinidad. BWIA also has a weekly flight to Barbados from London via New York.

Best bet for direct inter-island air connections is BWIA, which links Bridgetown with Trinidad, Tobago, Grenada, St. Lucia, Martinique, Guadelope, Jamaica, Puerto Rico, St. Kitts, Antigua and Bermuda.

In addition there is the Leeward Islands Air Transport, linking Bridgetown with St. Vincent and Dominica, and there is good old Air

BARBADOS

France, its largest network in the world spreading out to serve Barbados by way of Puerto Rico, St. Martin, Guadeloupe and Martinique.

A new terminal building at Seawell Airport includes shops & tropical bar surrounding floral patios and lily pond. Second floor has restaurant and balcony overlooking the field. In-bond shops have duty-free tourist merchandise.

By sea, Barbados is linked with New York via the Moore-McCormack Lines.

There are weekly sailings via Alcoa Steamship Company from New Orleans to Trinidad, where connection is made for Bridgetown.

Freighters of Canadian National Steamship Co. link Bridgetown with St. Vincent, Grenada, Trinidad, St. Lucia, Dominica, Montserrat, Antigua, St. Kitts and Bermuda.

The French Line serves Bridgetown, Trinidad, Martinique, Guadeloupe, Curaçao, La Guaira and Puerto Rico.

In addition to all this, Barbados is linked to Trinidad by three other companies, The Booth Line, the Dutch Line, and Elders & Fyffes Ltd., which last also has Kingston, Jamaica as a regular port of call.

As can be seen, getting to Barbados doesn't present any problem, but rather an *embarras de choix.*

 PASSPORTS, VISAS. Persons entering the island must be in possession of a valid passport or some other document satisfactorily establishing their nationality and identity. No visa is required of British, U.S. or Canadian citizens unless they plan to stay in Barbados for more than six months. A smallpox vaccination certificate is required for entering Barbados.

 CURRENCY. The Bee-Wee dollar is legal tender. American and Canadian dollars are accepted just about everywhere, or can be exchanged at any of the Bridgetown banks. English pounds are familiar enough in Little England, but U.K. travelers should check carefully with travel agent or bank on the latest restriction on importing pounds sterling into Barbados.

CLOTHING. Since the temperature, even in winter, has never been known to drop below 68 degrees, take lightweight clothes. Evening dress, optional for short stay visitors, is practically obligatory for winter visitors and residents who plan to participate in island social life. This being Little England, there are many local British families who dress for dinner. If you're invited out, better ask if it's "black tie". Tip: Barbados shops are bulging with attractive clothes, both formal and informal, at low prices, and they can make up tropical dinner clothes for you in a trice. Don't overpack.

 HOW TO GET ABOUT. Densely-populated Barbados has a network of public buses that will take you to almost any corner of the island. They have two advantages: they're dirt cheap and they provide the best introduction to local color. If you want to see the gregarious Bajuns at their informal best, take a bus; it's a circus. The disadvantage is that it's very slow. Not only are there many stops, but each one is an occasion for a more-or-less prolonged bout of local business and gossip. Once we even waited while the driver and his very pretty girl friend hopped out for a spot of tea. If you can't get out of high gear, avoid the busses, and don't take them if you have segregationist leanings.

For sightseeing out of Bridgetown, you will probably hire a taxi by hour or day, a self-drive or chauffeur-driven car. Rates are fixed and cheap; you can hire a little Hillman or Austin for as little as $28 a week. *Barbados Taxi Cab Service Ltd.* (Phone 2987) has drive-yourself cars, fully insured, in addition to 24-hour taxi service. *Dear's Garage Ltd.* has the same, on Roebuck St. in Bridgetown and with a branch in Hastings.

You can also arrange your transportation through the following recommended sightseeing tour operators, all in Bridgetown: *Johnson's Stables and Garage,* Coleridge Street; *United Taxi Owners Assn.,* Spry Street; *ABC Travel Agency Ltd., Robert Thom Ltd.,* and *H. B. Niblock Company.* The last three companies are on Broad Street.

HOTELS

Barbados has long been noted for the variety of its hotel accommodations, ranging from the Spartan adequate to the *grand luxe* and offering something for practically every taste and pocketbook. You have a wide choice. There are comfortable medium-priced hotels in Hastings that will remind you of places you've stayed at in Sussex, English to the last crumpet. You'll find American enterprises like the Coral Reef Club, the last word in luxury. Many of the hotels are designated as *Residential Clubs.* They are not clubs, but small-size luxury hotels of a residential type, rarely catering to long-term visitors, welcoming transitory ones. Service in Barbados hotels is generally a notch or two higher than on other islands, mainly due to the innate courtesy of the locals.

Rates fall off sharply in Barbados after the April 15 deadline, and it is possible to find modest seaside accommodations during the summer months for as little as $5 per day, everything included. Maximum off season rates, even at the most luxurious residential clubs, seldom if ever exceed U.S. $20 a day.

The Barbadians are not resting on their laurels in the hotel department. The situation is dynamic. A 380 acre resort has very recently been completed on the west coast with a 50-room hotel, beach and hillside cottages, and 45 acre, 9-hole golf course. The new 25-room *Royal Caribbean* is now in operation. In the meanwhile, here's our list of recommended hostelries.

Since there are no less than 37 of them, we give hotels alphabetically to facilitate reader reference, and follow this with an alphabetical listing of the residential clubs. All rates, unless otherwise indicated, are for American Plan, and quoted in U.S. currency.

Drinks in the drinks are served from Commander Nicholson's charter yacht "Mollihawk" to guests lazing in Marigot Lagoon off St.
Lucia. The picturesque Harbour Police of Bridgetown, Barbados,
look positively prim by comparison.

East meets West in Trinidad where this fanciful Hindu temple and its bearded, turbaned priest thrive like the Indian banyan transplanted in the tropics. Moslem mosques add another exotic note to the local scene.

BARBADOS

ABBEVILLE. On the beach at Worthing, three miles east of Bridgetown. An English boarding house type of place, owned and operated by A. Lamming, it has 10 rooms. Rates are $8 to $12 single, $16 to $23 double per day in winter. Summer rates range between $6 and $15.

BAGSHOT HOUSE. Also at Worthing, a very nice, very well run hotel with good plain food. There are 14 rooms. Mrs. E. Robinson is the manager, and most of her clients come back, the surest sign of a good place to stay. Rates: $12 single, $24 double in winter. Summer rates ranging from $9 single to a high of $18 double.

BLUE WATERS HOTEL. A new 30 room hotel just across the road from Rockley beach shares the shoreline with the Accra Beach Club and the Rockley Beach Club. Its owner, Pierre Maffei also built the Rockley. Mrs. Earle Smith is the manager. Rates are $17 single, $30 double, winter; $10 single, $20 double, summer.

BONNIE DUNDEE. Another newcomer to Barbadian hotels, the Dundee has 16 rooms, some air-conditioned, located on St. Lawrence Beach. Owner-Manager Errol Steele gives winter rates from $13 to $15 single and $22 to $26 double; summer rates are $11 to $14 single, $16 to $20 double.

CACRABANK HOTEL. Has an ocean-front setting at Worthing, a nice beach, a sun deck and sea breezes. Mrs. T. Corbin is the manager of this 24-room enterprise. They are famous throughout the isle for their Sunday smörgasbord dinner with curry and other English colonial touches. We were not wild about it, but that's a minority report. Rates are $12 to $15 per day single, $23 to $30 double in winter. Summer rates range from $6 to a high of $17.

CARIBEE. Formerly the Hotel Hastings, this 51-roomer is on the beach at the town of the same name, a suburb of Bridgetown. An observation deck overlooking the sea, a cocktail lounge, an attractive patio are among the amenities. Observation deck on roof makes scenic nightclub and fine convention hall. Manager is Mr. David Strawson. Rates are $14 to $18 single, $22 to $26 in the winter; summer are $10 to $14 single, $16 to $20 double (M.A.P.).

CRANE. On the beach at St. Philip, 13 miles from Bridgetown, this 25-room inn overlooks the sea from a cliff. Good surf bathing from a beach that's so uncrowded that you'll wonder what all this density-of-population talk is about. There's an outdoor casino ballroom. Special facilities here for fishermen. There are lots of good fish in the sea and on the dining room table of this attractive, well-run place. Mr. N. Goddard is your host. His rates are reasonable: $10 per day single, $28 double in winter. In summer they are even more inviting, $6 up to $17.50.

EASTRY HOUSE. A new development with swimming pool on the beach at St. Peter, about 10 miles from Bridgetown. The architecture is modern sanatorium, a little on the bare and bleak side, but the view is magnificent, the rooms are comfortable, and the food, which is billed as the "Cordon Bleu Cuisine" is good, especially when the manager, Mr. Horst Hohmann, an Austrian, lends a hand in the kitchen himself. There's dancing twice weekly in the Starlight Room, and a steel band holds forth on barbecue nights around the pool. There are 21 rooms, most of them luxurious double suites with private gallery sittting room. Rates, about the most expensive in Barbados, are $28 to $39 per day single. Prices drop as low as $23 for a single in summer.

EDGEWATER HOTEL. A nice old place, completely refurbished with clean new rooms and a charming swimming pool. It's at Bathsheba on the surfside (east coast) of the island and has the advantage of an isolated position. There are 20 rooms. Rates are $16.75-$20 a day single, $30-$34 double in winter. Lower summer rates.

HOTEL ROYAL ON SEA. Located on the beach at Hastings, this hotel has a pier with dining and cocktail terrace, a good place for dancing. Good meals and excellent management by A. M. Taylor account for the Royal's perennial popularity. There are 33 rooms, many of which have private balconies overlooking the sea. Winter rates are from $10-$12 per person. Summer rates dip to as little as $8 per person.

ISLAND INN. Owned and operated by a gracious host, Allen Martyr, this 20-room hotel has character and a delightful personal atmosphere. Near the sea at Garrison, just a mile out of Bridgetown, it is patronized by good-class English without money to throw around. Like most good values, Island Inn is popular. Book in advance. Rates in winter are $12 single, $20-$30 double. Summer rates are from $6 to $16.

MARINE HOTEL. Long-established and recently renovated, it is a local social center thanks to its ballroom and other amenities for big functions. The face-lifting hasn't spoiled its old-fashioned appeal and has expedited service from spanking new modern kitchens. Situated in its own garden in Hastings, the Marine has 120 rooms, the biggest in Barbados. Food is first class. The manager Mr. J. Zelinka is a German, and is probably the most professional hotelier on the island. Winter rates are $14-$17 per day single, $27 to $34 double. Summer rates range from $9.50 to $19 M.A.P.

OCEAN VIEW. An ocean-front hotel at Hastings, sandwiched between road and sea, this is a popular rendezvous with businessmen, who can always be depended on to smell good, hearty food a mile away. That's exactly what the Mitchell family provide, and it's excellent, as dozens of repeat clients will tell you. There are 40 rooms in this highly successful family enterprise. Rates are $12-$13.25 single per day, $24 to $31 double in winter. Summer rates from $9.50 to $19.

POWELL SPRING. Overlooking the beach at Bathsheba, this was a rather run-down looking place when last we saw it, but popular with local families because of correspondingly low-down prices. They were under $5 per person per day when last we looked in. Mr. Carter, the manager, doesn't like to publicise his prices. Guess he wants to look you over personally before telling. He has 23 rooms for rent.

FOUR WINDS CLUB. On the beach at St. Peter's, this small 7-room hotel is a beautiful house, loaded with enough character to make up for its doubtful plumbing and desultory cleaning. Another compensation: M. Griffith, the owner, is a superb cook. Note: The Four Winds blow on the European Plan; this means that breakfast is the only meal included in the rates. Winter rates are $15 per person.

KINGSLEY RESIDENTIAL CLUB. A real Barbadian place with few if any tourists, this small Bathsheba hotel has a large following because of its celebrated lobster lunches. The place has that casual don't-care-if I-fall-apart look. The 9 rooms are primitive but clean. A low-budget holiday haunt for islanders—and for you if you reserve early enough. Another highly-regarded specialty of the Kingsley kitchen is coconut meringue pie. Mrs. Ince is the manager. Her rates are $17 to $18 double, summer and winter.

PARADISE BEACH CLUB. On the beach at Black Rock, three miles north of Bridgetown, this is a big holiday camp with half a dozen attractice beach-front bungalows plus accommodations for 38 more in a guest house. The rooms are

BARBADOS

large, airy, well-appointed and modern in the Grand Rapids manner. The main lodge has dining patio, terrace and bar. The beach is unusually attractive. Lots of Venezuelan and American oil people come here for family vacations. The club, now managed by Mr. Fitzgerald is noted for its "jump-up" parties and other vigorous social activities. Rates are $26 to $30 double, in the winter.

MIRAMAR. At St. James on the beach, 8 miles north of Bridgetown, a charming hotel with an oceanfront and garden setting. Attractive dining room with adjacent cocktail lounge. Quiet, elegant, a bit on the formal side. The cuisine is so good that people drive out here for lunch. Mr. E. S. Bennett is the manager. There are 27 rooms, all with private bath. Winter rates are $25 single, $42 to $46 double. Summer $12 to $32.

SAM LORD'S CASTLE. On the sea at St. Philip, this is an island show place which you will probably visit on your sightseeing itinerary (See below: Exploring Barbados). Recently redecorated from top to bottom, it has not lost its romantic pirate's castle atmosphere. Under new management (Mr. K. G. Coombes); a new swimming pool and putting green have been built. Excellent French cuisine. A block of 10 rooms had been added to the other 17. Winter rates: $15 to $20 a day single, $30 to $40 double. Summer rates from $10 to $34.

ROYAL CARIBBEAN. New deluxe hotel right across from its big brother the Hotel Royal. There are 30 rooms, each with its own patio and an Esther Williams swimming pool beside which meals are served, and especially a very popular Sunday buffet. Mr. A. M. Taylor is manager. Rates are $14 single, $24 to $28 double, in winter.

SANDY LANE. New beachfront resort combining 18th-century elegance with 20th-century luxury. All 54 rooms have bath and face the sea. Private beach, golf, tennis. Mr. N. Behard is manager. Rates are: $28 single, $44 to $48 double, in winter. $18 to $38 in the summer.

SOUTH WINDS. Another new hotel, this one on the popular south coast. Built smack on St. Lawrence beach, it has 19 rooms plus an attractive restaurant and bar with ocean view. Owner-manager Russell Page. Rates are: $12 to $17 single, $22 to $28 double, in winter. $10.50 to $17 M.A.P. in the summer.

SUNSET LODGE. Among the brand new places, this one is unique. On the west coast near Eastry house, it has been made over from an old Plantation house, and very cleverly, too. Here you find beach side life with country house charm. Owner-manager is Owen Ellison. Winter rates: $14 single, $28 double. $9 single, $18 double, in summer.

ROCKLEY BEACH. Well-decorated, well-run, and an excellent value, this 20-room establishment is managed jointly with the Blue Waters Beach Hotel. It's on the sea at Rockley, three miles from Bridgetown. Good guitarist plays at the bar. Rates on application only.

SUPER MARE. A 12-room guest house on the sea at Worthing, run by Mrs. Parris, a Bajun woman who's so charming she could get Senator Eastland of Mississippi to advocate civil rights. Inexpensive rates: $6.50 single, $12 to $14 double in winter, without bath.

ST. LAWRENCE. Recently renovated, this 23-room hotel has the atmosphere of a good English pub. The cold buffet and West Indian lunches are just about tops in the island. There's a new air-conditioned wing, very well fitted out. A steel band plays for dancing on Wednesday nights. At St. Lawrence, four miles east of Bridgetown, this English inn is patronized by locals who know a good thing when they see it. Peter Morgan is the manager's name. His rates are $12 to $17 single, $24 to $28 double per day, less in summer.

SANDY BEACH. Ten or more bun-

galows plus a rambling lodge on
the beach at Worthing, near a golf
course. Some of the cottages have
kitchens, but you can get solid
English fare in the hotel dining
room. Mrs. Lampitt is the manager,
and her low rates appeal to a steady
budget-minded clientele, mostly
Canadians. Winter rates are $7
single, $16-$20 double. Also a new
wing of motels; rates on application.

SAN REMO BEACH. Five miles from
Bridgetown. On the beach, this
new development is moderately
priced. Winter rates are: $12 single;
$22 double.

WINDSOR. At Hastings. This terribly respectable 36-roomer has all
the earmarks of a provincial hotel
on the Sussex coast and dispenses
with such decadent frills as room
service. An English friend who
stayed there told us it was dull,
but we can't remember whether
his simile involved ditchwater or
dishwater. In any event, you get
the idea. We should add that there
is a cocktail lounge, but it's more
proper to sit up straight. The cuisine is it's bright spot: French. The
hotel, managed by A. Knight, has
a faithful clientele and reasonable
rates. They are $15 per day single,
$27 to $29 double in winter, $14.50
to $16 M.A.P. during summer.

Other recommended guest houses whose rates range between $8.00 and
$10.00 per person per day are:

*Sea View; Silver Beach; Stonehaven
Inn; White Sands; Brigade House;
Contentment; La Tropical; Mon-
treaux; Rhondda; Foster House;
Torrington; Blue Caribbean.*

RESIDENTIAL CLUBS

This term is very vague. It is employed by hotel keepers
who wish to preserve an illusion of selectivity in choosing
their guests. If, for example, one of them catered more or less
exclusively to members of the British peerage, and a drunken
Irishman staggered in, denouncing the Queen and demanding
a room, he would probably be told, "Sorry, old man; this isn't
just an *ordinary* hotel; it's a club." In other words the proprietor exercises his age-old English right to choose his own
company and to keep out people who for one reason or another might not be congenial to the other guests. To use a
favorite word of that great social arbiter, Miss Elsa Maxwell,
these clubs protect themselves from riffraff. For all practical
purposes, however, the residential clubs are merely luxury
hotels whose prices automatically exclude about 90 per cent
of the *hoi polloi*. If you have a clean shave, clean linen and a
clean tie (it doesn't have to be an old school one), you'll be
welcome at most of these "clubs". To show how vague the
club terminology is, five of the hotels listed above (Paradise
Beach, Sam Lord's, Four Winds, Miramar and Kingsley Residential Club) refer to themselves as clubs. The five listed below
are officially designated as clubs by the Barbados Tourist
Board, but remember they are hotels, very good ones for the
most part, and they wouldn't stay in business if it weren't for

tourists like you. Note: They only have about 103 rooms among them, and since their accommodations and amenities are apt to be among the best in Barbados, you are urged to make your reservations, especially for the winter season, well in advance.

ACCRA BEACH CLUB. The beach (at Rockley) is lovely, the bar is popular, and the food more than passable, but we found this favorite meeting place of local bank clerks and air-line personnel a rather weak facsimile of a fine beach club. Let's not carp, however. The 30 rooms and baths are clean and modern, and they certainly aren't expensive. Mr. and Mrs. A. S. Brooks, a young and appealing pair, manage the club. Rates in winter are $30 to $33 double per day.

BARBADOS AQUATIC CLUB. On the beach at Garrison, a mile from Bridgetown, the Aquatic used to be an elite place but had acquired a definite down at heel look the last time we saw it. The cheap shop-windows on the premises add to the impression. The place is a local yachting center. There's a private pier, a circular bar, snack-bar, and a row of 26 rooms. It's time for a major overhaul. Winter rates are $10.75 per day single, 21.50 to $24 double.

COLONY CLUB. On the beach at fashionable St. James, this is our personal choice for top honors among Barbados hotels. We spent two months convalescing here and have nothing but the utmost admiration for the way the place is equipped, decorated and managed by Peta Mitchell, who has turned a hotel hobby into an artistic way of life. This cottage colony grew from a beautiful clubhouse and is by far the most attractive of the clubs. All 23 rooms are luxuriously appointed; all have such plus values as dressing rooms and private patios overlooking the sea. The facilities include a private beach, tennis courts, and all equipment for aquatic sports from water skis to yachts. To add one more touch of gold leaf to the lily, we found here the most imaginative food, not only in Barbados, but in the whole British Caribbean area. Winter rates are $34.50 single, $46-$56 double. Sumer rates $20-$40.

CORAL REEF CLUB. Nearest neighbor to the Colony and on a par with it as a luxury beach resort. It's one of the leading residential clubs, and so popular as to make advance reservations mandatory. Its style and decoration seemed a bit on the a.b. side to us (angular and bleak), but that's a personal prejudice. We've talked to guests who have stayed in the deluxe double rooms and suites (there are 37 in all) of the cottages and main buildings, dined in the exclusive Bistro restaurant, and they have nothing but praise for food, service and accommodation. Among the equipment which the club has to assure you a happy holiday are three sailing yachts, two speed boats and a fishing boat. Managed by Mr. E. I. O'Hara, this place, like the Colony, is represented by Oliver-Kermit Hotel Associates, 521 Fifth Avenue, New York. You can make reservations directly through them. Winter Rates are $30 single per day; $40-$52 double. Summer rates range from $18 to $44.

FOOD, DRINK AND RESTAURANTS

Barbados' chief contribution to the taste buds of humanity is that famous light Barbados rum, forever amber, mellow and potent. You'll drink it neat, on the rocks, or mixed in the best Planters Punch you've ever tasted. Cocktail prices are a revelation, especially if you've been on the dollar-a-drink circuit. You can actually get a rum and coke in Barbados nightclubs for less than 30 cents. The local smart set prefers Scotch, but we'll take this Bajun vin du pays. Liquor price differentials, incidentally, are as follows—per bottle: Johnnie Walker Scotch $2.90; Gordon's Gin $1.90; Barbados Rum 90 cents.

The classic Barbados punch combines the local rum with lime juice, sugar, cracked ice and a dash of nutmeg on top. The famous Sangaree, which antedated rum as the favorite island drink, is still mixed at bars in Barbados. It consists of a wineglass of Madeira wine and half a teaspoonful of curaçao poured in a highball glass full of cracked ice, and completed by soda, a slice of fresh lime and grated nutmeg. If you want it sweeter, have it made with benedictine replacing the curaçao.

In the food line, there are a number of specialties. Outstanding is flying fish. There are more of these silver-finned creatures skimming the aquamarine waves around Barbados than you'll ever see on the road to Manadalay. Their flesh is moist and succulent, and the Bajuns transform them into a gastronomic delight by boiling, baking, frying, stuffing them or serving them up in a flying fish pie. However you eat them, their delicate nutty flavor is one of the taste thrills of the Caribbean. Another Bajun seafood specialty is the white sea urchin or *oursin*, which you may have eaten in France (dark). It was the Romans who first dared to open these spiky denizens of the deep and sample the orange-coral meat inside. The Bajuns call this venerable delicacy "sea eggs". They abound in Barbadian waters, and though their appearance is still enough to paralyze a provincial palate, take our word for it, they are delicious. Nor should you underestimate the ingenuity of Bajun cooks. We had been eating oursins, pardon us, *sea eggs* raw as hors d'oeuvre for years, but had to come to Barbados to have them sautéed in butter with onions. The result is worthy of the *cordon bleu*. Dolphin, salt fish cakes and "crab-in-the-back" are other Barbadian seafood specialties. Roast suckling pig is as highly regarded and as unctuously prepared here as it is throughout the rest of the Caribbean. The local creole "pepper pot" is worth sampling. As for island desserts, try the mangoes and paw-paws, either alone or in the various fancy dresses provided.

The backbone of the Barbados cuisine is, of course, English.

BARBADOS

But it's English with that dash of spice and flavor that perks it up above the mutton and marrow level of provincial British hotels. Chances are you'll fare better in the Hastings and Worthing of Little England than you would in their Big England namesakes. Mother country's cooking was never like this.

You'll do most of your eating in island hotels, many of which maintain the highest international standards of cuisine.

The Miramar is outstanding, and we recommend you try their Sunday Planter's Buffet Luncheon.

The *Beau Brummel Club* in Hastings and the *St. Lawrence Hotel* are celebrated for their creole dishes; the latter is a good place to try "pepper pot."

The food at *The Colony* is *hors de serie*, certainly the best on the island, with the *Coral Reef* a close runner up.

A honeymooning couple we knew provided us with the following indication of prices. They went to the Coral Reef Club, had a couple of rum cocktails, a big dinner with lobster cocktail, soup, fish, steak, salad, dessert and coffee; wine with their dinner, brandy afterward, and the tab came to $5 per person. Try ordering the same menu on the gay white way or in the fleshpots of Miami.

Apart from the hotel dining rooms, there are not many memorable places for lunching and dining. Bridgetown is not a gastronomic center.

You can go to the very popular *Flying Fish Club* for a drink, a snack and friendly conversation with island planters for whom this place is a rendezvous.

But the biggest and best Bridgetown rendezvous and the one you shouldn't miss is *Goddard's*. On Broad Street, it's a grocery store with restaurant, tea room, bar and barber shop upstairs. The long balcony overlooks the busy main drag. You can have a wonderful time sitting there and drinking in the atmosphere of Bridgetown along with a rum punch, tall and cool, costing all of 30 cents. You can get lunch here, tea and bread-and-but-ter and scones, and a supper of sorts all at prices comparable with that of the punch. (A haircut in the adjoining barber shop, incidentally, comes to 75 cents).

But the most significant thing about Goddard's is that blacks and whites and colors in between are lunching, drinking or supping happily at adjoining tables in an atmosphere of complete relaxation. No color bar here. Goddard's is an island institution.

Other popular restaurants are, the *Oasis*, the *Ecaf* in Bridgetown, the *Pied Piper* and *Fiesta* on the way to St. James.

NIGHTLIFE

There's dancing every evening in season at two nightclubs that have been planted in Barbados since the war and are flourishing in tropic soil.

First is *Club Morgan*, a big place with soft lights and sweet music, which can change to hot at the flip of a wrist. This is a smooth, New York type operation with these happy differences: a big dance floor instead of the usual postage stamp wrestling mat; fresh balmy air replacing the blue smog of a New York *boîte*; moon-drenched tropical gardens instead of four confining walls; a $1.25 entry fee

535

plus drinks that are less than half a buck instead of ... All this plus good entertainment has made Morgan's Club a favorite with vacationing Americans, Canadians, Venezuelans in addition to the local people out for a night on the town.

Newer, equally gay and equally cheap is the *Copa Cabana*, on the west coast between Paradise Beach and Colony Club. Excellent food, a superior calypso cabaret and good dancing to orchestra and vibrant steel band attract a gay international crowd nightly. The orchestra plays till the last guest leaves.

The *Breadfruit Tree* is on the beach road at Hastings. You dine by candlelight, overlooking the ocean, and dance to the music of a three piece orchestra. Open from 8 p.m. nightly.

There is also Thursday dancing at the *Royal Hotel;* Saturday night dancing at the *South Winds, Paradise Beach Club* and *Aquatic Club,* and Wednesday night dancing (dress is formal) at the *Colony Club.*

The *St. Lawrence Hotel* has a Wednesday night steel band session.

Bonnie Dundee, dancing Friday night.

You'll have no trouble finding congenial little bars in Barbados; the island abounds with all types. Just follow your eyes after dark in Bridgetown.

SHOPPING

Americans, Canadians and Venezuelans take advantage of low prices and favorable exchange rates to stock up on English and Scottish woolens and other British imports in Barbados. The shopping hub of Bridgetown is Broad Street. It is lined with department stores and specialty shops with woolens by the yard and British tailors who will make them up on the spot into men's and women's clothing. They're fast too; you can have a suit made in three days. Cost, as low as $60 including material, makes this the outstanding bargain of Barbados. Tip: Be explicit about the cut you want. Broad Street isn't Bond Street, just a reasonable facsimile. There are good ready-to-wear clothes in the shops too, well-tailored of sturdy English flannels and Scottish tweeds. Other imports from the mother country include cashmere sweaters, English china and silver, both sterling and Sheffield plate, and antiques.

Barbados is a great place for trinkets and souvenirs, including jewelry, made of Caribbean sea shells, tortoise shell and other tropical raw materials. These are apt to sound junky, but the Bajuns have a special way with such items and they come up with some striking baubles, bangles and beads. A lot of women who wouldn't be caught dead in sea shell earrings change their mind when they see the tasteful and cleverly-contrived local variety.

Akin to the jewelry in taste and feeling are the hand-embroidered linens and the hand-blocked skirts, sport shirts, blouses, table cloths, napkins and mats in Bajun motifs. These items are several notches above the usual souvenir stuff that are a drug on the Caribbean market.

You'll find baskets, sun hats, bags, and everything in straw work from Barbados and all the islands of the West Indies along with a good selection of other Caribbean handicrafts.

Modern and traditional pottery, the usual avalanche of silk, ivory and teak from the Orient, and tempting array of eatables and drinkables, including Barbados rum, round out the island list. It may not be Haiti, Curaçao or the Virgin Islands, but you'll find enough here, especially in the Ba Ba Blacksheep line, to cart away at least three bags full.

CAVE, SHEPHERD & CO. on Broad Street is the leading department store, and as good a place as any to survey the general offerings of Barbados both in the import and local division. In the latter, the store is richly equipped with Bajun and other West Indian handicrafts, attractively displayed on the ground floor. One of their novelties are island scenes created in balata rubber, a take-it-or-leave-it affair. We couldn't take it. Among the imported temptations: Wedgwood china, Liberty prints, English tweeds and doeskin, sea island cottons by the yard and made up into clothes, and wonderful cashmere cardigans and pullovers. Cave, Shepherd's tailors will make a suit to your measure too. Takes a week. The grocery department isn't Fortnum & Mason, but it's very good, full of cheerful salespeople and expert packers.

DA COSTA & CO. LTD., also on Broad Street has a fine selection of mohair, doeskins, garbadines, airborne tropicals, Irish linens, and a full line of Daks suits, slacks, shorts and skirts at way-below-U.S. prices. Tall gals should ask for Daks "slinkies", especially

created for long stems. Da Costa's tailors seemed to us to have a little more flair than some in other department stores.

WILLIAM FOGARTY LTD. is another Broad Street department store with a big line of imported English textiles, Liberty silks and cottons, china, doeskin gloves, sweaters and other accessories.

C. F. HARRISON & CO. is the fourth, not the least, in the quartet of Broad Street department stores. One of their outstanding departments is Ladies Ready-to-Wear Clothes.

C. B. RICE & CO. in Bolton Lane has made a specialty of tailoring for visitors since 1916, and they have it down to a science. Their skilled tailors and seamstresses will whip up a tropical suit for men or women in a trice, which is to say a couple of days, and at prices that are lower than ready-to-wear back home. They have fabrics and ready-to-wear stuff too, the latter from Austin Reed of Regent Street, for whom Rice is the Barbados agent.

THE LONDON SHOP on Broad Street is another place recommended for the quality of its tweeds and tailoring.

These six places, either shops or department stores, should be able to supply you with excellent samples of one of Little England's specialties, which is tailoring in Big England style. But don't hesitate to shop around; there are many others, some of them in the little back streets called "Gaps", and there prices will be even lower than the ones in the better-known places. Barbados is full of little dressmakers who sew a fine seam and a fast one too.

If you haven't got time for fittings and such, women will find plenty of ready-to-wear things in the department stores and in three Broad Street stores which specialize in this field: *Broadway Dress Shop, Modern Dress Shoppe* and *The Style Shoppe*. Don't let those silly terminal endings put you off; these shoppes are all good shops, tried, tested and recommended.

The Ideal Store in Bridgetown is tops for exclusive women's frocks, wonderful clothes from Italy, England, France.

There are at least a dozen good souvenir and gift shops in Barbados, most of them concentrated in the Bridgetown and Hastings areas.

West Indies Handcrafts at the corner of Bridge and Trafalgar Streets has long been famous for its wares, especially its one-foot-square fibre mats at 58 cents a piece; these can be made up into handsome rugs.

Two places you will not want to miss in the souvenir handcraft department are the *Women's Self Help Association* on Broad Street and the *Craft Center*, Garrison.

The English Shop (in Hastings and in Holetown) has as good a selection of holiday beach clothes for men, women, and children as we saw, also a superior line of costume jewelry, most of it locally made, much of it quite stunning.

Other souvenir and gift emporia are *The Turtle Shop* with branches in the Marine Hotel, Hastings, and Holetown, The *Cottage Gift Shop*, Aquatic Gap, Garrison, and the *Mayfair Gift Shop* at the Aquatic Club on Bay Street.

There are several stores specializing in gifts from the Orient. Among them: *Thani's Oriental Palace*, also known as *Kashmere*, on Broad Street next to the Canadian Bank; *Surti's Oriental Store* at High and Roebuck Streets; *Suliman I. Patel & Sons* on Lucas Street, and *India House* on Broad Street.

We found several reliable jewelers. Y. *De Lima & Co.* had an outstanding selection of bone china, silver, jewelry and watches both at their Broad Street store in Bridgetown and in the Hastings Village branch. *Alfonso B. De Lima* on Broad Street is equally good, and so is *Louis I. Bayley* in Bolton Lane, the local Rolex representative and *J. Baidini*, Broad Street. As for stationers, our personal favorite was *Roberts & Co.* on High Street where we found loads of American and British publications already in stock, so that we could browse, buy and read without the nuisance and delay involved in ordering.

You won't want to leave Barbados without having at least looked in at one of the big Wine and Spirit Merchants, stocked to the ceiling with enough stuff to fit out a fleet of ships. In the old days that's exactly what these grocers were: ships' chandlers, and their shops still have the spices, sauces and spirits dear to the hearts of seafarers, even if they sail on modern cruise ships.

GODDARD'S is that top favorite, island institution, more formally known as J. N. Goddard & Sons Ltd. This big, first class grocery with its upstairs restaurant, is a Broad Street landmark. You'll find curry and chutney, mangoes and cheese, whisky and rum and good English teas. The liquor department is well-stocked and efficient. The prices are enough to inflame your passion for ardent spirits: $2.50 a fifth for London gin; $3 and up for Scotch, 90 cents and less

BARBADOS

for Barbados rum. That last island specialty is not so easy to find at home, by the bye, and when you do find it, it's $7 a bottle. As for liqueurs, they have them in every flavor and every shade of stained glass. Goddard's is only one of the big food and wine centers.

COLONNADE STORES, also on Broad Street, is another and it's an excellent operation, beautifully-organized, well-stocked, staffed with the most helpful sales personnel.

If some rare spice or spirit still eludes you, try any of the other big grocers: *Alleyne Arthur & Co.* on High Street; those reliable ships' chandlers, *Hanschell, Larsen & Co. Ltd.* on Prince William Henry Street, or *Stansfeld Scott & Co. Ltd.* on Broad Street. Singly or among them, they can supply you with everything from A-1 Sauce to Zwieback.

SPORTS AND OTHER ACTIVITIES. Since Barbados is girdled by pink and white "granulated sugar" beaches with calm water on the west side, surf on the east, the island's *swimming* possibilities are hard to beat. Average water temperature is 77 degrees. Principal beaches are at Rockley, Worthing, Hastings, St. Lawrence, Maxwell's Coast, Crane and Bath-sheba. The last two, in the path of the trade winds, are for those who like to ride the Atlantic breakers or duck under them.

On the leeward side the water is usually as calm as a lake. South coast beaches (Worthing, Hastings, St. Lawrence, Maxwell's) are the rock-a-bye-baby type: a little motion, not too much. Best facilities: Accra Beach Club, Barbados Aquatic Club, Royal Barbados Yacht Club, Paradise Beach Club, Coral Reef and Colony Clubs, Miramar, Sunset Gardens, Sam Lord's and Crane Beach.

You can enjoy full membership in Aquatic and Paradise Beach Club for 36¢ per day (subject to change without notice). Visitors are always welcome, and there's always something going on at these places: races, water polo, dancing, aided, abetted or retarded by complementary activities at the bar.

Headquarters for *sailing* are at the democratic, everybody's-welcome Aquatic Club. And adjacent Barbados Sailing Club, as well as the staider Royal Barbados Yacht Club.

Sailing yacht "Carlotta" is available for charter, crew of nine, sails regularly on three week orbit (Barbados, Grenada, the Grenadines, Bequia, St. Vincent, St. Lucia, Martinique.) Take up to 10 people on fee basis per guest. Contact MacFadden, Colony Club Barbados.

The *fishing* is first rate. Barracuda, dolphin, king fish and flying fish are the principal catch. Fishing for the last affords a thrill special to Barbados. You can rent a motor launch or go with native fishermen in their small sailboats. The latter are very primitive when it comes to facilities; the toilet, for example in quite literally the "head" of the boat. You'll be more comfortable in a launch. Boats, guides and bait can be hired at reasonable prices; your hotel manager will arrange it. There seems to be an island shortage of rods and tackle, although they can be had. If you're a serious fisherman, bring your own. Even if you shrink from baiting a hook, you'll be excited by the flying fish, skimming the waters, sailing about, almost leaping into the boat. If fishing for them doesn't tempt you, enjoy it vicariously by watching the commercial flying-fish fleet come in at Tent Bay, near Bathsheba up on the breezy east coast. It's one of the sights of Barbados, just as eating these winged fish fresh from the sea is one of the gastronomic musts.

BARBADOS

There are good stables and horses, this being an English island, and good trails too for *horseback riding*. Your hotel can arrange for rental of a good mount at a fraction of what same would cost you in Central Park.

Golf is played on nine-hole course at Rockley Golf Club three miles from Bridgetown. Visitor green fees are $1.50 per day; weekly and monthly fees will be quoted on application. Incidentally, good golf equipment is considerably less expensive in Barbados than it is in the mother country or in those other offspring, the U.S. and Canada. Visitors are welcome at Rockley; no difficulty. Sandy Lane hotel has a 9-hole golf course.

Tennis is another matter. There are excellent courts at Royal Barbados Yacht Club and the Savannah Club (where exhibitions are held) and at some of the hotels. If you want to play, bring membership card from your tennis or country club at home, and arrange to contact one of the local tennis clubs through your hotel manager.

The three great spectator sports are *cricket, horse racing* and *polo*. There are three big race meetings a year, spring, summer, and autumn on the Savannah of Bidgetown. If you've never seen an island jump, this is your chance. The air vibrates to the rhythms of steel bands and hawkers' cries; the grounds are full of decorated food booths sizzling with those heavenly fried flying fish, and the whole place swarms with Bajun guys and dolls dressed to the gleaming teeth in finery fit for the king of sports. Ascot was never like this. Neither was Belmont or Santa Anita.

If you know and like cricket, you'll be impressed by the skill of the Bajuns in this department. Having adopted the sport from their white English brothers, they now surpass them at it. If you've never seen a match, take the opportunity to do it in Barbados. The general atmosphere of anxious excitement will give you one more insight into Bajun character.

Polo is becoming increasingly popular too in Little England. The season starts in July. Center for most of the spectator sports activity is the Savannah Club in Bridgetown.

It will also be your headquarters if you're a bridge fiend. It is played with great avidity here, at the Bridgetown Club and at the Royal Barbados Yacht Club. You need an introduction to penetrate these rather exclusive precincts. Temporary memberships at low rates can be arranged upon presentation of suitable credentials.

EXPLORING BARBADOS

Bridgetown, capital of Barbados, is best explored on foot, though there are plenty of taxis around if the tropical atmosphere has made you lazy. Take it easy. Despite the cooling trade winds which sweep over Barbados before they reach the rest of the West Indies, Bridgetown is a leeward pocket and can be very warm. Heat cannot mitigate its old-world charm, however. Many tourists, seeing the inner harbor known as the Careenage, are reminded of Venice because of the bridges spanning this Caribbean inlet, which does indeed look like a canal. On closer inspection, the harbor seems pure 18th-century English. When you see the tall masted schooners at the quay, when you see the colorful maubee woman selling

her spicy maubee-bark beer to the stevedores, above all when
you see the harbor police dressed as the tars of Nelson's fleet,
you're apt to whistle the opening bars of *H.M.S. Pinafore*.
The clock seems to have stopped here before Fulton's *Clermont*
first moved miraculously to steam. And that big sailing ship
you see, careened or heeled over on its side (hence the name,
Careenage), is being scraped clean of its barnacles, calked and
painted just as the clipper ships were.

The centuries mingle indiscriminately on the two bridges
with their stream of two-wheeled burro carts, bicycles,
pedestrians, midget English cars, and shiny red and blue
Barbadian busses, fortunately open because no walls could
contain the animated, overflowing crowd. Pause for a moment
on one of these bridges and savor the busy, vivid life of this
little capital of 30,000 souls. Every shade of human pigmentation will appear if you wait long enough. You'll see planters
and businessmen, impeccably turned out as though on their
way to lunch in the West End of London; uniformed school
girls, white, black and in-between; Venezuelan oil men; handsome Negro women, proud of carriage, high of head, balancing
a huge basket on the skull with more ease than a debutante
supports a book in a posture class; turbaned Hindus, Bajun
bucks, British matrons, Portuguese merchants, sailors and
stevedores of half a dozen nations and mixed races. The scene
is dominated by an officer of the law, a Bajun bobbie, resplendent in white jacket, Frank Buck helmet, red-striped,
superbly tailored blue trousers. The Careenage itself is
crowded with schooners from the Caribbean islands, unloading
the produce of the West Indies. The big international ships
would be an anachronism in this setting; they're out in Carlisle
Harbor, monsters of a later age, depending on the services of
tenders and other smaller fry. The deep-water harbor, under
construction, will be ready for the big ships in August 1961.

In this miniature capital, established when the Indians still
roamed Manhattan Island, history sometimes comes up with
some odd juxtapositions of style. The bronze statue of Lord
Nelson in Trafalgar Square, erected before the one in London,
overlooks the neo-Gothic Public Buildings, oddly decked out
with red awnings and green shutters. Inside are the chambers
of the oldest legislative body in the Caribbean. James I, first
of the Stuart kings, was reigning when the first Englishmen
reached Barbados. You can see this monarch's portrait in this
legislative building along with those of his successors. Barbados has always been at least as Royalist as the King.

Cromwell, who sent a fleet to establish Commonwealth authority over the recalcitrant colony, was a mere interloper.

The colorful native pottery market is here on Trafalgar Square and the War Memorial, honoring Barbadians who gave their lives for Britain in two world wars.

George Washington Worshipped Here

St. Michael's Cathedral, symbol of the Church of England transplanted, was first built in 1665. The present structure, constructed of coral rock, dates from 1831, the original church having been smashed up by hurricanes in that year and in 1780. The church's original memorial tablets go back to the 17th century, stone histories of colonial days. The verger says that George Washington came here to worship in 1751. There is no documentary evidence of this, but it seems more than likely. He was an exemplary young man of 19 at the time, and the episode of the cherry tree was a thing of the past. Washington came here from Virginia, accompanying his half-brother Lawrence who was afflicted with consumption. Barbados, it seems, was already noted for its beneficial climate. But there was smallpox in those days. George caught it here and carried its marks with him right into the Gilbert Stuart portrait. It was a mild case, immunizing him, say some authorities, to the ravages of this disease which were to decimate the ranks of his army during the American Revolution 21 years later.

One of the official "sights" of Bridgetown is the "George Washington House" on Upper Bay Street. It's an 18th-century house all right, and a nice one, but local historians doubt that G. W. really slept here. There is documentary evidence that America's first president did rent a house in Barbados for 15 pounds a month "exclusive of liquors and washings", but this was probably not the house. Washington loved Barbados; his enthusiastic description of the island, quoted in the introduction to this section, reads like an early example of tourist promotion.

Aside from the cathedral and "Washington's house", there are no special sights to see in Bridgetown. You'll savor this little town best by wandering through its winding lanes: Literary Row, Flower Pot Alley, poking around the old docks with their venerable stone warehouses and glass-enclosed turret lookouts from which the roadstead could be surveyed for the arrival of merchant friend or fighting foe. If you want to see the little native shops where the Bajuns, not the tourists go, slip over to Victoria Street, just a block north of Broad. If you want to spend a fascinating hour or more, briefing yourself on Barbados history and lore, take a cab to Garrison, a suburb just a mile and a half out of Bridgetown, and visit the Barbados Museum. There's a great miscellany of stuff here: old maps, prints, coins, Indian relics, domestic arts and crafts, and attractive exhibits of Barbadian fish, birds and other fauna.

The roads of Barbados are good, though narrow, and progress can be slowed down, pleasantly so in our opinion, by donkey carts and other primitive aspects of Bajun life and transport. Better allow a full day to swing around the island's perimeter and explore the interior, even though the whole place only measures 21 by 14 miles. The variety of scenery within so small a compass is extraordinary.

Driving south out of Bridgetown, you go through middle class beach resorts like those of the English Sussex coast: Hastings, Worthing, St. Lawrence; the very names are reminiscent of England. You drive through Christ Church, scene of the famous 19th-century "Barbados Coffin Mystery" in which coffins were switched around, stood on their ends, and disturbed in other ways inside a vault to which no one, presumably, had access. These ghoulish goings on caused such an uproar that the coffins were buried elsewhere on orders of the Governor. Tourists, either imaginative, indefatigable or both, still stare at "Chase's Vault", however, though it's been empty now for generations.

The Wild Atlantic Coast

The first part of your drive, through flat corridors of sugar cane, may strike you as tedious. When you come to Crane on the southeast coast, you'll change your mind. From here on the scenery is beautiful, getting more and more so as you drive north along the wildly-spectacular Atlantic coast, which, with its cliffs, plunging headlands, and sometimes turbulent surf, reminds many travelers of the coasts of Brittany and Cornwall. One of the show places here is Sam Lord's Castle, a beautiful early 19th-century mansion in the midst of an estate which overlooks the sea. Builder of the white stone castle was Sam Lord, a kind of landlubber buccaneer whose chief pastime was luring ships to the reef by hanging lanterns in the palm trees so that mariners, seeing them at night, thought they were the lights of ships anchored in a safe harbor. It was an old trick, practiced successfully in Cornwall and by the Nags Head bankers on the treacherous Hatteras reef. When the ships ran aground on the shoals, Sam Lord and slaves took possession of the cargoes, dispatching any sailors who had had the doubtful fortune to escape a gentler death by drowning. It must have been a lucrative business. Sam Lord imported Italian artisans to make his castle a thing of beauty; the plaster ceilings are their work and they are a joy to behold. The present owners of the castle, now a hotel, have kept it up in the style to which Sam Lord was accustomed. The place is furnished with splendid antiques, not the least of which are Sam Lord's mahogany four poster bed and a wardrobe in whose lavishly-carved doors we detected the fine Italian hand of the imported artisan.

Your next stop is Codrington College, which, despite its splendid avenue of palm trees, will remind you of Oxford. The flora may be tropical; the faces of the students black, but this is an English school in spirit and appearance, the oldest (1716) in the British West Indies. Just to the north is St. John's Church, 800 feet high and affording a sweeping view of the spectacular windward coast. The church dates from the 17th century. Its rosy stone exterior has the patina of age.

Where the Flying Fishes Play

Tent Bay, on the coast to the north, is the place to watch the Flying Fish Fleet come in. The hours are irregular, depending on the whim of the fish, but the catch is usually completed in the late afternoon toward 4:30 or 5. Just north of here is Bathsheba, which the natives accentuate on the first syllable. Here the Atlantic booms against the cliffs, dashing high on "a stern and rockbound coast", which is obligingly modified here and there to form stretches of beach where the swimming is exhilirating and still safe. Non-swimmers may want to visit the interesting pottery works at nearby Chalky Mount and watch the native potters at work.

North from Bathsheba, the views get even more spectacular as though they were in competition with each other. That from Hackleton's Cliff, 1,000 feet high, is hard to beat. But it is surpassed all the same by the panorama from Cherry Tree Hill, no parochial vision, but one of the great vistas of the world. Inland stretch Barbados' Scottish Highlands, where live the stand-offish "Redlegs". Below on the coast, Bathsheba looks like a toy village from this height. Mahogany trees clothe the landscape, and a surrealist touch is added by a score of old windmills, once used to grind the sugarcane. That this was prosperous sugar country is amply indicated by Farley Hill, a superb plantation house, partly rehabilitated by Hollywood to star in the film, *Island in the Sun*, but now again falling in ruins. All the techniques of modern stage and screen design were employed to re-create this picturesque relic of former grandeur. The result, with papier maché columns complementing the original façade of the house, is a fascinating combination of reality and make believe.

From Farley Hill, you can cut straight west across the island to Speightstown, the second "city" of Barbados, or you can make a loop to North Point at the top of the island and visit the fascinating Animal Flower Cave. This is actually a series of sea grottos which can only be visited at low tide. The animal flowers live in shallow pools left by the receding tide, strange, finger-petalled blooms that suggest the "Sensitive Plant" of Shelley. They recoil like sentient creatures from the touch of any intruder. Wear thick-soled shoes or sneakers for walking in these caves.

When you reach Speightstown you are on Barbados' celebrated "platinum coast". This is the leeward side of the island, the protected western shore, gently laved by the limpid, aquamarine Caribbean. The road follows the coast south into St. James Parish. The contrast between this and the eastern shore could not be greater. If the latter was Brittany, this is the Mediterranean, calm, brilliant, luxurious. Fortunately it is not so crowded as the Côte d'Azur. Wealthy Britons, Americans, Canadians who have built and are building here are making a conscious effort to keep their haven of refuge tranquil and uncluttered. They are succeeding. Exclusive hotels like the Colony Club and Coral Reef Club have done their part to preserve harmony with lovely tropical gardens and beautifully landscaped grounds surrounding the precincts of elegant beach resorts.

Center of the Platinum Coast is Holetown, more popularly and more elegantly known as St. James. Its church, one of the oldest in the West Indies, is as fashionable as the Abbey. Its font is dated 1684; its brazen bell commands that "God bless King William, 1696." In the town an obelisk marks the spot where Captain Catlin of the *Olive Blossom* is presumed to have landed in 1605, the first Englishman to set foot on the island. He had been driven off his course, and so may be said to have stumbled on Barbados. As the French say, he fell well, as have the current residents of this platinum strip at the west of Eden.

TRINIDAD AND TOBAGO

Calypso Cosmopolis and Crusoe's Island

Most southerly of the West Indies, these two islands became independent in August, 1962. Trinidad is the new government seat, while Tobago is its weekend resort. They could hardly be less alike. Trinidad is the teeming world in microcosm. Tobago is Crusoe's desert island. Trinidad is the Tower of Babel; Tobago is a treehouse. Trinidad is leviathan, Tobago a minnow swimming in the monster's shadow.

TRINIDAD

Once a part of the Spanish Main, Trinidad has the rough rectangular outline of a jig-saw puzzle piece; you can almost see where it should fit into Venezuela just a dozen miles away. The flora and fauna are not insular, but continental, thriving in complete indifference to the ageless caprices of the Orinoco. Nor is there anything insular about the human fauna of this colony. Her citizens have crossed half the oceans of the world to get here. The twain that Kipling said would never meet have met in Trinidad, making this island in many ways the most exciting of the Caribbean.

The rendezvous of races is Port of Spain, Trinidad's febrile capital. East Indians throng the streets, rubbing elbows with Syrians and Lebanese, Chinese, Japanese, Bengalese, half the races of the Near East and the Far. Red-fezzed Moslems, turbaned Hindus, dark women with jewels embedded in their flesh give the place an Arabian Nights air. The thousand and one races of Trinidad! They include the English, Spanish, French and Dutch, at peace after centuries of fighting for this rich island prize; Portuguese, Parsees, Madrassis; Americans and Venezuelans, their nostrils dilated with the smell of oil and pitch. Above all is what might be termed the "basic stock", those dusky descendants of African slaves emerging into the light of freedom as a new creative force in politics and art. Their tribal sense of rhythm, which the planters tried to suppress by forbidding the slaves to have drums, now expresses itself in three musical phenomena that have conquered the civilized world: calypso, limbo and steel bands. You will hear them all here at their best in the land of their birth.

The mingling of all these racial strains has left a physical mark on Trinidad and given a richness to its "national" life which few other islands can match. You will see every known costume and fabric worn in the streets of Port of Spain: saris, dhotis, Palm Beach suits, sea island cottons, Liberty prints, batik, madras, Japanese obis, Javanese sarongs, lace mantillas, Chinese split skirts and trousers, American aloha shirts. If you're a frustrated pukka sahib here's your chance to wear a pith helmet without feeling foolish. Anything goes on the head from a Borsalino to a basket of fruit.

The architecture of the city mingles the latest in flat slab and column construction with Victorian fantasies and the domes and minarets of Arabia. There are mosques and synagogues in Trinidad, Hindu temples, Buddhist shrines, the gray, steepled churches of England, a Catholic cathedral, a Benedictine monastery and just about every house of worship you can think of. The island is home to Jew and Gentile, Hindu and Moslem, the followers of Zoroaster and Mary Baker Eddy.

This wonderful diversity is reflected in island place names. Port of Spain replaces Puerto de España. Towns with Hindustani names like Fyzabad are cheek by jowl with English St. Mary's, Spanish San Fernando, Carib Siparia, pre-Carib Rampanalgas, French Plaisance and Roussillac. You drive from Pointe-a-Pierre to Waterloo by way of Claxton Bay and California.

Sense of Identity

Even more important than the diversity of Trinidad is its

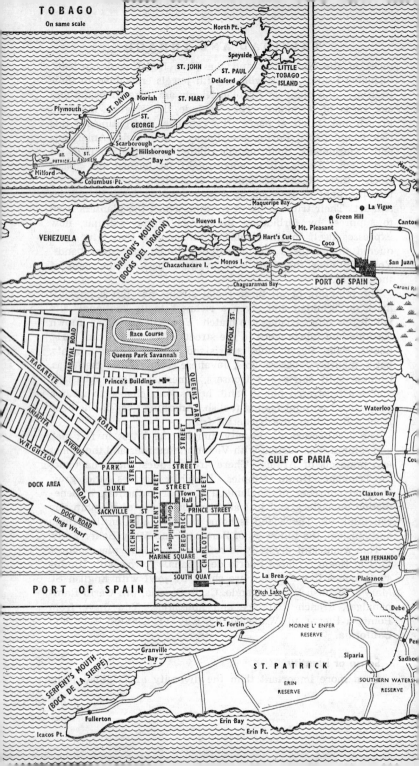

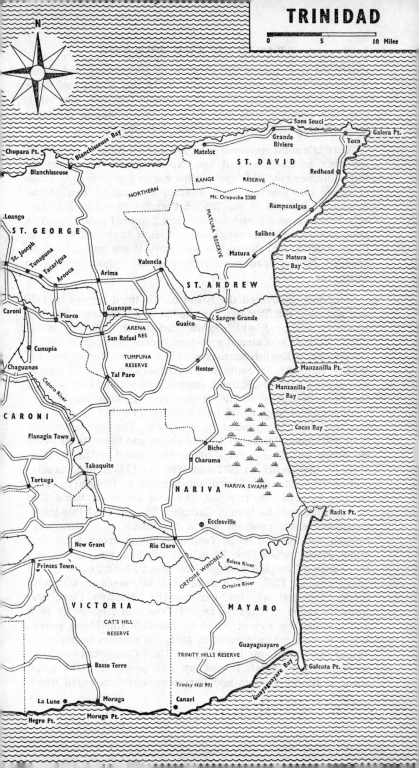

unity. As time passes, the children of many races and colors who make up the polygot population of this island feel more and more Trinidadian. They go to school together, they work and play together, and they all have two things in common: pride in their island and confidence in its future.

There is a solid economic basis for this confidence. Trinidad's revenues annually exceed her expenditures. Approximately thirty-six per cent of island income comes from the production of crude oil; the rest from asphalt, agriculture, one of the largest sugar mills in the British Commonwealth and Angostura Bitters whose secret formula is a Trinidad invention. The land suffered no impoverishment when it broke off from the Spanish Main, and the people who work it are industrious. In addition, Port of Spain is a commercial hub without peer in the Caribbean.

Columbus discovered the island on his third voyage in 1498 and named it La Trinidad for the three hills around the bay where he anchored, which symbolized the Holy Trinity to his pious mind. It was almost a century before the Spanish settled it. Two early English tourists were Sir Robert Dudley and Sir Walter Raleigh. En route to the Orinoco and his ill-starred search for El Dorado, Raleigh stopped just long enough to burn the Spanish colony to the ground and discover the strange viscous lake of pitch which now enriches Trinidad by contributing to the world's production of asphalt. The Spanish rebuilt their settlement, imported African slaves and began to cultivate the fertile soil. The thriving colony was raided by the Dutch in 1640, by the French in 1677 and 1690. In 1783 a royal proclamation from Madrid offered inducements to foreigners of all nations to settle in Trinidad, the sole condition being that immigrants must be Roman Catholic. The result of this initial Caribbean crash program was a big influx of settlers, augmented by many French families coming from Haiti and other places where the French Revolution was giving the black man all sorts of strange ideas about liberty, equality and fraternity. In 1797, the British, as usual, were at war with Spain. Trinidad was captured by His Majesty's Fleet, was formally ceded to England by the Treaty of Amiens in 1802, and became the richest jewel in Britain's Caribbean crown. When slavery was abolished in 1834, the negroes began cultivating the soil in small holdings and the Colonists brought in laborers from India. It was at this point that the great wave of Hindu, Moslem and Parsee immigration began which now accounts for nearly a third of Trinidad's 800,000 population.

The Bards of Trinidad

During World War II, the United States built three army bases and a naval base in Trinidad in a lend lease deal designed to protect the Caribbean and allied shipping from Nazi incursions. Among the visible results of this peaceful invasion: the beautiful "Sky-Line" highway to Maracas Bay, an increase in the mulatto population, and the immortal Calypso verses:

> "Since the Yankees came to Trinidad
> They have the young girls going mad
> The young girls say they treat them nice
> And they give them a better price.
> They buy rum and coca cola
> Go down Point Cumana
> Both mother and daughter
> Working for the Yankee dollar."

This direct and earthy commentary on recent events is typical of Calypso, those Negro folk ballads in 2/4 and 4/4 time which evolved here in Trinidad and have spread throughout the Caribbean, thence to New York, London, Montreal and Paris. It is impossible to date the emergence of Calypso as a folk art. Its wellsprings are in the melodies of Spain and the tribal rhythms of Africa. Even the origin of the name is obscure. Certainly it owes nothing to the classics, has nothing whatsoever to do with the sea nymph who kept Odysseus 7 years on her island of Ogygia, though it has been known to detain latter day travelers almost as long in Trinidad. The theory that Calypso is an anglicised corruption of the African word *kai-so*, meaning bravo, is as good as any. The important thing is that Calypso is the living expression of a very lively people; its warmth, vitality and rhythm are the essence of Trinidad.

The Calypso singers adopt high-sounding names: King Pharoah, Atilla the Hun, Lord Eisenhower, Lord Nelson and the like. They improvise on any theme: politics, sports, personalities, scandal, graft, the high cost of living, love and marriage, love without marriage, and every event of human life. The lyrics are frequently charged with coruscating sarcasm, *double entendre*, scandalous innuendo. More than one politician has been defeated at the polls because his shortcomings have been dinned into the electorate's ears by the devastating satire of Calypso.

Government officials have often been embarrassed by the

popular expression of disapproval explicit in Calypso. As early as 1897 a famous Calypsonian called Richard Coeur-de-Lion rebuked the Governor of Trinidad for his "rudeness" in dissolving the Port of Spain Borough Council in Calypso verses which echoed throughout the island. More recently, Atilla the Hun enjoyed a huge popular success with a typical mince-no-words Calypso: *Britain, Why Don't You Give Up The West Indies?* There is no doubt that Calypso has played its part in hastening independence, and will continue to reflect and shape the course of events in Trinidad.

World events are grist for Calypso's mill. A simple and memorable commentary emerged from all the uproar of Edward VIII's abdication:

> "Tis love and love alone
> That forced King Edward to leave the Throne."

Local happenings and island prejudices are equally inspiring. Trinidad's big-island contempt for the small islands comes out like this:

> "Yes, the product of Grenada is nutmeg
> Every woman in the place got bandy leg."

Often verging on the libellous and obscene, Calypso has had its ups and downs with the censors. But these folk ballads continue to "hold the mirror up to nature", to reflect the life of the most high-spirited of all the West Indians.

You'll hear Calypso singers and bands in the "tents", the three public halls of Port of Spain, in clubs, on beaches, in hotels and at parties in private homes. Like love, their magic spell is everywhere.

Steelbands and Carnival

No less ubiquitous in the Land of Calypso are the steelbands. It took the Trinidadians to add the fourth dimension of steel to the conventional orchestral categories of strings, woodwinds and brass. With an intuitive skill and taste that still amaze musicologists, they contrived new instruments out of oil drums, gas tanks, pots, pans and biscuit tins. Sounds tinpanny in the worst sense of the word. But the vibrant percussive effects which Trinidadians coax from these steel instruments have been compared to "melted gold and molten lava, the cross between the melody of a harpsichord and a clarion, an organ and a Hawaiian guitar." The steelbands have their origins in the Shango drums of slaves from the Yoruba and Madingo tribes of Africa, drums whose music was forbidden by the planters. As always in the rich cultural melting pot of

Trinidad, there were other influences in the development of this new musical phenomenon, notably the percussion instruments brought in by East Indian immigrants.

Whatever its ancestry, the Steelband as we know it today, was born on V-E Day in 1945, when the population of Trinidad grabbed garbage pail lids, empty cans and anything they could lay their hands on to beat out a victory march in the streets of Port of Spain. It wasn't long before the resonance of metal containers was being controlled by marking their surfaces into segments that would produce the notes of the scale. An uncanny sense of rhythm and tone guided the "untutored" ears of the steelband tuners. Within a year there were ensembles of "ping pongs", "piano pans", "second pans", "tenor kittles" and "tune booms". Within a decade steelbands had carried a new and fascinating musical art to the United States and Europe. With Calypso, steelbands have become a symbol of the irrepressible vitality of Trinidad. You'll hear the highly original music of both no matter when you visit the island, but the best time is after New Year's when all the island musicians start tuning up for the greatest Carnival of the West Indies.

Most carnivals, including those of Nice and Monte Carlo, are Sunday School picnics compared to the Carnival of Trinidad. For color, rhythm, fabulous costumes, and sheer, unrepressed animal spirits, it is unsurpassed. The excitement really starts right after New Year's in Port of Spain with the Calypso bands rehearsing new songs nightly before huge audiences in the "tents". One of these songs will be chosen by popular vote as the "road-march" of the Carnival, the greatest honor that composer, band and singer can hope to attain. Meanwhile, leaders of various costume groups are deciding on carnival themes, designing and sewing their elaborate costumes in secret. (The Trinidadian will save up for a whole year to afford his Carnival costume.)

In spite of all the preparation, the Carnival has a completely spontaneous air. By the Sunday before Carnival, the town is boiling over with excitement. Carnival opens at dawn on Monday with "Jour Ouvert", which the Trinidadians have gaily corrupted to "Joo-Vay". In the evening the top Calypsonian is proclaimed King, and the Queen of the bands and Carnival Queen are chosen. The whole place starts "jumping up", literally leaping straight into the air to the compelling rhythms of the steel bands, which are now outdoing themselves to win the accolade of public approval. The parades start with bands of Trinidadians up to 500 strong acting out some of the wildest and zaniest historical, Biblical, political pantomimes you ever saw in costumes and headdresses that would put the Ballet Russe to shame. The lid is off. The vibrant throbbing of the steel bands gets faster. The pace accelerates. And now it isn't just the paraders who are "jumping up". The spectators are doing it too, tourists and residents alike, caught up in this relentless, compulsive rhythm which transcends all questions of color, race and social position. We've seen American school marms and staid British dowagers unable to keep their feet still at the height of Trinidad's Carnival. The gaiety is more than infectious; it's irresistible. The celebration progresses from mere abandon on Monday to overmastering rapture on Tuesday morning and reaches throbbing, ecstatic climax on Tuesday night. By that time all notions of "the correct thing", all concepts of Anglo-Saxon reserve, anything formal or prim has been swept away by a primal tide. The dregs of decorum are dissolved in rum. Pandemonium reigns, a wild tumult in the streets and in the blood. Everybody is jumping high and higher. Suddenly it's midnight and Ash Wednesday. Carnival collapses like a punctured baloon. In the morning Trinidad goes back to the worries of a work-a-day world.

Somehow, even the aftermath is exhilirating. Carnival is calypsotherapy, a steel band purge. People have got the Old Nick out of their system, at least for another year, and there are smiles through the haze of hangovers. It's bad for business, a psychiatrist told us.

> 'Twas the greatest compliment that ever had
> Been paid to the Carnival of Trinidad.

PRACTICAL INFORMATION FOR TRINIDAD

HOW TO GET THERE. Trinidad, focal point in the Caribbean for air transport, is well served. From New York you can fly by *Aerolineas Argentinas, Varig Airlines,* or *Pan American Airways,* via Bermuda, Antigua and Barbados by *BOAC,* via Caracas by *Linea Aeropostal Venezolana.* From Miami you may take your choice among *British West Indian Airways* (direct or via Islands); *KLM Royal Dutch Airlines* (via Curaçao), *Pan Am.* (by way of Caracas), and *Varig Airlines.*

From Montreal take *Trans-Canada Airlines* or BOAC (via Bermuda, Antigua and Barbados).

Aerolineas Argentinas operates a twice weekly service between Buenos Aires, Rio or Sao Paolo, Trinidad, and New York.

TRINIDAD AND TOBAGO

From London, BOAC has a weekly flight to Trinidad, Barbados, Bermuda.

Island hoppers have a big choice. *BWIA* links Trinidad by air with Grenada, Barbados, St. Lucia, Martinique, St. Thomas, Guadelope, St. Vincent, Antigua, St, Kitts, Puerto Rico, Jamaica and Bermuda. *Leeward Islands Air Transport* links Trinidad with Anguilla, Antigua, Beef Island, Barbados, Dominica, Montserrat, Nevis, St. Eustatius, St. Kitts, St. Martin, St. Vincent. *Pan Am* offers flights from Puerto Rico, Martinique, Guadeloupe, Antigua, Haiti, Barbados, St. Thomas and St. Croix. *Trans-Canada* links Trinidad with Barbados and Antigua. *Air France* has twice weekly flights between Trinidad, Martinique and Guadeloupe, between Trinidad and St. Martin, Surinam and French Guiana. *KLM* connects Trinidad with Curaçao and Aruba three times weekly.

Saguenay Shipping has passenger service between Trinidad and Montreal. *Booth Lines, Pacific Steam Navigation Co., and P. and O. Orient Lines Passenger Services Ltd.,* call monthly from the home port of London, England, *Alcoa Steamship Company* has weekly sailings from New York, Baltimore, New Orleans and Mobile to Port of Spain. RNS also runs weekly boat service from New York and Gulf Port. *Moore-McCormack Lines* provide a monthly service between San Francisco and Port of Spain.

Federal Govt-Shipping Service serves Trinidad, Grenada, St. Vincent, Barbados, St. Lucia, Dominica, Antigua, St. Kitts, Montserrat, British Guiana, Jamaica. Ships of the *French Line* link Port of Spain with Pointe-a-Pitre, Fort-de-France, Kingston, Puerto Rico, Bridgetown, La Guaira. The *Potomac* links Trinidad to Grenada, St. Vincent, St. Lucia, Barbados.

Check with travel agent to see what lines offer stopover privileges at other Caribbean vacationlands en route to or from Trinidad. BWIA and Pan Am have these in summer along with reduced rates from $40 to $60 lower than regular fares. Intelligent use of stopover privileges can provide you with a lot of free island hopping.

PASSPORTS, VISAS. Neither are required of U.S., Canadian and U.K. citizens with return ticket providing they do not stay more than six months in Trinidad. Some form of identification such as a birth certificate is required, however. Non-U.S. citizens arriving from the U.S. and planning to return there must produce a U.S. Certificate of Income Tax Compliance and a U.S. re-entry permit.

CLIMATE. January through May is the dry cool season. June to December is wet, but the showers, though heavy, are intermittent. The trade winds do their usual air-conditioning act. But, despite tourist proclamations of delightful climate the year-round, the heat can be and often is in the 90's in summer. Compensations are low rates, rum punches, Angostura bitters, and cool relief when that evening sun goes down.

CURRENCY. The West Indian dollar, currently worth 59 cents, but American and Canadian currency are accepted almost anywhere at prevailing rates of exchange. You can bring in all the money you like but are not supposed to take out more than you brought in. You can make small economies by tipping in this money instead of your own currency. There is an exchange booth at King's Wharf.

TRINIDAD AND TOBAGO

HOW TO GET ABOUT. There are over 2,000 miles of good roads on which you will kindly keep to the left. Trinidad has a public bus system and 96 miles of passenger railroad out of Port of Spain. These provide the cheapest way of getting around and rubbing elbows with the natives, but it can be a jolting experience with olfactory overtones.

Taxi service is excellent. Rates are 75 cents W.I. for the first mile, 18 cents for each additional half mile. This is for one or two persons. For each additional person add 18 cents to the total tariff. Ingenious, wot? Taxis can also be rented at $3.60 W.I. an hour per four-passenger vehicle. These rates apply within the city limits.

If you want to drive yourself, your U.S. license is valid. The following reliable firms in Port of Spain have cars for rent: *Petter Rentals*, 89 Mucurapo Road; *Hub Taxi Service*, 30 Borde Street; *Henry Pain's Car Hire*, 92 Tragarete Road. This last organization also rents movie cameras and tape recorders. Rates for cars are around $15 W.I. per day ($9 U.S.).

Sightseeing tour operators in Port of Spain are: *Bacchus Taxi Service*, 8 Petra Street; *Battoo Brothers*, 67b St. Vincent Street; *Chippy's Taxi Service*, 44 Jerningham Avenue; *Hub Taxicabs Ltd.*, 30 Borde Street; *Sam's Taxi Garage*, 63 Richmond Street.

HOTELS. Trinidad, long satisfied with its oil-rich economy to the point of neglecting its visitors, is now turning its attention to the tourist potential with a program that should be a model for the rest of the West Indies south of Jamaica. More than $7,000,000 (U.S.) has been budgeted for a five year development plan. The multi-million dollar "upside down" Trinidad Hilton Hotel, a 260-room luxury resort, has recently opened its doors to the public. In the meantime the *Bel Air* and *Normandie* hotels have by this time completed extensive renovations, financed at least in part by Trinidad's wide-awake Industrial Development Corporation.

There is also a 120-room hotel coming in Tyrico Bay. To stimulate further development, Trinidad grants a ten-year tax holiday on all income derived from dividends and interest in approved hotel projects, and other tax concessions on new capital investment in tourist amenities.

ATLANTIS BEACH HOTEL. One of Trinidad's few beach resorts, it's on the southeast coast at Mayaro, a two hour drive from the capital. There are 17 rooms, some with balconies overlooking beach. T. D'Aguair is the manager, and he operates on the American Plan. Rates are $9 single, $16 double per day.

BAGSHOT HOUSE. An attractive guest house in the residential district of Maraval in Port of Spain. Well-stocked bar, and night-club, the Gay Cavalier. A spacious verandah overlooks two acres of lovely private gardens, and the hotel is within walking distance of the Country Club and its pool where Bagshot clients enjoy guest privi-

leges. There are 20 rooms with private bath. Dr. N. G. Sturm is the manager. Rates, American Plan, winter $9.60 to $13.50 single, $19 to $27 double; summer $9.60 single, $19.20 double.

BEL AIR. Near the terminal building at Piarco Airport, a modern 62-room operation with air-conditioned dining room, cocktail lounge. Steelbands and calypso singers are on hand to entertain Sunday nights. The manager of this enterprise is Mr. James Smith, and the service is absolutely top flight. Most of the amenities for a happy vacation or stop-over are available, including swimming pool and cabanas. The food is first rate. Sunday buffet

556

dinner here is an event with floor-show provided by Limbo and Bongo dancers. European Plan rates are in winter $8.40 to $9.60 single, $13.20 to $16.20 double. Air conditioning available on request.

BERGERAC. Twenty-six rooms and a swimming pool in the Maraval section of Port of Spain, near Golf and Country Clubs. American Plan. Summer $10.80 to $15.60 single, $18.30 to $24 double. Winter $15.60 to $16.80 single, $24 to $26.40 double. Mr. de Lima, the manager, will make attractive weekly rates if you plan a longer stay.

BRETTON HALL. A thorough face lifting has glamorized this 110-room hostelry in its own spacious grounds near Port of Spain's Queen's Park Savannah. New features include an attractive outdoor swimming pool and an air-conditioned night club, The Cyndiana Room, with nightly entertainment by outstanding local singers and dancers. There is also a beauty parlour on the mezzanine floor. I. N. Akow is the manager. The hotel operates on the Continental Plan (bed and breakfast). Rates are in winter $6 to $12 single, $12 to $21.60 double. All rooms have baths; air conditioning available.

FARRELL HOUSE HOTEL at Claxton Bay is a small luxury hotel in a restful setting. Swimming pool, garden terrace, putting green. Rates on application.

GULF VIEW APARTMENT. On the outskirts of Port of Spain, overlooking the ocean, this apartment-hotel has 12 suites, each of which can accommodate four persons. Air conditioning, balcony living rooms, ultra-modern housekeeping facilities plus maid and cook to whip you up an Armadillo stew at the clap of a hand. Continental Plan rates are in winter $10.20 to $15 single, $15 to $16.20 double. Catering is done on request.

NORMANDIE. A modern resort hotel, so up-and-coming that it doubles its room capacity between trips. There are now 60 rooms and suites, attractively furnished and air conditioned, with balconies overlooking a grand swimming pool. The hotel is in Port of Spain near the Botanical Garden. Excellent food with a French accent. Mr. Deguilhem is the manager. We regret but we must give two warnings: a) you will not sleep at all when there is dancing on the terrace restaurant on Tuesdays and Fridays. The steel band's din will penetrate under your blankets. b) the suites are overpriced. They are just large rooms partitioned by a screen. The rates are in winter $14.40 to $16.20 single, $20.40 to $24.60 double, $40.20 suites, Continental Plan.

PAN AMERICAN GUEST HOUSE. The second of the Piarco Airport Hotels, about half a mile from the terminal building. There are 44 well-decorated, over-air-conditioned rooms with bath, cocktail lounge, view of field. An efficient operation, but not as much fun as the rival Bel Air. European Plan rates: winter $8.40 single, $13.20 double. Has good American food, swimming pool.

QUEEN'S PARK. This is the dowager empress of Trinidad hotels; she's been here, overlooking the Savannah, since 1895 when the Widow of Windsor was still on the throne and the Duchess of Ditto had never been heard of. More British than Britain, more British even than Barbados, the Queen's Park is one of the landmarks of the West Indies. Conceived in a day when labor costs were cheap, the hotel has acres of public rooms including a roof terrace with grand view over the Savannah and bordering hills. Recent improvements include redecoration, air conditioning. Outside rooms are preferable; those on the interior patio are apt to be noisy. There are 130 rooms. Mr. J. B. Fernandes is the owner. European Plan rates $7 to $14 single, $11 to $20.50 double.

TRINIDAD AND TOBAGO

SIMPSON'S SHORELANDS HOTEL. This is Port of Spain's first seaside resort hotel, built in a residential area four miles west of the main business section. It is only a couple of hundred yards from the Trinidad Yacht Club. Small (only 12 rooms), the emphasis is on first class service and comfort. Every room has its own balcony and bath and the grounds feature the first salt water swimming pool in Trinidad. On a half acre plot with a sea frontage on the Gulf of Paria, the hotel has full facilities for water sports. Winter rates Continental Plan, $8 single, $14.50 double.

TRINIDAD HILTON. This multi-million dollar "upside down" luxury resort is Trinidad's largest modern hotel. Its 260 rooms were built on 20 acres of forested hillside provided by the government. The lobby is entered from the top and rear of the building and guests then descend to their rooms situated below the crest of the hill. Among other original notes: on the pool terrace at the top level of the hotel, the swimming pool is shaped like Trinidad, the wading pool like Tobago! A restaurant-night club, *La Boucan*, features distinctive European and West Indian cuisine plus entertainment. There is also a large ballroom, several private dining rooms, and noteworthy shopping arcades. Rates, European Plan, are $11 to $19 single; $16 to $24 and up for doubles, all with bath and terrace.

The accommodations so far listed are Trinidad's best to date. In addition to these there are a number of guest houses with which we do not have sufficient personal experience to warrant recommending them to American, Canadian and U.K. tourists. The guest houses often have desultory plumbing, conveniences and service. They do have the advantage of being inexpensive and of providing close daily contact with friendly Trinidadian fellow boarders.

The cheapest one that has come to our attention is *The Cosy Nook*, with rates as low as $3 per day European Plan. The following guest houses in Port of Spain will send rates on application; managers' names are in parentheses: *Cosy Nook* (W. Schwartz), *Dundonald Hall* (Mrs. H. C. Movat), *Fabienne's* (Mrs. E. L. Charbonne), *Nothnagel's* (Mrs. S. Nothnagel), *Stone's*, (80 Dundonald Street), *Roxburgh's* (Mrs. E. Roxburgh), *Tropical*, (3b Chancery Lane).

Pelican Inn, a 26-room hotel in a charming garden setting near the Savannah Park, is now under new management.

GASTRONOMY

The food is just as cosmopolitan as the island. There are standard British, American and Continental menus to which have been added Creole, Chinese and Indian specialties. Trinidad is famous for "the King and Queen of creole soups", *sans coche* and *calaloo*. The former is a fabulous ragout. Here's what's in it: fat pork, salted beef, pig tail, a couple of pounds of meat, onions, chives, split peas, butter, yams, dasheen, cush-cush, cassava, sweet potato, Irish potato, green plantain, coconut and green pepper. Something is missing. Ah yes, the dumplings! The "Queen of Creole Soups" is a mere broth by comparison. All calaloo requires is three bunches of dasheen leaves, two crabs, 12 okras, two onions, a bunch of chives, a clove of garlic and a couple of ounces of fat pork and salt beef.

Don't be afraid to try these wonderful soups. Deborah Kerr and Robert Mitchum survived a special Creole dinner served up to them on Tobago on the completion of the film, *Heaven Knows Mr. Allison*. Crab calaloo was only one of the courses on this menu. The film company also plowed through a peppery pigeon peas soup, stewed *tattoo* (an armadillo by any other name would taste as sweet), fried iguanas, *manicou* or possum stew, pork souse, green salad and *tum-tum*. Tum-tum sounds like an anti-acid, and that's what it ought to be after a meal like this. But in Trinidadian tum-tum equals mashed green plantains.

That pork souse mentioned above isn't a squiffed pig; it's a spicy creole dish garnished with cucumber, lime and onions, seasoned with hot pepper. Sometimes it's made with fish instead of pork. Served cold, it's a great picnic favorite, and calls for rum punch.

In addition to *armadillo* (whose tender, succulent meat bears no resemblance to its armored plate exterior), the Trinidadians are fond of venison, wild duck, *quenk* (the onomatopoetic word for wild pig) and *lappe*. The last, island hare, is considered the greatest of delicacies.

Try the *pastelles*, a kind of Spanish-island concoction of meat folded inside cornmeal and wrapped in a banana leaf. *Crab matete* is crabmeat and farina. Crab backs are crab meat taken from the shell, highly seasoned, then put back in the crab shell.

Among the Indian contributions are red hot curries and something called *roti*, which is like a king size crepe, rolled around a filling of chicken, fish or meat and seasoned to the palate-burning point.

Delicious bean-sized oysters are one of the specialties of the local seas. From freshwater streams comes the *Cascadou* or *Cascadura*, a fish that makes excellent eating, especially when stuffed. According to local legend, whoever eats the cascadura returns to Trinidad to end his days, a rather ambiguous phrase which does not make it clear whether one returns for that purpose or whether one can look forward to a happy old age in the Land of Calypso. In any event, the cascadura is symbolic, and you'll probably be tempted to take home one of the East Indian cascadura bracelets with its silver scales as a souvenir.

Rum is the national drink of Trinidad, and they serve it in many ways including the biggest Planter's punch you ever saw. The joys of rum and coca cola and gin and coconut water have both been recorded in calypso verses. The latter combination is especially recommended when the gin is poured into a freshly-cut green coconut and the mixture sipped from the shell in the shade of the very tree that produced the nut. Since Trinidad is the home of Angostura Bitters, there are lots of pink cocktails around. The secret formula of Dr. Siegert is applied here with a heavy hand, not by the drop as in more temperate climes, but by the spoonful. A kindred bitters, *Carypton,* is used to make the Trinidad specialty known as the green swizzle.

RESTAURANTS. The dining terrace of the *Hotel Normandie* gets our vote for top honors among Trinidad's restaurants. M. Deguilhem offers excellent French cooking plus a dash of Creole color here and there, and the combination is hard to beat. *Pan Am's Piarco Guest House* is by far the best in our opinion for good steaks, chops and other simple fare imported from the States daily by Pan American planes. The ice cream is wonderful.

The *Tavern-on-the-Green,* named after the one in Central Park, Manhattan, is good for outdoor lunching and dining; we had our first tattoo there, armadillo with a delicious sauce, and will go back for more anytime it's on the menu.

Speaking of restaurants with a view, the *Belvedere* is a joy, high upon a hilltop with Port of Spain's red and white rooftops beneath you. You lunch and dine on an open verandah with a million dollar vista at moderate prices.

La Boucan is the restaurant-night club at the new Trinidad Hilton. Dine in charming atmosphere and stay for the show.

The Cosy Nook on Abercromby Street is famous for its steaks. Pleasant and intimate atmosphere here; a good place, incidentally, to order calaloo.

There are so many Chinese in Port of Spain that you can hardly walk down the street without running into a Chinese restaurant. Among the leaders: *Lotus Restaurant, Kimling, China Clipper* and the *Ying King.*

You can count on good food at the *Trinidad Country Club* and *Trinidad Yacht Club.* If you want to get out of town and watch the big birds land and take off at Piarco Airport, the *Bel Air* has excellent food, well nigh perfect service, and moderate prices, a rare combination worth investigating.

The *Maravel Hotel* is also noted for its superb West Indian cuisine.

NIGHT LIFE. As befits a big international seaport, there's something doing every night in Port of Spain. The avidity of the average T'dadian for nightlife is extraordinary. Nightclubs throb with calypso and steel band rhythm throughout the year. In order to satisfy the local appetite for after-dark dancing and entertainment, the hotels stagger their dinner dancing and floor shows so that there's something going on practically seven days a week.

One of the newest and most elegant night places in Port of Spain is the *Penthouse Bar and Lounge* on the top floor of the new six-story Salvatori Building at the corner of Henry Street and Marine Square,

North. Dancing and floor shows nightly.

The *Trinidad Country Club* takes over on Tuesday with a bingo game that rivals roulette in excitement, and on Thursday with a supper-dance.

The *Normandie Hotel* has buffet dinner, floorshow and dancing on Tuesdays. On Thursdays there is an "Italian Night", and on Fridays there is dinner dancing with floor show. The *Bel Air* has dancing from 6 to 11 p.m. on Sundays, and so does the *Trinidad Yacht Club*. There is dancing and floor show on Wednesday and Saturday nights at the *Lotus Restaurant* on Henry Street.

For years night life in Port of Spain, apart from regular semi-formal dancing at leading hotels and restaurants, had been confined to a string of rather sordid dives along Wrightson Road, which, incidentally, has now dwindled down to one—the *Diamond Horseshoe*. But recently several more sophis-

ticated night clubs have opened their doors.

The *Cyndiana*, small pleasant bar in the Bretton Hall Hotel on Victoria Avenue where the piano or a small orchestra plays for dancing. There is a different attraction every night and food is also served.

The *Carnival Club*, a member club, is located on the corner of Saddle and Long Circular Road. The atmosphere is gay but intimate with low lighting and an excellent small combo that plays almost every night. If you are only in town for a short time and don't want to become a member, friends may get you in.

Capri-Ischia, Oddly named restaurant-cum-nightclub on the Long Circular Road in completely tropical jungle decor. Excellent steak dinners and good orchestra for dancing on Saturdays.

All of these clubs are air-conditioned, have well stocked bars and are open until 2 a.m. nightly and until 4 a.m. on Fridays and Saturdays.

SHOPPING

Port of Spain is one of the big bazaars of the West Indies. Its shops are stocked with goods from all over the world, and you'll be surrounded by hawkers the minute you step ashore. Look out for characters offering silver thread bangles in the streets. They'll sell you stuff at a quarter of the price originally asked, and your pride in the bargain will be vastly deflated when you examine your purchases more closely. All that glitters is not silver. Stick to the shops recommended below, and you won't be disillusioned. Most shops will deliver packages to the Tourist Bureau on the wharf as a convenience to cruise trippers.

Trinidad, though by no means a free port, does have bargains, especially for Canadians and Americans, thanks to the favorable exchange rate now prevailing. Among the outstanding buys are imported British fabrics: woolens, tweeds, Liberty printed cottons, silks and Irish linens. Men's and women's clothing can be made to order from these fabrics, and the whole operation, bolt to back, is skilful, swift and cheap. A man can get a tweed suit, material and work, for as little as $65 WI. Tropical fabrics are even less.

Recommended men's tailors are *Harry Clark, Ltd.* and *John Hoadley & Co.*, both in Marine Square; *Fitz Blackman & Co.* in Abercromby Street; and *London Fashion* and *Tip-Top Tailor*, both in Frederick Street, the main shopping avenue of Port of Spain. Tip-Top will make you a suit in six hours! For custom-made dresses, it's *Vanity Fair* at 43 Frederick Street.

At the same address and next door at number 45, you'll find *Gil's Lingerie Shop,* foaming with French and Madeira lace. Here you'll find some of the prettiest hand-made underwear in town plus various gift items that will have you throwing caution to the trade winds. There are some beautiful Italian silk ties, French brocaded evening bags and silk scarves, wonderful embroidered table linen from Madeira, France and Italy, good buys in native and Florentine straw, and French perfumes at prices as low as those in Curaçao can be obtained at *Stecher's,* just across the street, where you wil also find the aristocratic Piaget, Mido and International Watch Co., timepieces.

Speaking of perfumes, there is an even larger selection in Port of Spain's well-stocked department stores: *Stephens & Todd, Ltd.* at 8 Frederick Street, *J. T. Johnson, Ltd.* at number 13, and *William Fogarty, Ltd.* at 62 and 74 Marine Square. These three British em-

poria will give you a comprehensive view of Trinidad's merchandise.

Stephens & Todd are strong on English China (Denton, Minton, Wedgewood, Spode and Royal Doulton). They've also got some Limoges porcelain, Lalique glassware from Paris, and handcut English crystal. Their selection of local souvenirs is worth examining too.

Fogarty covers the same ground at 74 Marine Square (see their Marlborough china) while their Central Store (at no. 62) has a superabundance of tempting stuff from all over the British Empire: cashmere sweaters, doeskin gloves and suiting, Scotch and Irish tweeds, Irish linen sheets, tablecloths, napkins, Kent's shaving brushes, Dunhill pipes, Church shoes, and yards and yards of Liberty prints.

If Fogarty doesn't have it, *Johnson* will. The Dent's doeskin gloves are an outstanding buy here, and the selection of local dolls, ties and scarves are among the best of the Trinidad souvenirs. If you're getting shoppers' feet at this point, Johnson's has a delightful air-conditioned *Angostura Bar* upstairs in their Men's Shop.

Don't forget to visit the shopping arcades in the new *Trinidad Hilton.* They have a little bit of everything and charge the same prices as in town.

You'll have a grand time looking over the glittering crop of intricately-made East Indian filigree jewelry in Trinidad's shops. The celebrated cascadura bracelet and cunningly-contrived jewel boxes are among the most popular items in this island specialty.

The *Bombay Bazaar* at 14 Frederick Street has an excellent selection of these along with other Indian imports in ivory, leather, silver, teak, and brass.

Ursa's at 14 Frederick Street specializes in Oriental merchandise

from China and Japan, novelties, jewelry, statuettes, etc.

Lakhan's Tourist Center, The *Islamic Oriental Bazaar,* both on Western Main Road, St. James have good silver jewelry, ivory figurines and the like. But you haven't really

562

Mountain trails in Venezuela are eight-lanes wide

cased the local jewelry situation until you've browsed through *Trinidad Jewelry, Ltd.* at 17 Frederick Street. They have a wide selection of filigree jewelry in 9 carat gold as well as in sterling silver. There's some interesting butterfly-wing and Denton china jewelry here too, and a tempting selection of Trinidad charms for your bracelet.

Y. De Lima, three doors away at no. 23, also has a plethora of these and the East Indian jewelry that makes such a lasting souvenir of Trinidad.

For Trinidad handicrafts in straw, fibre and wood (including African figurines), start off at the Trinidad and Tobago Tourist Bureau at King's Wharf or the *Handicraft Shop* at Piarco.

Check the work at *West Indies Bible Institute* at 15 Carlos Street. Things to look for are those wonderful palm fiber tote bags, cleverly waterproofed in a manner invented by the Caribs. These are perfect for all the excess baggage you pick up in the shops.

Wood carving is the specialty at *V. Kacal*, 45 Frederick Street, but there's nothing exclusively insular about his point of view; ask to see his Czechoslovakian crystal.

The African figurines, carved from local Trinidad woods, are an outstanding bargain at *V. Wilson*; some of them are still as low as a dollar.

Among the island souvenirs that will delight both child and adult are the many dolls which reflect Trinidad's cosmopolitan culture. Steel band players, native limbo dancers, calypso characters like *Minnie of Trinidad*, sari-draped Hindu beauties, Moslem Hosein dolls: these are just a few of the colorful miniature personalities that you can take with you.

In the liquor department, you'll find rum at about $8 a case, top brands of Scotch at about $26. Too bad about Uncle Sam's limitation on duty-free import. In accordance with that customs restriction, Trinidad's stores have a nice neat rum package for you. Contents: one gallon.

Your best shopping bets for liquor are *Angostura Wine and Spirit Service* (at the corner of Marine Square and Frederick Street); *Fernandes & Co. Ltd.*, 27 Henry Street, *Hi-Lo Super Market* at the junction of Frederick, Queen and Chacon Streets and *United Grocers*, 26 Frederick St.

Trinidad, of course, is *the place* to buy calypso and steel band records. They are recorded right here on the island, hence free of import taxes.

Biggest selections are at *William Fogarty Ltd.*, 14 Chacon Street; *Sagomes Radio Emporium*, 44 Marine Sq.; and *Sports and Games Ltd,*. 28 Henry Steet. See also the offerings at the Tourist Bureau.

If you're really gone on steel bands, you can buy an actual playing-size pan for about $12. The *Handcraft Shop* at King's Wharf has them along with ceramic figurines of steel band players, steel band dolls, and steel band records. They are authentic souvenirs, for the steel band is the most striking symbol of creative Trinidad today.

SPORTS AND OTHER ACTIVITIES. The best *swimming* beaches are on the east coast on the other side of the island from Port of Spain. But Maracas Bay, 14 miles from the capital, has excellent swimming and the best *surf-boarding* in the Caribbean. The long, slow, continuous swells are just right for this sport. Maracas Beach is a beautiful long curve of glittering white sand, fringed with palm trees. Other out-

Old Holland in the New World: the Dutch Antilles

standing beaches are Las Cuevas, Manzanilla, Mayaro, Balandra and Toco. If you want pool swimming, the Trinidad Country Club's piscine is first rate.

Tennis may be played on top flight courts of Trinidad Country Club, Tranquillity Square Lawn Tennis Club, Marine Square Tennis Club and Colonial Tennis Club.

The *golf* course (18 holes) at St. Andrews Golf Club in Maraval, three miles from Port of Spain, is unsurpassed in the Caribbean. Three month visitor memberships are available upon introduction by a member of the club.

There's another 18-hole course at Pointe-a-Pierre and a 9-holer at La Brea's Brighton Golf Club.

Fishing is popular throughout the year. June through October is the best time for trolling for King fish and Spanish mackerel along the north coast, in the Gulf of Paria, and in Serpent's Mouth, one of the straits that separate Trinidad from Venezuela. Wahoo, Bonito, Skipjack, Red Fish, Barracuda and Tarpon are some of the denizens of the deep that haunt the waters around Trinidad and Tobago. You'll enjoy fly fishing, bait casting and spinning for mountain mullet and giant gobies in the streams along the north coast of Trinidad.

Mr. Jack Spratt, c/o Port of Spain Aquatic Club, Cocorite, has a cabin cruiser renting at $9 U.S. per hour. In Tobago, *Cecil Anthony* of Buccoo Point is a guide for reef fishing, spear fishing, lobstering and deap-sea fishing; he knows guides and has boats available. Motor boats and launches rent at $1.20 U.S. per person up.

See *Aquan & Correira*, Two Sea Lots, Port of Spain, to rent cheaper fishing boats with inboard or outboard motor. Trinidad Yacht Club is a helpful center for aquatic activities and will supply further information on boat charter.

Hunting offers exceptional thrills in Trinidad because of the wide variety of quarry. October 1 to December 31 is the season for armadillo (tatoo), lappe, and the peccary or wild hog which Trinidadians call quenk. Hunting license is obtainable from any Warden's office for $1.20 BWI per year. To bring firearms into Trinidad, you must apply to Commissioner of Police, Port of Spain. Give details of make, bore number of weapon, duration of your stay. Most frequently used are 12 and 16 gauge shotguns; .303 rifle for those tough-skinned alligators. You can buy equipment at *Sports & Games Ltd.*, 28 Henry Street, Port of Spain, and make contact with guides through this store. The season is year round for agouti, alligator (cayman), deer, manicou (opossum), mongoose and squirrel. November 1 to March 31 is the season for wild duck and other game birds.

Spectator Sports include *cricket*, which T'dadians follow with B'badian passion. This island has contributed some of the great batsmen and bowlers of the century, so good that they have inspired epic calypsos. The cricket season is from January to June.

Horse Racing, with at least 28 days of racing scheduled each year, is exciting and colorful. The big meets at Queen's Park Savannah in Port of Spain are held after Christmas and in June. The Easter meeting at San Fernando and the racing in May and August at the *Arima Race Club* are equally popular, bringing out huge crowds dressed to kill in all the fancy fabrics of the island.

The rich folklore of Trinidad has already been suggested in remarks on calypso and the Carnival. Remember that many races make up this fascinating island melting pot. An event worth a voyage is the Hosein Festival, celebrated by Trinidad's 50,000 Moslems who still bow toward

Mecca at the muezzin's call from the minaret. The festival starts 10 days after the appearance of the new moon in the first month of the Moslem calendar. Since both these events are variable, the date cannot be fixed. Sometimes it's in September. Last year it was in mid-July. Only Allah and The Trinidad Tourist Board at 48 East 43 Street, New York, know when Hosein (pronounced *hosay*) will take place. The festival honors two brothers, Hosein and Hassan, sons of Fatima and Ali, who were murdered in a holy war. Throbbing drums, whirling paper moons, colorful processions with "tadgeahs" of bamboo, tinsel, mirrors and multi-colored paper, mark the two day festival in Port of Spain, San Fernando, Arima and other centers where the Moslem population is large. Hosein has lost all traces of religious fanaticism, however, and it is typical of Trinidad that Hindus, Negroes and others now join in the general celebration.

If you get a chance to see the *Little Carib Company* of Trinidad, don't pass it up. This company of 31 talented West Indian dancers and drummers was organized by dancer-choreographer Beryl McBurnie, who has devoted her life to preserving authentic island music and dances. Their presentation of the Limbo, Bongo and Shango, West Indian dances of African inspiration, will give you a dramatic insight into the creative energy of a people. The company also performs the East Indian and Chinese dances which form another essential part of Trinidad's exotic culture. The Little Carib Company has appeared successfully in Canada and the United States. This group and other talented native sons and daughters participated in the first West Indies Festival of the Arts in Port of Spain in 1958. The festival was a resounding success.

EXPLORING TRINIDAD

Port of Spain with its twain-shall-meet flavor is best explored on foot. It is a big city, set between high hills and the curving shoreline of the Gulf of Paria. The view from the hills embraces a checkerboard of red and white roofs, one of the busiest harbors of the Caribbean, and the shore of the Spanish Main clearly visible across the Bocas or the Dragon's Mouths. At night the twinkling lights of Venezuela beckon romantically even to the weariest of travelers. By day, Port of Spain hums with the febrile activity of an international capital and seaport, and its 94,000 multi-colored citizens provide a passing show of rare, almost unique fascination. It is a dynamic city, preoccupied with its own importance and such civic problems as slum clearance which is tidying up what was once as abject a waterfront as one could find.

Best place to see the inhabitants in their native habitat is in the busy downtown section. Start at Queen's Wharf, walk one block north to Independence Square (formerly Marine Square), no square at all but a street, and mosey along Frederick Street, a perfect place for window-shopping and for people-gawking. By the time you've walked another block north to Queen Street you will have seen at least half of the United Nations on parade.

Beyond Queen Street on your left is Woodford Square. The big neo-Renaissance building facing you from St.Vincent Street is known as Red House. Built in 1906, it is the seat of the Government of Trinidad. The Anglican Cathedral of the Holy Trinity dominates Woodford Square from the south side. The Gothic spires of Oxford are no more British than this lovely monument of England-in-Trinidad. Step into the cool interior long enough to admire the carving on altar and choir stalls.

Religious architecture in Port of Spain is rich and as varied as the population itself. Worthy of mention is the Roman Catholic Cathedral of the Immaculate Conception which dates from 1816. Some visitors will no doubt be interested in seeing the distinctive religious buildings of the Eastern peoples in Trinidad. A large mosque is situated at the eastern end of Queen Street in Port of Spain. An even more impressive mosque, the Jinnah Memorial, can be seen from the Eastern Main Road near St. Joseph. A Hindu temple has recently been constructed in Port of Spain and small ones are to be found in many parts of the island.

Just three blocks east of Woodford Square is an interesting landmark in Port of Spain, the Angostura Bitters Factory. Established in 1875, this factory used to be open to visitors, but this is unfortunately no longer the case. Angostura Bitters is known all over the world, and every drop of it is made in Trinidad. The secret formula is, of course, closely guarded.

Back on Frederick Street turn right and walk seven blocks to the fashionable promenade of Port of Spain, the Queen's Park Savannah. This 200-acre lung with its racecourse and cricket fields is Trinidad's tropical version of St. James's Park, the Green Park and the Mall rolled into one. On the east can be seen the new Trinidad Hilton Hotel. On the south side, part of which is rather confusingly called Queen's Park West, are the venerable *Queen's Park Hotel* and its staid contemporary, The Royal Victoria Institute, built at the time of Queen Victoria's Diamond Jubilee. This is the Museum of Trinidad, guarded by Spanish cannon which date from Britain's capture of the island in 1797, and proudly displaying near its entrance the anchor which Columbus lost in Trinidad, dredged up 400 years later at Point Icacos off the southwest coast.

TRINIDAD AND TOBAGO

The Savannah

Surrounded by institutional buildings, the Savannah is so English you expect to see bowler hats and canes. But this is a land of turbans, pith helmets, straw hats and the bare heads of American tourists braving a midday sun that no mad dog or Englishman would go out in. You'll see the mixed children of a dozen races here, jiggling, I-got-rhythm negroes talking and gesticulating to themselves, the public of Port of Spain enjoying life. It's a wonderful place to watch the floating world of Trinidad.

The Savannah is also the best vantage point from which to explore the architectural diversity of the city. The west side, Maraval Road, is especially fascinating. Here you will find Stollmeyer's Castle, as Scotch baronial in appearance as Abbotsford, Balmoral in the tropics. Nearby is White Hall. Despite its nominal evocation of London, it's as Moorish as the Casbah. Once a sumptuous private residence, it served as American Army headquarters in World War II, and is now occupied by the Premier of Trinidad and Tobago. Also on Maraval Road is Roodal's Residence, so typical of the Second French Empire that you'd hardly be surprised to see the Empress Eugenie descending the stately perron. More Trinidadian in style and inspiration is the nearby pink and blue fantasy of Queens Royal College, but the chimes that ring out from its tower clock are authentically Westminster to the last leaden circle.

North of the Savannah on Circular Road are the Botanic Gardens and Governor General's House. The latter, beautifully situated within the precincts of the former, is L-shaped in honor of its first occupant, Governor James Robert Longden. The building combines arches and loggias in Italian Renaissance style with iron columns and railings of Victorian inspiration. Literary buffs will be charmed to know that Charles Kingsley lived in the guest cottage on Government House grounds and worked on his book, *At Last*.

The Royal Botanic Gardens are well worth spending some time on. They cover 63 acres and have been developing to their present impressive state since 1820. There are higly qualified licensed guides and the variety of trees and flowers is astonishing. Lotus lilies sacred to the Egyptians, the holy fig tree of the Buddhists, the bleeding "raw beef" tree, monkey pods, monkey puzzles, Indian and Chinese Banyans, Ceylon Willows are just a few of the exotics growing here. There is a spectacular orchid

house, a fernery, a nutmeg ravine, a riot of tropical flowers and
shrubs. You'll find the guides (they are walking encyclopedias
of garden lore and legend) at the entrance to the gardens, and
you will discover them indispensable. This is one tour that's
recommended even if you can't tell a caladium from a cactus.
The nearby Emperor Valley Zoo is an added attraction, providing
an excellent introduction to the fauna of Trinidad. Recently
enlarged, it now boasts some foreign elements, like lions, tigers
and American bison, which give the zoo an international flavor.

After all this flora and fauna, lunch and a view from
the Belvedere on Chancellor Hill may be in order. It's up
behind the Botanical Gardens, too steep and tiring a climb to
be taken without the assistance of a taxi. After lunch take a
taxi tour of the painted Hindu temples and gleaming alabaster-
white Moslem mosques of Trinidad. T'dadian taxi drivers,
about the politest and most intelligent in the West Indies, are
honest, and will take you to the most interesting places of
worship, ending with the Arabian Nights vision of the Jama
Masjid Mosque at the eastern end of Queen Street. A number
of temple-mosque-and-church tours are also offered by the
operators mentioned in *How To Get About*.

The Jama Masjid Mosque is within easy walking distance of
the Roman Catholic Cathedral, just two blocks away in Independence Square. Their proximity is one more indication of the
fabulous multicultural quality of Trinidad. As though to emphasize it, both cathedral and mosque are just a step from the
Eastern Market, most easily entered from Charlotte Street.
Don't miss this, and don't forget your camera. The stalls are
loaded with green, red and yellow peppers, both the hot and the
sweet variety; gourds, pumpkins, marrows, ginger root, cassava,
huge milk-white dasheen, purple egg plant, green and blushing
mangoes, bananas, plantains, lettuce, spinach, cress and figs.
The only thing more colorful than this home-grown produce
is the people who grew it, the people who are selling it, and
the people who are buying it. More than any market, mosque
or temple, the human race remains the crowning glory of Port
of Spain.

Around Port-of-Spain

Thanks to Pitch Lake and its inexhaustible supply of asphalt,
Trinidad has 2,000 miles of the best roads in the Caribbean.
They traverse mountains, plains, green valleys, sugar, cocoa
and coconut plantations, every possible variation of tropic
scenery. The island is large enough to provide motorists with

all day drives, small enough so that you can become acquainted with it in a short time. The following tours, with time duration suggested, can be taken either on your own or under the auspices of one of the Port of Spain sightseeing tour operators listed under *How To Get About*. All mileage indications are for round trip from Port of Spain.

Laventille Hills. An eight mile run to the east of Port of Spain by way of Belmont and Laventille, returning by the Eastern Main Road. High point of the trip is visit to the shrine of Our Lady of Laventille. At the top of this church stands an immense statue of Our Lady which is one of the landmarks of Port of Spain. It is illuminated at night on the 13th day of each month between May and October and can be seen from almost any part of the city. The panoramic view from this shrine is second to none. On the thirteenth day of each month between May and October there are special services in the chapel commemorating 3 apparitions of the Virgin to the children of Fatima, Portugal. Allow about an hour for this trip.

Fort George. Built by Governor Hislop in 1805, this fort is on a peak 1100 feet above Port of Spain. Formerly accessible only to hikers, it can now be reached by jeep road. Now a signal station, Fort George offers a series of uninterrupted views in all directions. The one to the west, overlooking the Boca Grande and the mountains of Venezuela is especially impressive. Although the round trip from Port of Spain is only 10 miles, better allow two hours for this.

Caroni Bird Sanctuary. Open only from July 1 to October 31, this 437-acre sanctuary is 7 miles from Port of Spain. Permits to visit it are issued free by the Trinidad and Tobago Tourist Board. There are about 6,000 Scarlet Ibis in this area, and a special "hide" has been constructed from which you can watch them. Best time to go is just before sunset when the birds come in in a blaze of color from their feeding grounds. The surroundings are fascinating in themselves, with lakes full of blue, mauve and white lilies, alligators resting on the mud-banks, oysters growing on trees. Tours by flat-bottomed boats may be taken. Charge is $9 for a three hour glide through this exotic wonderland. Better allow at least half a day for the entire excursion.

Western Main Road. A 16 mile trip past Cocorite and Point Cumana, (immortalized in the calypso, *Rum and Coca Cola*) to the United States Naval Base. You'll probably want to take photographs of St. Peter's waterside church en route. This is a level run between the hills and the sea, not spectacular but very lovely all the same. Allow a couple of hours if you want to get out and see the sights.

Morne Coco Road. A clockwise tour starting on the Western Main Road, thence via Four Roads to Petit Valley, over the Morne Coco Road to Maraval Village, and back to Port of Spain by the Saddle Road. Never more than eight miles from Port of Spain, you are far far from the madding crowd. Beautiful scenery, and out of this world by moonlight. Allow two hours for this leisurely 15 mile jaunt.

The Saddle. Another circular run, encompassing half the beauties of the island within a radius of 18 miles. The Saddle is a pass athwart the ridge which separates the valleys of Santa Cruz and Maraval. You'll see superb Samaan trees, one of which, the "great one" with a branch spread of one acre has to be seen—and photographed—to be believed. Luxuriant vegetation and splendid views of the Santa Cruz Valley characterize this trip. After descending from the Saddle, the road runs under vaulted arches of giant bamboo. Tour operators do this trip in two hours; it can be done more quickly.

The North Coast Road or *"Skyline Highway".* This tour—34 miles, three hours—is the most popular of all shore excursions with Caribbean cruise passengers. You go over the Saddle, then wind for seven miles through the Northern Range to Las Cuevas Bay. Driving about a thousand feet up, you have one splendid view after another, the grand climax being the hundred mile east-west sweep from Tobago to Venezuela. Take your swim togs. Mountain-hemmed Maracas Beach is a dream of white sand, limpid water and coconut palms. There are good cabin facilities for a nominal fee.

If you have time for only one Trinidad excursion, this Skyline Highway to Maracas should be it. If you haven't brought a picnic lunch, there are two small restaurants and a bar at Maracas Beach.

Blue Basin. This is the sort of idyllic dell where you expect to hear the horns of elfland. It's at the head of the Diego Martin Valley, reached via the Western Main Road, Four Roads, Diego Martin and the government-owned River Estate with its 16 miles of hibiscus hedge lining the road. A cool cascade tumbles into the fresh water pool of Blue Basin, and the swimming is divine. You have to walk half a mile from the car park at the end of the road to reach this enchanted spot. Don't wear high heels. The footpath is on the steep side, but the destination warrants the exertion. You can do this 20 mile round trip including the trail scramble in a couple of hours, but the best is to take a picnic lunch and make a real excursion of it. It was after a refreshing swim in Blue Basin that we ate our first pork souse, sitting on a rock (us, not the souse) and staring at that 300 foot waterfall. A memorable picnic in a setting worthy of Titania and Oberon.

Asphalt Jungle

The Pitch Lake. The contrast between this section of Dante's inferno and the fairyland of Blue Basin could hardly be greater. Pitch Lake is 105 acres of thick, hot, viscous grey pitch that the Trinidad Tourist Board has likened to "a magnified elephant skin". You can walk on this tough hide if you want to; the experience may remind you of your childhood when you couldn't resist taking a few gumshoe steps in fresh hot tar. The lake, which is 285 feet deep at the center, has, according to the Tourist Board, supplied 15,000,000 tons of asphalt to the world over the past 70 years and has paved the streets of the world from Lake Shore Drive to the Champs Elysées. It may be grey and ugly but it has a certain economic beauty which helps to keep Trinidad regularly in the black. You can see excavations in progress, huge slabs of the stuff being removed to pave the roads of Trinidad and the world. The level of the lake is said to be dropping six inches a year. At that rate it should be good for another half millenium, 570 years to be precise, by which time there will probably be interplanetary sources of pitch or a reasonable synthetic facsimile available.

The 130-mile round trip to Pitch Lake from Port of Spain will take you along the western coast through Couva, chief home of East Indian hand-made jewelry; Pointe-a-Pierre with its great oil refinery, the largest in the British Commonwealth; and San Fernando with its large East Indian population, the second city of Trinidad. Two short detours are interesting. The first, east of San Fernando will take you to Usine St. Madeleine, largest sugar refinery in the British territories. The second is south of St. Mary's to the Fyzabad oil wells and Siparia. Here in the church of La Divina Pastora is the celebrated Black Virgin of Siparia, clad in leather, surrounded by tokens of recognition from grateful former invalids who have been healed by her intercession. Some who have received her help and failed to recognize it with a contribution are said to have been fatally stricken as a result of this negligence. A fete and procession are held in honor of the Black Virgin in April of each year.

TRINIDAD AND TOBAGO

This tour, the ninth of our suggested itineraries, can not be done comfortably in less than a full day, say ten hours at the minimum. These excursions, especially the Pitch Lake and Skyline Highway outings, should give even the short-term visitor a memorable idea of the great scenic variety as well as the economic importance of Trinidad.

The Trinidad and Tobago Tourist Board lists a dozen more tours in addition to these, and will furnish all information on them upon request. Anyone staying longer than a few days in Trinidad will certainly want to explore the exhilirating east coast of the island with its splendid beaches of firm sand, fringed by green and silver coconut palms trembling in the trade winds, and washed by the white-capped breakers of the Atlantic endlessly rolling in. At low tide these beaches become a thoroughfare, an unimaginably beautiful super highway stretching from Manzanilla Point south to Guayaguayare Bay. North of Manzanilla Point is the perfect half-mile crescent of Balandra Beach. On the northern coast in the Toco district there is a series of lovely beaches and secluded coves, linked together by rugged headlands plunging down to those sparkling blue waters which are here disputed between the Atlantic and the Caribbean. One look at this undeveloped coast, now being made accessible by the construction of the North Coast Road, will convince you of Trinidad's almost limitless tourist potential. Barring an atomic cataclysm, sun worshippers will probably be coming here long after Pitch Lake and the oil wells are dry.

TOBAGO

Twenty-one miles northeast of Trinidad, Tobago is the 30th and poorest ward of the bigger island. But she is a beautiful stepchild, possessed of all the raw materials for a happy holiday. Twenty-six miles long by seven wide, the island has verdant mountains, beautiful white beaches, deep azure bays, almost all the exotic flowers and trees that can grow in the tropics, and more exotic birds per acre than any other land.

Plowing southward from Grenada to Trinidad, Columbus must have sighted this fish-shaped island lying to port on his third voyage in 1498. He may have been snoozing, however, for there is no mention of the island in his log. Even more remarkable, he failed to give the place a name. Subsequent Spanish colonists called it Tobago from the Indian word *tabaco*, meaning the Y-shaped pipe with which the natives inhaled tabaco, pardon us, tobacco smoke.

TRINIDAD AND TOBAGO

In the 18th century when Sugar was King of the Caribbean, Tobago raised cane with the best of them, producing as much as half a million gallons of rum in 1793. This will explain why four nations and assorted buccaneers battled for more than a century over this rich little prize. The Spanish, the Dutch, the French and the English all laid hands on Tobago at one time or another, but the British were the most tenacious. Although the French got it under the terms of the Treaty of Amiens in 1802, the English seized it the following year at gunpoint, of course. This shotgun wedding was legalized in 1814 when the Congress of Vienna tried to tidy up the world.

The great sugar plantations are no more. Tobago imports its rum today from Trinidad, and ekes out a living on cacao, copra, lime juice and tourists. The last, grown from American, English and Canadian stock, bids fair to become the island's most important crop.

Tobagonians are fond of telling the world that their land is Robinson Crusoe's island. Since Daniel Defoe never set foot on any isle but England, and since Alexander Selkirk, the flesh-and-blood prototype of Crusoe was actually marooned on the Pacific island of Juan Fernandez, Tobago's claim would seem to be grounded more in the realms of gold than in the swamps of science. But do not underestimate the power of poetic truth. You will see Crusoe's cave on Tobago, and you will agree that this isle, whose dazzling splendors were south-sea-island enough for *Heaven Knows Mr. Allison,* is a more suitable place for R. Crusoe and his Man Friday than Juan Fernandez. If there are doubts about the identity of Crusoe's island home, there can be none when it comes to those other romantic explorers, The Swiss Family Robinson. Their tree house was right here on Tobago. Mr. Walt Disney has recorded the fact on color film. And seeing is believing.

Swiss Family Robinson, Robinson Crusoe: both names evoke a mental image of the tropics just discovered, still unspoiled. Tobago is about as close as one can come to a realization of that romantic picture. This is perhaps the secret of its charm for the traveler. The climate, averaging between 80 and 84 degrees, is cooler and less humid than that of Trinidad. Another attraction is the economic factor. Off the sea lanes of the big cruise ships, this little sea-girt paradise was until recently one of the least expensive of West Indian resorts. Tobago is all heaven and this too, but it is not inexpensive any longer.

TRINIDAD AND TOBAGO

PRACTICAL INFORMATION FOR TOBAGO

HOW TO GET THERE. Unless you are traveling by private yacht, all entry is from Trinidad. There are flights every hour on the hour in the new air shuttle service from Piarco Airport in Trinidad to Crown Point Airport near Scarborough, Tobago, by *British West Indian Airways Ltd.* Flight time is 25 minutes. Round trip fare is $22.50 WI. Two government coastal steamers ply the sea route between Trinidad and Tobago, providing service four times weekly from Port of Spain to Scarborough, including the new car ferry, *Bird of Paradise.* The trip takes 6 hours. Round trip fare is $13 WI. Note to bad sailors: this trip can be uncomfortably rough.

PASSPORTS, VISAS. Same as for Trinidad. Tobago is a ward of the bigger island, and there are no more formalities involved than if you were going from New York to New Jersey.

HOW TO GET ABOUT. Public buses, surprisingly modern and very cheap, make several daily trips from one end of the island to the other.

Taxis are plentiful and cheap, about $2.50 BW per hour. Sightseeing tours are arranged by your hotel. Hotels will also arrange for self-drive cars at prices as low as $8 to $10 per day. There are 220 miles of good road. Driving is to the left. Your own driver's license is valid in Tobago. Bicycles and horses may also be rented.

HOTELS. Until recently Tobago was a haven for escapists longing for the simple comforts without too many frills. Those days are gone forever. New hotels have sprung up which are as slick and streamlined as any on the major tourist islands, although so far they are smaller. They tend to be crowded on weekends by Trinidadians on regular visits to their resort "colony". All prices are slightly less in summer.

ARNOS VALE BEACH HOTEL. About a mile from Plymouth, six from Scarborough, this is an attractive, recently-built "Bermuda Guest House" hotel, with central building and adjacent cottages overlooking a palm-shaded beach. Beach House is well equipped with bar, showers, lockers. Week-end lunches served right on beach are a popular feature. A sail boat, car service and riding horses are available for guests. There are 20 bedrooms, each with its own private bath and veranda. Mr. and Mrs. Cooke run the show, and provide excellent meals. Rates are $20 to $22 single, $34 to $38 double.

BACOLET INN. A mile from Scarborough, this is a nice old-fashioned bungalow guest house, superbly situated on a spit of land that juts out into the sea and has its own beach of hard white sand. *Curlew Cottage* has several double rooms with private bath and veranda overlooking the ocean, hot water and sundeck. You dine on a lovely big open porch with a splendid view up and down the coast. There are 25 rooms. W. Mendes is the manager. His rates are $7.50 single (with semi-private bath shared by two rooms); $14 double, $30 for a suite. Horses available for riding about Bacolet's 1250 acre estate.

BIRD OF PARADISE INN. At Speyside on the northeast coast, just opposite Bird of Paradise Island. The setting is first rate and so is the food. There's a private beach. A well-run small hotel (14 rooms) owned by E. Lau. Rates are $9 to $15 single; $18 to $30 double.

TRINIDAD AND TOBAGO

BLUE HAVEN HOTEL. The Blue Haven is situated on a promontory at Scarborough, jutting into the Atlantic. There's a good beach, a paddling pool for kids, a barbecue terrace for eating al fresco. Service and all the basic comforts plus these extras: steel bands, twin engine cruiser for deepsea fishing, covered and open launches for visiting Buccoo Reef and trawling for shells. There are 43 rooms and baths, many with private balconies and air conditioning. The rates are $18 single; $30 to $36 double.

CASTLE COVE BEACH HOTEL. Half a mile from Scarborough on the beach, this is an intimate, well run place. Its dining room features Chinese as well as West Indian and American dishes. There are 10 rooms with bath. A. Zeller, the manager, will arrange for self-drive cars, bicycle rental, and conducted tours to Buccoo Reef, Bird of Paradise Island, and other points of interest. Rates are $10 to $12 a day single, $20 to $24 double.

CROWN POINT HOTEL. Superbly situated on Crown Point at the south-western tip of Tobago, this is a modern luxury hotel with swimming pool and air conditioning. Jacob Straessle is the manager. There are 37 exquisitely decorated rooms and three suites, all with private bath and lovely views over the Caribbean south toward Trinidad. There is European cuisine supervised by an outstanding Swiss chef and West Indian dishes served in a relaxed atmosphere. Rates are $21 per day single; $36 to $39 double: Tobago's most expensive accommodations; in fact, in our opinion it's overpriced.

DELLA MIRA GUEST HOUSE. A pleasant 11-room hostelry in Scarborough, efficiently run by N. T. Miranda whose rates are the lowest of the recommended hotels on the island: $6 to $9 single, $11 to $15 double.

HOTEL ROBINSON CRUSOE. A mile from Scarborough, this top favorite has a beautiful view across the bay to the capital and enjoys the natural air conditioning of Atlantic breezes. It's the social center and informal club of island residents, giving visitors a chance to meet the local British and American settlers. A big comfortable veranda lounge overlooks a good swimming beach. There's a pleasant dining room and well-stocked bar. T. Gomes is the manager and owner, and guests are unanimous in praise of his personality and professional aplomb. The food is good at the Robinson Crusoe, and there's dancing come Saturday night. Rates are $15 to $18 single; $24 to $27 double.

Note: The cheapest way to enjoy a longer stay in Tobago is to settle down in a furnished cottage, many of which come with the services of a servant. There are a dozen or more of such cottages, some running as low as $90 a month. A list of these accommodations will be furnished on request by the Trinidad and Tobago Tourist Board, 48 East 43 Street, New York 17, New York.

FOOD, DRINK AND RESTAURANTS. The cuisine similar to Trinidad's is British, American and Creole plus some notable seafood specialties: lobster, conch and jackfish. Rum is the "comfortable waters" of Tobago. Other than hotel dining rooms, there is only one restaurant, the *Swiss Inn*, former Alma Guest House. The Sunday beach luncheon at the *Arnos Vale* is a delightful, delicious and delovely super-picnic: five courses, hot and cold. It's open to the general public. Hotel *Robinson Crusoe* is about the best place for calaloo and other Creole food. *Castle Cove Hotel* does well by West Indian dishes too and serves the best Chinese food in Tobago.

575

TRINIDAD AND TOBAGO

NIGHTLIFE. Wholesome and healthy. There's dancing at the *Robinson Crusoe Hotel* on Saturday nights, and the *Bluehaven* has steelband music and limbo dancers at their barbecue suppers. There are two small nightclubs, *The Swallow* and *La Tropicale.*

SHOPPING. You won't find the myriad shops of Trinidad, but latterday Crusoes can fill their requirements and their bags too in Scarborough's stores. Merchandise for sale is similar to that found in Trinidad shops but the choice is likely to be much narrower. Prices, on the other hand, tend to be lower. East Indian fabrics and jewelry are outstanding buys.

Miller's Stores Ltd. in Market Square has everything from soup tureens to fishing poles.

Joseph Sabga & Sons is another department store, specializing in dry goods.

William Fogarty Ltd. of Port of Spain has a branch here in Scarborough where you will find the same low prices prevailing for French perfume and fine English goods.

For native goods and handcrafts you have a choice between *Fitz Blackman* and the *Tobago Tourist Bureau Shop;* both are on Main Street and Market Square.

Try *James A. Scott & Co.* for hardware; *Sports & Games Ltd.* for fishing and snorkeling supplies. *Miller's* will be your headquarters for film, post cards and the like.

For rum, bitters and other "ardent spirits", it's *Young's Grocery* on Burnett Street.

SPORTS AND OTHER ACTIVITIES. The golden beaches and blue green bays which ring this island are a standing invitation to swim, sun-bathe and picnic. You'll find coves so solitary that you really will feel like Crusoe. In addition there are the excellent hotel beaches, the popular *Aquatic Club* at Pigeon Point Beach where temporary memberships can be arranged, and beatiful stretches of sand and clear water at Man o'War Bay, Courland and Mt. Irvine Bays.

Snorkeling is the outstanding specialty of Tobago, especially over the celebrated Buccoo Reef, an underwater wonderland that has few equals. Your hotel will arrange for you to visit the reef, which must be timed to coincide with low tide. A boat takes you out to the reef in Buccoo Bay, and you can explore the submarine gardens through glass bottom boxes or with snorkel or diving mask, usually supplied by your hotel. Even non-swimmers can enjoy this experience, wading knee deep in water of incredible clarity. You become so absorbed in gazing at these exotic coral gardens and their schools of many-colored striped and spotted fish that you forget about time and the problems of the world above the surface. The great danger, even for the already tanned, is over-exposure to the blazing tropic sun whose power is amplified here by reflection. It is imperative to wear an old shirt and pants on this expedition as well as a broad-brimmed hat. There's no other shade; you have to supply your own. You must also wear sneakers or other shoes to protect your feet from the razor sharp coral.

The trip by motor launch to Buccoo Reef costs $7 for two hours, three persons or more pay $2.50 W.I. each.

When it comes to *reef fishing, spear fishing, lobstering* and *deep-sea fishing,* the man to see is Cecil Anthony of Buccoo Point. An outstanding sports fishing guide, he has caught tarpon up to 87 pounds, bone fish up

576

to 14 in Tobago Waters, which he knows like the back of his hand. He will personally guide you in his own boats to the best fishing grounds. Cost is $5 W.I. for a four-hour trip. You can bring your own tackle (duty-free at customs), rent it from Mr. Anthony for about $1.65 (rod, reel and bait), or buy equipment in Scarborough.

Arnos Vale and Bluehaven Hotels have boats for hire, and most hotels can make arrangements for charter. If not, C. Anthony.

Horseback riding is one of the pleasures of Tobago. Good mounts can be hired through your hotel. Arnos Vale Hotel, Bird of Paradise Inn and Bacolet Guest House have horses and bridle paths on their own large properties. Northwest Tobago is ideal for hiking and horseback riding, but if you want to do some reconnoitering a la Robinson Crusoe, better get a local Man Friday as a guide. You'd be surprised how easy it is to get lost on a small island.

Go to your hotel manager or the Warden's office in Scarborough for all information on *hunting* (duck, waterfowl, heron, etc.).

Chief spectator sport is *horse racing* at the Tobago Turf Club. There are two unnual meets, in March and in November, with people and horses coming over from Trinidad to compete with the local products. Feeling, color, excitement, just about everything is sky high at these two day meets. Check with Tobago Tourist Bureau for precise dates, and come if you want to see the high jinks.

Goat racing, a one-day only event in Tobago, takes place at Buccoo Point at Easter.

Tobago has its *Carnival* at the same time as Trinidad's. It's gay enough, but still just a faint echo of the goings on to the south. It isn't for Carnival that people come to Tobago.

EXPLORING TOBAGO

Scarborough, a town of 15,000, is one of the quietest places under the sun. Its official sights are few. There is a native market with its usual air of color, heat and sound, open every day, but buzzing a little louder, blazing a little brighter on Wednesdays and Saturdays. You can walk or drive up the hill to Old Fort George. From this height, 430 feet, you will have a grand view of town, bay and countryside and the great sweep of the blue Atlantic stretching 21 miles southwest to Trinidad, clearly visible like a ship on the horizon. Nothing remains of the old French fort, but you can see the ruins of the old barracks and an old mortar near the lighthouse, a silent reminder of Tobago's days of violence. The impression of past history is deepened as you descend the hill past a row of silent cannon trained toward the sea and enemies long forgotten. Below the General Hospital you will see another relic of the past, the old prison. Here in 1801 after a revolt of the slaves, the ringleader and 38 of his associates were imprisoned. To terrorize the negroes into submission, the governor pretended to hang all 39 of the prisoners from a gibbet on the prison walls. The townspeople watched 39 hangings, the slaves terrified into submission, the planters appalled at such reckless destruction of their property. But only one man, the ringleader, was really executed, his body being strung up again and again from the gallows.

Using Scarborough as a starting point, a number of delightful excursions can be made to all parts of the island. Allow a full day for the trip to Charlotteville and Man o'War Bay on the northern coast. This run will take you on the Windward Road along the Atlantic Coast, through lovely valleys, up steep hills, through groves of coconut and cocoa, and along mountain ridges affording matchless views over the beaches, bays and reefs until you come to Speyside. This is a delightful fishing village, set on the superb crescent of Speyside Bay. Behind it the green profile of Pigeon Peak rises 1800 feet, Tobago's highest mountain, dominating the entire northern end of the island.

Speyside is the jumping off place for a wonderful island in the mouth of the bay, a star-shaped island with three names: Little Tobago, Ingram Island and Bird-of-Paradise Island. The last is the least official and the most firmly established by popular usage. It was here that Sir William Ingram brought those gold-plumed exotic birds of paradise from New Guinea in 1909, and it is here alone that you can see them in the Western Hemisphere. The island is now a 450-acre bird sanctuary, reached by a boat from Speyside. Guides will meet you on the island and conduct small groups along the trails where you are most likely to see these extraordinary cockerels flashing about with their great sprays of golden plumage. Silence is also golden in these precincts. The birds are timid, and you're more likely to get a glimpse of them if you use the stealthy Indian approach. Many other exotic birds may be seen here. Hawks and other birds of prey are shot on sight. Admission to the sanctuary is 30 cents U.S., the money helping to maintain America's rarest wild birds in their natural state.

Speyside is the terminus of the Windward Road. From here you cut northwest across a narrow neck of the island to Charlotteville, Tobago's biggest town, and Man o'War Bay, one of the finest natural harbors in the Caribbean. Forty fathoms deep at the mouth, ten fathoms just off shore, it could accommodate any number of cruise ships. Our prediction is that some day it will. The south side of the bay is graced by a long sandy beach. Above it on the hillside the white houses of Charlottevillle nestle like pigeons come home to roost. Pigeon Peak rises grandly behind the whole scene, verdant, majestic, silent. *A Government Rest House* is situated on the palm-fringed beach at Man o'War Bay; you'll go a long way before you find as perfect a setting as this for a swim and a picnic.

Not such a long way at that. Pigeon Point on the north-western shore, already mentioned under Sports, is even better, if the truth be told, and Store Bay at the western end of the island, is merely excellent. To quote Commander Alford's charming book, *The Island of Tobago*, "It is the sort of bay with white sand and clear green waters that you dream about on cold nights in northern climes."

Store Bay is the base for a difficult mile-and-a-half hike to "Robinson Crusoe's Cave." It can only be reached by foot. "A local descendant will take you there," writes Commander Alford, "but it is only fair to warn you that there is not very much to see!" This advice, coming from a staunch exponent of the theory that Robinson Crusoe slept here, was enough to discourage us. Instead of slogging off to the Robinson Crusoe Cave we rolled in the direction of the Robinson Crusoe Hotel and a king-size planter's punch. Man cannot live by romance alone.

THE THREE GUIANAS

Surinam — Bee Gee — La Guyane Française

SURINAM₁

BY

ALBERT HELMAN

(One of the best-known novelists of Holland, Albert Helman is from genuine Surinam stock. In the civil service of his native country as advisor on cultural matters of the government, he has published a large number of books and articles in the Guianas and the Caribbean region.)

Between the wide curves of two of the world's most impressive rivers, the Orinoco and the Amazon, in the northeastern part of South America, is a vast territory called Guiana. Surinam is the heart of this region. Although it was discovered by the Spaniards as early as the end of the 15th century, it took about hundred years more before the Dutch settled on what they used to call in those days "the Wild

Coast". The old colony often changed hands between the French, the English and the Dutch, but has remained exclusively Dutch since 1816. Many are the characteristics which the Dutch impressed on this otherwise typical part of tropical America, and these characteristics are still there, in spite of the fact that Surinam has an exceptionally cosmopolitan population and is nowadays an autonomous part of the Kingdom of the Netherlands.

Mostly known as "Dutch Guiana", its ancient and official name is "Surinam", an Amerindian word, meaning "Rocky Rivers", a most appropriate designation. Its capital "Paramaribo" also bears an Amerindian name. So do most of its rivers, animals, plants and popular implements. It remains essentially "the Wild Coast", a partly unexplored country, covered by virgin forests, dense and mysterious, sometimes almost impenetrable, but always luring the hunter, the fisherman, those who love the unconventional adventure, and especially the curious who are eager to meet the last representatives of some of the strangest people on earth. In short, Surinam is decidedly not the country for common tourists, but rather for the happy few who seek a never-to-be-forgotten, rare and exquisite adventure. These super-tourists will be fully rewarded.

Only a very small part of the country, the coastal belt in the North, is inhabited. There you will see neat Dutch polders, surrounded by high tropical forests. There too you will find the old plantations, haunted by whisperings from the past, and everywhere you will meet a mixed rural population: Negroes and Creoles, East Indians and Javanese, each retaining their ancestral ways of life, and striking attire, but living together in harmony and peace.

In the coastal belt too is the capital, Paramaribo, on the banks of the wide, impressive Surinam-River. More than a third of the entire population of the country live in this picturesque city, the heart (and brain) of a country that thrives on agriculture, forestry, and the mining of bauxite. A day's journey into the interior will take you to the main mining-town Moengo, a modern American creation, not far from the French border in the East and from the lovely little village of Albina. Near the British border in the West is Nickerie, the second town of Surinam, in the midst of a prosperous agricultural district. All these places are accessible by river, but can also be reached by air.

The coastal belt is low and partly marshy. This explains the frequent occurence of polders. More to the south there is a broad belt of Savanna land, sloping upwards and changing into a hilly wilderness, inhabited only by the nomadic Amerindians, who still live as in the days before Columbus, and by the Bush Negroes, the descendants of escaped slaves, who have retained their original customs for centuries, brought over from the dark heart of West-Africa.

All these different groups, who occasionally visit the coastal towns, can also be met in their natural surroundings. Travel by boat to the Bush-negro and Amerindian villages is one of the thrills of the Caribbean. The Bush Negroes are boatmen "par excellence" in the interior, knowing exactly how to take the many rapids in the rivers as soon as the hilly part of the country is reached. Fortunately they are completely reliable, and cheerful company too!

With all its exuberant tropical vegetation, its beautiful landscapes, especially at dawn and at sunset, and its delicious nights, Surinam can compete as a tourist attraction with many other better-known countries. In addition its population gives it a flavor which is absolutely unique. First of all, it is still inhabited by the South American aboriginals, Indians belonging to the Arawak and Carib groups, with their different sub-tribes, such as the Oayana, the Wama, the Trio and the Warrau, each with their own language and tribal customs. Some have adapted themselves to the western way of life and have become sedentary; they can easily be reached in their small villages, consisting of low, palm-roofed huts. They sleep and sit in hammocks, the women weave and bake their pottery in open kilns, the men dedicate their timeless days to hunting and fishing. In preparation of their feasts the women chew the cassava-cakes, which are their main fare, and spit the masticated stuff in a trough, where it ferments in a short time and becomes a clear alcoholic beverage, the "tapana". This is the stimulant for their dances and prodigious demonstrations of prowess.

In the interior many nomadic clans are scattered. They still live to a great extent in the Stone Age, using bow and arrow for both hunting and fishing, and crossing the rivers in very primitive boats, made from bark. They go almost completely naked, except on special occasions when they wear their colorful and costly feather head-dresses and submit themselves to the wasp- or ant-ordeal. For these severe tests they wear a kind of wicker-work waistcoat, the inner side of which is buzzing with living wasps or crawling with half-inch ants. Thus clad, they perform the ritual dances of their ancestors, seemingly oblivious to the torture of sting and bite, proudly exhibiting their endurance to pain. Even small boys have to submit periodically to this proof of growing manhood. A normally taciturn lot, they are a physically beautiful people with strong athletic bodies. They are skilful hunters, often tipping arrows and spears with the well-known deadly poison "curare", extracted from a rather common jungle-plant.

Slaves That Got Away

When in the course of almost 300 years many thousands of slaves were brought from Africa to supply the labor refused by the freedom-loving Amerindians, the recalcitrant Negroes regularly escaped to the forests and settled in almost inaccessible places above the rapids in the river-laced depths of the jungle. These Bush Negroes still inhabit the same places, which only recently can be reached without real danger. They still live according to their age-old African traditions, a sturdy and good looking people with no inclination whatever to hide their physical beauty. Open, friendly and talkative, they appreciate the benefits of western culture, without being influenced in their primitive way of life. Many of their huts display the fine wood-carvings for which they are famous and which also adorn their furniture, implements and boats. They have a special skill in felling and burning out big trees, and their boats made in this way are strong and reliable, especially in the rapids, where they exhibit a rare ability as boatsmen and conquerors of the wilderness.

The Bush Negroes also carve their drums—never to be touched by any female—and as soon as the sound of a drum or rattle is heard, their feet start to move in a most dexterous way. For them most dancefeasts are competitions between men or between women, where they try to out-dance each other, accompanied by the songs and the rhythmic noises of the onlookers. For gaiety, wit and practical jokes, they are unsurpassed by any of the other population groups.

The more adapted negroes of the towns and coastal settlements have not yet lost all African habits. Ready to dance when any kind of music is made, they often feast on the occasion of a birthday or a funeral, and sometimes indulge in magic dances, in which some of them become "spirited",—temporarily possessed by some strange deity. Outwardly they have adopted many western characteristics, however, and this is still more the case with the creole population of mixed ancestry. A large group is almost completely westernized and even Americanized. In the more accessible parts of the country you will find them speaking English like any good Dutchman.

Asiatic influence is very strong in Surinam, in fact stronger than in any place in this hemisphere. You may happen to meet a procession of white-clad, turbaned men and beautifully veiled women, jingling with silverware. The men carry a model mosque, all made from tinsel and coloured paper. A flute and a drum precede the merry crowd which bursts into song. These are Mohammedans of East-Indian origin, celebrating the Tadiyahfeast. They have quite a number of real mosques for worship, wherever they live in the country. You will also find numerous Hindustani who venerate one of the many-limbed or phallic deities of Hinduism. These "real" Indians keep cows, but never will kill any of these animals, which are sacred in their religion. They plant long poles, bearing a pennon, in front of their dwellings as a token of sacrifices poured on the naked skin of Mother Earth. They work harder than anyone else on Mother Earth too, but when having a good time they are the most richly-adorned and most colorful group of Surinam's little League of Nations.

At night, even in your hotel, you may hear from afar the mellow sounds of metallic music. This is the famous "gamelan", played by the Javanese. By day you will encounter everywhere their slender, elegant women, still wearing the sarong as in Indonesia and ready to greet you with a lovely smile. You will meet the Chinese in many shops, and if you are interested in dry goods, you certainly will have a good talk with some of the Lebanese merchants who have brought the color of the Near East to this part of America. The main racial divisions of Surinam are: Creole, about 115,000; Hindustani, about 93,000; Indonesians, about 43,000; 4,000 white Europeans; 4,000 Chinese; 33,000 Bush Negroes; 5,000 Amerindians.

The important thing is that all these population groups, whilst retaining so many of their proper characteristics, nevertheless intermingle in a most natural way during all the activities of commercial, industrial and rural daily life. As there are no real minority problems, no major sources of friction, they are drawing nearer from day to day, and soon will become the one and unified people which is needed in this young, growing country with its very old, diversified components.

THE THREE GUIANAS

PRACTICAL INFORMATION FOR SURINAM

WHEN TO COME? The main rainy season is from April to August. November to February is the most agreeable part of the year. But, although the climate is moist and tropical, it is cooled by the north-east trades, and monthly mean temperatures range from only 79 to 83 degrees. Even in the wet season, showers are interspersed with long periods of sunshine.

Popular feasts in the capital and smaller towns are celebrated about the end of August, at the *Konferjari*, where all the different races meet and frolic, mostly in the evening. There is also a yearly Trade Fair in Paramaribo, with many attractions, but on no fixed dates; check with your travel agency. Almost the whole year there is occasion to assist at some native festivity,—in the capital the frequent *Ferjari-oso*, creole dancing-parties; some Javanese *Slamatan* in the outskirts, with genuine Indonesian dances and gamelan-music; or a Hindustani wedding, very ceremonial, with display of gorgeous costumes and sometimes stage-plays. In the interior the Bush Negroes easily arrange a dance-feast at night for generous visitors. Attending Amerindian dances is a matter of chance,— but you may have luck!

HOW TO GET THERE. *By Air.* KLM has 3 flights a week from New York, and 5 from Miami to Curaçao. From there, KLM flies propeller planes 3 times a week to Paramaribo, plus an additional weekly jet service. Pan American has one weekly jet service from New York via Antigua, Barbados, Trinidad and British Guiana. You can also fly from Paris on Air France by way of Puerto Rico, Fort de France (Martinique) to Paramaribo.

By Ship. Alcoa has freighters with accommodations for 12 passengers leaving New York monthly for the Guianas. Alcoa also has weekly passenger sailings from New Orleans, and Alcoa's air-conditioned cargo ships take passengers on frequent trips from Trinidad to Surinam, plying up the Cottica River to Moengo right through the jungle and the Bush-Negro villages: one of the most exotic voyages the Caribbean offers.

PASSPORTS, VISAS. All aliens should have a valid passport, but no visa is required. U.S. citizens, staying for less than 60 days, need no passport but should have birth certificate or naturalization certificate. All temporary visitors should also have a vaccination certificate (not more than three years old) and a through or return ticket.

171.5
13.0
201.0
———
385.5

CURRENCY. The Surinam Guilder, also called a Surinam Florin (and abbreviated Sfl.) is the legal tender here. It is divided into 100 cents. Present exchange rate is approximately fl. 1.86 to the U.S. dollar. Hotels and many shops accept U.S. currency travelers checks at the official rate of exchange.

HOW TO GET ABOUT. Plenty of taxis available in Paramaribo and some U-drive cars. You drive on the left side of the road. There is excellent interior transportation by Beechcraft (seating 10) and other planes of Surinam Airways between Paramaribo and Nickerie, Coronie, Moengo and Albina. Other points in the interior can also be reached by plane. The Surinam Navigation Company has coasters traveling to Nickerie and other points on the coast. Local travel bureaus arrange visits to just about any accessible spot of this area.

THE THREE GUIANAS

HOTELS

PARAMARIBO

SURINAM TORARICA. This three-story, 81-room hotel is the first truly luxury resort of Surinam. Built by the Condado Caribbean Hotel Corp. (of Puerto Rico fame) on a $2 million budget, it is located near the river on the outskirts of Paramaribo. Its elegant facilities include a swimming pool, an attractive dining room, a night club and a gambling casino. All rooms, private and public, are air-conditioned. Summer rates are: $11 to $15 single, $15 to $19 double. In winter a single room is $15 to $19, a double is $19 to $23, European Plan. For Modified American Plan, add $7 per person; for full American Plan, add $10. All rates include private bath and 10% service charge.

The opening of this superb hotel is a giant step towards qualifying Surinam as a Caribbean holiday destination of major interest for those who are attracted by the really exotic and unusual background, yet prefer to take their adventures in maximum comfort.

PALACE HOTEL, Oranjeplein 6. Best in town. 32 rooms with private bath. Partly air-conditioned. Facing the splendid main plaza, solid and quiet. Bar, restaurant. Rates are: $12 to $18 single, $22 to $27 double, A.P.

HOTEL VERVUURT, in city center; 29 rooms, private bath, hot and cold water. Partly air-conditioned. Roof-garden. Rates are: $9-$11 single, $12-$18 double, A.P.

KERSTEN HOTEL, Steenbakkerijstraat 27. Well-tended; 27 rooms with private baths; lies in the center of the commercial district. Bar, garage. Rates are: $7.50 single, $13 double. Air-conditioned: $11-$15, A.P.

LASHLEY HOTEL. Watermolenstraat 48. 12 rooms, some with private bath. Rates are: $5-$11 single, $9-$20 double. A.P.

OUTSIDE PARAMARIBO

MOENGO, mining center on the Cottica-river; *The Government Guest House* charges $6.50 single, $9 double, A.P.

ALBINA, opposite French St. Laurent on the Marowijne River. Moderate accommodation in the *Government Guest House,* 3 rooms.

CORONIE, center of coconut plantations area. Only accomodation is in the *Government Guest House.* 5 rooms, 3 baths. Satisfactory.

NICKERIE, thriving agricultural town. *Government Guest House,* adequate, *Pension Sjiem Fat,* 10 rooms. *Hotel Dorien,* 10 rooms.

WAGENINGEN, interesting modern private settlement. Hotel *De Wereld,* 6 rooms, 4 baths. 2 rooms with private bath. Very well tended.

 RESTAURANTS. Due to its varied population, you can find in Paramaribo either American, Creole, Chinese of Indonesian food. Meat, poultry, fish and vegetables are the foundations of most dishes, and rice in different forms generally will be a substantial part of the menu. Creole dishes like *pom* (poultry and ground tayer-roots) or *pastey* (poultry and vegetables) can be recommended, as well as the Indonesian *rijsttafel* (a long series of small items) and *nasi goreng* (baked rice and minced poultry). As preparation of these dishes is rather elaborate, they will have to be ordered well in advance. Recommendable are: *Park Club* (Oranjeplein), *Country Club* (Anton Dragtenweg 75), *Hong Kong* (Keizerstraat 51) for Chinese and *Pomo* (Gravenstraat 77) for Indonesian food. *Madura* for Indonesian dishes.

USEFUL ADRESSES. *American Consulate General,* Noorderkerkstraat 3, 3024, open 8-1. *British Consulate,* Kromme Elleboogstraat 9, 2148, open 8-1.

Historic Colombia and one of its sons

THE THREE GUIANAS

Rotary Club, Palace Hotel; Lions' Club, Park Club. *Tourist Board and Information office:* Tel. 3733, 10 Kerkplein.

 SHOPPING. Once you have met Amerindians and Bush Negroes, either in Paramaribo or in their own settlements, you'll be eager to acquire some specimens of their native arts and crafts. Amerindian sets of bows and arrows, cotton hammocks, small objects in wickerwork are available, and their ceramic jugs and animals of striking design are unusual buys. It is not easy to bargain for them in the settlements, especially if you are in a hurry. Shops in the capital offer a choice, and you will be better off there. This is also the case with the wood-carvings of the Bush Negroes, which display an extraordinary skill, fashioned from one single piece of wood into an intricate stool or bench. Their round trays are highly prized as beautiful geometrical ornaments. Smaller objects are combs, ladles and cudgels, used to beat their laundry. The ornamental paddles are rather bulky, but very handsome; the carved or painted gourds on the other hand weigh almost nothing and are inexpensive. The curio shops in Paramaribo have these in stock, together with necklaces from all kinds of seeds and kernels.

Numerous stores have gold and silverware, mostly in classical East Indian designs, at moderate prices, and here is your chance to buy original nuggets of natural gold, priced according to weight. Some shops also sell fine and light-weight East-Indian saris (long scarfs) and Chinese textile products, carved Oriental boxes and cheaper jewelry. Javanese bamboo and wickerwork objects are sold in all of the local markets at very reasonable prices.

ENTERTAINMENT. Besides cinemas, which show American and East-Indian films, there is little entertainment outside of Paramaribo. In the capital agreeable evenings can be spent at the *Park Club* and the *Country Club*, where you can wine, dine and dance.

 SPORTS. Swimming can be arranged through Tourist Board at *Oase, Dolfijn,* and *Kwie Kwie,* three private clubs. An 18-hole golf course is located three miles from Paramaribo on the airport road. Bicycling is getting to be almost as popular as it is in Holland, and bikes can be rented easily in the capital. Hunting for tapir, deer, pingo and pakira (wild hogs), alligator and wild duck is one of the big attractions of Surinam. Make arrangements through Travel Bureaus. Fishing for tarpon and the voracious but tasty pirén (piranha) is another Surinam specialty. Lawn tennis is popular. Outstanding spectator sports are soccer and cricket.

EXPLORING SURINAM

Paramaribo, a city of 110,000 people, has an extensive surface, hugging the left bank of the Surinam River, where it nears the Atlantic Ocean after confluence with the Commewijne River. From the harbourside, where the Central Market is a daily meeting-place of all races and shades of the population, the town expands in all directions, leading to the poorer outskirts with their slums and to the richer residential and villa-districts with their flowering gardens and white-washed dwellings.

North of the port-area is the oldest part of the town, with

587

Formal and informal elegance in the Guianas

or Javanese peasants, cultivating rice, citrus and vegetables. A long road, following the Suriname River upstream, passes the lovely settlement of *Domburg*, leads after about 20 miles to *Paranam*, mining settlement of Alcoa, and to the interesting mining center of the Biliton-Company. Mining is also in full operation on the opposite side of the river at Paranam, in the Rorac-fields. On both banks of the river old plantations, still active, can be visited by boat, either from the capital or from Paranam where bauxite is shipped to Trinidad for transshipment to the U.S.A. and Canada.

Opposite the capital, on the right bank of the Surinam River, accessible by hourly ferry boat a series of plantations can be reached, the settlement of *New Amsterdam* with its old fortresses, strategically erected at the confluence of the Surinam and Commewijne Rivers. Fifteen miles away is the large sugar-estate of Mariënburg, gateway to many sugar and coffee plantations and the happy hunting-grounds of their hinterland.

Jungle Cruises

The Surinam Travel and Tourist Bureaus arrange many interesting sight-seeing trips into the jungle interior of this fascinating land. English-speaking guides are provided. Among the tours are a half-day trip by car to the Indian villages near Onverwacht and an equally short tour of the Botanical Gardens, and the charming Javanese village of Domburg on the Surinam River. A one day tour by motorboat will take you to the "Jewish Savannah" with its old cemetery and ruined Synagogue, after which you go on foot to an Amerindian village. If you want to watch the fascinating process of mining gold, take the full-day motor coach and rail trip to Goldplacer De Jong. A similar excursion can be made to Kabel Station, the railway terminal, after which you proceed by "corjaal" through the rapids to Ganzee, the largest Bush-Negro village in the country. Return to Paramaribo is by motorboat.

A great tourist favorite is the voyage up the Cottica River to Moengo where the American Aluminum Company has its plant. There are twice-weekly scheduled trips by the Surinam Navigation Company whose comfortable boats make the round trip in two days. Alcoa's air-conditioned bauxite ships do it in two. You can save time by flying back to Paramaribo by Surinam Airways. But most tourists are so fascinated by the voyage through the jungle, past the Bush-Negro villages and into the heart of this strange and primitive land that they are happy to stick to the river. You'll see the Djukas as God made them, often without benefit of clothes, paddling their canoes, dancing on the river banks, and living the ancient tribal life they brought with them from the jungle of Africa to the jungle of Surinam.

If you have the leisure for it, the most rewarding voyage of all is the three day tour to Stoelmansisland, an island in the Marowijne, largest river in Surinam. You travel by plane and by "corjaal" which your boatman brings through the rapids with the greatest of ease. From this point the unique gold mines of Benzdorp may be visited for a day. On this trip you will come into close contact with dozens of Bush-Negro and Amerindian settlements. It is an unforgetable exotic voyage into another time, another culture, another world.

BRITISH GUIANA

BY

WILLIAM CURTIS

(Co-editor of the French editions of Fodor's Modern Guides, assistant editor of the "Jet Age Guide to Europe", Mr. Curtis is a British travel writer with a special interest in British Guiana and the Central American scene.)

One of the Latin American chips off the Old World block is British Guiana, the only English-speaking country along the Spanish Main. It derives its name from an Amerindian word that means "Land of the Waters". Originally there were five Guianas, denoting the eminently hydrographic character of this part of the world: Spanish (now Venezuela), Portuguese (now Brazil), Dutch (now Surinam), French and British. A navigable river was so important to the adventurers who first explored the coastline between the Orinoco and the Amazon that they gave the native name of each river to the surrounding country. Thus the three counties of British Guiana: Essequibo, Demerara and Berbice take their names from the rivers that flow through them, and so do all the outlying districts.

The shores of Guiana were sighted by Columbus in 1498 but he never landed there. Later on, exploration of this region was stimulated by the search for the fabled golden city of El Dorado which went on for over a hundred years, but neither Sir Walter Raleigh nor Alonzo de Ojeda was able to find it. No wonder—it never existed. The Dutch, more patient and sedate, established several permanent settlements there but were evicted by British privateers toward the middle of the 18th century. The French got into the fray and the Colony changed hands several times until a financial settlement—shortly after the Napoleonic wars—left it in Britain's hands. Place names like Hampton Court, Vreed-en-Hoop (Peace and Hope), La Bonne Mère vividly reflect British Guiana's chequered history.

Bee-Gee is the fond abbreviation by which the six peoples who inhabit Guiana call their country. Anglo-Saxons (and there are records of 70 American families having emigrated here in the 1830's), Portuguese from Madeira and the Azores, Africans who were brought here to work the sugar-cane plantations, Chinese to keep the wheels of commerce turning, indentured East Indians to labor the ricefields, and the remaining Amerindians: all are groping their way toward a common destiny, self-government and eventual independence.

The recent, 1961 elections were won by the left-wing politician Jagan who was voted into power by an East Indian majority (against an equally radical negro minority) on a platform of immediate independence. Jagan's victory is likely to doom the "British" nomen preceding the country's name. It also spells a period of political unrest in the near future. Lacking facilities in any case, Guiana thus remains of minimum interest to tourists.

PRACTICAL INFORMATION FOR BRITISH GUIANA

HOW TO GET THERE. *By Air.* Pan American has two weekly flights from New York and Trinidad, en route to Brazil. British West Indian Airways has daily flights from Trinidad. BOAC operates from Barbados and KLM touches down thrice weekly on its way from Curaçao to Surinam. British Guiana Airways operate scheduled services from St. Vincent, connecting with the other Windward Islands and with Martinique. Air France arrives from Martinique-Barbados. Cruzeira Do Sul has weekly flights from Manaos, Brazil.

By Sea. ALCOA's modern passenger-freighters regularly call at the capital, Georgetown, sailing from New York, Baltimore, New Orleans and Mobile. Saguenay Steamships, sailing from Montreal also have passenger accommodations on their cargo ships. U.K. ports of embarkation for the Colony are Liverpool (Booker Line) and London (Harrison Line). Many schooners are plying between the West Indian islands and British Guiana.

PASSPORT, VISAS, CURRENCY. All visitors must hold a round-trip ticket. American and Canadian tourists are exempt from passport and visa requirements provided their stay is to be not more than 3 months. British and other Commonwealth subjects should carry passports but don't need a visa. The Bee-Wee dollar is legal tender but U.S. and Canadian dollars

THE THREE GUIANAS

are readily accepted everywhere. Most of the coins are British, however, these are gradually being replaced by a local coinage ranging from 50 to ½ cent pieces. While visitors are allowed to bring in only 10 pounds sterling or $48 in BWI currency, there is no limit to the amount of U.S. and Canadian currency you may bring in. To take it out again you show the declaration form which you filled out when entering the country.

CLOTHING. Temperatures range between 75-85°, tempered by northerly breezes. Light tropical clothes for both sexes. Not-too-provocative shorts and slacks may be worn by women. Informality is the keynote though jacket and summer dress are expected to be worn at dinner. To explore interior, khaki-drill shorts or breeches, bush shirts and light raincoats are recommended. A special warning to those who want to visit the Rupununi savannah country: be sure to bring shirts with long sleeves and long trousers or slacks. There is a little fly called *pium* and its bite itches terribly.

HOW TO GET ABOUT. Only about ⅓ of the 260 miles of main highways (all in the coastal region) are hard surfaced, the remainder consists of burnt clay. Car-hire rates are reasonable and gasoline (petrol) costs about 80 beewee-cents a gallon. There are two single-track railroads—one (61 miles) connecting the capital with Rosignol, opposite New Amsterdam. The other (20 miles) leads to Parika on the east bank of Essequibo River. You can continue from there 30 miles upriver—to Bartica—by steamer service. A coastal service connects Georgetown with Morawhanna, right on the Venezuelan border. Because of the many rapids and waterfalls, inland navigation is undeveloped. The farthest you can get is from New Amsterdam to Arima, 130 miles up the Berbice River.

There are landing-strips all over the country. British Guiana Airways operate several internal services. Those of tourist interest: 1. a one-day excursion to fabulous Kaieteur Falls, at a cost of some 60 local dollars, basket-lunch included. Seating is limited; inform your ship's purser of your intended trip or book by cable with British Guiana Tourist Committee, Georgetown, if arriving by plane. 2. Week-end charter flights to the Orinduik Falls, near the Brazilian border; approximate cost BW 44, with a minimum of 25 passengers. 3. Visit to Wichabai, "capital" of the Amerindian tribes, in the Savannah country. 4. Freshwater fishing expedition to Karanambo.

If you are on a cruise, and while your ship is cargo-loading, you may undertake the following collective motorcar excursion (minimum four persons): Visit of the Amerindian model village at the B.G. Museum - Stabroek Market - Botanic Gardens - Carib Hotel for refreshments - visit to B.G.'s largest sugar plantation - en route you can photograph Mohammedan mosques and Hindu temples. This will take about six hours and cost you some 12 BW dollars.

A more ambitious trip—taking up a full day—will run you across plantations to River Demerara where you embark for Kamuni Creek, right in the Guiana jungle. Short ramble ashore. Lunch and refreshments on board. Cost: 15 BW dollars if there are at least 12 participants. Notify your ship's purser four days before arrival or cable to Tourist Committee if arriving by plane.

Concerning game-fishing and duck shooting or combined fishing and jaguar safaris contact Louis Chung Tours, P.O. Box 231, Georgetown, B.G.

THE THREE GUIANAS

 SPORTS. The outstanding sport in British Guiana is fishing, be it of marine or the freshwater type. In the Rupununi district you might make a catch of rare and fantastic fish like the giant arapaima, the man-eating piranna or you may join one of the schooners who do their fishing for red snappers and groupers by hand line about 100 miles offshore. You can do some estuarine and coastal fishing by hiring an outboard motor-boat. The types caught are snook, bashaw, queriman and scaleless skin-fish.

 SHOPPING. Georgetown's colorful Stabroek Market, where you can see Guiana's all six races engaged in noisy transactions, is good hunting ground for native straws and curios but if you are not good at bargaining better visit the government-sponsored *Sales Centre* at 6 High Street where you'll find attractive hand-bags, souvenirs from tropical woods, stuffed baby alligators and beautiful filigree silver jewelry. Some of the finest fruit-cured rums in the Caribbean come from British Guiana. If you want to take home a bottle or two, ask for *Houston's* or *d'Aguiar's*. In the textile line the locally-manufactured shirts and pajamas, made of English poplins and zephyrs are a good buy; look for *Windsor, Esquire* or *Carib* labels. The eau-de-cologne of the Caribbean, *Limacol* is manufactured in British Guiana.

 HOTELS AND RESTAURANTS. The Guianese table, if there is such a thing, is the heritage of six different cuisines. Do not expect food to compare with the best international standards. There are the English dishes—all the roasts, minced meats and potato chips;—the Indian dishes with their variety of *curries*. The Chinese have brought the mysterious blending of sweet and sour pork and the *chow-mein* and *low-mein*. Africa has contributed *foo-foo* and *metemgee*; Christmas is celebrated with Portuguese garlic-pork. And even if you don't fancy the Amerindian preparation of roasted queen ants you're sure to like their pepperpot!

Pleasantly situated the *Tower* is probably the leading hotel in the Colony. Suites and most of the rooms have private baths; air-conditioning; swimming pool; dancing on week-ends at the *Cactus Club* restaurant. Doubles (air condition de luxe) are $11-$24 per day on the Continental Plan, which includes breakfast. The *Park* is restful, rather Victorian in atmosphere. Doubles are $11-$20 per day, American Plan; $7-$17 European Plan. Preferred by "open-air types" (settlers from the interior, mining engineers, etc.), the *Woodbine* has clublike, genial drinking conditions. Single with bath are $9.50-$17, Continental Plan. At the *Palm Court* fairly good food is served in pleasant surroundings. Doubles are $11-$19, Modified American Plan. The *Carib* has Saturday night dancing. There are

several Guest Houses such as *Trent House*, 72 Main Street, *Roraima* and *The Grill* which are considerably cheaper BW $6 to $10, American Plan.

In the country Bartica is best served with hotels: *Moderne, Berner's Croft* and *Kaira*. The *Strand* in New Amsterdam is very simple. At Lethem, in the Rupununi region, the *Melbro*, right at the end of the airstrip, is a Brazilian-style hotel.

The Government *Rest House*, with the District Commissioner's blessing and if there are unoccupied rooms available, will accept you as a paying guest. Near Wichabai, at Dadanawa Ranch, the Rupununi Development Company has a guesthouse, try and arrange for an invitation.

All hotels in the Colony have

restaurant services and bars. In the capital there are a few restaurants which serve American, Continental(?), Chinese and Indian food: *Betty Brown's*, *New City*, *Green Tureen*, *Waterloo* are among the more popular places.

EXPLORING BRITISH GUIANA

Georgetown is the best-preserved Georgian city in wooden architecture anywhere in the Caribbean and it boasts the highest timber building in the world, St. George's Cathedral. The beauty of this garden-city of some 125.000 inhabitants is basically due to the Dutch, who laid out those wonderful wide avenues with canals down the middle, as a reminder of their homeland. Most of the older, green-shuttered houses were built on stilts, 8-10 feet off the ground to avoid flooding. "Mudland", as the inhabitants derisively call the coastal area, is now protected by dikes just like those in Holland but modern structures are built low in the usual manner. The great fires of more than ten years ago cleared out most of the center of Georgetown and allowed brand new modern shops to be built which, by the way, are excellent. But if you want to see real local color, visit Stabroek Market, a kaleidoscope of races. It's difficult to say who steals the picture, the people or the produce they sell.

The capital has a few sights of its own to offer. You can see a variety of strange tropical flowers in its Botanical Garden and the finest existing collection of palm trees; lotuslike lilies and the majestic Guianese Victoria Regina, the world's largest leafed aquatic plant which can easily support a five year old child on its fronds. Feeding the manatees—gentle seacows— has become a tourist ritual. The Zoological Park has a typical collection of the Colony's animals, birds and reptiles. The museum contains some interesting exhibits of Amerindian arts and crafts; in its aquarium you can tease with impunity the terrible man-eating perai, the electric eel and other monsters of the deep who are best met under these circumstances.

The Jungle

The narrow coastal belt—often below sea-level and *poldered* in the Dutch manner—is scenically the least interesting, though 90 per cent of the country's half million inhabitants live here. It's the highlands of the farther interior you should visit. They are covered with tropical forests of lofty trees, tangled bush ropes (*lianas*), great thick vines and rapids and waterfalls of great beauty. A trip inland to these curiously-shaped mountains is most rewarding. See the lovely Kanaku mountains, the

Savannah and its picturesque *vaqueros* rounding up cattle, the river scenery of the Rupununi and the way of life of the Amerindians, hardly touched by civilization. These children of a lost world, though primitive, have ceased to be dangerous long ago and their poisonous blow-guns belong to the distant past and have become museum exhibits. However, you can still see them hunting birds and shooting fish with their out-size bows and arrows. It's a joy to watch them at work: Amerindian archers rarely miss....

In the very heart of British Guiana is one of the wonders of the world, Kaieteur Fall, terrifying in its grandeur, fascinating in its beauty, five times the height of Niagara. Its greatest attraction is the ever changing clouds of prismatic hues. And if you are lucky you will see the Kaieteur martin birds flying home to the under-shelves of rock behind the curtain of water. Kaieteur is a corruption of native words meaning „Old Man's Fall". A local ballad tells of an old chieftain who offered himself, for the good of his tribe, to Makonaima, the Great Spirit. This he did by paddling his canoe over the mighty waterfall. His craft, turned to stone, may be seen at the foot of Kaieteur whenever a drought has reduced the volume of water. The small Grumman sea-plane always lands on the Potaro river above the falls. Its take-off from the brink of the cataract never fails to thrill visitors.

Farther on, some 190 miles from Georgetown, are the Orinduik Falls on River Ireng at the Brazilian frontier. You can reach this beauty spot by charter plane which takes you there for a week-end outing in less than two hours. There are more falls and rapids on the Essequibo river, not far from Bartica where three great rivers meet. This attractive little town is the base for visiting the gold and diamond mines that Raleigh missed. Important timber operations also go on here.

Within easy access of Bartica are the ruins of Kijk-over-al, the look-out island fortified by the Dutch in the 17th century, and Fort Island, sighted about ten miles upstream from Georgetown. This was the seat of their government. The remains of Fort Zeelandia are among the most impressive ruins on the Spanish Main.

The Savannah Country

The Rupununi savannah is an outdoor man's paradise. The settlers who live there all hope for a bigger and better future but at present the actual castles belong to the ants! These giant cone-shaped hummocks of earth are a startling feature of the grasslands. It used to take six gruelling weeks of paddling or walking up the cattle trail to get there—today it can be done in an hour and a half, by plane.

The sparse Amerindian population consists of the Macushi, Wapishana and Wai-Wai tribes. The latter are a hardy, remote and primitive people. Hunting dogs play an important part in their lives and are treated with great respect. The Indians rest and sleep in tiny hammocks that can spread out to incredible size, owing to the way they are woven. Part of the hammock folds over the sleeper in lieu of a blanket. These cleverly-woven "beauty rests" impressed Columbus. They are wonderful souvenirs. The Guiana Amerindians are very international. Before they can speak English, they have already learned Portuguese. They are natural musicians, play banjo, mandolin or guitar very quickly and their music is purely Brazilian. In the little border town of Lethem there is a *fiesta* at the slightest excuse and many Brazilians come across the border with their pretty senhoritas to help liven up the proceedings.

All through the dry season—October to May—is fishing time in the Rupununi but don't get hurt by the sting-ray; the shock of the electric eel is tame beside its nasty sting. Amerindians will teach you how to shoot the giant arapaima fish or the turtle with bow and arrow; they'll look after you while you scoop up in your net the razortoothed perai or a man-sized alligator; they'll paint themselves all over when they accompany you on a jaguar or puma hunt and they'll teach you a little song you might hum nostalgically once back at your office. It goes something like this:

"I can shoot Arapaima well
I can hold a tiger by his tail
And choke an Anaconda
I am an Indian marksman."

Sometimes, when the pressures of this atomic age get too great, you'll wish you were too.

FRENCH GUIANA

Like so many of France's overseas possessions, French Guiana is a country whose tourism is on the agenda for future development. At the present writing it remains a place for "unaccommodated man", a tropical jungle of wild and primitive beauty, so thick at times that the rays of the sun have never filtered to its depths. The trees of this jungle drip with wild orchids, echo with the chatter of monkeys and the raucous cries of brilliantly-colored birds. The forest, dense and mysterious, is watered by a fan of rivers spreading out from south to north: the Maroni, the Mana, the Sinnamary, Approuague and Oyapock. A trip up any these rivers by motorized dugout canoe is far from a luxury cruise, but it's a travel experience that's hard to beat for sheer exoticism.

Some of the greatest explorers of history reconnoitred along the Guiana coast. Columbus was here in 1498. So was Alphonse d'Ojeda, Jean de las Cosa, and that Italian navigator whose name became an eponym for the whole New World: Amerigo Vespucci. In the following century a rumor swept through Europe like a brush fire: there was a city in the heartland of Guiana whose streets were paved with gold. Manoa del Dorado was its name, and it was ruled by the last of the Inca Emperors. A hundred prows turned toward the Orinoco. Such soldiers of fortune as Sir Walter Raleigh and Laurence Keymis penetrated the steaming jungles of Guiana. In 1598, the latter found not El Dorado, but the French, already ensconed and extracting dyes from the dark trees of the tropic forest.

In 1604 the French contingent was reinforced by De Rivardière and a group of colonists. Several other French companies followed, leaving the province of Normandy for richer virgin territory between the Orinoco and the Amazon. There *was* gold in the soil of Guiana, though no golden city existed, and there was sugar, spice, bauxite and endless stretches of forest whose trees promised an inexhaustable supply of timber, oil of rosewood and other essential gums.

Since the land was rich, it was coveted. The Dutch grabbed it from the French toward the end of the 17th century. No sooner had the French reconquered it than the English got into the act. They ravaged the countryside in 1667, then left to ravage somewhere else. The Dutch seized Inini and the territory east of the Maroni again, but Admiral d'Estrées recaptured it for France in 1676. Although the French had to give up the rich prize between the Amazon and the Oyapoc by the treaty of Utrecht in 1713, they held onto what is now French Guiana except for a brief period from 1808 to 1816 when the English and the Portuguese occupied it.

Now a department of France, the territory of French Guiana consists of the coastal arrondissement of Guyane, facing the Atlantic between 54 and 56 degrees of west longitude, and the interior arrondissement of Inini, stretching south to within two degrees of the Equator. There are about 36,000 French Guyanese, the majority of whom live in the coastal capital of Cayenne. The population is composed of French officials and businessmen, indigenous Guyanese, French creoles and a smattering of the ubiquitous Chinese. French culture has flourished under the hot equatorial sun, and the government boasts that French Guiana has the lowest illiteracy rate in all of South America.

Devil's Island

What they cannot live down is that palmy little rock, Ile au Diable, about six miles off the coast among the Iles du Salut. This is the infamous Devil's Island, scene of one of history's most notorious prisons. It was abolished after World War II but the spectre of Devil's Island still haunts the popular imagination like a symbol of horror. The persistence of this image even penetrates official places. When our man Friday called at the French Embassy in Washington to check on some historical information about Guiana, the charming young girl behind the desk in the library said, "Mon Dieu, who wants to go there? It's the *bagne!*" (*Bagne* is the worst word for prison in the French language.) This from an intelligent young French girl who was a child when Devil's Island ceased to exist as a prison! It is obvious that the French will need a public relations program to turn this tropical hell into a tropical paradise. There's nothing either good or bad but thinking makes it so.

In the meantime French Guiana offers tourists the offbeat attractions of a rich tropical land whose historic colonial monuments only serve to emphasize the enduring splendors of nature, primitive and unspoiled.

Approaching by air or by sea, you will sense this grandeur as soon as you glimpse the Iles du Salut and the verdure-clad crags of the island of Cayenne in the midst of whose luxuriant vegetation rises a touch of metropolitan France, the territory's capital. This city of 20,000 has been laid out with that unerring French instinct for urban planning which has resulted in the handsome promenades of the Place des Palmistes and the Place des Amandiers. Curiosities of the capital include the official residence of the prefect, built in the 18th century by the Jesuit fathers. Also, not far from the island's Rochambeau Airport is found one of the most exotic small zoos in existence, noted for its collection of magnificent tropical birds. A taxi will take you along the coast for an interesting tour of the summer homes of Cayenne's leading citizens, and it is just a few miles

THE THREE GUIANAS

to the jungle with its superb groves of bamboo which meet overhead to form cool archways of golden green.

Cayenne is the hub of all activity, center for sea bathing, cockfighting, fishing, and point of departure for hunting safaris. The local museum is worth visiting and so is the Botanic Garden, a wonderful place to study the flora of the equatorial jungle. Speaking of which, you will notice the giant double palms of the Place des Palmistes. These are a specialty of Guiana, not found elsewhere.

There are a number of interesting excursions from Cayenne. Fort Diamant, built in 1652, is the New World's best-preserved example of a genuine feudal castle. Fort Trio with its double tower is another monument of European military architecture transplanted to America.

The "Tour de l'Ile" excursion will enable you to appreciate the magnificent scenery of French Guiana's rugged coast, swift rivers and dense forests. The Montagne de Mahury provides hikers with a rare opportunity to climb among the orchid-draped trees of an equatorial forest to the three lakes of Mount Rorota. Most impressive—and most rugged—of all are the river trips into the heartland of the luxuriant interior province of Inini.

You may visit Iracoubo with its melancholy tombs of France's political deportees. Then there are the lovely Iles du Salut and Devil's Island, which brings us back to the spectre which still haunts French Guiana.

PRACTICAL INFORMATION FOR FRENCH GUIANA

 HOW TO GET THERE. There are air services to Cayenne's Rochambeau airport by Air France, and Pan America World Airways, connecting with the main north-south Caribbean flights of these carriers. PAA Clipper will fly you from New York to Cayenne by way of Port of Spain, Trinidad, British Guiana and Surinam, as will Air France.

Cayenne is a port of call for ships of the Compagnie Générale Transatlantique.

PASSPORTS, VISAS. Same as for the French West Indies.

CURRENCY. The French new franc, 4,83 to the American dollar at this writing.

 WHEN TO COME? Best weather is in February and March. Rainy season—and it's torrential—is from January to the end of July, with a short dry season in March. Average temperature is only 80 degrees, but the humidity makes it worse than this would seem to indicate.

THE THREE GUIANAS

WHERE TO STAY. The leading hotels of Cayenne are the *Hotel des Palmistes* on the *place* of the same name and the *Hotel du Montabo*, which has just undergone important renovations. We cannot recommend the Palmistes. The Montabo is perched on the top of a hill overlooking the town of Cayenne. It has an open-air lounge with a view on the sea, as well as a swimming pool. 15 of the 30 large rooms of this hotel are air-conditioned and equipped with telephone. All the rooms have showers and their own balcony. The rates are $6 or $9 (European Plan) depending on whether or not you have air-conditioning. Your meals should run to between $2 and $4. The hotel is under the expert management of S.I.T.O.

VENEZUELA

Criollos in Skyscrapers

BY

ROBERT H. MILLER

(Writer for "The Daily Journal" in Caracas and correspondent of "The Financial Times" of London, Mr. Miller can also add twenty years of residence in and around Venezuela to his impressive list of qualifications as a competent interpreter of "Little Venice".)

Christopher Columbus discovered Venezuela on August 1, 1498 on his third voyage to the New World. Attracted by a strong current of fresh water that flowed far out to sea from the mouth of the Orinoco River, he made landfall that day at a place the Indians called Macuro and claimed it for Spain. This point is now called Puerto Cristóbal Colón in memory of this intrepid voyager.

Venezuela received its name, according to historians, from Americo Vespucci, who, while sailing together with Alonso de Ojeda on Lake Maracaibo (approximately 4,907 square miles) at the beginning of the 16th century, associated the sight of Indian canoes gliding silently between houses built on piles

601

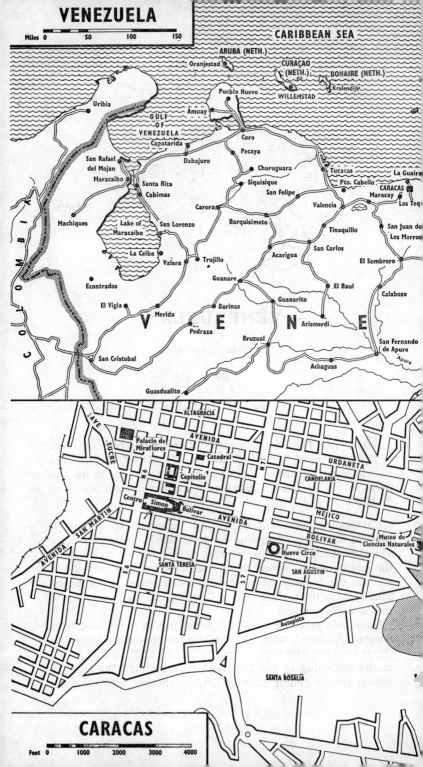

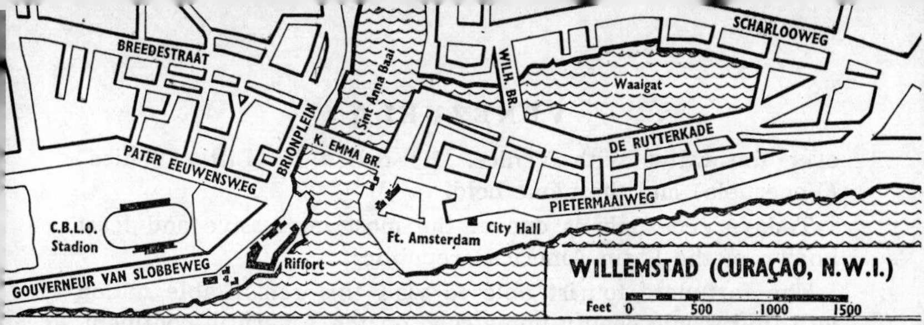
BREEDESTRAAT
Sint Anna Baai
WILH. BR.
SCHARLOOWEG
Waaigat
BRIONPLEIN
K. EMMA BR.
DE RUYTERKADE
PATER EEUWENSWEG
PIETERMAAIWEG
C.B.L.O.
Stadion
City Hall
Ft. Amsterdam
Riffort
GOUVERNEUR VAN SLOBBEWEG
WILLEMSTAD (CURAÇAO, N.W.I.)
Feet 0 500 1000 1500

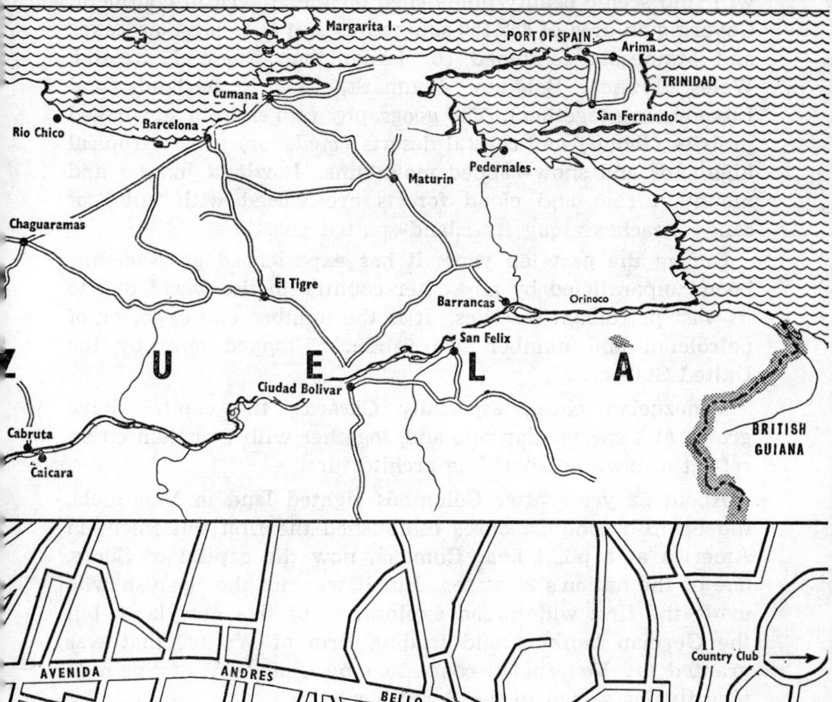
Margarita I.
PORT OF SPAIN
Arima
TRINIDAD
Cumana
San Fernando
Rio Chico
Barcelona
Pedernales
Maturin
Chaguaramas
El Tigre
Barrancas
Orinoco
San Felix
Z U E L A
Ciudad Bolivar
BRITISH
GUIANA
Cabruta
Caicara

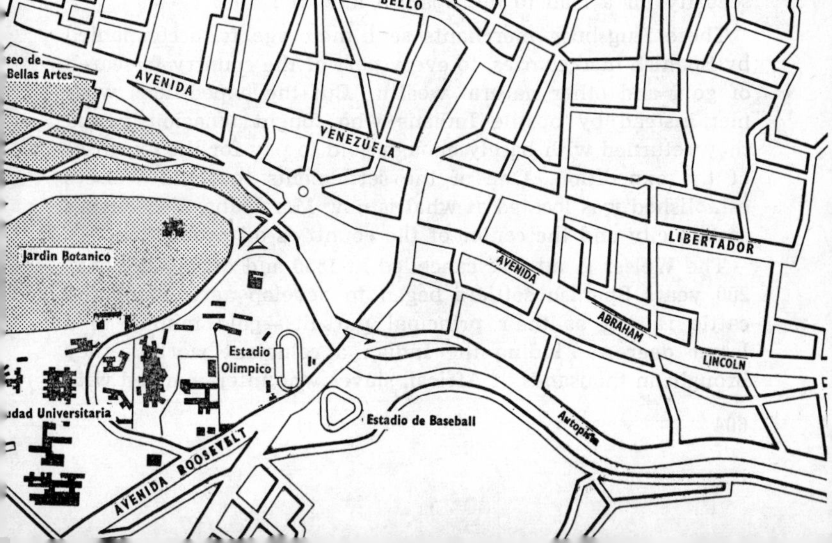
Country Club
AVENIDA
ANDRES
BELLO
seo de
Bellas Artes
AVENIDA
VENEZUELA
LIBERTADOR
Jardin Botanico
AVENIDA
ABRAHAM
LINCOLN
Estadio
Olimpico
udad Universitaria
Estadio de Baseball
Autopista
AVENIDA ROOSEVELT

VENEZUELA

over the water with Venice. He called it "Little Venice" (Venezuela) and the name held.

Today, Venezuela is one of the most impressive and least known of the Latin American republics.

The fortunate tourist able to visit this remarkable nation will find scenic beauty unmatched on the American continent. Covering an area of 352,150 square miles, it is as large as Texas and Minnesota combined (or larger than England, Ireland, Wales, France, Belgium, Denmark, The Netherlands and Luxembourg together). The geography ranges from sun-baked prairies (*llanos*) and coastal deserts (*médanos*) to sub-tropical highlands and snow-capped mountains. Lowland jungles and mountain rain and cloud forests are varied with miles of sandy beaches along its island-spotted coastline.

During the past ten years it has experienced an economic boom unparalleled by any other country in the world due to its vast petroleum reserves. It is the number one exporter of petroleum and number two producer, topped only by the United States.

Venezuelan cities, especially Caracas, the capital, have grown at a spectacular rate and, together with Brazilian cities, reflect a new and sparkling architecture.

About 22 years after Columbus sighted land in Venezuela, the Spanish conquistadores established the first settlement in America at a point near Cumaná, now the capital of Sucre, one of the nation's 20 states. But it was not the Spanish who made the first widespread exploration of this new land, but the German banking and trading firm of Welser, that was granted the Venezuelan concession by Charles V of Spain as security for a loan to the Spanish monarch.

These Augsburg merchants sent their agents, accompanied by Spanish mercenaries, to every part of the country in search of gold and other natural wealth. But the expeditions were met instead by hostile Indians who fought tenaciously and they returned with barely enough gold to pay for the expenses of the expedition. One of the settlements that the Welsers established was located at what is now Maracaibo, Venezuela's second city and the center of the country's oil production.

The Welser grant was cancelled in 1556 and during the next 250 years Spanish settlers began to develop agriculture and cattle raising as their principal pursuits—gold mining to a lesser degree. Finding the Indian a reluctant worker, they brought in thousands of African slaves who inter-married with

Indians who, in turn, mixed with the Spaniards and formed the present *criollo* or Venezuelan type of today.

The beginning of 1800 saw the Venezuelan becoming increasingly dissatisfied with Spanish rule. Young criollo intellectuals, schooled abroad in France and the United States, returned to their homeland where discrimination against the criollo was beginning to mount and served as a springboard for the struggle which eventually ended in independence from Spain.

A brief, unsuccessful revolt was stifled by the Spaniards in 1796 and another in 1806. General Francisco Miranda brought the country under a short-lived independence in 1811 when Spain was occupied defending itself against invasion by Napoleon. However, Spanish forces overwhelmed the colonists, captured Miranda and reestablished Spanish rule.

It was at this dark hour that Simón Bolívar, Venezuela's Liberator and one of South America's greatest heroes, rose to fill Miranda's place as the head of downtrodden Venezuelans. This remarkable figure, who set aside the life of ease and wealth into which he was born, was directly responsible for the liberation of five Latin American nations from under the yoke of Spain—Peru, Bolívia (named for him), Ecuador, Colombia and Venezuela. Bolívar also exerted great influence over the whole independence movement from Mexico to Chile.

Invincible in war, Bolívar found that the enormous task of replacing three centuries of Spanish colonial rule with an independent republican form of government was overwhelming. His dream of uniting Venezuela, Colombia and Ecuador into "Gran Colombia" was sabotaged by his own lieutenants. Disillusioned and penniless, Bolívar died in Santa Marta, Colombia on December 17, 1830 age 47. Foreseeing years of anarchy ahead, he wrote in despair: "All who have served the revolution have ploughed in the sea."

One hundred years of dictatorial rule and internal strife followed after the death of Bolívar. The land, rugged and poor, presented formidable obstacles to agricultural development and the Venezuelan lived under the poorest of conditions until the advent of petroleum. The first commercialization of oil was made in the State of Táchira in the 1870's but it was not until the mid-1920's that oil in the Maracaibo Lake basin began to flow in sufficient quantities to influence the national economy. Foreign oil companies began to enter during the dictatorship of Juan Vicente Gómez and since that time billions of dollars have been poured into the Venezuelan oil industry.

VENEZUELA

The present-day Venezuelan, known locally as *Juan Bimba* (Mr. Average Man) is one of 7,500,000. His principal recreation is conversation and his slang-filled Spanish is dotted with borrowed English phrases like "O.K." or "alright." Although he is a nationalist, he does not hate the foreigner, usually referring to him light-heartedly as *Musiú* (moo-see-óo) from the French *monsieur*. The Venezuelan is fond of baseball, television, *bolas criollas*, dominos and soccer football.

PRACTICAL INFORMATION FOR VENEZUELA

WHEN TO GO. Venezuela is best enjoyed between the months of November and April, the best months being December, January, February and March. At this time there is a minimum of rainfall, the countryside is green and the climate is most agreeable everywhere.

TRADITIONAL EVENTS. While Venezuela has its traditional events, such as the "Diablos de Yare" and the "Bailes de San Juan" each year, these events have not yet graduated to the level where accommodations are provided for tourists. As there are so many everyday things of interest to see in this country, there is no need for a tourist to schedule his trip to take in such events.

 HOW TO GO. Venezuela is on the crossroads of practically all steamship and airlines serving the South American continent. To name a few: Pan American, Delta, VIASA, KLM, VARIG, all serve Venezuela from the United States, departing from New York, Miami, New Orleans, Houston and Los Angeles. KLM, Air France, VIASA, Iberia, Alitalia, Avianca and BOAC all have direct services to Europe from Venezuela. All of the above-mentioned airlines, with the exception of Delta, continue to other parts of Latin America. Delta serves Jamaica from Venezuela on its U.S.-Venezuela route. Steamship lines touching Venezuelan ports are the Grace Line, Alcoa and P&O from New York, New Orleans and Miami. Venezuelan Line (New York, New Orleans, Baltimore, Houston, Philadelphia). Other lines from Europe are the Pacific Steam Navigation, French Line, KNSM, Italian Line, Hamburg Amerika Line, Spanish Steamship Line and Portuguese Steamship Company, all with passenger accommodations.

Ship passengers whose destination is Caracas will disembark at La Guaira and be driven to the capital on what is the most spectacular highway in the world. This unforgettable mountain drive, still a thrill though no longer dangerous, is one of the most rewarding extra bonuses of the sea voyage.

PASSPORTS, VISAS. All consulates are authorized to issue tourist cards up to 30 days to nationals of the following countries: the United States, Canada, Western Germany, Holland (metropolitan), Sweden, Belgium, Norway, Denmark, and England. You will need proof of nationality (passport or birth certificate, a round-trip ticket or ticket to another country, four frontview photographs (4 by 4 inches), a smallpox vaccination certificate

VENEZUELA

(issued within the past three months). Carriers duly authorized by the Venezuelan government may also issue tourist cards up to 8 days upon presentation of the documents listed above. As an extra bonus, this 8-day tourist card will be automatically extended for 12 additional days upon arrival in Venezuela, by the immigration authorities.

WHAT TO TAKE. If you are planning a trip only to Caracas, take the type of clothing you are accustomed to wearing in spring or early summer. Caracas is a sophisticated city and does not look willingly on clothes generally described as "cruise line". If your trip takes you to the beaches, the latest in beach wear is in order. Nothing scandalous is tolerated and shorts are not permitted outside of the bathing area.

On trips to Maracaibo and other coastal cities, the lightest summer clothing is recommended. Men wear shirts and trousers only.

If you are going to rough it in the interior, then bring along leather boots and khaki breeches, long-sleeved shirts or blouses, a sun helmet or rag hat, rain gear, mosquito netting and some insect repellent. The rest you can obtain locally and it is usually better that you do so because the latest inventions for jungle travel are generally found to be impractical when put into use either by yourself or local people who have never seen them.

If you like golf, bring clubs. Anglers will find plenty of equipment here if anything goes wrong with their own. Hunters must first be sure to get a permit from the Venezuelan Consul in port of origin before attempting to bring a gun into the country. Rifles are usually not allowed. Single and double-barreled shotguns get permits with little difficulty. No pistols. Cameras and used portable radios may be carried without problem. Pictures may be taken anywhere in the country except around military installations or major airports.

WHAT WILL IT COST? A typical day in Caracas, first class, can go as high as $40 to $50 for room, food, transportation and odds and ends. However, this day can be enjoyed for as low as $15 if one stays at modest hotels and eats in modest restaurants, takes buses and walks.

TRANSPORTATION. Buses reach every part of the city for either 25 or 50 céntimos and run almost 24 hours a day. Buses are nearly every color of the rainbow (the illiteracy rate still being high) and each color represents a different route. "Por puestos" (jitneys) cover most Caracas areas for either 50 céntimos or one bolívar. Taxis charge a minimum of 3 bolívares but, as they have no meters, arrangements should be made before entering. The usual fare from the Hotel Tamanaco to the center of town is 5 bolívares and to the airport 35 bolívares. From the center of town the fare to the airport is 20 bolívares. No tipping in cabs.

MONEY. The bolívar (Bs) is worth about 22 cents U.S. Conversely, $1.00 equals Bs 3.35; however, bolívars can be easily converted into dollars at the rate prevailing in the market, which fluctuates from Bs 4.54 to Bs 4.58 per U.S. dollar. There are no restrictions on importation of currency. U.S. and Canadian dollars are exchanged easily everywhere. The bolívar is divided into 100 céntimos and the coins are as follows:

5 céntimos (puya) - a nickel or copper coin the size of a dime U.S.

VENEZUELA

12½ céntimos (locha) - a nickel coin the size of a quarter. (Note: this coin can be confused with the bolívar as it is the same size. The difference is that the edges of the locha are *not* milled while the bolivar has milled edges, and on one side the face of Bolivar.)

25 céntimos (medio) - a silver coin, half the size of a dime.

50 céntimos (real) - a silver coin about the size of a dime.

1 bolivar - a silver coin about the size of a U.S. quarter.

2 bolivares - a silver coin slightly smaller than a U.S. fifty-cent piece.

5 bolivares (cachete or fuerte) - a silver coin slightly larger than a U.S. dollar.

Venezuelan paper money is in the following denominations: Bs 10, Bs 20, Bs 50, Bs 100, Bs 500.

 TIPPING. Usually 10 per cent on top of restaurant bills (which is normally added by the waiter to the bill). It is also customary to add another 5 % to this which is left on the table. It is also the custom to tip chambermaids and others who render services in a hotel. No one is annoyed if you do not tip, as it is a new custom brought to Venezuela by European immigrants over the last ten years.

 TELEPHONES. Fully automatic, although somewhat reluctant. Hotels charge 25 céntimos per call made from rooms. Pay phones are still a novelty and are being installed in Caracas and Maracaibo for the first time. For long distance, call 06 and long distance complaints 41.20.63. For long distance in the Caracas area, dial 00 and for complaints 41.55.94. The 06 number has English-speaking operators. 03 is for information, 05 for numbers out of order and 09 and 43 for the time.

MISCELLANEOUS. Drive-yourself cars are available from "Fiesta Car Rental" telephone 334861. The charge is approximately $11.00 per day. gasoline included for a Chevrolet or similar make, and slightly less for a small European car. Special rates by week or month.

Electric current in Caracas is 50 cycle, 110 volt and in Maracaibo 60/110.

Mail is rapid to New York and Europe. A 5-gram letter to the United States is 40 céntimos and to Europe either 60 or 80 céntimos depending on the country. All America Cables has an office in Caracas and others in Puerto La Cruz, La Guaira and Maracaibo. The Government radio is connected with the RCA service overseas. Both have English-speaking attendants and charge current world rates for messages. Interior telegraph service is bad and not recommended. Interior radio service is good. Mail to the interior is bad unless letters are sent "expreso" at an extra charge. Urban delivery of letters in Caracas usually takes three days.

Weights and measures are on the metric system.

HOTELS

The visitor has a choice of four first-rate hotels strategically located throughout the city. Accommodations are on a par with good U.S. hostelries, although the service is considerably less efficient. Prices range from $9.00 to $100.00 per day European plan, depending on the degree of luxury sought by the visitor. The six major hotels offering English-speaking personnel are as follows:

VENEZUELA

CARACAS

HOTEL TAMANACO. Urbanización Las Mercedes. Located on the southern side of the Valley of Caracas with an unexcelled view. Accommodations range from the presidential suite to simple rooms. The hotel has a large swimming pool, night club, restaurant, grill, bar, shopping and social centers. Several rooms and suites have private flower-decked terraces. Single rooms begin at $14 per day, doubles $21, European plan. Tel. 33.37.11. This is one of the pearls of the *Intercontinental* chain.

HOTEL AVILA. A quiet deluxe hotel in Urbanización San Bernardino with charm, quiet and comfort in the shady, wooded hills on the north side of the Valley of Caracas. Dining room, bar, banquet and conference rooms, sun terrace and swimming pool. No night club. Rates begin at $11 daily single, $19 double, European plan. Telephone 55.61.11.

HOTEL EL CONDE. Esquina El Conde in the heart of downtown Caracas. This is a businessman's hotel and offers excellent cuisine in its main dining room and breakfast grill. Drinks are served in an air-conditioned bar and rooms may be had with or without air-conditioning. Rates begin at $10.50 single, $15 double, European plan per day. Telephone 81.11.72.

HOTEL POTOMAC. Urbanización San Bernardino. This is a family type hotel just outside of the perimeter of downtown Caracas and one block off the city's main commercial avenue. The address is Esquina de Avenida Caracas y Avenida Vollmer. Excellent meals are served in a large dining room or on the terrace, and it has a popular bar. Rates begin at $9 single, $15 double daily European plan. Tel. 55.40.81.

HOTEL HUMBOLDT. This re-opened hotel, and one of the world's most spectacular, the Humboldt towers in majestic glass and steel from the green crest of Avila Park, 7052 feet above sea level. There is a spectacular view of the bay and city below. Access to the Humboldt is by cable car from the heart of Caracas, or by picturesque mountain road (cable is faster) and either way the view is stupendous. The hotel tower is a wonder of engineering, 14 floors high with 75 suites arranged in circular pattern so that all have balconies and views. The hotel is well equipped with all that you need for a two-day or two-month stay. An indoor swimming pool and skating rink make sports possible the year round. Rates: European Plan $12 and up single, $13.50 and up double.

MACUTO-SHERATON. This Venezuelan luxury hotel, 20 miles from Caracas was built at an estimated cost of $30,000,000. It includes 16 different types of imported marbles. Fully air conditioned, it features 1500 feet of natural beach; two swimming pools, lanais and cabanas, golf and marina facilities at the adjacent Carabelleda Golf & Yacht Club, a roof top night club, three dining rooms and four bars, and the grandest ballroom in Venezuela. Rates are surprisingly economical; from $9.50 single, and $14.50 double, E.P.

Other smaller hotels are:

		Rate	Phone
TIUNA. Av. Urdaneta, Esquina Pelota		from $7.50	82.51.12
MARA. Av. Urdaneta, Esquina Pelota	,,	7.50	81.10.51
BIDASOA. Ibarras a Maturín	,,	3.60	82.17.07
CRISTAL. Pasaje Asunción, Sbna. Gde.	,,	7.50	71.91.31
COMERCIO. Puente Soublette	,,	5.50	41.91.41
SAVOY. Avenida México 192	,,	5.00	55.26.31
VENEZUELA. Pedrera a Gorda 64	,,	6.60	41.45.92

These hotels are all European plan, modern buildings, clean and safe for tourists.

VENEZUELA

FOOD AND RESTAURANTS

Venezuelan food, contrary to expectation, is not fiery hot. However, a condiment known as *guasacaca* and another called *picante* can be applied to any dish. Most of the dishes have an overtone of cumin and saffron, often colored a reddish-yellow with *onoto* (used by the Indians to paint their faces) and, when well prepared, have a delicate flavor. Some of these dishes are:

Parilla Criolla—Native barbecued beef served with *yuca* or *hallaquitas* (see continuing food vocabulary for explanation).

Carne Mechada—A sort of hash made with jerked meat, served with rice, fried or baked plaintains, black beans, yuca and hallaquitas.

Hallaca—This is the most advertised native delicacy. It is basically a type of tamale, except that it is wrapped in a banana or plaintain leaf instead of corn husk, is flat instead of round, is *not* hot (like a Mexican tamale) and the ingredients inside the corn-meal covering include meat, spices, olives, raisins and other odds and ends. There are chicken, pork and beef hallacas, each with a flavor all its own. Although available the year around, they are particular favorites during the Christmas and New Year holidays.

Hervido—A soupy stew made with chunks of chicken, beef or fish and native vegetables and roots.

Sancocho—The same as *hervido* except that the chunks are larger and the dish is considerably more primitive. The vegetables used are auyama, tomato, cabbage and whole sections of corn on the cob. The roots are ocumo, ñame of batata and yuca. It must be eaten with a knife, fork, spoon and the fingers. The latter are generally licked when finished.

Pelao—A native chicken and rice dish which, according to legend, must be prepared with a stolen chicken over an open fire in the woods by those who stole the chicken. This can be a very tasty dish provided the participants do not forget the spices. A more refined version of this dish is called *Arroz con Pollo* and can be eaten under respectable circumstances.

Other tasty dishes are *asado* (native roast), *empanadas* (a meat-filled turnover), *lapa* (native guinea pig) and tapir in various forms.

Many of these dishes are accompanied by native breads. Of these, the two principal ones are *casabe* and *arepa*.

Casabe—a tasteless unleavened slab in the form of a cartwheel and quite as large, made of bitter yuca from which the bitter (and poison) juice has been removed. It is sun-dried usually on a thatched roof and later baked over a charcoal fire on an iron slab about three feet in diameter. The nearest thing it can be compared with is rye crisp.

Arepa—a primitive corn meal bun, made over a charcoal fire, crisp on the outside when hot and mealy-soft on the inside. Arepas should be eaten hot, with or without butter, and lately have been used for making sandwiches called *tostadas,* eaten mainly as late snacks at night.

It is recommended that these dishes be obtained in a reputable place for, when they are good they are delicious, but when they are bad they are horrible. Some of these places are *Venezuela (Parque El Pinar), El Campo, Rio Chama,* Caracas; *Hotel Maracay, Salón Aragua,* Maracay, *Estado Aragua* (Sunday noon buffet, especially).

IN THE CAPITAL. Caracas has a large variety of restaurants for all tastes and pocketbooks. It can be generally said that the price of food in Caracas is similar to that charged in New York, Los Angeles or Washington. The price of liquor is slightly higher. In addition to restaurants good food can also be obtained in the dining rooms and grills of several hotels, among which are the Tamanaco, Avila, El Conde and Potomac in Caracas, the Maracay in Maracay, the El Lago in Maracaibo and the hotels in the Andes.

Note: Prices shown with each description are for full meals. All of these restaurants serve a la carte.

Toni's. Edificio Gran Avenida, Plaza Venezuela. Telephone 54.33.06. Heading the list, Tony's is a smart restaurant in the New York or Continental manner, with music for dancing and occasionally a top entertainer. Tony's has an intimate bar just off the main dining room and special parties are attended in the wine cellar. Expect to pay $12 upwards per person.

Monseignor. Edificio Capri, sur Plaza Altamira. Telephone 33.42.74. Continental, French-style restaurant, with bar and piano music. Excellent cuisine. Prices begin at about $10 per person.

Centro Venezolano - Americano. Av. Francisco de Miranda, Chacao. Telephone 37.28.33. While this is really an educational and social organization, it has developed perhaps the best steak house in Caracas. Here, also, one may find several of the native dishes mentioned elsewhere in this section. Decor is "caney" style—a rustic shelter open to tropical gardens.

La Carreta. Calle Real Dos Caminos, Santa Eduvigis. Telephone 37.16.64. This is one of the best places in Caracas to find a native style meal. Located slightly out of town, it is an old hacienda-type house that has been converted into a restaurant. Also among the popular dishes here is the famous parrillada Argentina, a barbecued assortment of beef, sausages, liver and kidneys, all served directly from a hot charcoal brazier alongside the table and eaten from a table board. Prices here run from $5.00 up.

El Pinar. Parque El Pinar, El Paraiso. Telephone 24.448. This restaurant, operated by the "Pro-Venezuela" organization, serves only typical food. See a list of specialities in another part of this chapter. Prices run from $5.00 up for a full meal.

Tarzilandia. 10° Transversal de Altamira. Telephone 33.28.80. Set in a tropical rock garden at the foot of Pico El Avila, the highest of the coastal range, this rustic semi-outdoor restaurant specializes in charcoal-broiled meats. Here, as in most of the other restaurants specializing in beef, they use Santa Barbara beef from the State of Zulia (Maracaibo), which is the tenderest and choicest in Venezuela. Prices start at $5.00.

Pepe's. Baruta. Telephone 33.53.11 and ask for extension 27. A Bavarian-style pension, lunch and dinner is served inside or in the garden by Pepe himself in leather jerkins. Excellent sauerbraten, knackwurst and other Germanic dishes are all made right in Baruta. Prices are moderate; from $4.00 up per person per meal.

Montmartre. Also in Baruta (telephone the same number as Pepe's and ask for Montmartre for Extension 26). A gay, montmartresque restaurant found in an old colonial type house. Baruta is about ten minutes by car south of Plaza Chacaito in Caracas. Decorated in typical Parisian left bank style. The food is superb. There is music and dancing and, from time to time, entertainment. Prices for a full meal start about $10 per person.

El Dragon Verde (The Green Dragon). Av. Maturín, Los Cedros. Telephone 71.84.04. This restaurant specializes in Chinese and Russian food. Considered the best in its category in Caracas, prices run from $7.00 up. There is a bar on the main floor. The Russian restaurant is downstairs and the Chinese section is on the terrace.

The Steak House. Primer Transversal de La Castellana. Telephone 33.13.73. Run by an American restaurateur, the Steak House serves American cuts, charcoal broiled or grill-fried. Considered one of the best steak houses in Caracas. Meals start at $5.00 per person.

Other good restaurants in the $2.00 and up category are *El Tyrol* (Austrian); *El Faisán de Oro* (Hungarian); *Paprika* (Hungarian); *El Rincón de Baviera* (Bavarian); *Danubio Azul* (Yugoslav); *Ivo's* (Yugoslav); *Hector's Quasimodo* (French-Italian); *Mazola* (Italian) and *Frisco's* (German). American snacks, short orders and counter meals may be had at the *Automercado Las Mercedes* (a super-market with restaurant).

 NIGHTLIFE. Caracas nightlife is loud, brassy, flashy and vigorous. At the *Naiguatá* in the Hotel Tamanaco for example, we had the benefit of not one, but two hot Latin-American orchestras. When one stops, the other takes right over without a single moment of interruption. Samba, rhumba, cha cha cha, merengue, are the order of the night, occasionally slowing down to a rhythmic bolero. The noise is deafening. Conversation impossible. Big international floorshow with a strong Argentine accent. Liquor flows and you pay through the nose for all the frenetic gaiety. Other big places are *Todo Paris, El Trovador, Ninoska, River's.* Quieter (no floor show) are *Maxim's, Le Mazot, Picolino, Mucuruba, Le Garage.*

World-famous celebrities are often presented in the Naiguatá. Cover charge on these occasions runs from $6.00 to $9.00 and a bill for an evening usually runs from $35 up.

VENEZUELA

ENTERTAINMENT. Rarely a week passes without a worthwhile event taking place in Caracas in the concert or entertainment field in Caracas. The Nacional and Municipal theaters house a continuous stream of concerts, ballets, plays, operas, operettas and others types of attractions, with both local and important talent. Smaller theaters throughout the city present local companies in plays in Spanish, English and French. It is not a rare sight to see world famous names on Caracas billboards.

CULTURE. The museum of fine arts and the museum of history are the two most important homes of Venezuela's past. Added to this is the Bolivarian Museum, which houses all of the personal effects and documents of Simón Bolívar. Many galleries exhibit paintings and sculptures by local and foreign artists and there are many musical recitals and poetry readings, a popular cultural enterprise in Latin America.

SPORTS. Venezuela has just inaugurated South America's newest, largest, most modern and most expensive race track. Called "La Rinconada", it sports everything from an air-conditioned box for the president to a swimming pool for horses. Escalators take spectators to their stands each Saturday and Sunday as fans pack in to play the pari-mutual or the "five and six". This latter game began in Venezuela and has spread to Colombia and Puerto Rico. It consists of a betting system wherein should the bettor correctly pick the winners out of five or six races listed, he will be awarded a slice of the pot. The amount varies from very low to very high depending on the number of winners, but it is not uncommon for a better to parley a four-bolivar ($1.20) bet into hundreds of thousands. The highest single winning on record was slightly under Bs 1,000,000 (over $300,000).

Bullfighting in season is another popular spectator sport. The season usually runs from November through March and world famous matadores perform in Caracas and Maracay bull rings. Prices for a bull fight in Caracas run from $10.00 in the sun to $20 in the shade. This is more than bull fights cost anywhere else in the world.

Watersports are available less than an hour from Caracas on the Caribbean. Good deep-sea fishing is beginning to attract angles and a tournament is held each year for marlin.

Boxing and **baseball** are two very popular spectator sports in Venezuela and events of this nature can be seen the year around. Wrestling (called "lucha libre") is a weekly event.

EXPLORING CARACAS

Caracas, Venezuela's capital, is located about 12 degrees north of the equator. Founded in 1567 by Diego de Lozada, it was christened Santiago de León de Caracas, after its patron saint.

VENEZUELA

The hub of business, cultural and every major activity in the country—except the oil industry,—the capital is nestled in a long, narrow valley in the coastal mountain range just nine miles from the sea as the crow flies. At 3,164 feet above sea level, Caracas has one of the world's best climates. Springlike the year around, the temperature averages 64° with a high of 80° during April, May, September and October during the day and a low of 56° at night during January and February. The rainy season generally occurs from April through September, with a small rainy spell during part of November. The rest of the year, while it may rain once or twice, is usually dry. The best months are from December to March.

The population of Caracas is cosmopolitan, the result of heavy immigration during the past ten years. The faces of Italians, Spanish, Portuguese, central Europeans and North Americans are as familiar a sight as those of the criollo on the streets of the city.

Modern architecture has brought about a change in the character of the city. Apartment buildings now outnumber the old colonial house, fast disappearing. Four and eight-lane speedways cut the length and width of the valley and Caracas, which 15 years ago enjoyed the sedate pleasure of an unhurried existence, is now a bustling metropolis choked with traffic.

Due to its topography, the visitor will find that Caracas is bordered to the north by a high, green chain of mountains that run the length of its long corridor-like valley, and to the south by lower hills. The original center of Caracas is still the center of town, both geographically and commercially, and retains much of its colonial flavor.

Arriving from the airport on the *autopista* (super highway), the tourist enters Caracas through its western industrial area. Riding along the Avenida Sucre, he joins Avenida Urdaneta at Miraflores Palace and the Secretariat Building, Venezuela's seat of government, and will find himself on a modern thoroughfare lined on either side with new office buildings.

To the north, in the shadow of tall blue mountains, lies the old colonial section called San José and La Pastora. Its narrow, sloping streets lead down to the heart of the city at Plaza Bolívar, a beautiful square shaded by tall trees and flanked by the old cathedral, the archbishop's residence, the historic *Casa Amarilla* and the municipal council building. Off to one corner is the capitol building, built in 90 days by President Guzmán Blanco in 1890 and used today entirely by Congress. This splendid building with its golden cupola has a beautiful tropical patio with orchids hanging from the trees.

Sharp Contrast

Contrasting sharply with this colonial scene are the twin towers of Centro Simón Bolívar rising 30 floors above the street. This building complex, costing over $180,000,000, is a mammoth commercial and business area, criss-crossed with underground ramps for automobiles and pedestrians, shops, restaurants and recreational area. A large seven-block commercial and residential development flanks this area, replacing with modern buildings what was once one of the world's worst slums.

Several blocks north of the Plaza Bolívar, the National Pantheon rises in tribute to the heroes that have found their final resting place therein. It is here that the remains of Bolívar are entombed.

Leaving the colonial center of the city, the tourist becomes aware of the ultra-modern development of Caracas. Through San Bernardino, he heads east along Avenida Andres Bello, winds through the Country Club, enters La Castellana, Altamira and other sumptuous residential areas. Returning back along the Avenida Francisco de Miranda, he will find himself in a smart shopping area and, leaving this, he will see Plaza Venezuela where water in a huge fountain spills over five giant statues. South of the plaza is University City, a 400-acre center of learning dotted with futuristic buildings, halls and student residences. West of the plaza is Parque Los Caobos, a bower of mahogany trees that once gave shade to coffee when is was a plantation. The museums of fine arts and science are located at the western end of this park where the visitor may view a large collection of Indian lore or Venezuelan art as he chooses.

South of the main center of the city, broad avenues take the visitor to the Circulo de las Fuerzas Armadas (Officer's Club), considered one of the most extravagant in the world. This remarkable center of recreation is flanked by the Military School, also one of the continent's largest and best equipped.

Undergoing its tremendous transformation, Caracas presents a startling and often bewildering picture to the tourist. In the eastern part of the city, where peons drove cattle just ten years ago, sophisticated Caracas residents now sip coffee and cocktails in chic sidewalk cafes in the best continental manner.

The hillsides are filling up with fine homes as dozens of

urbanizing concerns cut into the once rugged and impenetrable barriers. During the last year, however, an interesting phenomenon has also developed: that of the illiterate peasant, unaccustomed to city dwelling, who has found his way by the thousands into town. He has covered thousands of acres of choice hillsides with shanties. This phenomenon is considered temporary by government authorities and is expected to disappear as the acute housing problem of the underprivileged classes is corrected.

A complete bird's-eye view of the valley of Caracas can be had from the heights of Mount Avila just behind the city. It can be reached by cable car—the longest in the world—from the coast or from the city itself. The tourist will find a large dining room and recreation center at the top, an ice-skating rink, a luxury hotel and swimming pool. Paths winding down into cloud-forest country lead to the community of Galipan, Caracas' flower-growing center just a mile or two away.

EXPLORING THE REST OF THE COUNTRY

Venezuela wears its major cities like a string of pearls along its coast. It is in this area that the majority of Venezuela's citizens live and it is here that most of the industry, agriculture and commerce is carried on. Nevertheless, the criollo proudly points west, south and east and declares that "this is the real Venezuela."

Los Llanos. The city of San Juan de los Morros, gateway to the *llanos* (plains) lies about 75 miles southwest of Caracas. The typical llanos lie in the State of Guárico but spread over into the states of Barinas, Portuguesa, Cojedes, Apure, Anzoátegui and even Miranda. The vast plains stretch as far as the eye can see and are rich in Venezuelan folklore. They are to Venezuela what the Far West is to the United States.

The national dance of Venezuela, the *joropo*, is from the llanos. The locale of Venezuela's most famous novel, *Doña Bárbara* by Rómulo Gallegos, is also laid here. Skilled horsemen ride its 108,989 square miles just as they did during the wars of independence. Stoutly independent, the *Llanero* (plainsman) has persistently remained outside the influence of the currents of progress. His life is cattle raising. Hardened by outdoor life, he rises before dawn and, with only a cup of black coffee in his stomach, spends the day in the saddle until sunset, when he climbs into his hammock to sleep after a spartan evening meal.

VENEZUELA

The Llanero has two enemies. The first is the capricious weather with its alternate floods and droughts and the second is *el tigre*, the jaguar which stalks his cattle. Naturalist Ernst Schaeffer says "... the jaguar is the classical animal of the llanos. I know no other one that excites the same way and causes so much terror among young and old, among brave and cowardly. He is not spoken of in other than the singular as if one were dealing with one of those ancient Indian gods that has retreated before the invasion of unbridled greed, riotous music of the radio and the reek of gasoline into the heart of the deep jungle ..." The Llanero frequently hunts the jaguar with nothing more than a lance while out hunting deer and other game on the broad expanse of his plains.

The Llanero shows his horse-riding prowess during frequent rodeos. The chief event is called *toros coleados* in which a Llanero on horseback gallops past a steer, grabs it by the tail and flips it off its feet. Rodeos are accompanied with huge *parrillas* or *asados* (barbecues) with dancing to joropo music. The typical dress of the Llanero on these occasions is the white linen *liquiliqui* (pronounced leeky-leeky), a simple two-piece suit with military collar and studs, a Stetsontype hat and low-heeled boots. The music is played by a *conjunto* composed of *cuatros* (four-stringed instruments about half the size of a guitar), a harp (miniature size without pedals) and maracas.

No other landscape in Venezuela seems to produce such a profound impression on the imagination as do the llanos. A short stay, or even a single day in the region is an unforgettable experience.

HOTELS

LLANO ALTO, at Barinas in the high prairies beside the Santo Domingo River is one of the chain of fine government hotels found throughout the country. An ideal spot for sportsmen, there are horses available for riding the many trails nearby, excellent fishing and hunting. Guides are available and the game bagged in the area sounds like a run down of animals at the zoo with pumas and deers leading the list. The Llano has adult and children's swimming pools, playroom for children and a ballroom. There are 31 rooms and 17 cabin accommodations. Rates: European Plan, $8.95 single, $11.94 to $19.40 double.

TRUJILLO, is another comfortable government hostelry in the capital of Trujillo State, 3,300 feet above sea level. Built in 1955, the 30 room hotel is well appointed with bar, grill, dining room, swimming pool, shops and a handsome park. Numerous tours are arranged for guests to neighboring places of scenic and historical interest. Rates: European Plan, $7.46 single, $11.94 to $17.91 double.

VENEZUELA

Los Andes. The Venezuelan Andes rise like islands out of the tropical lowlands that surround them. Located in the southwest angle of the country, no other place in Venezuela offers such an opportunity to see varied landscapes in such strong relief.

This region of snow-capped mountains, sparkling rivers and high lakes makes up the states of Táchira, Mérida and Trujillo. In the state of Mérida, which produces the best coffee in Venezuela, the leading and largest city is its capital, also named Mérida. This city of tiled roofs is a colonial gem which houses the University of the Andes, one of the oldest in the Western Hemisphere, founded 170 years ago.

Lofty Pico Bolívar pushes its white summit 16,144 feet into the sky. It is the highest point in Venezuela and, along with a half dozen other peaks over the 15,000-foot level, forms the Sierra Nevada National Park in the heart of the Venezuelan Andes.

Folklore of the region is maintained in the colorful clothing of the Andean farmer which they use during yearly festivals. The "Andino" (Andean) is astute, tenacious and a hard worker. He is strong because his environment will not allow the weak to survive and he is either a friend or an enemy because he is straightforward and does not split loyalties. The Andean likes politics, discipline and strong rule and the Andes have supplied most of Venezuelan's political and military leaders. Juan Vicente Gomez and Marcos Pérez Jimenez, Venezuela's last two dictators, also came from the Andes.

In the cool mirrors of Andean lakes, fishing is nearly an obligation. Most of these lakes are easily accessible and offer excellent trout for the angler. Snow sports are also available nearby, with skiing on snowy slopes nearly on the equator.

PRADO RIO is one of a number of Government hotels in the scenic Andes area. This one, located at the foot of the Sierra Nevada near the city of Merida at 5,280 feet above sea level, is built in ranch style with 13 rooms in the main building and 42 single and double cabins in the surrounding area. Swimming pool, play room for children, soda fountain and bar are all in the main building. Fishing is good here if you like angling for trout in mountain streams. Tours are arranged for visits to mountain lakes nearby and to points of interest in Merida, a picturesque city founded in 1558. Rates: $7.46 single, $11.94 to $19.40 double, cabins from $17.91.

AGUAS CALIENTES in Urena is located not far from the Columbian border in one of the most picturesque parts of Venezuela. Visitors can take the thermal baths here from sulphur and iron water springs with temperatures from 82°F to 123°F. Water for the hotel comes from cool rock spring water which also fills the hotel pools. Rates:

VENEZUELA

European Plan, $6.57 single, $10.45 double with a Presidential Suite at $22.39.

EL TAMA, a large government hotel near San Antonio in western Venezuela. There are 98 rooms, all with private bath and terraces and 15 suites. "El Condor" diningroom specializes in Venezuelan and international cuisine. Their large Olympic Pool meets all standards for official swim meets. Special interest tours are arranged for guests including visits to villages where native handicrafts are made.

Rates: European Plan, $7.46 single, $13.43 double.

MORUCO, is 7000 feet high in the Andes in Santo Domingo with an impressive mountain view a cool, refreshing climate year round. Attractive rustic architecture on the Swiss chalet style makes this place especially restful. Trout fishing, riding, and many open air sports are arranged by the hotel staff. A glass enclosed swimming pool with heated water allows swimming in all seasons. There are 21 rooms Rates: European Plan, $8.36 single, $13.43 to $19.40 double.

Western Venezuela. Western Venezuela holds the pot of "black gold" that brought wealth to the nation. Its largest city is Maracaibo, capital of the State of Zulia and oil capital of the country. It is located at the head of Lake Maracaibo which, in effect, is not so much a lake as it is a river, according to geophysical experts. Hundreds of rivers drain from the Andes and the Santa Marta mountains which surround it and settle in the lowest part, forming the huge body of fresh water. This water flows northward and drains into the Caribbean Sea. The water around the city of Maracaibo itself is slightly brackish.

Maracaibo received its name, according to legend, after a battle between the Conquistadores and an Indian tribe led by their chief, Mara. Upon defeating Mara and his tribe, the Spaniards jubilantly cried out "Mara cayó" (Mara has fallen) which finally became Maracaibo. The name is today synonymous with oil.

The "Maracucho" (slang name for a native of Maracaibo) does not apologize for his weather. It is hot, very hot. But he likes his city and state. Despite the heat, the Maracucho is active and agressive in business, preferring to make money rather than to dabble in politics. He loves sports, is an avid baseball fan and fond of giving his children elaborate names. Recently a girl baby was named Laika Sputnik González.

Not far from Maracaibo are two of the most fascinating Indian tribes in the country. They are the Goajiros, a nomadic, cattleraising tribe, and the Motilones, fierce killers.

The Goajiros, maintaining a thin veneer of Spanish Catholic teaching, are all named Gonaléz. They are of medium height, copper complexion and have jet black, straight hair.

When dressed for visiting, the male wears a large, many-folded breechclout, a bright mantle, immense sash, a necklace and headband of feathers. The woman wears a sack dress of calico, sometimes with holes only for head and arms, a "puna" —long strings of colored beads that pass over both arms and cross each other on the breast and back. These are held by a "sirapo," a belt of black beads. These beads are collected from childhood and some Goajiro girls have as many as 100 turns of beads around their waists, ankles and wrists. They paint their faces various hues to protect them from the sun and mosquitos.

The Motilones have remained hostile to the white man since first discovered during colonial times. They are constantly at war and not more than a dozen tribes are reported to be in existence. The name "Motilone" is now synonymous with any wild Indian of the region. They make frequent raids on white settlements and attack all who try to enter their territory. They use an awesome weapon: a six-foot bow from which they shoot six-foot arrows capable of penetrating a bullet-proof vest that would stop a .45 calibre bullet. They shoot the bow while lying on their backs and use their legs to support the bow and often shoot at low-flying airplanes. More than one pilot has landed to find a large arrow impaled in the wings or fuselage of his plane after flying over the area. This region is not recommended to tourists.

CUMANAGOTO a government hotel in Cumana, doorway to eastern Venezuela, and one of the most modern in Venezuela. Ten minutes from the airport and connected to Caracas by excellent roads, the hotel has its own beach facilities nearby and a pool at the hotel. Tours are arranged into Cumana which has many spots of historic interest. Rates: European Plan, $8.36 single, $13.43 to $19.40 double with a Presidential Suite at $44.78.

Eastern and Southern Venezuela. This, the biggest and most sparsely populated area of Venezuela, represents what many believe to be the economic future of this already wealthy nation. Made up of five states (Anzoátegui, Monagas, Sucre, Nueva Esparta and Bolívar) and two territories (Delta Amacuro and Amazonas), the area covers some 208,000 square miles of plains, seacoasts, jungles, savannah and highlands—59 per cent of the total area of the country.

It was here that Columbus first landed and the Spanish made their first settlements. Today's principal seaport is Puerto La Cruz, the gateway to Eastern Venezuela. The beaches along this coast are unexcelled. Dotted with islands and inlets, the water is incredibly blue and the sands on the beaches range from pure white, through pink to golden and black. Other coastal cities are Cumaná, founded in 1520, the first Spanish settlement in America (then called Nueva Granada) and Carúpano, established in 1647. The area of northeastern Venezuela is still very primitive and, except in the highly developed petroleum area in the states of Monagas and Anzoátegui, there are no facilities for travellers.

Margarita Island

The island of Margarita, principal island in the island-state of Nueva Esparta, lies 18 miles off the coast directly north of Cumaná. The other two islands of this group are Coche and Cubagua. On Cubagua are found the ruins of *Nueva Cadiz* destroyed in 1550. Margarita is on the way to becoming a tourist attraction in the Caribbean. Settled by the Spaniards in the 1520's, the towns of Pampatar, Porlamar, Asunción, Juan Griego and El Tirano sprang into being. It was a haven for pirates along the Spanish Main and several well-preserved forts remain as silent witnesses to the island's historic past.

Lack of natural water, except for a few springs, has limited the population and growth of the island of Margarita. However, by the time you read this book, an 18-mile undersea aqueduct will be bringing water from the Carinicuao River in the State of Sucre to the islanders. Property values have risen recently and three new hotels have been built in expectation of new interest in this island as a tourist resort.

Margarita is the home of pearl fishing in the Americas. Its people have plied this trade for almost 500 years. Fishing is the only other important industry, plus limited salt processing. All of the salt in Venezuela comes from the sea and is harvested in Araya, Coche and Margarita.

BELLA VISTA is a luxury hotel on Margarita Island, easily accessible by regular airline service from all parts of Venezuela. There is a private protected beach and many other luxury resort features including the intimate *El Bambu* night club. The *Salon Paraguachoa* is available for private parties. There are 49 rooms all overlooking the ocean and suites are also available. The island is rich in local color, archeological treasures and picturesque fishing villages for those who like to explore. Rates: American Plan, $8.96 single, $17,91 double.

MIRANDA, a charming government hotel with a background of sand dunes and the Caribbean on one side and historical sights and sites on the other. It is located in the city of Coro, on the ocean within easy driving distance or flying time from Caracas. There are 59 rooms, nine suites, all air-conditioned. Swimming pool, tennis courts and a playground area. Interesting tours to the ruins of San Pablo fortress, Taratara on the Coro-Cumarebo road and to excavations of ancient Indian civilization at Piritu can be arranged through the hotel staff. There are also tours to

621

the Cathedral of Coro, the first on the continent where services were held, and to the old colonial houses in the town. Rates: European Plan, $7.46 single, $11.94 to $17.91 double.

Bolívar and the Orinoco

The capital city of the State of Bolívar is Ciudad Bolívar. Located on a mound of boulders, which form the heart of the old city, it lies 240 miles upstream from the mouth of the Orinoco River. It was formerly called Angostura because this is the narrowest part of the lower Orinoco, only 2/3 of a mile wide—but over 300 feet deep. Much Venezuelan history was written in Angostura and it was once the capital of Venezuela. It was also the original home of Angostura Bitters, which later moved lock, stock and barrel to Trinidad where, during the early days, it was easier to do business.

Ciudad Bolívar is the commercial center for the entire Orinoco River system. Its greatest activity is during April and May before the rainy season and when the rivers are at their lowest. Expeditions set out into the vast wilderness to collect chicle, balatá and tonka beans. Other groups go southward into the Gran Sabana to hunt diamonds and gold.

In recent years iron ore has become the second national staple of Venezuela. Two principal world companies, Bethlehem Steel and United States Steel both have subsidiary companies operating major mines in the eastern part of the State of Bolívar along the south bank of the Orinoco River where it joins the legendary Rio Caroní. Other mineral products from the state are gold, manganese and, more recently bauxite.

Perhaps the most romantic part of Venezuela is found in the Gran Sabana. This area, about the size of Germany, is a tropical highland that begins midway down the state and runs to the Brazilian frontier. It is dotted with small communities with Indian or Spanish names, the most important of which are Santa Elena, Icabaru, Kanavayén, Paraitepui and Luepa.

Truncated mountains rise from 7,000 to 10,000 feet like giant sentinels from the rolling savannah. One, Roraima, became the setting for Conan Doyle's famous novel "The Lost World." But the more famous one in recent years is Auyan-tepuí from which drops the world's highest waterfall—some 20 times higher than Niagara. These falls were discovered in 1937 by Jimmy Angel and are called Angel Falls.

Tourists may make the trip to Auyan-tepuí in about a week from a starting point at Canaima, a rustic resort development near its base. The trip must be made by outboard canoe up the Carrao River for 3½ days and overland on foot for one more to reach the base of the falls. It takes two or three days to come back.

These tours may be made by writing to Rudy Truffino, Canaima, Estado Bolívar, Venezuela, who will give particulars. Rudy guides all travellers in the region and makes up his party of bearers from native Indians in the region. The usual price is $240 per person in parties of 4 or more for the trip.

For those who want to see the jungle at its best but cannot stand the strain of a safari, the camp at Canaima is comfortable, running some $15.00 per day all inclusive. There are native-type huts with hammocks or beds and, more recently, Avensa, the airline that serves Canaima, has installed several prefab houses along the natural river lagoon at the foot of Hacha Falls facing this picturesque resort. All-inclusive weekend from Caracas and return $85.

Green Mansions of the Amazon

Puerto Ayacucho, the capital of the territory of Amazonas, still retains a frontier spirit found in very few towns today. Located near the northern extremity of the territory on the east bank of the Orinoco River, it is the typical tropical town that foreigners expect to see.

While the Government has constructed modern administration buildings, a hospital, school and a hotel in recent years, the remainder of the town is built in the traditional fashion that characterizes the region. Despite its location in the deep tropics, the town is clean, the water is good and its people are healthy. Malaria, yellow fever, small-pox, etc., have been completely eradicated.

Puerto Ayacucho is the gateway to the land of "Green Mansions" typified by Hudson and recently made into a moving picture which was filmed in part on location here and in Canaima. A well-surfaced dirt road leads south to a town called Sanariapo where it ends, some 40 miles distant. From that point on, the more hardy visitor may engage canoes and continue on to Brazil through a joint waterway called the Casiquiare Canal which empties into the Rio Negro which, in turn, flows into the Amazon River. This canal was first recorded by Alexander Humboldt, the famous German explorer and naturalist.

Just outside of Puerto Ayacucho is a settlement of Piaroa Indians who live in typical "churuatas" or community houses made of palm fronds. A Franciscan mission nearby also tends several communities of Indians of various races and Protestant missions dot the interior of the area.

This area is accessible to the tourist by air from Caracas via Linea Aeropostal Venezolana, or by river boat from Ciudad Bolívar via CAVN (Compañía Anónima Venezolana de Navegación). Round trip by air is approximately $100 and by boat from Ciudad Bolívar the same. The boats are of modern construction (made in Scotland) and specially designed for the river. They have small but clean two-berth staterooms in first class with a wash basin and closet in the room. The ports are screened and each cabin has an electric fan. There are separate baths for men and women passengers. The food is abundant and good, cooked in native style and with many native dishes. The trip upriver takes a week or eight days. Downstream it takes from 3½ to four days. One can combine the air and river trips to save time. Departures of the boat are approximately the 7th and 23rd of each month from Ciudad Bolívar. The return dates of the boat are more speculative, but usually half-way in between the two dates mentioned. One way fare on the boat is approximately $62 all-inclusive.

For the angler, fishing in the upper Orinoco and its tributaries is superb. Indians use the net and with a single throw can take from one to two dozen fish of as many different varieties.

The hunter will also find an interesting field for deer, lapa, tapir, jaguar, nutria and, if he chooses, boa constrictor and anaconda.

It might be well to advise the stranger that dangers in this area, as depicted in moving pictures, are greatly exaggerated. In short, the dangers are no greater than they would be in crossing a street in New York.

Central Venezuela. Returning now to the central part of the country, in the area of Caracas, we find many beaches and resorts, easily accessible and enjoyable. Most of the beaches for the city of Caracas are private clubs where Caraqueños (natives of Caracas) swim, sail, fish and water-ski. About 35 miles east of La Guaira, the main seaport for Caracas, is Los Caracas, a popular resort development and one of the most modern of its kind anywhere.

Passengers arriving by ship to La Guaira are greeted by majestic mountains rising from the sea. The hillsides are dotted with pastelcolored houses, for there is no level land available for anything except the port works. The port itself is compact, functional and modern.

West of Caracas, along a super highway, are the cities of Maracay and Valencia. Maracay, the capital of the State of Aragua, is primarily an agricultural community. In late years, however, it has become the principal training center for the air force. There are three airports in this fast-developing area.

Near Maracay, a paved road will take the visitor high into the maritime mountains to the north and into one of the most fascinating areas of the country from the scientific point of view. The Henri Pittier National Park, named for the naturalist

Stars over Tobago.... a resonant steel band.... a
bevy of creole beauties.... rum at the clap of a hand:
You'd never take it today for Robinson Crusoe's land.

An Indian rests amidst the stark beauty of his native mountains while international society lounges on the poolside terrace of the Hotel Tamanaco in Caracas: the Venezuela story is full of stunning contrasts.

of the same name, covers 210,000 acres of mountain forest land. It can be divided into three sections: rain and cloud forests, jungles and wastelands. In this area are found the largest variety of insects, flora and fauna as well as ornithological specimens of any similar area in the world.

Farther west, and skirting the shores of Lake Valencia, one reaches the city of Valencia, capital of the State of Carabobo and center of Venezuela's growing industry. The port for Valencia is Puerto Cabello, near which the nation has developed a petrochemical industry, a major dry dock and thermoelectric complex for central Venezuela. It is also the hub of a new railroad system which is gradually taking form in the nation and a major oil company has built a large refinery there. There are also many fine beaches near Puerto Cabello.

South and west, along the Pan American highway, are the towns of San Felipe, Barquisimeto and Carora, all engaged in an agricultural and cattle-raising economy.

So much for a thumbnail sketch of this nation, whose vast wealth seems almost like a 20th-century realization of the conquistadores' longed-for El Dorado. It is a strange and wonderful land, encompassing the most modern of cities with the most primitive of Indian villages, still inhabited by indigenes who will attack any white intruder into their territory. A country where Jaguars zip along the super highways and jaguars stalk their prey in the jungle, Venezuela is a place of vast variety, discovered long since by tourists but still only half explored.

MARACAY is in the beautiful valley of Las Delicias, only 70 miles from Caracas. It is a luxury hotel in a tropical setting with golf course, riding club, swimming pool, Turkish baths and an auditorium in a separate building. A dream resort spot. Rates: European Plan $12.00 single, $17.00 to $25.00 double.

DUTCH WEST INDIES

ABC and the Three Little S's

You can't beat the Dutch. From the Caribbean colonial grab bag they plucked a paltry 366 square miles, much of it so arid and rocky that nobody else wanted it. Then, with typical ingenuity and hard work, they turned it into the richest holding in the West Indies. In plantation days they supplied the whole of South America with slaves. What other people dismissed as cactus, they exported as medicinal aloes to the tune of two million florins a year. In the 19th century they scratched around and found some gold. In the 20th they found a different kind, not even on their own property, and proceeded to turn the viscid oils of Venezuela into liquid gold in the largest refineries in the world.

The energy that built the dikes of Holland built the refineries of Aruba and Curaçao. The Dutch cleansing passion that scrubs the tiles of Delft brightens the streets of Willemstad, Oranjestad and Philipsburg. Dutch hospitality, expansive at home, expands even further in the Caribbean. Dutch West Indian architecture keeps the traditions of gabled Haarlem, but doesn't hesitate to take a plunge now and then in the pioneer spirit of renascent Rotterdam.

DUTCH WEST INDIES

On some of the islands, even nature conspires to arrange a landscape by Hobbema or Ruysdael. On precipitous, conical Saba, the crater of an extinct volcano suddenly flattens out to accommodate the toy village of Bottom, replete with tow-headed peasants tilling fields and cows grazing in green pastures. At Willemstad, St. Anna Bay, leading to the land-locked port, narrows obligingly to the exact proportions of a Dutch canal. You might be sailing into Amsterdam. In short, the Netherlands Antilles are floating fragments of Holland, moored in a bluer sea, burnished by a brighter sun. You'll be meeting old friends here or making new ones, depending on whether or not you already know the Dutch.

There are two groups of islands forming the Dutch West Indies, known as the leeward and the windward islands from their comparative positions. The leeward group consists of three islands, Curaçao, Aruba and Bonaire. They are very close to the Spanish Main. Aruba, the westernmost island and the final link in the long Antillean chain, is only 15 miles from Venezuela.

The 3 Little S's

The three windward islands are Saba, Sint Maarten and Sint Eustatius. About 550 miles northwest of the ABC group, they are situated in the upper portion of the Leeward Islands group, thus achieving the distinction of being the Dutch Windwards of the Leewards. To clear up another small confusion, only half of Sint Maarten is Dutch. The other half is French, and they call it Saint Martin.

The Dutch Windward Islands, once very prosperous, are smaller and economically much less important than the ABC group. They are different in other ways too. They are more mountainous, more lush, not industrialized. There is a surplus of women over men because of the employment of the latter in the refineries of Curaçao and Aruba. Conversely, there are more men than women in the ABC group. The reader may interpret this information according to his own lights.

What the two groups do have in common is political autonomy, and the trade winds. The Antilleans have the same rights of citizenship as Hollanders at home. They elect their own legislature, called the "Staten", on a basis of universal suffrage. The governor is appointed and paid by the Crown. He ratifies legislation and represents the mother country in the joint conduct of foreign and defense affairs, in consultation with the Council of Ministers. It works out very well. Economic affairs are attended to by the Minister of Economic Affairs, as part of the Home Rule. The official language is Dutch.

The dialect of the people on the three largest islands is a mixture of Dutch, Spanish, Portuguese and English with a dash of African. It's called Papiamento. Sounds hard, but you'll be surprised at how much of it you can understand, especially if you've studied a little Spanish. It's a living language, still in a state of flux. There's plenty of room for improvisation. Try it; you may add a new word or two. Do you have to know it or Dutch to get along? Not at all. As one Curaçao businessman put it, "We are Dutch; therefore we all speak English!" Newspapers are published in Dutch, in Spanish and Papiamento. This will give you some idea of the cosmopolitan character of the Dutch West Indies, whose capital island, Curaçao, is the most cosmopolitan place in the whole Caribbean.

CURAÇAO

Curaçao, with 173 square miles and about 130,000 inhabitants, is the largest and most important of the Netherlands Antilles. Discovered, not by Columbus, but by Alonso de Ojeda in 1499, it was first occupied by the Spaniards in 1527. In 1634 the enterprising Dutch arrived under the auspices of the Netherlands West India Company, banished the Spanish Governor and 400 assorted Spaniards and Indians to Venezuela, and set up a Dutch colony. Ironwilled Peter Stuyvesant was appointed governor of Curaçao in 1643. A year later, while leading an expedition against St. Martin, he was shot in the right leg. The leg was amputated and buried in Curaçao. You'll see a fine statue of this intrepid Dutchman in Willemstad, at Peter Stuyvesant College. He jabs a staff into the ground as though he had just claimed the whole New World for Holland, and his expression is enough to explain how he got the better of all the Indians of Manhattan. When confronted by this statue, it is customary to ask which of the legs is the wooden one. The answer: they are both bronze, an indication of local wit.

Jews, fleeing from the persecutions of Spain, found refuge among the tolerant Dutch, as did the American Pilgrim fathers. Many Jews settled in Curaçao, enriching the community with their own highly-developed culture. See below: Exploring Curaçao.

Although rocky and arid, Curaçao flourished during the Colonial period as an entrepot and a center of the Caribbean slave trade. With the abolition of slavery by King William III in 1863, Curaçao went into the economic doldrums. Half a century later, in 1915, the rich oil fields of Venezuela's Lake Maracaibo were discovered. The following year, Royal Dutch Shell began construction of one of the world's biggest oil refineries in Curaçao. The daily fleets of tankers have been bringing the crude oil from the shallows of Lake Maracaibo ever since. The oil is refined in Curaçao and shipped in ocean-going tankers to the farthest corners of the earth. The chief result: great prosperity for Curaçao and nearly half a century of influx of all the workers, merchants, and soldiers of fortune that a prosperous center attracts like a lodestone to itself. Denizens of half a hundred nations now mingle in the streets of Curaçao and Aruba: Spanish, Portuguese, Hindus, East and West Indians, Caribs, Negroes, Jews, Venezuelans, Javanese, Americans, Dutch, Chinese. There is a sizeable colony of the last, of the Nationalist persuasion, in Willemstad; a former consul of China promptly opened a grocery when the Dutch government recognized the Communist regime.

Some side results of the oil refinery: (1) a localized green Eden where the Shell Oil Colony waters the arid soil of Curaçao with the water ballast in returning tankers; (2) a very bad smell on the days, fortunately rare, when the trade winds do not perform their salubrious function of blowing the fumes out to sea. When the wind blows from west to east, which it is perverse enough to do for a week or more every year, the citizens of Willemstad pay through the nose for their prosperity. Our old friend Sydney Clark reported a candid Dutchman as saying, "During that week, the city doesn't have a bad smell; it *stinks*." A polite euphemism for the reek is to say that it smells of garlic, the realistic answer to which is: No, it smells of money.

The Shell Oil Company town looks like American suburbia with its nicely-landscaped, red brick houses, golf club, hotel, and all the other amenities for a self-contained life. The gardens, as has been noted, are far greener than the average run of shrub and lawn you see on this dry island. Water is the island's biggest problem. There's a sea-water distillery, whose capacity is constantly being increased, but at a price. Outside the Shell colony, only the high-income groups can afford the high water bills, 50 to 60 guilders a month, which a garden exacts.

The government is bringing running distilled sea water into their splendid new bungalow communities for low-income groups. These are for people with incomes below $150 a month. With two and three rooms, gas, refrigerators and even washing-machines, they are a far cry from the usual native shack that blights the Caribbean landscape.

The use of color is typical. You will be struck by it the minute you arrive in Curaçao, whether you land at Dr. Albert Plesman Airport at Hato (a million dollar gem, worthy of comparison with Schiphol in Amsterdam) or whether you sail into the marvelous harbor of Willemstad through the channel flanked by the narrow gabled houses of 17th-century Holland and the fabulous Hotel Curaçao Intercontinental of the 20th century. The combination of bright primary colors, harmoniously blended with pastels and unified by the overall pale red of the tiled roofs usually lifts the spirits of even the satiated tourist. The story goes that a governor of Curaçao sensitive of eye and dazzled by the glare of tropic sun on Willemstad's white buildings, ordered all houses to be painted in other colors. Whatever the reason, the staid, sedate dignity of the Dutch architectural style has been vivified by the brush in the best operetta tradition. The result is a captivating stage set of story book buildings in blue, red, lemon yellow, lilac, pistachio, and a Neapolitan slice of strawberry, chocolate and vanilla. If your eye doesn't respond to this, it is quite possible that you have been color blind from birth.

PRACTICAL INFORMATION FOR CURAÇAO

HOW TO GET THERE. *By Air.* From New York by *KLM Royal Dutch Airlines* and *Pan American World Airways*, both of which also have direct flights from Miami to Dr. Albert Plesman Airport at Hato. KLM also provides direct inter-island connections between Curaçao and Aruba, Bonaire, Cuba, Jamaica, St. Maarten, St. Kitts, and Trinidad. Pan Am links Curaçao directly with the Dominican Republic, Puerto Rico, Trinidad, Miami and New York. VIASA and Guest Aerovias Mexico S.A., also call frequently at Curaçao.

By Sea. The *Grace Line* has a weekly service (4½ days) from New York to Curaçao and, in addition, makes Willemstad its chief port of call on regularly-scheduled 12-day luxury cruises. *The Royal Netherlands Steamship Company* has six-day passenger-carrying freighters which ply between New York and Curaçao. There are regularly-scheduled sailings from New Orleans (5 days) on ships of the *Royal Netherlands Steamship Company*, and besides these sailings a number of lines link Curaçao with such west coast ports as Vancouver, Seattle, San Francisco and Los Angeles. Among them: the *Johnson Line, Italian Line, Hamburg-American Line, Fred Olson Line, Hanseatic Vaasa Line, Inter Ocean Line* and *Osaka Shosen Kaisha Line.*

The inter-island Motorship *Antilia* runs once a month, linking Curaçao with Bonaire, the Dutch Windward Islands and St. Kitts. It is also fairly easy to island hop to Aruba and other islands on one of the transatlantic liners or cargo vessels that sail in and out of Willemstad harbor. There

SUN, SEA, SAND, AIR
BONAIRE

Timeless in its beauty, Bonaire, the Flamingo Island of the Netherland Antilles, is a paradise for water sports and fishing enthusiasts. Daytime exploring, sailing by moon-light, beautiful hours of self-discovery.

See your travel agent, or write:
BONAIRE INFORMATION CENTER
1270 Ave. of the Americas, N.Y. 20,

QUIET
ST. MAARTEN
ST. EUSTATIUS · SABA

THE TEMPTING CORNER OF THE CARIBBEAN

Near Puerto Rico and the U.S. Virgin Islands, unmatched for tranquil beauty and historical interest, the Windward Islands of the Netherland Antilles offer an easy pace: rambling tours on horse back, fishing, and superb cuisine.
Of special interest:
The half French, half Dutch flavor of romantic St. Maarten.

See your travel agent, or write:
NETHERLANDS WINDWARD ISLANDS INFORMATION CENTER
1270 AVE. OF THE AMERICAS
NEW YORK 20, N.Y.

WELCOME TO CURAÇAO

Sophisticated, colorful Curacao welcomes you in many languages. The most cosmopolitan island of the Caribbean offers you the treasures and moods of the whole wide world at free-port prices. Lovely bays, beaches and lagoons for fishing and swimming, luxurious hotels, marvelous food . . . against a fascinating background of Dutch history and architecture.

Come to the excitement of this crossroads for the world.

For information, see your travel agent, or write:
CURAÇAO INFORMATION CENTER, 1270 AVE. OF THE AMERICAS, N.Y. 20, N.Y.

were more than 6,000 of them last year, an average of about 17 ships per day.

PASSPORTS, VISAS. Transit passengers staying 24 hours or less in Curaçao (this includes most cruise passengers) need only some proof of identity. Tourists from the U.S. do not need passport or visa but must show birth or naturalization certificate or re-entry permit in addition to vaccination certificate and ticket out of Dutch territory. British and Canadian citizens need passports.

CURRENCY. The guilder or florin (names are interchangeable) is the Dutch Antilles unit of money, subdivided into 100 cents. It is issued in all denominations including a square nickel which delights amateurs of numismatics. The official rate of exchange is 1.87 florins to the U.S. dollar, and many stores accept U.S. currency at an exchange of two florins to the dollar. So if you figure the florin as half an American dollar, you won't be far off. Travelers checks are accepted everywhere.

HOW TO GET ABOUT. By foot in the town of Willemstad, which is divided into two sections, the Punda (shopping area) and the Otrabanda ("Other Side" another shopping center) by the famous Queen Emma pontoon bridge. There are good public buses for trips to the airport, suburbs, or out into the country; terminals are at Wilhelmina Square on the Punda side, Brion Square on Otrabanda. There are plenty of taxis. The drivers have an official tariff chart. Fare from the airport to Willemstad is $4 per cab.

There are a number of well-organized sightseeing tours offered by *Taber Tours*, *Palm Tours*, ranging from $3.30 per person for a 1½ hour tour to $18 for a full day's trip. Comfortable American passenger cars are provided with well-informed, English-speaking guides. There are interesting harbor sightseeing tours, sponsored by *Taber Tours* and *Palm Tours* are is $3.30 for a 1½ hour tour. You can rent a drive-your-self car at *Taber Tours*. Large American cars $12 per day, $72 per week, compacts $9 per day, $54 per week. *Isa Sales & Agencies*, Jeep Gaides $7 per day, $42 per week. *Palm Tours*, Large American cars $10 per day, $60 per week. European cars (Volkswagen) $8 per day, $48 per week. *P.B.C. Machines & Services*, European cars (Austin) $5.50 per day, $33 per week. You can get a temporary Curaçao driver's permit at Police Headquarters merely by showing your own driving license.

HOTELS

Curaçao, always one of the top flight stations on the Caribbean cruise parade, has, up until recently, been content with the brief layover of cruise ships discharging hundreds of passengers for a gander at Willemstad and a few hours' shopping spree in the city's bargain shops. With the erection of the 125-room Hotel *Curaçao Intercontinental*, the recent inauguration of KLM's nonstop flight from Idlewild, and increased inter-island air service, tourists are now being tempted to stay longer, visit other islands in the Dutch West Indies.

DUTCH WEST INDIES

HOTEL CURAÇAO INTERCONTINEN-TAL. Another link in the superb Intercontinental chain, worthy of comparison with the *Tamanaco* in Caracas, the *Tequendama* in Bogota and the *Hotel del Prado* in Barranquilla. Seldom has there been such a happy combination of site and architecture as in this hostelry built right into the old water fort at the entrance to Willemstad harbor. The ramparts of the old fort have been left intact, now serve as a promenade for guests. The hotel, with its perforated loft and long red roof, is ultra modern, yet blends beautifully with the traditional Dutch architecture of Willemstad. It looks as though it had grown organically out of the fortress. A beautiful pool and deck grace the upper promenade. A waterfall cascades to the open terrace below from which, through a series of ingenious portholes in the walls of the pool you have an underwater view of the swimmers. The hotel is air-conditioned throughout, has lovely tropical gardens, indoor and outdoor dining rooms, the first gambling casino in the Dutch West Indies, and an attractive shopping arcade in what used to be the storage vaults of the old fort. George Markicos is the manager of the Curaçao Intercontinental, a gracious and competent host.

Since our last visit, the hotel indeed made many improvements. The bath towels are soft and fluffy. Top talents from the hemisphere and Europe succeed each other every other week. The night shows are so successful the management decided to have the night club enlarged till now it seats about 175 people; a new dance floor was made and a revolving stage was built. Also, an attractive Snack Bar is a new feature on the terrace by the swimming pool which provides service for snacks, sodas, drinks, etc. in a pleasant, informal atmosphere. Plans for expansion include a 7-floor Tower in the Sea with a "Marina", a supper club and an open-air Charcoal Pit. The Hotel Curaçao is fast being brought up to same level of perfection as the Tamanaco and Tequendama operations. The *Curaçao Intercontinental* operates on the European Plan. Rates are $13 to $19 single; $17 to $23 double. Mid December to mid April rates are $2 per room higher.

PISCADERA BAY CLUB. A mile and a half from Willemstad, this is an outstanding beach resort hotel with just about every facility to make the tourist happy. If you've got kids with you, this is somewhere over the rainbow for you and for them. There's a special beach, pool, playground, dining room and kitchen for them with a trained nurse in charge of it all. Adults have a private beach, tennis court, access to the nine-hole Shell Golf Course. There are 64 rooms and suites, some air conditioned, many with private terraces. Rates are a little complicated because of variety of accommodations and a fluctuating managerial policy. Both an American Plan and a Modified European Plan, or what we call the Continental Plan, meaning room and breakfast with no other meals, are available. Rates American Plan are $18 to $19.50 single, $29.50 to $30.50 double. Continental Plan $11 to $12.50 single, $16 to $17 double. Suites with sitting rooms and deluxe suites are also available. The meals, incidentally, are gargantuan. One of Piscadera Club's specialties is that dainty Indonesian delicacy known as Nasi Goreng, diced pork, ham, shrimps and vegetables served up with about ten pounds of fried rice. Have this for lunch, and Hemingway's title, "Death in the Afternoon" will take on a new meaning in your life. G. Vergeer is the manager of this generous establishment.

HOTEL AMERICANO. Right at the Otrabanda end of the Queen Emma pontoon bridge, this is an old

632

timer. Its venerable Dutch veranda is like a mezzanine overlooking the animated harbor with the pontoon bridge swinging back and forth at the toot of a whistle, and the front rooms afford private box seats on the same spectacle. Aside from this and its proximity to the shops, you may find the *Americano* a little on the dull side. The cook knows how to grill lobster and fish, however, always a compensation, and you won't be staying more than a day or two in any event. There are 45 rooms; air conditioning is available; add $2 per person. American Plan rates are from $12 to $13.50 daily single, $24 to $27 double. European Plan: $6 to $8 single, $10 to $13 double. B. G. Santine is the manager.

THE AVILA. A 45 room hotel, pleasantly situated on the ocean and with a nice swimming pool. Despite its Spanish name, it specializes in French food, and very good it is, served up under the coconut palms. There is a bar in the form of the bow of a sailing vessel called the Schooner-Bar. Mrs. P. H. Maal is the manager, and she will provide you with free car ride into town, though it's really close enough to walk. Her rates: American Plan, $14 to $19 single, $23 to $28 double; Modified American Plan, $12.50 to $17.50 single, $20 to $25 double; European Plan, $8.50 to $13.50 single, $12 to $17 double. You pay for that

French cuisine, voyez-vouz? Typical native dishes can be obtained on order.

BELLEVUE. A 42-room hotel, which used to be a government guest house, this will appeal to the budget-minded. Overlooks the busy Schottegat with its bustle of ships, and charges $8 to $12 per day, full American Plan single; $15 to $19 double. The manager, Mr. C. van Oosterhout, also takes clients on the Continental Plan, for which rates are $5.50 to $8.25 single, $11 to $13 double. You can have air conditioning at $1.10 extra per day for a double room.

HOTEL SAN MARCO. Located on Columbusstraat, right in the shopping district of Willemstad, new and air-conditioned. It has a cocktail lounge and roof garden, and features international cooking with an Italian accent. Mr. C. d'Angelo is the manager. There are 25 rooms with bath. American Plan rates are $13.50 single, $23 double. European Plan rates: $9.45 single; $12.20 double.

KLM HATO HOTEL. Run by Royal Dutch Airlines with their customary royal attention to efficiency and cleanliness, this provides 20 rooms with shower at the Curaçao Airport. Continental Plan only. Rates are $8 per day single, $12 double. That includes an ample Dutch breakfast.

At Santa-Martha Bay, about 24 miles from town, a 35-room resort hotel by the name of *Coral Cliff Hotel* is being built. As attraction it will have a radio ham station, which may be used by all radio-hams carrying their original (not photostat) licenses as such. There will be a small observatory for amateur star-gazers. Yachting facilities in the beautiful inland bay are also to be constructed. We expect the hotel to open in December of this year. The Santa Martha estate with its restored estate house can be considered as one of the most scenic spots of Curaçao.

FOOD

The basic cuisine of the Netherlands Antilles is Dutch with Indonesian and Javanese complements, and it tends to be on the heavy side, especially for the tropics. Nevertheless, the Dutch are a strong race, as you will agree when you see them plow through something called *honde portie* ("a hound's portion"). This is a Javanese dish consisting of a pile of rice slightly smaller than Mount Everest, topped by two fried eggs and surrounded by steak, potatoes (lots of them in case you're suffering from a starch deficiency), assorted vegetables, the whole seasoned with curry powder, soya sauce and several kinds of Javanese spices including a pimento paste that will make you breathe fire. First time we ever saw this dish served, it was set down before a Dutch family of four, and we concluded that it was for the entire family. We were wrong; it was just a single portion. Three more of the same followed, and the family, including two pretty, pink-faced daughters, polished it off with gusto and then ordered an apple tart with *slagroom* (whipped cream.) As has been said before in a different context, you can't beat 'em. Another dainty Indonesian dish to set before the tourist is the celebrated Javanese *rijsttafel,* or rice table. This consists of the usual mountainous portion of rice with which you consume anywhere from 20 to 40 assorted side dishes, all as exotic and mysterious as their East Indian names. *Erwtensoep* is a famous Dutch pea soup, about as thick as that oil that comes in crude from Maracaibo, then thickened a little more with pork fat and sausage. It may sound like hell, but it's heavenly. Don't plan to eat anything else with it, however; it's two meals in itself. Then there's *gevulde kaas,* filled cheese, usually of the Edam variety (the kind that looks like a bomb), stuffed with meat and baked. After which, it's *gevulde* you. But you don't have to subsist on rich soup, cheese and rice dishes in the Dutch West Indies. There are Dutch steaks, simple, slimming, and savory. There is boiled beef. There is "dried beef", which is actually the meat of the local goat, dried and salted. The nearest thing to a national dish of the Netherlands Antilles is *funchi,* which has been called the Caribbean tortilla. It's made of cornmeal and will remind you of cornmeal mush. It's served with meat or fish, has a nice texture, and seems to have been made to soak up those rich Dutch gravies.

The cosmopolitan character of Curaçao is reflected in its food. You can find French and Italian cuisine, good Chinese food and plenty of typical American meals. The menu of the *Curaçao Intercontinental*, for example, often features a twelve ounce U.S. choice sizzling steak, and the only difference between this steak here and in New York is that it's described on the menu as *"solomo de res (12 oz.) importado de EE.UU."* for the benefit of the South and Central American patrons.

Papas O'Brien are O'Brien Potatoes; there are even Irish over-tones to the cooking of Curaçao. As for seafood, we've always found it good here, whether from Caribbean waters or imported. High among the local gastronomic pleasures are fish soup and fresh fried fish. The snail-like crustacean from the karko or concha shell is considered a great delicacy by the natives. Best in demand are the wahoo, the dolphin and the red snapper.

DRINK

First there's the imported beer from Holland, and the locally brewed *Amstel*, it couldn't be better, unless it came from Germany, and even that is open to argument. Then there is Holland Gin or *jenever* (juniper). The Dutch down this neat like *schnaps*. It's almost as colorless as our gin, perhaps a shade on the tawny side, and it tastes much different. Actually it has more taste. Try it and see. Don't try to mix a martini with it; the results are appalling.

Finally, in the liquor department, there's the liqueur that made Curaçao famous, *Curaçao* itself. It is, of course, the grand specialty of the island, made from local oranges. It is the peel of this bitter orange that supplies the oil for this famous liqueur. A single orange supplies enough of this potent essence to make 24 bottles of Curaçao. The local Senior distillery may be visited (See below: Exploring Curaçao), but a lot of the liqueur is now being made abroad from exported Curaçao oranges. Interestingly enough, many other Caribbean islands have tried to duplicate this liqueur, but only Curaçao has been able to produce this special orange. Leave it to the Dutch to find gold in that arid soil. The good news about Curaçao is the local price: $2 to $4 a bottle. Low prices are also a happy characteristic of Holland-made beer and gin and of other imported spirits. (See below: Shopping).

RESTAURANTS

Old Dutch Tavern is located on Columbusstraat in the center of town. The old Dutch setting is attractive, the Dutch beefsteaks are tops, there's a wide range of Dutch specialties on the menu, and the generally high quality justifies the generally ditto prices.

Chunking, upstairs on Wilhelminaplein and comfortably air-conditioned, has good American and Chinese food, and so does the *Formosa* on Helfrichplein.

Fort Nassau, with a picturesque decor and old Dutch antiques is on a 200-foot hill and specializes in Dutch cuisine.

Another restaurant with excellent Chinese food, perhaps the best in town, is the unlikely-named *Lido* on Helfrichplein. It has a first class bar, an à la carte menu, air conditioning, and fast service; good place for lunch.

The *San Marco* at corner of Columbusstraat and Passaatstraat is best for Italian food, prepared by Italian chefs. *Lam Yuen Restaurant* has excellent Chinese food. This restaurant is located at Schottegatweg Oost 152.

The *Piscadera Bay Club* is another pleasant place for breezy lunching and dining *al fresco*.

Don't overlook the pleasures of the *Aerovista* restaurant at Dr. Albert Plesman Airport. Here you'll find the national lunch of Holland, the famous "Dutch Coffee Table" with at least one warm dish, cold meats, cheese and fruit. Try *rolpens*, minced beef with fried apples, if it is on the menu. And don't hesitate to order turbot, Dover sole or any other fish from the faraway North Sea, here or in the other restaurants of Curaçao, for these are flying fish, flown in fresh by the big silver birds of KLM. (Manager Mr. Pierre D. Spijkermans).

Ritz is the name in Willemstad for modern snackbars and soda fountains. There are three of them, on Breedstraat (P), Heerenstraat, Hendrikplein.

NIGHTLIFE

Smartest place in town for dining, dancing and gambling is the *Hotel Curaçao Intercontinental*. You will enjoy the floor show which has considerably improved.

The local gentry like the *Piscadera Bay Club* for a social evening on the town, and that's about it.

The *Chobolobo Club* is a nightclub popular with natives. There is canned music most of the time. Sometimes there's a weekend floorshow but the big show here is the view of the oil refinery under the glare of its own flames like a vision of Dante's Inferno.

The *Bahia Nightclub*, overlooking the Pontoon Bridge from the Kelber Building in Punda, has nightly dancing, mostly to canned music. The atmosphere is air-conditioned and native.

SHOPPING

Two factors combine to make Curaçao a haven for shoppers. First of all, the import duty on all goods except tobacco and alcohol is only 3.3 per cent, which is practically tantamount to making Curaçao a free port. Secondly, the cosmopolitan character of the city is reflected in a staggering array of merchandise. It is displayed in a wide variety of shops, ranging from those with a sleek, streamlined Fifth Avenue atmosphere to some which will remind you of a bazaar in old Bagdad. Almost all of the shops are concentrated in Punda, the oldest quarter of Willemstad, a section that seems to have been invented for happy tourist browsing. The chief shopping streets are Heerenstraat, Breedestraat and Madurostraat. Caution: you can't walk two yards down any one of them without seeing something you've just got to have. Heerenstraat has recently been closed to traffic and made into a pedestrian mall; the roadbed has been raised to sidewalk level and covered with pink inlaid tiles. So far, this promenade is unique in the Caribbean.

The range of bargains extends alphabetically from Antiques

to Zulu Sculpture and includes Swiss watches, French perfumes (all the great names plus some you never heard of), china, porcelain, silver, crystal, cameras, binoculars, Oriental silks, ivories, enamelware, straw goods, diamonds and other precious stones and jewelry, Latin-American handicrafts, Indian brass and cloisonné, Spanish shawls, Dutch tiles, Delftware, Saba and Madeira lace, English cashmere sweaters, music boxes, imported clothing, rare stamps, and more whisky, wine and rum than you could sample in a lifetime. If you don't see it, keep looking; if it exists and can be sold, they'll have it in the shops of Punda. If by any chance they don't, there are more shops with excellent bargains in the Otrabanda. Curaçao is a place where you will want to shop about and find your own buys. Most of the prices are fixed and there is little room for bargaining over prices that are already way below what they are at home. Nevertheless, some of the merchants keep the instincts of the bazaar, and a regretful negative on your part may prompt a sudden lowering of the price on theirs. Once this happens, you can haggle to your heart's content.

The shops listed below are just a few dozen which our own buyers have checked and found not wanting from the point of view of goods and service. This list should be augmented by the results of your own researches.

SPRITZER & FUHRMANN LTD., with three shops, are probably the leading island jewelers. Their air-conditioned three story headquarters on Breedestraat can satisfy most of your yearnings in the watch, silver and jewelry department. Expensive, 18-carat gold, hand-crafted Swiss watches, such as Piaget, sell here for less than half what they cost in the U.S. There's some beautiful Dutch and Danish silver in the sterling department, lovely Delftware and other porcelains in the china shop. A girl's best friend, diamonds, can be bought here at Amsterdam prices, and the stones are beautifully cut. If you want to go whole hog, there are spectacular chokers, tiaras and other Grand Opera openers in diamonds, rubies and emeralds. The prices for these, from $10,000 and up, are big, but not so high as those in Paris and New York.

THE GOLDEN TANKARD (Gouden Beker) on Heerenstraat, has Girard, Ulysse Nardin, Mido, International, Juvenia and other big-name Swiss watches at the lowest prices we've come across. Their selection of modern European sterling flatware, tea and coffee sets may change some of your decorating and serving ideas. There's a collection of gems that would make a buccaneer's eyes bug: rubies, diamonds and other shiny stones, either loose or set in 14 and 18 karat gold. Less precious, almost equally effective are the Brazilian aquamarines, amethysts and topaze mounted in gold. Ask to see the gold rings, earrings and bracelets, designed and made by H. Stern in Rio de Janeiro. Among other tempting items here: Saint-Louis crystal from Paris.

GOSEN'S, at 27 Breedestraat, is the third, though not the least, of the big watch-and-jewelry three of Curaçao. This is the place to buy that permanently-sealed Rolex Oyster you've been saving for at a little more than half the U.S. price.

THE YELLOW HOUSE, La Casa Amarilla, has been pleasing tourists since before the turn of the century with its complete line of French perfumes, Beauvais and Petit Point bags, embroidered Indian and Madeira linen. They also have clothing, cashmere sweaters, Panama hats. Their liquor department is excellent: a large assortment including the local Curaçao, and you can avoid payment of any local duty by ordering your choice of liquor delivered from their bonded warehouse to your ship. There is no delivery charge.

JULIUS L. PENHA & SONS INC. are strategically located at the corner of Breedestraat and Heerenstraat, just in front of the pontoon bridge. They have all the leading brands of heady French perfumes at those heady prices, about a third of the New York cost. Excellent selection of Alligator and leather handbags, Viennese petit-point and French beaded evening bags. If you've got sculpture-lovers on your Christmas list, check Penha's collection of Balinese woodcarvings. Little girls? There are dolls here from the four corners of the earth. Men? Cashmere sweaters and socks, and a good selection of shirts, ties, sports jackets, belts, pipes and wallets.

EL LOUVRE at 12 Heerenstraat is distributor for Caron, the greatest of French perfumes, Schiaparelli, Balenciaga and other haute couture scents. Their bonded warehouse is chock full of treasures like 15-year-old Scotches, 20-year-old French brandies. They also have the complete gamut of Kodak photographic supplies.

EL CONTINENTAL, at 24 and 26 Heerenstraat, is a delightful gift shop. Jack and Max Fruchter, who run it, have assembled a wonderful assortment of Dutch and Danish silver, Swedish and French crystal, Murano glass, Hummel figurines,

English bone china and Delft Blue to tempt their customers. They also have Kislav gloves at bargain prices, French perfumes ditto, English woolens and cashmere sweaters, and some beautiful linens. There is also a wide selection of Zodiac watches here.

FANNY'S SHOP, at 3 Hendrikplein, three blocks straight ahead from the pontoon bridge, is one of the best places for fine china and crystal, for hand-embroidered linens, both the kind you put on the table and the kind you put on yourself. She has some lovely gift items in jade and ivory, a wide selection of cameras, binoculars, and perfumes, some exquisite Persian rugs, and a selection of gift articles from Israel, which seem to be one of her outstanding specialties.

LA ESTRELLA, 30 Heerenstraat, also has Israeli art objects including some unusual handmade sweaters and stoles. You can also find Dutch national costumes here and wooden shoes. See the selection of colorful Mexican and Guatemalan fabrics made up in shirts, skirts and tablecloths. There's also a good standard line of liquors and Swiss watches in this store.

M. DIALDAS & SONS is a department store smack in the center of Heerenstraat. They claim to have more than a thousand varieties of merchandise in this air-conditioned emporium. Among them: a wide selection of Irish, French, Madeira and Hongkong linens; some lovely bags in Petit Point, a complete assortment of French perfumes, and Juvenia, Borel and Favre Leuba watches and clocks.

EUROPA, another department store at 3 Breedestraat, has a splendid array of crystal: Swedish Orrefors, Belgian Val-Saint Lambert, Dutch Leerdam. They also have a big china department featuring Limoges porcelain, English bone china and modern Dutch and Swedish ceramics. This is the place for the

DUTCH WEST INDIES

handsome Swedish stainless steel "Gense" tableware and ebony Isolite, inlaid with handcut sterling silver. If you're looking for Haagsche hopjes and other toothsome imports from Europe, try Europa's candy department.

PALAIS ORIENTAL, with two shops at 29 Heerenstraat and 37 Breedestraat, is well known for its big selection of Chinese curios and linens at low prices. They also have a good selection of bags: leather, alligator, beaded, and petitpoint, and French perfumes.

ORIENTAL ART PALACE, at 10 Heerenstraat behind a facade of red and white checked tiles, has a huge selection of Indian brassware, silver, and fabrics, including some lovely saris and scarves. Lots of ivory figurines and Chinese objets d'art. But despite the name of Mr. Boolchand Pessoomal's establishment, he also has such items as French perfumes, English Cashmere sweaters, Italian silk ties, Dutch dolls, Swiss watches, clocks and music boxes, and Guatemalan sport shirts.

ORIENTAL STORE at 5 Heerenstraat specializes in fine linen, hand-embroidered tablecloths from Hong Kong, Madeira, Italy. Scrumptious Venetian lace ones, too. The prices are the lowest we've seen yet.

Another place for fine hand-embroidered Irish and Hong Kong linen table cloths is the *New Amsterdam Store*, Helfrichplein 14. They also carry a handsome gift line. Mail orders accepted.

EL GLOBO, 17 Heerenstraat and 8 Breedestraat, is the place for German and Japanese cameras and binoculars, and the prices are real bargains. Among the brands they carry: Bauer, Bolex, Contax, Exakta, Leica, Minox, and Rolleiflex. They've made arrangements for repair services in the U.S.A. should anything go wrong with equipment purchased here. Ask for their free catalogue, comprising everything in the camera line from Agfa to Zeiss.

This is merely a random sampling of Curaçao's shops. Camera buffs will want to look in at *El Globo*, 48 Breedestraat, where they do Ektachrome color developing.

If you are interested in local handicrafts, don't fail to see what they have at *Home Industry*, Plaza Piar, near Hotel Curaçoa intercontinental, especially in lace, pottery, basketry, and Saba draw work.

If you are looking for recorded island and Caribbean music there are several shops selling records both in Punda and in Otrabanda. Among the largest are *La Bonanza*, having a shop both at 10 Breedestraat (Punda) and at 33-35 Breedestraat (Otrabanda).

For *Curaçao liqueur*, it's *Senior & Co.*, the local maker of this potent orangeade. Visitors are welcome to the spic and span distillery housed in an old Dutch setting in scenic Chobolobo estate. Curaçao comes in three colors: green, orange and white. At Senior's, you can sample them all amidst a pleasant discussion of how much of which ingredient makes what. You can buy as much as you want; there are no export restrictions, but remember that Uncle Sam only allows a gallon of liquor in duty free.

At the airport, cigarettes and liquor can be bought in bond at *Spritzer & Fuhrmann*.

SPORTS AND OTHER AMUSEMENTS. There's *swimming* at Piscadera Bay Club, at the public pool near Rif Stadium, at the Avila Hotel, at Knip Bay, at Santa Cruz beaches, and at Westpunt Bay and several other bays and beaches. Check on coral bottom; you may have to wear shoes.

Spear-fishing and the more conventional kind with hook and line are good at Spanish Water and Knip Bays.

DUTCH WEST INDIES

Boating, both motor and sail, can be arranged through the Asiento Sailing Club of the Shell Oil Company at Brakkeput, and local agencies, Taber, or Palm.

The *tennis* courts at the Curaçao Sport Club, Piscadera Bay, and the Van Engelen and Kwiek Clubs are all available to visitors.

You can play *golf* on the nine-hole course of the Shell Golf Club, near the refinery, upon payment of a $2 green fee, caddy $1, rent clubs $2.

Bowling at the Curaçao Sport Club.

Two business and social clubs of Curaçao welcome visitors, the *Club de Gezelligheid* and *Societeit Curaçao,* providing a good chance to get to know local people. There are four cinemas: *Roxy, West End, Cinelandia,* and the *Caribe.* If you're in Curaçao for Christmas or New Years, you'll see the burgers of Willemstad painting their houses for the occasion; that's one reason they always look so new. April 30 is the Queen's Birthday; it's celebrated with donkey races, music, picnics, and, of course, the inevitable Dutch scrub-up that makes the Netherlands Antilles the neatest, cleanest land in the Caribbean.

EXPLORING CURAÇAO

The chief diversion of Willemstad is watching the *Koningin Emma Brug* or Queen Emma pontoon bridge swing open to let ships pass into and out of the harbor, which it does on an average of 30 times a day. It may sound like a form of idiot's delight, but it is amusing none the less to watch people scrambling to get across this floating bridge so as to avoid the 15 or 20 minute wait or the trip by ferry which ensues if you don't make it on time. The bridge, which moves under your feet and actually makes some people seasick, was first built in 1888. It was the American consul, Leonard Ben Smith, who designed and built the bridge, not without a certain opposition from the conservative 19th-century burgers of Willemstad. It used to be a toll bridge: two cents if you wore shoes, one cent if you were shod in sandals or barefoot. The economic principle of this graduated toll was obvious enough: tax each according to his ability to pay. But the authorities forgot the foibles of human nature. The proudest of barefoot poor begged, borrowed or bought sandals for the privilege of paying two cents to display an elevated standard of living. Meanwhile wealthy American tourists were gaily kicking their shoes off and crossing the bridge barefoot as a lark. The toll was abandoned, so shod and shoeless, all are treated the same.

Almost as colorful as the pontoon bridge connecting the gabled shops and houses of Punda with those of Otrabanda, is the native schooner market on the little canal leading to Waaigat, a small yacht basin on the Punda side. Dozens of sailboats from Aruba, Bonaire, Venezuela and other Caribbean places tie up at the Ruyterkade, and the quay is full of local consumers who have come down to examine the wares of these floating markets. The produce, mostly fruit, vegetables, dried meat, fresh fish, fabric and clothing is draped on the boats with all the garish color of a Venezuelan fiesta. Merchants and customers of every shade from satinwood to mahogany are as vivid as the produce, and the smells are as strong as the colors. So are the sounds. Only a Caspar Milquetoast would fail to haggle here. One golden-colored East Indian boy assured us that the place was full of smugglers. "They hide gold and precious stones in the oranges," he said, indicating a boatload of the golden fruit, whose proprietor suddenly began to look like the Thief of Bagdad. We were tempted to make an offer for the entire cargo, but restrained ourselves.

Willemstad is a tourist's dream, for nearly everything is within short walking distance of the center of town. One highlight is the beautiful old Dutch Reformed Church, built in 1769. It has a cannon ball, fired by the English in 1804, still embedded in its walls. The Mikve Israel Synagogue, oldest in the Western Hemisphere, should not be missed. Built in 1732, the building is an outstanding example of 18th-century Dutch architecture. The interior is dignified and rich with the white sand, symbol of the wandering in the desert before the Jews reached the Promised Land, covering the floor like a thick carpet. The 24-candle brass chandeliers which hang from the mahogany ceiling are replicas of those in the Portuguese Synagogue in Amsterdam. The natural complement to this venerable place of worship is the Beth Haim (House of Life) Jewish Cemetery just west of the town. Consecrated before 1659, it is the oldest Caucasian burial place still in use in the New World. It occupies three acres, and contains about 2500 graves. The carving on some of the 17th and 18th-century tombstones is among the most impressive sculpture of its kind in America, a touching record in stone of a persecuted people who escaped and flourished under the Dutch flag in America.

A Local Hero

Even if you wanted to, you could not miss the statue of Pedro Luis Brion, which dominates the square called Brionplein right at the Otrabanda end of the Emma bridge. Brion, born in Curaçao in 1782, was a terrible thorn in the flesh of the English who tried to seize Curaçao on a number of occasions. As chief of militia of Curaçao, 23-year-old Brion administered a decisive defeat to the English in 1805. In 1814 he joined the great liberator Simon Bolivar, and was instrumental as Admiral of the Colombia Fleet in winning freedom for Colombia and Venezuela. His statue here in Brionplein is a monument without a tomb. His mortal remains are in the National Pantheon of Caracas, having been transferred there from a Curaçao grave at the request of the Venezuelan president in 1881. His claim to veneration by still a third country is explicit in a quotation from Bolivar, inscribed on the monument in Curaçao: "Colombia owes half her blessings to Brion."

Another point of tourist interest on the Otrabanda, but farther out on Leeuwenhoekstraat, is the Curaçao Museum, a former military hospital carefully restored as a fine example of Dutch architecture. Its gardens, containing specimens of all the island's plants and trees, are worth a visit in their own right. The museum is furnished with lovely old antiques, paintings of the colonial epoch, and objets d'art which recreate the atmosphere of an earlier day. Occasional exhibitions of paintings and other works of art are held in this museum.

Of more recent vintage is the Franklin D. Roosevelt House, splendidly situated on top of Ararat Hill on the Punda side, overlooking the city and the sea. It has the distinction of being one of the few examples in the world of a gift by the local population to the United States instead of the usual *vice versa*. A handsome house, it was built in 1950 and presented to the American government as the official residence of the United States Consul General in the Netherlands Antilles. The generous Dutch, grateful for America's war time protection of Curaçao and Aruba, wanted to make the place bigger and more pretentious, but were restrained. After all, it's only a Consulate General, not an Embassy. The panorama from Roosevelt House is magnificent. Even the huge complex of the Shell Oil Refinery looks like something in F.A.O. Schwarz' window from this vantage point.

That refinery, by the way, employs about 8,000 people and produces 390,000 barrels of oil a day, the economic life blood of thriving, cosmopolitan Curaçao. Whether this refinery or the Lago Oil and Transport Company on neighboring Aruba (See below) is the largest in the world, is a subject for friendly argument between the two islands. The Curaçao refinery is big enough to test the energy of the most avid sightseer; you'll find that out when you visit it.

Outside of Willemstad, the arid, cactus-spiked landscape of Curaçao has a charm of its own, but is generally less appealing to visitors than the old world Dutch capital. Some of the cacti rising twenty feet and more into the air, are spectacular. The dividivi tree, sculpted by the trade wind, flings its branches out dramatically at right angles on the leeward side of the trunk. Flaming Flamboyant (or Royal Poinciana) trees punctuate the dry countryside from time to time, and you'll see a few picturesque thatched native huts that have not yet succumbed to the aggressive new order of modern housing developments. You'll see families weaving straw, women pounding cornmeal, native fishermen casting their nets, primitive gestures which are as old as time, far removed from the smell of oil. Boca Tabla, a fantastic grotto carved by the relentless hammering of the sea, is the sight of the north coast. Since you can't see it without the help of a guide, it might be best to take *Taber Tours* or *Palm Tours* to West Point, which includes this phenomenon. This tour, which can be taken in a single afternoon, goes to the farthest western point on the island accessible by car. A bay, the remains of an old slave settlement, a fishing village and a pleasant beach await you at West Point. En route, you travel through the interesting countryside of the interior, passing a number of handsome old colonial estates. There's a stop for a swim at Knip Bay. The route back from West Point is along the rugged northern coast. After you've marched around in sneakers or some other thick-soled shoes to protect your feet from the sharp coral while inspecting nature's handiwork at Boca Tabla, you'll be glad to see the narrow houses, the gabled roofs and the gay colors of man's construction again. Willemstad, before and after all, is the high point of Curaçao.

ARUBA

Flat, arid Aruba, floating in the sea 45 miles west of Curaçao, was an economic ugly duckling for centuries, ekeing out a subsistence on the exportation of aloes. In 1929, fateful year, the Lago Oil and Transport Company, a subsidiary of Standard Oil of New Jersey, built a refinery at Sint Nicolaas on the southern end of the island. It wasn't just another refinery; it was the biggest in the world, capable of producing more than 400,000 barrels of oil per day, employing up to 10,000 people, representing more than a score of different nationalities. The result? In three decades tiny Aruba (19.6 by 6 miles) has achieved one of the highest standards of living in the West Indies, has reduced its illiteracy rate below that of the United

States, has become a factor in modern world economy. The ugly duckling now vies with Puerto Rico for the title of proudest industrial swan in the Caribbean Sea.

New Yorkers, approaching Aruba from the south, are apt to do a double take. The cluster of towers rising from the sea suggests the silhouette of lower Manhattan. These are the chimneys of Esso Town. By the way, Aruba's resort area is 14 or 15 miles from the refinery. Even near the refinery there is no problem, thanks to the trade wind that whisks smoke and fumes out to sea.

No archives mention the exact date of Aruba's discovery. Alonzo de Ojera claimed the island for Spain in 1499. Potsherds and clay pottery collected on Aruba from excavations, hieroglyphics left in the caves, are evidence that the island was inhabited by the Arawak Indians. Aruba is one island where the Indian population was not exterminated. Although the Spanish deported the virile Indians to work the mines of Hispaniola, the island enjoyed a special dispensation from the usual horrors of Spanish colonial policy. Charles V promulgated a decree forbidding further settlement of foreign colonists in Aruba with the result that the virile Indians remained a free people, sharing their island with a small Spanish garrison. When the Dutch took over in 1634, they maintained this "closed area" principle on into the 19th century. Aruba thus had the status of an unofficial "reservation" for the Indians.

Of the 57,500 persons living on Aruba today, 36,000 (nearly two-thirds) are descendants of the indigenous Indians. There is a striking difference, therefore, between the natives of Aruba and those of polyglot Curaçao. You may not see any pure-blooded Indians, since neither the Spanish nor the Dutch were exactly averse to enjoying themselves in the most basic way, but the Carib strain is very marked in the majority of the natives, golden of skin, Mongoloid of cheek and eye. They are a strong race, hard working, and have a knack for technical work. In addition to this preponderant combination of Carib-Spanish-Dutch, there are colorful smatterings of 40 other nationalities, including Chinese and *Indian* Indians. The native language as on Curaçao is Papiamento, with English, Dutch and Spanish widely spoken and understood.

Aruba is now vying with other Caribbean islands to become one of the most popular vacation spots in the Caribbean tourist area. She has decked herself out with a new five million dollar hotel, the *Aruba Caribbean,* replete with pool, casino and free-port shopping arcade, and this is just the first step

DUTCH WEST INDIES

in a concerted plan to build Aruba into a top-flight resort. Air conditioning will lick the problem of September and October heat, which, frankly, can be oppressive when you're only 12 degrees from the equator. The climate is considered the finest in the Caribbean; although rainfall is scant, the days are pleasantly cooled by the northeast trade-wind always present; you'll even want a blanket at night.

The basic attractions of Aruba are different from those of other Caribbean islands. There is little rainfall (drinking water is distilled from the sea), and you'll find no lush, verdure-clad mountains here. You will find giant cactus, aloes, the dividivi trees with their branches flowing west like hair blown in the trade winds, umbrella-like kwihi trees, and the kibra hachi tree, a sunburst of glorious yellow blossoms. You'll find strange, monolitic rock formations, caves adorned with Indian inscriptions, green parakeets, beautiful beaches, and a pastel-colored "free port" shopping capital, Oranjestad, as neat as the Netherlands, as Dutch as a dyke.

PRACTICAL INFORMATION FOR ARUBA

(Currency, clothing, retail merchandise prices, tourist formalities are the same as for Curaçao).

HOW TO GET THERE. *KLM Royal Dutch Airlines* has three flights per week in each direction between Aruba and New York, by way of Curaçao. KLM also flies to Aruba from Miami five times weekly. There are direct inter-island connections by KLM between Jamaica and Trinidad. You can also fly via KLM between Aruba and Caracas, Maracaibo, Baranquilla. *Trans Caribbean Airways* has three flights weekly from New York-San Juan by DC-6Bs. Construction will begin next year on a new terminal building for Aruba's Princess Beatrix Airport. The runway will be extended to 9,000 feet to accommodate the largest jets.

Both the *Grace Line* and *Royal Netherlands Steamship Company* have ships that link New York with Oranjestad. You can sail from New Orleans to Aruba on *Alcoa* Steamship boats as well as those of Royal Netherlands. If you're in Curaçao and would like to make the 45 mile voyage to Aruba, a delightful way is by the weekly sailing of the motorship *Niagara*.

HOTELS

ARUBA CARIBBEAN HOTEL-CASINO. Designed by Morris Lapidus, who did the Fontainebleau and Eden Roc hotels in Miami, this eight-story building was completed in 1959 right on the shore of Palm Beach, a sweeping stretch of white sand and clear water which has already become one of the best known strands in the Caribbean. Native tiles, stone, straw, bamboo and other exotic woods have been used in a conscious effort to make the Papiamento Dining Room, Bali Cocktail Lounge and other public rooms reflect the Dutch, Portuguese, Spanish, English, Arowak and East Indian motifs which permeate island culture. The hotel has a gaming casino, run by imported experts from Nevada; a large swimming pool, deck, outdoor circular bar, barbecue area and open-air dancing terrace in the area between the hotel and the sea. Operated by Condado Caribbean Hotels Inc., the Aruba Caribbean has a beauty parlor, gift center, free-port shopping arcade and all the amenities of a self-sufficient beach resort. There are 120 air-conditioned rooms plus 20 de luxe cabanas. All have private terraces. Modified European Plan rates are from $23 to $27 a day single, from $28 to $32 double. Suites are available from $35. These are winter rates, operative from December 16 through April 15. Summer rates are $13 to $17 single, $17 to $21 double with suites starting at $25.

BASI RUTI. A very attractive small resort hotel on Palm Beach, ten minutes' drive from Oranjestad. The hotel seeks to combine the luxury and comfort of a modern hostelry with the friendly hospitality of a country club. The results are most successful. There's a gift shop, terrace on the sea, indoor and outdoor bar. Swimming, water skiing, spearfishing, deepsea fishing and trolling are the diversions by day; dancing at night. There's a golf course three minutes

away. Basi Ruti has 15 rooms, all air-conditioned. American Plan Rates are $20 per day single, $30 double in winter. Same accommodations on the Continental Plan in winter are $12 single, $18 double. Summer rates are A.P. $16 single, $26 double, C.P. $10 single, $16 double. Manager is D. Moroso.

THE STRAND. Once the chief hotel of Aruba, and still a charming place to stay. It overlooks the Caribbean, half way between Beatrix Airport and Oranjestad. It has both mechanical and trade winds air conditioning; most of the rooms are cross-ventilated. The managers, Mr. F. Wong and Mr. S. Mason, provide their guests with good Dutch food and service. There are 32 rooms, bar, dining room, night club.

SCALA. Right in Oranjestad with 24 air-conditioned rooms, Dutch cleanliness, Dutch meals and Dutch management (J. van Gyn). Rates are $13.50 per day single, $24 per day double, American Plan. Continental Plan rates (and the breakfast is Dutch) are $9.50 single, $16 double.

ASTORIA. 12 air-conditioned rooms with private bath, owned and managed by Mr. Wong Hong; located in a quiet section of San Nicholas. Excellent Chinese food. Continental plan rates (room and breakfast): $9.33 per day single; $13.60 double.

RESTAURANTS

All hotels maintain the hearty Dutch reputation of the groaning board; every day is Thanksgiving.

Of the independent restaurants, *The Trocadero* is recommended. Here you can lunch or dine at leisure on a porch overlooking Schooner Harbor, or, if you prefer, in the attractive Dutch dining room.

If you're feeling strong enough to wade through 40 plates of a Javanese *rijsttafel*, go to *The Bali*, a

most attractive floating East Indian restaurant in the harbor; it recently won a citation as most interesting restaurant in the Caribbean.

Basi Ruti has good Italian food. Recently opened is *De Oude Molen*, an authentic Dutch windmill reconstructed on the Palm Beach area, and rebuilt into a restaurant specializing in Dutch Food. You'll have the feeling of being in Holland. *Uchee's Place* is the name in Oranjestad's mainstreet for a modern snackbar.

In Sint Nicolaas, your best bets, beside Marchena, are the *Astoria*, the *Roof Garden, Charlie's,* the *Lido and Premier,* and the *Chesterfield*. The last, despite its veddy English name, is a Chinese restaurant. Visitors can also lunch at the *Esso Club* in the Lago Colony.

NIGHTLIFE

When the well-heeled burghers of Oranjestad want to raise a little dust (they're usually busy keeping it down!), they go dancing at the Capri Room of the Strand Hotel.

The *Klompen Klub* is the nightclub of the Aruba Caribbean Hotel, and there's plenty of klomping around there when darkness falls. The Aruba Gaming Casino, Las Vegas in the tropics, is close by.

The *Bali Bar* of the Aruba Caribbean Hotel is one of the most popular night spots with continental music.

There's occasional outdoor dancing at the Palm Beach Club.

The *Lido* in Sint Nicolaas is the first of a number of small nightclubs that are trying their wings in that bustling, burgeoning town.

SHOPPING

Just as good and just as cheap as in Curaçao, Nassaustraat is the main shopping drag of Oranjestad, and many of its stores are branches of shops in Curaçao. By the same token, many of the shops in Sint Nicolaas are branches of the shops on Nassaustraat.

There's a very nice gift shop at Beatrix Airport if you have a few guilders to get rid of before leaving Aruba. That little airport, by the way, is one of the beauties of the Caribbean; it's even a pleasure to *meet* a plane there.

There are no less than eight department stores in Oranjestad. That fact may inspire or exhaust you, depending upon your temperament, but no one of them is as big as a single floor of Marshall Field or Macy's.

Largest is *The Aruba Trading Company*. You'll find almost anything you want here including a wide selection of French perfumes at French rather than American prices.

If you really want to case the "big stores", you can also drop into *Fuchs and Gelbstein, La Linda, Manhattan Store, El Paraiso, La Moderna, Casa Matias,* and *Gottfried Department Store,* whose collective names are a commentary on tiny, cosmopolitan Oranjestad.

For jewelry and luxury goods, your best specialty shops are *Spritzer & Fuhrmann, I. Kan* (that's not a pun), *The Pearl of the Orient,* and *Raghunath*.

The *Aruba Peasant Shop* (both in Oranjestad and Sint Nicolaas) has a staggering array of handicrafts from the West Indies and half a hundred countries around the world. You'll love browsing through all the hand-woven, hand-painted, hand-carved, hand-embroidered, hand-fired and hand-hammered articles in this international bazaar.

If you want more, there's *WIMCO, The Pearl of the Orient,* and *Palais Oriental;* all three have branches in Sint Nicolaas. There are many liquor stores. As in Curaçao, you avoid payment of duty by having your purchases in this department sent to the ship from bonded warehouse.

Cameras? Binoculars? *Neme's, Bonke, Aruba Trading,* and *I. Kan* have all of these things. The exclusive agent of Zodiac watches is *N.V. Kan.*

Whitfield's souvenir and resort shop, *Mario's* liquor store, *Playalux* (ladies shop), *Bon Bini* gift shop, *De Wit's* stationery, bookstore and souvenirs.

 SPORTS AND OTHER AMUSEMENTS. *Swimming* on the northwest coast beaches is excellent. Palm Beach with its gradual slope is perfect for children and beginners. For surf swimming, go north to Andi Couri and Boca Cruz beaches. Water temperature fluctuates between 70 and 75 degrees all year round.

Fishing, sailing, water skiing are all popular. Palm Beach is the center for the last. The Yacht Club at Lago is open to visitors by permission; so is the Aruba Boating Club at Oranjestad.

Visitors may also play *golf* on nine-hole Eagle Golf Club course or at Lago's Aruba Golf Club.

The local tourist bureau or your own hotel can arrange for you to play *tennis* at the Caribe Club, Eagle Club, Tivoli Club or Lago Club.

Sports flying is becoming increasingly popular in Aruba; headquarters is the Aruba Flying Club.

Interesting linguistic note: you can borrow books in 14 different languages from the Government Library on Wilhelmina Street in Oranjestad.

Unusual Spectator Sport: Walk down Lloyd Smith Boulevard along Schooner Bay in Oranjestad to watch the fishing boats and market. Sharks are very seldom seen; the waters of the west coast where the good beaches are, are free of them.

Aruba Tours and *De Palm Tours* offer a number of island-wide tours: Oranjestad, San Nicholas (oil-town), Pirates Castle, Indian caves, Palm Beach, Ghost Town (scene of 19th-century gold mining operations), Schooner Harbor and the native fruit market.

You can also make your plans through the *Aruba Tourist Bureau* in Oranjestad and *Maduro Tours.*

They will find you taxis with English-speaking drivers who operate at fixed rates. They will also arrange for the rental of a drive-yourself car if you want one.

EXPLORING ARUBA

Your first explorations will be on foot in the miniature capital of Oranjestad. With its picture book deep-water harbor and its traditional Dutch houses, this town of 11,000 is a peripatetic delight. The blending of the old with the new, the multi-colored houses with their roofs of red tile, above all the sparkling Dutch cleanliness of Oranjestad and its waterfront will appeal to your eye and your sense of propriety. The Dutch, here as well as in Curaçao, have proved that you don't have to be dirty to be picturesque. Other Caribbean ports take note.

Take your camera to record this gentle riot of pastel and primary colors and to shoot the fishing boats and the native

The Dutch colonial pageant ranges from Bush Negro huts in Surinam to the de luxe Curaçao Intercontinental Hotel, from whose rampart promenade you can almost touch the ships that call at busy Willemstad.

From the ruined tower of Old Panama's colonial cathedral to the terraced sundecks of the new El Panama Hotel, five centuries of architecture have left their mark on the world's most strategic isthmus.

market with its fruits, vegetables and gleaming fish exhibited in stalls against the intricate pattern of masts and rigging produced by the schooners tied up at the quay. As in Curaçao, much of the produce is sold direct from the sail boats, mostly Venezuelan, which come from the Spanish Main just 15 miles across the water.

Walking from the Grace Line docks along Lloyd Smith Boulevard, you'll see the Trocadero Restaurant on your left; it often has an exhibition of local art and photography if you want to see the island through native eyes. Just beyond, on your right, you'll see the exotic, prize-winning Bali houseboat restaurant. Continuing up the boulevard, you will pass several government office buildings, then reach Oranjestad's newest civic development: Wilhelmina Park, which was created in 1955 to celebrate the visit of Queen Juliana and Prince Bernhard of the Netherlands. The statue of Queen Mother Wilhelmina, unveiled by her daughter, was sculptured of white marble in Florence, Italy by Arnoldo Lualdi. The Governor's House, flying the flag of the Netherlands, completes this civil ensemble. Beyond lies a residential section, worth a stroll for its attractive houses, both old and new, and its gardens, glowing with many varieties of flower, shrub and tropical plant.

You can drive the full length of the island from Sint Nicolaas at the southern tip to the California light at the northwestern end. The island is less than 20 miles long. Two of its outstanding physical features are visible from almost every vantage point. One is the 550-foot Hooiberg or "haystack" dominating the flat country side which the natives call the "cunucu" (countryside). The other notable silhouette is that of the strange, bell-shaped ovens which are used to process the island stone with which Aruba's houses are built.

The island is dotted with these houses, painted in the primary hues of the rainbow, solid, neat, immaculate, in striking contrast to the ratty shacks which often mar other Caribbean landscapes.

Strange geological formations impart a unique quality to the "cunucu" of Aruba. Most impressive are the huge monoliths of solid diorite, each weighing several thousand tons. They are scattered about indiscriminately, playthings of some vast primordial force. The most impressive of these granite boulders are at Ayo where they are held in a delicate state of balance or set one on top of the other in so precarious a manner that one hesitates to approach them. Yet they remain fixed. Geologists have not yet explained the origin and the evolution of these rocks, nor the strange fact that many of them are hollowed out with the cavity always on the side turned away from the prevailing trade wind. A night drive through this weird, boulder-strewn area is like a preview of the manned Lunik alight on the moon. The origin of the diorite blocks may be shrouded in mystery, but one thing is certain: they furnish the Arubans with excellent building material. The rock formations reach a bizarre climax at Canashito Hill where an extra note of tropical exoticism is added by the presence of large flocks of brilliant green parakeets.

Even more interesting than the exterior rocks of the "cunucu" are the caves and grottos, many of them, like Quadirikiri Cave, decorated with drawings and symbols etched in red pigment by Indians long before Aruba was "discovered." Done with a surprising sophistication of line, these petroglyphs may be as old as those of Altamira or Lascaux, going back to the dawn of man's adventure on the earth. The symbols have not been transcribed; their meaning remains as unfathomable as the forces which moved and carved the giant boulders.

There was gold in this rocky soil, discovered in stream beds in 1825. Mining operations went on for a century, although the process was difficult, usually involving smelting. You can see the remains of one of the old gold smelters at Balashi. Although the mining company paid a 50 per cent stock dividend as recently as 1910, the industry gradually disappeared. Gold had come to Aruba in another form, and the wage scale paid by the refineries made smelting uninteresting by comparison. Nuggets still turn up now and then and are traded in small quantities. So if you've always wanted to take a fling at prospecting, here's your chance to try it in Balashi, Aruba's gold-mining ghost town.

Unless you have friends or business in the Lago Colony, you probably won't visit Sint Nicolaas and the southeastern quarter of Aruba. Most of the North Americans on the island live here in a self-contained model community with its own schools (staffed by American teachers), its own church, hospital, golf course, country club, tennis courts, bowling alleys, beaches and commissary. They even have their own Aruba Flying Club, mentioned above under sports. Among other amenities of the colony: gardens, which have been painstakingly cultivated on dirt brought in from the other end of the island. The trade winds normally blow the refinery fumes away from the Colony and Aruba. You won't want to be around when this cosmic ventilating system goes into reverse. For permission to visit the Lago Colony, apply to the tourist bureau or to the public relations department of the Lago Oil & Transport Company. They made Aruba what it is today, and they're quite pleased with the results.

BONAIRE

Bonaire, second largest of the ABC group of the Dutch West Indies, is the Island of the Flamingoes, the breeding and nesting place of thousands of these beautiful pink birds. Hatching season is usually March or April, and the sight of the flamingoes, sitting on their pie-shaped nests and tending their babies attracts more and more bird lovers each year. Late afternoon is the time for bird watching, a pastime which is rewarded on Bonaire not only by the flamingoes but by many thousands of herons, snipe, tern, pelicans, green parrots, parakeets and other birds of brilliant hue. Myriads of rainbow-colored tropical fish attract almost as many tourists to the coral reefs off Bonaire, both spear fishermen and those who are content to study marine life without disturbing it. Snorkels, glass bottom boats and boxes are available for the latter.

Forty miles east of Curaçao, 60 miles north of Venezuela, Bonaire is much like its two sister islands in flora, or rather the relative lack of it. The island, flat and dry in the south, becomes hilly in the north, rising to a height of 784 feet at the summit of Mt. Brandaris. There are about 6,000 persons inhabiting Bonaire's 112 square miles. The women outnumber the men 3 to 1, the latter attracted by the high wages of the refineries on Aruba and Curaçao. Those who remain at home are occupied in the manufacture of salt and charcoal, fishing, raising sheep and goats, and drying aloes, which are a pharmaceutical export.

Capital of Bonaire is Kralendijk, a tiny town of 1,000, as Dutch as its name. It's painted orange, pink, and green. When you see it with its neat gardens, Liliputian harbor, pink fish market, and midget boats supplying it, you'll want to have the whole village wrapped as a gift to take home.

PRACTICAL INFORMATION FOR BONAIRE

HOW TO GET THERE. You reach Bonaire by *KLM Royal Dutch Airlines* via Curaçao; there are daily flights. It takes exactly 20 minutes from airport to airport. You can also come by sea from Curaçao on the new motor ship *Niagara* sailing every Friday for Bonaire or almost every day by smaller boats. Fare is $8 one way, $13.50 round trip.

HOTELS. *The Flamingo Beach Club* is a good hotel for tourists. Its screened veranda overlooks the bay of Bonaire, less than a 10-minute walk from the center of Kralendijk. It has 19 bungalows, each with twin beds, bath and porch, some are air-conditioned. Three square Dutch meals are offered a day to the guests and they will be met at the airport if advance notice of arrival is given. The hotel has a private pier, a glass bottom boat and supplies its guests with water skis, plus a 35 horsepower boat and driver to pull them along. Cost for this is $10 an hour. Rowboats are free. A Chris Craft cabin cruiser and a motorketch are also available. Rates are $12-$15 a day single, $22-$26 double, American Plan. Slightly more luxurious than the *Flamingo*, the 30-room *Hotel Bonaire* should be open by the time you read this.

SHOPPING. There are some small shops in this toy capital, with a nice selection of souvenir articles and imported items, free port prices. But you won't be doing that kind of shopping here. You'll be more tempted by Mr. Heitkönig's hand-made or hand-painted souvenirs of tortoise shell, coral, concha-shells and paintwood tree at his store on the waterfront. Incidentally, he also has everything you need for the special bliss of getting out of this world and into the silent sanctuary of a submarine garden.

SPORTS. The best fishing season in Bonaire is from September until February. Then the waters jump with bonito, tuna, wahoo, barracuda, sailfish, kingfish.

Cars, with or without drivers, are available and can be arranged for either through the hotel or by the Bonaire Tourist Bureau at Kralendijk. There are good roads, and you have that wonderful away-from-it-all feeling as you drive to the deserted salt ponds, the old Fontein Plantation, the Indian-inscribed grottos of Spelonk and Boca Onima. You're far from the travelled track here, and the only tourists you'll meet will be those like yourself who are trying to get away from other tourists.

Final Note: If Bonaire attracts you chiefly as a bird watcher's paradise, check as far in advance as you can with the local Tourist Bureau as to the best dates to come. They know what the flamingoes have been up to.

THE DUTCH WINDWARD ISLANDS

The Dutch Windwards are three dots in the sea north of St. Kitts and the Leeward Group. The largest dot, Sint Maarten, is shared by the French, who call their half of it Saint Martin. The other dots, Saba "The Rock" and Sint Eustatius, nicknamed Statia, are entirely Dutch.

SINT MAARTEN (ST. MARTIN)

The Netherlands part of St. Maarten (to compromise on the name) comprises 16 of the island's 37 square miles. Columbus discovered the island on St. Martin's day in 1493. *He*, of course, called it San Martino. He didn't choose to go ashore, having already had a taste of Carib reception committees elsewhere. French pirates arrived in 1638; the Spanish dropped in briefly in 1640. In 1648, according to local legend, French and Dutch prisoners of war, brought to the island to destroy Spanish fort and buildings, had hidden themselves on the island and met each other when the Spaniards left. They agreed to divide the island and sent word to their countrymen to that effect. (St. Eustatius and Guadeloupe.) It was then that the frontier was established by a walking contest. A Frenchman and a Dutchman, starting at the same spot, walked around the island in opposite directions. It was agreed that the boundary line would be drawn straight across the island where they met. The Frenchman walked faster, but the Dutch portion, though smaller, turned out to be more valuable, thanks to important salt ponds. In 1948, a monument was erected at the border to commemorate three centuries of peaceful relations between the two countries. Except for the monument, you wouldn't know there was a border. There are no barriers, no guards, no customs inspectors, no formalities. When will the great world catch up with this tiny island?

The Dutch portion of the island is in the south. There's a big, beautiful, land-locked bay in the western half of the island, called Simson Lagoon. Here there is a small white fishing settlement. The airport is here, served twice a week from Curaçao by *KLM*, and three times weekly by *Caribair, Air France* and *Leeward Island Airlines*. The Simson Lagoon lowlands area is also the center of a big housing and hotel project, covering more than 2,000 acres with 15 miles of superb water frontage. Erik Lawaetz, a Virgin Islands realtor who landed on St. Martin in 1955 because he had been swept off his course, fell in love with the green valleys, forested hills and unspoiled beaches of the island and started this "Island Gem Development". If you have always dreamed of a beach or bay-front homesite in an ideal tropical setting, this may present a chance to realize that dream. For information write to *Lawaetz Land Development*, Christiansted, St. Croix, U.S. Virgin Islands, or to their New York Office in the Roosevelt Hotel, Madison Ave at 45 St. If you want to realize the dream independently and more cheaply write the tourist bureau about lots for lease by the Government.

There are 2,760 people inhabiting the 16 square miles of Dutch Sint Maarten. The island, indented by several fine bays, is hilly, rising to 1200 feet at the top of Flagstaff Hill. Philipsburg, the diminutive capital, is one of the most oddly situated towns in the world. It's strung out on a sandbar like a string of coral beads between Great Bay and Great Salt Pond.

DUTCH WEST INDIES

PRACTICAL INFORMATION

HOW TO GET THERE. By *KLM Royal Dutch Airlines* from Curaçao twice weekly on Monday and Thursday. By *Caribair* 3 times weekly from Puerto Rico and St. Thomas. By *Air France* from Puerto Rico, Antigua and Guadeloupe, 3 times weekly. By *Leeward Islands Air Transport* from Antigua, Montserrat, St. Kitts, St. Eustatius, Anguilla, and Puerto Rico, 3 times weekly.

The government motor vessel, *Hertha*, links Sint Maarten, Saba, St. Barthelemy and Sint Eustatius with St. Kitts on regular weekly voyages. There is also a once-a-month voyage from Curaçao on the coastal steamer *Antilia*, stopping at Aruba, Bonaire, Sint Maarten, Saba and Statia.

HOTELS. St. Maarten is gaining in hotel facilities. Three new small hotels, *Hunter's House* on the ocean at Point Blanche (recommended for couples), *Mary's Fancy Inn* at Cul-de-Sac (8 rooms and a swimming pool), and *Sea View* in Philipsburg (12 rooms, ocean swimming) all opened in 1961. Three more hotels are in the planning stages. Even the old pioneer, *Little Bay Hotel*, has expanded with 20 new rooms.

THE LITTLE BAY HOTEL, built in 1955, was the first to exploit the natural advantages of this lovely Caribbean island for the benefit of tourists. It's right on the Caribbean at Little Bay, has 42 comfortable rooms with private bath in three good-looking and well-appointed modern pavilions. There's a charming dining room, dining terrace and cocktail lounge, also a "free port" souvenir and gift shop. The meals are in the Dutch tradition; you won't go hungry. Rates, American Plan, are $30 to $32 single; $40 to $44 double. In the summer, they drop to $17-$24 single; $27-$30 double. You can dance at the *Little Bay* to a Steel band, and there's a program of entertainment for the guests.

THE LIDO GUEST HOUSE, at the foot of the pier near the center of Philipsburg, offers five modernly-appointed rooms, three with bath. Accommodations are simple, but, this is Holland, immaculate. There's a bar, a cocktail lounge, a spacious dining veranda, overlooking the Great Bay Beach and the Caribbean. American Plan rates are $14 to $16 single, $20 to $24 double.

PASANG-GRAHAN. Also in Philipsburg on Great Bay Beach. A former government guest house with wide verandas, lounge, cocktail bar, dining room, and 12 attractively-appointed double bedrooms, all with private bath. The bedrooms are in two pavilions on the beach. Griffin Vass manages this hotel, and it's Netherlands spic and span. Rates are $16 to $18 per day single, $24 to $28 double, American Plan.

Chief diversions of this little paradise are *swimming, fishing* and *horse-back riding*. The last is especially popular on island-bred horses from the French side, many of which are exported for racing in the British islands. A local boy, also on horseback, accompanies you like a page if you want to explore the island. There's plenty of fishing tackle, also boats for hire in Philipsburg if you want to go after some of the game fish which swim the island waters.

It's fun to browse in the little shops of Philipsburg, where the usual low-duty prices apply. You'll find some lovely old Dutch silver, a good selection of Holland Delft and liquid bargains in perfumes and alcohol. Some of the well-known shops in Curaçao, such as Spritzer & Fuhrmann, have recently opened branches in Philipsburg.

Sightseeing? Except for crumbling old Fort Amsterdam, the 17th-century historic "sight" of Sint Maarten, there's nothing but the scenery and the people. But these should be enough. You won't see happier, friendlier dark faces in the Caribbean than the ones on these natives, products of a relaxed and easy-going administration. You'll see them tending their cattle, goats, chickens, donkeys in a bucolic atmosphere far removed from the jet age. If you want to bounce over some pretty country roads, flanked by stone walls crawling with pink honeysuckle, this is the place for you. There are plenty of licensed taxis and cars for rent.

Sint Maarten is a beautiful island, already in the process of "development", but still "unspoiled". If you want to commune with nature, swim, sun, fish, ride and relax, this is for you.

SABA

That first a is long, as though you were a sheep doctor: "Say Ba." Topographically, the island is the most unusual of the whole Caribbean fleet. The whole place is an extinct volcano, rising abruptly from the sea without a single beach. It comprises five square miles, most of them running straight up and down. It's 28 miles south of Sint Maarten, 17 miles northwest of Sint Eustatius, and when you approach this cone from the sea, you'll swear that it's uninhabited, that not even Crusoe's man Friday could survive here.

As the Cunard Line is fond of pointing out, getting there is half the fun. In the case of Saba, it's an adventure. You have to go by sea, either on the *Hertha* or the *Antilia*. There are only two points where you can land, Fort Bay and Ladder Bay. Fort Bay is for calm weather. As you nose in, you see that there are inhabitants after all, for the Sabans come out in little boats and take you through the churning surf to shore. There you are met by a jeep, which takes you at an angle approaching 90 degrees "over the top" to Bottom. Bottom, so named because it's on the bottom of the crater, is the principal village, and it has the never-failing, unexpected charm of a Dutch village, with gabled roofs, chimneys, gardens and all, plunked down on a plateau in the midst of tropic seas. If the sea has been acting up and it's too rough to land at Fort Bay, you will be taken to Ladder Bay. After which, you climb "The Ladder", 530 steps up to reach the Bottom. However you approach it, it's doubtful if you'll ever forget this many-colored capital with its burgeoning gardens and surrounding green fields. Its population is about 1000.

The island has no industry of its own so many of the men are away in Aruba and Curaçao, working in the refineries, sending money back to Saba. The women, who outnumber the men, produce exquisite hand-made lace, embroidery and drawn work, which you can buy here or in the shops of Curaçao.

About 60 per cent of Saba's population is white, said to have descended from Caribbean seafarers, who may have found in Bottom the snug harbor of their dreams. In any event, the sea is still in the blood of their descendants. Native born Sabans are found in the navies and merchant fleets of half the countries in the world.

From Bottom, your trusty jeep will take you to even tinier villages: St. John, Windwardside, Hellsgate; you could easily imagine them under a Christmas tree, especially Windwardside with its red-roofed white houses. At 1800 feet, Windwardside is 1100 feet higher up than Bottom; it clings to the crest of the volcano, cooled by the never-failing trades, on top of the world with a vertiginous view of the Caribbean. From Zion Hill on Hellsgate, you can look over a sheer drop to the sea, the kind of view that has you holding your breath. Incidentally, if you are the type to despise the luxury of a jeep, you can explore this precipitous terrain on horseback, burroback, or your own two feet.

WHERE TO STAY?

You can find lodging and good Dutch board at the *Government Guesthouse* in the Bottom, a neat two story house with four bedrooms, two baths. The rates, $6.25 to $8 per person per day, include three meals. There's an even smaller guesthouse in Windwardside. The friendly Sabans—they've been called "the nicest people in the world"—will provide you with simple accommodations in private homes as well. You should reserve space in advance by writing to the Lieutenant Governor's office in Sint Maarten, or to the Administrator of Saba, N.W.I.

Saba is a delightful target for a one day's excursion, charming and certainly unusual. There are presently plans for an airstrip on Saba. If that materializes, the tourists will not be far behind and with them the hotels and restaurants now lacking.

SINT EUSTATIUS

With an area of 11.8 square miles, Statia, as she is called is the second in size of the three Windward sisters, the smallest in population. Viewed from Saba, the island looks like two barren cones. It is actually two extinct volcanoes, connected by a valley. Oranjestad, the capital, clings to the side of the higher cone.

Once known as the "Golden Rock" of the Caribbean, Statia is a silent shell of her former glory. A neutral port in the 18th century, Statia was a bustling point for the transshipment of arms, food and clothing to the beleaguered American revolutionists, fighting Britain's colonial blockade. As many as 200 ships crowded into Statia's harbors on a single day in those momentous times. Behind the harbor, sugar, tobacco and other crops flourished in Statia's still fertile soil. A population 20 times the size of today's prospered.

Statia's downfall resulted from a libertarian gesture which should endear this spot forever to Americans. When, on November 16, 1776, the United States Brig *Andrew Doria* entered the harbor flying its brand new flag, the Statians, full of enthusiasm for the American cause, fired from Fort Oranje the first salute ever accorded by a foreign power to the Stars and Stripes. This overt championing of the rebel cause infuriated British Admiral Rodney, a vindictive old sea dog if ever there was one. Five years later when England declared war on Holland, he captured Statia, but kept the Dutch flag flying to lure unsuspecting ships into the harbor. These were seized, their cargoes confiscated and auctioned off to the tune of $3,000,000. After that, this ruler of the King's Navee, looted the island and burned everything he wasn't able to carry away with him.

Statia never recovered. Her sights today are ruins: the roofless Dutch Reformed Church, the crumbling fort, the yellow brick and rubble of the Jewish Synagogue, the dilapidated warehouses which once played their role in American history.

Statia's principal activity today is agricultural. The Netherlands Government take an active part in promoting it. Chief products are yams and sweet potatoes, exported for the most part to Curaçao.

For the tourist, Statia offers a rendezvous with American history in a little-known corner of the Caribbean.

WHERE TO STAY?

There is little else but peace and quiet and there are no hotel accommodations except for four rooms in the *Government Guest House* in Oranjestad. Rates are $6.25 per person a day, and rooms should be reserved by writing to The Administrator, St. Eustatius. The food is Dutch and therefore copious.

COLOMBIA

Emerald of the Spanish Main

This beautiful country, the only South American republic
with a Pacific and a Caribbean waterfront, never fails to dazzle
visitors with its soaring green mountains, its lush jungles and
fertile deltas, its quiet Indian villages and bustling ultra-
modern cities. It is Switzerland, Colonial Spain and Contemporary America, all rolled into one and washed by the emerald
Caribbean. The range in altitude, from sea level up to 18,000
feet, offers a corresponding latitude of tourist pleasures. Within the space of a few days you can enjoy deep sea fishing,
mountain climbing in the Andes, swimming, snorkeling, a big
game safari, or a leisurely cruise into the heart of a tropical
jungle. Even Europe would be hard put to it to match the
16th-century walled city of Cartagena, combining the charms
of quaint narrow streets and balconied houses with the amenities of a glittering beach resort. And if you tire of the lazy
life of beach and palm, Bogotá, Colombia's exhilarating two-
mile-high capital, is less than two hours away by plane. It's almost 20 degrees cooler here, the bracing temperature averaging
a delightful 58 degrees the year round.

COLOMBIA

There are 14 million Colombians, mostly of European stock but there is a strong Indian and mestizo flavor. The country is intensely Spanish, inhabited by a people of deep and ancient culture, and proud that its capital city is known as "The Athens of America". Shopping in that Athens is a tourist pleasure, for a favorable rate of exchange makes prices low, and the quality of merchandise is high. You will find bargains in emeralds and golden jewelry, so abundant that it will make you think of those mythical Indian treasure cities that lured so many of the *conquistadores* to glory and the grave.

Long before the discovery of America the Colombian territory was inhabited by natives of different races, temperaments and languages. Among the principal groups were the Andean, who lived in the mountainous interior, and the Caribs, who lived along the northern coast.

What is now Colombia was discovered by Spanish and Italian sea captains—among them Columbus, Alonso de Ojeda, Juan de la Cosa, Rodrigo de Bastidas and Amerigo Vespucci—who sailed into the Caribbean in the late 15th and early 16th centuries. These and other explorers founded the coastal cities and those of the interior which still exist and thrive: Santa Marta in 1525, Cartagena in 1533, Bogotá in 1538 and others. An effort had been made by Ojeda to found a settlement at Cartagena as early as 1500 but the Spaniards were driven off by fierce Indians and the effort was abandoned.

From the 16th century to the beginning of the 19th, Spain governed Colombia through a system of viceroys, *presidentes* and *oidores* but as early as 1781 movements toward independence from the mother country were under way. Declarations of independence from Spain were made in Bogotá on July 20, 1810, and in Cartagena on November 11, 1811.

A period of open struggle, which was echoed up and down the length of the continent, culminated on August 7, 1819, in the Battle of Boyacá, 100 miles northeast of Bogotá, which marked the final defeat of Spanish forces in the New World. The life of the new republic began under the presidency of the great Liberator, Simón Bolivar, and the vice presidency of Francisco de Paula Santander, called "the man of laws". Until 1830, Colombia, Venezuela and Ecuador were joined in a union called *Gran Colombia* but in that year the nations divided to go their separate ways.

A number of civil wars occurred in Colombia during the 19th century following the gaining of independence, for administrative, political and religious reasons. Out of these

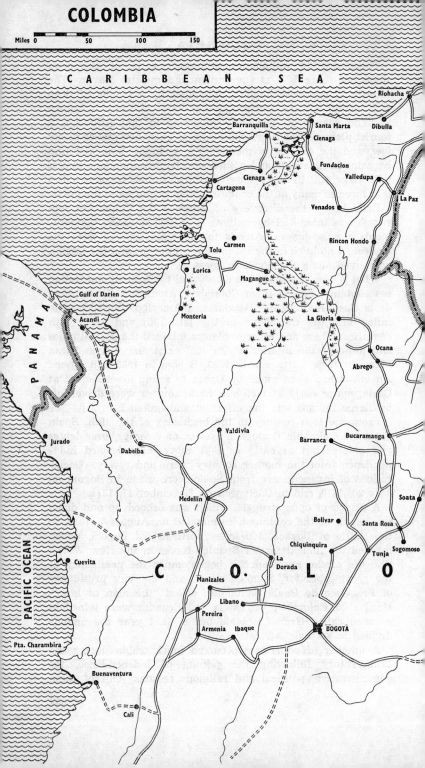

COLOMBIA

Miles 0   50   100   150

CARIBBEAN   SEA

Riohacha

Barranquilla   Santa Marta   Dibulla
Cienaga

Fundacion
Cienaga   Valledupa
Cartagena   La Paz

Venados

Rincon Hondo
Carmen
Tolu
Lorica
Magangue
Gulf of Darien
Monteria   La Gloria

Acandi   Ocana

Abrego

P
A
N
A
M
A

Valdivia

Bucaramanga
Barranca
Dabeiba

Jurado

Soata
Medellin
Bolivar   Santa Rosa

Cuevita   Sogomoso
La   Tunja
C   O   Dorada   L   O

Pta. Charambira

Manizales
Libano
Pereira
Armenia   Ibaque   BOGOTA
Chiquinquira

PACIFIC OCEAN

Buenaventura

Cali

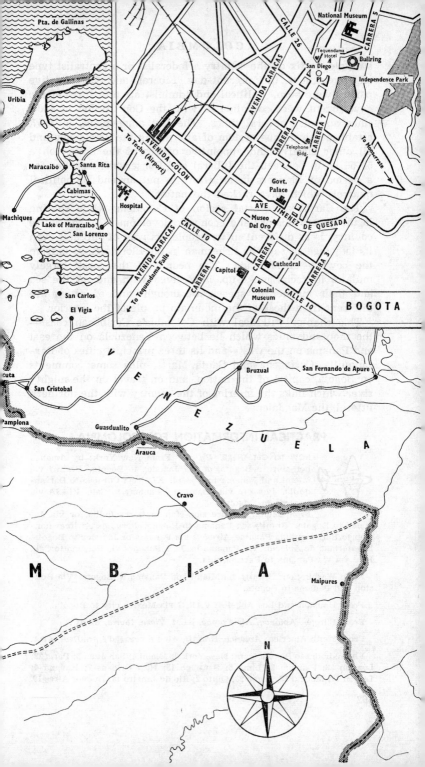

Pta. de Gallinas

Uribia

Maracaibo   Santa Rita

Cabimas

Machiques

Lake of Maracaibo
San Lorenzo

San Carlos

El Vigia

cuta

San Cristobal

Pamplona

Guasdualito

Arauca

Cravo

M B I A

Bruzual   San Fernando de Apure

Maipures

N

BOGOTA

National Museum

CARRERA 5

CALLE 26

AVENIDA CARACAS

Tequendama
Hotel

San Diego
Pl.

Bullring

Independence Park

AVENIDA COLON

To Techo (Airport)

CARRERA 10

CARRERA 7

To Monserrate

Telephone
Bldg.

Govt.
Palace

Hospital

AVE JIMENEZ DE QUESADA

CALLE 10

Museo
Del Oro

CARRERA 7

CARRERA 3

To Tequendama Falls

AVENIDA CARACAS

CARRERA 10

Capitol

Cathedral

Colonial
Museum

CALLE 10

V E N E Z U E L A

COLOMBIA

struggles to fix on the country a federalist or a centralist type of government the present-day Liberal and Conservative parties were born. Political and administrative features of the government were consolidated with the Constitution of 1886, since amended several times. The last amendment, in 1957, established a unique system of alternating the presidency and all other elective and appointive offices of the nation on a 50-50 basis, between the Liberal and Conservative parties for a period of 16 years in an effort to put an end to political quarrels which have racked the nation.

The Caribbean coastal region of Colombia, while sharing in the general history and economic development of the entire country, is as different in its people, its way of life and even its language as, say, the fisherman in the Florida Keys is from the cowboy of Montana. The people of the coast, largely mulatto in racial make-up, have lived with and on the sea and their manner of speech, of thought and of action are different from those of the mountain people of the interior.

This chapter will deal with Colombia's Caribbean coast— the thousand miles which lie between Venezuela on the east and Panama on the west—and its three principal cities of Barranquilla, Cartagena and Santa Marta, plus some comments on Bogotá, capital of the nation, and on travel on the mighty river which links the interior of the country with the northern littoral, the Magdalena.

PRACTICAL INFORMATION FOR COLOMBIA

HOW TO GET THERE. *By air.* From New York: by *Avianca* non-stop to Bogota, or via Jamaica to Bogota. *Braniff* via Miami and Panama to Bogota. *KLM* via Curaçao to Barranquilla. *Panagra* via Miami and Panama to Cali. *VIASA* via Caracas to Bogota.

From Miami: *Vianca* non-stop to Barranquilla, or via Jamaica to Bogota. *Braniff* via Panama to Bogota. *Peruvian Airlines* non-stop to Barranquilla. *Panama Airways* via Panama or Jamaica to Bogota. *Ecuatoriana de Aviacion* via Panama to Cali. *Panagra* via Panama to Cali. *Pan Am* via Panama to Barranquilla.

From Washington: *Braniff* via Miami and Panama to Bogota. Via Houston and Panama to Bogota.

From Houston and Los Angeles: *VARIG* via Mexico city to Bogota.

From Europe: *Avianca, Air France, KLM, Viasa, Iberia, BOAC.*

From South America: *Avianca, Braniff, Air France, Panagra, Real, APA.*

Flying hours to Bogota from: New York 6; Miami 4; San Juan 3; Paris 22; London 23; Panama 2; Lima 6; Santiago 15; New Orleans 7; Havana 4; Lisbon 17; Madrid 12; Rome 23; Quito 2; Rio de Janeiro 14; Buenos Aires 19.

662

COLOMBIA

By ship. The following maritime companies regularly serve Colombian ports with both passenger and combination passenger-freight vessels: *Grace Line, Hamburg-Amerika Line, French Line, Knutsen Line.*

By car. Since the Darién Gap, which lies in southern Panama and north-western Colombia, still remains open in the Pan American Highway it is impossible to drive one's car into Colombia from Panama at the present time. Engineering studies, however, are going forward and in the not-too-distant future the last link in the tremendous Alaska-to-Tierra del Fuego highway may be completed and in operation.

WHEN TO COME. Since Colombia is a tropical country with its capital lying less than 800 miles north of the equator, climate is very largely a matter of altitude. Temperatures range from an average of about 83° F. along the Caribbean coast to a chilly 55° F. average in the capital city, perched in the Andes at an altitude of 8,660 feet.

Although seasons as such do not exist, Colombians call their rainy seasons, which come approximately from February to April and from October to December, "winter" and the remainder of the months "summer".

Rainfall, however, is never excessive nor continuous, except in such coastal areas as the Pacific coast department of the Chocó where rainfall averages an inch a day.

The Caribbean coast of Colombia is rich in festivals of all kinds—music, folklore, sports, religious and commercial—and the *costeño* is generally regarded by his more sober brothers of the Andean highlands as rather more given to fun-making and the lighter things of life than is proper. He has been described as "expansive, conceited and vehement.... His life opens on the limitless horizon of the sea, and his African descent confers on him the fatuity and conceit which is one of the characteristics of that race. His feelings are skin-deep, free, for he has nothing to hide and this makes him thoughtless of the future, generous and spendthrift."

Cartagena celebrates its independence from Spain on *November 11* with a week of merrymaking, parades and dancing. It also sponsors weeks devoted to folklore, music and international films and Colombia's representative to international beauty contests, such as that to choose "Miss Universe", is always selected in Cartagena.

Barranquilla's carnival season, famous throughout the hemisphere, is held the week before Ash Wednesday.

International tennis matches are scheduled there in *March* and international fishing competition is held in *May*.

Santa Marta, oldest city in the Western Hemisphere, also observes the week before Lent with a carnival and merry-making similar to that of Barranquilla. During the month of *July* Santa Marta presents a "Fiesta del Mar" with regattas, beauty contests, water-skiing exhibitions and street dances. In late May and early June the International Flower and Textile Festival is held in Medellin. However, this is more than flowers and fabrics—bullfights, parades, concerts, street dances, gala balls (open to visitors) and art shows are all part of the hectic activity. Medellin, incidentally, is the "orchid capital of the world".

The Ibague Festival, in Ibague, is usually held in the last week of June. This is Colombia's largest folklore, and includes auto races, horse shows, shooting contests and art shows, as well as the traditional dance and music events.

oldest airline in the Americas and second oldest anywhere. It operates daily flights connecting all important cities of Colombia, including those of the Caribbean coastal area. Other airlines conducting internal flight operations are *Taxader* and *Aerotaxi*, plus *Helicol*, an Avianca subsidiary, specializing in short helicopter flights.

A good highway connects Santa Marta on the east with Cartagena, crossing the Magdalena River by ferry and passing through Barranquilla en route. In times of high water or discontinuance of the ferry for other reason, travelers may go from Barranquilla to Santa Marta by a round-about route of approximately 150 miles but the roadway is badly maintained and the trip is not recommended. East of Santa Marta in the Guajira Peninsula roads are usually passable except during rainy periods.

Highway transportation is maintained between the coastal cities and the capital and other cities of the interior, moving from Cartagena south through Medellín but much of the highway is rutted, with dirt and gravel stretches, and light cars are subject to damage from the wear and tear of the trip. Buses, often ancient vehicles with wooden seats and space in the rear for baggage and farm produce, provide transportation between coastal towns and cities but tourists wishing to travel by highway in the area may make use of private cars available for hire at reasonable rates. Taxis, both in the Caribbean cities and the capital are plentiful with rates at about US $0.15 per mile. City bus fares are approximately US $0.02.

The Magdalena River is the main artery of Colombia and navigation is carried on from Puerto Berrio, 130 air miles from Bogotá, to Barranquilla and Cartagena, using sternwheel steamers similar to those formerly used on the Mississippi and other American rivers. Time of travel is about three and a half days downstream and about seven days for the trip up, depending to a large extent on the level of water in the Magdalena. Deluxe accommodations on a well-outfitted steamer from Barranquilla to Puerto Berrio, usual point of disembarkation for Bogotá, is about US $50 per person. The new *Ferrocarril del Atlantico* (Atlantic Railway) now connects the Caribbean coast of Colombia with the interior. Covering 625 miles of varied terrain and climate, the railroad climbs from the sultry warmth of Santa Marta on the Caribbean to the bracing nip of lofty Bogotá, high in the Andes, running parallel to the Magdalena River most of the way.

HOTELS

Generally speaking, Colombia's hotels are among the best values in the Caribbean area. Prices are relatively low, and service is excellent. In the face of increasing tourist business, hotels of the coastal area are often short of space. It is advisable to reserve well in advance. A five per cent tax is added to hotel bills throughout Colombia to help promote tourism, but prices are so low that it's quite painless.

The opening of Intercontinental's *Tequendama Hotel* transformed Bogotá from a provincial to an international capital. It introduced one of the smoothest and efficient hotel operations ever seen, and set the tone for future hotel developments. Its manager, Gus Romea, top notch Spanish-American hotel man

COLOMBIA

is responsible for the magnificent personalized service here. Latest news on the Colombia hotel picture comes from New York with the signing of the construction contract for the new Bogotá Hilton Hotel, a four million dollar, 300 room tower which will occupy 30 acres of the new 300-acre Capellania tract between Bogotá and the new international El Dorado airport.

BARRANQUILLA

EL PRADO. Oldest hotel in the Intercontinental chain, this delightful hostelry is everything a South American hotel should be, full of Spanish colonial atmosphere plus the superlative service characteristic of the Intercontinental operation. There are 200 rooms, swimming pool, tennis courts. The food here was the best we came across in the whole of Columbia. Dinner dancing and entertainment provided by charming young Colombians dancing the native *cumbia*. European plan rates are $8.50 to $12 a day single, $12 to $15 double.

If the El Prado is full, you will have your choice among four secondary hotels: *The Central, The Astoria, The Genova* and *The Victoria*. Their chief appeal will be to the budget-minded traveler, for American plan prices are as low as $4 and $5 per person per day.

BOGOTÁ

TEQUENDAMA. Absolutely top flight de luxe hotel (see above), has 650 rooms, two excellent restaurants with international cuisine. The center of the capital's busy social life. European Plan rates are $9 to $12 a day single, $13.50 to $16.50 double. A new wing has made this 17 story hostelry the largest in South America.

CONTINENTAL. Centrally-located, first class superior hotel with 248 rooms. European Plan rates: $5-$7 single, $7-$10 double.

RESIDENCIAS STEVES. First class superior, 125-room apartment hotel with modern efficiency kitchens, in spite of which factor rates are only about $10 single, $14 double.

RESIDENCIAS SANTA FE. Charming pension; private baths. $5 single.

The *Granada, San Francisco* and *Residencias Doña Marina* are three moderately priced hotels. There are also many small hotels and pensions where you can find decent accommodation and food at rock bottom prices.

CARTAGENA

DEL CARIBE is a de luxe hostelry on the Bocagrande Peninsula of this glittering resort. Has night club, casino, swimming pool, beach and private dock to accommodate guests who want sailing and fishing trips. There are 130 rooms, mostly air conditioned. European Plan rates are $6 a day single, $11 double without air-conditioning.

HOTEL CASINO. Ready this winter. Air-conditioned, guest rooms, casino, beach and swimming pool.

SAN FELIPE. Charming hotel in old walled section of city. American Plan: $5 single, $9 double.

FLAMINGO. New 35-room air-conditioned hotel, directly on beach. $7 single, $12 double.

BAHIA is a modern excellently appointed hotel with a view of the bay of Cartagena. Rates here are also the same as Del Caribe's.

The *Playa, Plaza Bolivar* and *Quinta Avenida* are all first class establishments with American Plan rates at $8 single, $12 double.

COLOMBIA

SANTA MARTA

TAMACÁ. Completed in 1959, this is a luxury resort hotel on El Rodadero Beach, about 30 minutes from Santa Marta. Eighty rooms, good restaurant and bar. Rates are same as El Caribe in Cartagena.

TAYRONA. A popular favorite on the boulevard which rings the lovely Bay of Santa Marta. Thirty-six rooms; superior food and service. American Plan rates: $11 single, about $20 double.

MIAMI. Good 40-room hotel on the bay. $10 single, $20 double.

RODADERO MOTEL. New 35-room motel on Rodarero Beach; 15 min. from town. European Plan rates are $7 single, $12 double.

FOOD AND DRINK

At principal hotels, nightclubs and luxury restaurants the menu is international and French, Italian, Spanish and American dishes are quite usual. All sorts of liquors and drinks are also found. Colombia also has varied domestic dishes that can be obtained in all typical hotels and restaurants. Almost every city has a special dish.

The Colombian liquors are "aguardiente" and rum produced in different areas under the direct control of the State. Both are distilled liquors extracted from sugar cane and among them "Viejo de Caldas", "Medellin", and "Cundinamarca" rums are worth mentioning.

Among the varied typical dishes the following are found:

Viudo de Pescado (fish), favorite dish on the Atlantic coast and in the departments of Huila, Tolima and in almost every town on the great rivers.

Fríjoles (kidney beans) prepared in Antioquia and Caldas; *Arepas* (corn griddle cakes) of common use in Antioquia, Caldas, Santander and Valle. *Peto* (soup) made out of a special white corn with milk. *Lechona*, a special dish prepared with sucking pigs, principally in warm climates. *Tamal*, originally from Santander but eaten all over the country, consisting of a preparation of flour, meats and vegetables cooked and wrapped in banana or wild leaves that give it a special taste. *Tortoise eggs* and *fried ants* can be obtained in Santander. Bread is made in Colombia with different kinds of flour and, apart from the common bread there are the typical *pan de yuca, pan de bono, pan de queso, almojábanas* and *garullas*.

Among sweets or desserts the best are *arequipe*, made of milk and sugar; *bocadillos veleños* made of *guayaba* juice, a typical Colombian fruit.

Typical dishes in Colombia are *ajiaco con pollo*, (potatoes and chicken soup), *longaniza* (a mixture of different meats), *ensalada de aguacate* (avocado salad) with or without chili,

COLOMBIA

papas chorriadas (potatoes covered with cheese, onions and butter) and *cuajada con melado* (milk curd with cane syrup or "panela").

Pears, apples, peaches, *curubas*, figs, strawberries and black-berries are found in cool climates. In medium and warm climates, pineapples, avocados, mangos, *chirimoyas*, papayas, *guanabanas*, medlars, oranges of different kinds, *zapotes*, coconuts, *anones*, exotic bananas, *granadillas*, watermelons, cantaloupes, *guayabas*, gooseberries, tamarinds, lulos, pitayas, etc. From these fruits, juices and refreshments most agreeable to the palate are made. Due to good refrigeration and transportation facilities, fruits of all climates can be obtained in any city.

RESTAURANTS AND NIGHT CLUBS

BARRANQUILLA. Best for dining and dancing is the *El Prado*, a vivacious social center with good food, music and talented local entertainers. *La Camelia* is also popular for dancing. *Brandes* has excellent German cooking; the *Steak House* boasts succulent steaks.

CARTAGENA. The leader for after dark amusement is the *Del Caribe*. Outstanding for seafood is the *Club de Pesca* (Fish Club), picturesquely situated in old Fort de San Sebastian. There's Saturday and Sunday dancing in the bar of the *Club Cartagena*. *La Capilla del Mar*, despite its Spanish name, specializes in French cuisine and seafood.

SANTA MARTA. There are a number of excellent grills and restaurants in this charming resort. It's a toss-up between the grillrooms of the *Tayrona* and *Tamacá* for the best food local diversion. Chances are you'll see some good Andino dancing at either place. Runners-up, and very close behind, are the Grill *El Rodadero*, Grill *Santa Marta*, *Hosteria Bella Vista*, *Restaurante Panamerican* and *Restaurant Mi-ramar*. The *Punta Betin* restaurant is on a high cliff overlooking the entire city and bay of Santa Marta.

BOGOTÁ. Here in the capital the hours are very Spanish indeed; you'll be sitting down to an *early* dinner at 9 p.m. There's a grand choice of restaurants.

Our own favorite is the glamorous Monserrate Dining Room of the *Tequendama Hotel* which has top notch food and music for dancing. The same hotel's coffee shop is very elegant. *Temel*, at Carrera 8A No. 15-65, is a big cosmopolitan Bogotá favorite for exquisitely prepared food in the international manner. The *Gran Vatel* in the home of one of Columbia's presidents and *Verner's* are also excellent restaurants, located less than five minutes walking distance from the Hotel Tequendama.

You'll find good French cooking at *Leon's Grill*, *Koster*, and *Restaurante Cyrus*. For Spanish and Colombian food, it's *As de Copas* at Carrera 13, No. 59-24. Best Italian food in town is at the Pizzeria Napolitana, Calle 17.

Gayest nightspots, in addition to the Tequendama's Monserrate Room, are *Grill Colombia*, *La Casbah*, *Grill Europa* and *La Pampa;* the last features food and music with an Argentine accent; the others are international in style.

668

COLOMBIA

If you've always longed for an emerald, here's your chance. These fabulous green gems are one of the great specialties of Colombia, and you get them here, the genuine article, not far from the mines. Exportation and prices are government controlled, and you can get these jewels here cheaper than anywhere else. Queen of the mines is the Muzo emerald, a stunning gem of purest ray serene, with a price range beginning at about a thousand dollars a carat.

When you are buying in this league, you'll do well to stick to reputable shops like *Bauer, Dita's* (in Hotel Tequendama), *Kling* (Carrera 7a), *Krauss & Co.* or *Compania Colombiana de Esmeraldas.* Get a certificate from the seller, authenticating the jewel and noting the purchase price. From Muzo, queen of the emeralds, you descend to lesser breeds like Chivors. But these are still genuine emeralds all the same, and they are very effective, especially when well set by a clever designer. Inexpensive emeralds set in gold can be bought for as little as $40. You'll find them at *Martha Bauer's* and other jewelry shops along with wonderful trinkets in 18 carat gold and silver. The ones that are made to sew onto the clothing of a saint's statue, sell for as little as half a dollar!

The old Indian and Spanish skill of craftsmanship persists in hand-hammered silver and hand-worked tortoise shell and gold, also in copper and palm ivory, which resembles the real McCoy. Standards of taste and workmanship are as high as prices are low.

You'll find excellent leatherwork and all sorts of tempting items in alligator, crocodile and snakeskin. The Colombians also have a way with straw, called *toquilla* and *iraca,* and with *agave,* a tough native fibre from which they make hats, shoes, handbags and even umbrellas. Particularly good ladies' shoes and handbags can be obtained in Medellin.

Men strike it rich in Colombia shops. Beautiful linen shirts are as little as $4. You can get a made-to-measure suit in silk or wool for $40 and up. Top quality shoes and hats are as low as $8. You'll find these and all the accessories you can think of, including terrific bargains in alligator belts, at the *Men's Shop* in the Hotel Tequendama, at *Bambuco's* and at *Daniel's,* all in Bogotá.

Daniel's is also a leader for women's fashions. Which leads us to one of the unique buys of Colombia: the famous *ruana,* the striking native poncho hand woven from handcarded Colombian wool. An oil in the wool of native flocks makes

COLOMBIA

these colorful garments well nigh impermeable to rain, and they're as warm as toast. There's enough diversity in style and color so that you'll want more than one of these pull-over stoles or short capes, especially since the average price is only ten U.S. dollars. You'll find these all over Colombia. In Bogotá, you might orient yourself on ruanas and other native bargains at *Valdiri,* the big department store.

If you're an admirer of pre-Colombian artifacts and jewelry, you'll find the real thing here along with some very skilful imitations. Don't despise the latter. Fashioned by hand, they make excellent souvenirs of this fascinating country, and you can actually find small charms and objects in 18 karat gold in the dollar and up department!

 SPORTS. On the coast. Sports on the Caribbean coast of Colombia are largely those related to the sea.

Fishing is excellent the year 'round for such species as marlin, sawfish, shad, dolphin and tuna. An international fishing competition is held in Barranquilla in May of each year.

There is good *skindiving* at Los Rosarios Islands and this sport is becoming more popular in the clear tropical waters but visitors should consult local authorities before practicing it, since both sharks and barracuda have caused a number of deaths among local divers in recent years. Beaches all along the north coast are of white sand shelving gently into the water and *swimming* is the most popular sport.

Water skiing, boating and *sailing* are common pastimes and the visitor may make arrangements to participate in these sports through his hotel or tourist agency.

Both Barranquilla and Cartagena have *golf* courses for which guest cards may be arranged.

Tennis is a very popular sport among *costeños* and an international tournament, which draws worldwide tennis figures, is held each March at the Country Club in Barranquilla.

In the field of spectator sports, *baseball* is extremely popular on the coast.

For the more active sportsman, the Sierra Neveda, which begins some 30 miles east of Santa Marta, offers an experience in *mountain climbing* with peaks that go up to nearly 19,000 feet.

Hunting for ducks along the coast or for such game as jaguar, tapir and other wild animals may be arranged. Also available by arrangement are safaris into the *Llanos* or the Amazon basin to established hunting camps.

In Bogotá, visitors may play *golf* at the *Bogotá Country Club* (two 18-hole courses), *Los Lagartos* and *San Andrés* by arranging for guest cards at their hotels or tourist agencies. All three clubs have *tennis* courts.

Covered pools for swimming are located at the Bogotá Country Club, Los Lagartos and the Club Militar.

Sailing and *water skiing* are practiced at Los Lagartos and at the Bogotá Yacht Club on Lake Muña near the city. *Hunting* expeditions and trout *fishing* in mountain lakes may be arranged locally. Spectator sports include *bullfighting* in the Circo Santamaria (February and March), *soccer,*

COLOMBIA

basketball and *polo* at the Polo Club de Santa Fé where international matches are often held. *Horse races* are run every Sunday afternoon at the Hipódromo de Techo with parimutuel betting as in the United States.

 ELECTRIC CURRENT. In all of Colombia, except the cities of Bogotá and Armenia, electric current is 110 volts 60 cycles AC. In these two cities current is 60 cycle alternating but 150 volts. The Hotel Tequendama in Bogotá, as well as a number of other new buildings, has been converted to 110 volts. Transformers should be 110-150 volts 60 cycles AC with standard U.S. flat plugs.

 TIPPING. The standard tip in Colombia is 10% of the bill. Taxi drivers are usually not tipped.

USEFUL ADDRESSES. *Barranquilla*, Consulates, *American*, Edificio Banco de la República, tel. 11650; *British*, Calle 30 No. 43-54.

Bogotá, Embassies, *American*, Edificio Seguros Bolívar, tel. 420-060; British, Carrera 8a. 15-46, tel. 411-051; *Canadian*, Carrera 10 No. 16-92, tel. 430-065. *Automobile Club.* Touring Club de Colombia, Cra. 6 No. 14-86, tel. 414-100. *Travel Agencies.* Colombian Tourist Bureau, Cra. 5 No. 14-15, tel. 419-577; Exprinter, Cra. 6 No. 14-64, tel. 415-704; Allen & Mary Lowrie, Calle 19 No. 7-30, tel. 432-547; Wagons Lits-Cook, Hotel Tequendama, tel. 419-250; Empresa Colombiana de Turismo, Edificio Banco del Comercio.

Cartagena, Vice-consulate, *British*, Edificio Andian.

Santa Marta, Vice-consulate, *British*, Paseo Bastidas, Calle Cangrejal.

EXPLORING COLOMBIA

The Caribbean coast of Colombia stretches from its juncture with Panama on the Gulf of Darién eastward to its boundary with Venezuela on the Península of Guajira—approximately 1,000 miles of deeply-indented coastline, curving sand beaches, modern port cities and fishing villages. Beginning with the trio of cities which dominate the north coast, the visitor finds himself deep in an atmosphere reminiscent of the Spanish Main, the Inquisition and the 19th century wars for independence.

Cartagena is a walled city with many well preserved relics of its exciting history at every turn: the huge stone fortress of San Felipe de Barajas; the half-ruined monastery of La Popa towering above the city, capping a massive headland visible for many miles at sea; the twin forts of San Fernando and San José of the harbor entrance at Bocachica; the Palace of the Inquisition, established in 1610; the walls of Las Bovédas, 26 feet high and 70 feet wide; the Jesuit church of St. Peter Claver, the "slave of the slaves"; the market beside which *goletas* dock to unload fruits and vegetables; plazas in which more than 400 years of history have taken place, and narrow, winding streets.

Eighty-five miles to the east is Barranquilla—30 minutes by

671

plane and two hours by modern highway—largest and most modern of the trio of coastal cities in which the chief interest for the tourist is in the life of the streets and the Magdalena River, principal artery of travel and commerce in Colombia until fairly recent times. Barranquilla's new jet airport, to open in the winter of '61-'62, will link Colombia's Caribbean Coast to all major cities in the U.S. and Canada.

A 20-minute flight by plane or an hour and a half by car across the Magdalena River ferry and through the great salt marshes which border the coast bring the traveler to Santa Marta, 60 highway miles east of Barranquilla. Oldest city of the New World, Santa Marta is called "the Pearl of the Americas" because of the beautiful half-moon bay on which the city fronts. Of principal interest to the tourist is the *Quinta de San Pedro Alejandrino*, three miles southeast of the city, where Simón Bolívar, liberator of five South American countries, died on his way into exile in 1830; the colonial Cathedral and the Church of San Francisco, dating from the same period, and the Sierra Nevada, a snow-capped range of mountains independent of the Andes, 30 miles to the east, in which Colombia's highest peak, the *Pico Cristóbal Colón*, rises to 18,960 feet above sea level and immense banana plantations stretching south.

One hundred miles east of Santa Marta, reachable both by plane and by highway during the dry season, is Riohacha, capital of the Territory of Guajira and former pearling center raided by Sir Francis Drake in 1596. The Peninsula of Guajira is arid and scarcely settled, the nomadic Indians who inhabit it living on cattle raising, pearl fishing and salt production.

A short distance southwest of Cartagena, reached in about two hours by launch from the city, are the *Islas del Rosario,* a cluster of small islands where many residents of the coast and the interior have built villas and summer homes. Among the attractions of the archipelago are beautiful coral reefs and colorful tropical fish.

Two hours north by plane from Cartagena are the Colombian islands of San Andres and Providencia, discovered by Columbus on his first voyage, popular among Colombian and other tourists because of their status as duty free ports where luxury items from all parts of the world may be bought at bargain prices. The islands also are popular because of their beautiful white beaches, rolling surf, and relaxed, informal atmosphere, and the frequent *puentes* (holidays of three or more consecutive days) find hundreds of highland dwellers taking advantage of air excursion rates to visit them.

Sixty-five airline miles directly south of Cartagena, reached by a passable highway (130 miles) or by combination of plane to the town of Sincelejo and by car the remaining 25 miles, is Tolú, a small fishing town on the handsome Gulf of Morrosquillo. Lodging in Tolú is not deluxe but perfectly acceptable to the traveler looking for an out-of-the way spot where he can fish, swim in warm, blue tropical surf and invite his soul in peace and confort. South along the gulf beach, within sight of Tolú is Coveñas, the Caribbean terminal of the trans-Andean oil pipeline from Colombian fields on the Venezuela frontier.

Many tourists visiting the Caribbean coast of Colombia take advantage of convenient airline schedules to visit Bogotá, the nation's capital, two hours flying time from Barranquilla and from Cartagena. Others, who have the leisure to enjoy a slower means of transportation, take a paddlewheel river steamer in Barranquilla and go up the Magdalena River to Puerto Berrio where they change from sternwheeler to railroad car, or airplane reaching Bogotá in a week or so, depending on the vagaries of a river that sometimes strands boats on sandbars for days at a time. The cost for this trip is not prohibitive.

The Caribbean Coast

Barranquilla is a modern industrial city of some 400,000 and Colombia's second port, although in recent years silting of its Magdalena River entrance has caused concern to port authorities. The city, founded in 1721, is located ten miles from the river's mouth of the west bank of the Magdalena and is the principal port of entry for visitors arriving either by plane or ship from the north.

Barranquilla normally holds little of interest for the tourist beyond hunting or fishing, of which there is an abundance in the area, or merely observing the busy port and lively activity in the streets of the city. There is a handsome Cathedral in the Plaza Bolivar before which stands a statue of Columbus. The municipal market, located on the Caño de las Compañias, a side channel of the Magdalena, is vivid and noisy. Overlooking the city from the northeastern heights is the select residential suburb of El Prado, not far from which is the Country Club with tennis courts, golf links and a swimming pool.

COLOMBIA

Normally a lively, happy city, Barranquilla becomes in the week before Lent each year what its inhabitants call *una ciudad loca*—a "crazy city" in which crowds fill the streets day and night dressed in exotic costumes and masks. There are parades of floats and folklore dances and music, a battle of flowers, beauty contests, an acquatic festival and finally the night before Ash Wednesday, the burial of "Joselito Carnaval" the spirit of the celebration, for another year. Also observed by the *Barranquilleros* is the annual feast of San Roque on August 16.

Fifteen miles from Barranquilla eastward to the Caribbean shore is the beach resort of Puerto Colombia. Once used as the port of Barranquilla when the Magdalena became heavily silted, Puerto Colombia now serves only for the recreation of residents and visitors. Other nearby bathing resorts include Pradomar, Salgar, Sabanilla, Galerazamba and Santa Veronica, while 18 miles southwest are the excellent thermal springs of Usiacuri.

Fascinating Cartagena

One of the most fascinating cities of the Western Hemisphere, Cartagena de Indias, to give it its proper name, lies 30 minutes by air or two hours by highway west of Barranquilla on the Caribbean coast. A city of 185,000, commercial Cartagena deals largely in platinum from the headwaters of the Atrato and San Juan Rivers, coffee from the Sierra Nevada and oil products piped from Barrancabermeja 335 miles up the Magdalena.

But it is not commercial Cartagena that interests the tourist but rather the city founded in 1533 by Don Pedro de Heredía, which still largely remains locked behind its massive walls on the island of Tierra Bomba. Actually the city is no longer an island since one of the two original entrances into its bay— Boca Grande—was walled up by the Spaniards after the attack by Sir Edward Vernon in 1741. The other entrance—Boca Chica—is now the only passage into the bay from the sea, guarded by two ancient and derelict forts, San Fernando and San José. During the days when pirates of all nations harassed the Spanish Main, Cartagena was guarded by a massive chain stretched between these two forts. Launches run regularly from the city to San Fernando where facilities for picnicking and sea bathing exist.

Towering over all of the many forts which guarded the approaches to Cartagena is the powerful fortress of San Felipe de Barajas, 135 feet above sea level. Begun in 1634 under Philip II of Spain and completed in 1735 in the reign of Ferdinand VI, the enormous fortifications cost the Spanish crown so much that Philip, so the story goes, once went to the window of his palace in Madrid looking for them in the belief that anything so costly should be visible across the ocean.

After the interior of the country was settled, wealth of all kinds flowed into Cartagena for shipment to Spain, wealth which soon invited pirate attacks in spite of the sturdy defenses of the city. Cartagena was sacked by Henry Morgan, by Sir Francis Drake and by other freebooters but an imposing fleet and powerful British army under Admiral Vernon failed before its stubborn resistance in 1741. Vernon was accompanied by a brother of George Washington in this attempt; Mount Vernon in Virginia is named in his honor.

During the wars for independence, Cartagena was captured by Spanish loyalist troops under Pablo Morillo after a prolonged siege in 1815 which gained it the title of "the Heroic City" or, as Colombians refer to it, "La Heroica". Simón Bolívar used Cartagena as his base in the Magdalena compaign in 1811.

Cartagena is divided by 17th century walls into the "old" and "new" city. In the "old" city houses are in the Iberian style: thick walls, high ceilings, central patios and gardens, narrow streets and crooked for protection during assault, balconies of many varieties.

Other sites of interest to the visitor to Cartagena include the Paseo de Mártires, a wide promenade flanked by the busts of nine patriots executed by Morillo after he took the city; the Plaza Bolivar with an equestrian statue of the Liberator in the center and flanked by the Palace of the Inquisition, a good example of colonial baroque architecture, which was built in 1776; the Cathedral, built in 1538; the Jesuit Church of St. Peter Claver, in which the body of the saint lies in a chest under the main altar; the half-ruined 17th century monastery of La Popa from which the best view of Cartagena is obtained; the walls of Las Bovedas, wide enough for automobile use in sightseeing tours, and the colorful and noisy market surrounded on three sides by the waters of the bay.

November 11, the anniversary of the city's declaration of its independence from Spain, is the city's principal celebration and the population parades the streets in fancy dress and masks. Another feast of great popular participation is that of the Virgin of la Candelaria (Candlemas) on February 2 when pilgrims from many parts troop up the 500-foot height of La Popa bearing lighted tapers.

Pearl of the Americas

Fifty airline miles northeast of Barranquilla—20 minutes by plane or an hour and a half by highway—is Santa Marta, the "Pearl of the Americas", which was founded in 1525 by Rodrigo de Bastidas, one of the early *conquistadores*. Located at the mouth of the Manzanares River, Santa Marta lies on a deep bay protected on both flanks by ancient forts. In spite of these, however, the city was sacked a number of times by pirates in the 16th and 17th centuries.

Santa Marta, with its deep water allowing ocean-going vessels to lie alongside its docks, is increasing in importance as a commercial port. Its principal export is bananas, brought to dockside by a railway from the widespread plantations of various fruit companies spread along the base of the Sierra Nevada de Santa Marta to the south and east.

It was to Santa Marta in 1830 that Simón Bolívar, the liberator of half the countries of South America, came penniless and broken in health on his way to voluntary exile after his dream of a *Gran Colombia* had shattered on the petty political machinations of his colleagues. He was given refuge at the plantation of the Marquis de Mier y Benítez, called "San Pedro Alejandrino", where he died on December 17 at the age of 47. The plantation, now a national shrine, no longer shelters the hero's remains, which were removed to Caracas in 1842, but the simple room in which he died and his few pathetic belongings may still be seen. The plantation is three miles southeast of Santa Marta on the road leading to the Sierra Nevada.

This compact range of mountains, highest of which reaches 18,960 feet, is snow-covered the year around. Coffee plantations which grow a fine grade of mild coffee are found on its flanks with banana plantations spreading out below. It is possible to reach the summit of the range but it is advisable to use local guides in any attempt at climbing.

Aside from the beautiful Bay of Santa Marta, points of interest in and near the city include the bathing resort at Punta de Betín, the Rodadero and Gaira beaches, the fishing villages of La Concha and Taganga, the Cathedral and the Church of San Francisco.

From the Caribbean coast it is a 750-mile two-hour flight

COLOMBIA

to Colombia's capital, Bogotá, situated high in the Andes at 8,660 feet in a long flat valley surrounded by peaks. With 1,180,000 inhabitants in its Special District, which is similar to the District of Columbia in which Washington is located, Bogotá is the first city of Colombia—politically, numerically, commercially and culturally.

The city was founded in 1538 by Gonzalo Jimenez de Quesada, who fought his way up the Magdalena River valley to find the sedentary kingdom of the Chibchas spread over the cool plateau which was once the bed of a prehistoric lake. Forces of Francisco Pizarro arrived at the site of Bogotá, coming up from Perú, soon after Quesada had begun his settlement, followed shortly after by German adventurers who forced their way over the eastern cordilleras from Venezuela.

The Plaza Bolivar, around which the original town of Bogotá grew, is at the heart of the city and around it spreads what is left of the old quarter with its narrow streets and massive mansions with their barred windows, carved doorways, tiled roofs extending over the sidewalks. In this area worth the visitor's attention are the Palace of San Carlos, home of Colombia's presidents; the house of the Marquis of San Jorge, the Observatory, the Conciliary Seminary of San José, the Municipal Palace, the Capitol, the Churches of San Ignacio, Santa Inés, San Augustín and San Francisco, and the Teatro Colón.

The Gold Museum in the vaults of the Banco de la República contains works of art and ornaments made by the Chibchas and other natives before the arrival of the Spaniards. Emeralds of great value are among the collection's treasures.

The University City, site of the *Universidad Nacional*; the Quinta de Bolivar, the National Museum, the Colonial Museum and the Luis Angel Arango Library are all worth the visitor's time. Other churches of interest are those of San Diego, opposite the Hotel Tequendama, Santa Clara, Santa Barbara and Veracruz. A splendid view of the city and of the *sabana* of Bogotá may be obtained from the peak of Monserrate, site of a much venerated shrine, which is reached from the eastern edge of the city by both a funicular railroad and cable cars in a matter of minutes.

Excursions from Bogotá may be made to the Falls of Tequendama, a half-hour southward from the city; to the Salt Cathedral of Zipaquirá, 40 minutes to the north by car; to the Archeological Park at Facatativá, 40 minutes west, an ancient fortress of the Zipa Indians who left a number of still undeciphered hieroglyphics carved and painted on boulders and in caves, and to a number of small towns and villages along the way to the *tierra caliente*, the hot country along the Magdalena River. Visitors who have a yen to know how the business end of bullfighting feels may arrange a visit to a ranch where fighting bulls are bred. Try your cape work on a fighting calf—all without bloodshed on either side, of course.

Information about trips on the Magdalena River may be obtained from the offices of the *Naviera Fluvial Colombiana* either in Bogotá of Barranquilla, or from *Allen and Mary Lowie*, Apartado Aereo 7262, Bogota, Colombia. The leisurely trip by paddle steamer, a sort of Latin-American Life on the Mississippi, is highly recommended. You can almost reach out and touch the green jungle gliding past. Food and service are good. Beer is 10 cents a bottle; scotch, 45 cents a shot. Fare for a 12-day round trip from Barranquilla is approximately $80. If you're looking for a low cost relaxation and luxury, this is it.

PANAMA AND THE CANAL ZONE

Corridor of Six Continents

BY

WILLIAM CURTIS

Panama, the youngest among the Central American republics, is a curious blend of the historic, the modern and the primitive. For the historians there are vestiges of the Spanish conquest and skirmishes with British buccaneers, for the engineering enthusiast there's the top attraction of the "Big Ditch", for the sportsman the promise of a country whose very name means "abundance of fish" (panamá), for the photographer a riot of color, and for everywoman an emporium of exotic treasures at bargain prices.

In reality there are three Panamas; the landscaped town of the ten-mile wide Canal Zone, controlled by the United States; the noisy international glitter of ultra-modern Panama City, the steaming tropical jungle where the Indians perpetuate

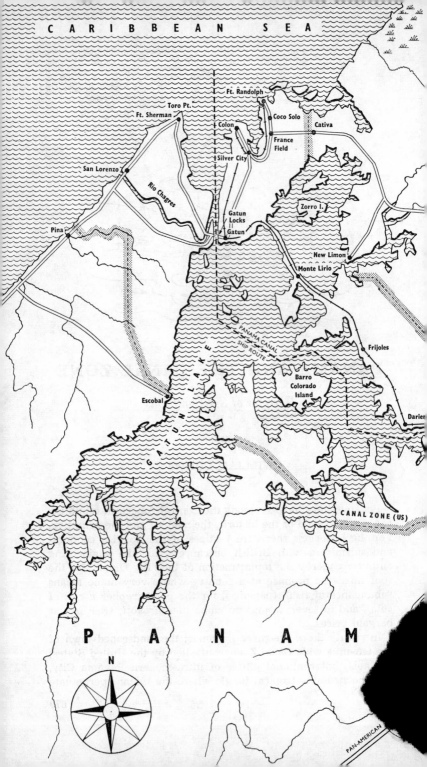

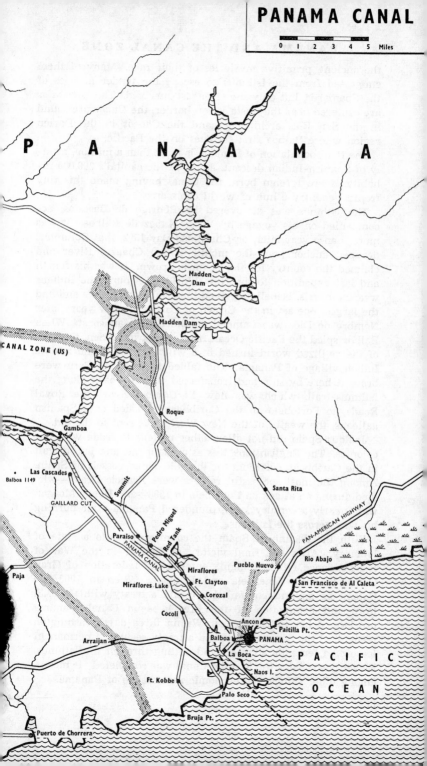

the ancient, primitive mysteries of their race. Many of them emigrated from the Isthmus to escape the tender mercies of the Spaniards, but only the strongest survived. The *Guaymies* are centered near the Costa Rican border, the *Cunas* are found in the San Blas archipelago and the *Chocós* in the Darién region where Balboa first set eyes on the Pacific.

The total population of Panama is more than a million, mostly of Spanish-Indian descent. Many of the capital's 200,000 inhabitants are foreign born, the Canal having made this tiny tropical country a hub of world commerce.

The Isthmus was discovered by Rodrigo de Bastidas, accompanied on his voyage by Vasco Nuñez de Balboa. It was more than a year later, on Christmas Day 1502, that Columbus dropped anchor near the mouth of the Chagres River and claimed the country for the Spanish Crown. It was his fourth and last expedition to the New World. He found the Indians wearing pearls. Isabella received these fabulous jewels and had the largest one set in the Crown of Castile. A few years later Nombre de Dios was founded on the Caribbean coast. When Balboa spied the Pacific Ocean from a peak in Darien, the eyes of the civilized world turned in a wild surmise to the remote Indian village of Panamá. The fabled treasures of Peru were brought here by ship and transferred on mule-back along the Isthmus-trail, which was now *El Camino Real* (the Royal Road), to Portobelo on the Caribbean. Loaded onto Spanish galleons, the wealth of the New World was sent to the old.

Jealous Spain did not allow other nations to trade with her colonies. The English took this as a challenge, and lay in wait in the Caribbean corridors for the gold-laden vessels of Spain. Among the most successful raiders were Francis Drake—who died during an attack on Portobelo in 1596—and Henry Morgan who, nearly a century later, plundered Panamá after burning his way across the Isthmus.

With the decline of Spain the country fell into a state of lethargy. After the final victory of Bolivar in the War of Independence (1819) Panama entered the federation of Gran Colombia with Venezuela and Ecuador. When in 1903 the Colombian government failed to ratify a treaty with the U.S. to permit completion of the French-begun Canal, Panama proclaimed her independence. Within three days Washington recognized the new republic and a treaty secured a permanent lease of a ten-mile strip of land cutting through the Isthmus. Eleven years later the 51-mile Canal was completed. It meant, among other things, the economic renaissance of Panama.

PANAMA AND THE CANAL ZONE

PRACTICAL INFORMATION FOR PANAMA AND THE CANAL ZONE

WHEN TO COME. Climate tropical; temperature practically uniform the year round: from 73° to 81° in the Pacific area, from 73° to 84° on the Atlantic side. Nights are generally much cooler. In the interior, temperatures sometimes drop to 41°. At about mid-day it rains for a couple of hours during the rainy season which lasts from April to December. Best months to come—mid-December through March. Summer is pleasant, avoid October-November.

Two outstanding events which make it an excellent time to visit Panama are the four-day *Carnival* which ends on Ash Wednesday and the *Semana Santa* (Holy Week), the religious festival before Easter.

Clothing. Thinnest possible cottons and cool evening dresses for women, tropical suits for men. Evening clothes are much worn in better hotels and night-clubs. Thin raincoat a necessity during rainy season, short topcoat recommended for stay in mountains. Dry cleaning and laundry efficient.

Health aspects. Excellent medical services, good standard of hygiene in principal cities. You can drink water and milk freely in all but the you, nevertheless. Food, including green vegetables and fresh fruit, safe everywhere.

most primitive villages. Take water bottle and chlorine tablets with

HOW TO GET THERE. *By Air.* Tocumen, about 18 miles from Panama City, is a buzy international airport also convenient to Cristobal and Colon (five hours from New York). From New York, Braniff International and Pan Am. offer regular same-plane service via Miami; Pan Am also flies via Santo Domingo. Panama is well served by Pan American from San Francisco, Los Angeles, and from Miami, Houston, New Orleans. Other flights to Panama include: from New Orleans: TACA. From Dallas: Braniff. From Miami: APA (Aerovias Panama Airways) both direct and via Kingston; Braniff; VIP Airlines; LACSA; LAN-Chile or Ecuatoriana de aviacion. From Mexico: Guest or Pan Am. From Central America: Pan Am, LACSA, TACA. From South America: Avianca, Panagra, Braniff, KLM, Varig, LAN-Chile, Ecuatoriana.

By Sea. It takes about five days to come from New York to Cristobal, the principal Caribbean port. Both Balboa (Pacific side) and Cristobal are visited by ships from all over the world. Many Caribbean cruise ships (e.g. Grace Line, Furness) call at Cristobal. Ships from over 700 companies pass through the canal; some freighters accept a limited number of passengers. Among the lines serving Panama regularly are: United Fruits, American President Lines, Moore-McCormack (all U.S.). British lines include Pacific Steam Navigation Co., Royal Mail, Furness Withy & Co., Cunard, the New Zealand Shipping Co., Shaw, Saville. Others are Holland-America Line, French Line, Italian Line, the Japanese O.S.K. Line and Scandinavian Knutsen and Johnson Lines.

By Land. The inter-American Highway will soon be a reality. Between San Jose, Costa Rica, and the Panama border, only a few bridges must be completed to provide a year 'round route.

COLOMBIA

Deep sea, lake and river fishing, water skiing, golf, tennis, skin-diving, hunting, sailing and other sports are practiced on the coast the year 'round. Baseball is popular on the coast.

Bogotá has bullfights most of the year but the principal season, during which outstanding Spanish and Mexican toreros appear, is in *February* and *March*. Outstanding *corridas* also take place during the Cali and Manizales *ferias* late in *December* and *January* respectively.

A national agricultural and cattle fair is held during the first week of *August*. Independence Day *(July 20)* and the anniversary of the decisive battle of Boyacá *(August 7)* are usually occasions for showy military parades and popular observances of all kinds.

Horse racing, with parimutuel betting as in the United States, takes place every Sunday afternoon. Other spectator sports regularly practiced are polo matches, soccer games and cock fighting.

Tejo, a game in which flat stones are tossed at explosive caps, is widely played in the highlands.

TRAVEL DOCUMENTS. The Colombian Government gives Tourist Cards to U.S. citizens wishing to visit Colombia for a maximum visit of 90 days. Cards are valid for 4 years. Tourist Cards may be obtained at the airlines or at any Colombian Consulate upon presentation of two passport-size photographs, a smallpox vaccination certificate, proof of citizenship (i.e. voter's registration card, birth certificate, passport, naturalization papers, etc.) and round-trip ticket. Tourist Cards are issued immediately, free of charge.

Canadian citizens must present the same documents; however, they must have a valid passport. Cards for Canadian citizens are valid for 90 days and must be used within 60 days of issuance.

These Tourist Cards issued for 90-day periods are not sufficient for foreigners who wish to work or carry on any sort of business in Colombia. Tourists who wish to stay in Columbia more than 90 days, or businessmen who desire to work will need a special visa given by Colombian consulates with a charge of US $5.

CURRENCY. Monetary unit is the Peso which is currently exchanged at 9 to the American dollar. Ergo, the peso equals 13 cents. American and Canadian money is accepted in all tourist centers.

WHAT TO WEAR. With climate in Colombia depending pretty largely at what altitude one may be, what a traveler brings with him will depend on where he intends to go in the country. On the coast the climate is warm, averaging about 83° F., and sport shirts and slacks for men and cotton dresses and shorts for women are recommended. In the better hotels coats and ties for men and dresses for women are expected at meals. In Bogotá, which has a perpetual spring-like climate, lightweight woolen suits for men and wool suits and dresses, sweaters and skirts for women are needed. Fur jackets or stoles and light topcoats are often worn in the evening. Regardless of where you are, a raincoat is often a handy thing to have in Colombia.

HOW TO GET ABOUT. Colombia, faced with the extremely difficult problem of transport in a country which is almost as vertical as it is horizontal, has developed one of the best air transportation systems in the world.

Avianca, owned by private Colombian citizens is the

Best shops: *Casa Fastlich*, 161 A-venida Central and El Panamá Hotel; *Nat Mendez*, 15 Calle "J"; *Tahiti*, 137 Ave. Central; *Casuela* and *Perret* at Colón, Front Street.

French perfumes may be bought at the El Panamá lobby shops, *Cyrno's Gift Shop*, 16 Tivoli Avenue and *Motta's*. They carry just about everything: Panama hats, Royal Crown Derby and Doulton china, oriental specialties and duty free liquors. Motta's Shops are located at Colón (44 Front St.), Tocumen Airport, Hotel El Panamá and 476 and 844 Avenida Colón at Panama City. Other reputable liquor stores: *Silvestre & Brostella*, 6 Avenida Cuba and Esquina Calle 27 Este. *Bonded Liquors* Inc. sell at both Tocumen Airport and Hotel El Panamá.

Silverware and gift items can be bought in confidence at *Mercurio's*, Avenida Central, who are also jewelers. *Porras*, across from Internacional Hotel, sells not only silver but cameras as well. So does *International Photo* at 155 Avenida Central, *Madurito*, at n° 100 and the *Camera Shop* at the El Panama Lobby.

A galaxy of English and Continental china and porcelain dinnerware can be found at *Shaw's*, 14 Tivoli Avenue, Panama City and Front Street, Colón; *Dagmar*, also in Tivoli Avenue (and El Panamá Lobby) specializes mainly in Scandinavian ceramics, furniture and sterling silver. *Surany's* is a good gift-shop in Front Street, Colón, *Morrison* in Panama City, corner 4th of July and "J" Street. For embroidered linen visit *Galeria Panamá*, 17-85 Avenida Central or *Nueva India* at no. 115 in the same street. The latter sells also Oriental goods and so do *Bombay Palace* and *Sun of India*, almost next door to it. In Colón it's *Flor de Bombay*, 43 Front St. who is tops in this line.

For ladies' apparel and accessories you'll shop at the best department store, *Chambonnet y Quinta Avenida* or at *Sarah Fashions*, Via España, opposite El Panamá Hotel. A good bet for tropical clothing and fine haberdashery is the *American Bazaar*, with three shops in the capital and if your fishing tackle is incomplete, see *Unisport*, just across from El Panamá Hotel or *Mauricio*, 47 Avenida Central.

Whether it's fishing, hunting or just an exploration trip to San Blas Islands or the Darién province, Jungle Jim at El Panamá Hotel will fix you up. Give him plenty of advance notice, if possible.

 SPORTS. Many hunters are attracted by the wildlife found in Panama, specially in Chiriqui and Darién provinces, where the big game such as jaguar, puma-tiger, wild boar and ocelot are abundant. Less risky are the mule deer, peccary and the *conejo pintado* (painted rabbit). Guides are available and you can hire horses and tents locally. If you don't want to wander far afield, take a launch at Gatún Lake, to take you into the jungle just outside the Canal Zone. There is plenty of waterfowl and shooting alligators is merely target practice. A license is necessary and in order to bring your gun into Panama you need a permit from the nearest Panamanian consulate.

Some of the best fishing grounds in the world are in this area. The Pacific side of the Isthmus, the Chiriqui Lagoon off the Archipelago of Bocas del Toro and the waters along the San Blas coast are best for deep-sea fishing. Among the big-game fish there are the giant tarpon, sailfish, tuna and marlin, to mention a few. Fishing is good during all the year but the season from May to November proves most satisfying.

For more modest purses boats complete with crew, tackle, bait and food are available on a daily basis. Two of the best known clubs welcome non-residents: the Panama Canal Tarpon Club in Colón, and the Pacific Sailfish Club in Balboa. For freshwater fishing go to the Chiriqui River, which is teeming with rainbow trout. Another good place is Bambito, near El Volcàn Barù.

Surf bathing and water-skiing are popular sports on the beaches near Panama City, such as Santa Clara, Gorgona, and Río Mar. You can hire sailing boats practically everywhere along the coast. There are six golf courses on the Isthmus. Panama Golf Club's fine links are open to tourists without much formality.

Among spectator sports baseball holds first place, closely followed by horseracing on Presidente Remon racetrack. Also on the outskirts of the capital is La Macarena arena where bullfighting is taking place. Cock-fighting on Sundays and during *fiestas* is followed with great enthusiasm by the people of the interior.

USEFUL ADDRESSES. (in Panama City). *U.S. Embassy*, Avenida Balboa at 37th Street; *British Embassy*, Via España 120, who looks after Canadian nationals as well. Travel bureaus: *Boyd Brothers*, Via España 120, tel. 3-7428; *Tivoli*, at n° 8, tel. 2-0465. Both have comprehensive sightseeing programs. Car-hire: at El Panama, Internacional and Roosevelt hotels. Riding: *Club de Equitacion*, Old Panama, tel. 3-0279. Trail rides with or without guides.

EXPLORING PANAMA

As a tourist sight, the greatest curiosity is the Panama Canal. Entering from the Atlantic side, your ship sails across Limon Bay, past the giant moles which mark the actual entrance. On your left you'll see the silhouetted buildings of Colón (Spanish for Columbus) and its twin city, Cristobal. Colón is a busy port where you can see all sorts of craft, from luxury liners to Indian dugout canoes. Shopping in Front Street is an exciting adventure for ladies, nightclubbing for gentlemen. If you want to flee Colón's almost perpetual local rain, take the hourly bus toward Panama City. You pass Mt. Hope Cemetery, marking the graves of the many Frenchmen who died of yellow fever while trying to build the Canal under Ferdinand de Lesseps. This brilliant diplomat, promoter of the Suez Canal, failed in his second enterprise because of climatic conditions, the dishonesty of his collaborators and his inability to raise new funds. Some six miles farther on is Fort Davis, the largest on the Isthmus. You continue toward Gatún Locks, the largest structure in the canal, where you can usually see a ship being raised or lowered. Gatún Lake has several arms which stretch right into the jungle. Alligators glide through the water and you hear the mysterious whispers, cries and snorts of unseen animals nearby.

You can make a pleasant side-trip by crossing Gatún Locks via the Sea Gates, thence over the jungle road to the ruins of

PANAMA AND THE CANAL ZONE

San Lorenzo, which once guarded the vital Chagres river. When Columbus anchored his ships at the mouth of this broad river, he never suspected how close he was to that passage to the Indies, which he sought in vain.

While Boyd-Roosevelt Highway is the quickest way across the Isthmus the trip through the Canal is the more spectacular one. It takes about eight hours and there is never a dull moment: you see the operation of this engineering miracle at close range, pass through a series of locks, the famed Gaillard Cut, and into lovely lakes, always amid lush, tropical scenery. On reaching the Pacific terminal you see three cities, Balboa Panama and Ancon, almost welded into one, though only Panama City is outside the U.S. Canal Zone.

The Capital

The strategic importance of the Isthmus accounts for Panama City's turbulent history. For centuries it has been the transfer point and clearing house for commerce in the New World. When Morgan captured and sacked the city in 1671, the present capital was founded a few miles up the coast at a spot which could be more easily defended. After the peace treaty between Spain and England and because of the ever present danger of yellow fever—now eradicated by American medical science—the city declined rapidly until gold was discovered in California. Two steamship lines operated to Panama, one from New York and one from California and prospectors used every means of travel across the Isthmus, even Indian *cayucos* to paddle up the Chagres river. Since the completion of the Canal, Panama City has become one of the great crossroads of the world, a thriving, bustling capital where people from every nation meet.

The capital is justly famous for its pre-Lent four-day carnival when you can see the national costumes from the various regions of the country, some of them heavy with beautiful embroidery. There is much gaiety, with parades, floats and dancing in the streets all night. This is the time to watch the native dances, the *tamborito*, the *cumbia* and others.

The city itself, overlooking the Pacific Ocean, offers a variety of architectural attractions. Modern buildings are standing next to antique churches, broad promenades straddle ancient fortifications. Most of the interesting places to visit are within an area of about half square mile. On the small fortified peninsula lies the Plaza de Francia with a monument dedicated to the ill-fated French and highlighting the history of the

Canal. From the esplanade above, you have an excellent view of the Bay. Next to the National Theater and the Church of San Francisco is the Colegio La Salle where the great liberator and idealist Simon Bolivar proposed in 1826 a United States of South America which never materialized. The President's palace is a pseudo-Moorish building; its *patio* can be visited at certain hours. Avenida Central, studded with shops, cafés and nightclubs runs through the oldest section of town and passes four important *plazas* on its route. Facing the Plaza de la Independenzia is the twin-towered cathedral which is as old as the city itself (1673). In an adjacent street is San José Church, which contains a gold altar, a priceless masterpiece of Spanish baroque colonial art. It was saved from Morgan's men by a quick-thinking monk who covered the gleaming gold with a coat of paint.. Note San Domingo's unsupported flat arch. Firm and immovable since the fire of 1737, it helped to prove that Panama was free of earthquakes an argument that tipped the scales in favour of Panama over Nicaragua when the Canal route was decided.

Only about five miles away lies "the greatest city in the New World", Old Panama. It was founded in 1518 by Pedro Arias, a nobleman from Avilá, nominated as governor by the Spanish Crown. It was used as a base for expeditions to various parts of the west coast of Central and South America and all the wealth gathered in these regions was brought here. The city was connected with the Caribbean harbor of Portobelo by a 50 mile, stone-paved road over which fabulous treasures were carried by pack animals. The landmark of these ruins is the impressive square tower of the Cathedral. This once flourishing city is now being gradually restored by the Panama government. At the farthermost tip of Panama City, extending into the blue Bay of Panama, lies "Las Bovedas" the old dungeons, which at different times have been a protective bastion, prisoners' gaol, and lovers lane.

When in 1671 the pirate Morgan sacked the original city of Panama, the inhabitants moved to the present site which seemed to offer better protection from invaders. They encircled the new city of Panama with a wall, part of which still remains, and took advantage of the jut of land which rose high on a rocky cliff for their fort. Here was built Las Bovedas, which bustled with activity. A twenty-four hour vigil was kept to protect the steady stream of gold and precious stones which flowed from the countries to the South across the Isthmus of Panama to Spain. And it must have been a noisy place, for the guards' steady tread on the parapet could not dim the cries of the prisoners in the dungeons below when the high tide carried the sea knee-deep into their very cells.

With the passing of time the dungeons were no longer used and Las Bovedas became only a military garrison for troops when Panama was under the rule of Colombia. It was from here that in 1903 that the signal was given the Panamanians and Colombian gunboats that the Colombian generals had surrendered and the new Republic of Panama was born.

Through a treaty with the United States to protect Panama and the Panama Canal from attack, troops were no longer needed in Panama, and Las Bovedas lost its military aspect. The parapet has since become the popular place for the evening walk or "paseo". Many a romance has bloomed there.

TABOGA ISLAND

Fast launches make the round trip to Taboga Island twice daily, sailing from pier 17, Balboa. The journey which takes little over an hour is in itself a sightseeing tour. Once at the "Island of Flowers"—as the tourist posters call it—you can spend a leisurely day swimming, sightseeing in the picturesque and friendly native village or just lazing on the beach. An ex-president of the Republic called it "The Island of Health and Beauty". Tourists and residents of Panama and the Canal Zone find here an ideal place for vacationing and it's a fisherman's paradise. The newly built *Hotel Taboga* offers all modern conveniences. A popular spot with honeymooners with its palm groves and heavy surf, Taboga represents all the allure of a tropical setting most tourists from northern climes hope to find.

The Island is also renowned for its sweet, fragrant pineapples which are cultivated everywhere. The quality of this fruit is so fine and so delicate that it is impossible to export them. This is because of the enormous quantity of juice they contain which begins seeping through the thick husks before they are hardly ripe.

The most beautiful flowers of the tropics show their colors on the steep hillsides of the little streets of Taboga; roses, jasmines, daisies and lilies grow everywhere in great abundance, virtually wild under the bright Isthmian sun.

East of the Canal

Portobelo, about twenty miles from Colón, is today a ghost

town, coming to life once a year when the Feast of the Black Christ is celebrated. His life-sized statue, made of *bolo*-wood which does not float, was miraculously washed ashore in 1658, coming probably from a Spanish galleon sunk by pirates. Ever since, the statue is carried through the town on the evening of October 21 in a slow, dancing procession to the accompaniment of some rather weird music. The populace then celebrates in the streets far into the night. Portobelo's moss-covered ruins are the former fortifications of this once flourishing port. The Customs House which dates from 1611 is the only structure that weathered time and the repeated attacks of such English plunderers as Henry Morgan and William Parker. While charter planes bring you quickly to Portobelo from Panama City, little effort is made to take tourists to Nombre de Dios, another historic site farther east.

There are daily excursion flights to the Caribbean coast facing a multitude of small islands (San Blas), inhabited by the Cuna Indians who spend most of their life on and in the water. A fastidious race, their women adore colorful clothes, make-up and a large golden ring in the nose. Many of them have plantations on the mainland and they'll readily paddle you out to their island villages. The Cunas have a strict color bar and refuse to intermarry or corrupt their ancient way of life. Cuna women are the *acknowledged* bosses of the family and supervise all trading which is done mostly by barter.

The Darién Jungle is a great adventure for those who are not afraid to rough it for a few days. Here you'll meet again those stocky Cunas—of the continental variety—and the tall Chocós who live in the Sambu River Valley. Some fifty miles southeast of Panama City lie the atolls, known as Pearl Islands. In pre-Columbian times the region was an important pearl-fishing center. Native divers still search for these lustrous gems, but deep-sea fishing, among the best in the world, provides a surer means of livelihood today.

A Trip to the West

The towns in the region extending toward the Costa Rican frontier retain much of the charm of the Spanish colonial era. A good road, part of the Panamerican Highway, takes you from Panama City to David, chief city of Chiriqui province. Leaving the capital you pass through Balboa, headquarters of all canal operations. A place to visit in Balboa is the Orchid Garden where over 400 varieties of this lovely plant can be seen. In less than two hours you reach Chame, known for its superb beach, Gorgona. A bit further on, San Carlos offers river as well as sea bathing. From here you should make a side-trip to the picturesque mountain village of El Valle, fast becoming a fashionable resort, a lovely and comfortable stopover for the night. Back on the highway, we proceed to Santa Clara, a modern seaside resort. Penomé and Natà were important Indian settlements long before Spanish colonization. Some nine miles out of El Roble turn left to visit Ocú where you'll see the inhabitants, *montunos* wearing their traditional dress, the men in richly-embroidered, homespun fringed suits and the women in brightly-colored full skirts, the *tumba hombre* (men throwers) and blouses trimmed with handmade lace. Both sexes sport the famed handmade Panama hat. The men usually carry the all-purpose *machete*, a razor-sharp knife with an 18 inch blade, used to cut grass and jungle undergrowth, to cultivate crops and even for shaving and haircutting! But no fear, they are shy and friendly folk. During the Feast of San Sebastian, which lasts nearly a week (January 19-24) there is plenty of gaiety with bullfights, cockfights and dancing in the streets.

Some 300 miles from the capital lies David, third largest city in the Republic and a good center for excursions and for hunting and fishing expeditions all the year round. The mountain village of Boquete, nestling on a ridge of the multi-peaked Volcàn Barú, is easily reached by car or narrow-gauge railroad. Here is a terrestrial Paradise. Whole fields of Easter lilies dazzle the eye. In addition are strawberries, coffee fincas running as high as 7000 feet up the slopes of the volcano, groves of oranges, a perpetual harvest of vegetables, all due to the temperate climate in this unique and delightful spot where the winds of the Atlantic meet the soft Pacific breeze. A perpetual fine mist is thus created refracting the glory of the sun in as many as seven rainbows at a time. This hauntingly beautiful region can be explored on horseback. Sure-footed native ponies will take you to the other side of the volcano and a virgin land of giant trees and rushing mountain streams, nature undefiled, a beautiful and unexpected Eden between the Pacific and the Caribbean Sea.

its typical buildings adorned with stilted balconies, constructed of local hardwood; painted in bright colors. From the spacious Oranjeplein you may continue in the direction of the river to see old Fort Zeelandia, established about 1650 by Francis Willoughby, Lord Parham, but taken and rebuilt as early as 1667 by the Dutch, who gave it its present name. The population still say "the Fort", meaning the whole city of Paramaribo.

Fifty steps farther to the North is the old "Barracks 1790", a typical colonial building of stone imported as ballast by the sailing vessels of the ancient West Indian Company. Opposite there is an entrance to the peaceful Palm-garden, from which you can reach again the Oranjeplein at the beginning of one of the oldest and principal streets, the Gravenstraat. Flanking this street are centuries-old buildings: the Roman Catholic Cathedral, an artful wooden construction, and in the mahogany-shaded part of the street, the old Portuguese-Sephardic Synagogue and the Government Hospital. Continuing up this street, you'll find the Art-Centre (C.C.S.) with its Library, well-provided with English books. Opposite is the old Oranjetuin-Cemetery with its historic tombs.

Parallel to the Gravenstraat are a number of other picturesque mahogany-shaded streets: Herenstraat, Wagenwegstraat and Keizerstraat. Their cross-streets all lead to the commercial district, of which Dominéstraat is the busiest, and its parallel, the Maagdenstraat ("Virgin-street") the most picturesque with its high palm-trees in two rows. Never ask why the latter street leads to the point where Heiligenweg ("Saint's Road") and Knuffelgracht ("Petting ditch") happen to meet! Protestant churches of different denominations rise amidst this shopping center, whilst at the end of the Jodenbreestraat, connecting the former-mentioned streets with the harbor, is a second, large Synagogue, that of the Ashkenazi community.

From here the city fans out, ending in the fresh and open district of Zorg-en-Hoop, where, amidst modern villas, the Ethnological Museum displays fine specimens of native arts and crafts together with many historical documents, engravings and rare books about the country. From here it is only a hundred paces to Paramaribo's airport. In the same area large modern school-buildings and three brand-new churches (Catholic and Protestant) show a growing taste for the latest fashion in architecture.

In the outskirts of Paramaribo, either to the south or to the west, are agricultural districts, mainly occupied by Hindustani

PANAMA AND THE CANAL ZONE

 PASSPORTS, VISAS. The only entry requirement for visitors is a Tourist Card (US $2) and two passport-size photographs. The card is valid for 30 days and issued by your transportation company. The traveler must have a vaccination certificate and a round-trip ticket or transportation to another country. You are advised to check; these regulations are subject to change. You could also obtain a tourist visa at any Panama consulate which is valid for 90 days at a cost of US $5. (To citizens of the U.S., Mexico, Columbia, the Netherlands, Sweden, Norway and Denmark, it is issued free of charge by virtue of existing agreements).

CURRENCY. The monetary unit is the *balboa,* written B. This is divided into 100 centavos and is on a par with the U.S. dollar. U.S. currency, legal tender in the Canal Zone, circulates freely in the Republic.

 HOW TO GET ABOUT. In all the larger towns there are taxis or cars for hire at reasonable rates. The Panamerican Highway is just about ready to push right into Panama City and in a good state of repair. Some of the secondary roads are also good. Both railroads, (the one in Chiriqui province, the other between Panama City and Colón) may soon close down. The Panameña de Aviación links all principal cities of the country and there is a network of small airfields, convenient for hunting and fishing party charter flights. Rates for air travel are very reasonable. Balboa and Cristobal, both in the Canal Zone, are international harbors. There is a fast *expreso* bus service linking the two. From Balboa, two daily launches leave for Tobago Island and return the same day (extra service on weekends). The round trip costs only $2 per person; it is about one hour each way. Sea travel by coastal vessels is cheap but not too comfortable. Puerto Armuelles in the Gulf of Chirikui, Almirante and Bocas del Toro in the Caribbean serve fruit traffic. Aguadulce, in the Gulf of Panama, is another port serving coastal trade. A quaint innovation are Panama's "micro-taxis", a fleet of small cars with fares considerably less than standard models.

HOTELS

With the exception of the more modest establishments, prices are nearly the same as in the U.S. Best hotels operate on European Plan Basis.

PANAMA CITY AND CANAL ZONE

EL PANAMA. The usual Hilton luxury and efficiency; 300 air-conditioned rooms with private terraces overlooking the Pacific Ocean. Dinner dance under the tropical stars. You'll swim, tan or play tennis at its Cabaña Club, surrounded by 15 acres of tropical gardens. You can try your luck at the air-conditioned Casino-in-the-Sky. There is a miniature golf course, duty-free lobby shops in the lobby arcade, and guests have privileges at the nearby Panama Golf Club and Riding Club. If you are the adventurous type, Jungle Jim will despatch you on jaunts you'll never forget. Summer rates are: $10-15 single, $15-20 double; Suites (2 rooms) $25-$30. Winter rates are: $13-20 single, $19-$26 double. Suites $35-40. European Plan.

INTERNACIONAL. Newly renovated; now a luxury hotel. All rooms with air-conditioning and private bath. Dancing, bar. Rates: $9 and up.

LA SIESTA. New 100-room hotel with swimming pool, just two minutes away from Tocumen airport. Ideal for honeymooners.

HOTEL LUX. The newest hotel in

Panama. All rooms with air conditioning and private bath. Rates, single $9-$10; double $12-$13; suites $12-$16.

Other hotels include: *Colón, Colombia, Ambassador* (air-conditioned rooms), *Roosevelt, Central. Pension Mexico* is a guest-house in avenue of same name.

At Ancon, the former Tivoli Hotel is now a U.S. *Government Guest House.* Only those with Canal Zone privileges can stay there.

You dock and shop in Colón. The leading hotel here is the *Washington,* overlooking Limon Bay. Has swimming pool. Others include: *Astor, Carlton, Imperial* and *Plaza.*

IN THE COUNTRY

AGUADULCE (Coclé). *Internacional.* A possible overnight stop.

BOCAS DEL TORO (in province of same name). *Copa.* Not tested.

BOQUETE (Chiriqui). 30 miles from David, 4000 feet up. *Panamonte Inn,* quiet life, excellent cuisine. Open Dec. 1 to Sept. 1. Runner up: *Wing.* Another 1000 feet up, *Bambito Fishing Lodge,* is simple, inexpensive.

CERRO CAMPANA (Panamá). A solitary mountain hotel 40 miles from the capital, the *Posada San Antonio* is nearly 3000 feet up. Call 2-2134 in Panama City for reservations.

CERRO PUNTA (Chiriqui). A mountain resort. *Casa Chipre, Pension Chonguita* and *Pension Felicita* are modest guesthouses.

CHITRE (Herrera). *Florida, Santa Rita, Plaza.*

DAVID (Chiriqui). Vacation center, at the base of El Volcán Barù. *Nacional,* up-to-date; all rooms with private bath. Swimming pool.

EL VALLE (Coclé). Mountain resort, good stopover—if you can get a room. *El Greco, Club Campestre.*

OCÚ (Herrera). Town of "montunos". *Posada San Sebastian,* for short stay.

SAN CARLOS BEACH (Panamá). Bungalow accommodation: *Rio Mar.*

SANTA CLARA BEACH (Coclé). Bungalow accommodation: *Casino Santa Clara, Cabanas Phillips, Geneva.*

SANTIAGO (Veraguas). Stopover on Panamerican Highway, en route for Chiriqui Province or Costa Rica. *Magnolia, Del Moral, Plaza,* all moderate.

SAJALICES (Panama). *Parque Villa Real.* Not so royal as its name implies.

SAN BLAS ISLANDS. (One hour by plane from Panama City). *Hotel San Blas;* water skiing, surf boarding, skindiving, big-game hunting *and* the Cuna Indians thrown in. For reservations contact Jungle Jim, Hotel El Panamá Hilton, Panama City.

TABOGA ISLAND (Panama). *Hotel Taboga.* 30 rooms with beautiful view on Panama Bay.

RESTAURANTS. French, Spanish and American food can be had in all restaurants and hotels. Some of the native cooking is reminiscent of the creole cuisine of Haiti and New Orleans. There are Oriental restaurants as well as beer-gardens with hearty teutonic fare. Some like it hot, so try the piquant fish appetizer, *ceviche,* marinated in lime juice. Another cocktail-hour delicacy is *patacones de platano,* or fried yucca. *Sancocho* is a Panamanian stew with chicken, meat and all sorts of vegetables. Another national dish is *tamales* a sort of pie, only moderately seasoned and wrapped up in banana leaves. Other good pies, filled with meat or chicken or cheese are *carimañolas* and *empanadas. Arroz con pollo,* a universal Latin-American dish has a delicious local twist. Meals cost about the same as in the States.

PANAMA AND THE CANAL ZONE

The *De Lesseps Room* at the Hotel El Panamá Hilton is crowded with smart people. Service and cuisine are tops and so are prices. The *Skychef,* Hotel Internacional, has excellent food, coupled with soft music. On the transisthmian highway, next to Riba-Smith Supermarket, *Lee's Stake House* specializes in charcoal broiled steaks. Opens at 4 pm.; piano, bar. Good food is served at *Jardín El Rancho* and *Jardín Atlas;* both are of the beer-garden type. In the suburb of San Francisco de la Caleta: *Club Nautico* for seafood and the best *paella* in town; *Brisas del Mar,* also popular. *Panamar* is another seafood restaurant, at the end of Calle 50. For Spanish food visit *Iberia,* next to National Bank. Half an hour's drive to *Lo Panameño,* a small, typical, thatchroofed place, famous for its native dishes. At Colón try the *Washington* and the *Monaco Gardens Club,* both beautifully located and quite reasonable.

NIGHTLIFE. Most nightclubs follow the standard pattern; they are noisy and glittery. A few have floor shows, most of them serve food. With few exceptions they come and go; check whether the place of your choice is still running.

Nice in every way is the *Bella Vista Room* at El Panamá Hilton. Second choice in Panama City is *Maxim's,* quite luxurious, good floorshow. *Boite "W"* is a restaurant plus nightclub. Good runner-up is *Grill El Sombrero. Balboa Breezes* on Avenida Balboa at 26th. Street is a recent venture.

For good dining and dancing try the *Bahia* in front of the bay. There are two shows nightly. A good place for dining is the *Skychef,* open 5 p.m. to 11 p.m.

The *Strangers Club* is the number one smart place in Colón. The other night spots are on the honky tonk side, if that's the kind of fun you're looking for.

 SHOPPING. Panama has a real tourist bait: it makes possible the importation of goods from all over the world, free of duty. Amazing bargains can be had on some products, often at half the U.S. price. Liquor sold is among the cheapest in the Western Hemisphere. Danish silver, English bone china, Swiss watches, French perfumes, German cameras, Italian silks and Irish linen sell at savings of about one-third and more. Local craft is also represented: leatherware, alligator skins; *bateas,* hand painted trays in native aztec or contemporary design, mahogany bowls, and other souvenirs. With the exception of the leading shops, bargaining is a much favored practice; about one-third off the price asked for is an acceptable deal for both parties. Colón is supposed to be cheaper than Panama City but that's a myth. The two principal shopping streets in the Republic are Avenida Central in Panama City and Front Street in Colón.

Watches. Don't simply ask for a Swiss watch, there are scores of cheap makes in that country. Here's a list of outstanding names in alphabetical order: Audemars-Piguet who make some of the thinnest existing watches; Consul 30 jewels; Clarenzia 42 jewels; Jaeger-Le Coultre for the successful man's fiancée; Juvenia "Slim" chronowatches; Longines "Calendar" with date-reading; Marvin's assortment of "Seven Wonders"; Movado "Kingmatic" super-waterproof; Mido "Powerwind"; Piaget, the ultimate in daintiness; Rolex, a sturdy topnotcher; Vulcain "Cricket"wrist alarm-watch; Zodiac "Glorious", with diamond-cut hour batons; Zenith "Captain", with date register.